so take me
someplace far away

CLOVER

1

I WANT HAPPINESS

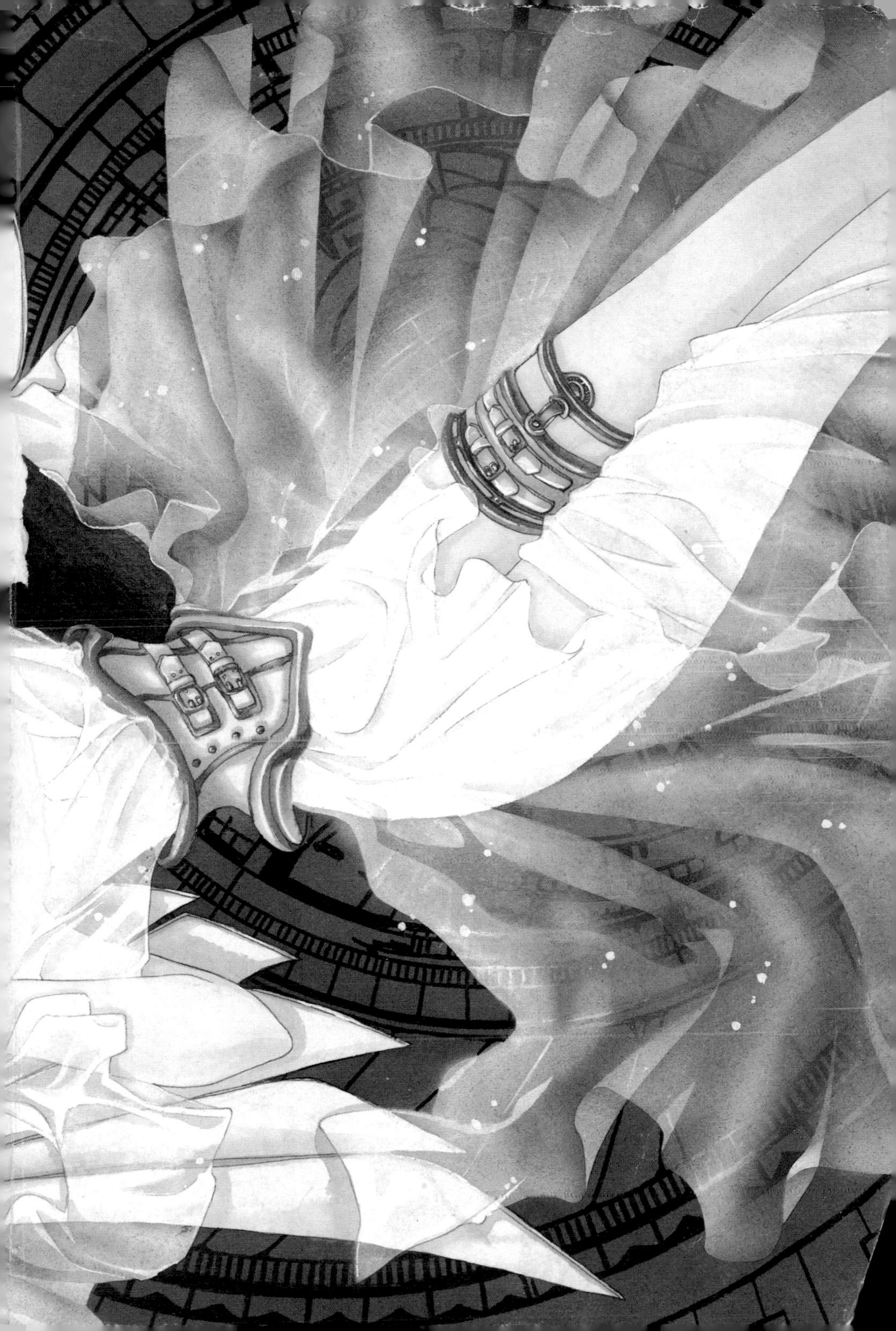

They say
A four-leaf clover
brings happiness

But
Don't tell anyone

Where the clovers
Bloom white flowers

Or how many leaves
From its stem extend

A four-leaf clover

I only want your happiness
But I cannot be yours

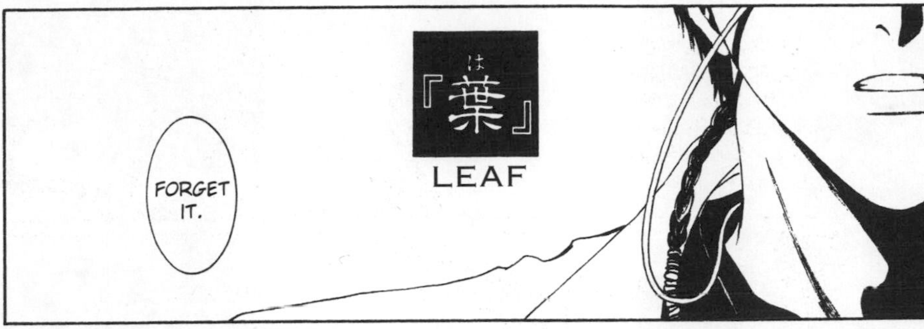
『葉』
は
LEAF
FORGET IT.
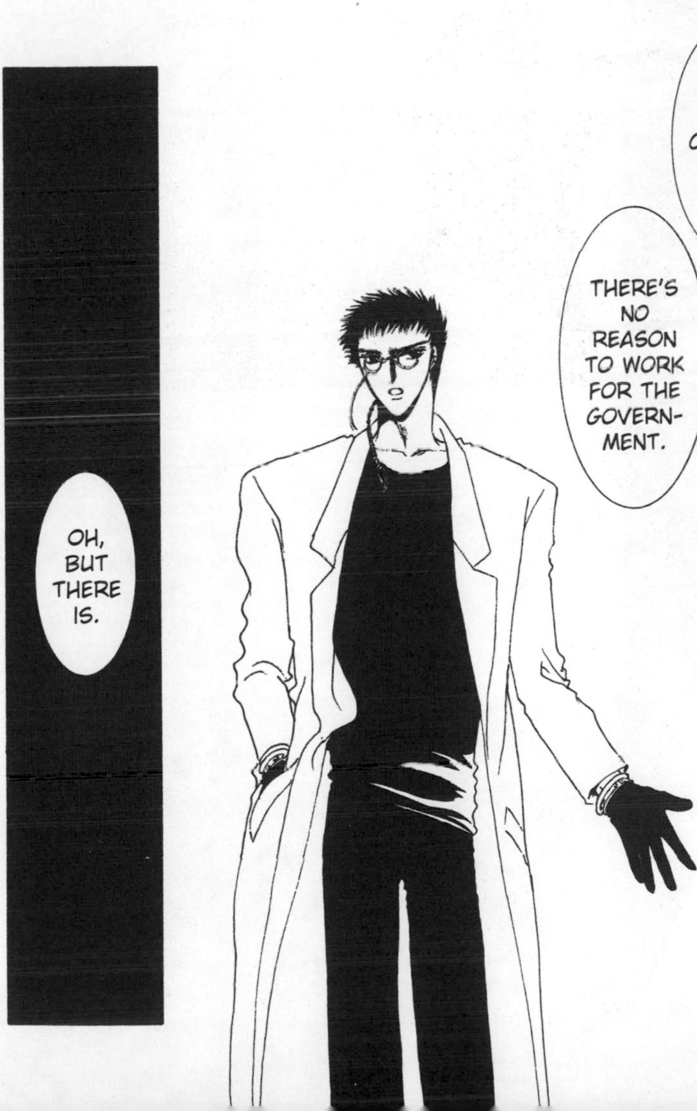
I'M A CIVILIAN NOW.
THERE'S NO REASON TO WORK FOR THE GOVERN-MENT.
OH, BUT THERE IS.

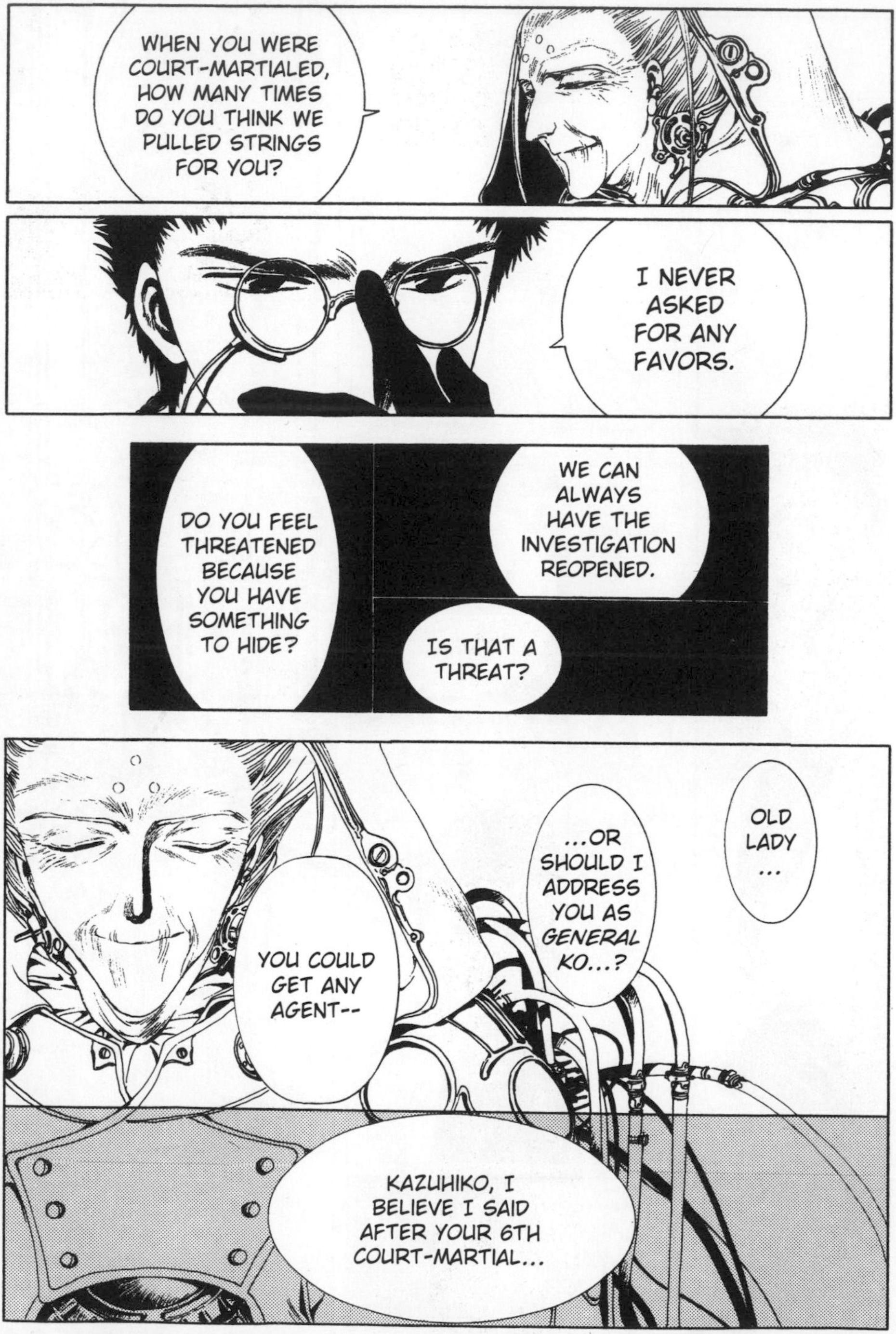
WHEN YOU WERE COURT-MARTIALED, HOW MANY TIMES DO YOU THINK WE PULLED STRINGS FOR YOU?
I NEVER ASKED FOR ANY FAVORS.
WE CAN ALWAYS HAVE THE INVESTIGATION REOPENED.
IS THAT A THREAT?
DO YOU FEEL THREATENED BECAUSE YOU HAVE SOMETHING TO HIDE?
OLD LADY ...
...OR SHOULD I ADDRESS YOU AS GENERAL KO...?
YOU COULD GET ANY AGENT--
KAZUHIKO, I BELIEVE I SAID AFTER YOUR 6TH COURT-MARTIAL...

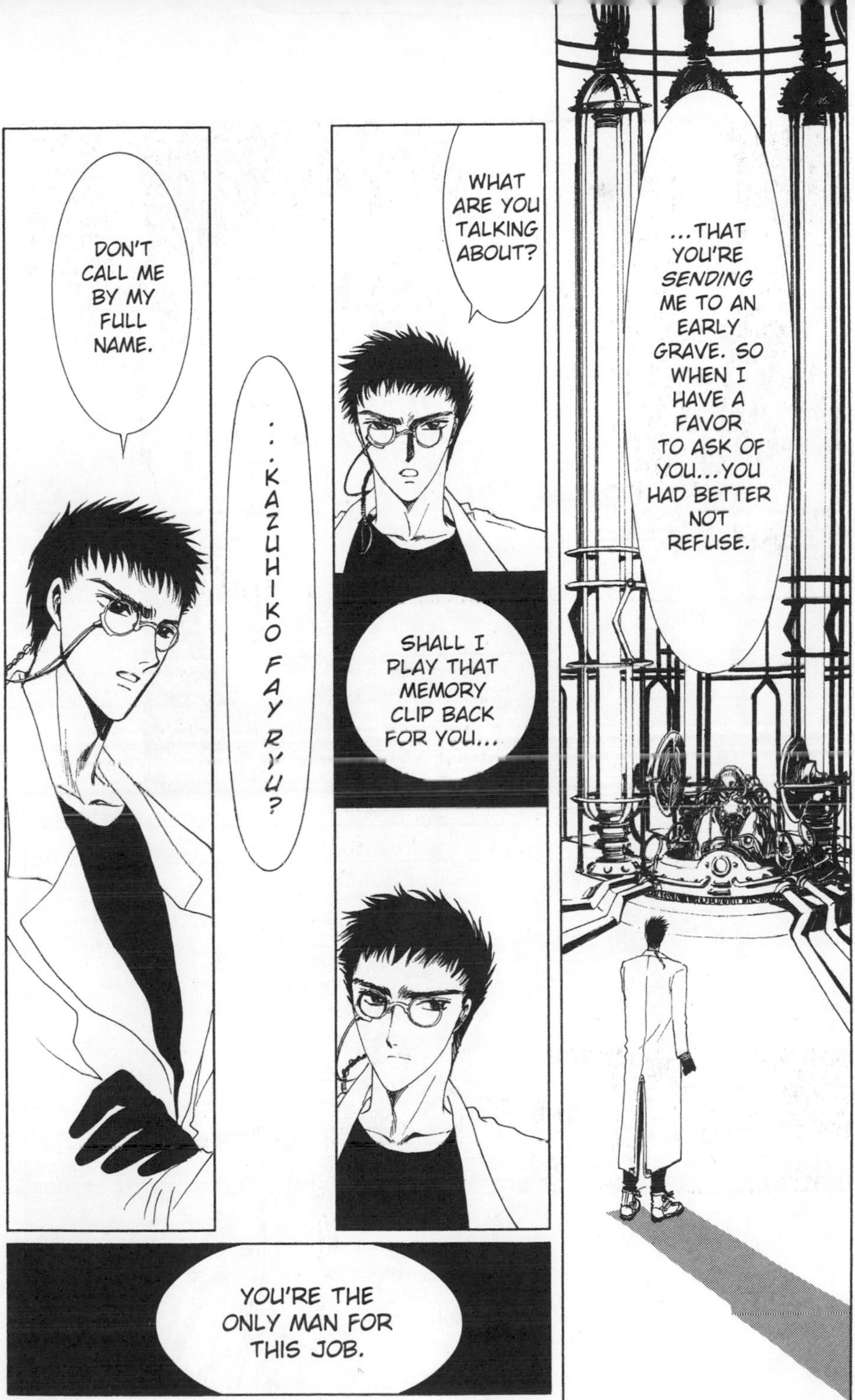
...THAT YOU'RE SENDING ME TO AN EARLY GRAVE. SO WHEN I HAVE A FAVOR TO ASK OF YOU...YOU HAD BETTER NOT REFUSE.
WHAT ARE YOU TALKING ABOUT?
SHALL I PLAY THAT MEMORY CLIP BACK FOR YOU...
...KAZUHIKO FAY RYU?
DON'T CALL ME BY MY FULL NAME.
YOU'RE THE ONLY MAN FOR THIS JOB.

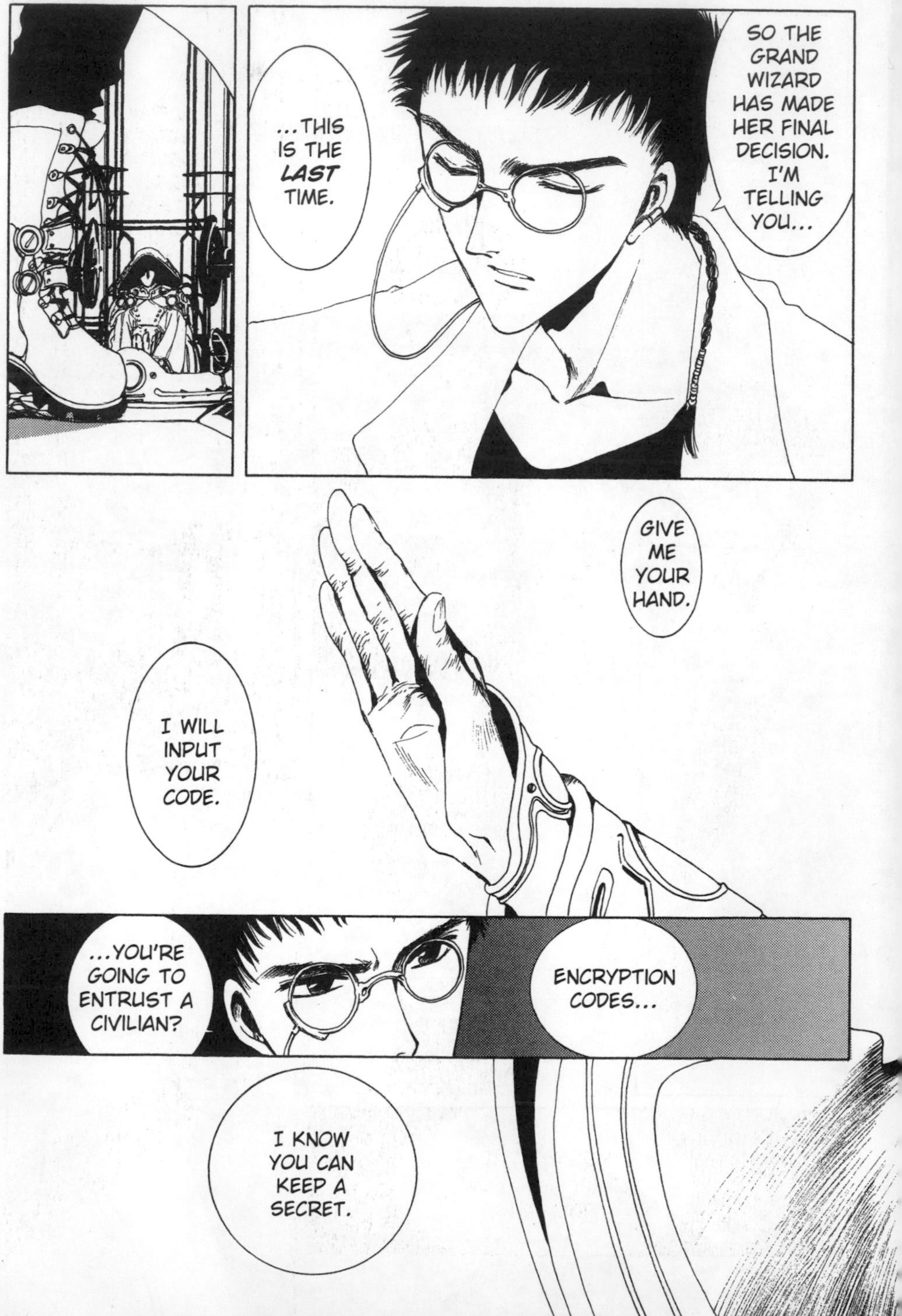
SO THE GRAND WIZARD HAS MADE HER FINAL DECISION. I'M TELLING YOU...
...THIS IS THE *LAST* TIME.
GIVE ME YOUR HAND.
I WILL INPUT YOUR CODE.
ENCRYPTION CODES...
...YOU'RE GOING TO ENTRUST A CIVILIAN?
I KNOW YOU CAN KEEP A SECRET.

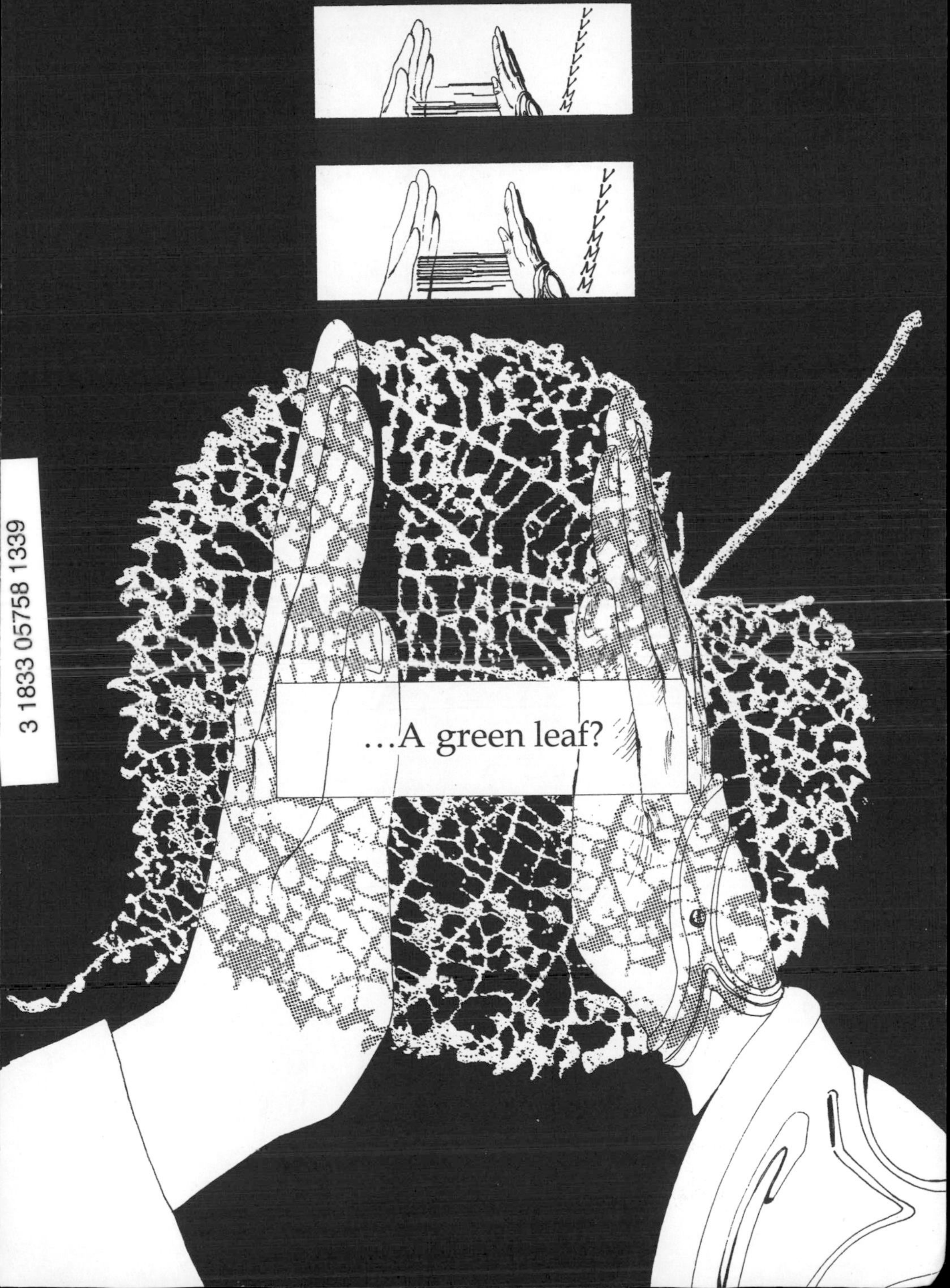
VVVVVVVMM
VVVVMMMM
…A green leaf?

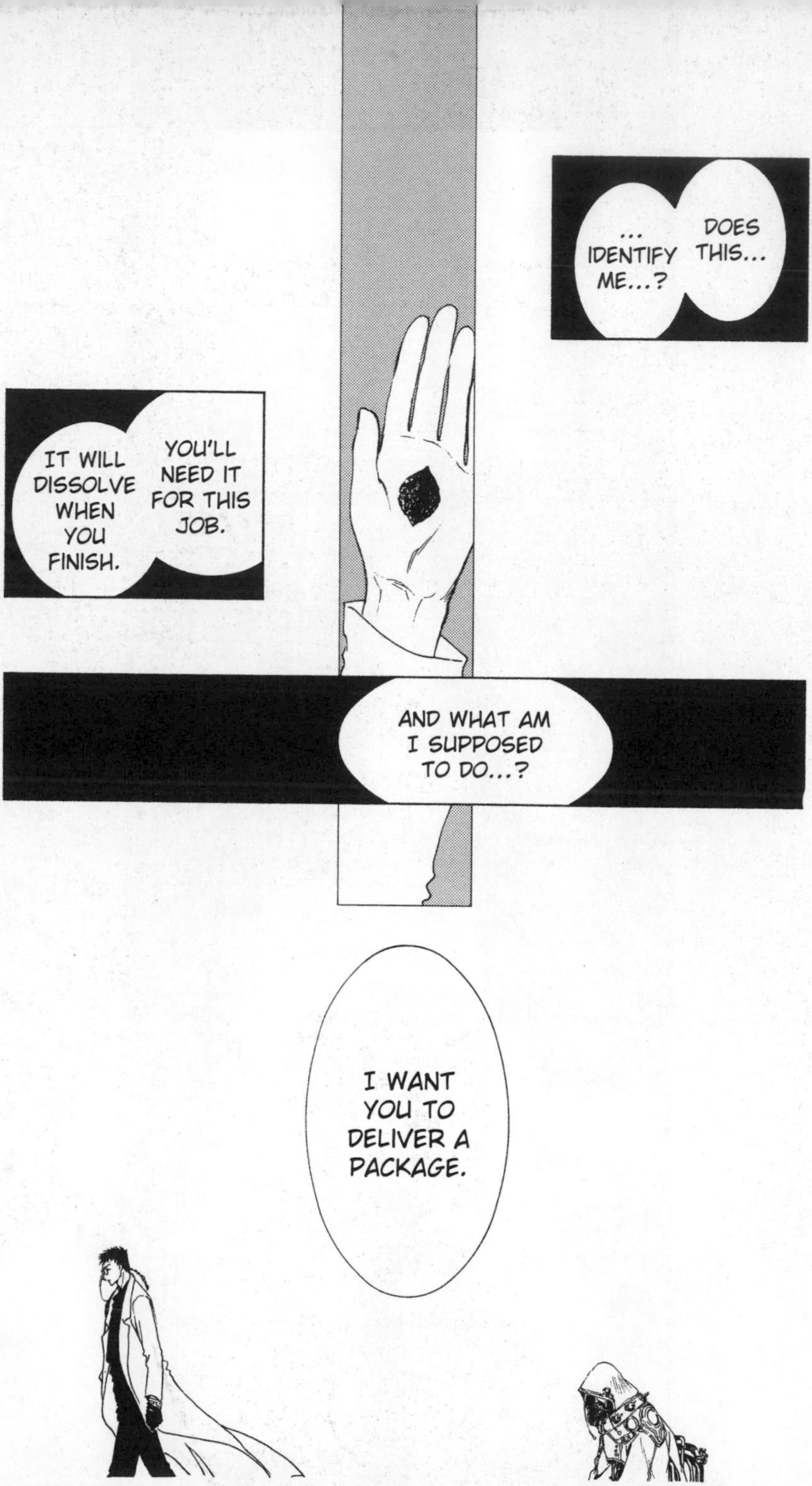
DOES THIS...
... IDENTIFY ME...?
YOU'LL NEED IT FOR THIS JOB.
IT WILL DISSOLVE WHEN YOU FINISH.
AND WHAT AM I SUPPOSED TO DO...?
I WANT YOU TO DELIVER A PACKAGE.

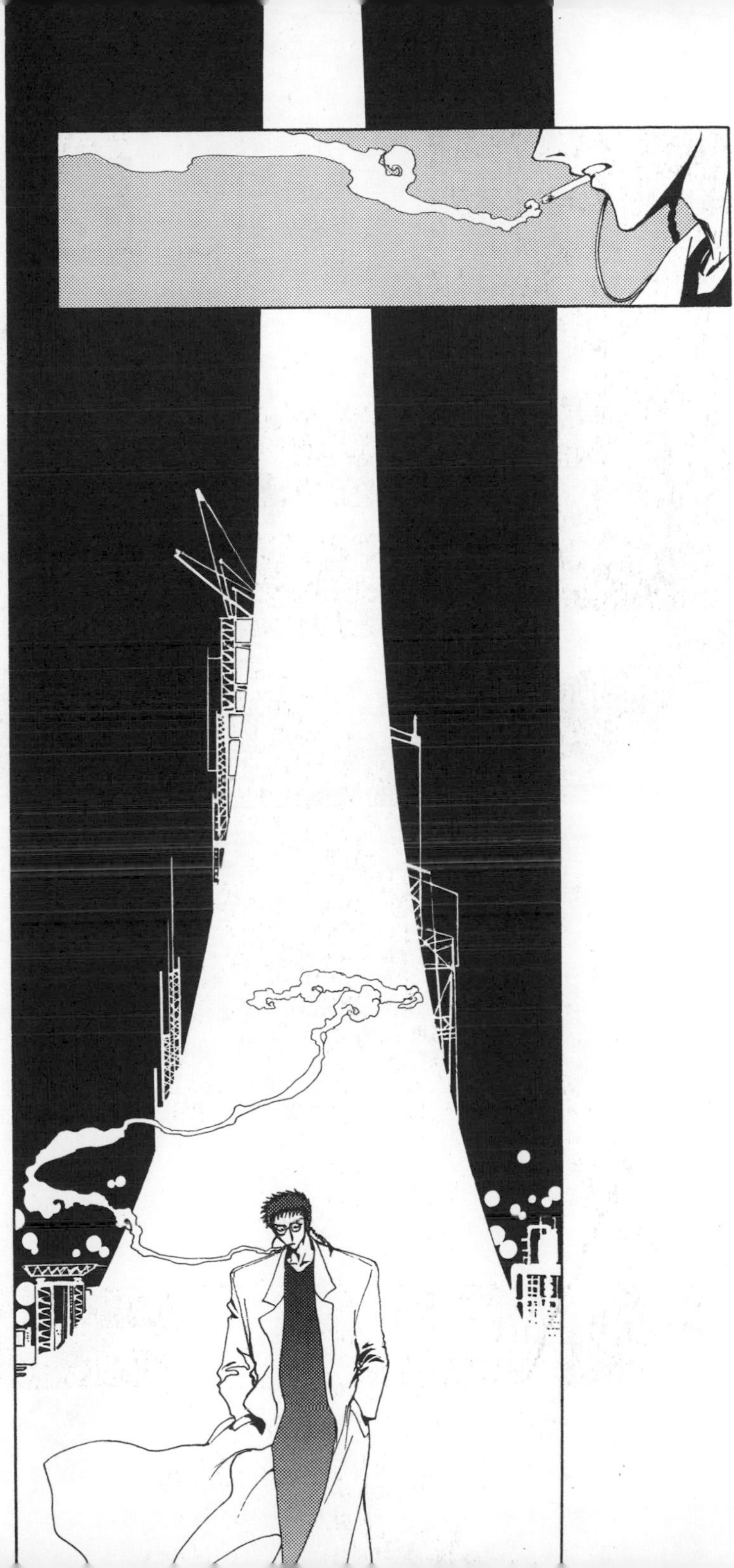

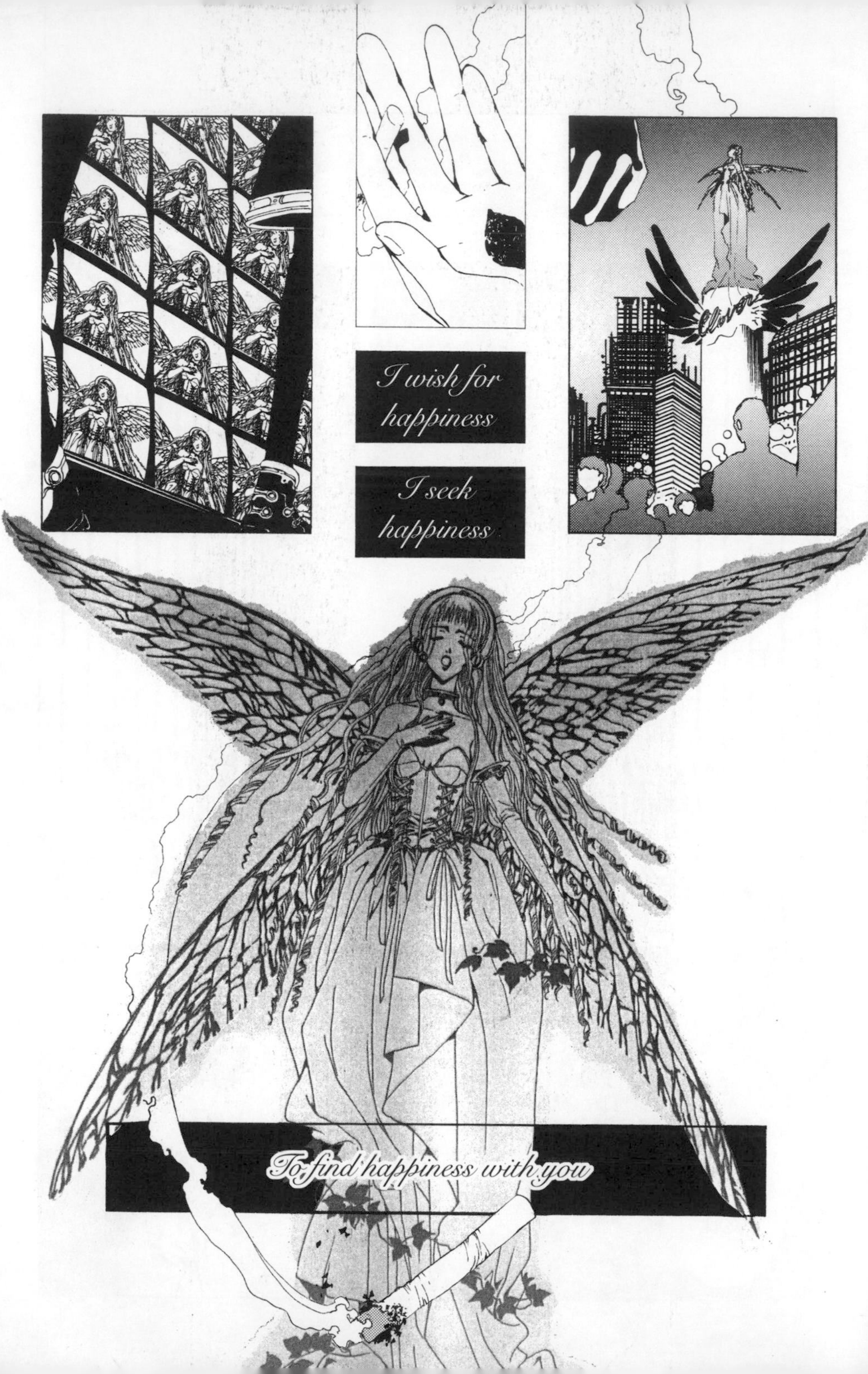
I wish for happiness
I seek happiness
To find happiness with you

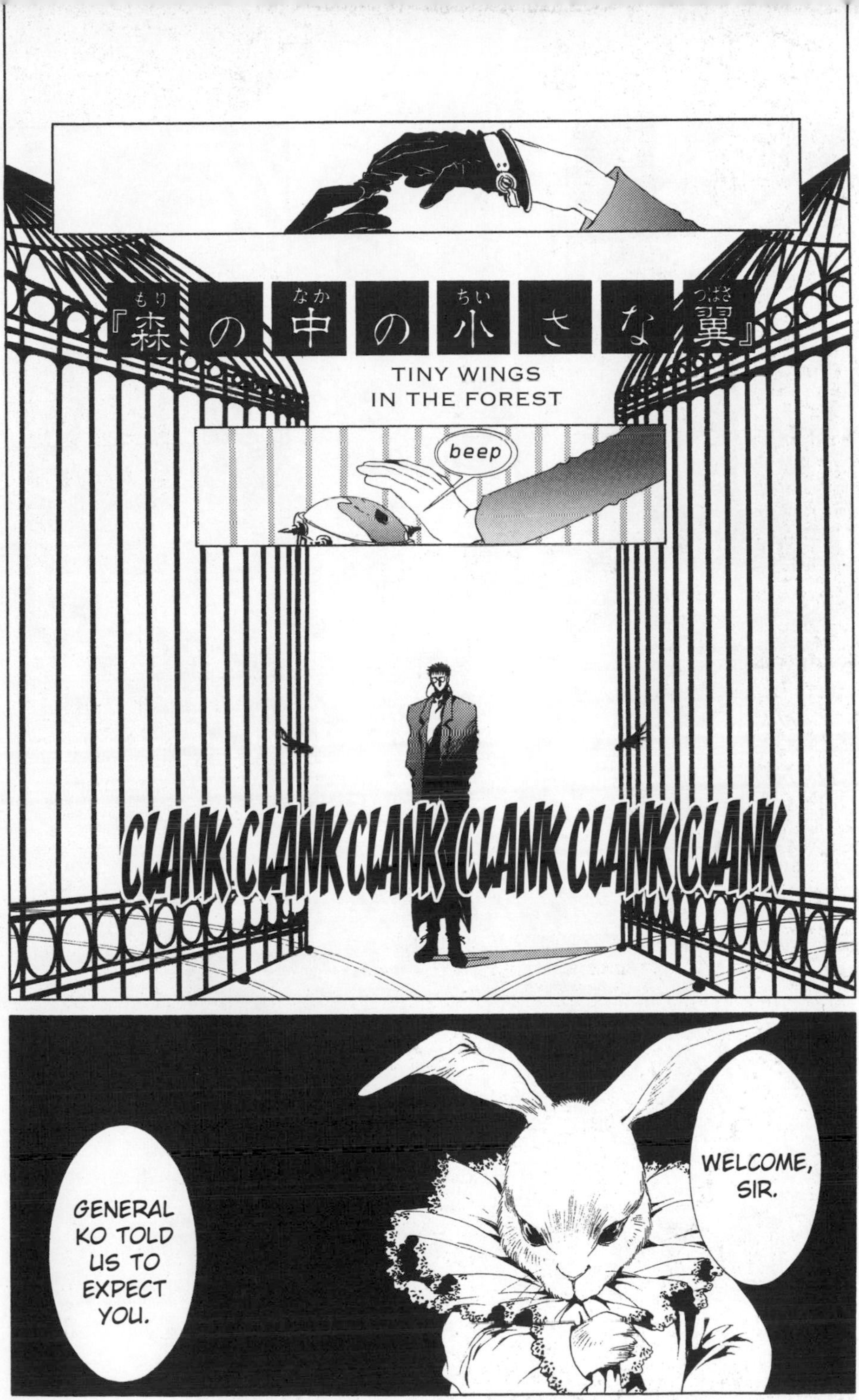
『森の中の小さな翼』
TINY WINGS
IN THE FOREST
beep
CLANK CLANK CLANK CLANK CLANK CLANK
WELCOME, SIR.
GENERAL KO TOLD US TO EXPECT YOU.

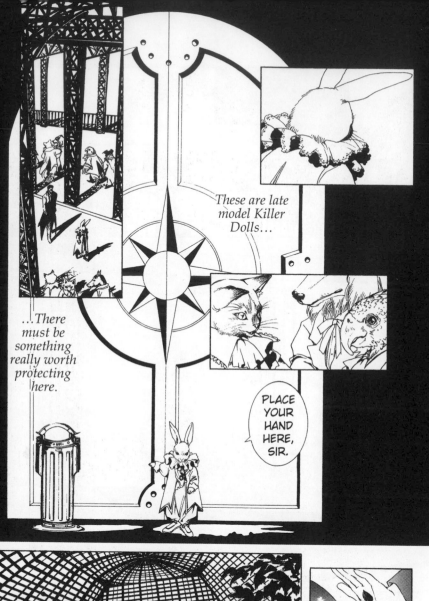

These are late model Killer Dolls...

...There must be something really worth protecting here.

PLACE YOUR HAND HERE, SIR.

klank

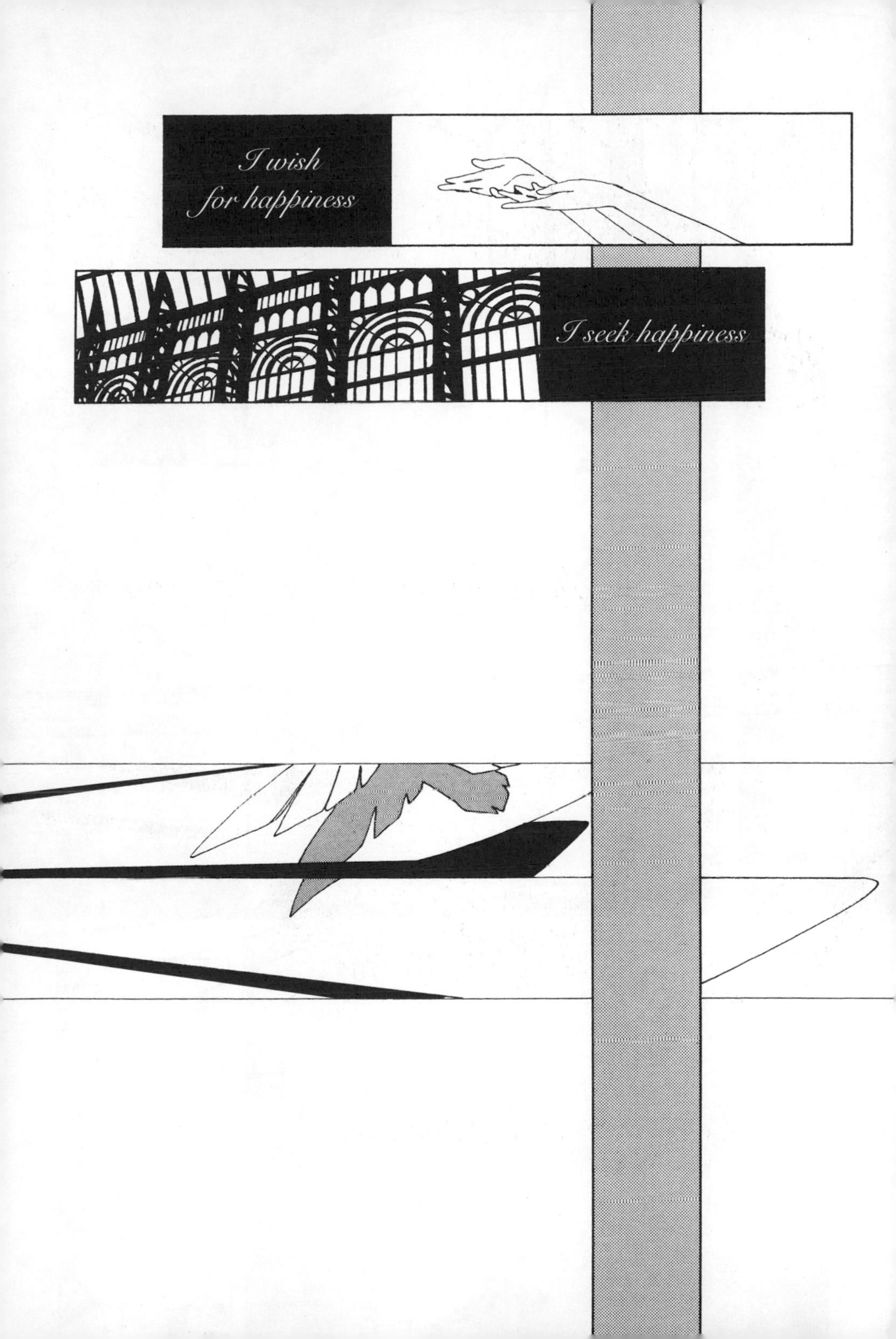
I wish for happiness
I seek happiness

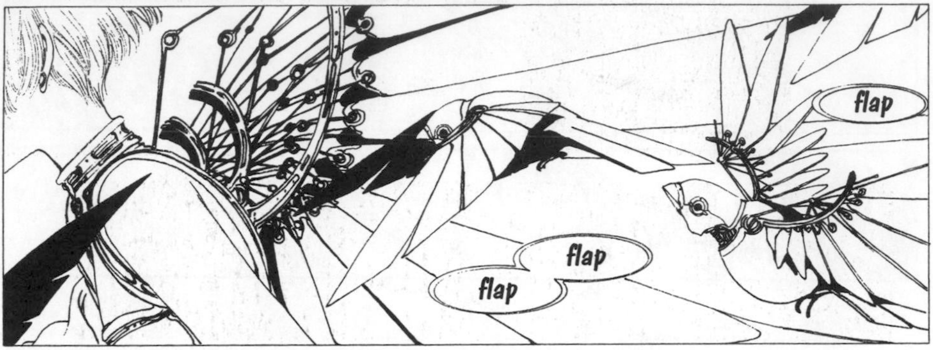
flap
flap
flap

To find happiness with you

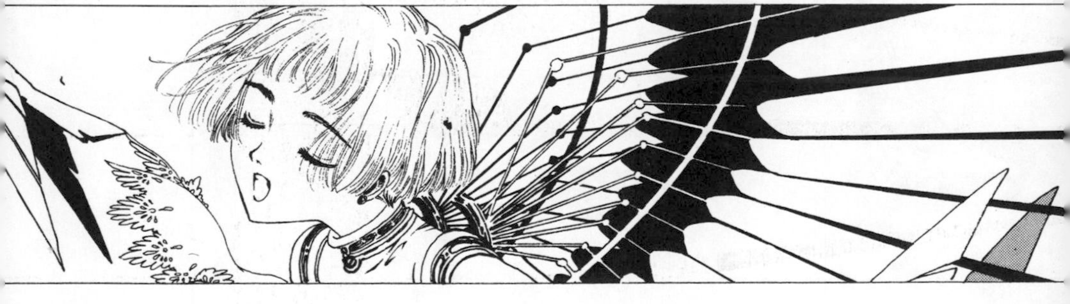

To be your happiness

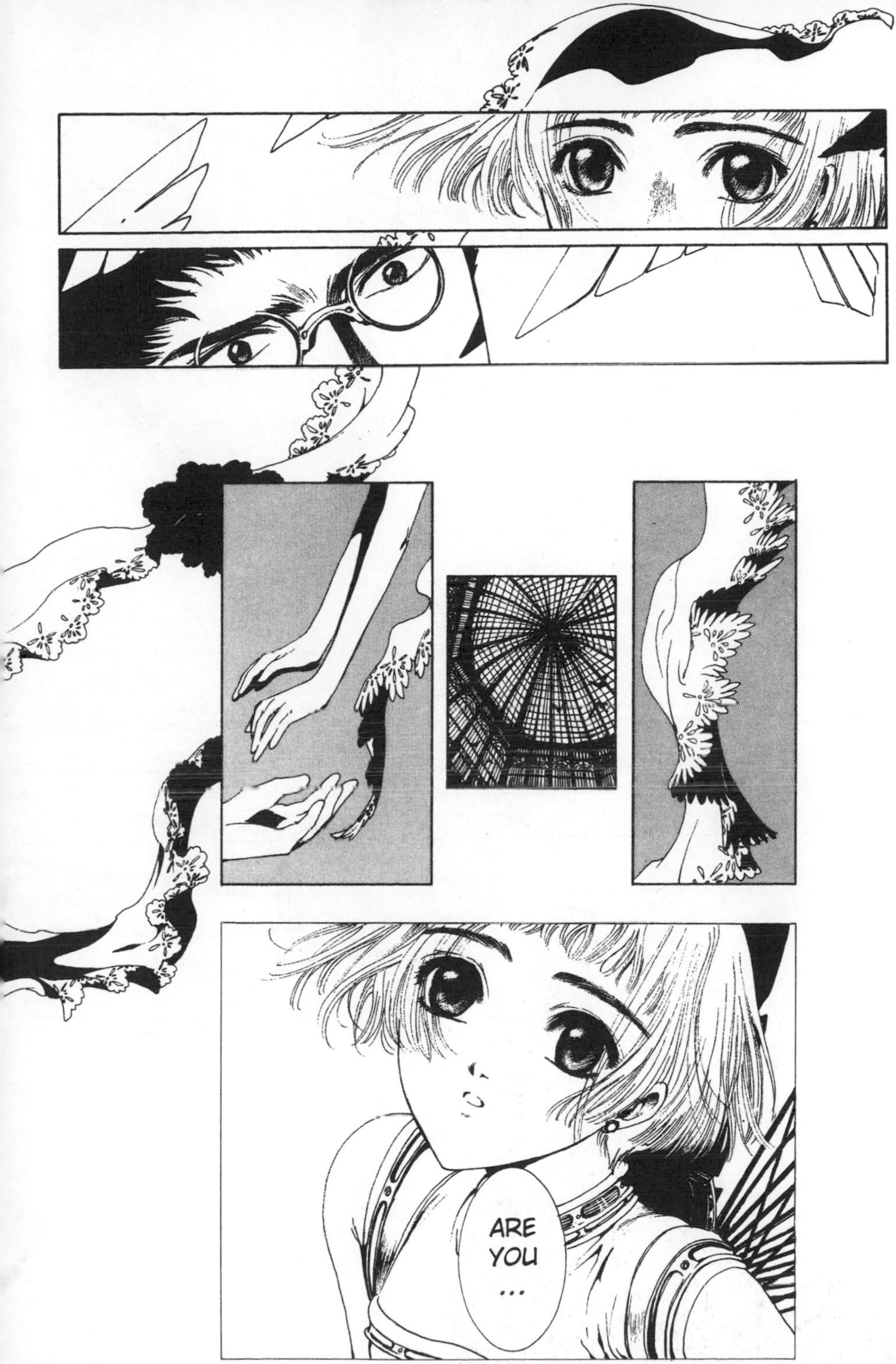
ARE YOU ...

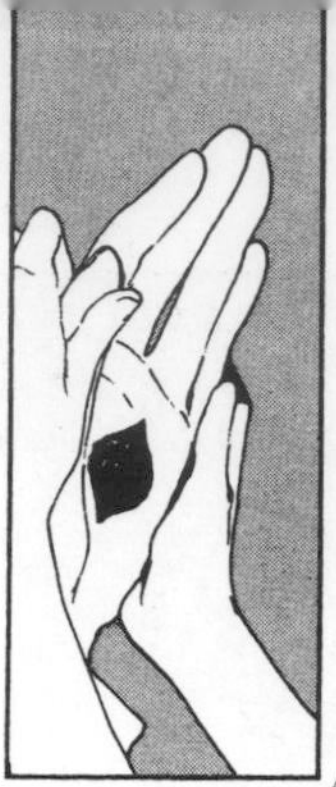
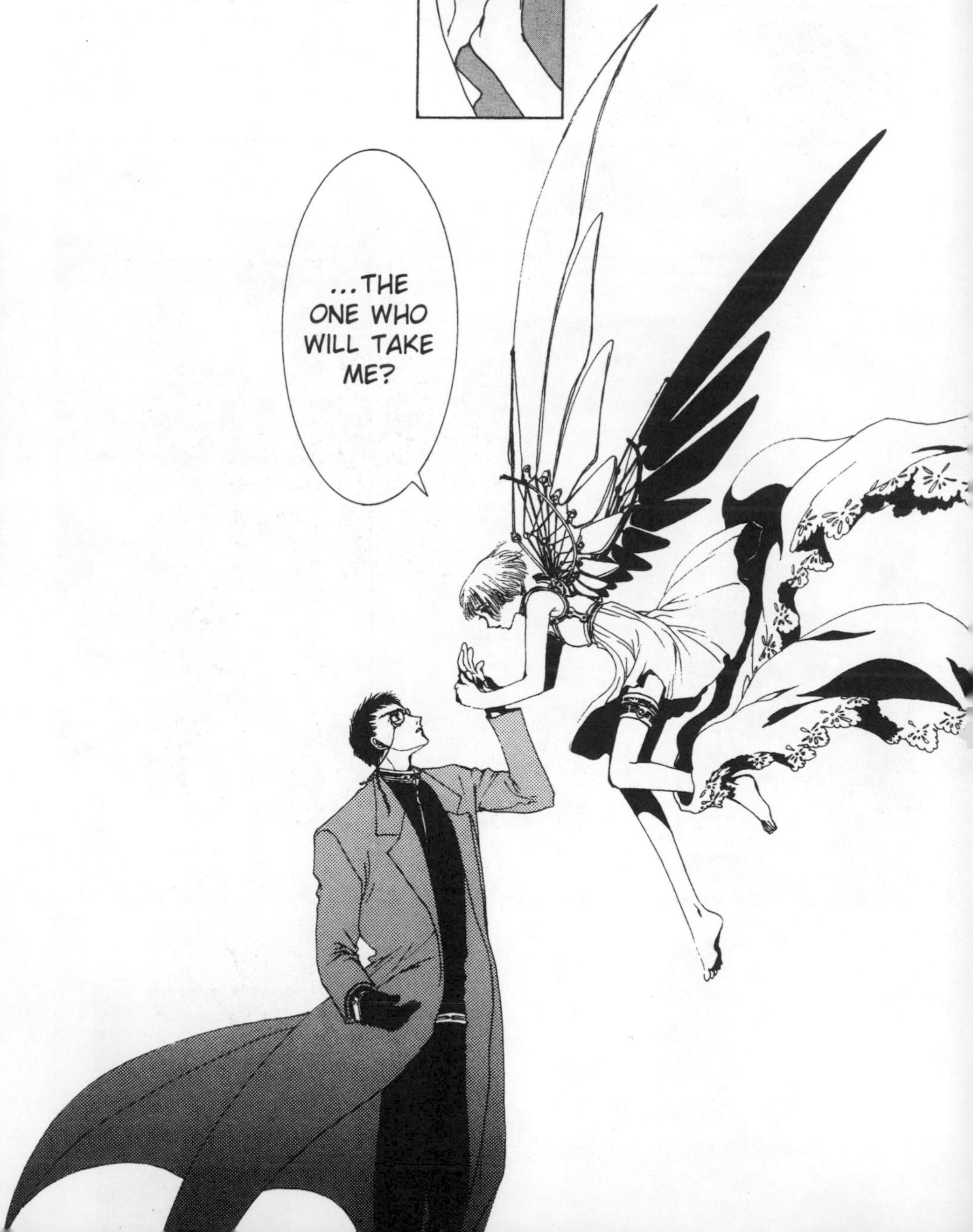
...THE ONE WHO WILL TAKE ME?

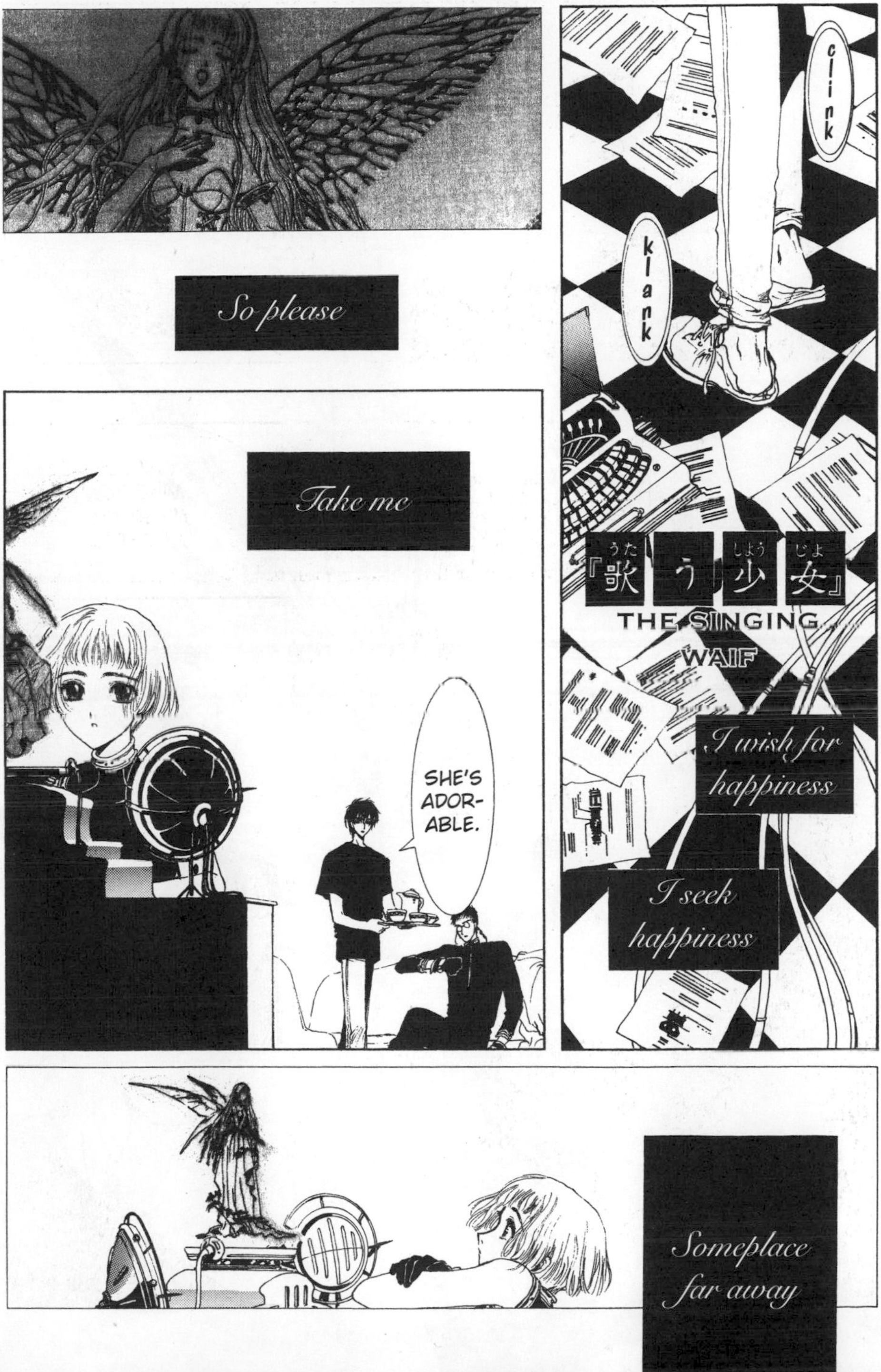
clink
klank
『歌う少女』
THE SINGING WAIF
I wish for happiness
I seek happiness
So please
Take me
SHE'S ADORABLE.
Someplace far away

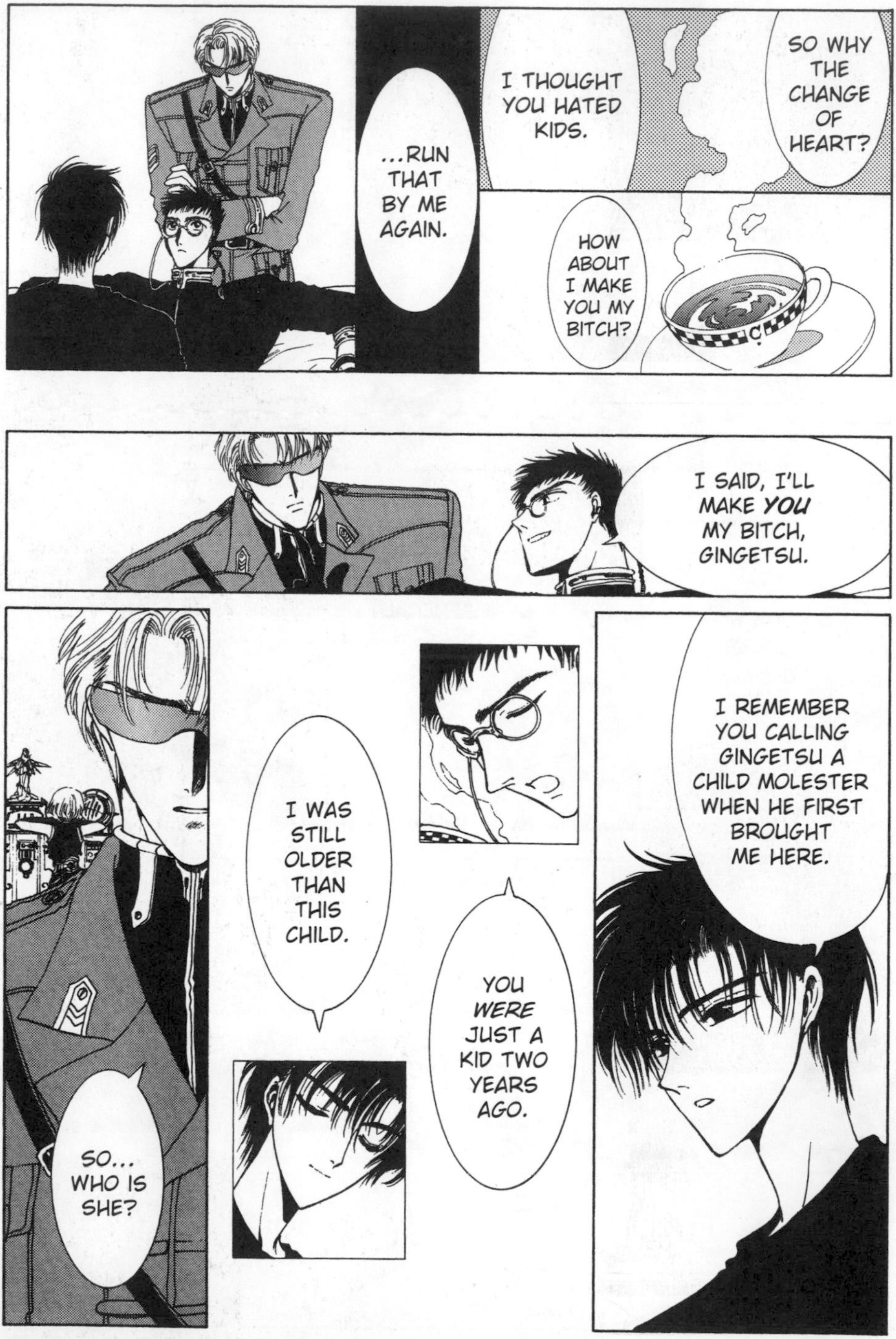
I THOUGHT YOU HATED KIDS.
SO WHY THE CHANGE OF HEART?
HOW ABOUT I MAKE YOU MY BITCH?
...RUN THAT BY ME AGAIN.
I SAID, I'LL MAKE *YOU* MY BITCH, GINGETSU.
I REMEMBER YOU CALLING GINGETSU A CHILD MOLESTER WHEN HE FIRST BROUGHT ME HERE.
YOU *WERE* JUST A KID TWO YEARS AGO.
I WAS STILL OLDER THAN THIS CHILD.
SO... WHO IS SHE?

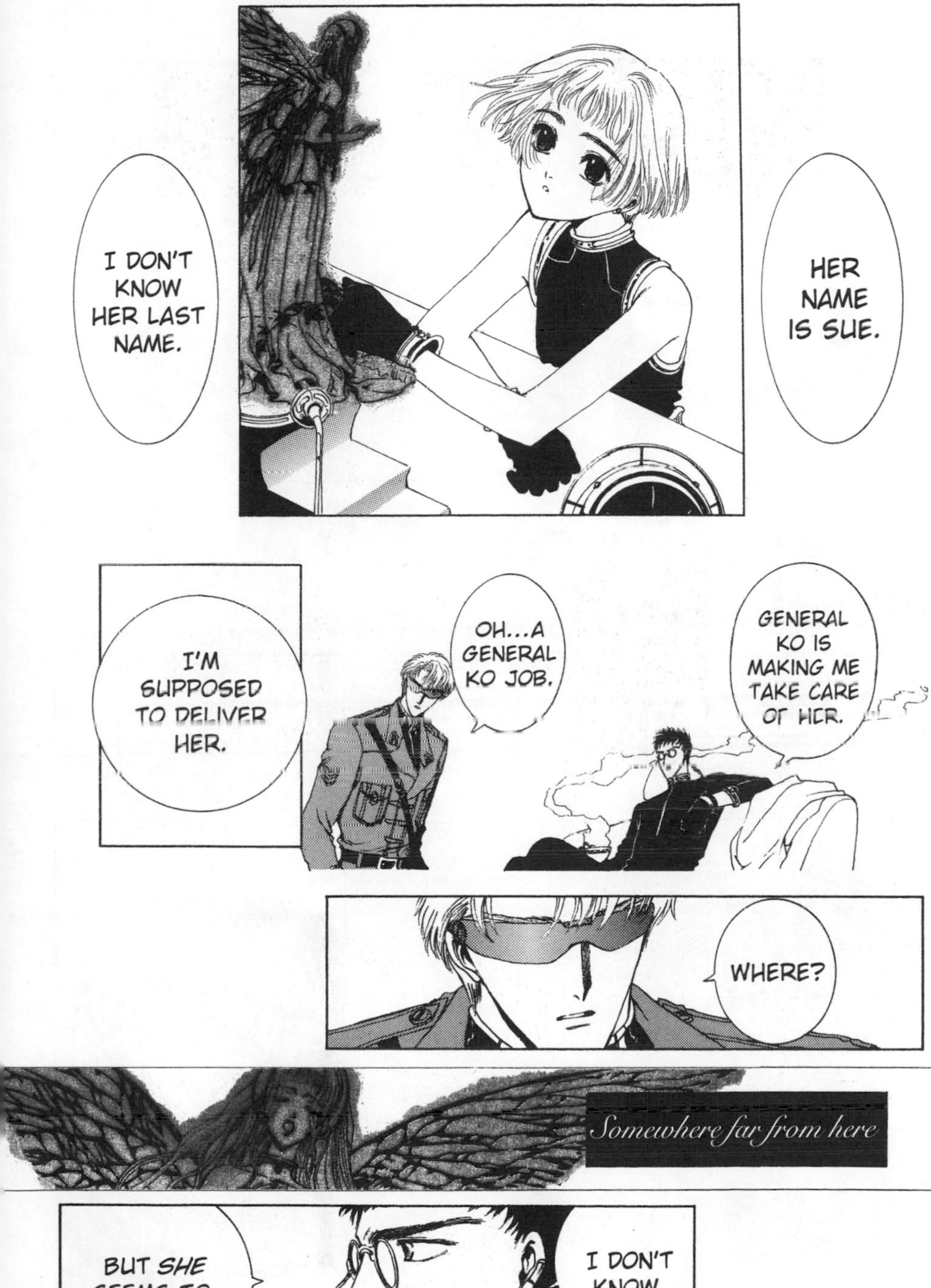
HER NAME IS SUE.
I DON'T KNOW HER LAST NAME.
GENERAL KO IS MAKING ME TAKE CARE OF HER.
OH...A GENERAL KO JOB.
I'M SUPPOSED TO DELIVER HER.
WHERE?
Somewhere far from here
I DON'T KNOW.
BUT SHE SEEMS TO.

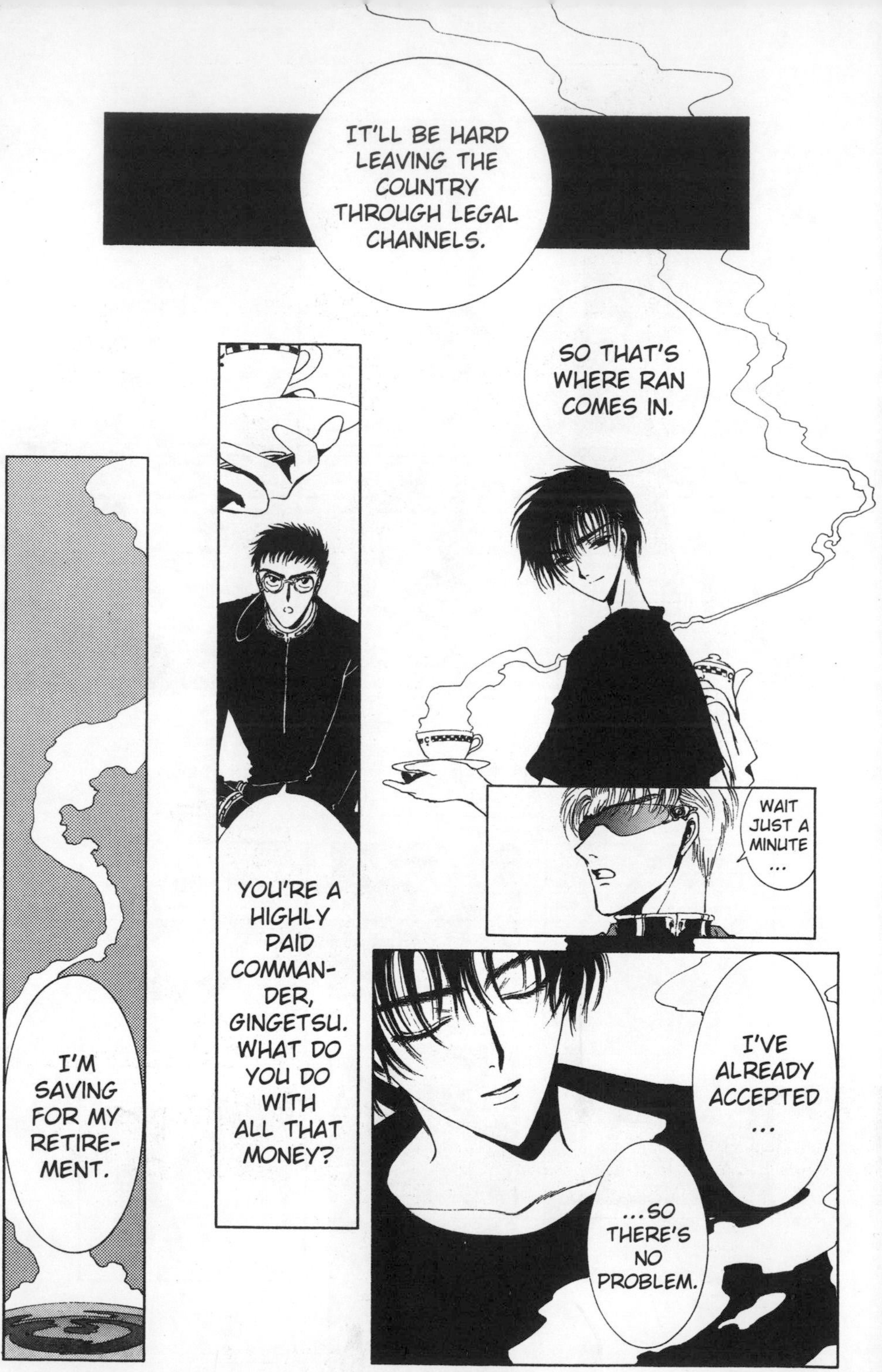
IT'LL BE HARD LEAVING THE COUNTRY THROUGH LEGAL CHANNELS.
SO THAT'S WHERE RAN COMES IN.
WAIT JUST A MINUTE ...
I'VE ALREADY ACCEPTED ...
...SO THERE'S NO PROBLEM.
YOU'RE A HIGHLY PAID COMMANDER, GINGETSU. WHAT DO YOU DO WITH ALL THAT MONEY?
I'M SAVING FOR MY RETIREMENT.

YES.

DO YOU WANT TO LISTEN TO THE SONG AGAIN?

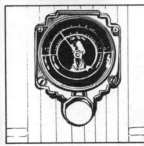

click

Take me away

An unbreakable spell A never-ending kiss An endless dream Eternal happiness

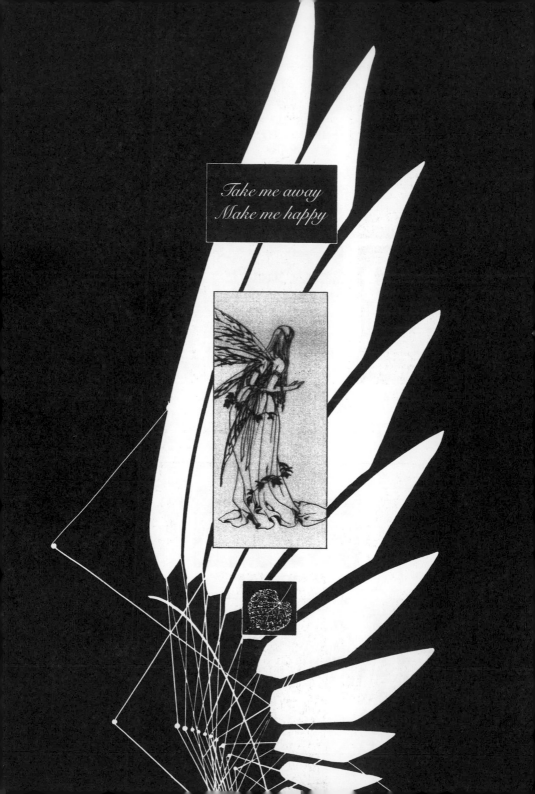

Take me away
Make me happy

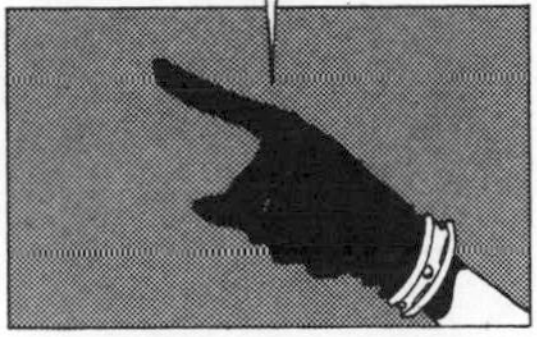
WE'RE GOING TO FAIRY PARK.
THAT PLACE? IT'S RUN DOWN.

『鳥籠』
とり かご

BIRDCAGE

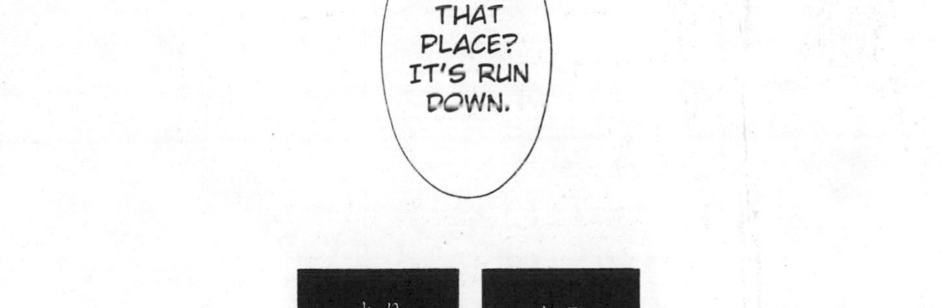
RAN HERE ...
... MODIFIED THIS TELE-PORTER.

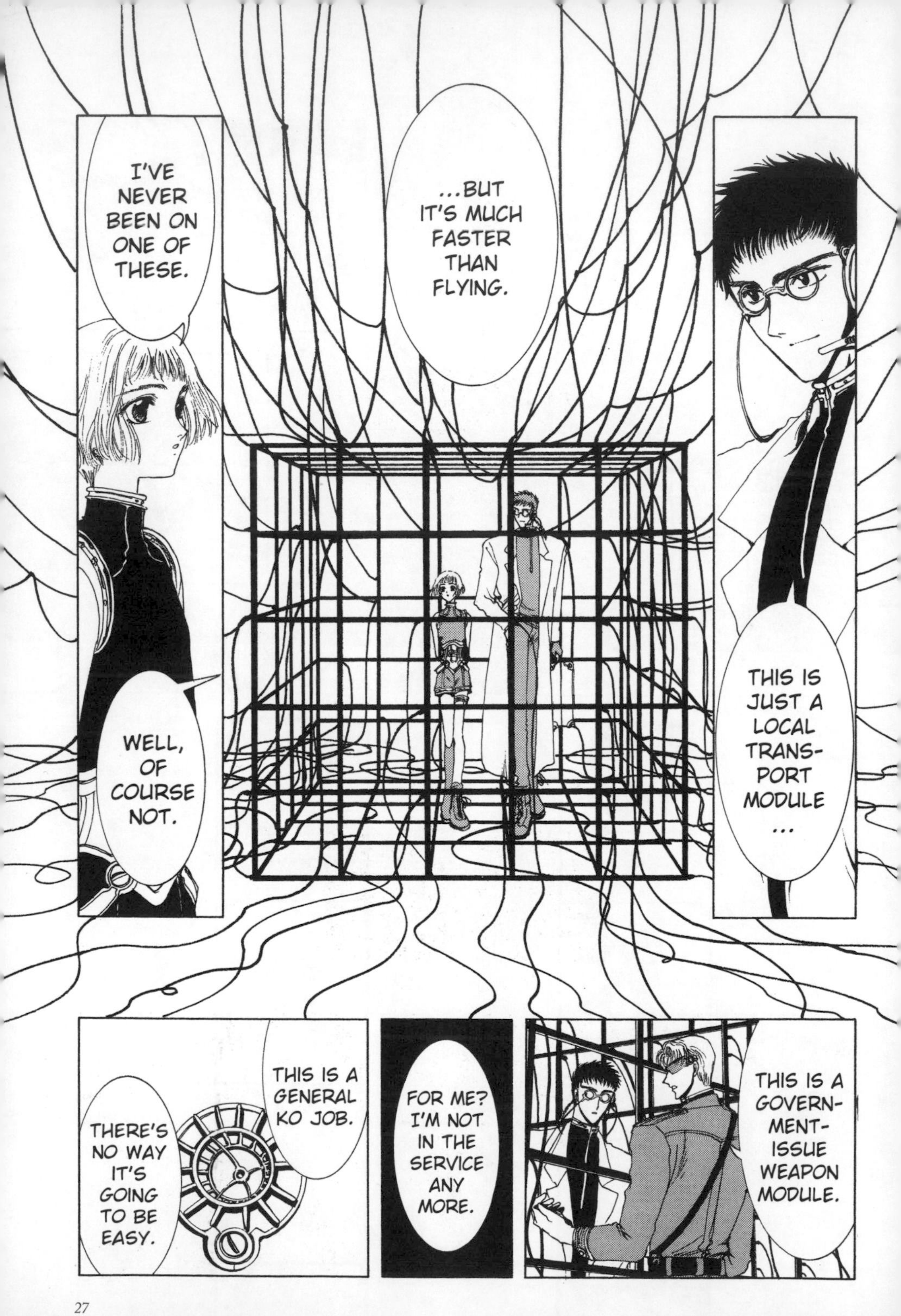
THIS IS JUST A LOCAL TRANS-PORT MODULE ...
...BUT IT'S MUCH FASTER THAN FLYING.
I'VE NEVER BEEN ON ONE OF THESE.
WELL, OF COURSE NOT.
THIS IS A GOVERN-MENT-ISSUE WEAPON MODULE.
FOR ME? I'M NOT IN THE SERVICE ANY MORE.
THIS IS A GENERAL KO JOB.
THERE'S NO WAY IT'S GOING TO BE EASY.

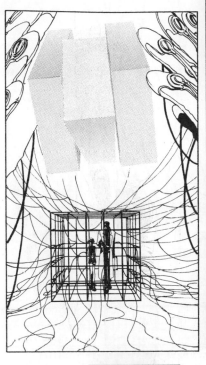

CAN I *HOPE* IT'S EASY? THE LAST JOB, I LOST MY RIGHT HAND.

...THANKS, THOUGH.

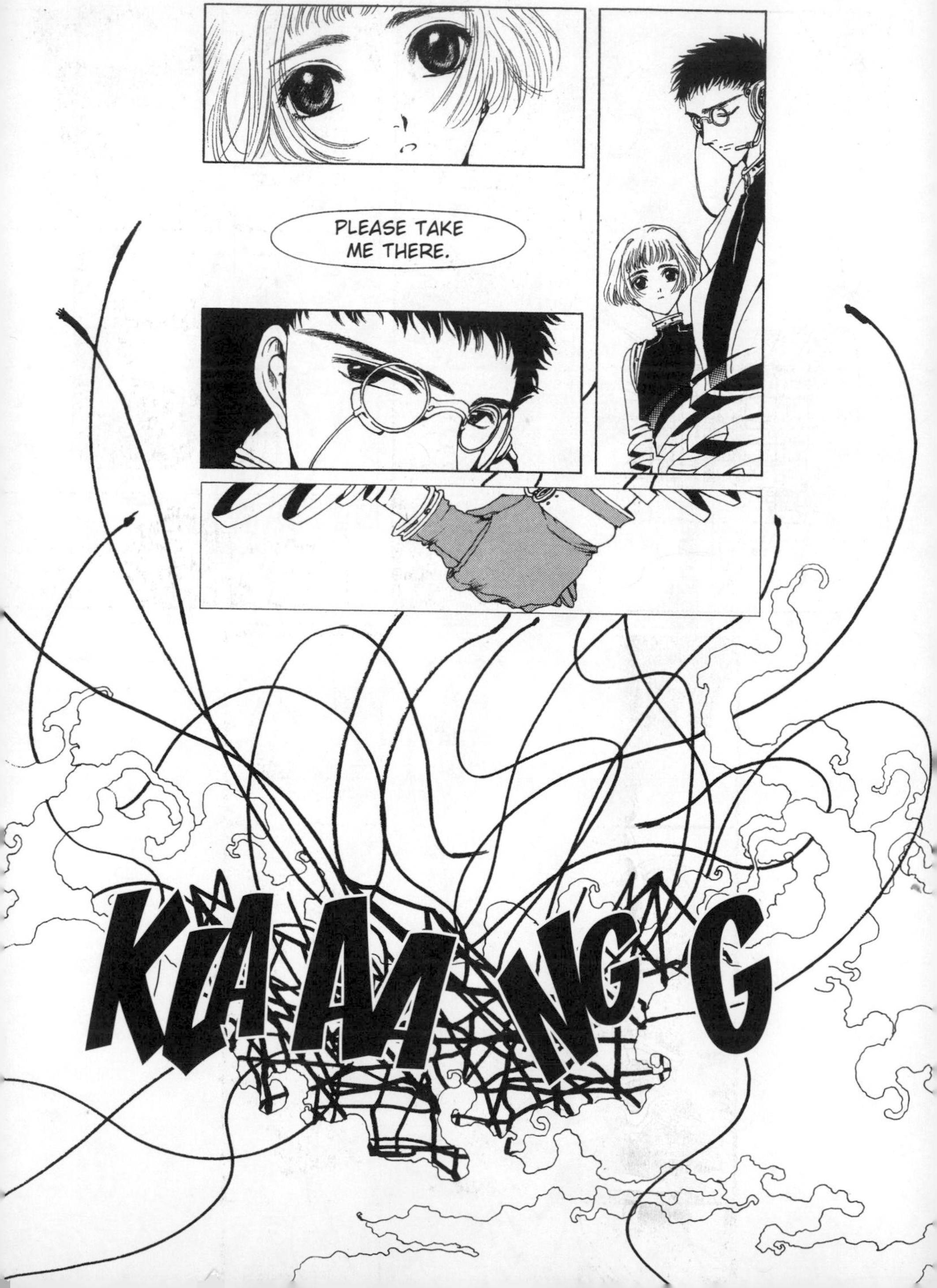
PLEASE TAKE ME THERE.
KLAAANG-G

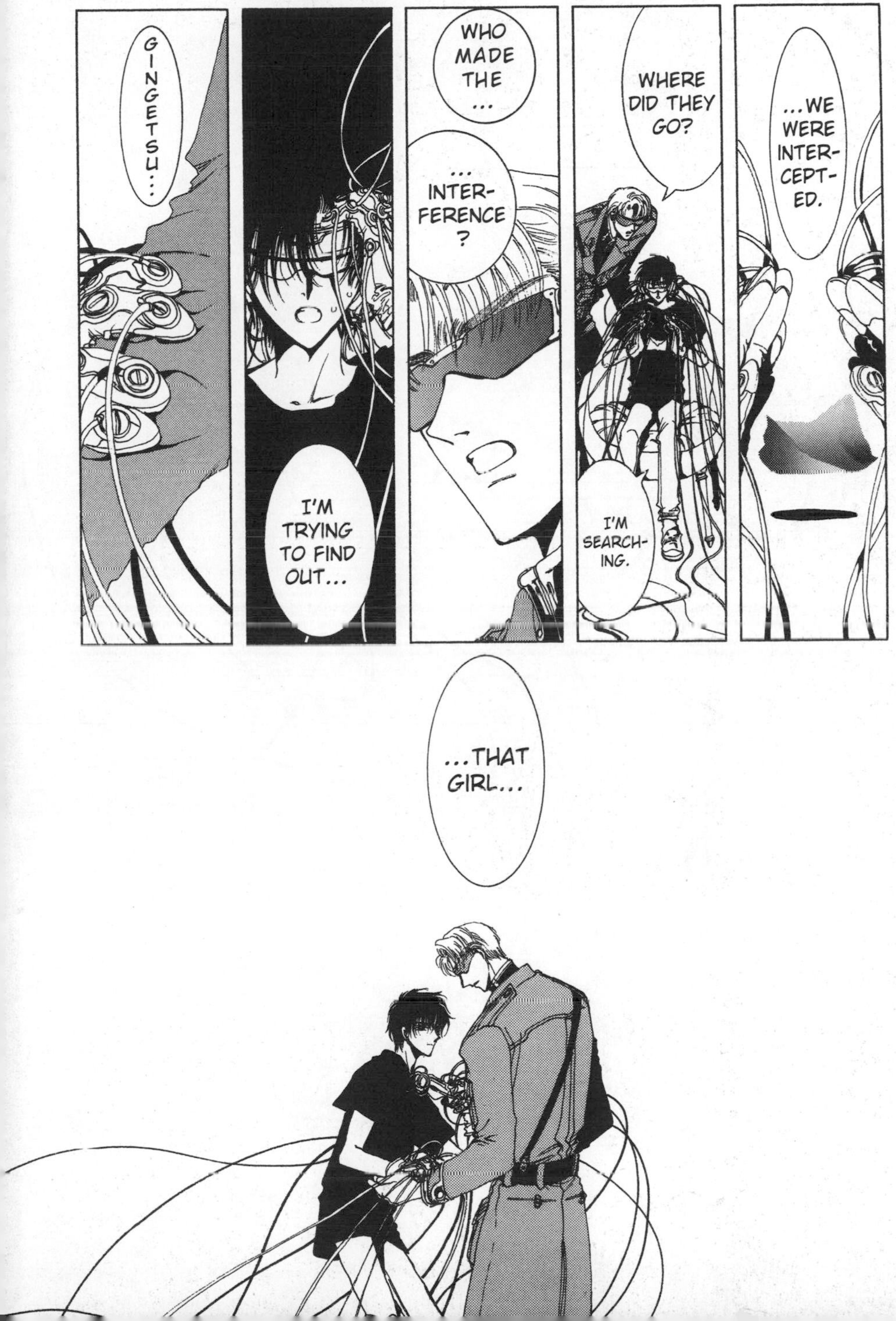
...WE WERE INTERCEPT-ED.
WHERE DID THEY GO?
I'M SEARCH-ING.
WHO MADE THE ...
... INTERFERENCE ?
I'M TRYING TO FIND OUT...
GINGETSU...
...THAT GIRL...

Take me
Somewhere
far from
here

A green
leaf?

Take me
away

An unbreakable spell
A never-ending kiss
An endless dream
Eternal happiness

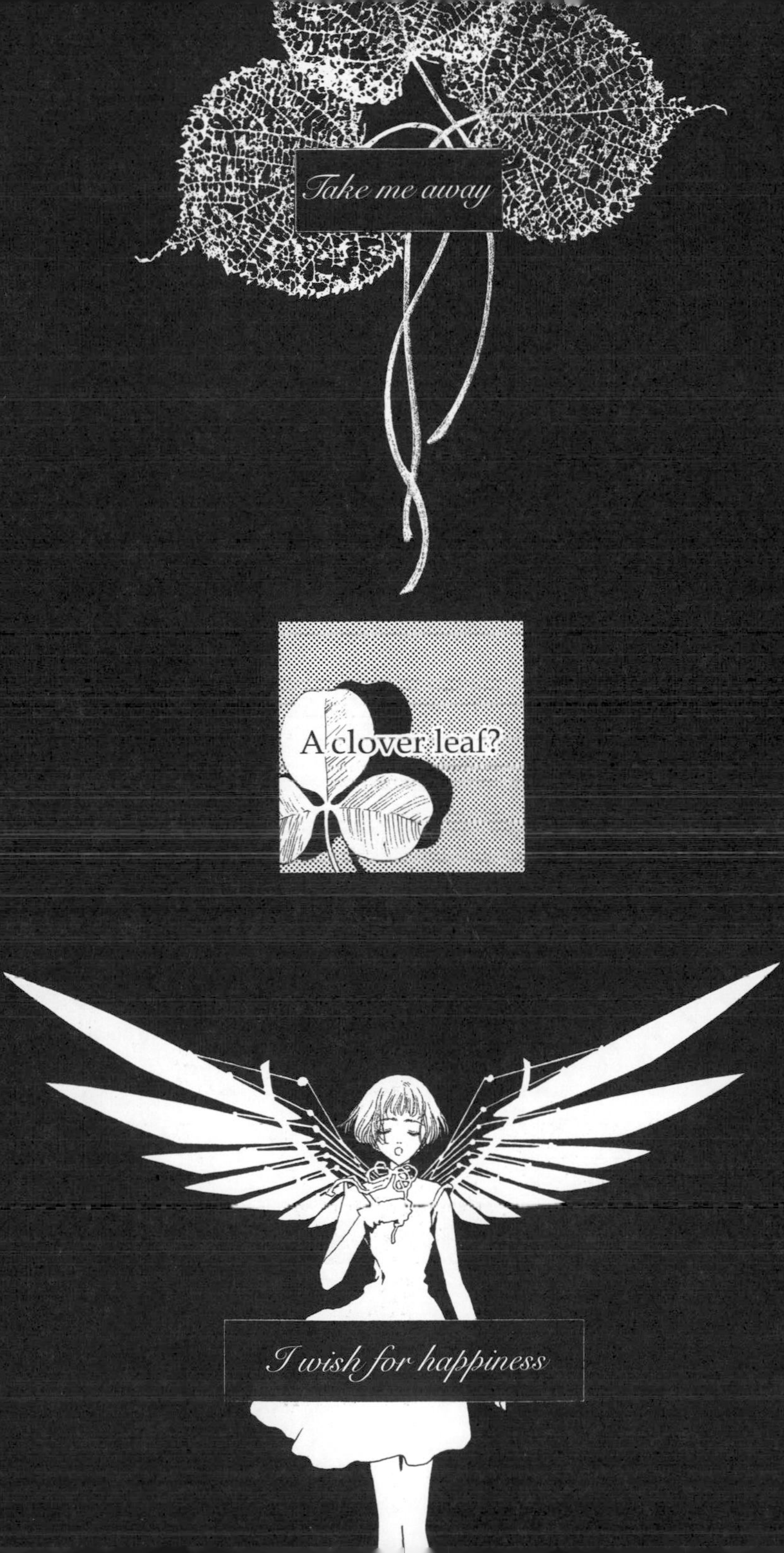
Take me away
A clover leaf?
I wish for happiness

A MAZE

『迷

IS THIS IT?

路』

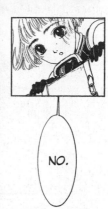

NO.

DON'T MOVE.

PEFANG

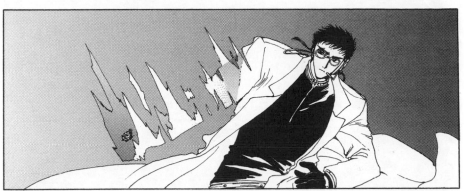

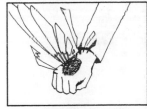

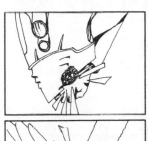

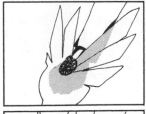

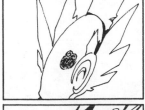

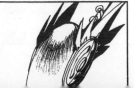

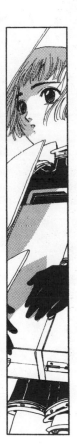

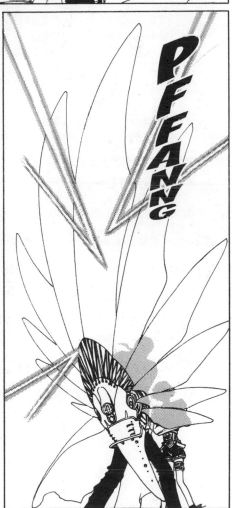

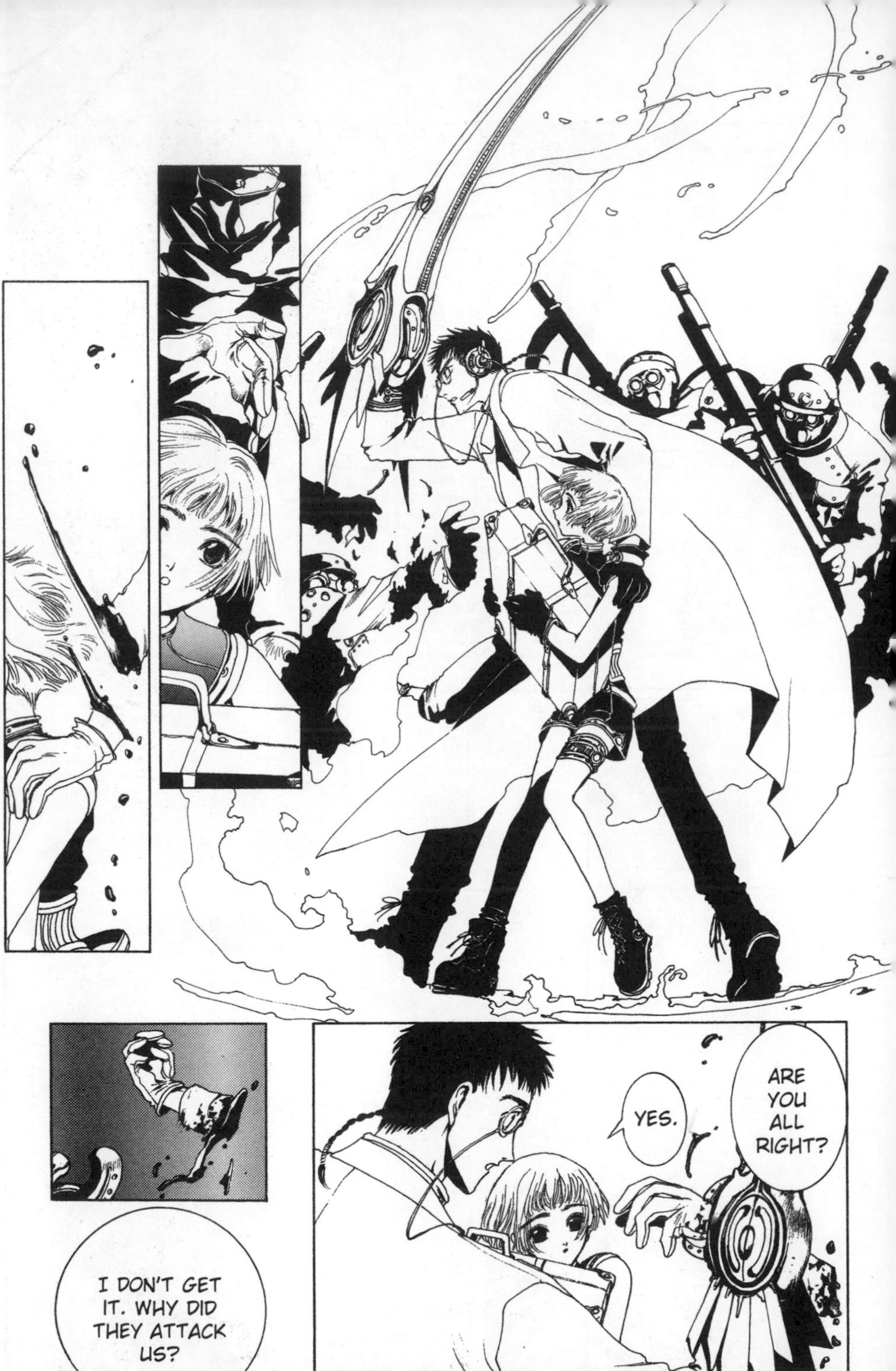
ARE YOU ALL RIGHT?
YES.
I DON'T GET IT. WHY DID THEY ATTACK US?

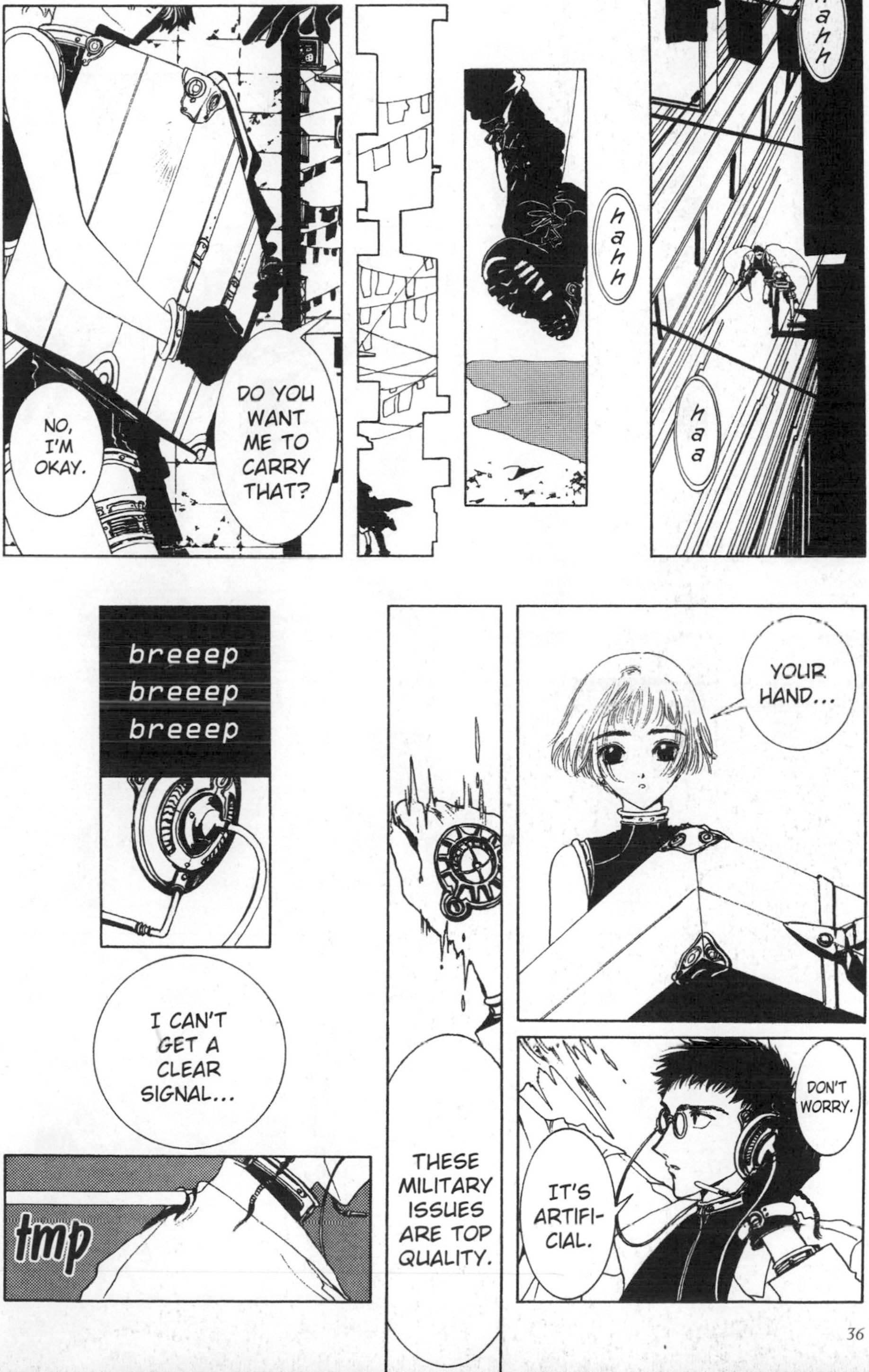
hahh
haa
hahh
DO YOU WANT ME TO CARRY THAT?
NO, I'M OKAY.
YOUR HAND...
DON'T WORRY.
IT'S ARTIFICIAL.
THESE MILITARY ISSUES ARE TOP QUALITY.
breeep
breeep
breeep
I CAN'T GET A CLEAR SIGNAL...
tmp

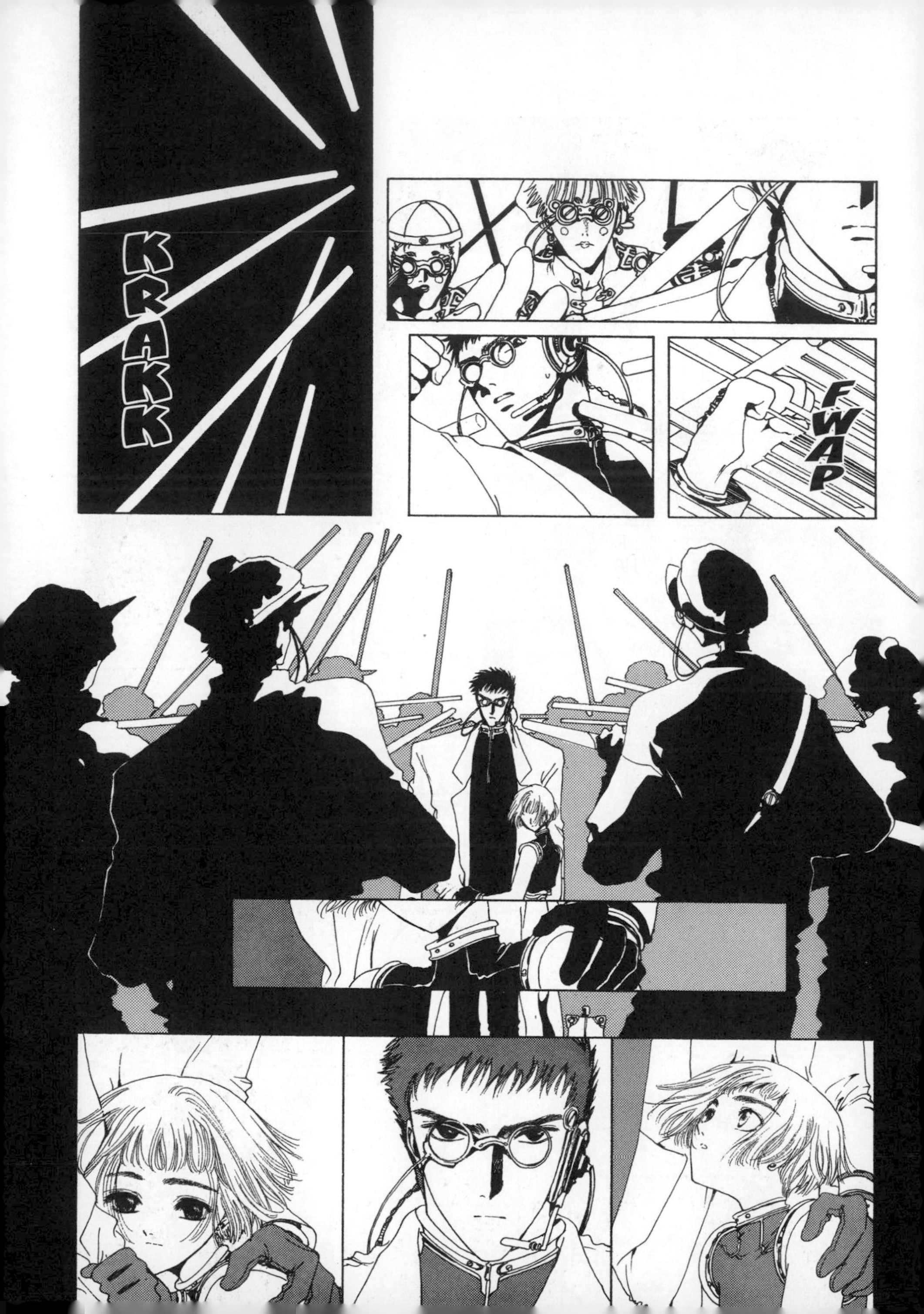
FWAP
KRAKK

THE CAT

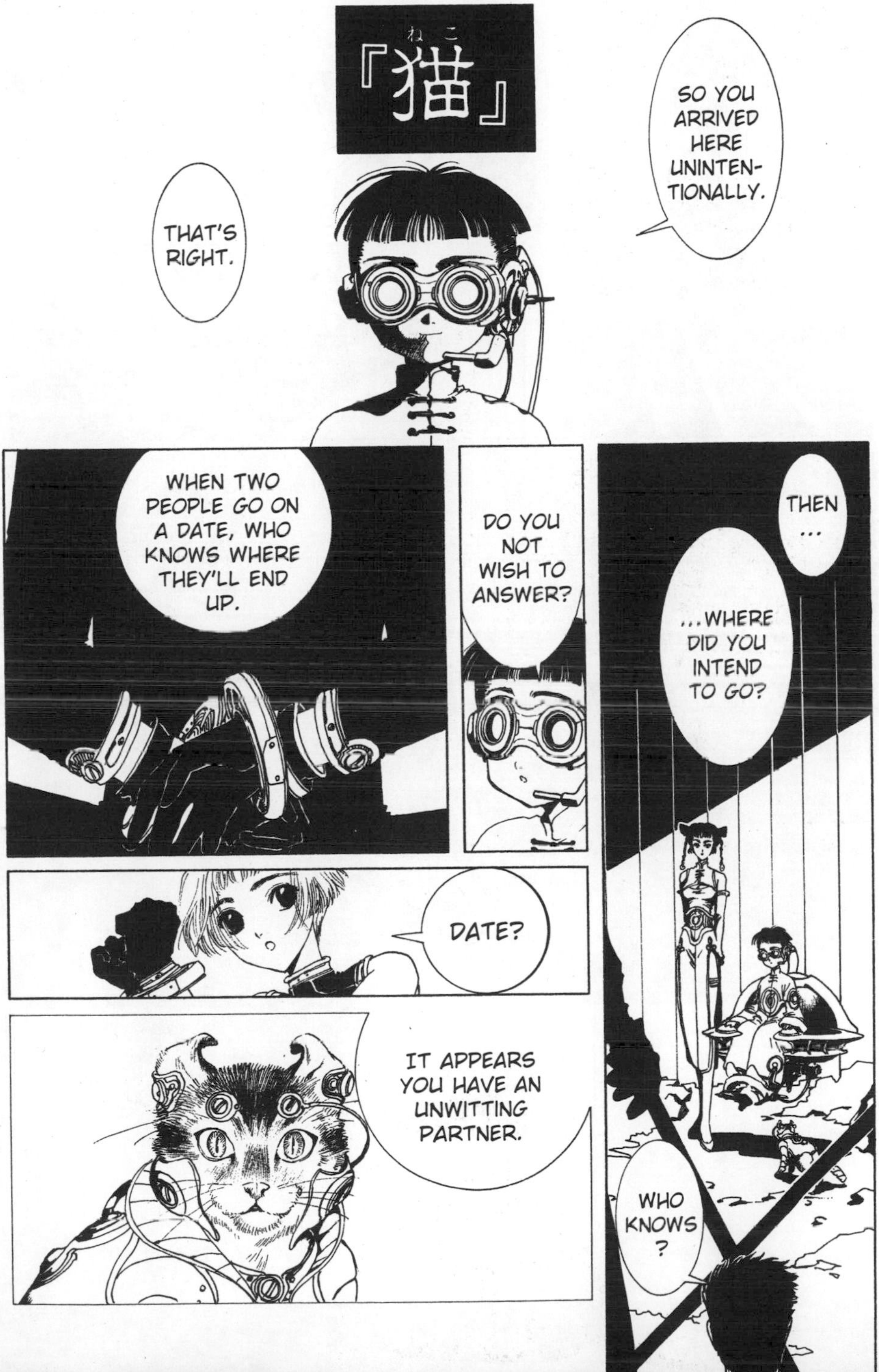
『猫』
SO YOU ARRIVED HERE UNINTENTIONALLY.
THAT'S RIGHT.
THEN ...
...WHERE DID YOU INTEND TO GO?
WHO KNOWS?
DO YOU NOT WISH TO ANSWER?
WHEN TWO PEOPLE GO ON A DATE, WHO KNOWS WHERE THEY'LL END UP.
DATE?
IT APPEARS YOU HAVE AN UNWITTING PARTNER.

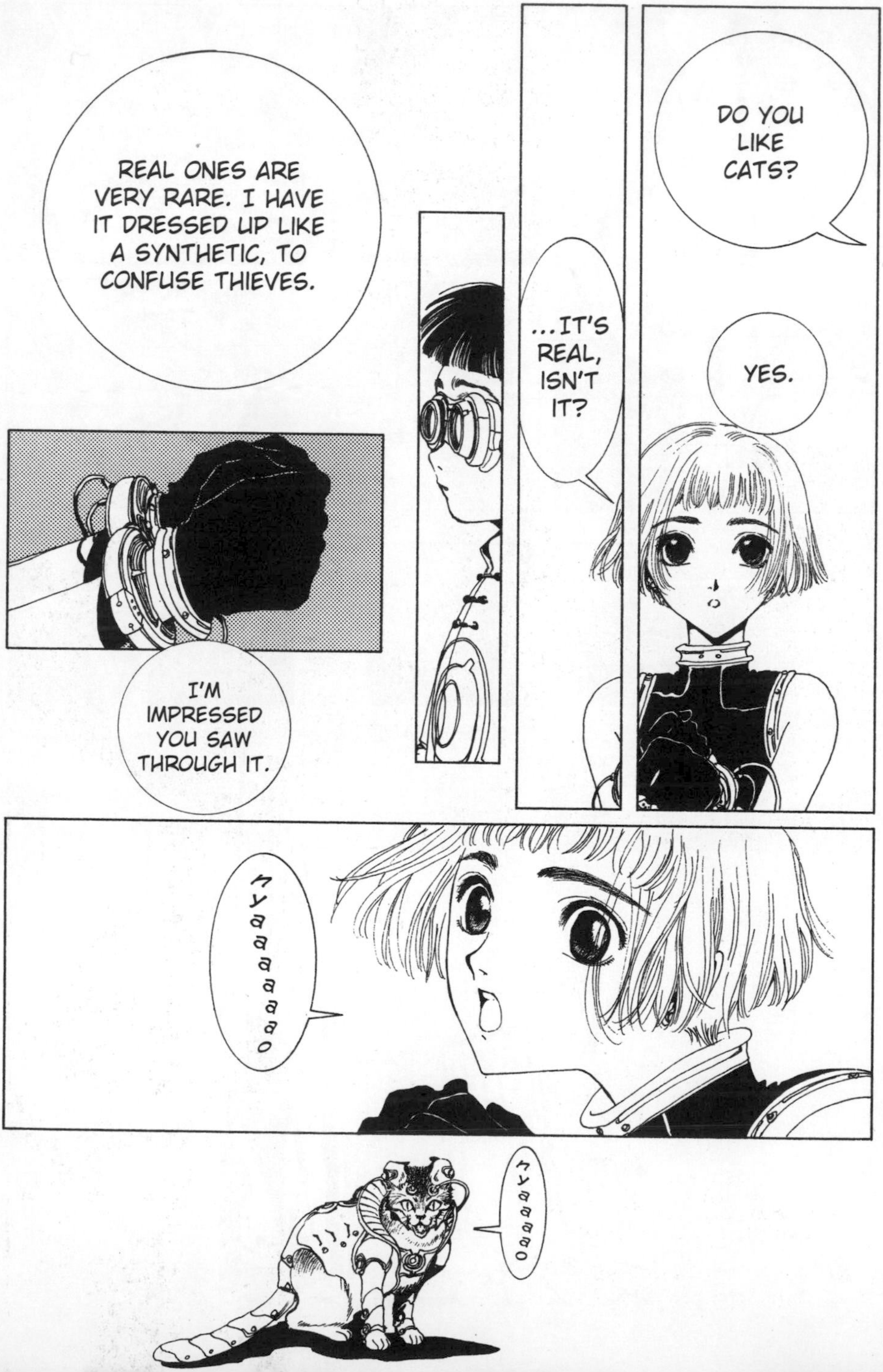
DO YOU LIKE CATS?
YES.
...IT'S REAL, ISN'T IT?
REAL ONES ARE VERY RARE. I HAVE IT DRESSED UP LIKE A SYNTHETIC, TO CONFUSE THIEVES.
I'M IMPRESSED YOU SAW THROUGH IT.
nyaaaaaao
nyaaaao

YOU WILL BE OUR GUESTS WHILE WE INVESTIGATE FURTHER.

AH, WE'RE IN KIND OF A HURRY--

TAO FA...
...PLEASE SHOW OUR GUESTS THEIR ROOMS.

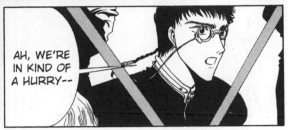

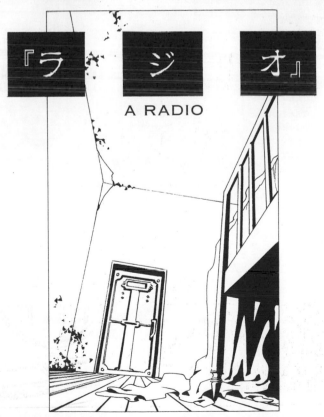

『ラジオ』
A RADIO

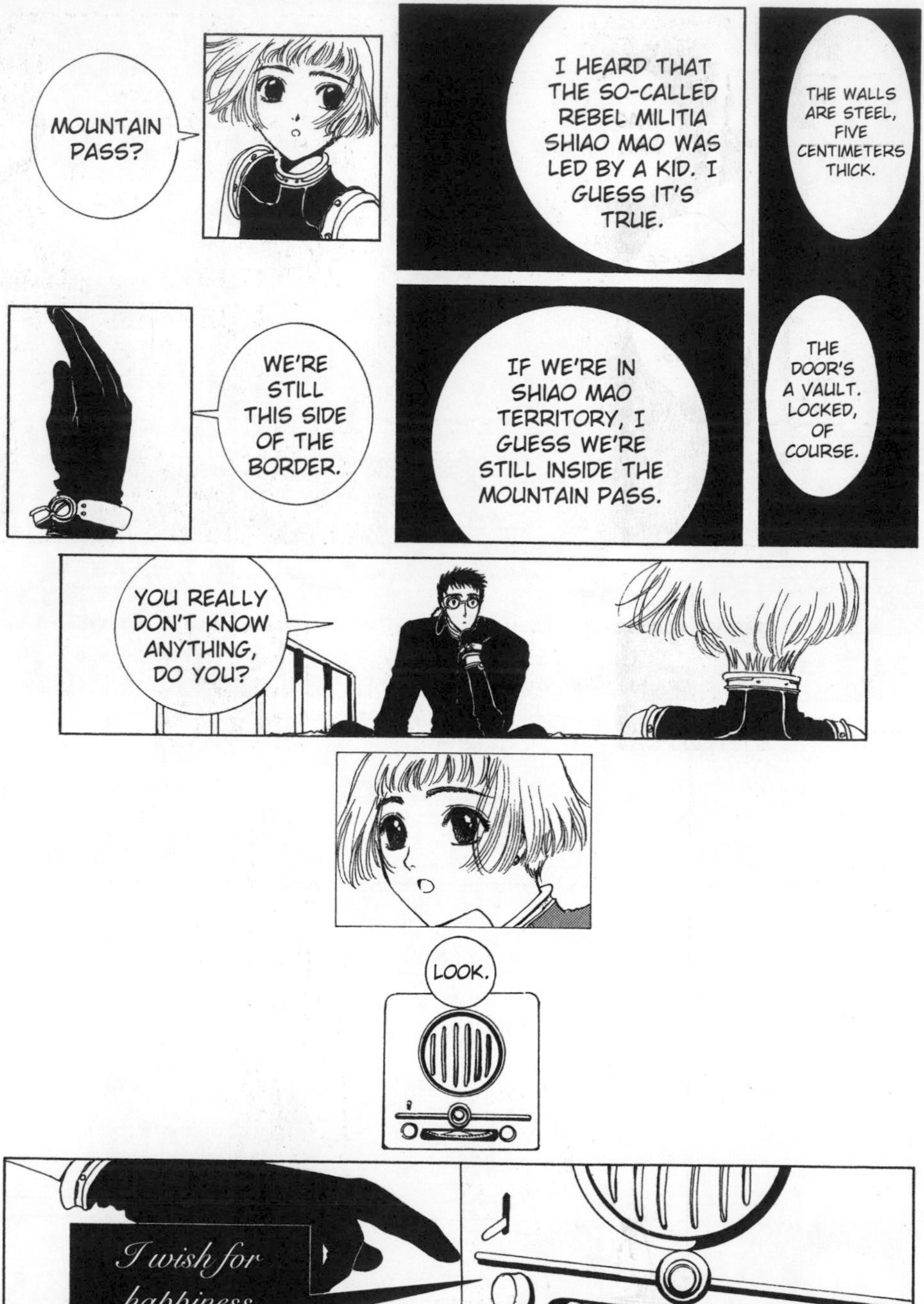
THE WALLS ARE STEEL, FIVE CENTIMETERS THICK.
THE DOOR'S A VAULT. LOCKED, OF COURSE.
I HEARD THAT THE SO-CALLED REBEL MILITIA SHIAO MAO WAS LED BY A KID. I GUESS IT'S TRUE.
IF WE'RE IN SHIAO MAO TERRITORY, I GUESS WE'RE STILL INSIDE THE MOUNTAIN PASS.
MOUNTAIN PASS?
WE'RE STILL THIS SIDE OF THE BORDER.
YOU REALLY DON'T KNOW ANYTHING, DO YOU?
LOOK.
I wish for happiness

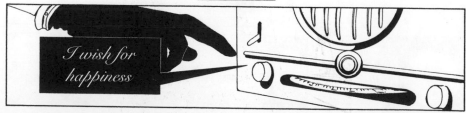

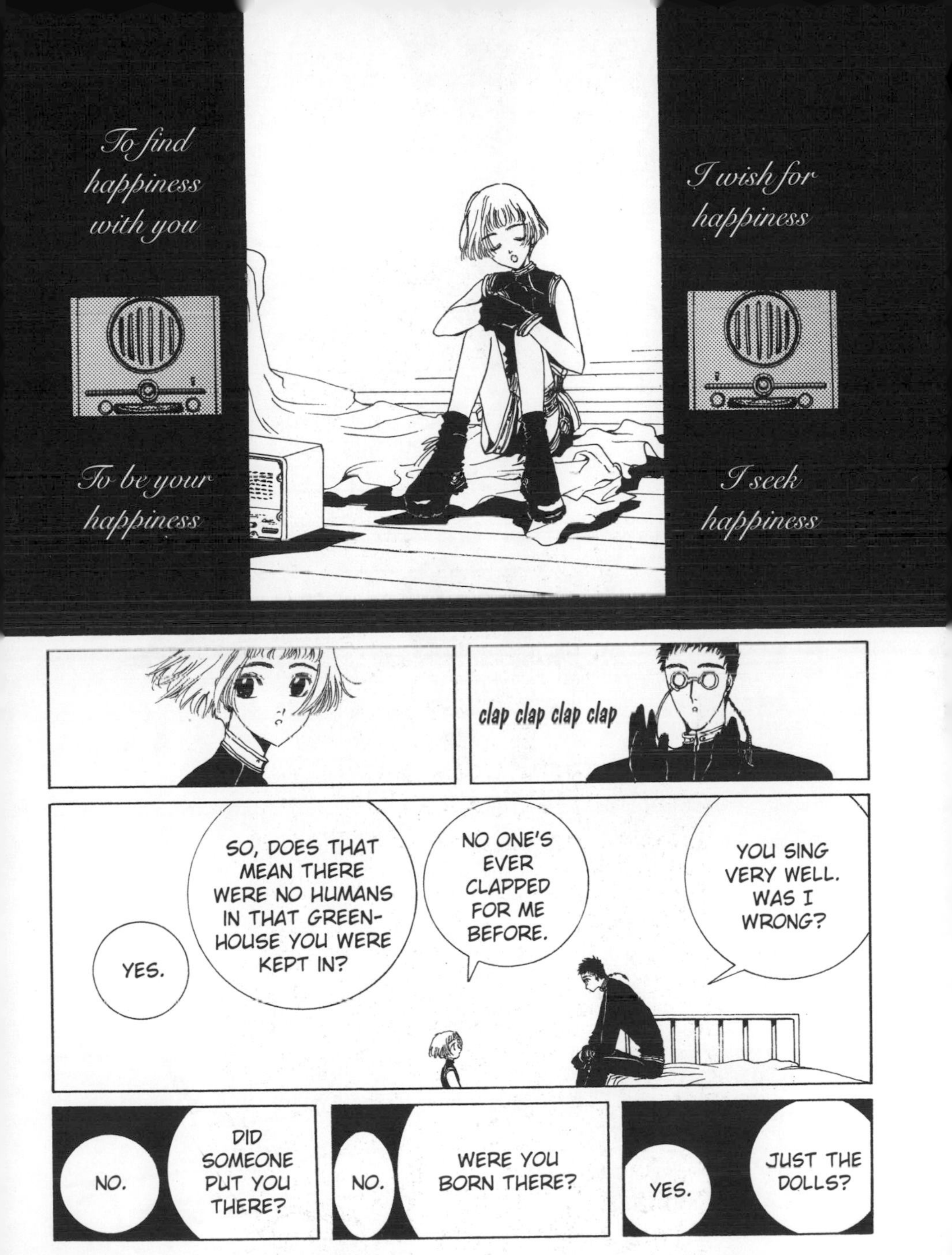
I wish for happiness
I seek happiness
To find happiness with you
To be your happiness
clap clap clap clap
YOU SING VERY WELL. WAS I WRONG?
NO ONE'S EVER CLAPPED FOR ME BEFORE.
SO, DOES THAT MEAN THERE WERE NO HUMANS IN THAT GREEN-HOUSE YOU WERE KEPT IN?
YES.
JUST THE DOLLS?
YES.
WERE YOU BORN THERE?
NO.
DID SOMEONE PUT YOU THERE?
NO.

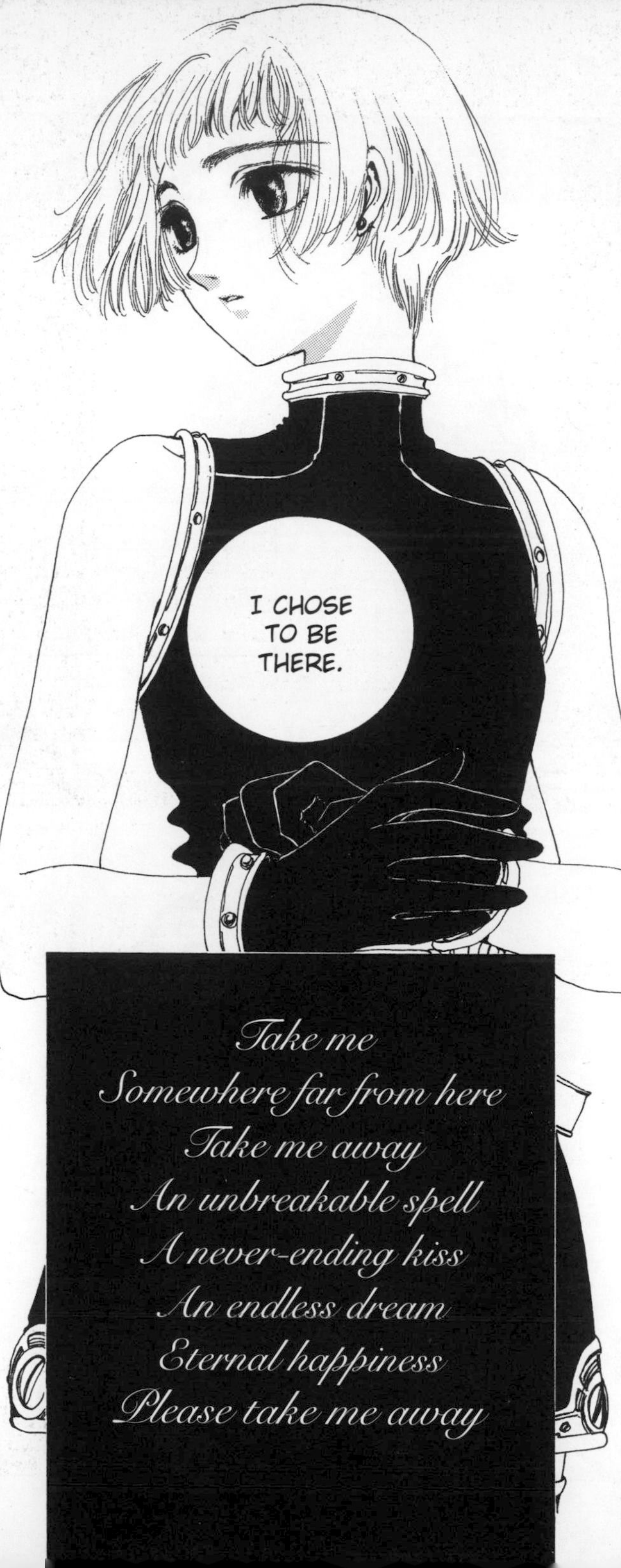
I CHOSE TO BE THERE.
Take me
Somewhere far from here
Take me away
An unbreakable spell
A never-ending kiss
An endless dream
Eternal happiness
Please take me away

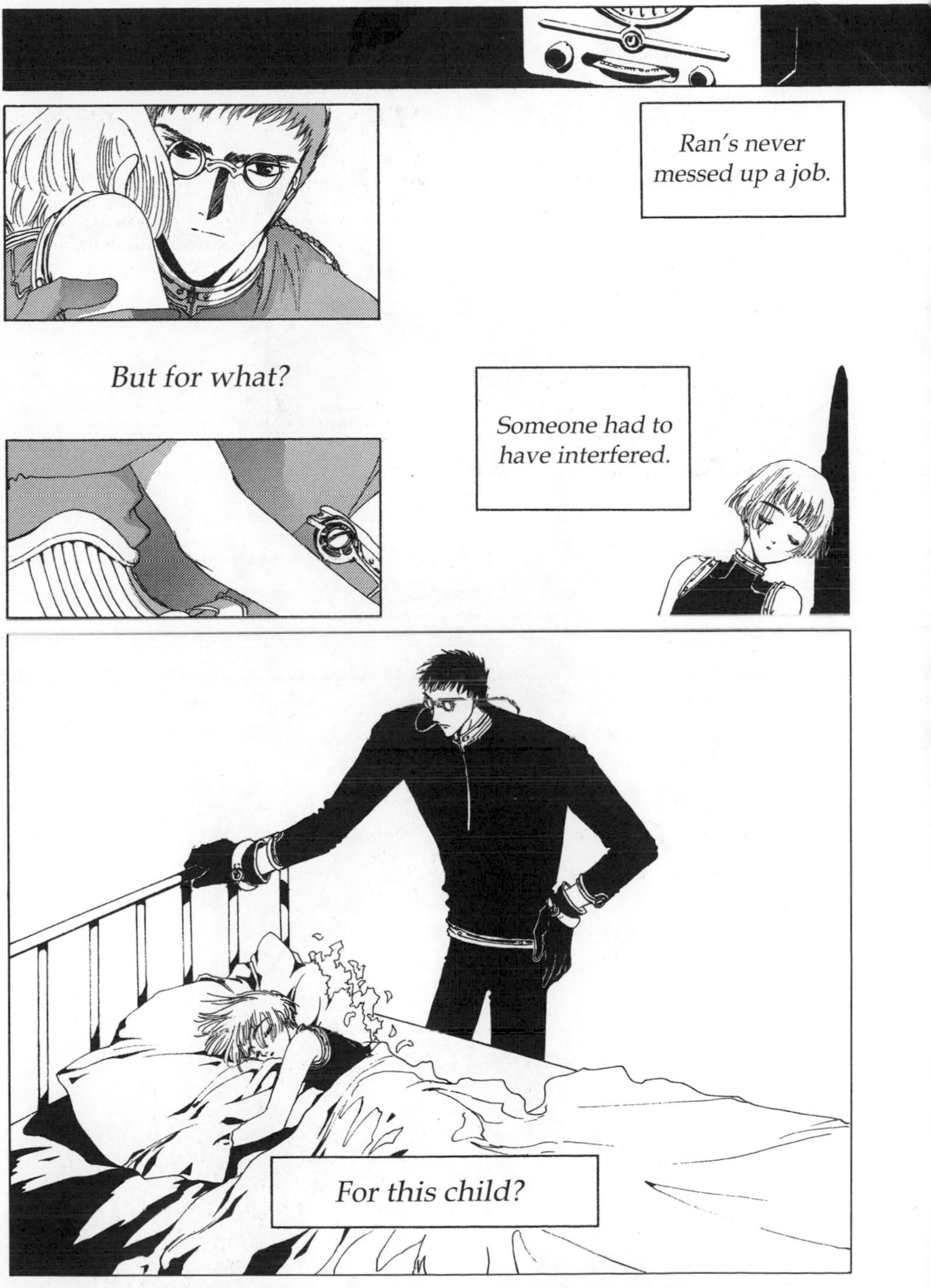
Ran's never messed up a job.
Someone had to have interfered.
But for what?
For this child?

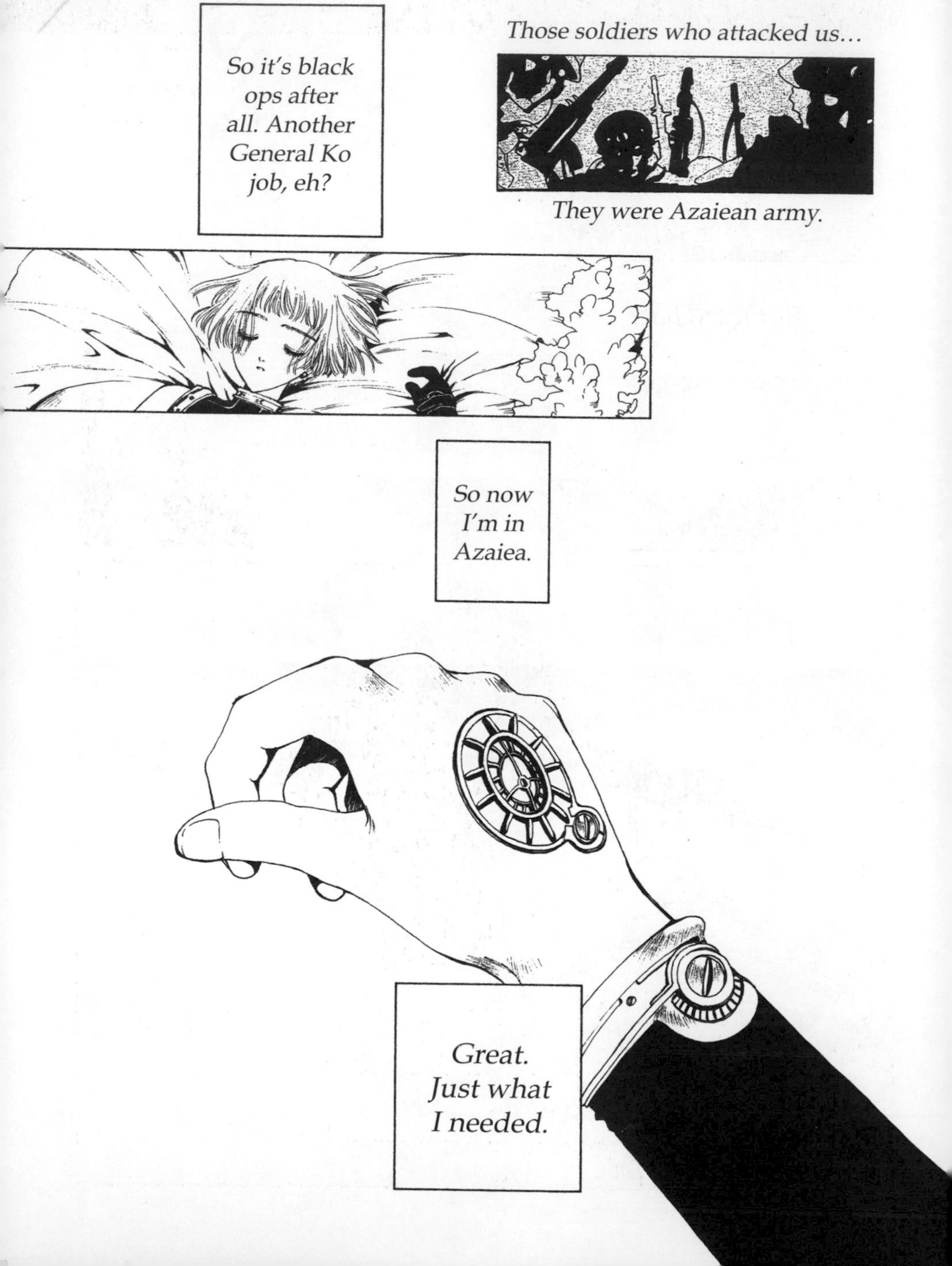
Those soldiers who attacked us…
They were Azaiean army.
So it's black ops after all. Another General Ko job, eh?
So now I'm in Azaiea.
Great. Just what I needed.

A TRACE

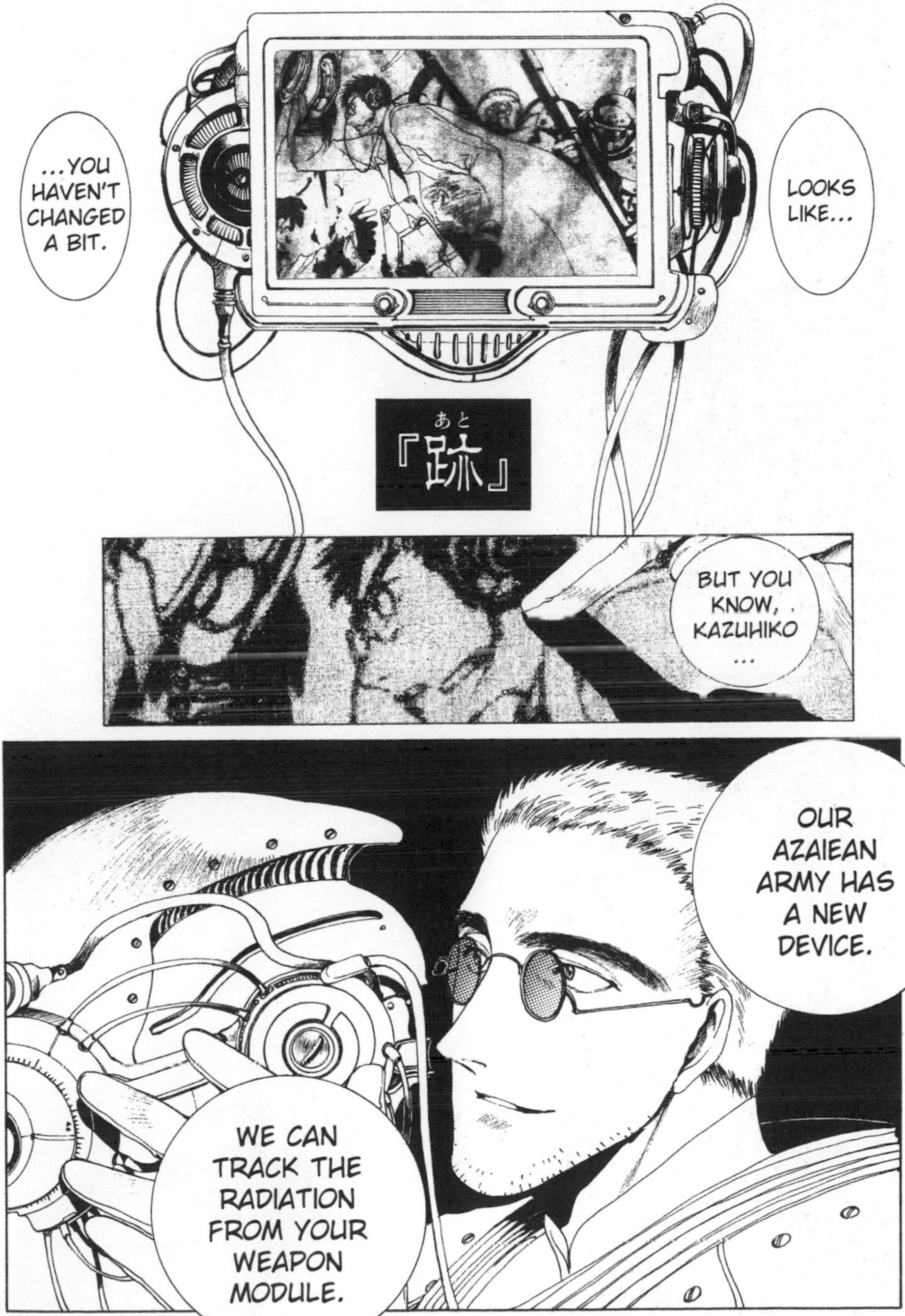
LOOKS LIKE...
...YOU HAVEN'T CHANGED A BIT.
『跡』(あと)
BUT YOU KNOW, KAZUHIKO ...
OUR AZAIEAN ARMY HAS A NEW DEVICE.
WE CAN TRACK THE RADIATION FROM YOUR WEAPON MODULE.

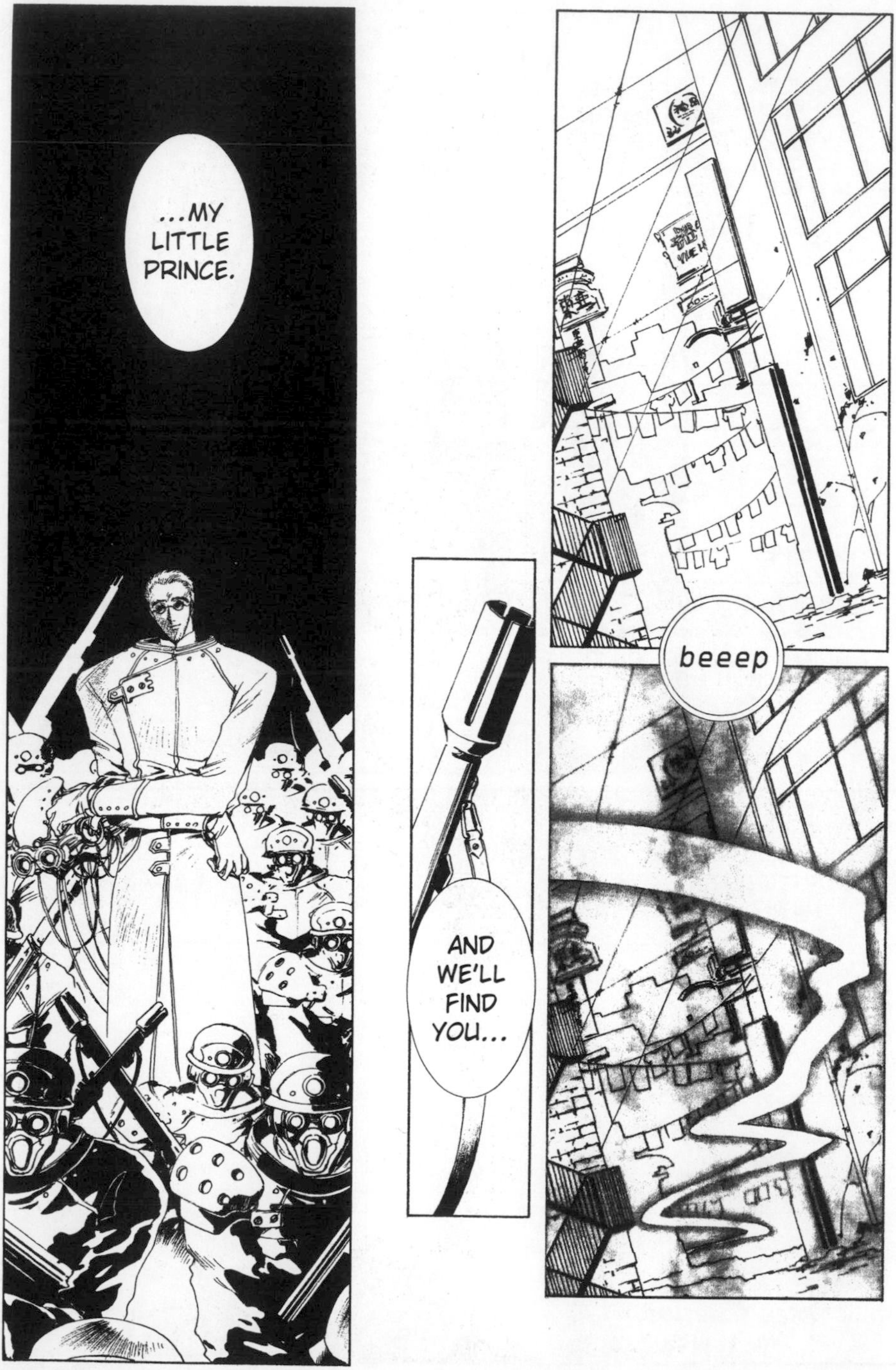
beeep
AND WE'LL FIND YOU...
...MY LITTLE PRINCE.

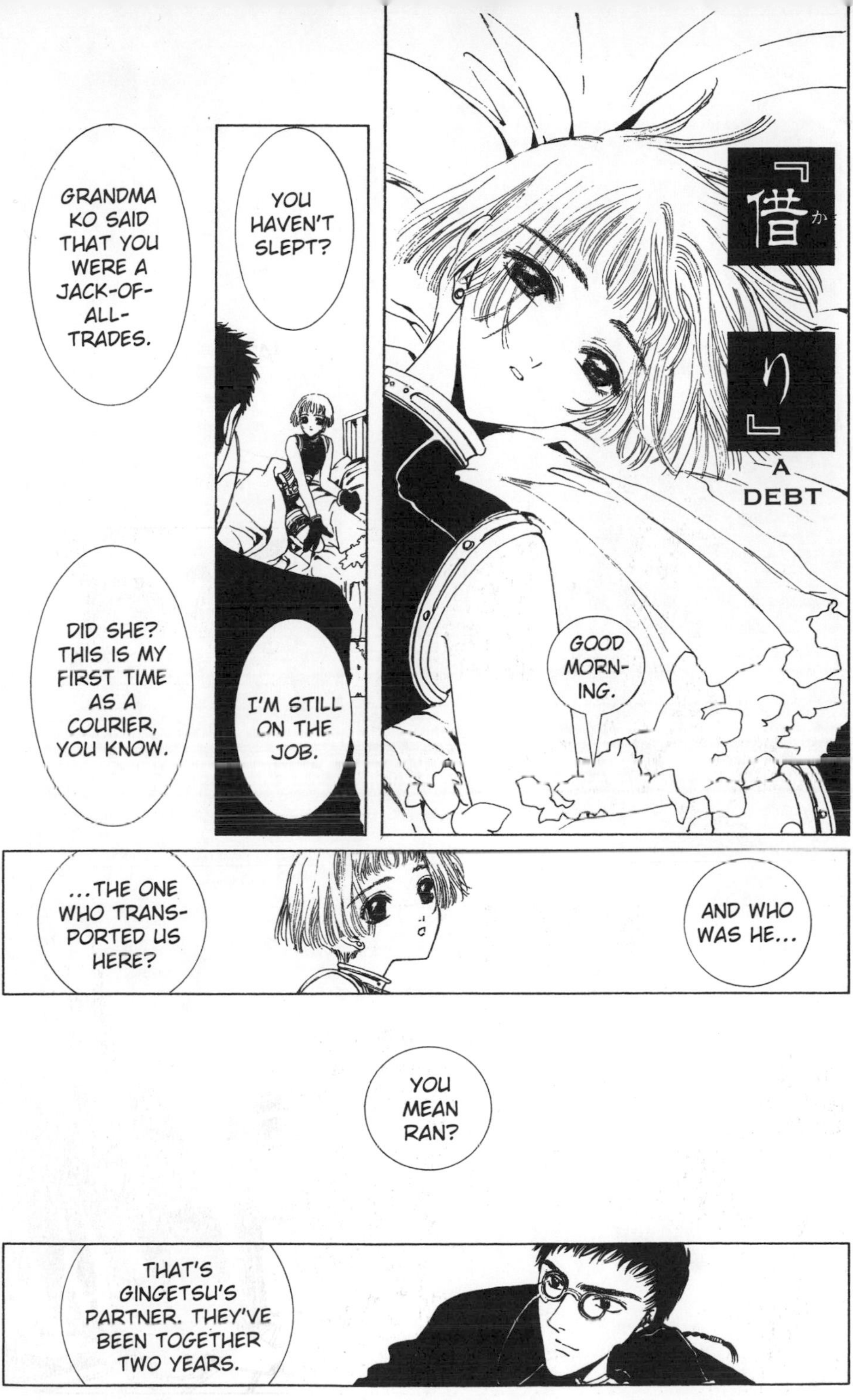
『借り』
A DEBT
GOOD MORNING.
YOU HAVEN'T SLEPT?
I'M STILL ON THE JOB.
GRANDMA KO SAID THAT YOU WERE A JACK-OF-ALL-TRADES.
DID SHE? THIS IS MY FIRST TIME AS A COURIER, YOU KNOW.
AND WHO WAS HE...
...THE ONE WHO TRANSPORTED US HERE?
YOU MEAN RAN?
THAT'S GINGETSU'S PARTNER. THEY'VE BEEN TOGETHER TWO YEARS.

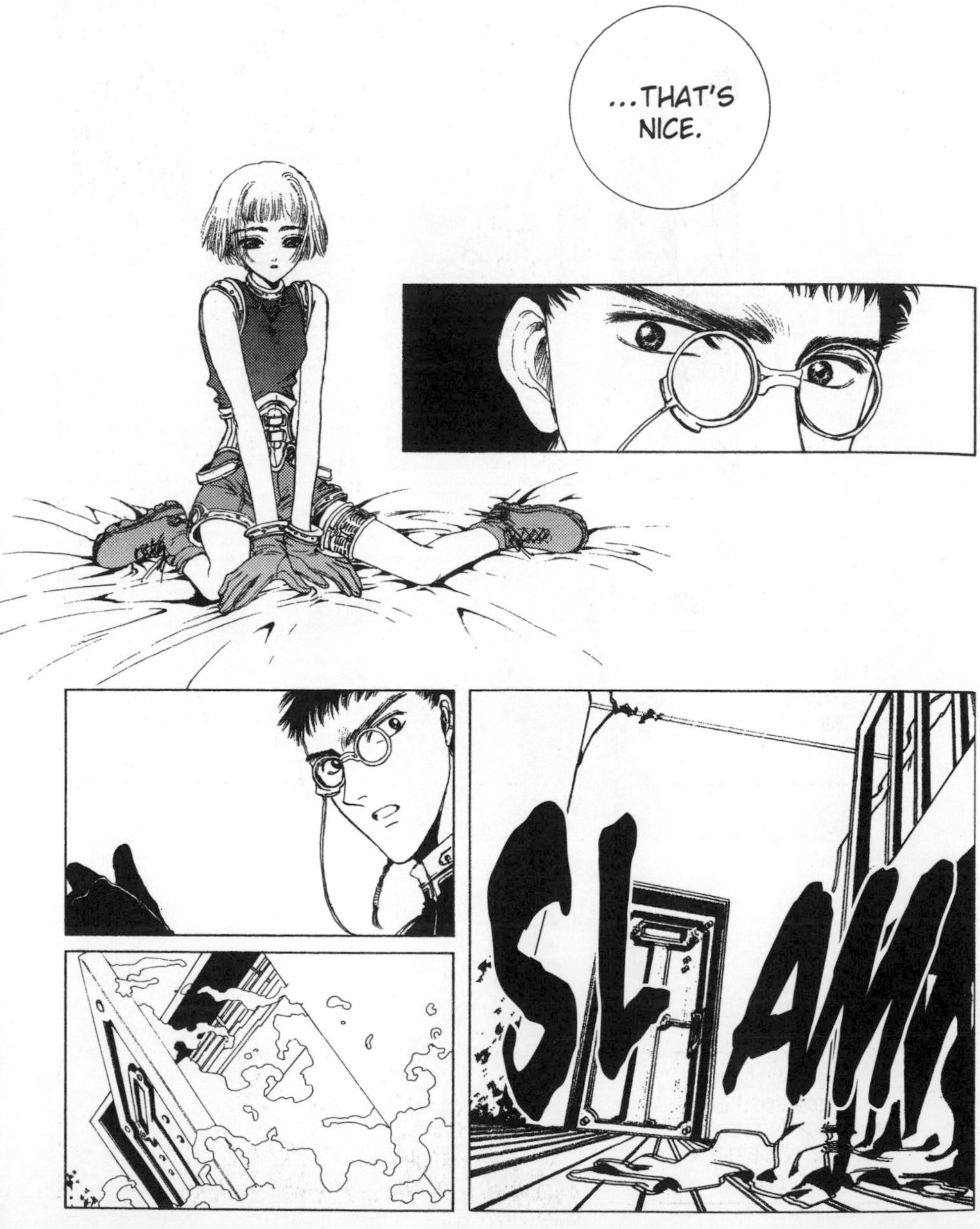
...THAT'S NICE.
SLAM

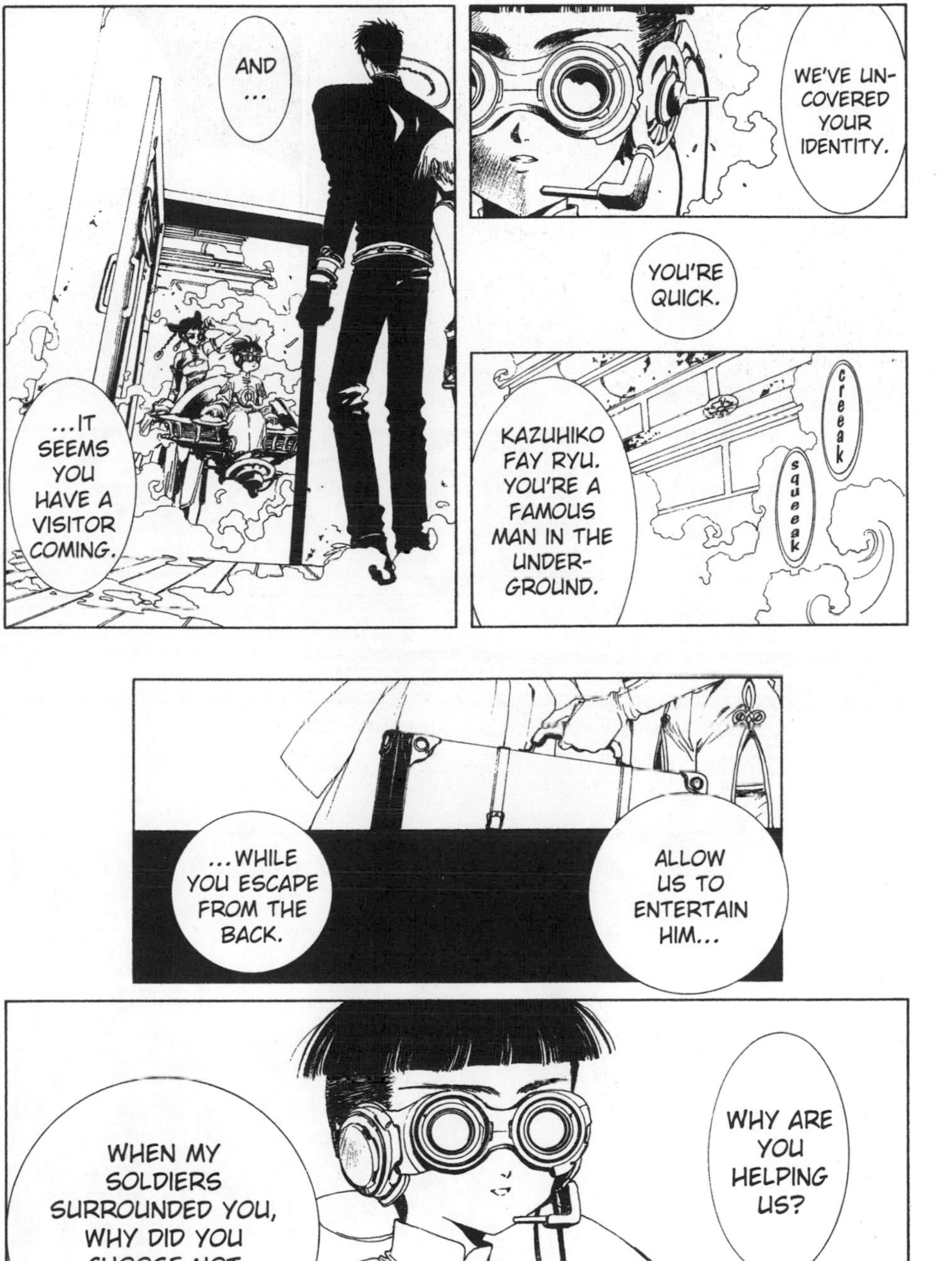
WE'VE UN-COVERED YOUR IDENTITY.
YOU'RE QUICK.
creeak
squeeeak
KAZUHIKO FAY RYU. YOU'RE A FAMOUS MAN IN THE UNDER-GROUND.
AND ...
...IT SEEMS YOU HAVE A VISITOR COMING.
ALLOW US TO ENTERTAIN HIM...
...WHILE YOU ESCAPE FROM THE BACK.
WHY ARE YOU HELPING US?
WHEN MY SOLDIERS SURROUNDED YOU, WHY DID YOU CHOOSE NOT TO FIGHT?

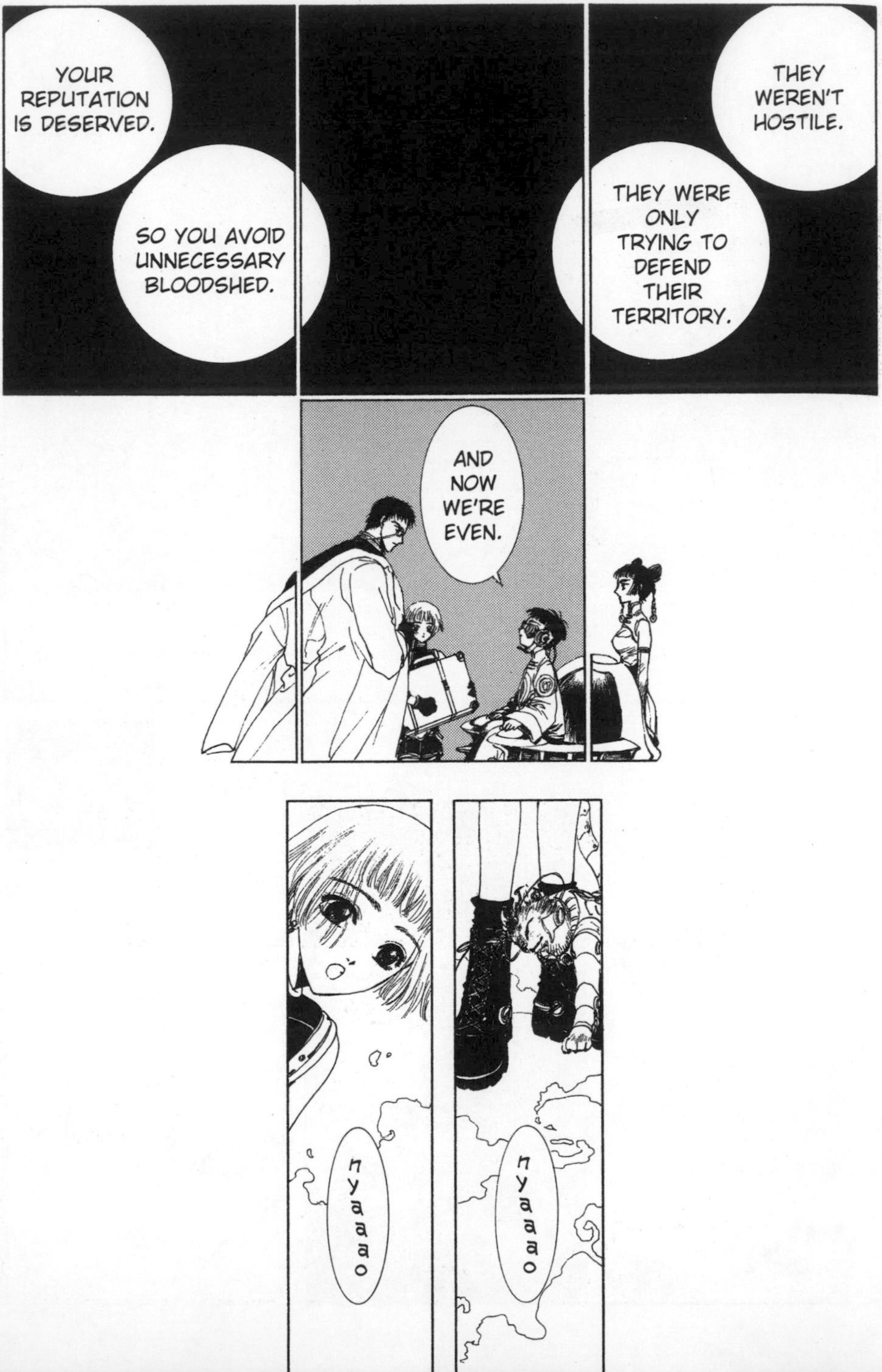
THEY WEREN'T HOSTILE.
THEY WERE ONLY TRYING TO DEFEND THEIR TERRITORY.
YOUR REPUTATION IS DESERVED.
SO YOU AVOID UNNECESSARY BLOODSHED.
AND NOW WE'RE EVEN.
nyaaao
nyaaao

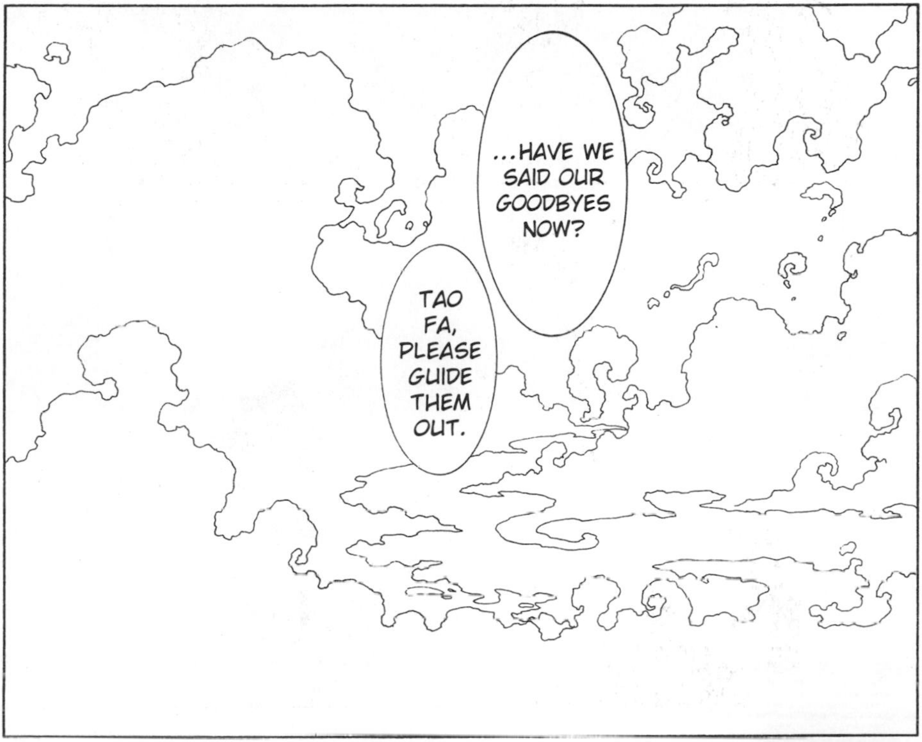
...HAVE WE SAID OUR GOODBYES NOW?
TAO FA, PLEASE GUIDE THEM OUT.

A FLOWER 『花』

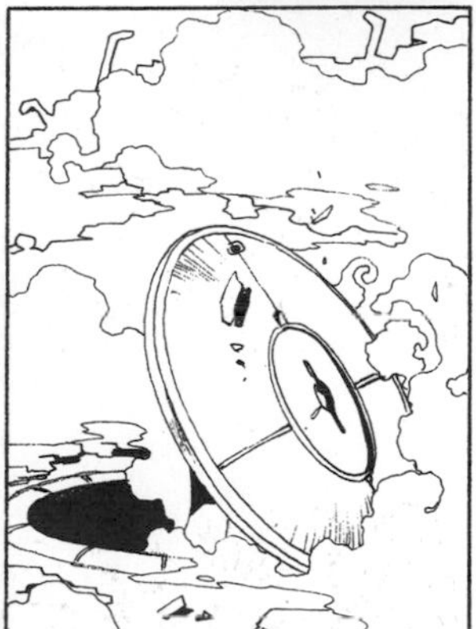
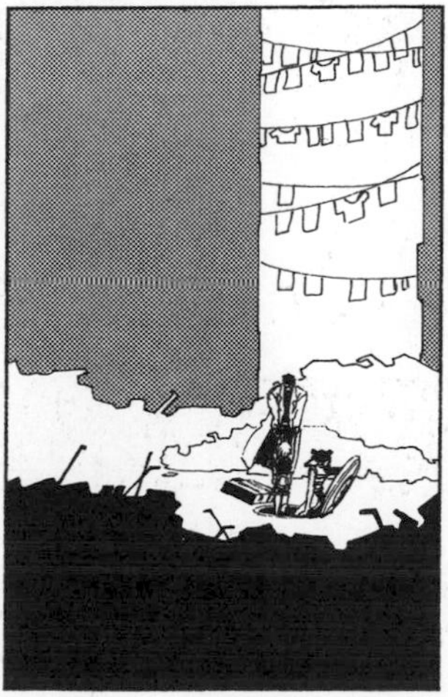
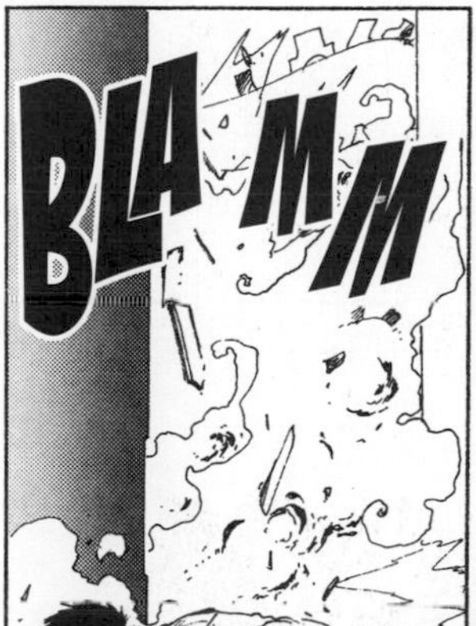
BLAMM

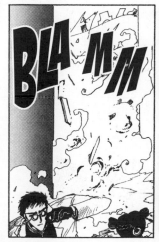

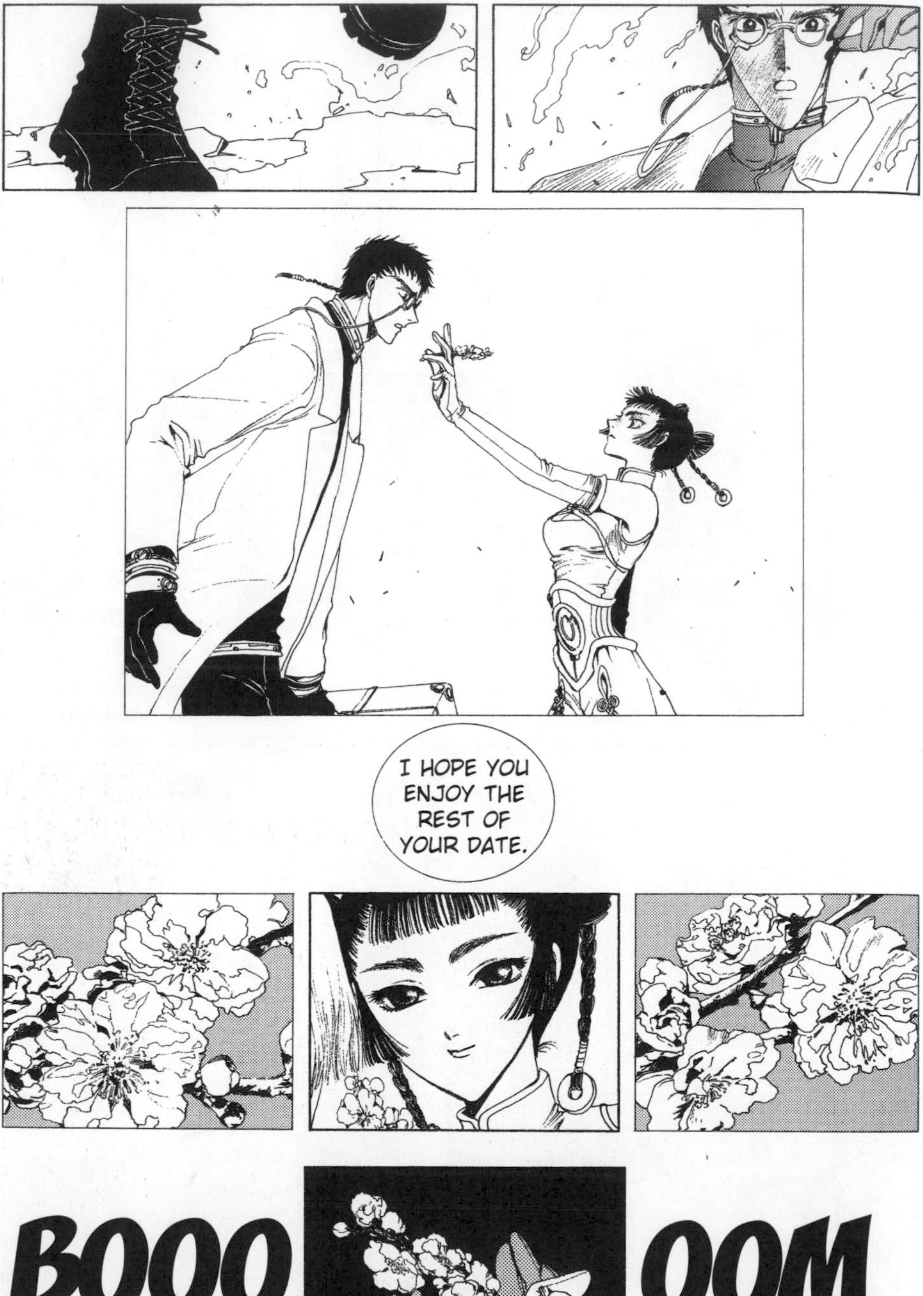
I HOPE YOU ENJOY THE REST OF YOUR DATE.
BOOO OOM

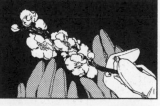

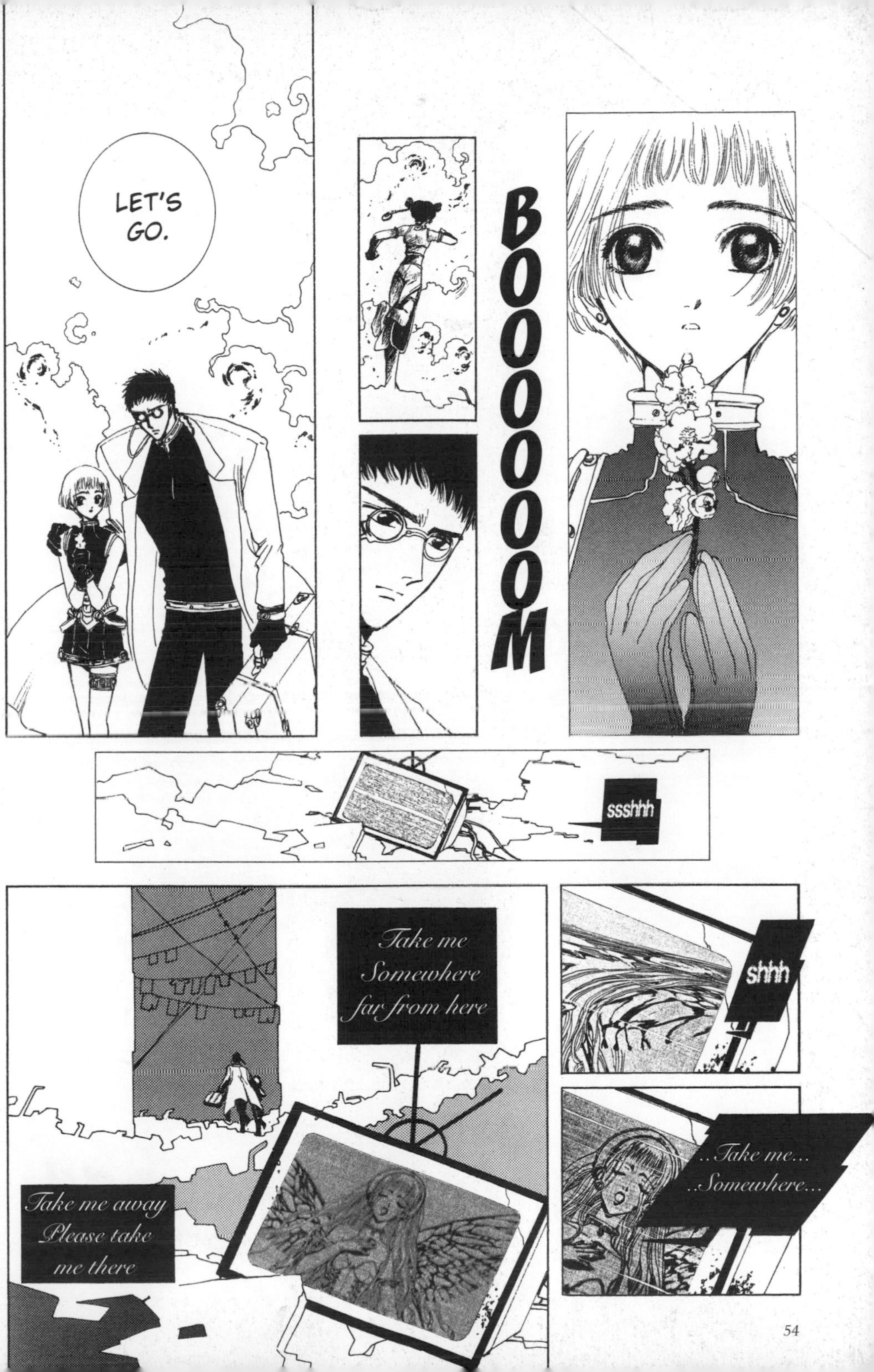
BOOOOOOOM
LET'S GO.
ssshhh
shhh
..Take me...
..Somewhere...
Take me Somewhere far from here
Take me away Please take me there

The birds
sing a song
In a foreign
tongue
In a place
where wings
Are not enough

A place
Not reachable
alone

So please
Take me
Somewhere far
from here

To be your happiness   To find happiness with you

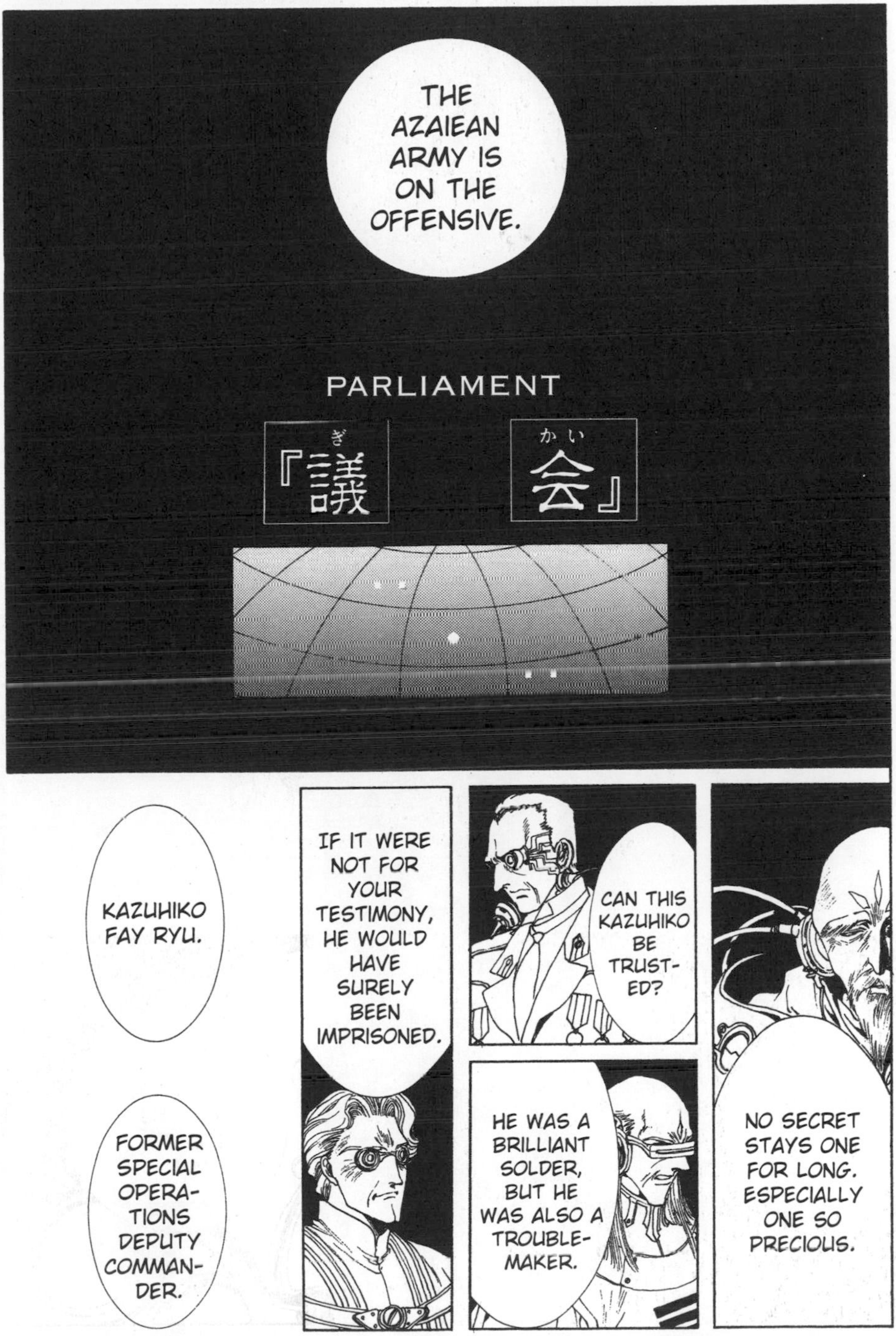
THE AZAIEAN ARMY IS ON THE OFFENSIVE.
PARLIAMENT
『議会』
NO SECRET STAYS ONE FOR LONG. ESPECIALLY ONE SO PRECIOUS.
CAN THIS KAZUHIKO BE TRUST-ED?
HE WAS A BRILLIANT SOLDER, BUT HE WAS ALSO A TROUBLE-MAKER.
IF IT WERE NOT FOR YOUR TESTIMONY, HE WOULD HAVE SURELY BEEN IMPRISONED.
KAZUHIKO FAY RYU.
FORMER SPECIAL OPERA-TIONS DEPUTY COMMAN-DER.

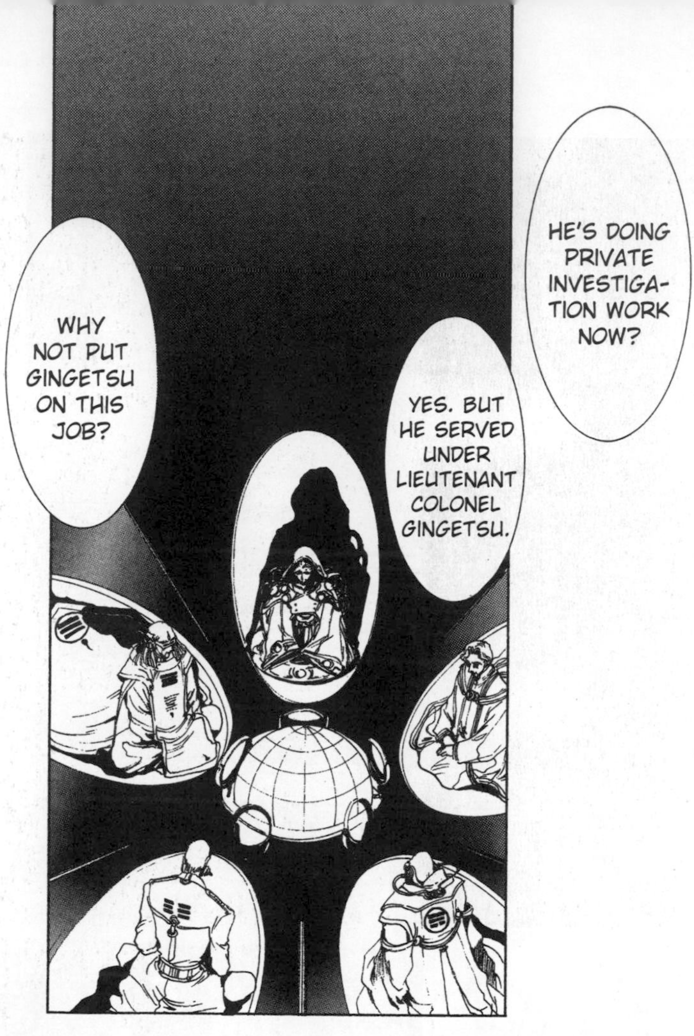
HE'S DOING PRIVATE INVESTIGATION WORK NOW?
YES. BUT HE SERVED UNDER LIEUTENANT COLONEL GINGETSU.
WHY NOT PUT GINGETSU ON THIS JOB?

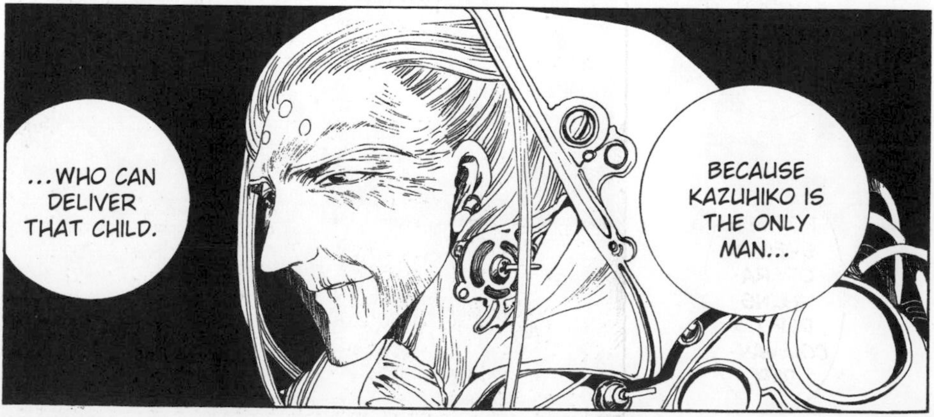
BECAUSE KAZUHIKO IS THE ONLY MAN...
...WHO CAN DELIVER THAT CHILD.

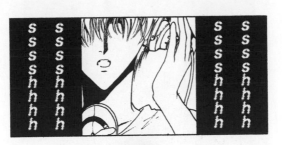

KAZUHIKO...
SSSShhhh
SSSShhhh
SSSShhhh
SSSShhhh
KAZUHIKO...

『クローバー』

CLOVER

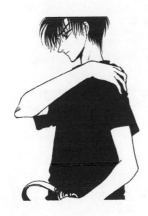

"FOUR LEAF CLOVER?"
...SO THERE IS SUCH A THING.

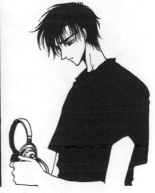

『電話』

A TELEPHONE

sssshhhh
sssshhhh
sssshhhh
sssshhhh

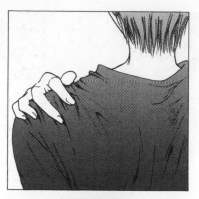

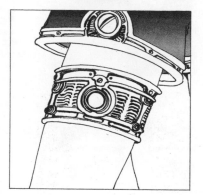

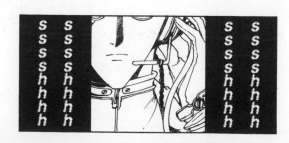

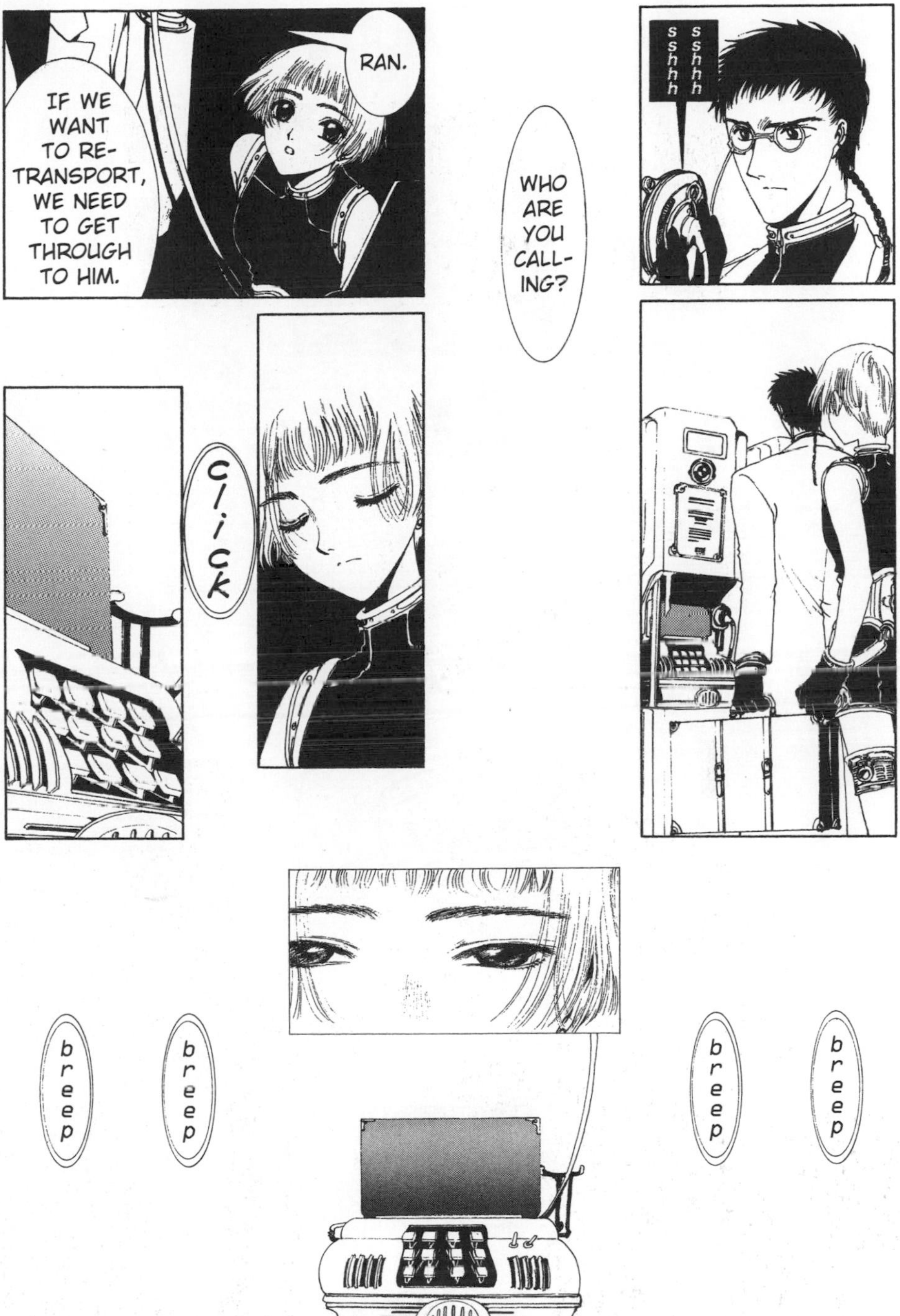

sshhh sshhh
WHO ARE YOU CALLING?
RAN.
IF WE WANT TO RE-TRANSPORT, WE NEED TO GET THROUGH TO HIM.
click
breep
breep
breep
breep

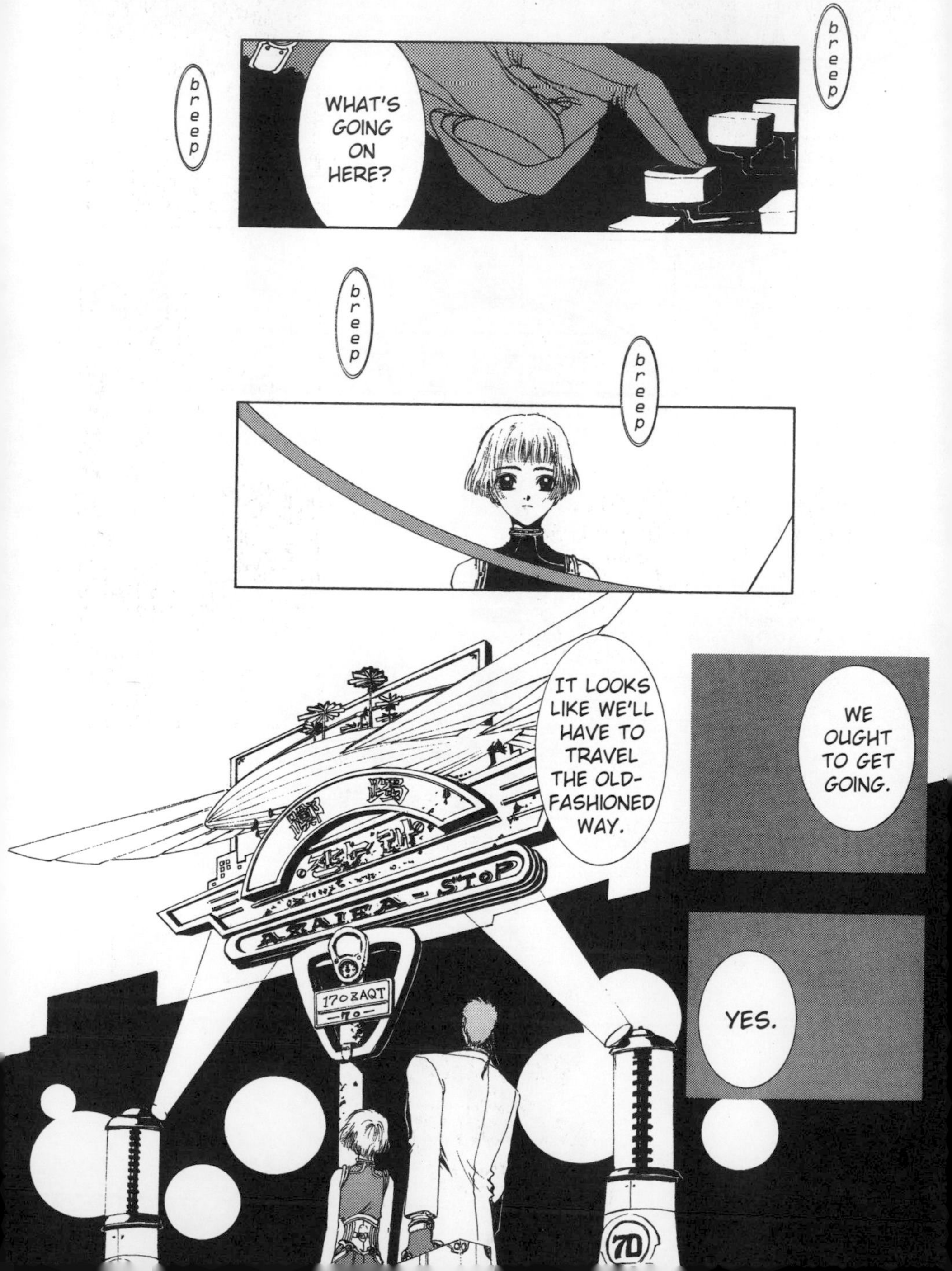
breep
WHAT'S GOING ON HERE?
breep
breep
breep
WE OUGHT TO GET GOING.
YES.
IT LOOKS LIKE WE'LL HAVE TO TRAVEL THE OLD-FASHIONED WAY.

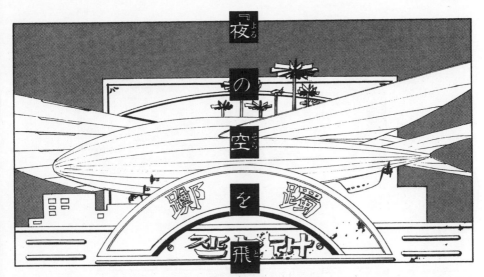

『夜の空を蹴飛ばす羽のはえた魚』

WINGED FISH THAT FLIES THROUGH THE NIGHT

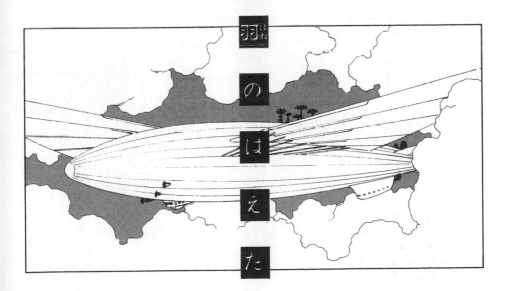

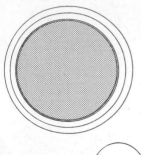   

YES.

YOUR FIRST TIME RIDING ON ONE OF THESE?

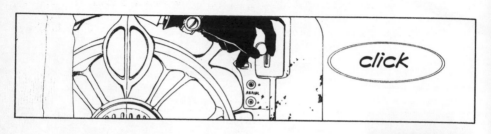

click

I wish for happiness

I seek happiness

To find happiness with you

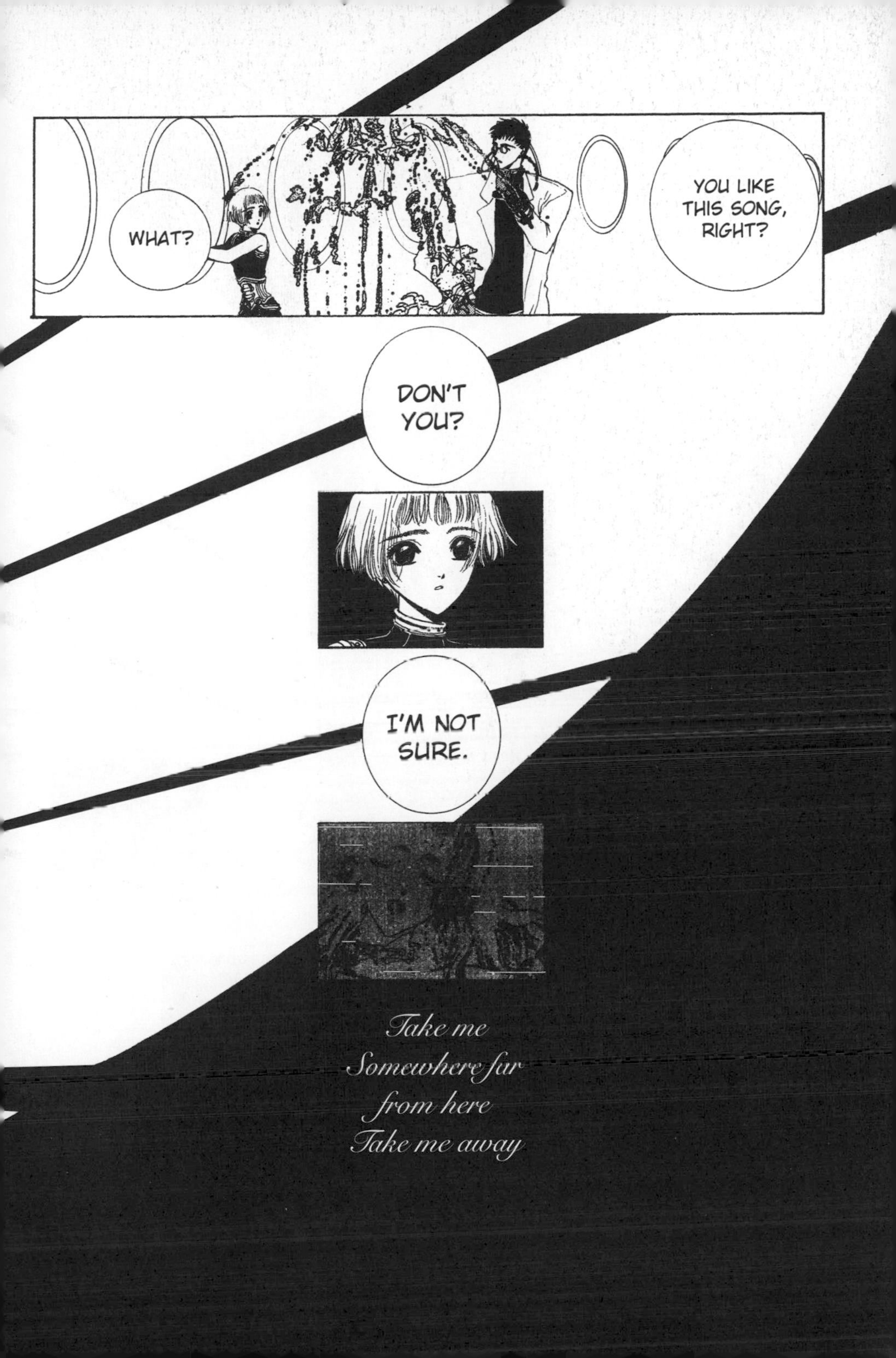
YOU LIKE THIS SONG, RIGHT?
WHAT?
DON'T YOU?
I'M NOT SURE.
Take me
Somewhere far
from here
Take me away

The birds sing a song
In a foreign tongue
In a place where wings
Are not enough
A place
Not reachable alone

So please
Take me
Somewhere
far from here

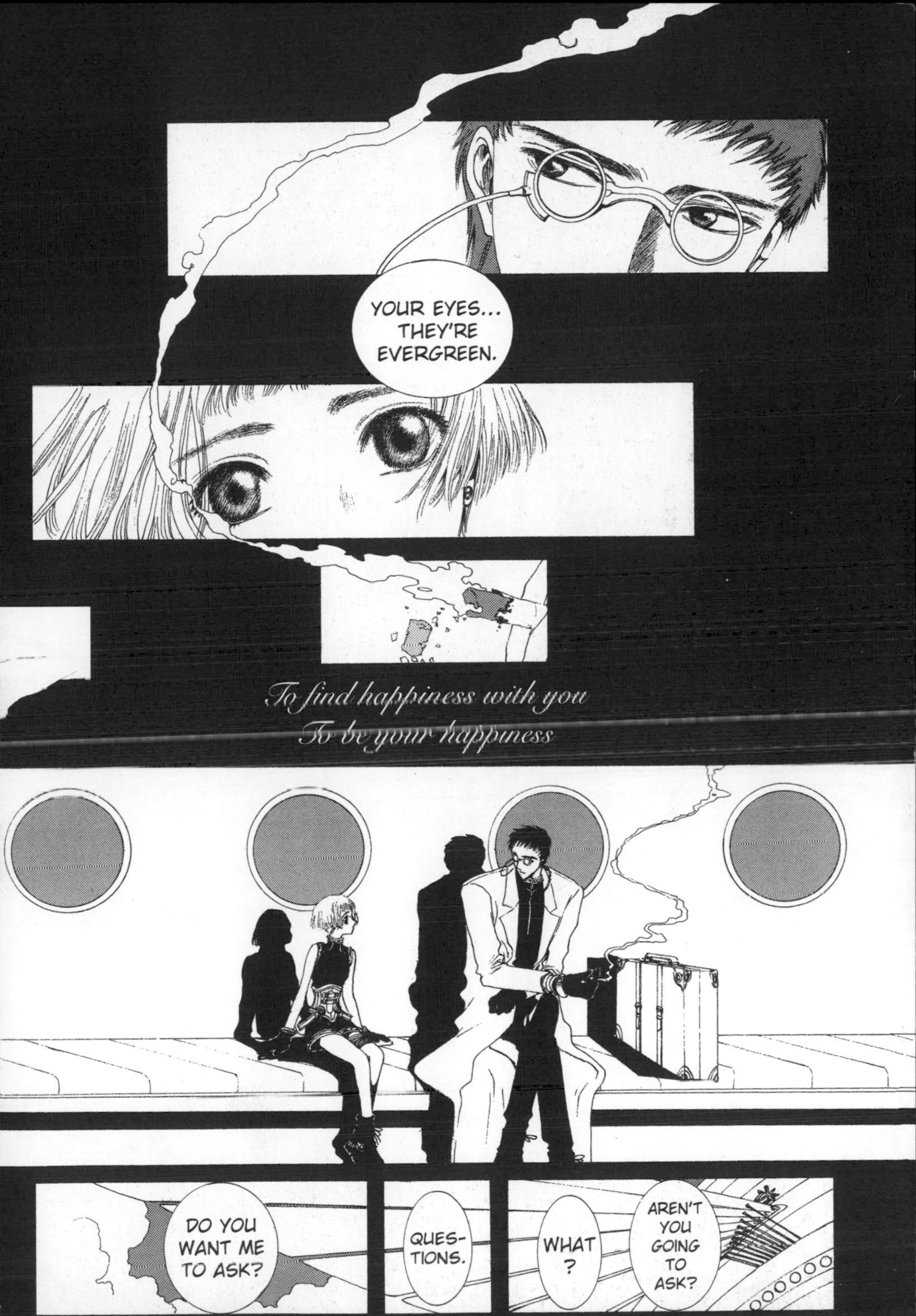
YOUR EYES... THEY'RE EVERGREEN.
To find happiness with you
To be your happiness
AREN'T YOU GOING TO ASK?
WHAT ?
QUES-TIONS.
DO YOU WANT ME TO ASK?

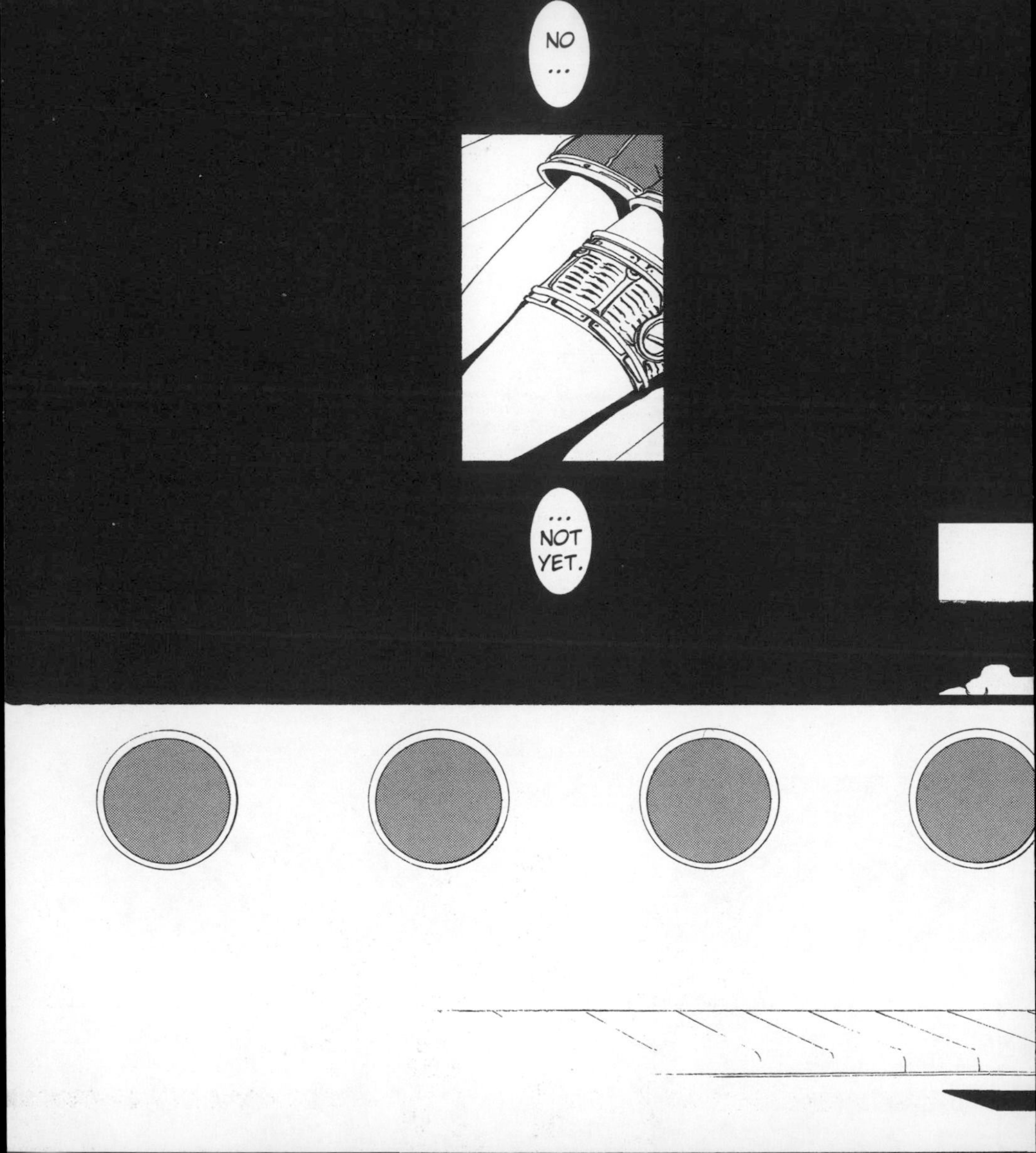
NO
...
... NOT YET.

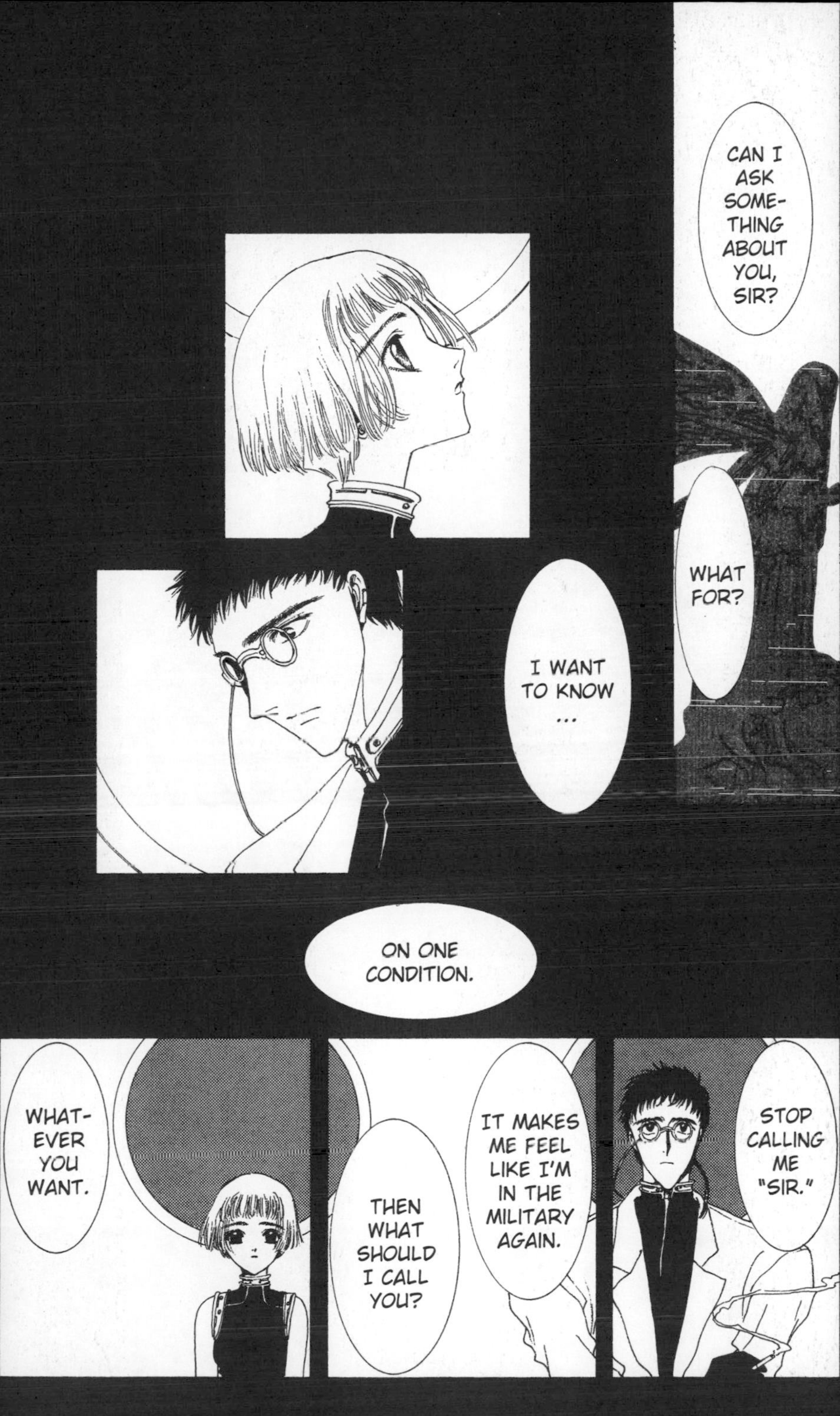
CAN I ASK SOME-THING ABOUT YOU, SIR?
WHAT FOR?
I WANT TO KNOW ...
ON ONE CONDITION.
STOP CALLING ME "SIR."
IT MAKES ME FEEL LIKE I'M IN THE MILITARY AGAIN.
THEN WHAT SHOULD I CALL YOU?
WHAT-EVER YOU WANT.

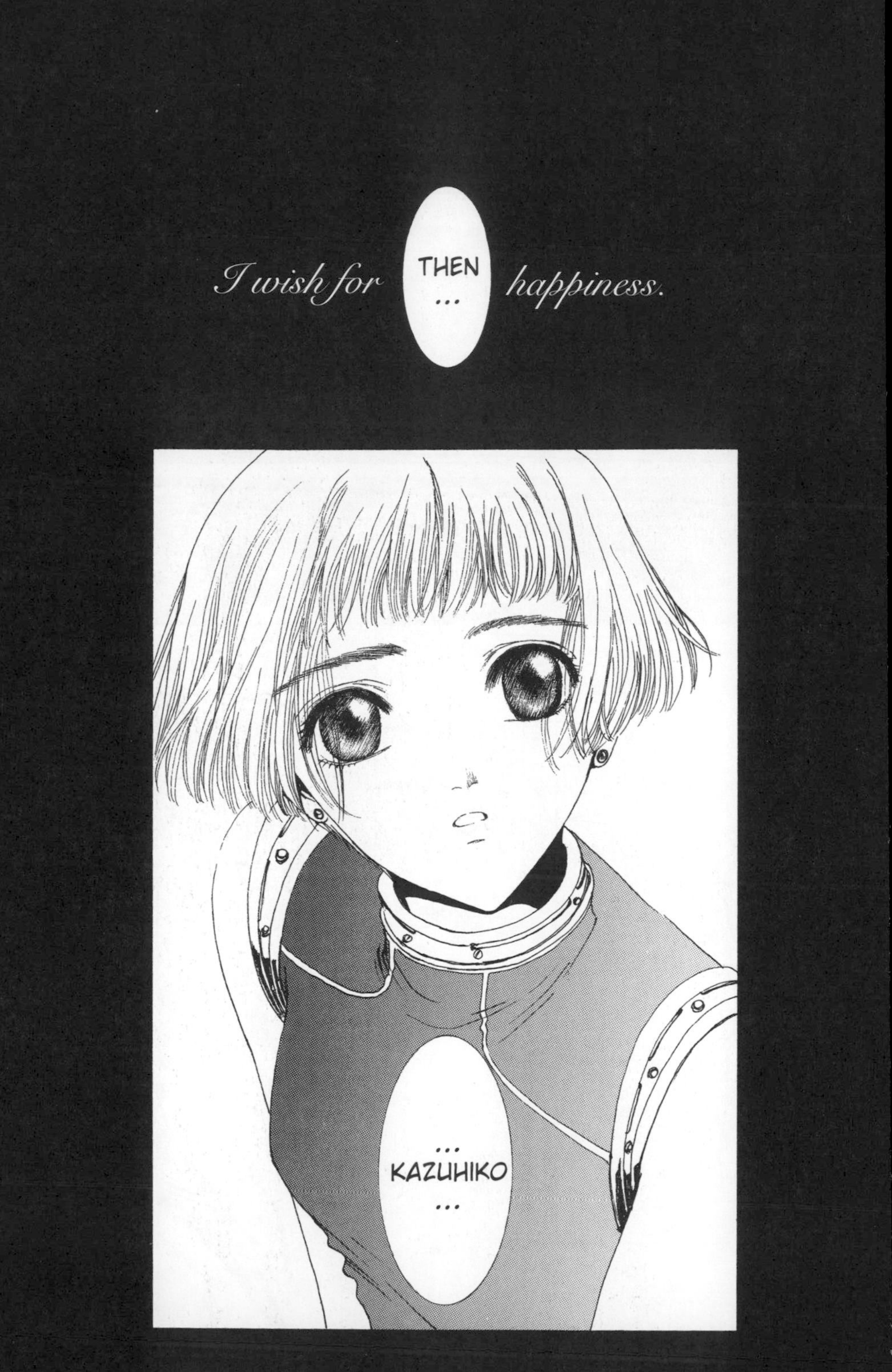
I wish for happiness.
THEN ...
... KAZUHIKO ...

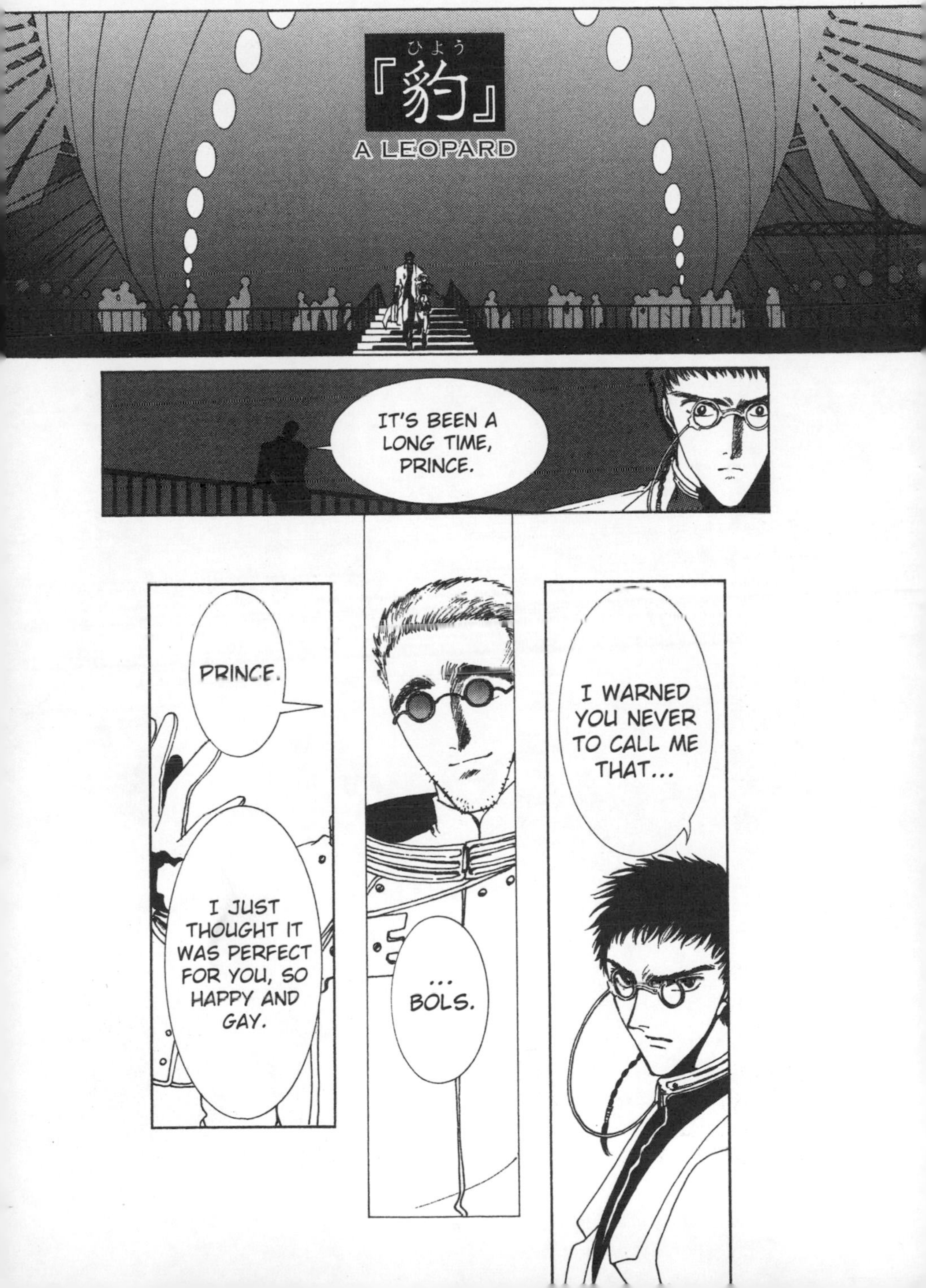
ひょう
『豹』
A LEOPARD
IT'S BEEN A LONG TIME, PRINCE.
I WARNED YOU NEVER TO CALL ME THAT...
... BOLS.
PRINCE.
I JUST THOUGHT IT WAS PERFECT FOR YOU, SO HAPPY AND GAY.

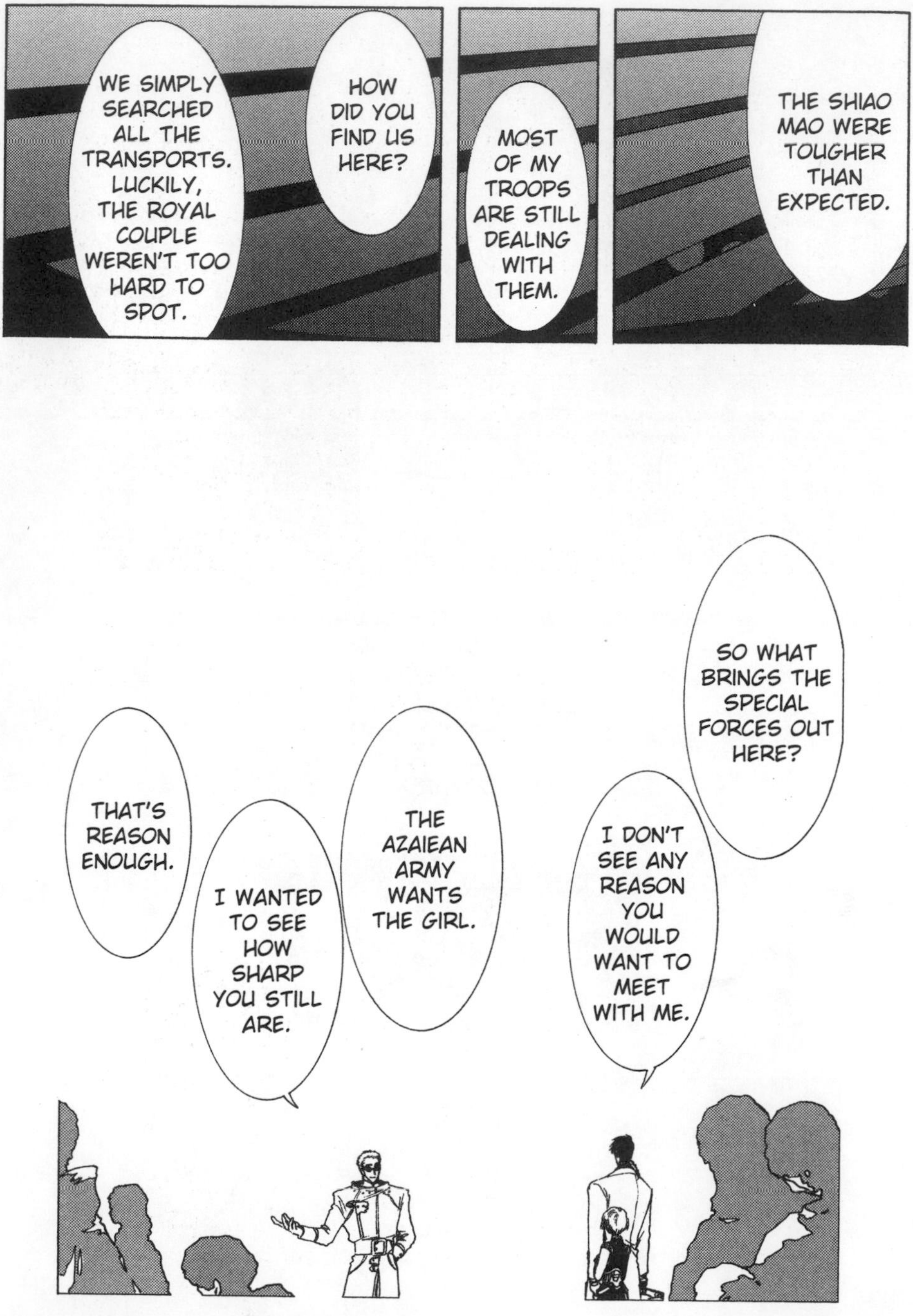
THE SHIAO MAO WERE TOUGHER THAN EXPECTED.
MOST OF MY TROOPS ARE STILL DEALING WITH THEM.
HOW DID YOU FIND US HERE?
WE SIMPLY SEARCHED ALL THE TRANSPORTS. LUCKILY, THE ROYAL COUPLE WEREN'T TOO HARD TO SPOT.
SO WHAT BRINGS THE SPECIAL FORCES OUT HERE?
I DON'T SEE ANY REASON YOU WOULD WANT TO MEET WITH ME.
THE AZAIEAN ARMY WANTS THE GIRL.
I WANTED TO SEE HOW SHARP YOU STILL ARE.
THAT'S REASON ENOUGH.

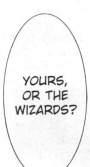

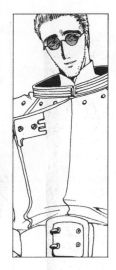

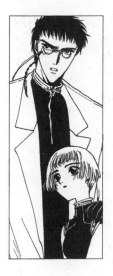

THIS GIRL IS MY RESPONSIBILITY.

YOURS, OR THE WIZARDS?

I'M SURE THE OLD BLIZZARDS OF THE PARLIAMENTARY COUNCIL WOULD BE THRILLED TO HEAR YOU CALL THEM "THE WIZARDS."
BUT I HEAR THOSE RELICS CONTROL MOST OF THE UNDERGROUND THESE DAYS.

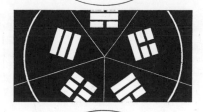

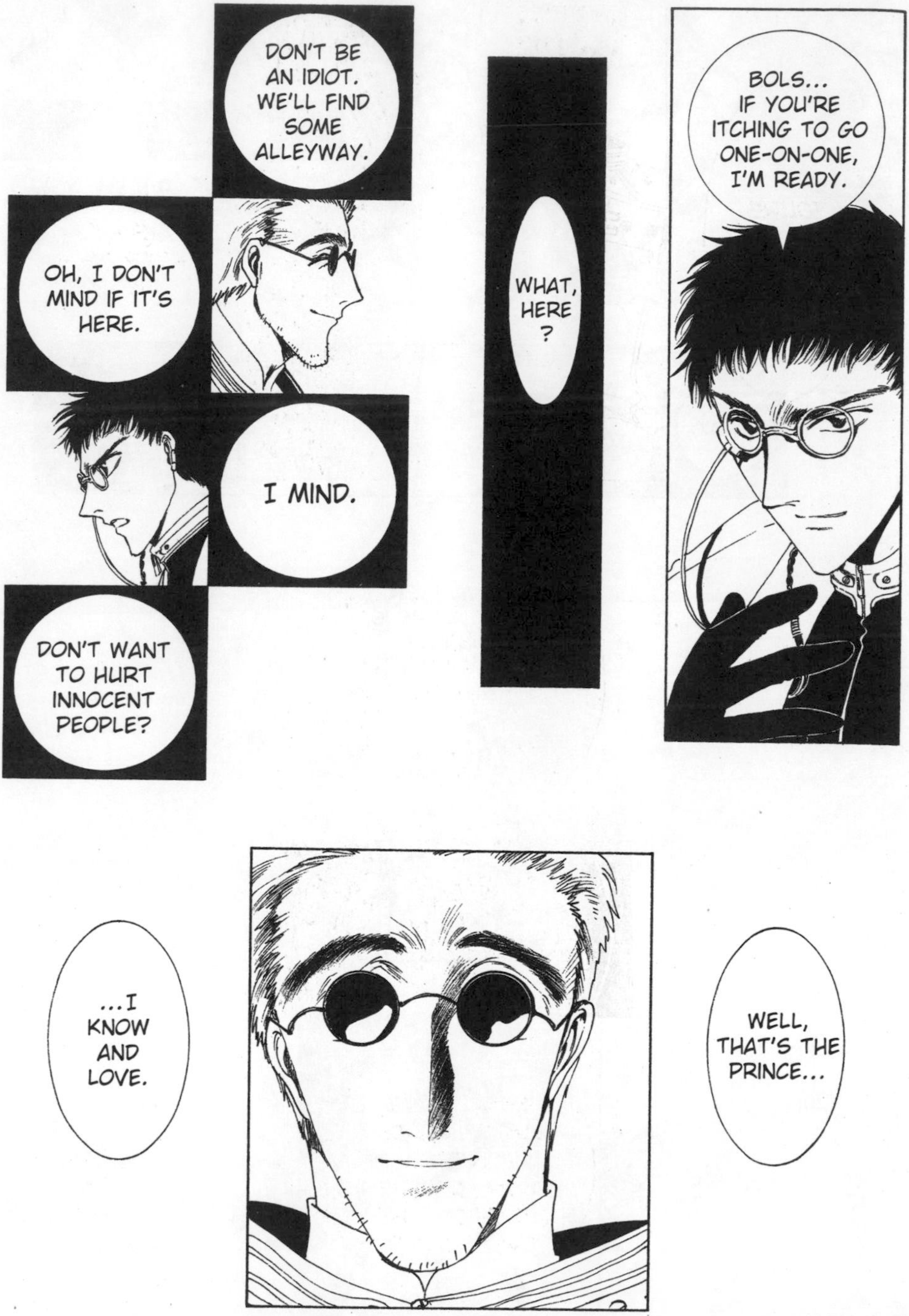
BOLS... IF YOU'RE ITCHING TO GO ONE-ON-ONE, I'M READY.
WHAT, HERE?
DON'T BE AN IDIOT. WE'LL FIND SOME ALLEYWAY.
OH, I DON'T MIND IF IT'S HERE.
I MIND.
DON'T WANT TO HURT INNOCENT PEOPLE?
WELL, THAT'S THE PRINCE...
...I KNOW AND LOVE.

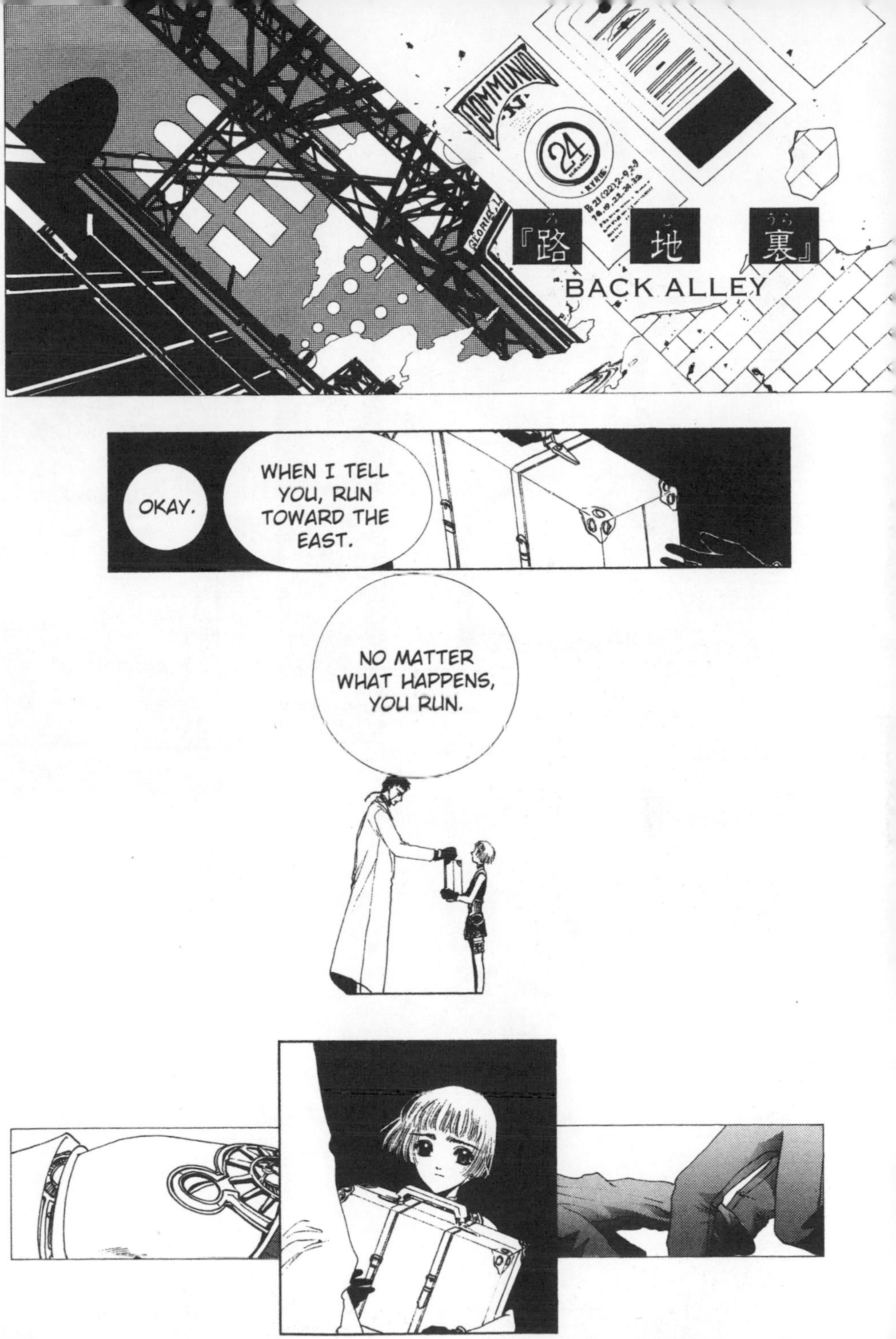
『路地裏』
BACK ALLEY
WHEN I TELL YOU, RUN TOWARD THE EAST.
OKAY.
NO MATTER WHAT HAPPENS, YOU RUN.

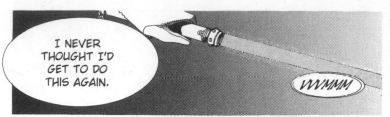

I NEVER THOUGHT I'D GET TO DO THIS AGAIN.

VVVMMM

SO NO ONE WANTS TO PLAY WITH YOU...?

VVVMMM

THAT'S BECAUSE EVERYBODY HATES YOU, BOLS.

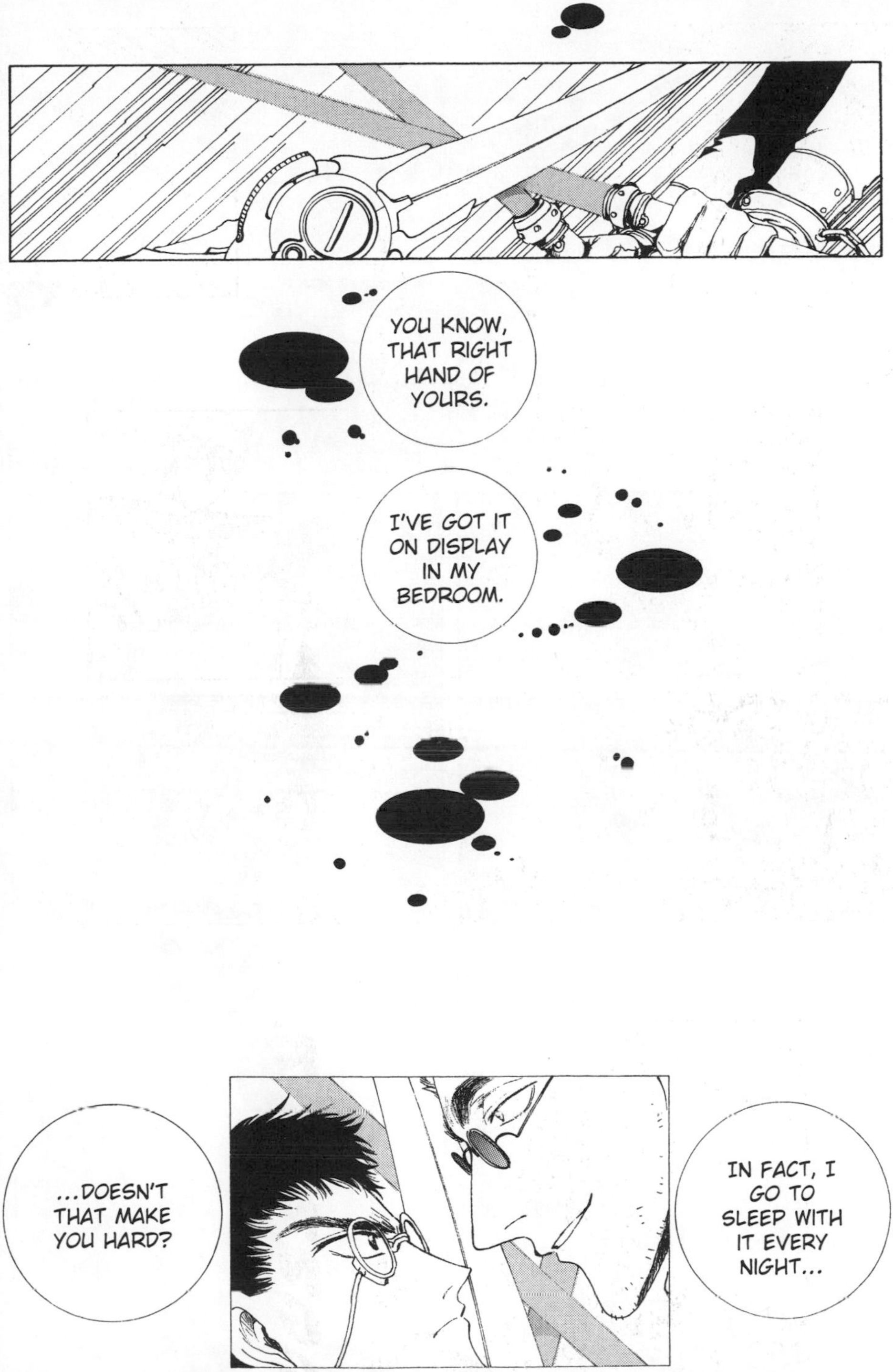
YOU KNOW, THAT RIGHT HAND OF YOURS.
I'VE GOT IT ON DISPLAY IN MY BEDROOM.
IN FACT, I GO TO SLEEP WITH IT EVERY NIGHT...
...DOESN'T THAT MAKE YOU HARD?

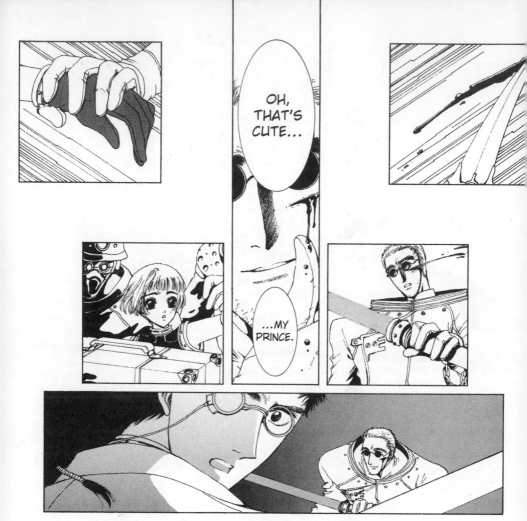

OH, THAT'S CUTE...

...MY PRINCE.

KLANNGG

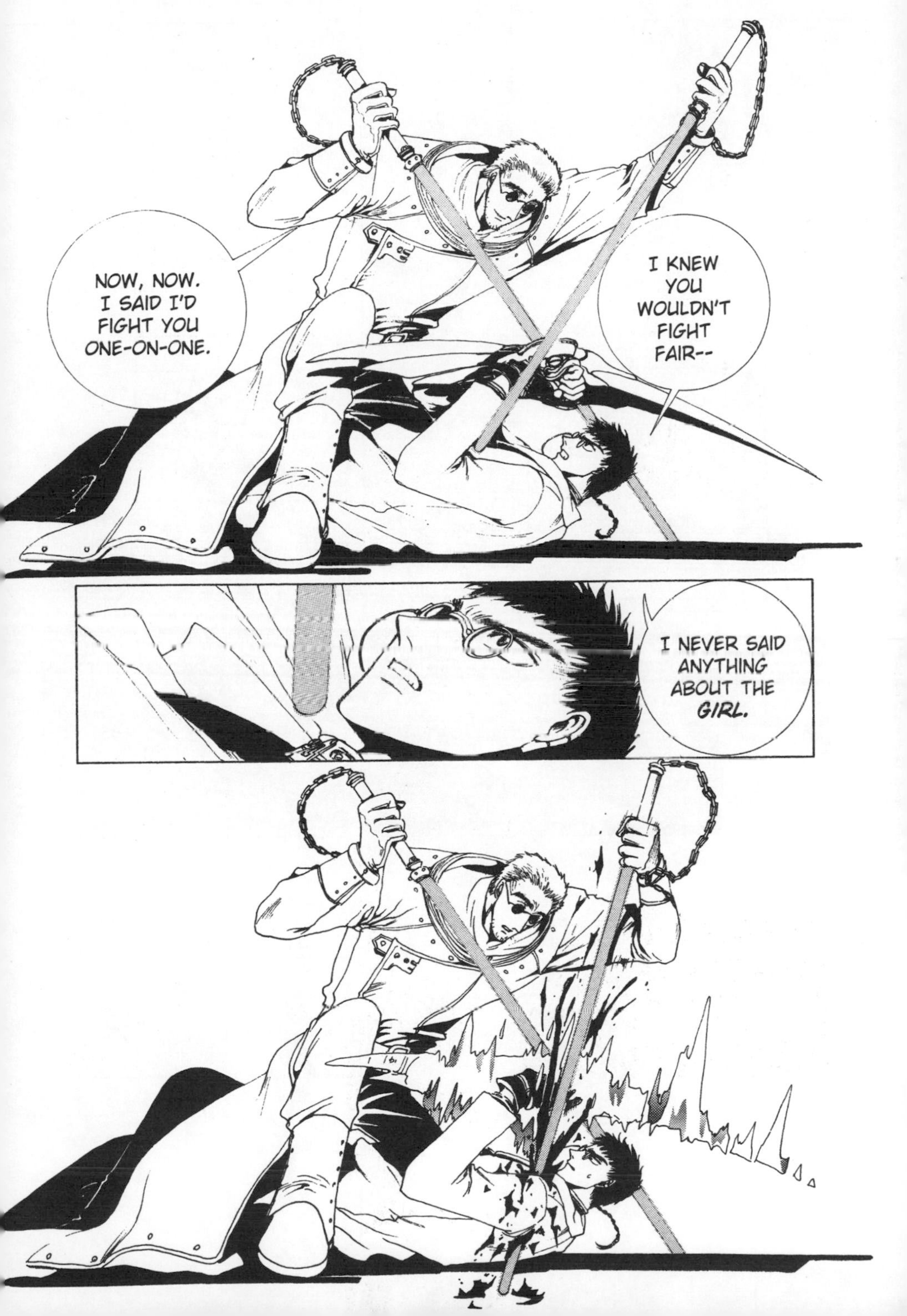
I KNEW YOU WOULDN'T FIGHT FAIR--
NOW, NOW. I SAID I'D FIGHT YOU ONE-ON-ONE.
I NEVER SAID ANYTHING ABOUT THE *GIRL.*

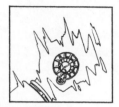

WEEEEEEE

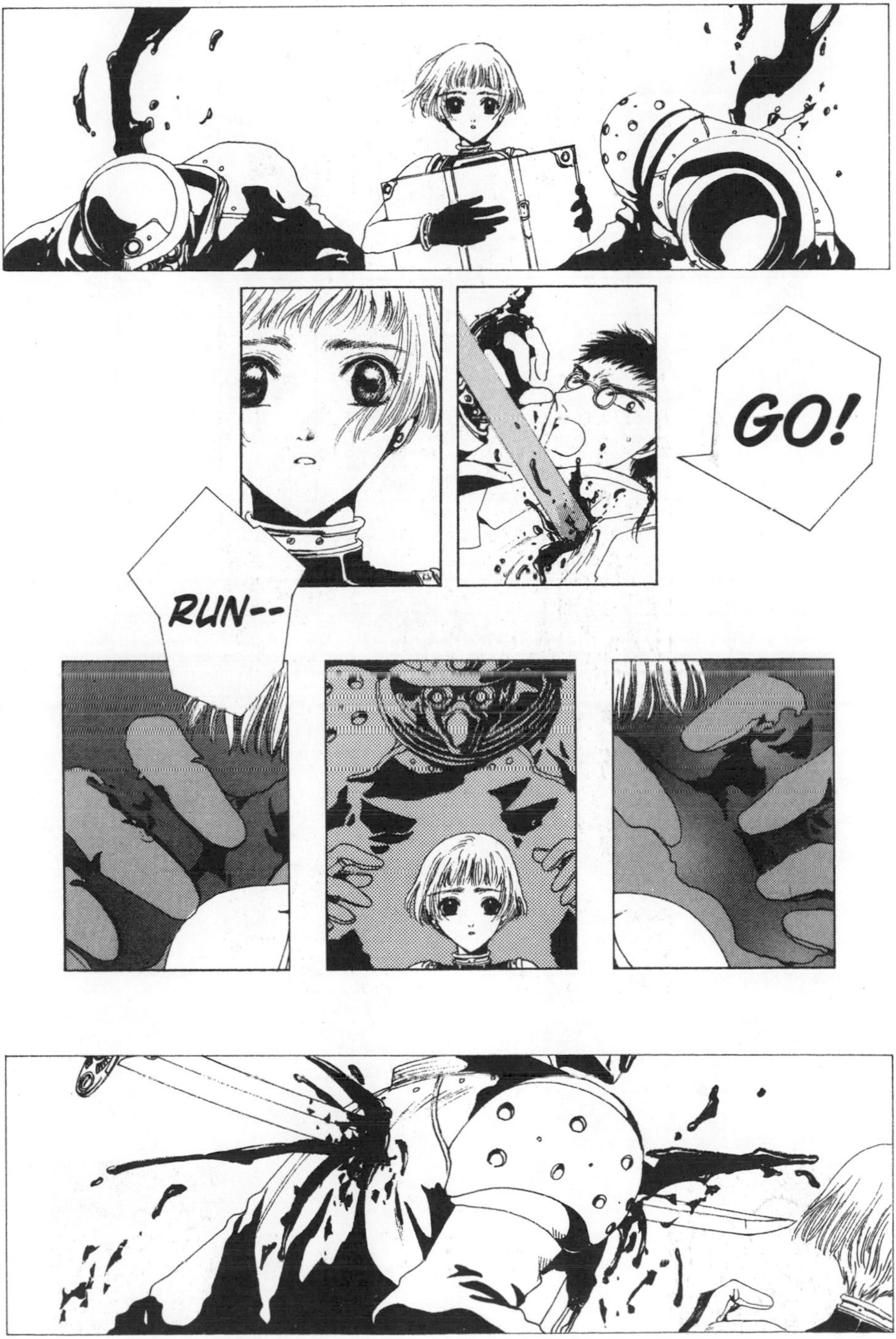
GO!
RUN--

...
GINGETSU
?

『傷 THE SCAR 痕』

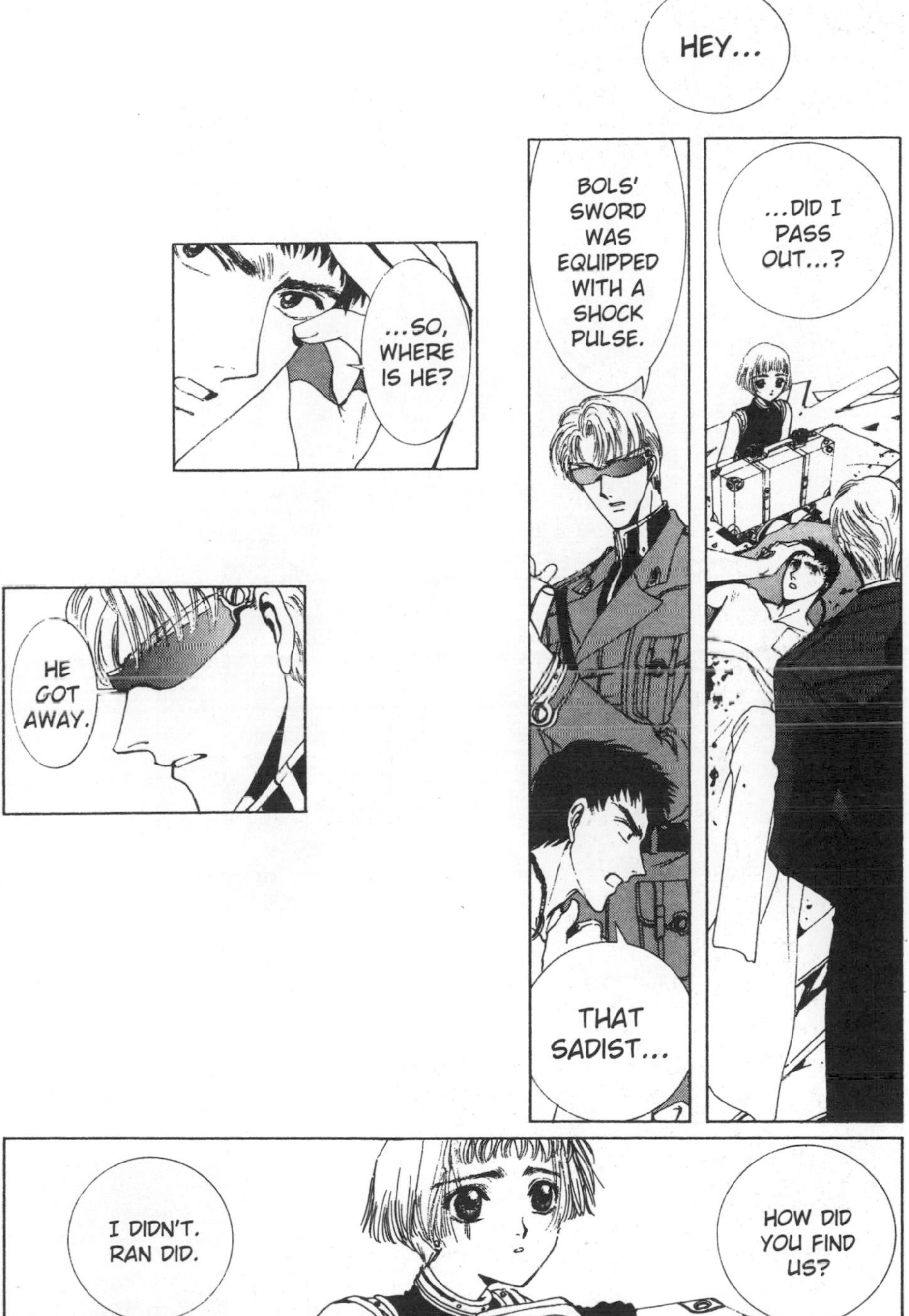
HEY...
...DID I PASS OUT...?
BOLS' SWORD WAS EQUIPPED WITH A SHOCK PULSE.
THAT SADIST...
...SO, WHERE IS HE?
HE GOT AWAY.
HOW DID YOU FIND US?
I DIDN'T. RAN DID.

I HATE THE TASTE OF THESE PAIN-KILLERS.
THEN DON'T TAKE THEM.
WHY DIDN'T YOU RUN WHEN I TOLD YOU?

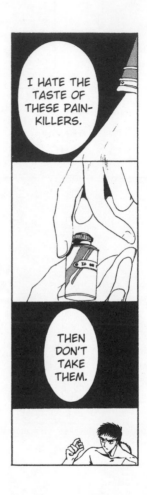

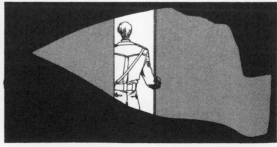

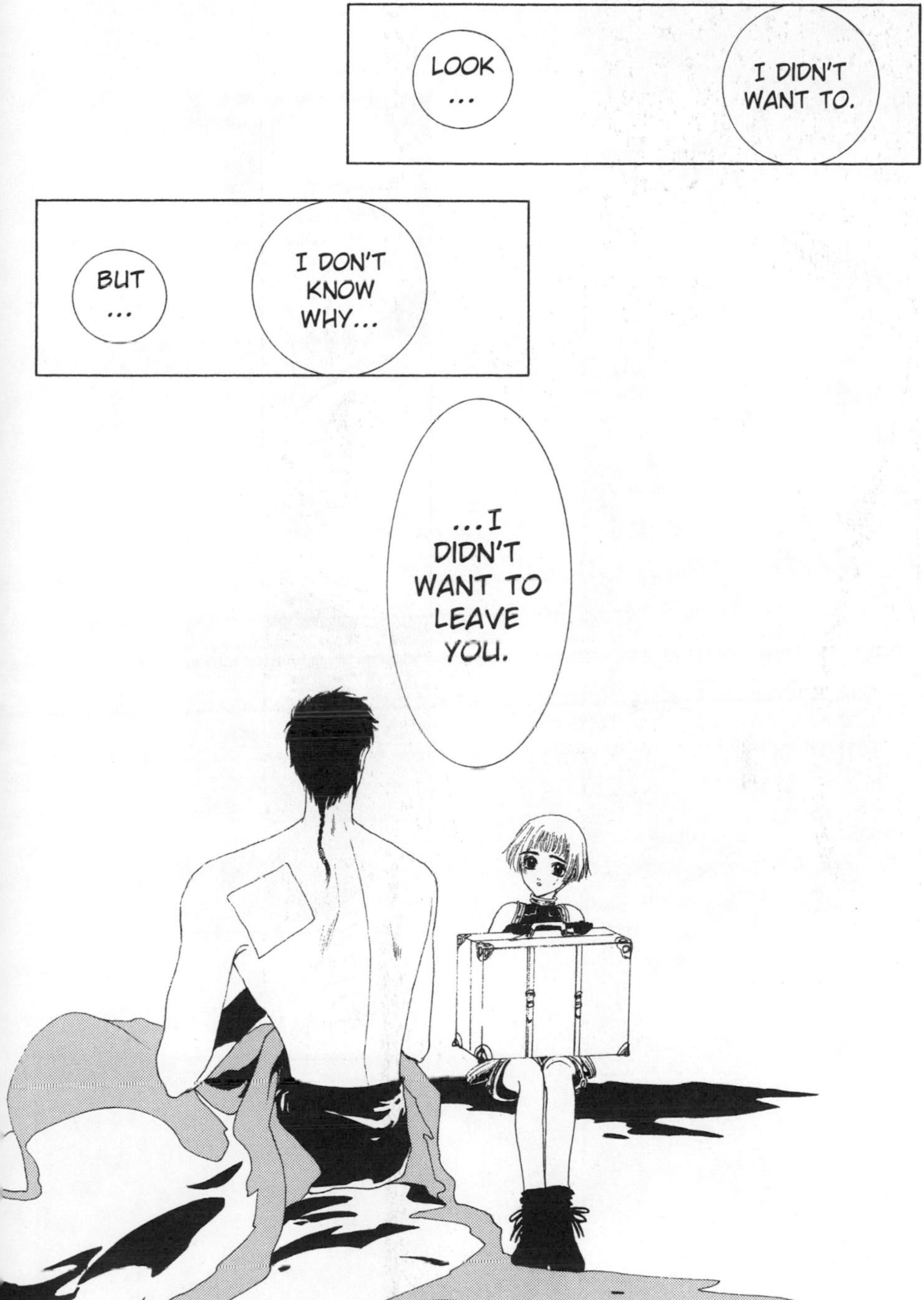
LOOK ...
I DIDN'T WANT TO.
BUT ...
I DON'T KNOW WHY...
...I DIDN'T WANT TO LEAVE YOU.

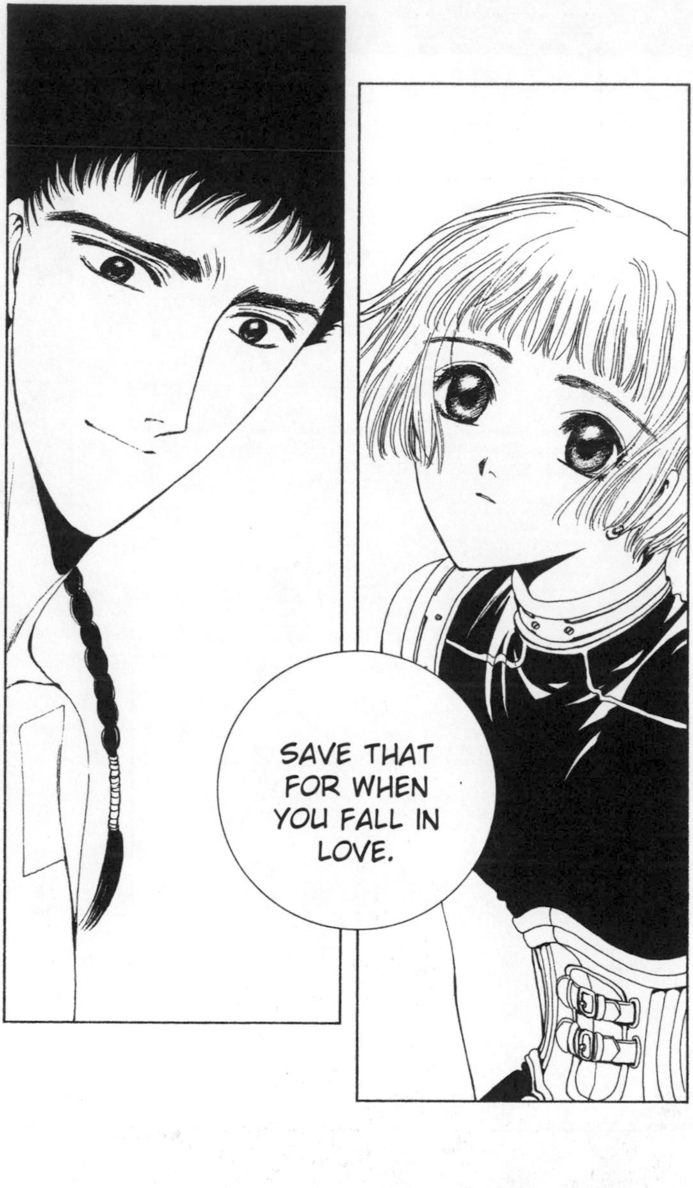
SAVE THAT FOR WHEN YOU FALL IN LOVE.

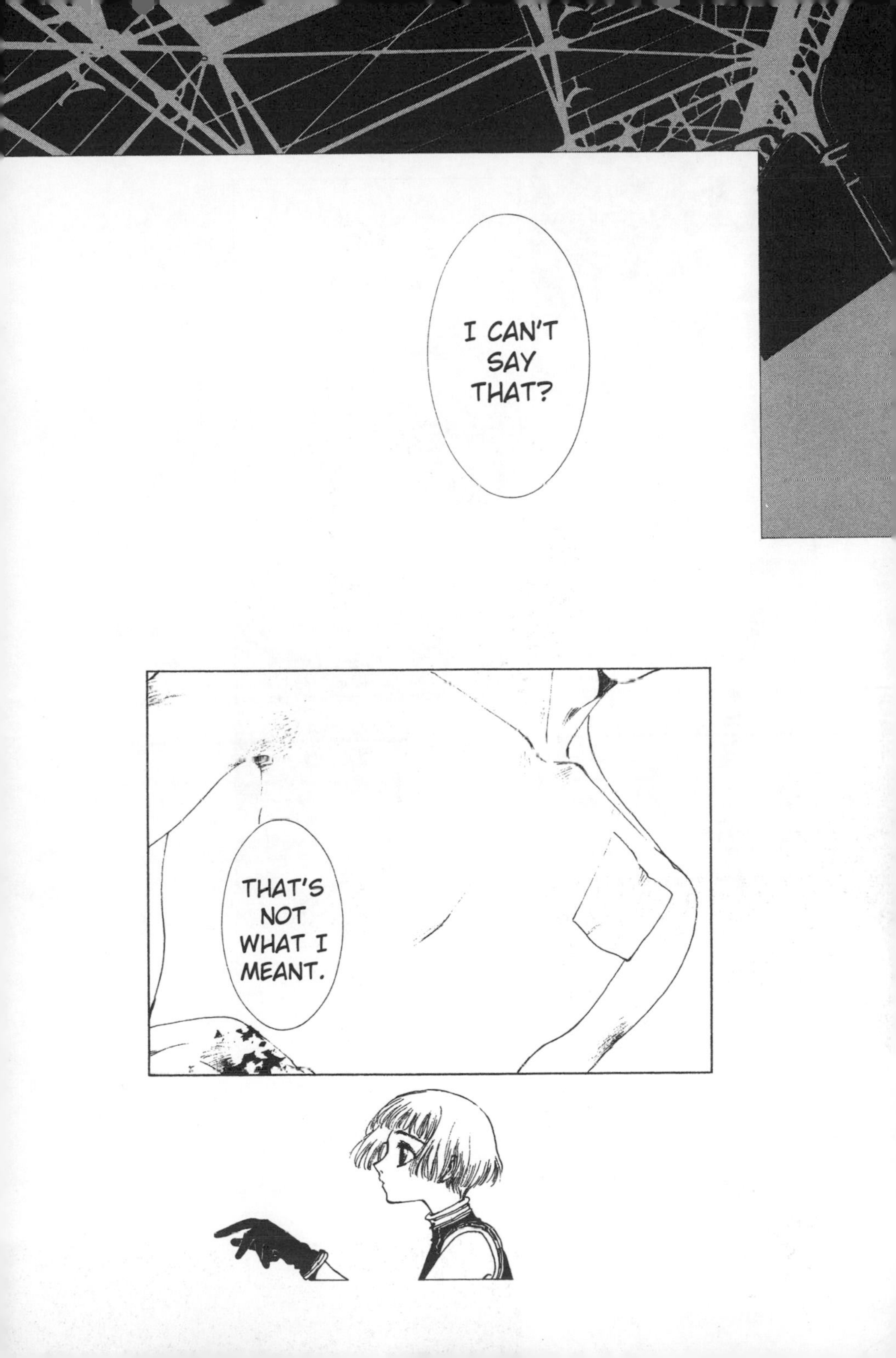
I CAN'T SAY THAT?
THAT'S NOT WHAT I MEANT.

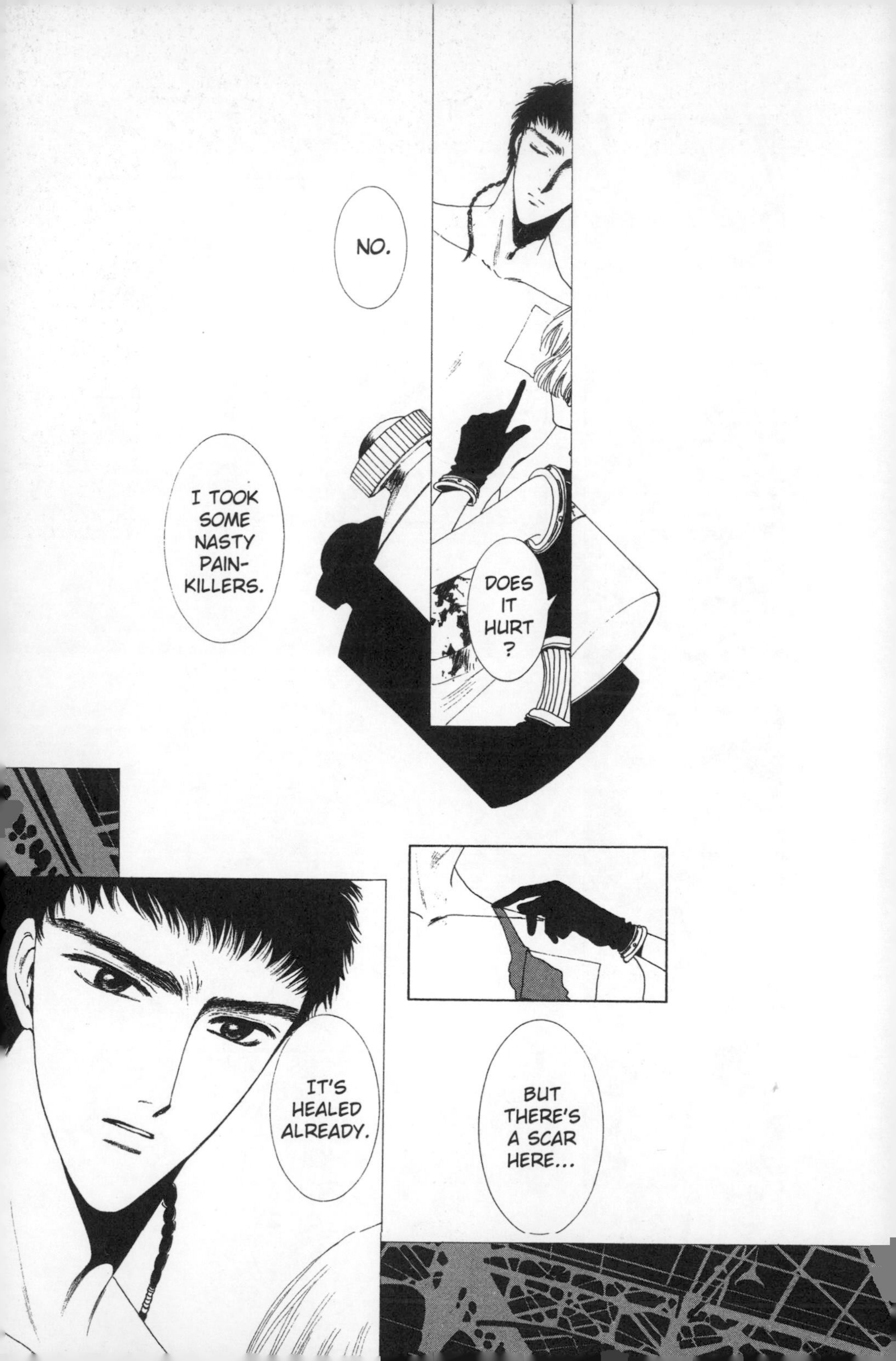
NO.
I TOOK SOME NASTY PAIN-KILLERS.
DOES IT HURT?
BUT THERE'S A SCAR HERE...
IT'S HEALED ALREADY.

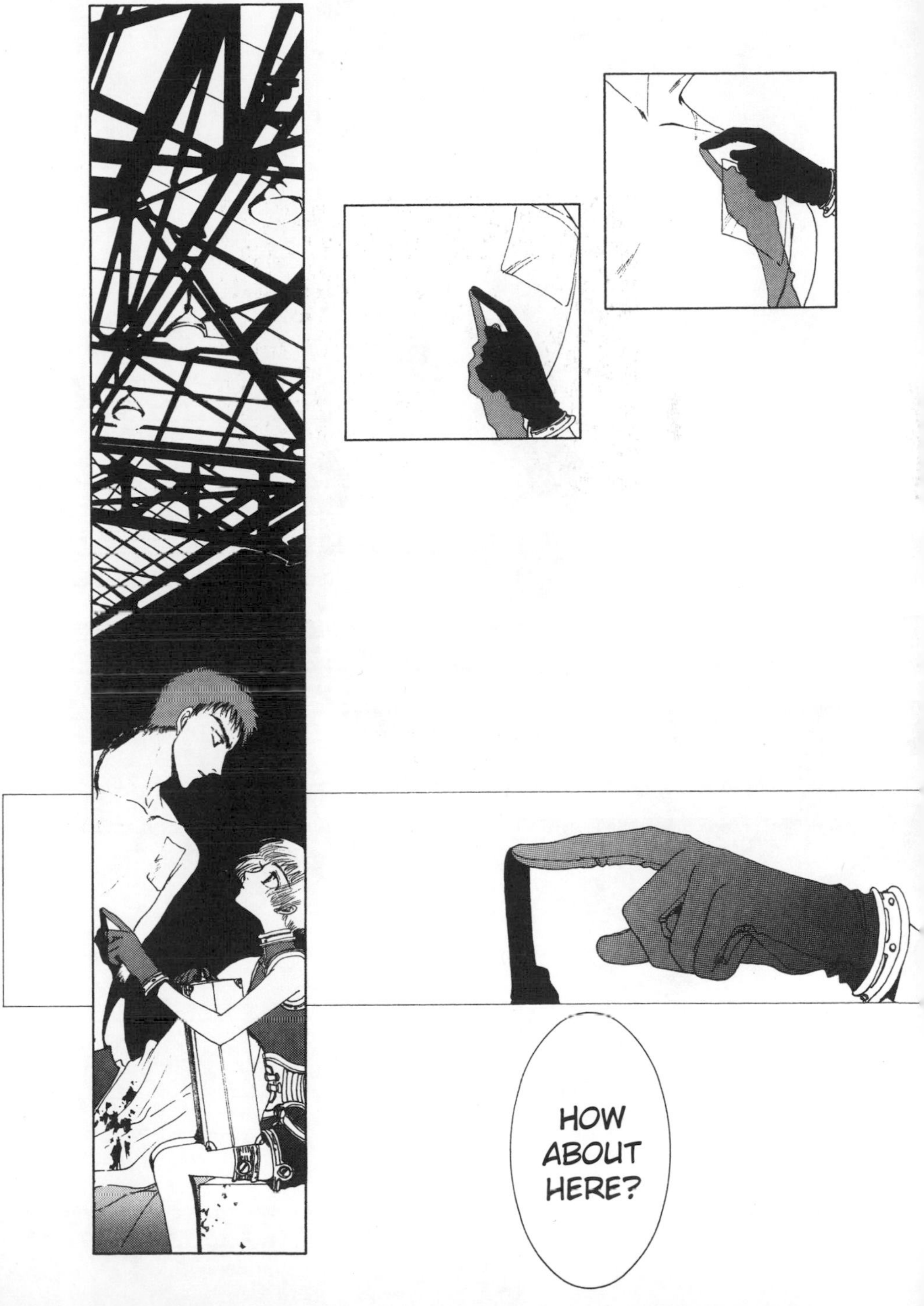
HOW ABOUT HERE?

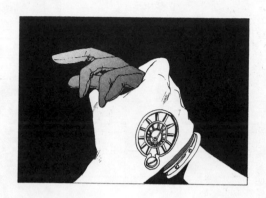

...WHO KNOWS.

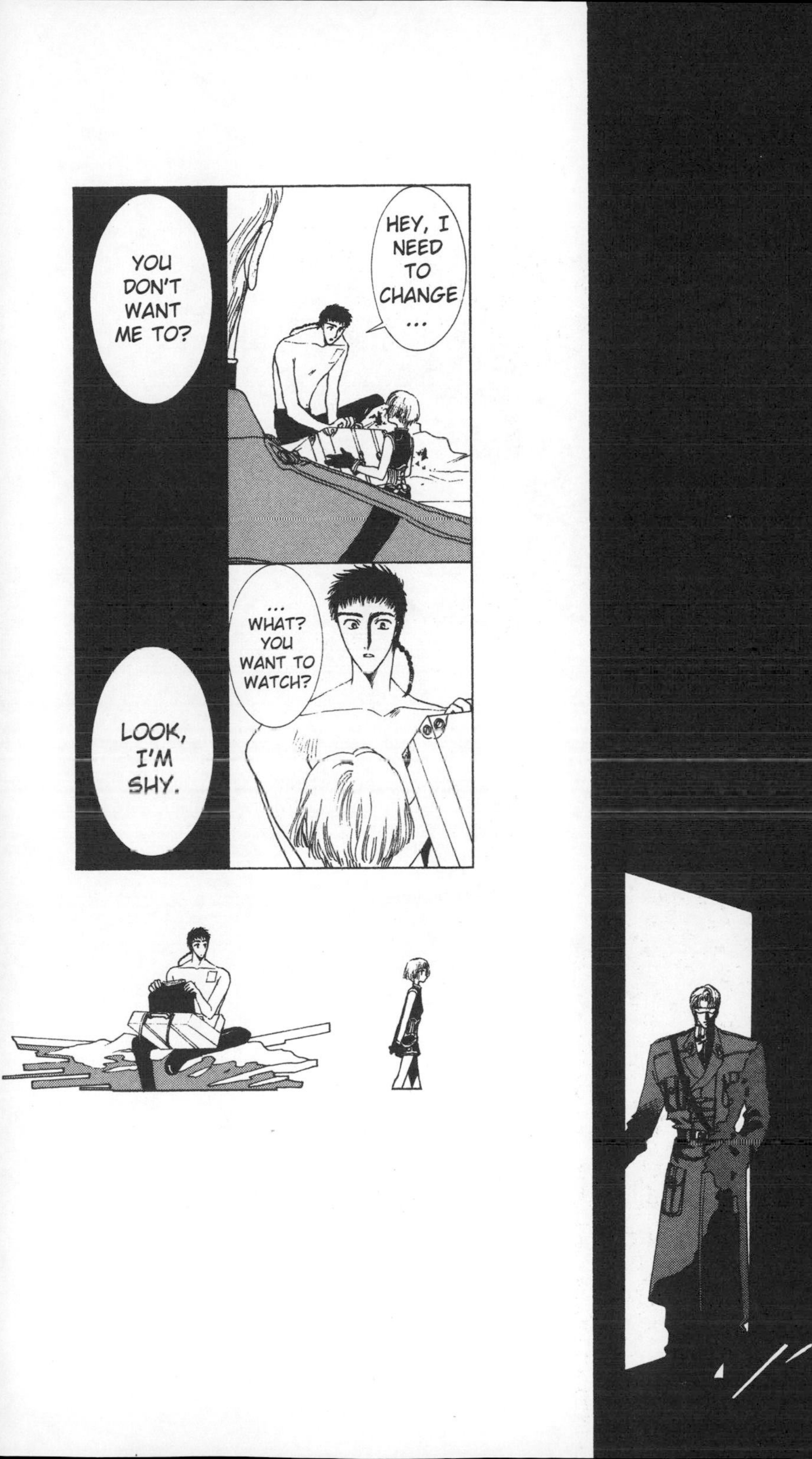
HEY, I NEED TO CHANGE ...
YOU DON'T WANT ME TO?
... WHAT? YOU WANT TO WATCH?
LOOK, I'M SHY.

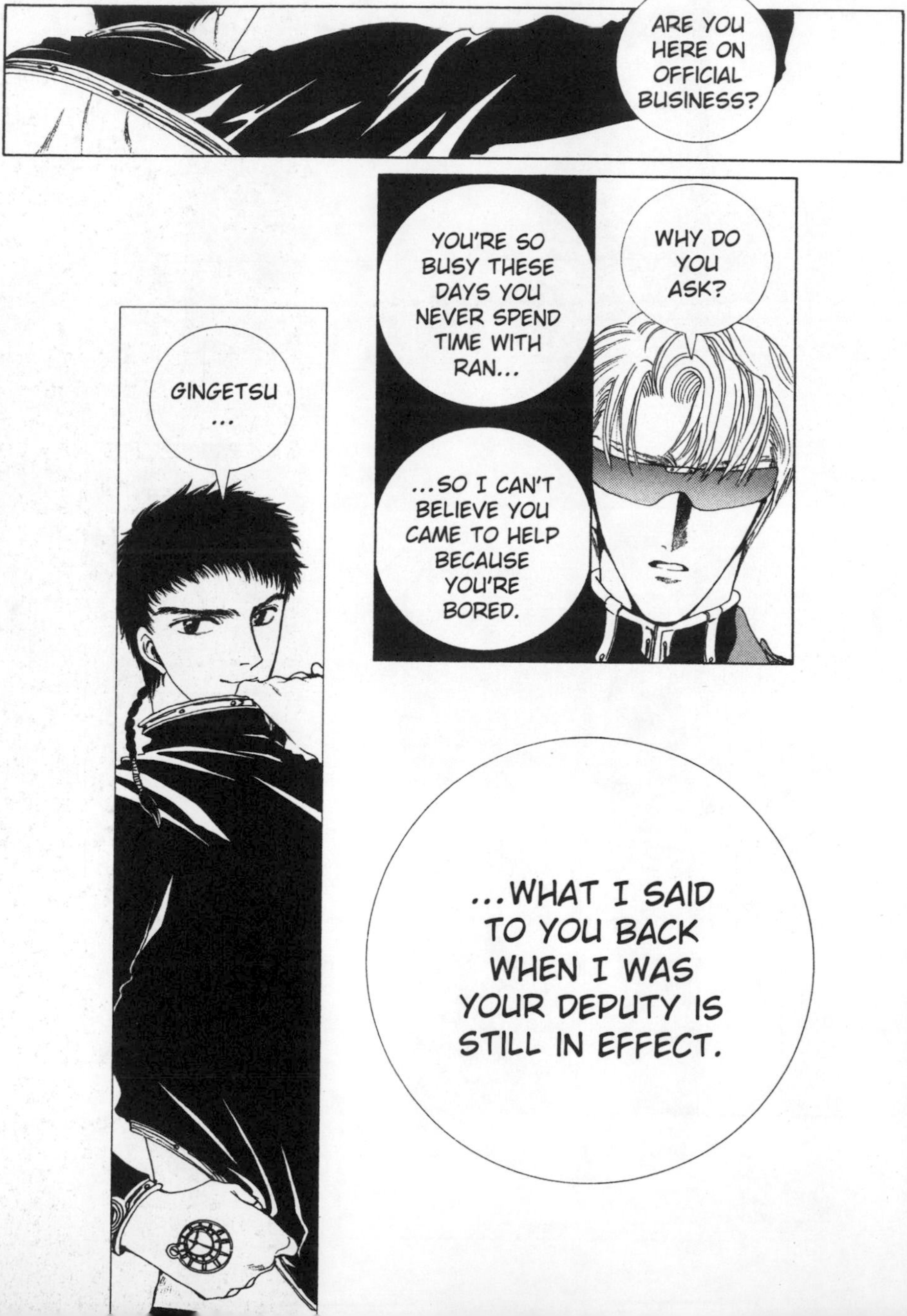
ARE YOU HERE ON OFFICIAL BUSINESS?
WHY DO YOU ASK?
YOU'RE SO BUSY THESE DAYS YOU NEVER SPEND TIME WITH RAN...
...SO I CAN'T BELIEVE YOU CAME TO HELP BECAUSE YOU'RE BORED.
GINGETSU...
...WHAT I SAID TO YOU BACK WHEN I WAS YOUR DEPUTY IS STILL IN EFFECT.

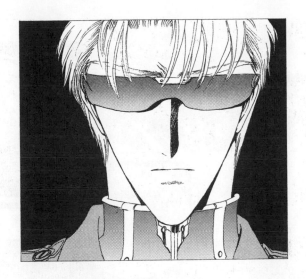

BOLS'S MEN ARE
WATCHING THE
TRANSPORTS...
FROM HERE,
YOU DRIVE.

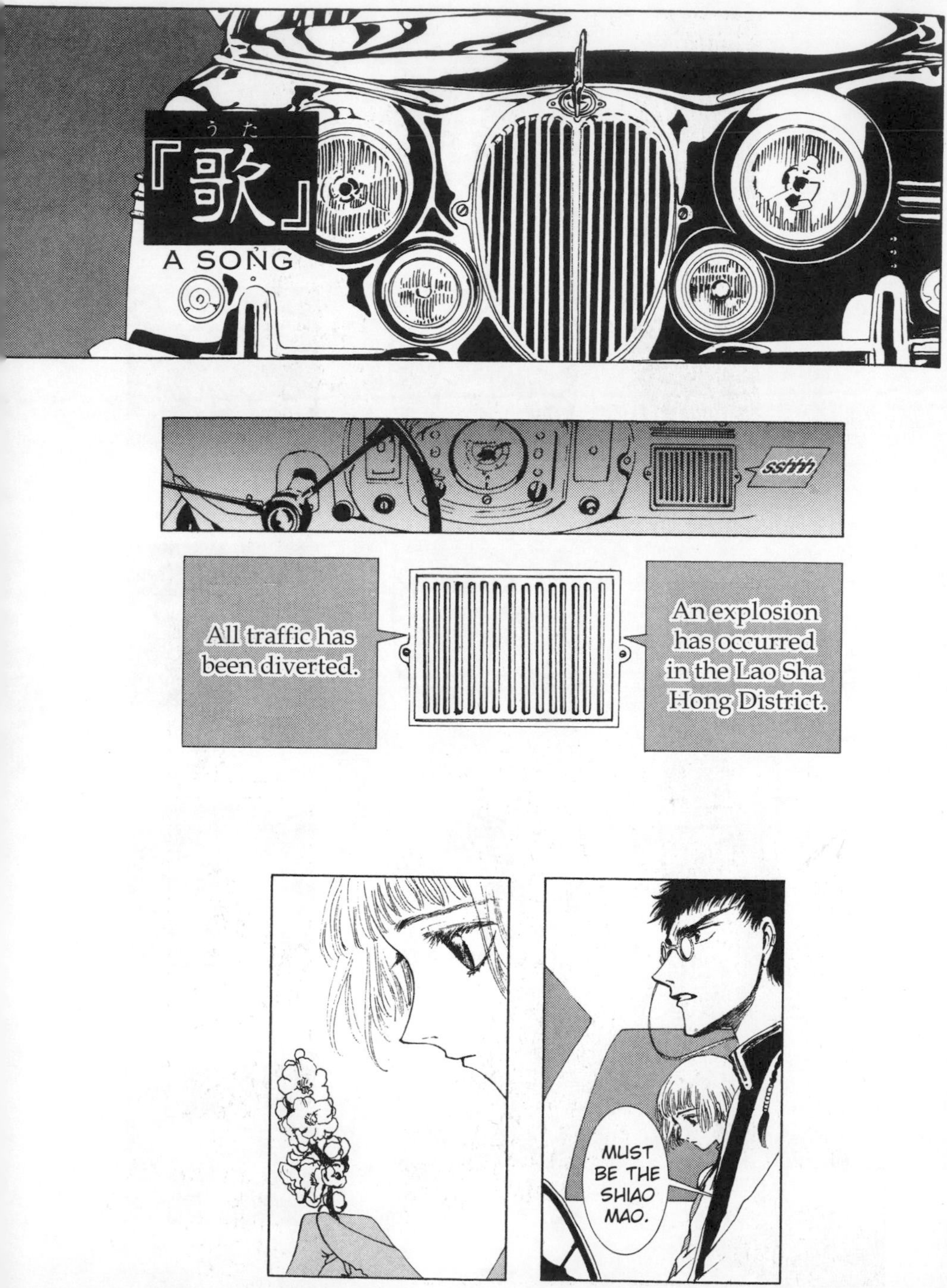
うた
『歌』
A SONG
sshhh
An explosion has occurred in the Lao Sha Hong District.
All traffic has been diverted.
MUST BE THE SHIAO MAO.

I wish for
happiness
I seek
happiness

So take me
somewhere
far from
here

I wish for
happiness
I seek
happiness

Take me
Somewhere
away from
here

Please
Take me

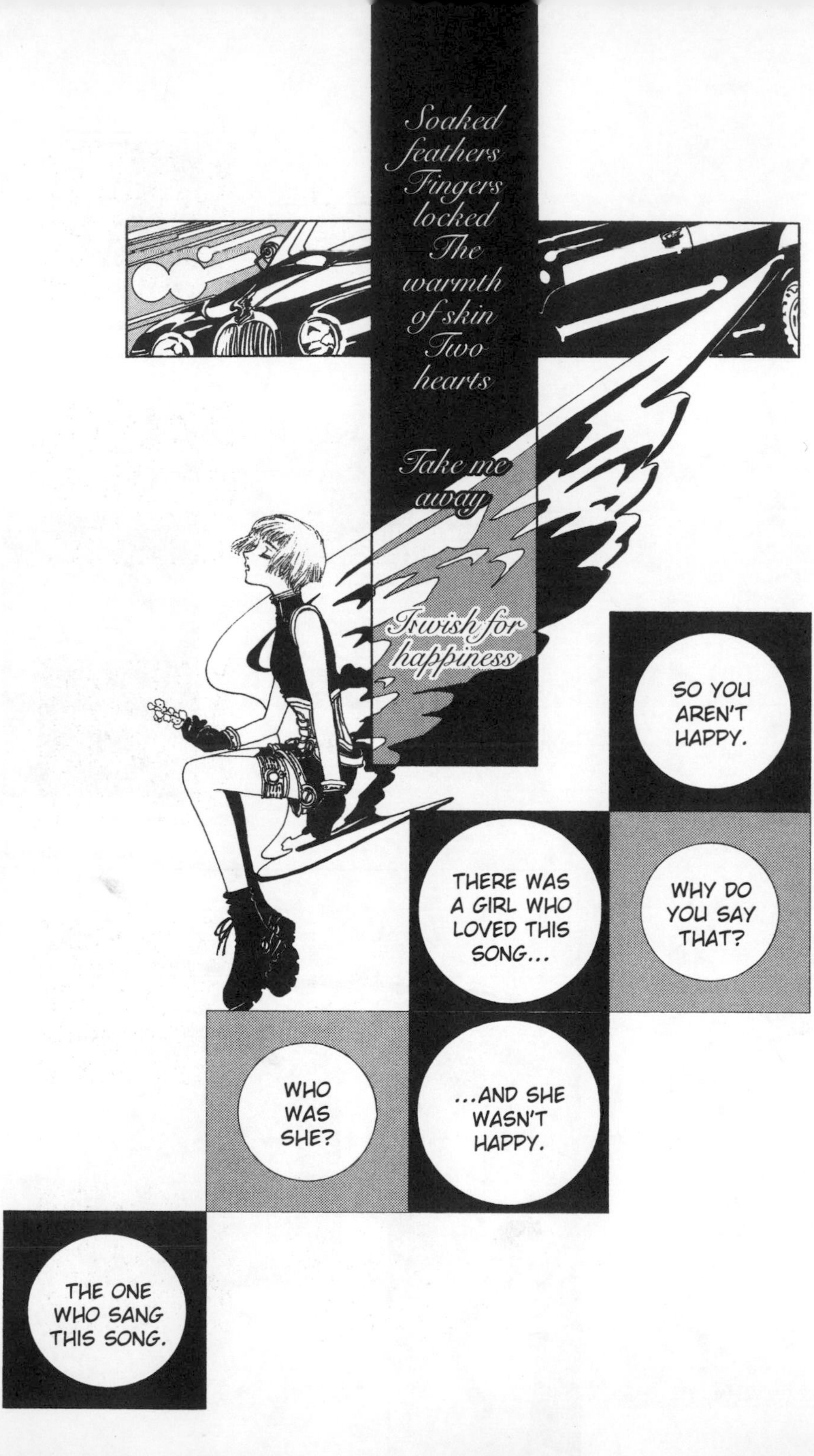
Soaked feathers Fingers locked The warmth of skin Two hearts
Take me away
I wish for happiness
SO YOU AREN'T HAPPY.
WHY DO YOU SAY THAT?
THERE WAS A GIRL WHO LOVED THIS SONG...
...AND SHE WASN'T HAPPY.
WHO WAS SHE?
THE ONE WHO SANG THIS SONG.

To find
happiness
with you

To be your
happiness

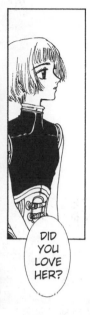

DID
YOU
LOVE
HER?

SOME-
THING
LIKE
THAT.

EVEN
NOW?

SHE'S
DEAD.

NO.

I wish for
happiness

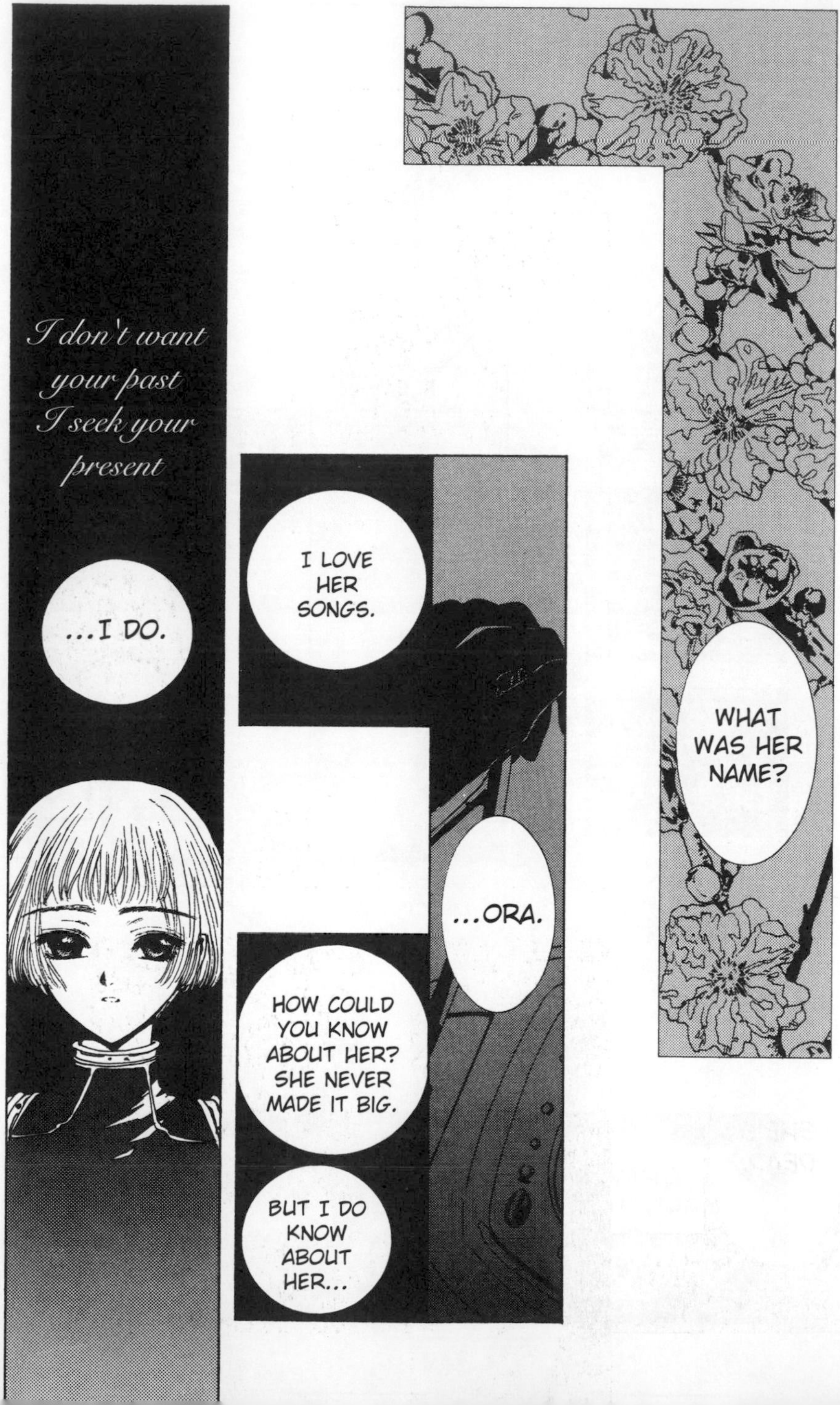
WHAT WAS HER NAME?
...ORA.
I LOVE HER SONGS.
HOW COULD YOU KNOW ABOUT HER? SHE NEVER MADE IT BIG.
BUT I DO KNOW ABOUT HER...
I don't want your past I seek your present
...I DO.

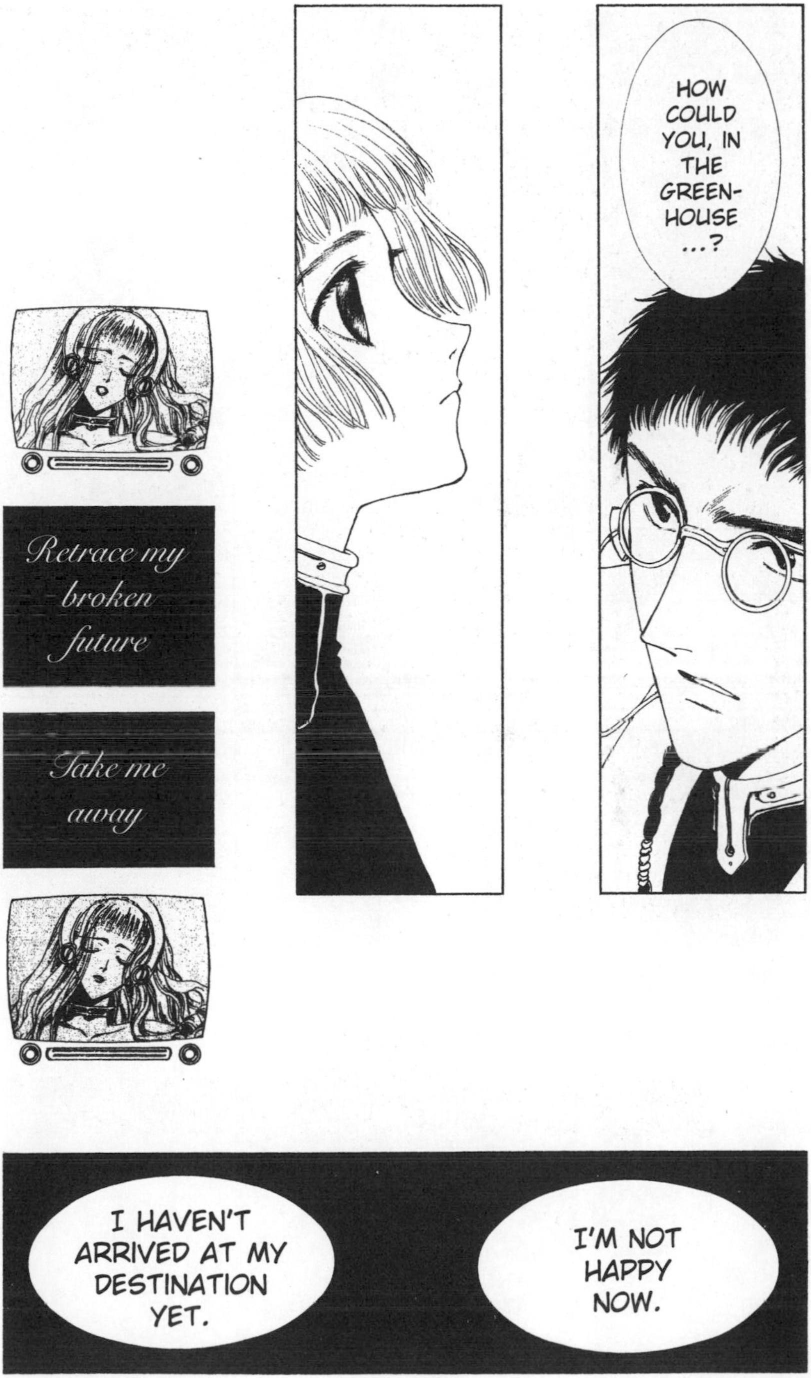
HOW COULD YOU, IN THE GREEN-HOUSE ...?
Retrace my broken future
Take me away
I'M NOT HAPPY NOW.
I HAVEN'T ARRIVED AT MY DESTINATION YET.

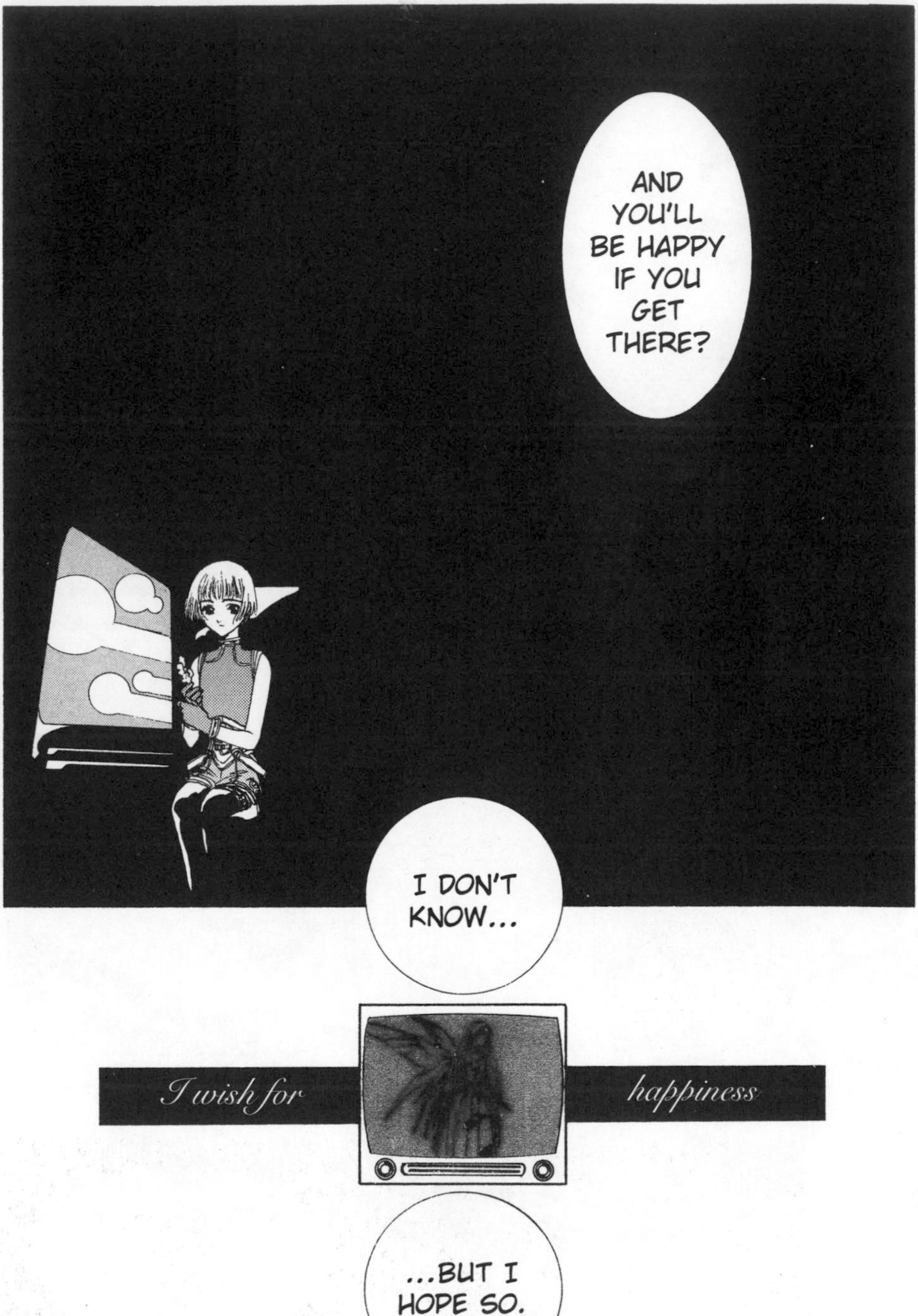
AND YOU'LL BE HAPPY IF YOU GET THERE?
I DON'T KNOW...
I wish for happiness
...BUT I HOPE SO.

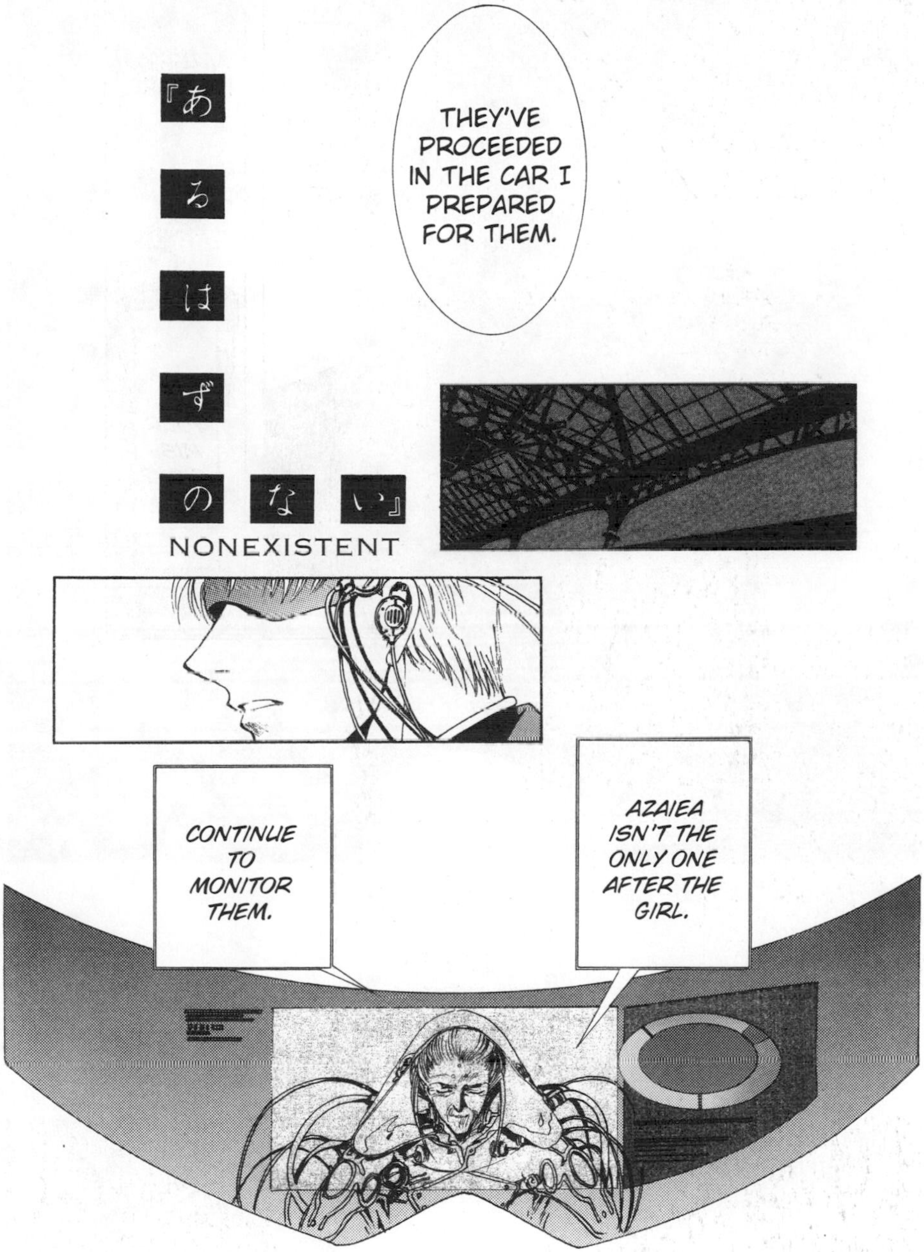
THEY'VE PROCEEDED IN THE CAR I PREPARED FOR THEM.
『あるはずのない』
NONEXISTENT
AZAIEA ISN'T THE ONLY ONE AFTER THE GIRL.
CONTINUE TO MONITOR THEM.

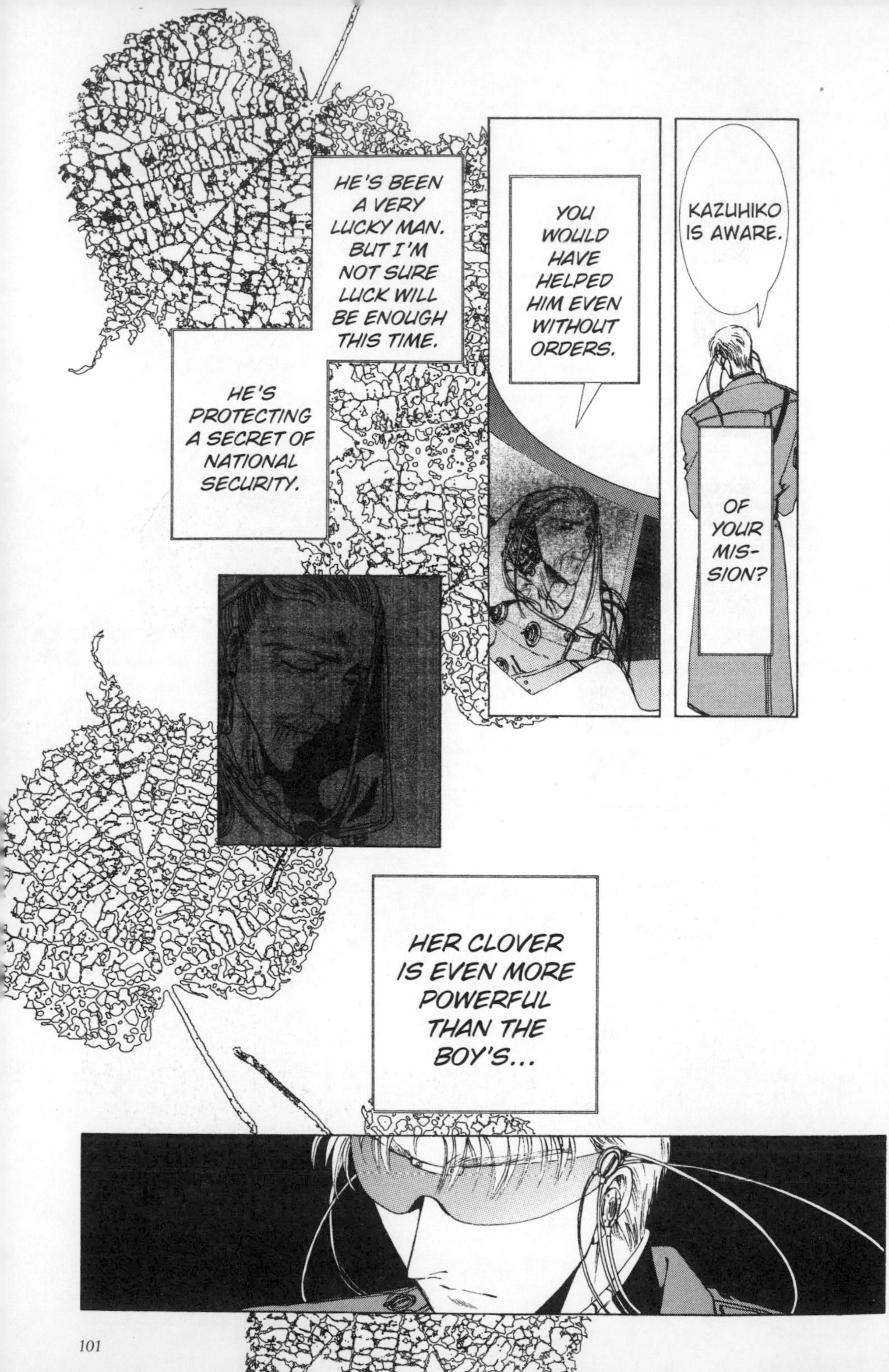
KAZUHIKO IS AWARE.
OF YOUR MIS-SION?
YOU WOULD HAVE HELPED HIM EVEN WITHOUT ORDERS.
HE'S BEEN A VERY LUCKY MAN. BUT I'M NOT SURE LUCK WILL BE ENOUGH THIS TIME.
HE'S PROTECTING A SECRET OF NATIONAL SECURITY.
HER CLOVER IS EVEN MORE POWERFUL THAN THE BOY'S...

I NEVER
KNEW IT
EXISTED
UNTIL NOW...
A FOUR-LEAF
CLOVER.

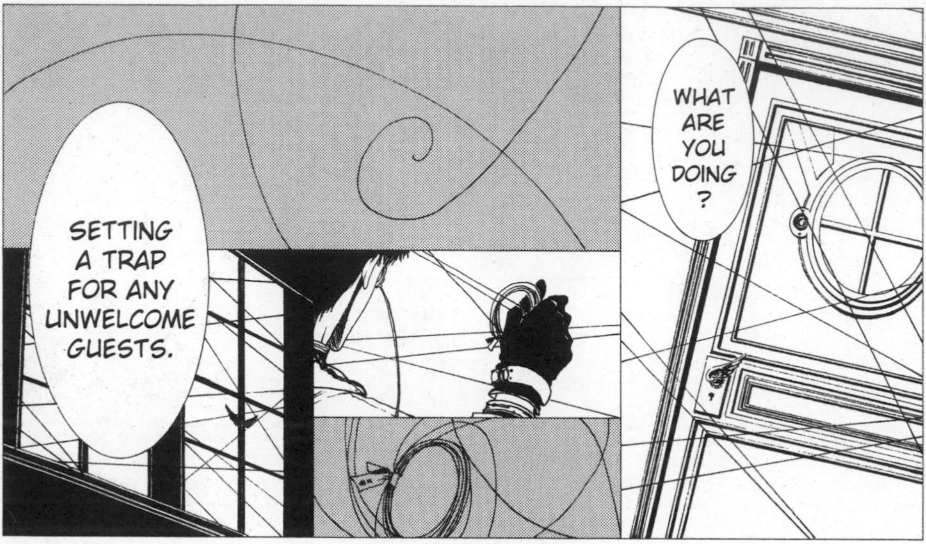
WHAT ARE YOU DOING?
SETTING A TRAP FOR ANY UNWELCOME GUESTS.

GOODNIGHT

『おやすみ』

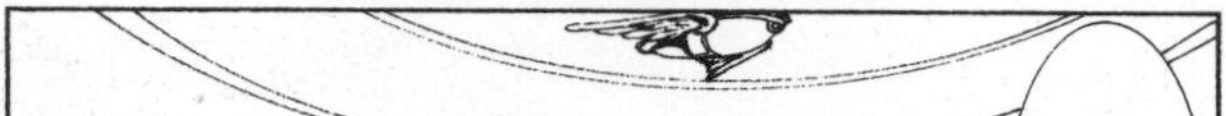
THIS PLACE IS NICE.
LESS LIKELY TO GET ATTACKED HERE.

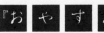

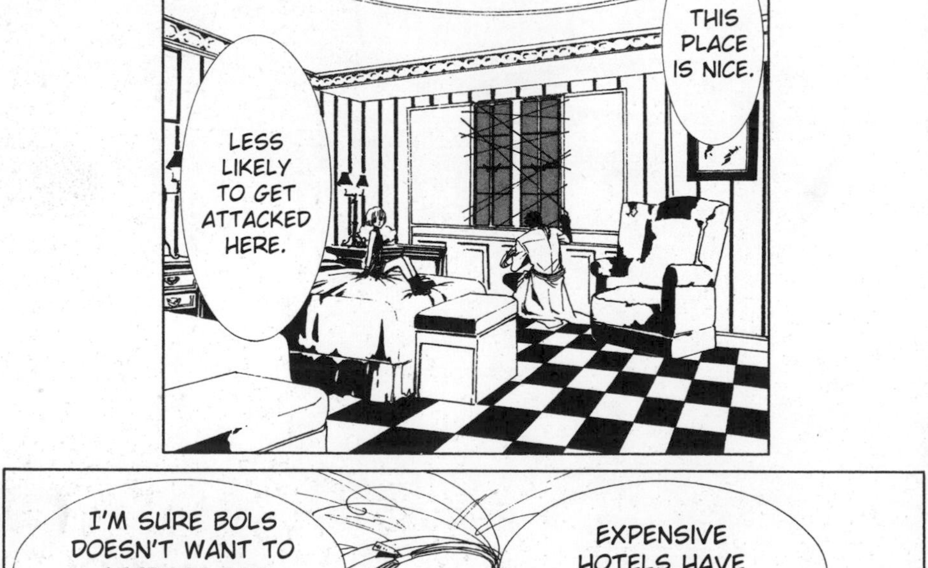
EXPENSIVE HOTELS HAVE BETTER SECURITY.
I'M SURE BOLS DOESN'T WANT TO ATTRACT TOO MUCH ATTENTION IN PUBLIC.

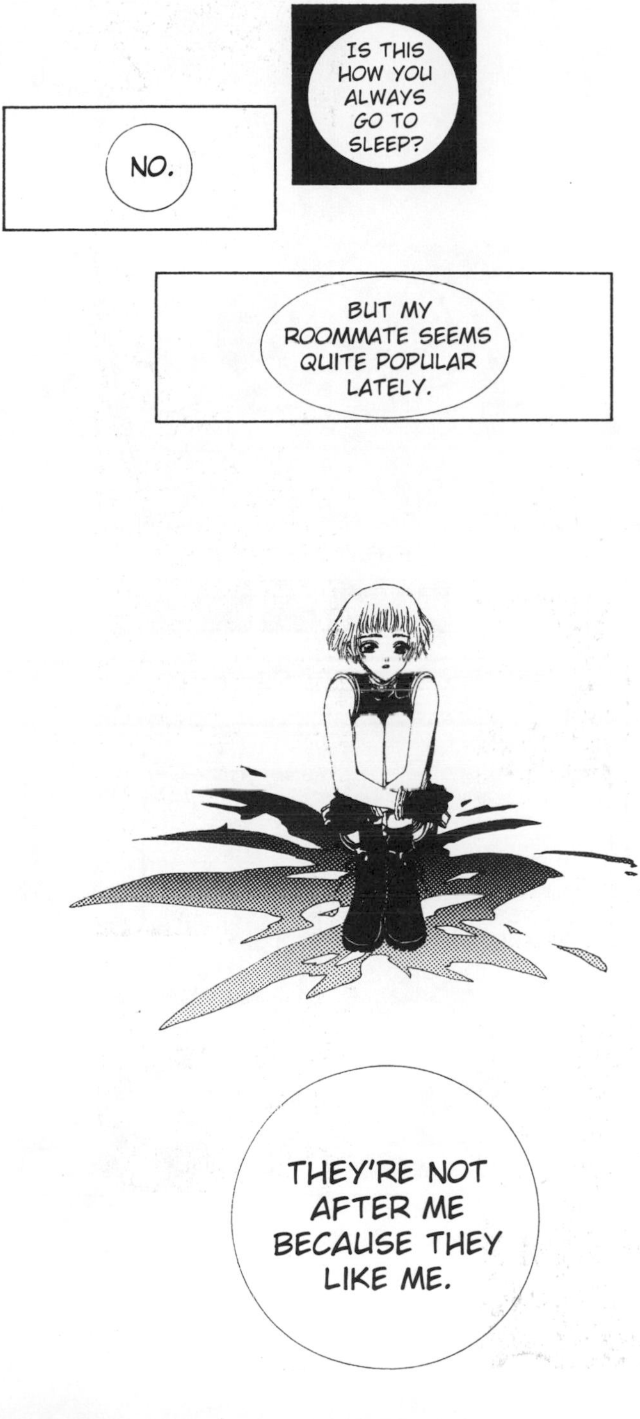
IS THIS HOW YOU ALWAYS GO TO SLEEP?
NO.
BUT MY ROOMMATE SEEMS QUITE POPULAR LATELY.
THEY'RE NOT AFTER ME BECAUSE THEY LIKE ME.

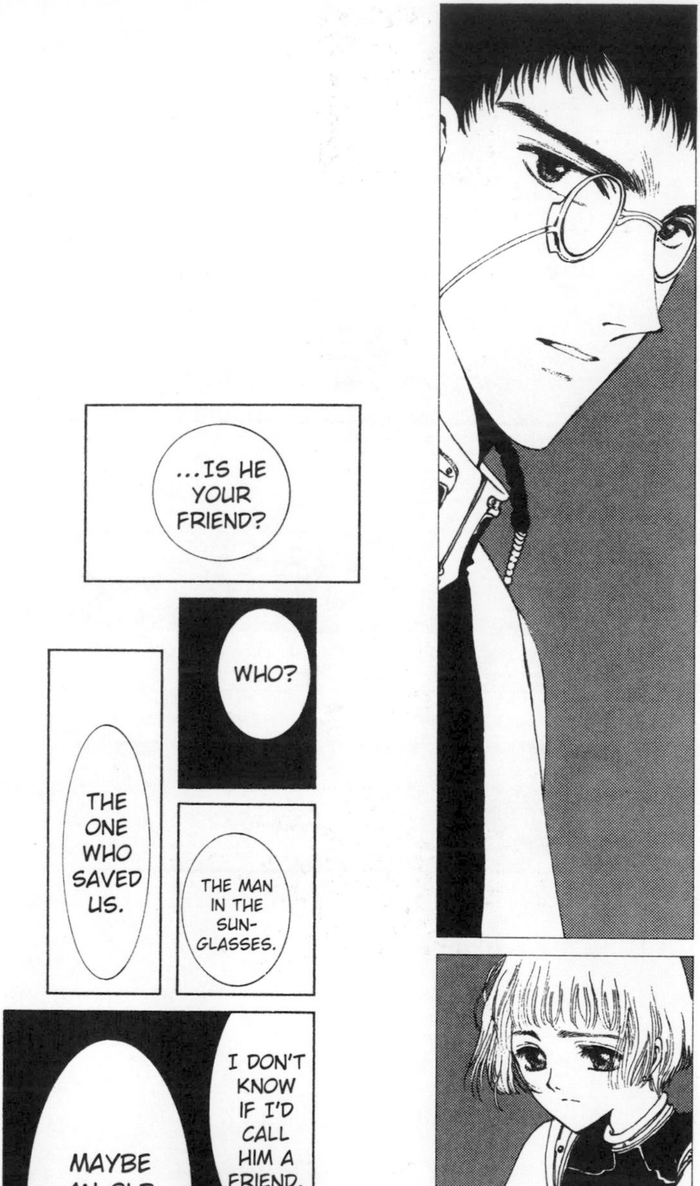
...IS HE YOUR FRIEND?
WHO?
THE MAN IN THE SUN-GLASSES.
THE ONE WHO SAVED US.
I DON'T KNOW IF I'D CALL HIM A FRIEND.
MAYBE AN OLD MILITARY ASSOCIATE.

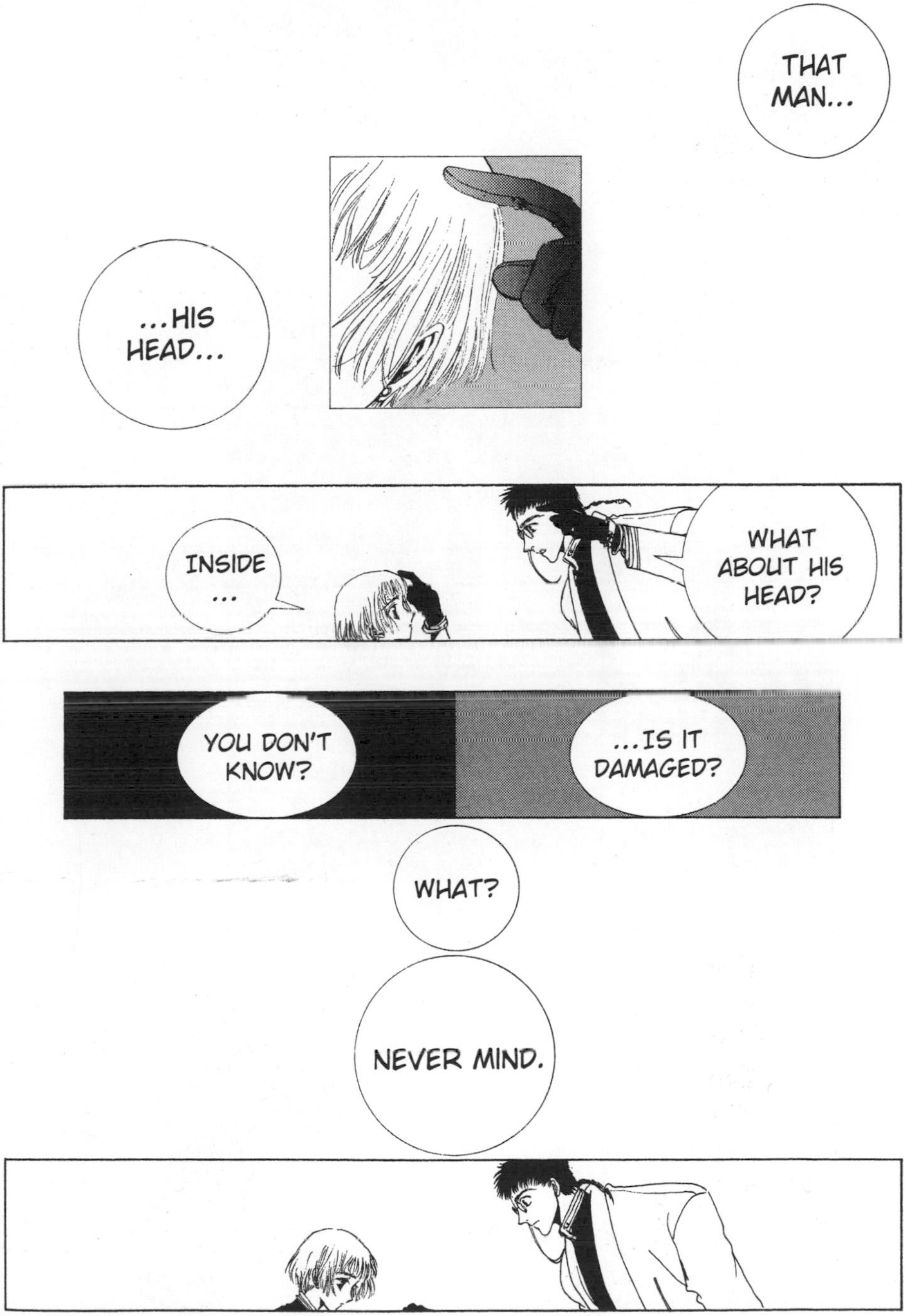
THAT MAN...
...HIS HEAD...
WHAT ABOUT HIS HEAD?
INSIDE ...
...IS IT DAMAGED?
YOU DON'T KNOW?
WHAT?
NEVER MIND.

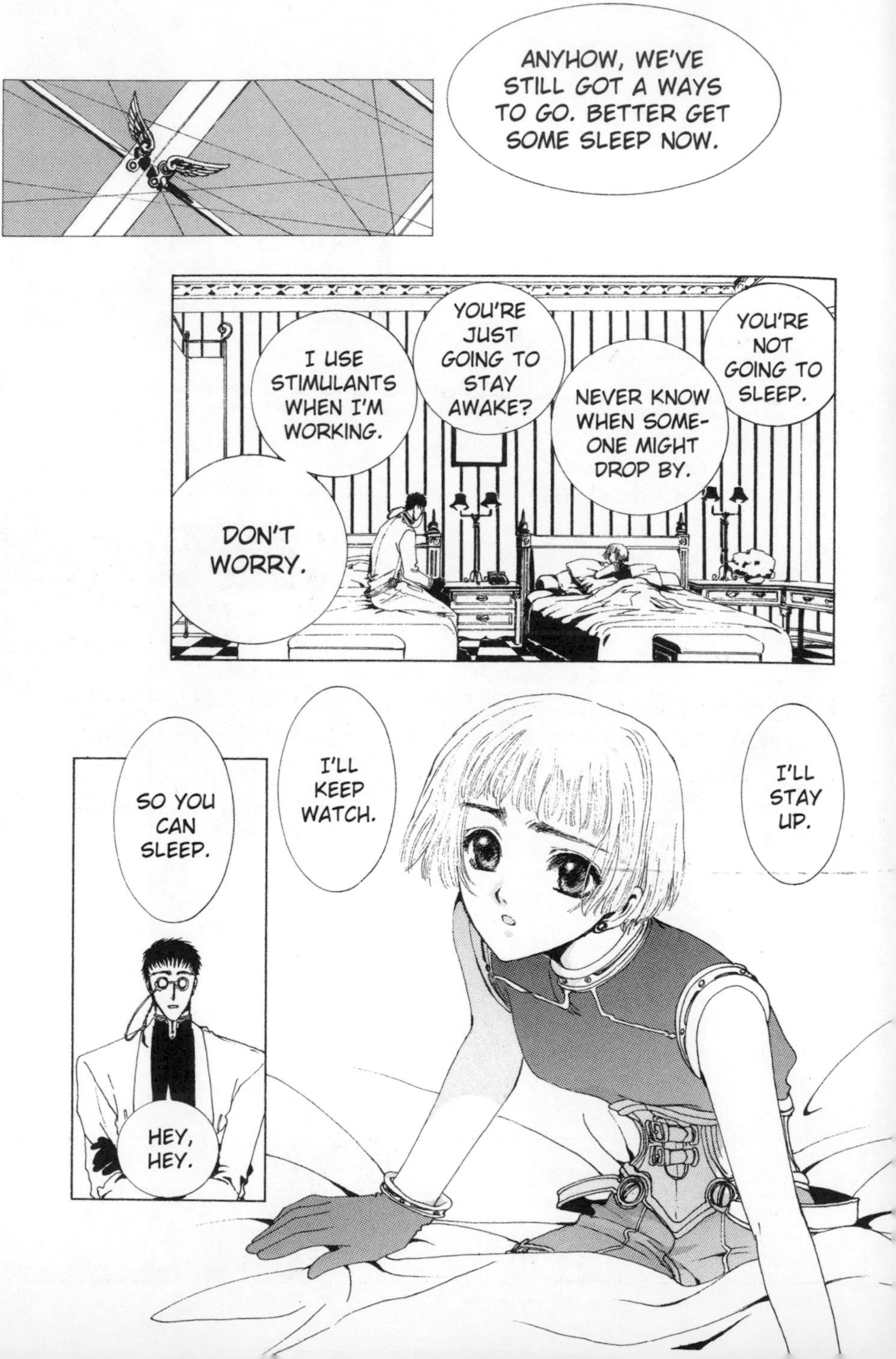
ANYHOW, WE'VE STILL GOT A WAYS TO GO. BETTER GET SOME SLEEP NOW.
YOU'RE NOT GOING TO SLEEP.
NEVER KNOW WHEN SOME-ONE MIGHT DROP BY.
YOU'RE JUST GOING TO STAY AWAKE?
I USE STIMULANTS WHEN I'M WORKING.
DON'T WORRY.
I'LL STAY UP.
I'LL KEEP WATCH.
SO YOU CAN SLEEP.
HEY, HEY.

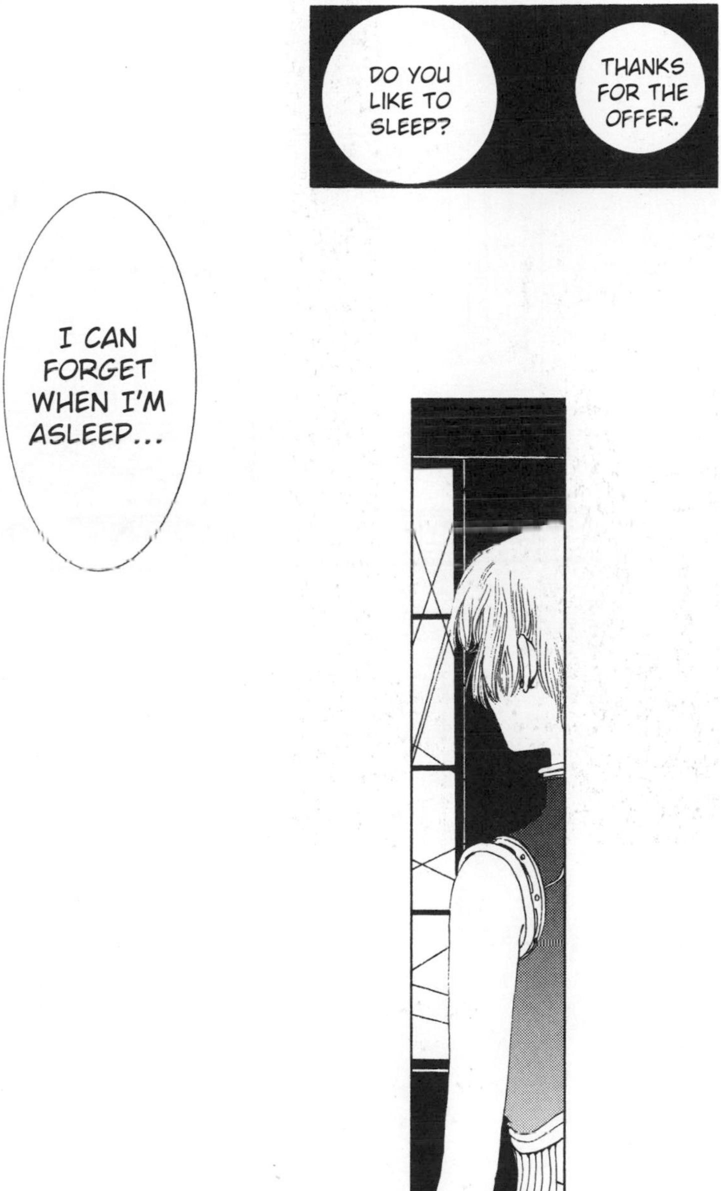
THANKS FOR THE OFFER.
DO YOU LIKE TO SLEEP?
I CAN FORGET WHEN I'M ASLEEP...

...
FORGET
I'M
ALONE.

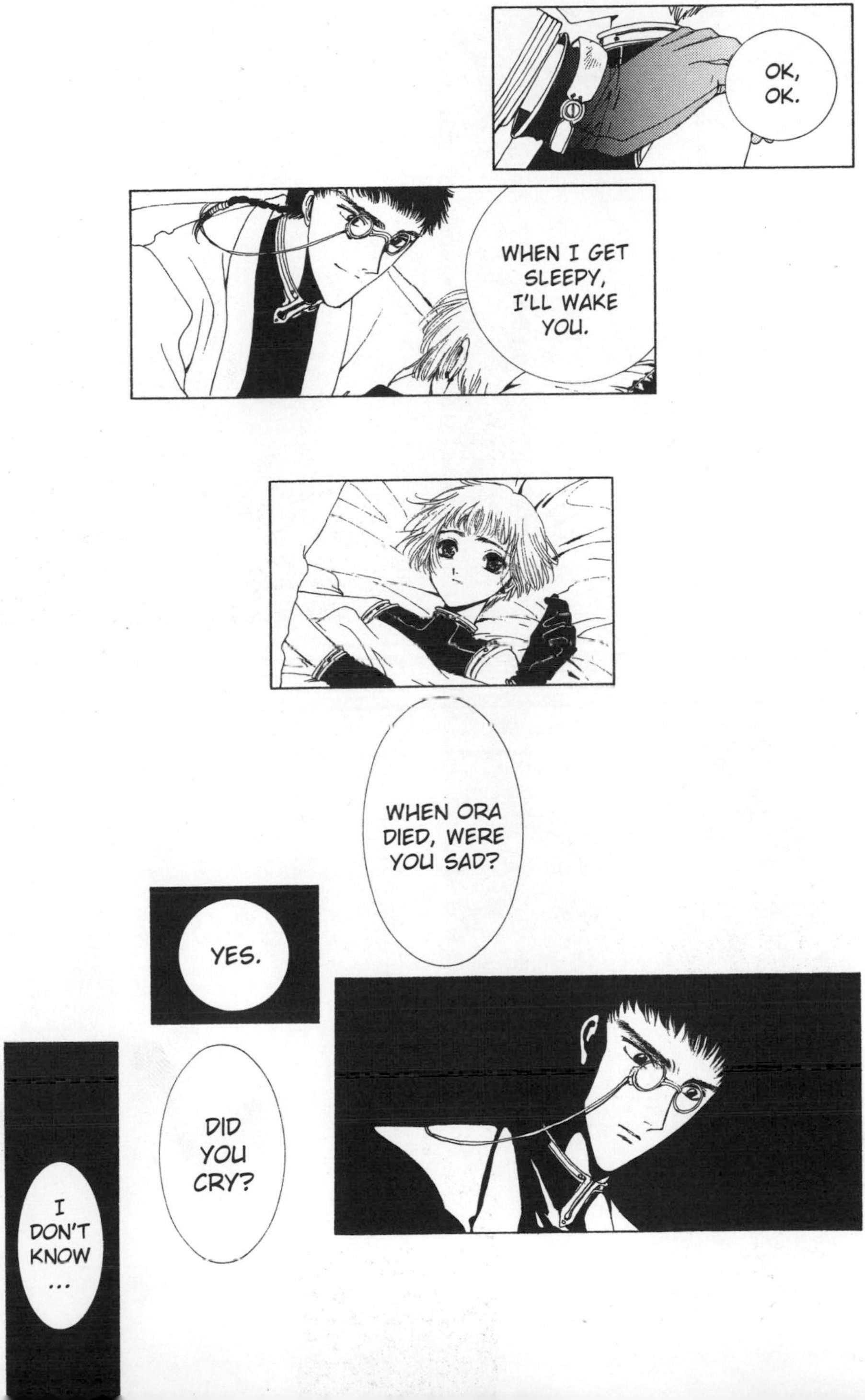
OK, OK.
WHEN I GET SLEEPY, I'LL WAKE YOU.
WHEN ORA DIED, WERE YOU SAD?
YES.
DID YOU CRY?
I DON'T KNOW ...

WHEN I DIE, NOBODY WILL CRY FOR ME.

WHY?

BE-CAUSE I'M ALONE.

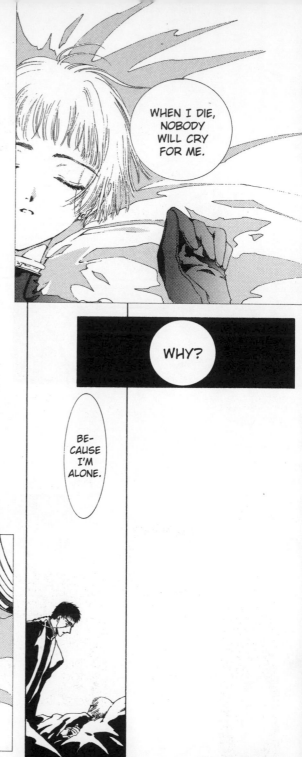

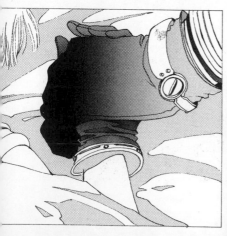

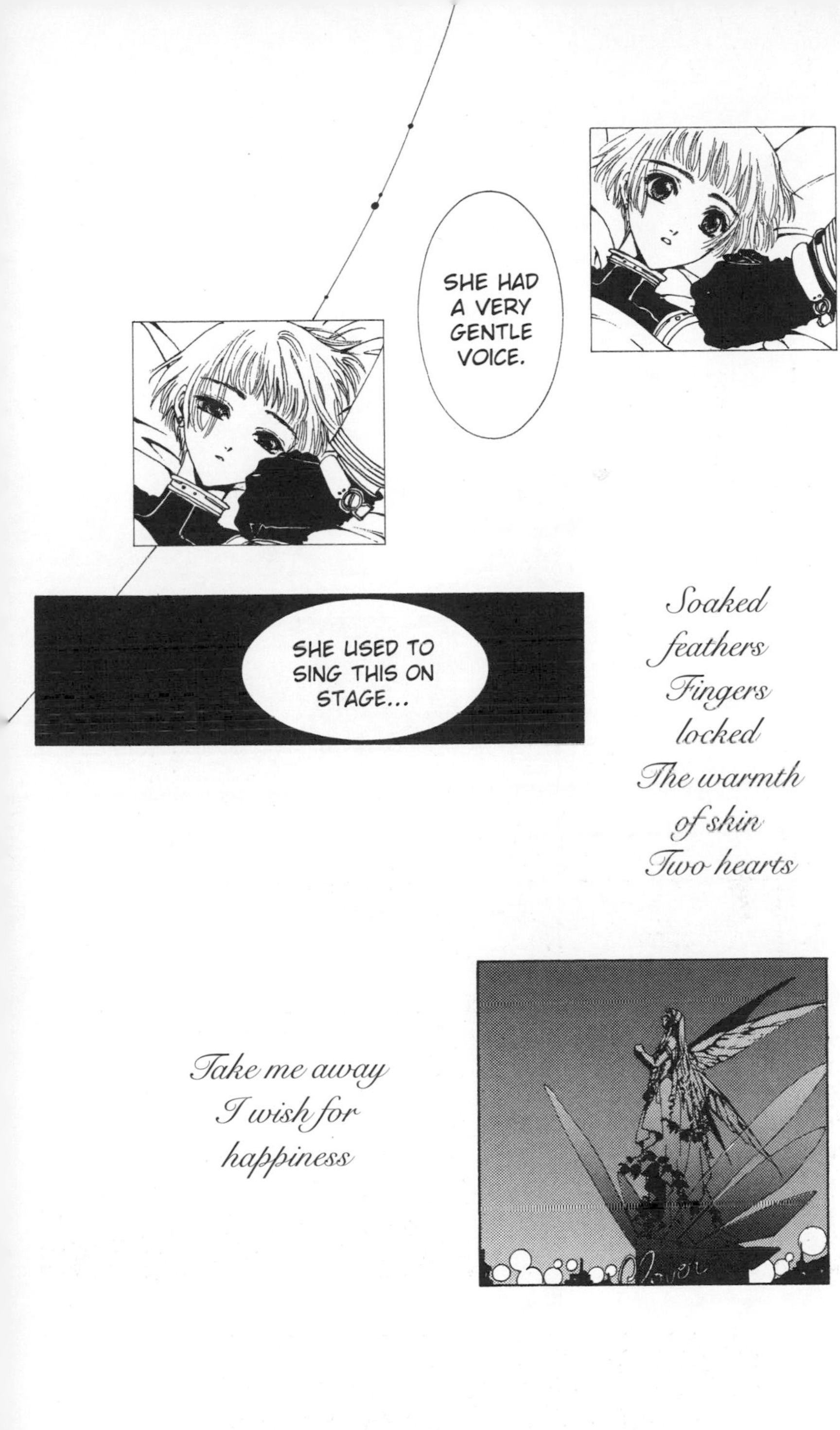
SHE HAD A VERY GENTLE VOICE.
SHE USED TO SING THIS ON STAGE...
Soaked feathers Fingers locked The warmth of skin Two hearts
Take me away I wish for happiness

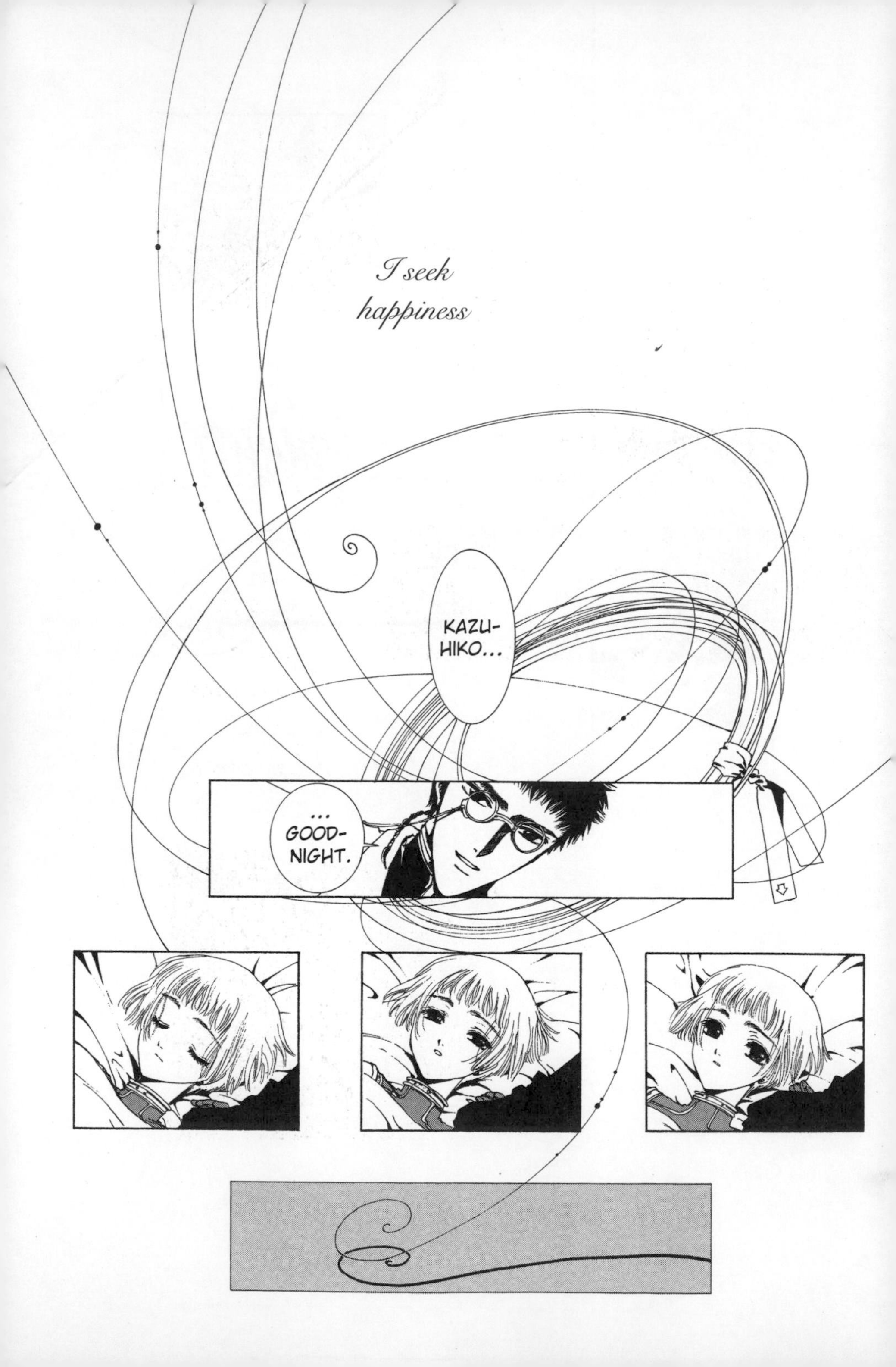
I seek happiness
KAZU-HIKO...
...GOOD-NIGHT.

...TO FAIRY PARK...

WE'D BETTER GET THERE BEFORE I RUN OUT OF STIMULANT...

PSHHHTT

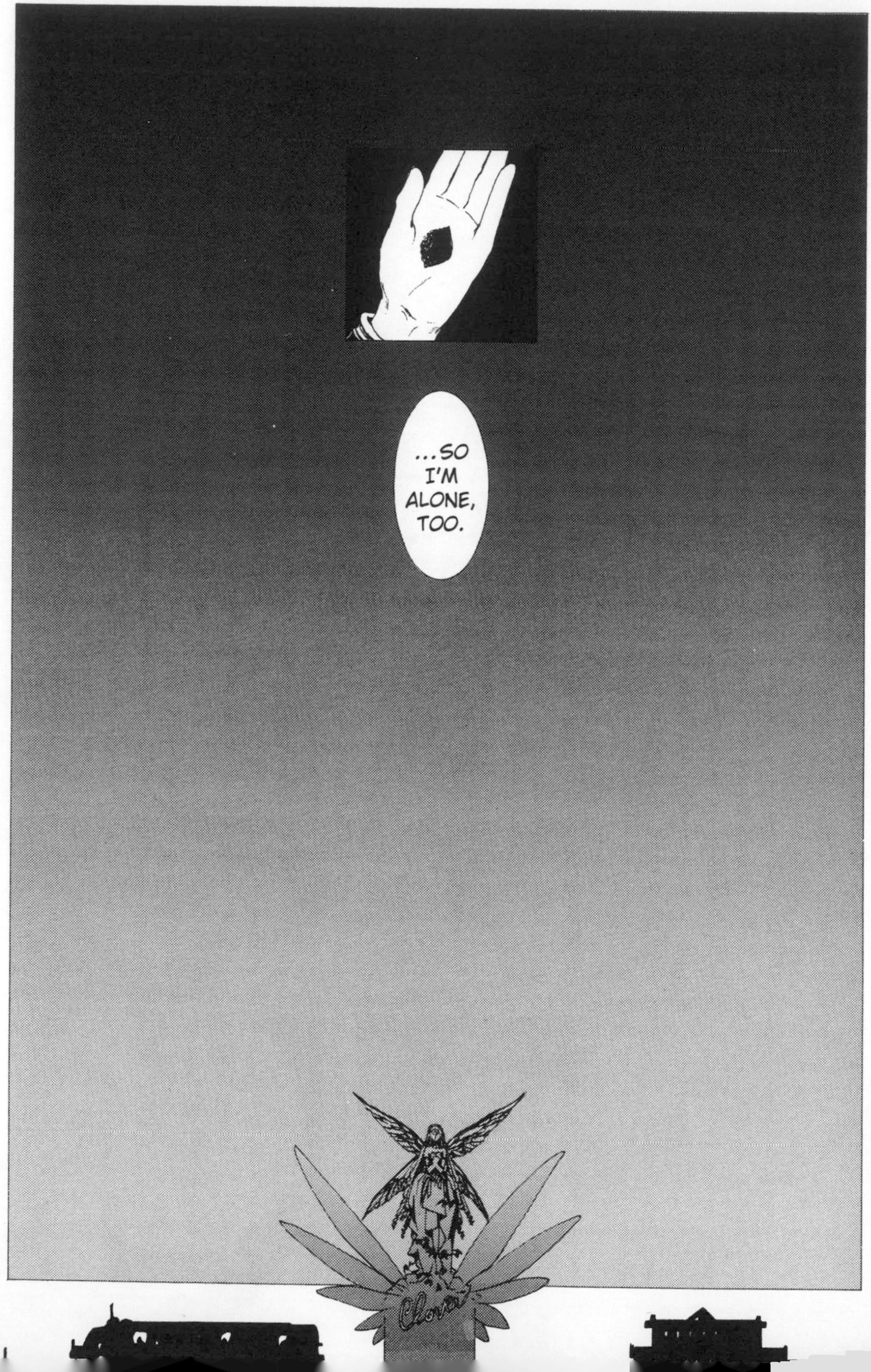
...SO I'M ALONE, TOO.

『追 つい
PURSUIT

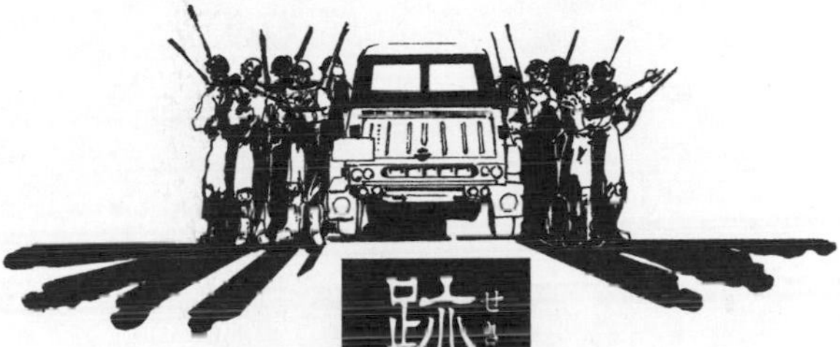

跡 せき』

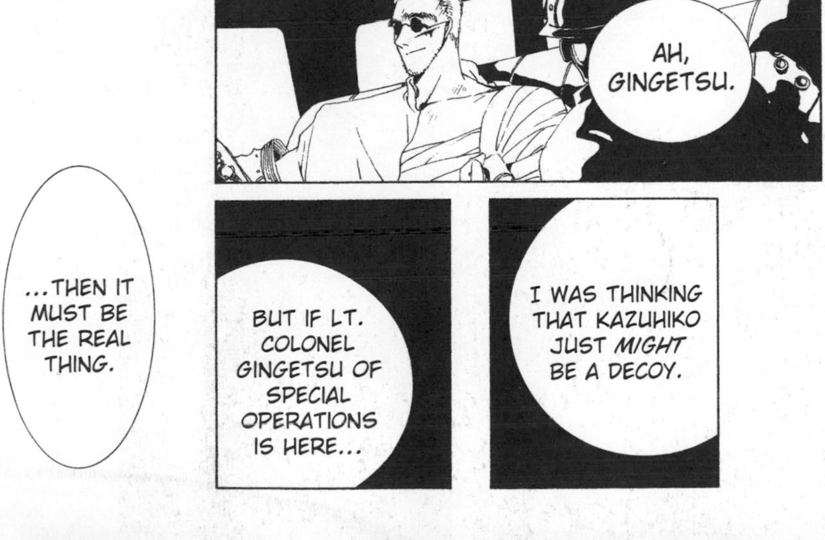
AH, GINGETSU.
I WAS THINKING THAT KAZUHIKO JUST *MIGHT* BE A DECOY.
BUT IF LT. COLONEL GINGETSU OF SPECIAL OPERATIONS IS HERE...
...THEN IT MUST BE THE REAL THING.

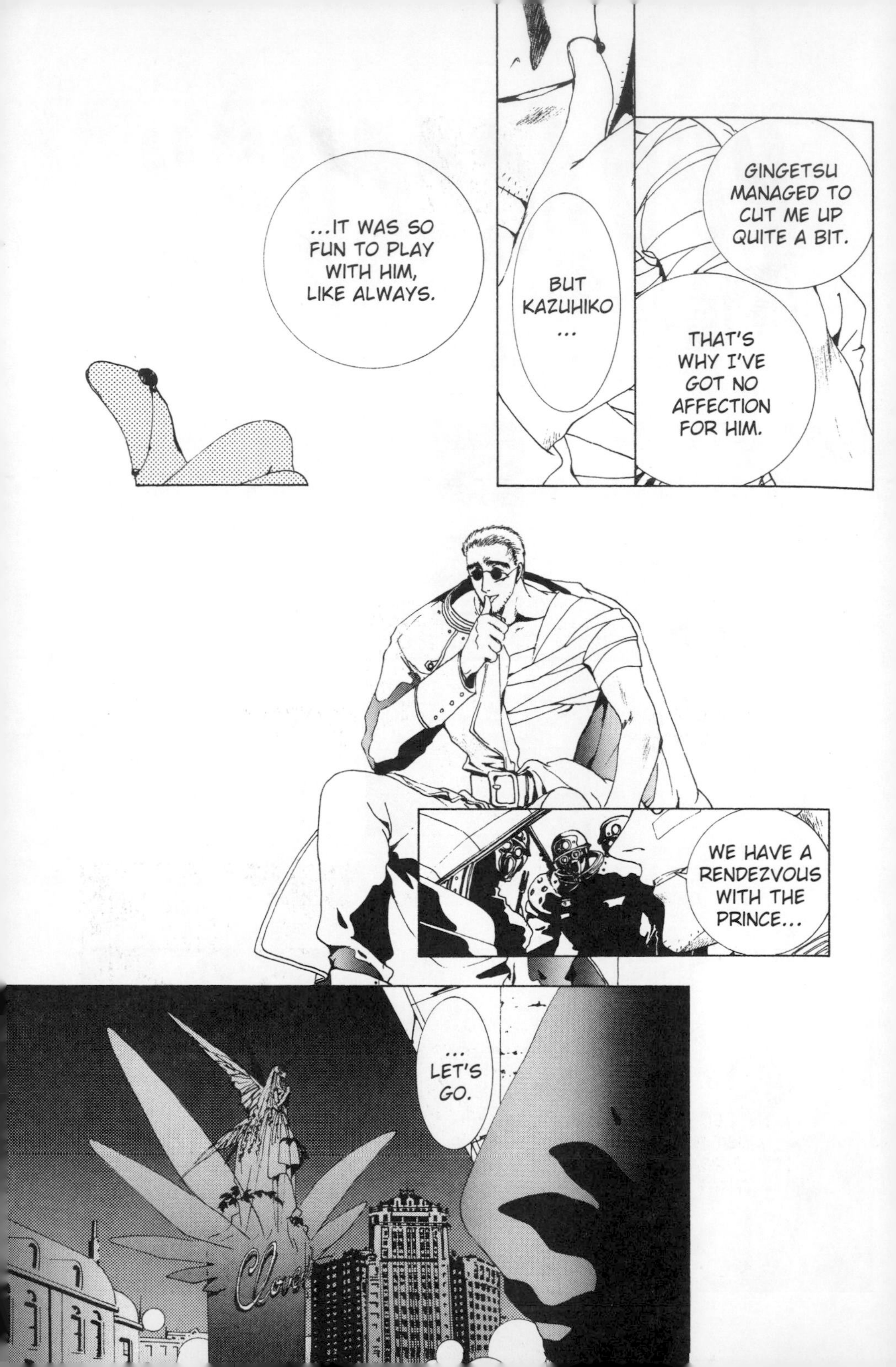
GINGETSU MANAGED TO CUT ME UP QUITE A BIT.
THAT'S WHY I'VE GOT NO AFFECTION FOR HIM.
BUT KAZUHIKO ...
...IT WAS SO FUN TO PLAY WITH HIM, LIKE ALWAYS.
WE HAVE A RENDEZVOUS WITH THE PRINCE...
... LET'S GO.

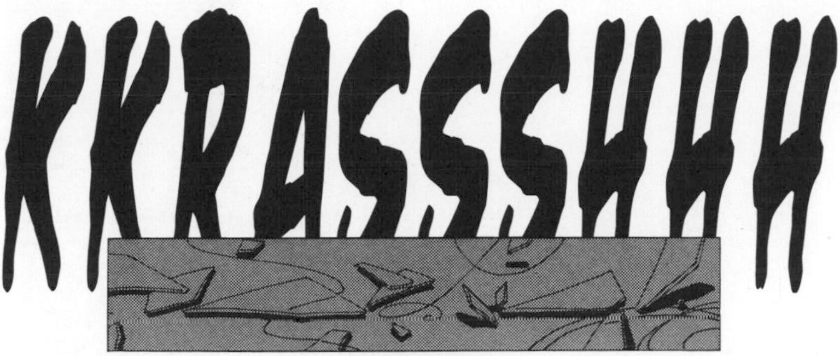
KKRASSSHHH

『羽根』

FEATHERS

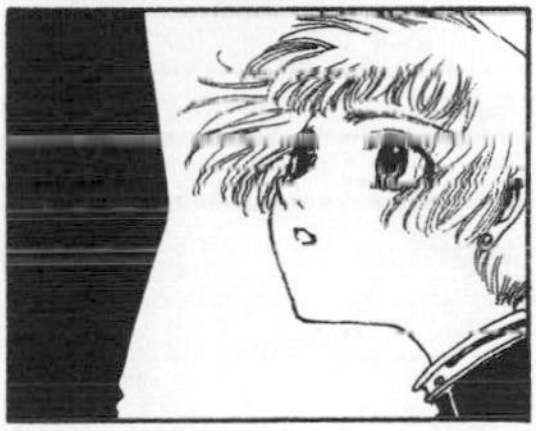

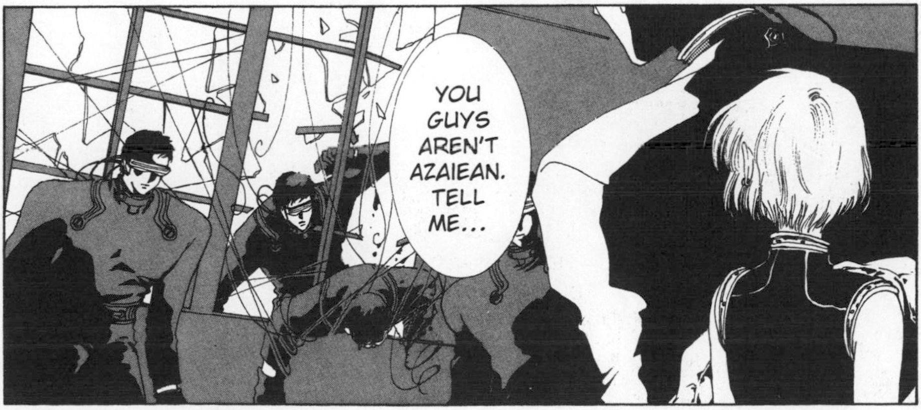
YOU GUYS AREN'T AZAIEAN. TELL ME...

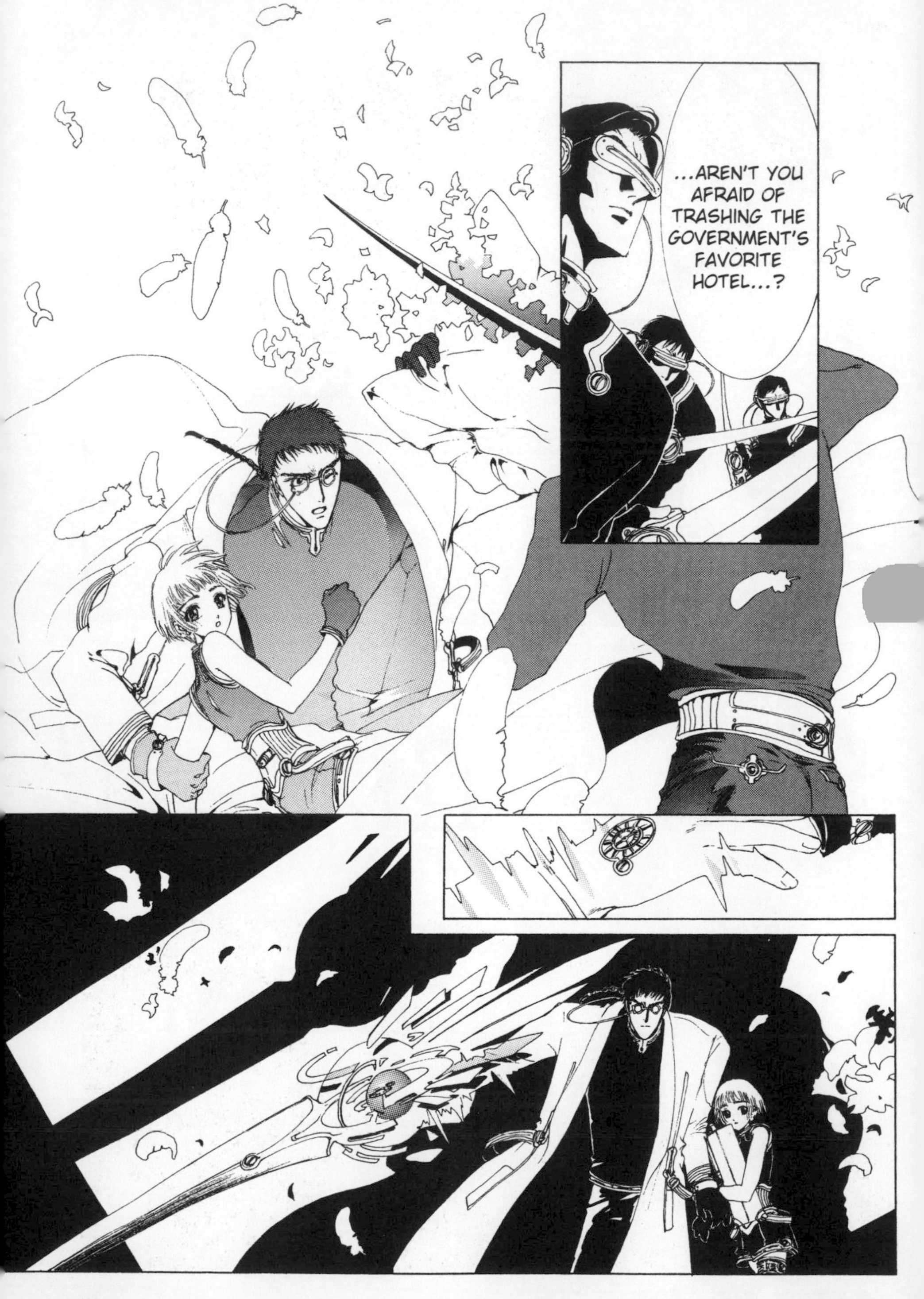
...AREN'T YOU AFRAID OF TRASHING THE GOVERNMENT'S FAVORITE HOTEL...?

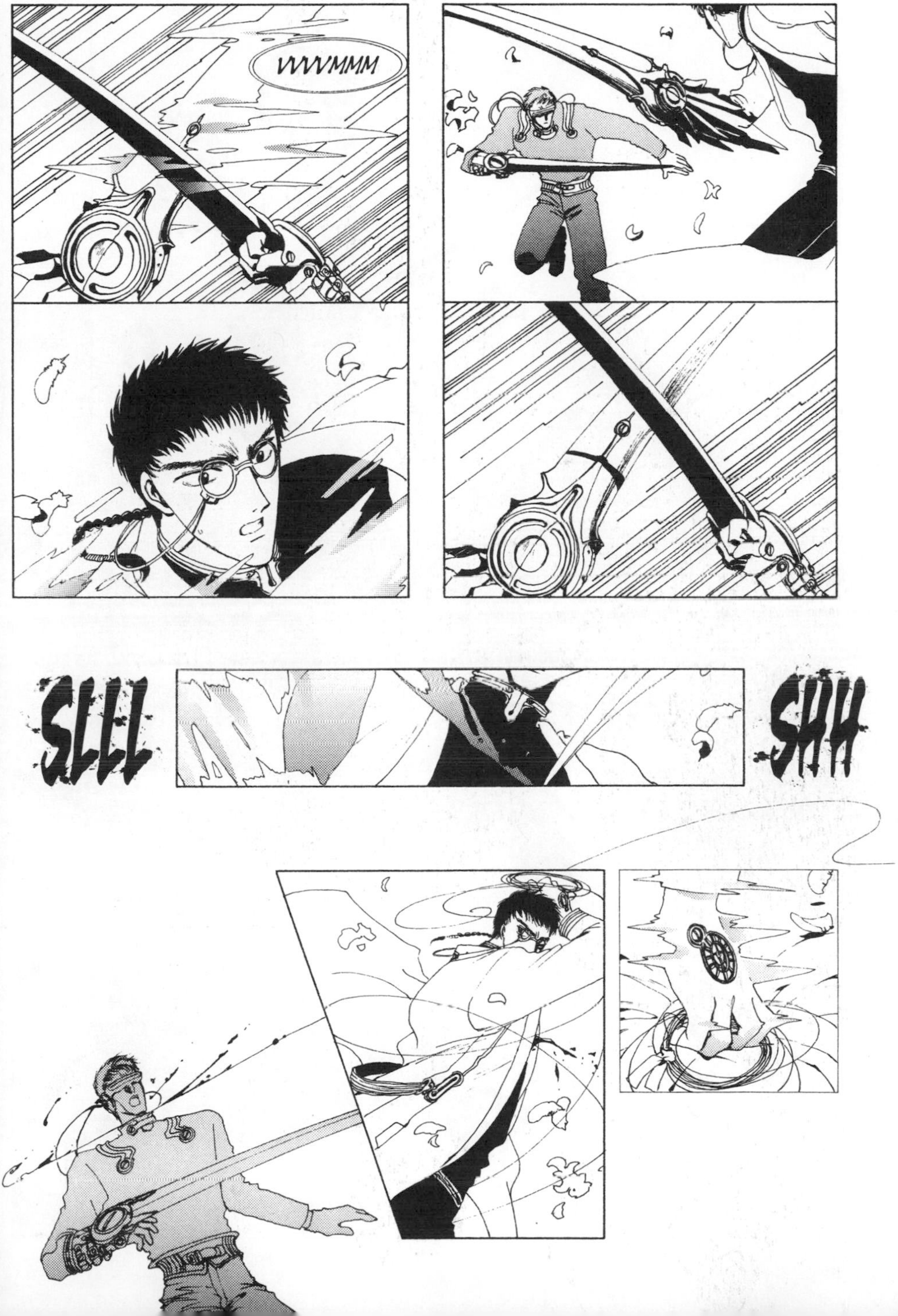
VVVVMMM
SHH
SLLL

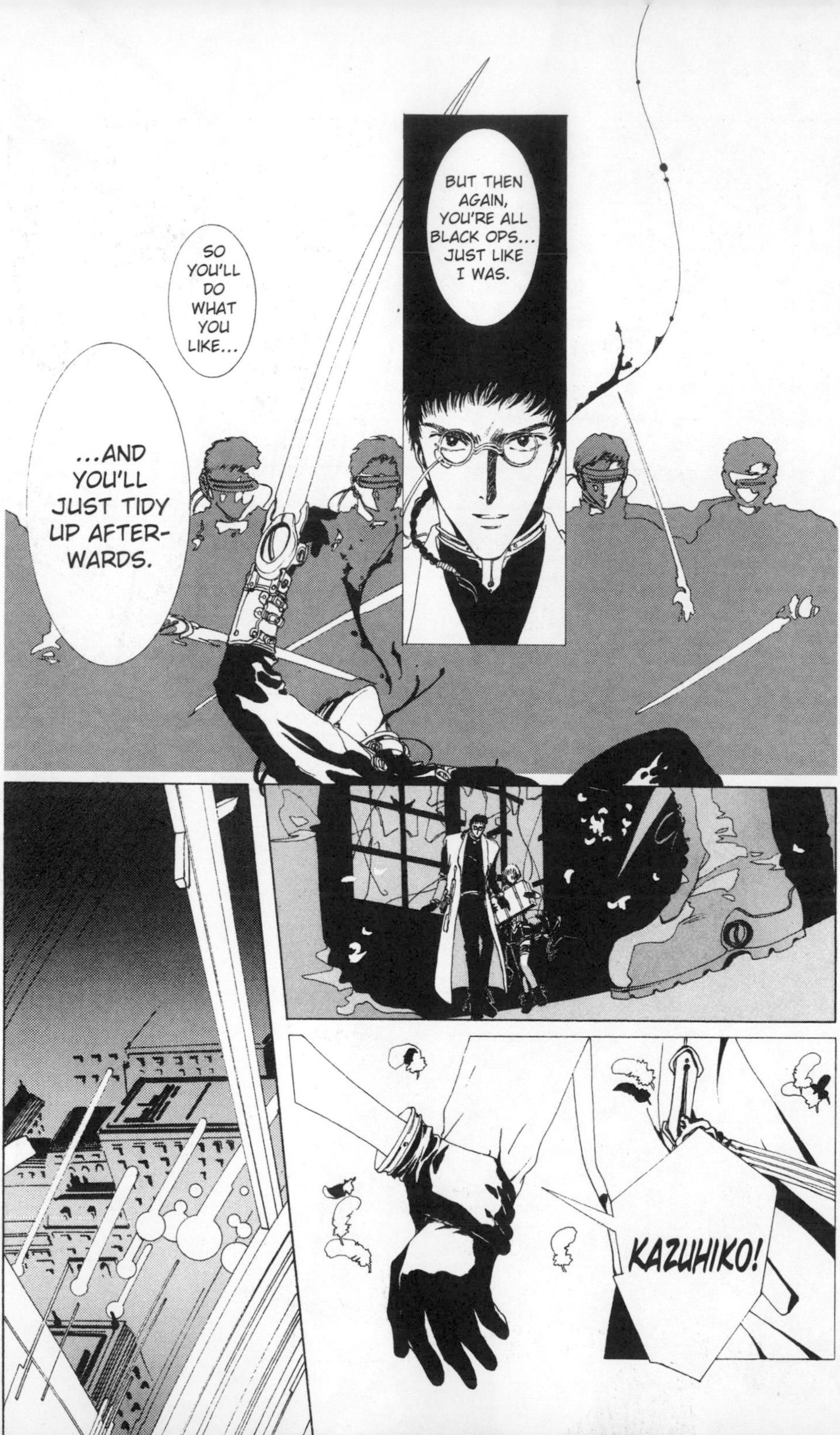
BUT THEN AGAIN, YOU'RE ALL BLACK OPS... JUST LIKE I WAS.
SO YOU'LL DO WHAT YOU LIKE...
...AND YOU'LL JUST TIDY UP AFTER-WARDS.
KAZUHIKO!

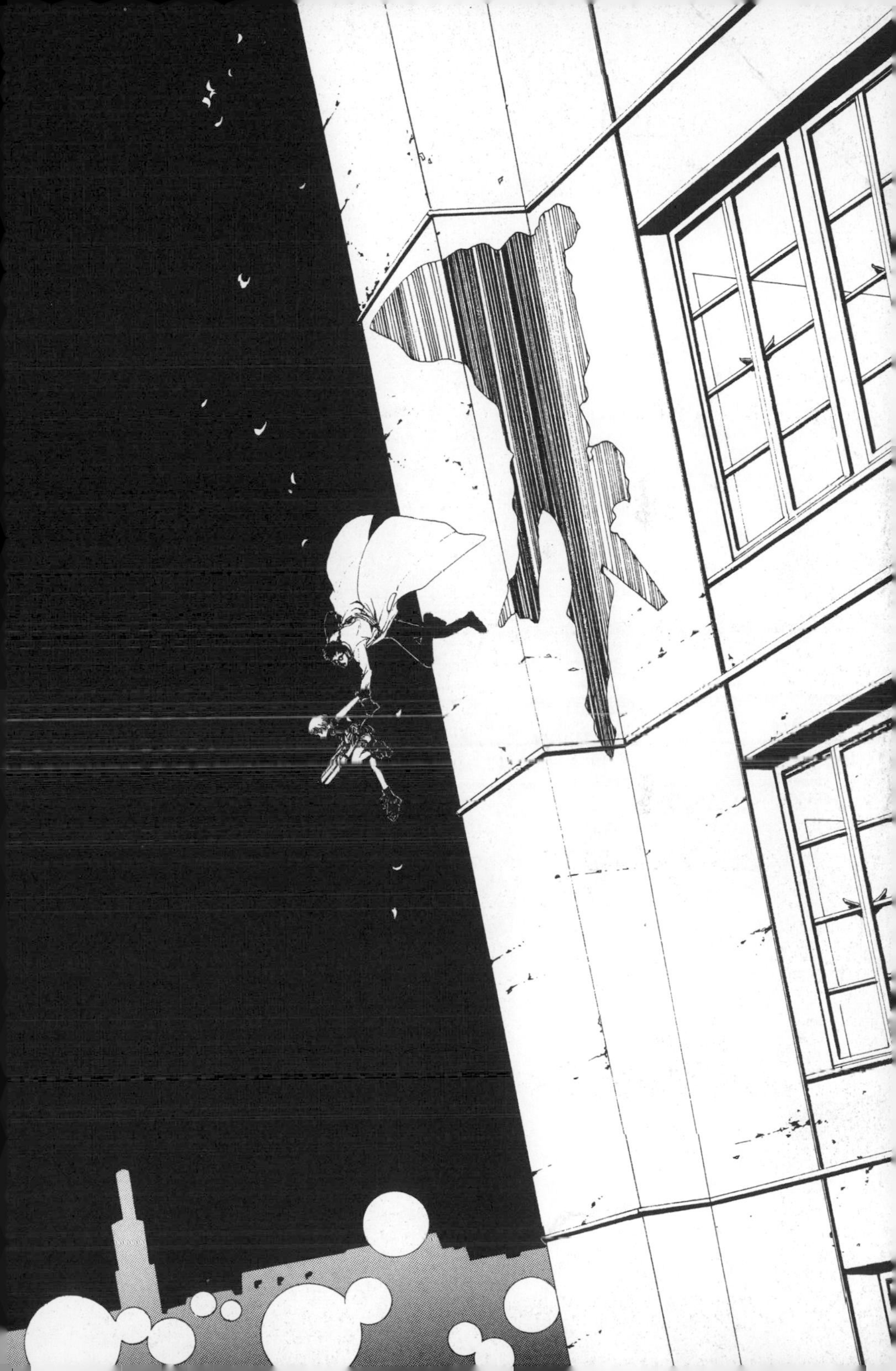

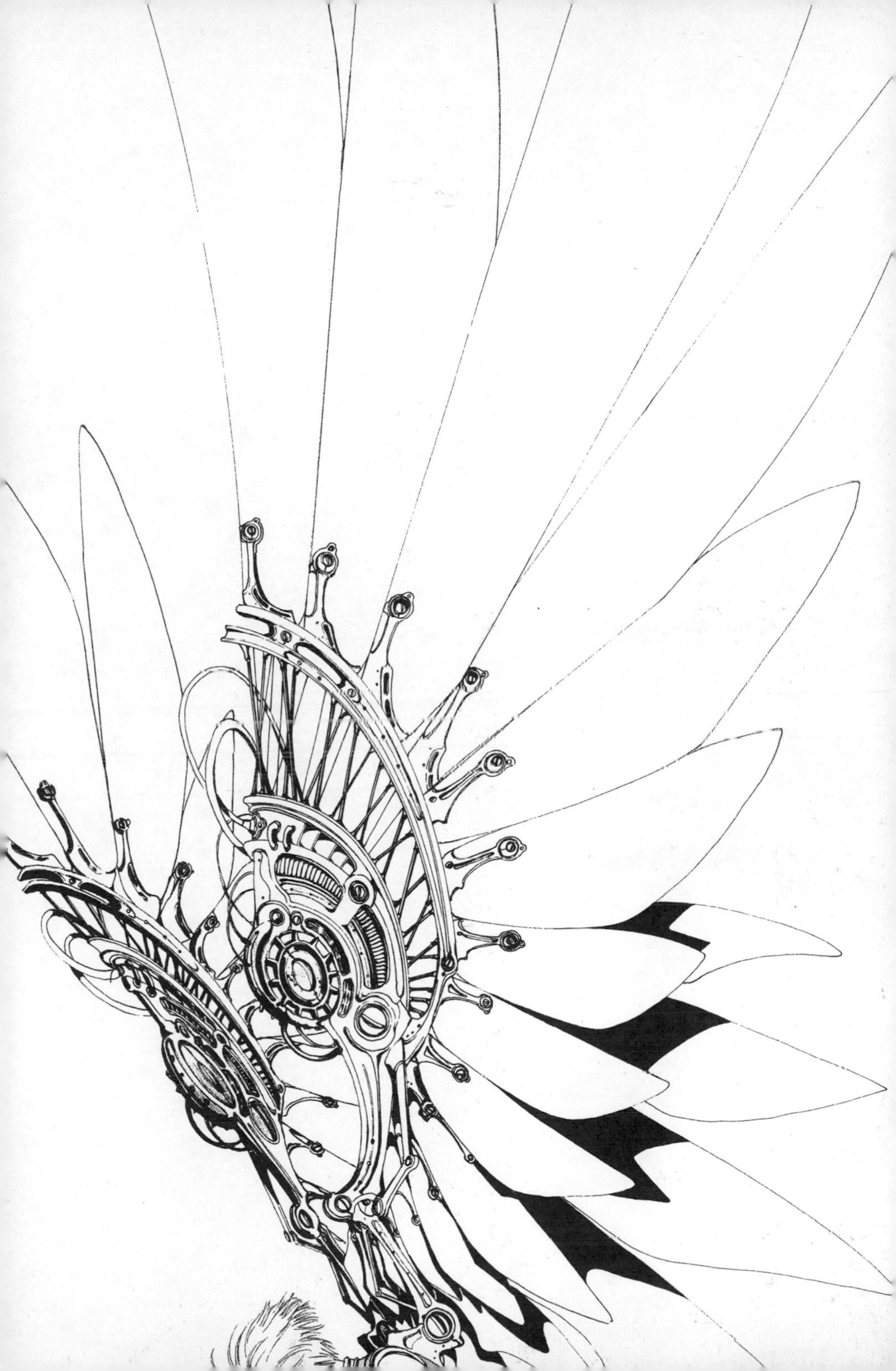

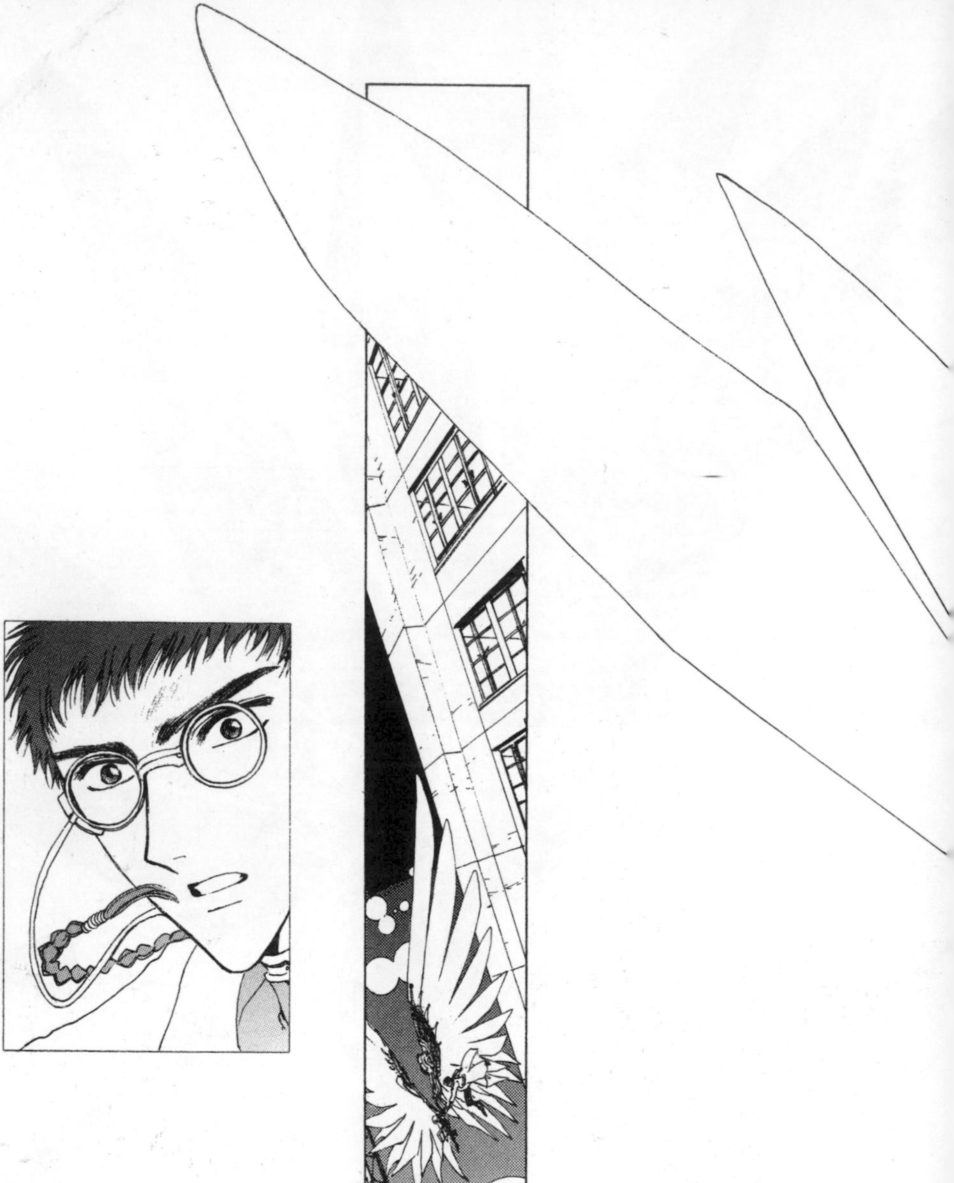

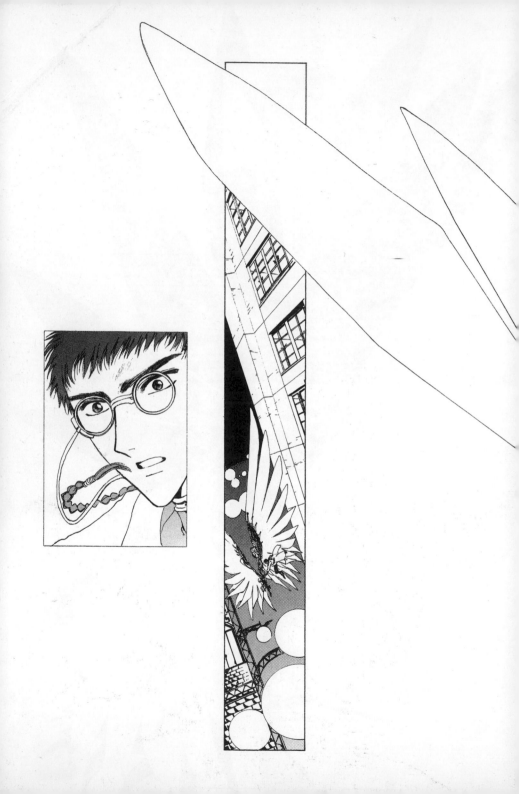

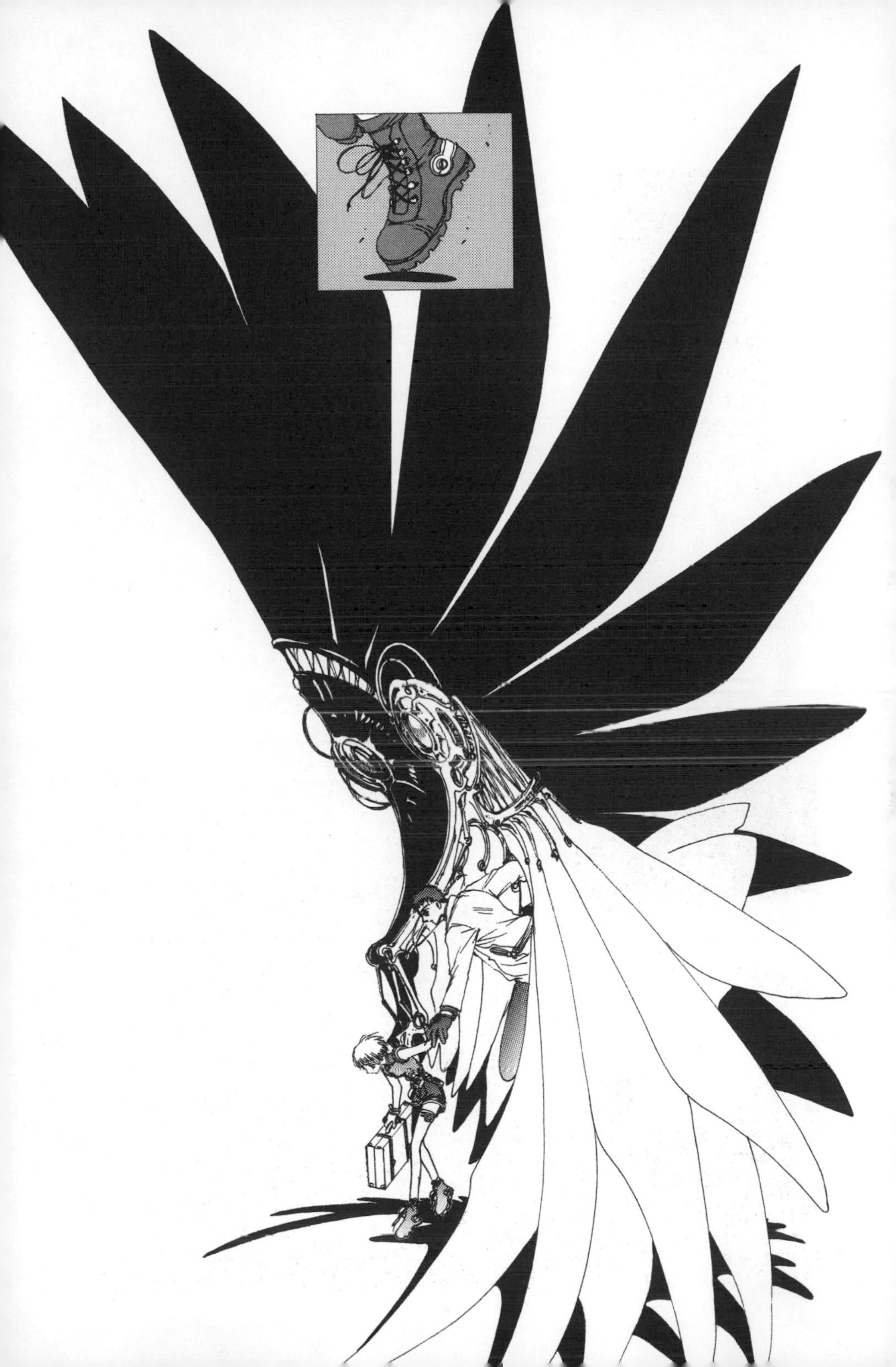

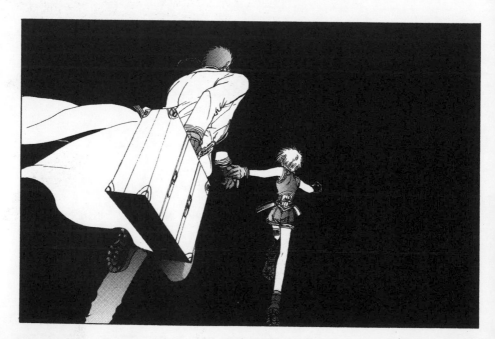

WHITEOUT

『ホワイトアウト』

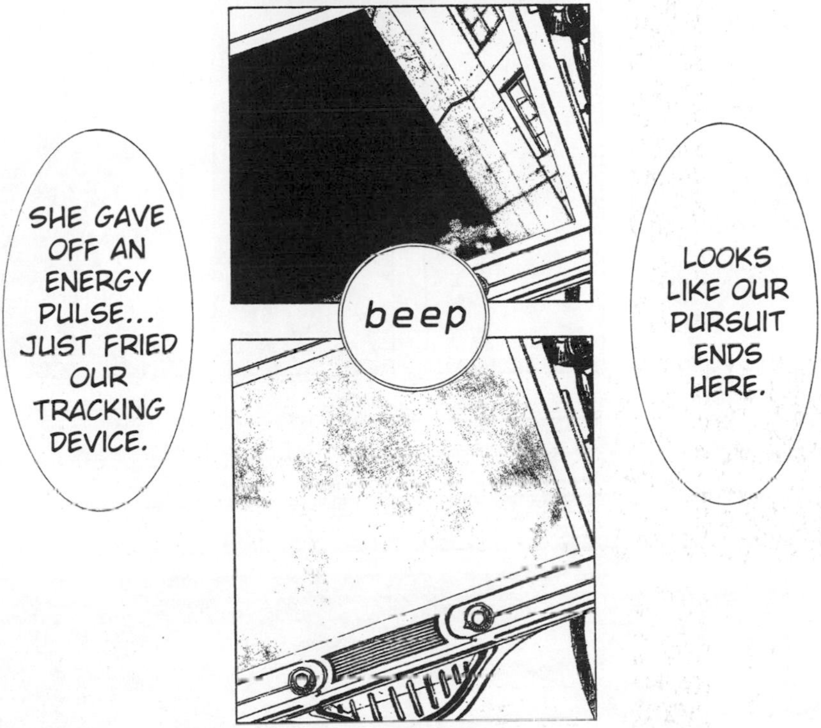
LOOKS LIKE OUR PURSUIT ENDS HERE.
beep
SHE GAVE OFF AN ENERGY PULSE... JUST FRIED OUR TRACKING DEVICE.

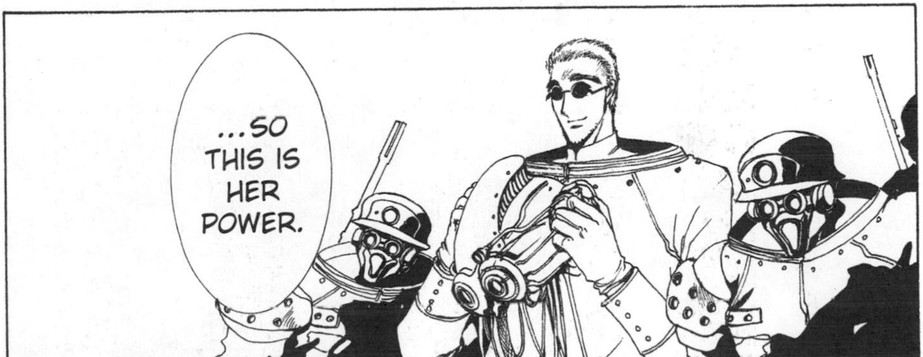
...SO THIS IS HER POWER.

『お
な
じ
だ
け
ど

THE ONE AND

RAN.

RAN!

fzzzt

bzzzt

お
な
じ
じ
ゃ
な
い
』

NOT THE SAME

THE TRACKING DEVICE ON RYU'S WEAPONS MODULE SEEMS TO HAVE MALFUNC-TIONED.

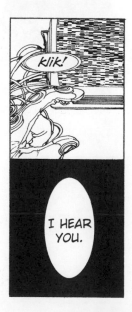

klik!

I HEAR YOU.

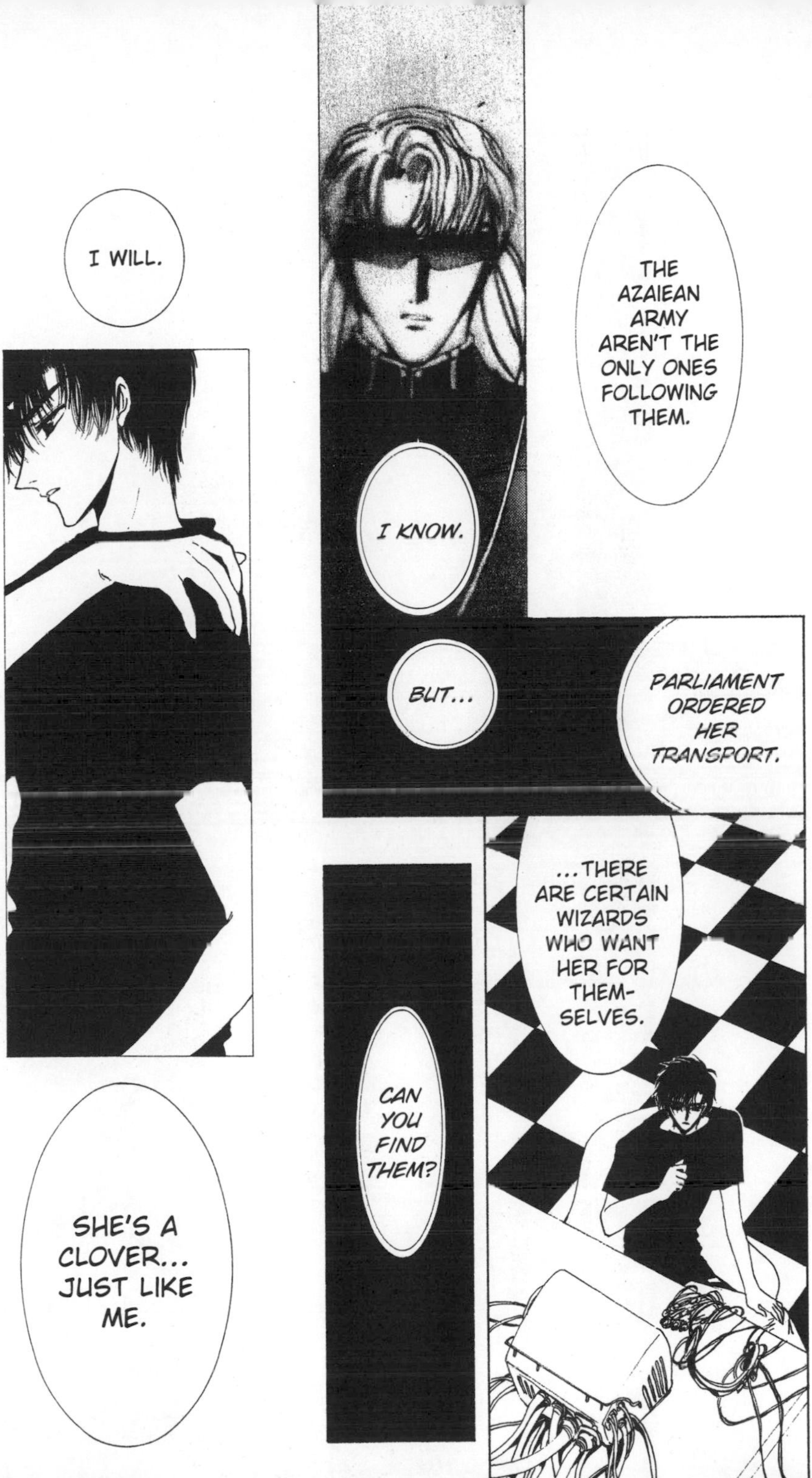
THE AZAIEAN ARMY AREN'T THE ONLY ONES FOLLOWING THEM.
I KNOW.
PARLIAMENT ORDERED HER TRANSPORT.
BUT...
...THERE ARE CERTAIN WIZARDS WHO WANT HER FOR THEM-SELVES.
CAN YOU FIND THEM?
I WILL.
SHE'S A CLOVER... JUST LIKE ME.

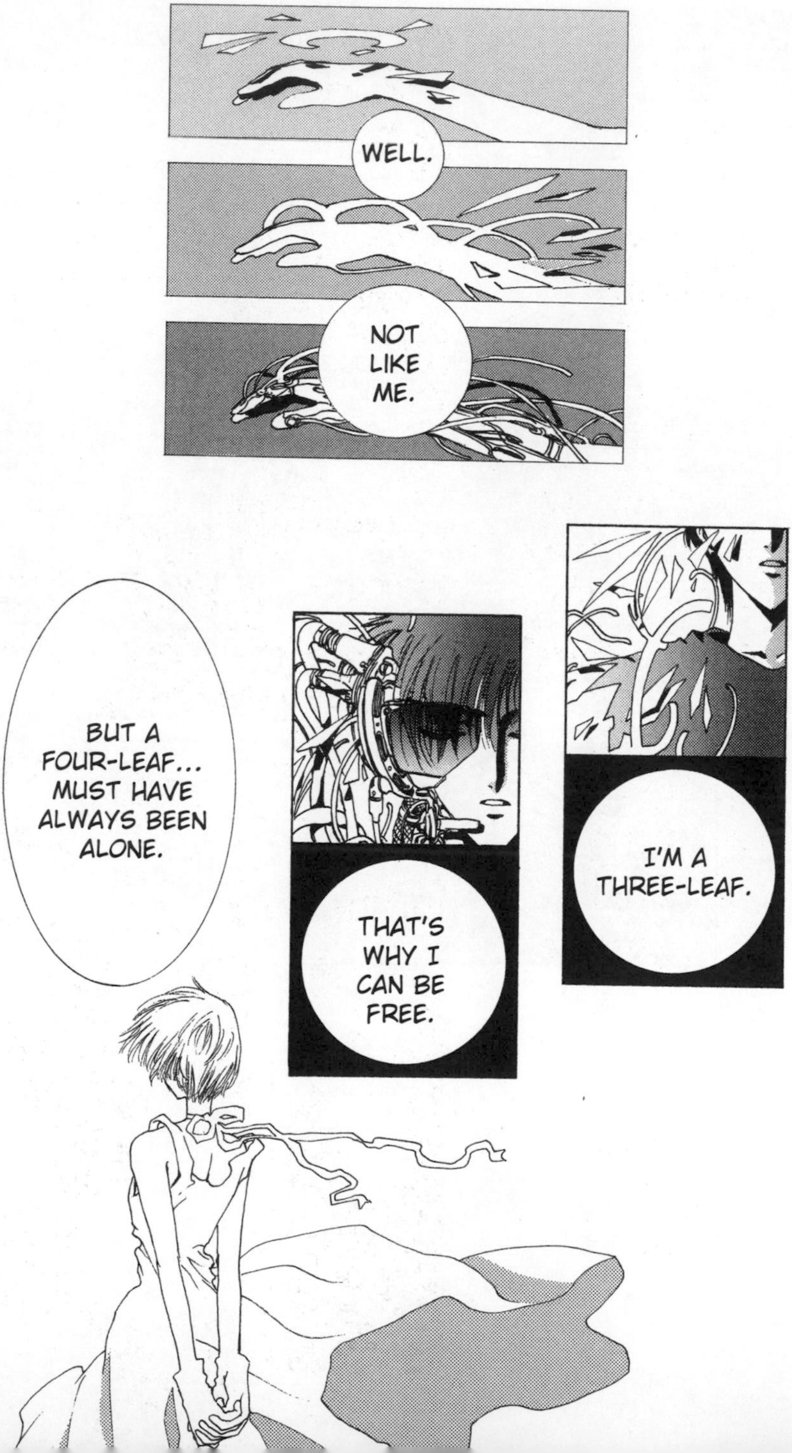
WELL.
NOT LIKE ME.
I'M A THREE-LEAF.
THAT'S WHY I CAN BE FREE.
BUT A FOUR-LEAF... MUST HAVE ALWAYS BEEN ALONE.

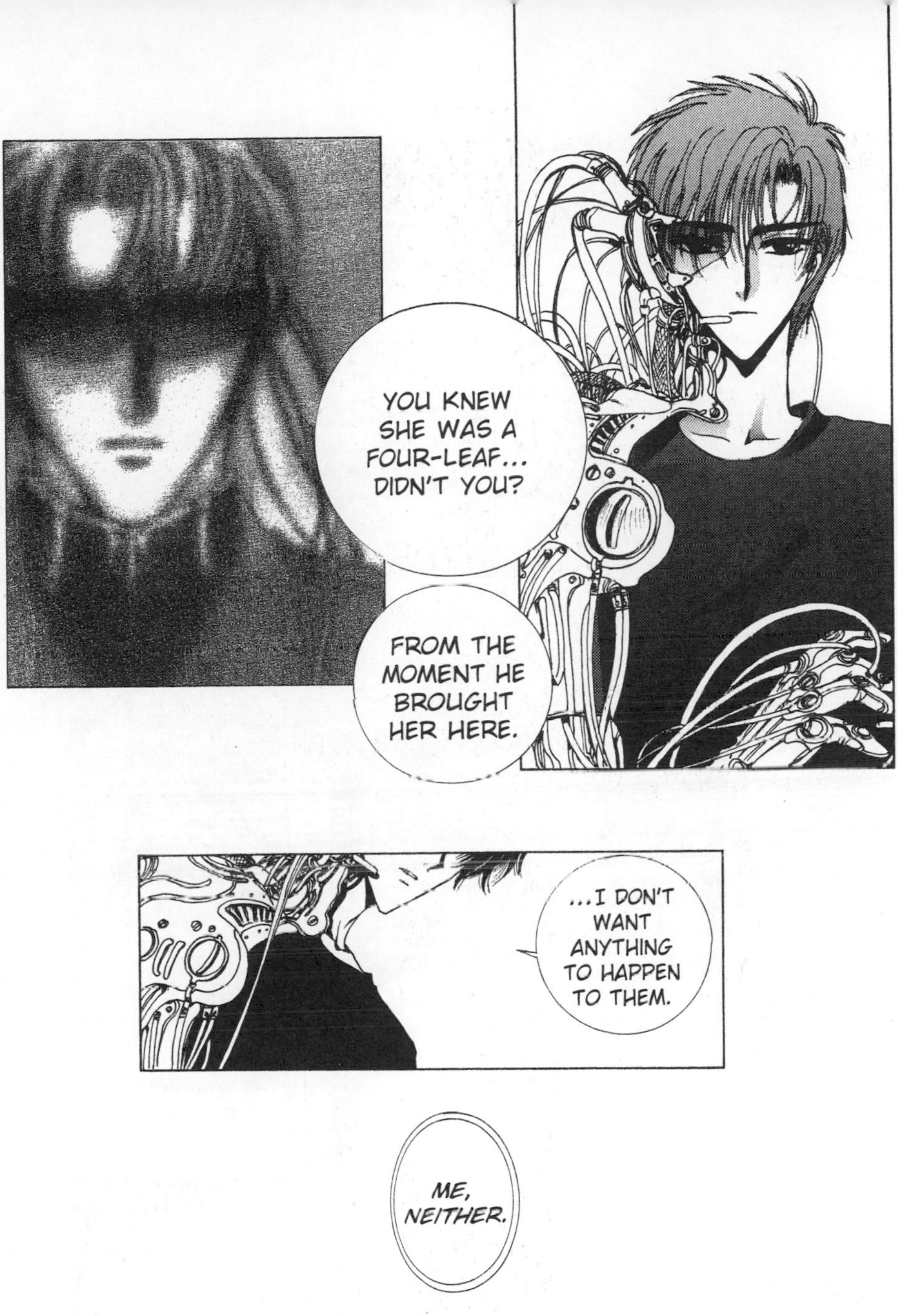
YOU KNEW SHE WAS A FOUR-LEAF... DIDN'T YOU?
FROM THE MOMENT HE BROUGHT HER HERE.
...I DON'T WANT ANYTHING TO HAPPEN TO THEM.
ME, NEITHER.

NIGHT

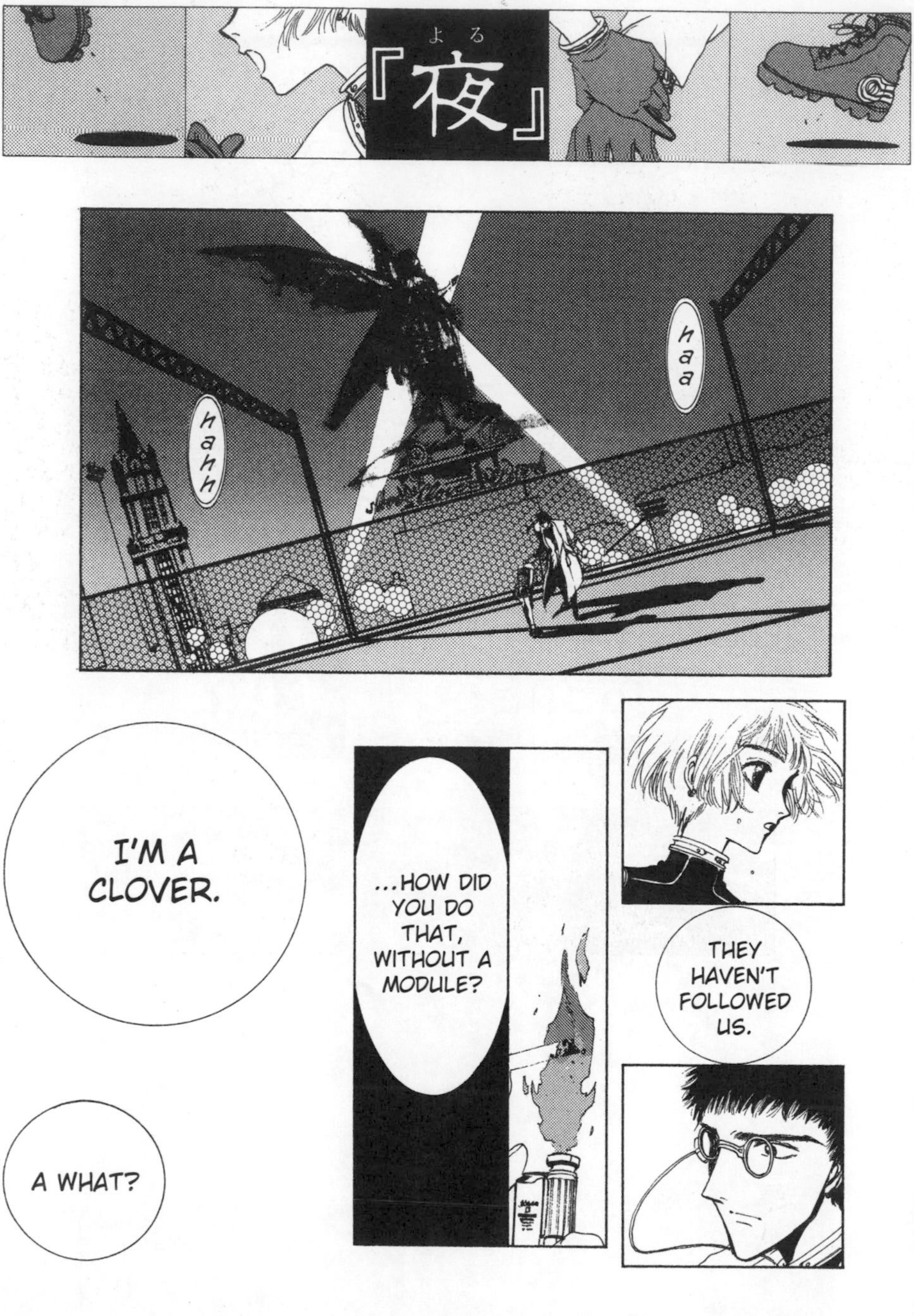
よる
『夜』
haa
hahh
THEY HAVEN'T FOLLOWED US.
...HOW DID YOU DO THAT, WITHOUT A MODULE?
I'M A CLOVER.
A WHAT?

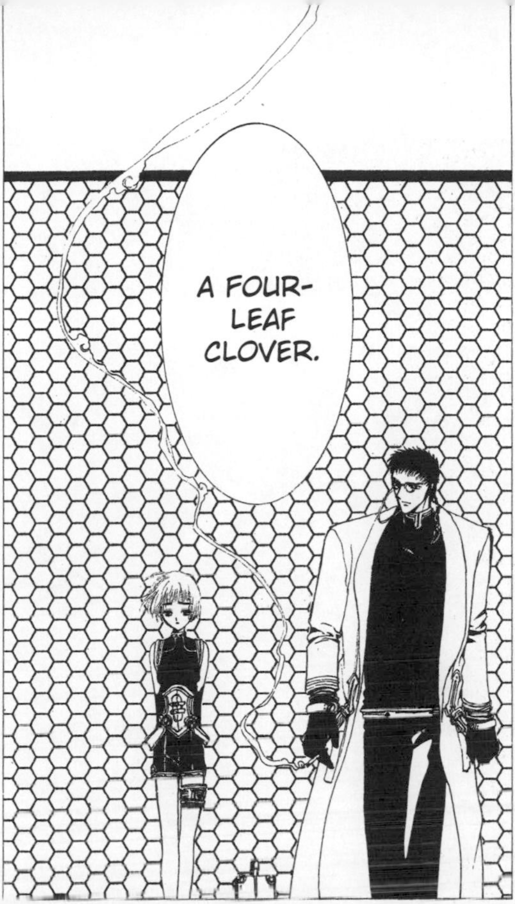
A FOUR-LEAF CLOVER.

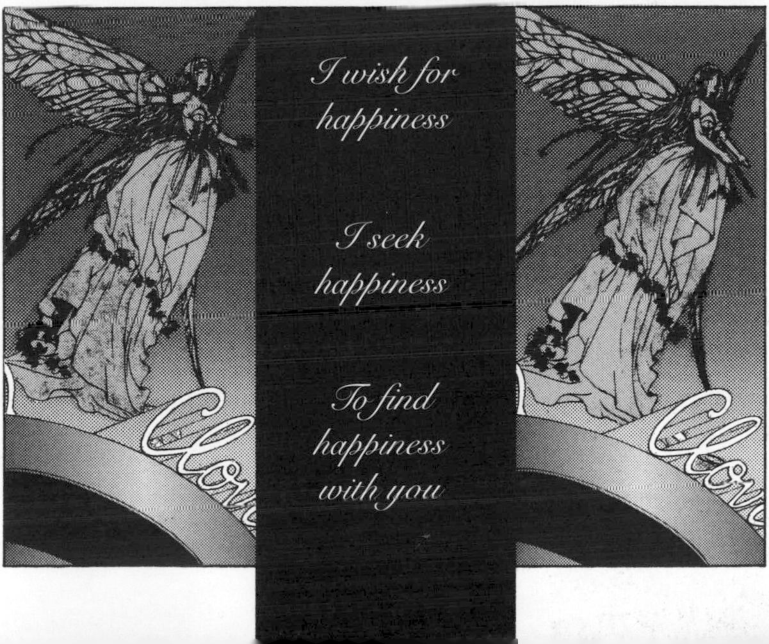
I wish for happiness
I seek happiness
To find happiness with you
Clover
Clover

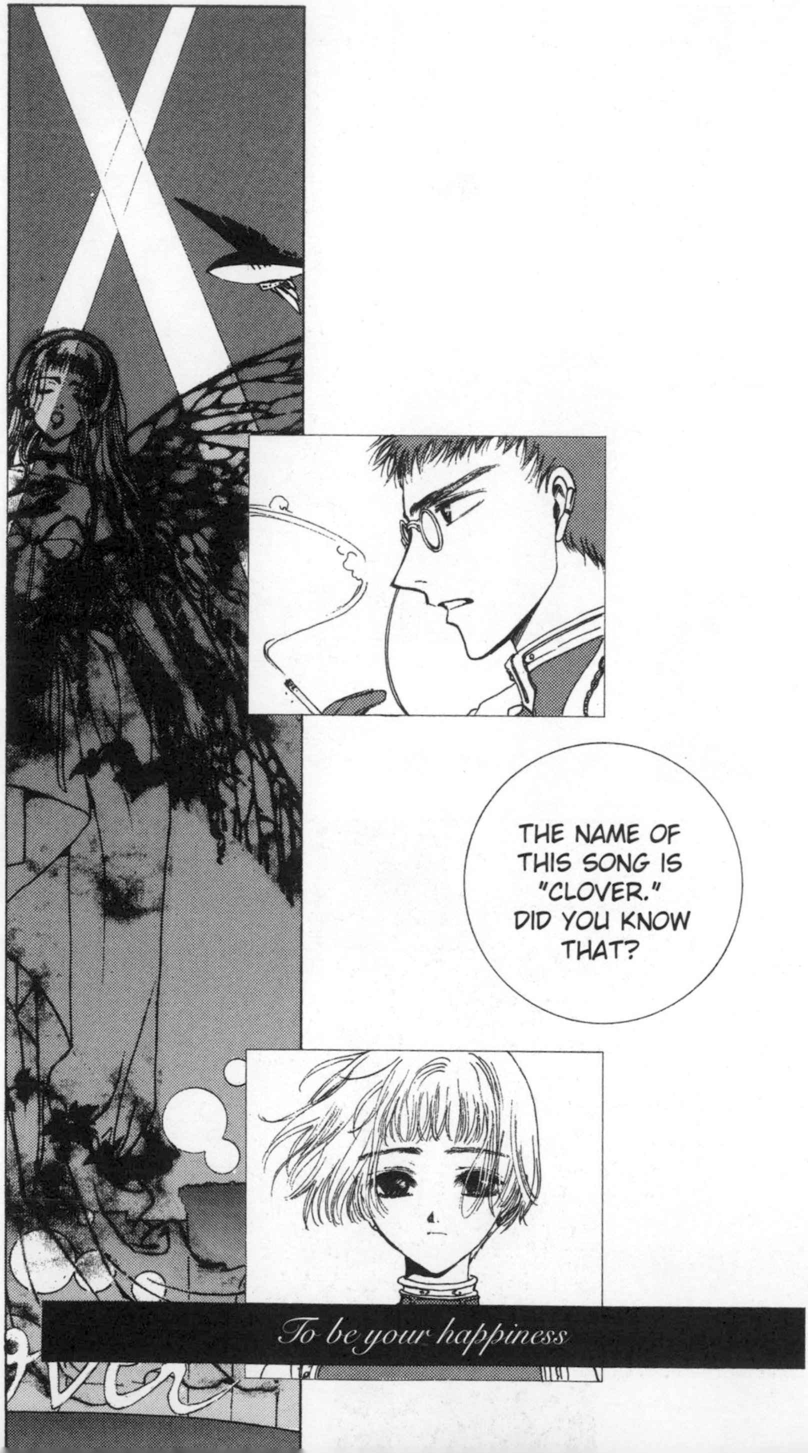
THE NAME OF THIS SONG IS "CLOVER." DID YOU KNOW THAT?
To be your happiness

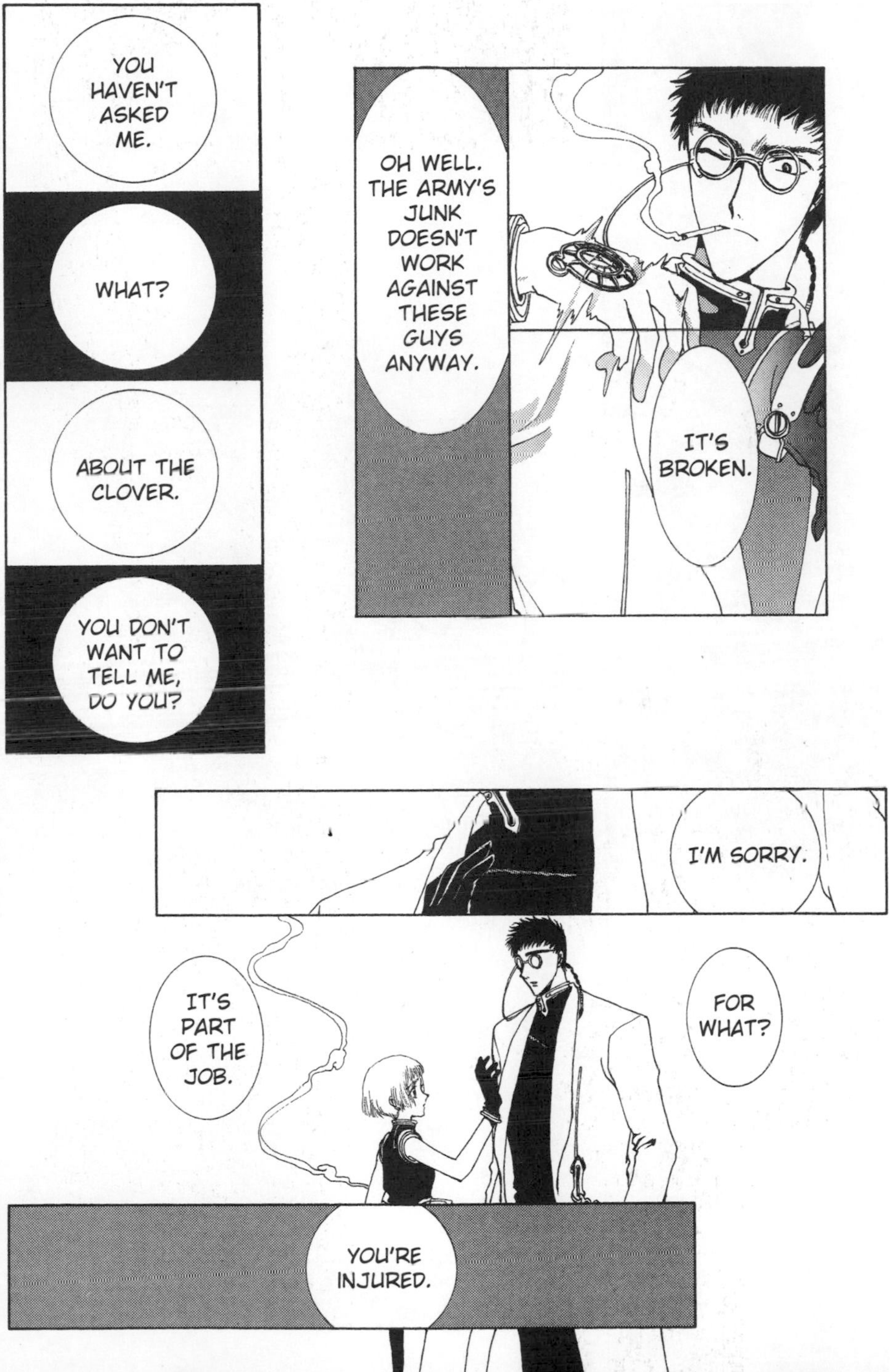
IT'S BROKEN.
OH WELL. THE ARMY'S JUNK DOESN'T WORK AGAINST THESE GUYS ANYWAY.
YOU HAVEN'T ASKED ME.
WHAT?
ABOUT THE CLOVER.
YOU DON'T WANT TO TELL ME, DO YOU?
I'M SORRY.
FOR WHAT?
IT'S PART OF THE JOB.
YOU'RE INJURED.

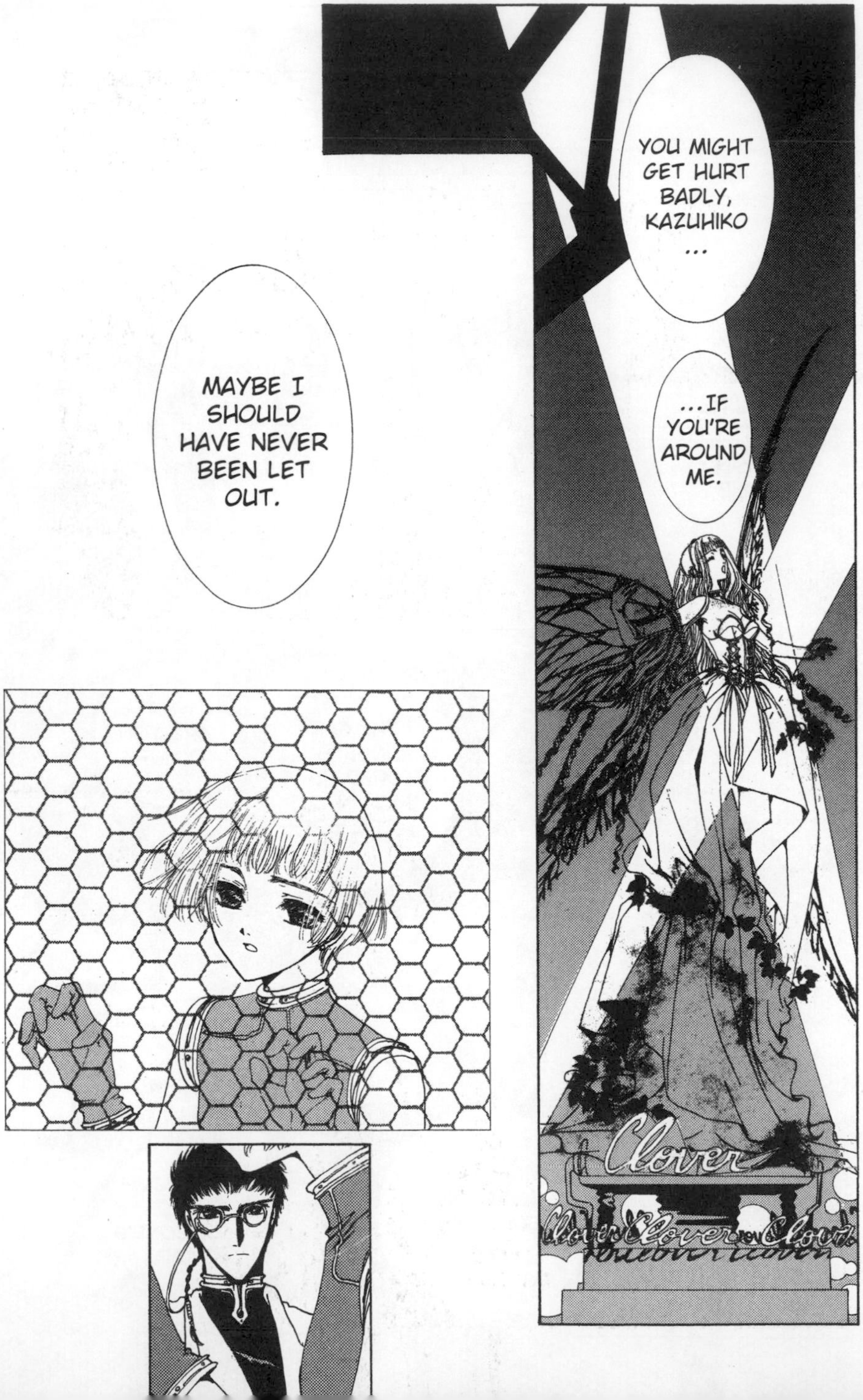
YOU MIGHT GET HURT BADLY, KAZUHIKO ...
...IF YOU'RE AROUND ME.
Clover
MAYBE I SHOULD HAVE NEVER BEEN LET OUT.

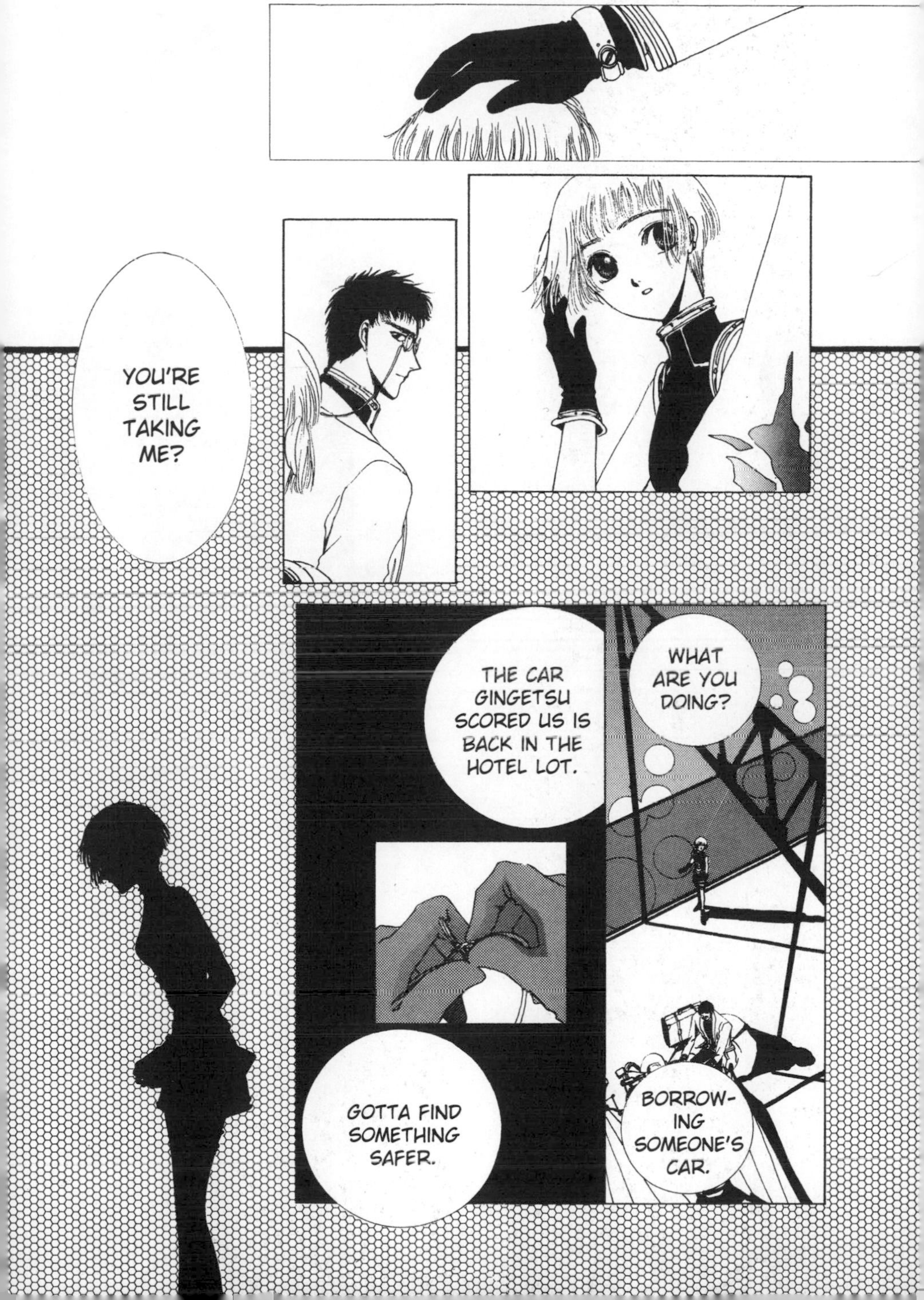
YOU'RE STILL TAKING ME?
WHAT ARE YOU DOING?
BORROW-ING SOMEONE'S CAR.
THE CAR GINGETSU SCORED US IS BACK IN THE HOTEL LOT.
GOTTA FIND SOMETHING SAFER.

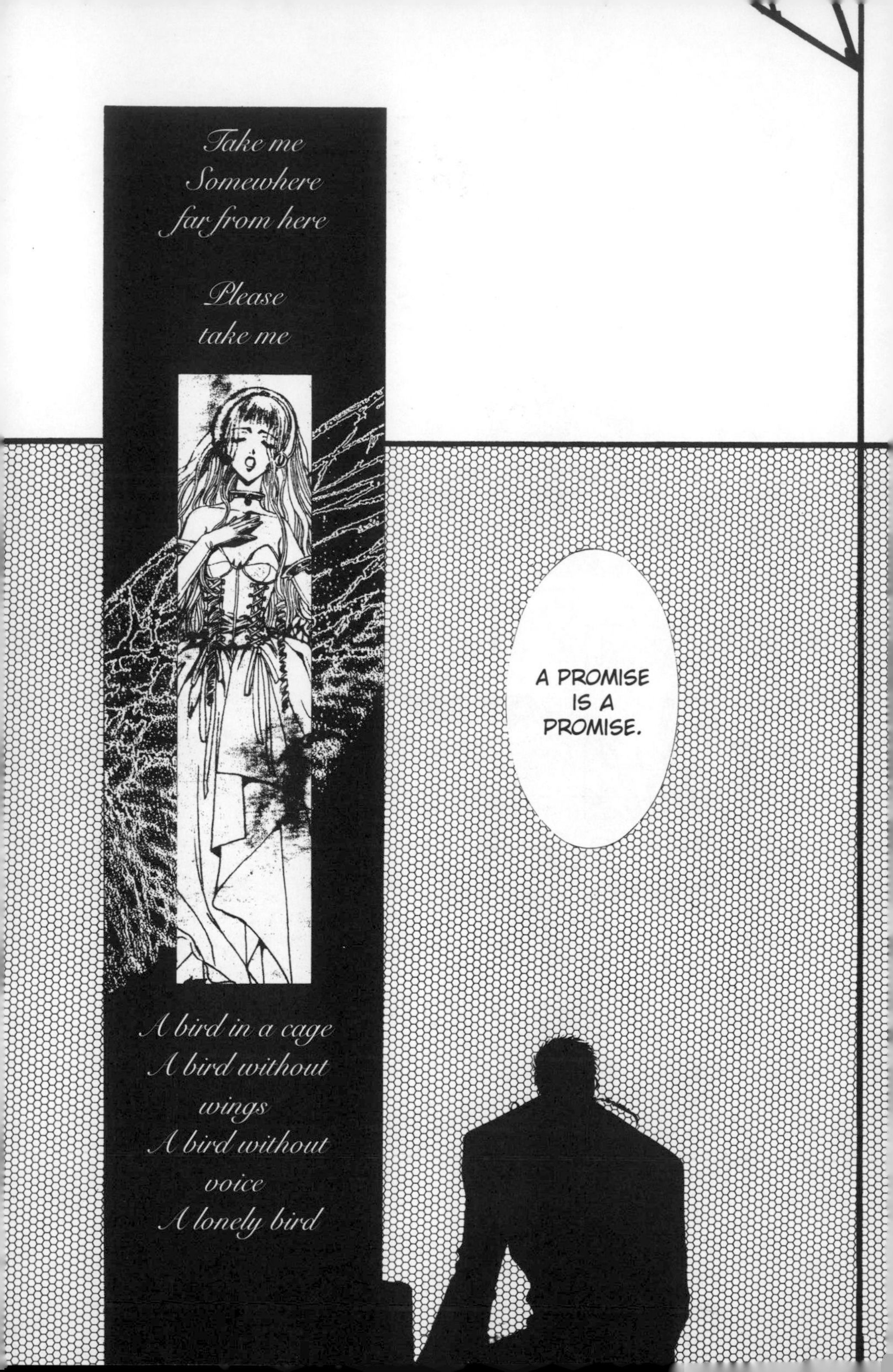
A PROMISE IS A PROMISE.
Take me Somewhere far from here
Please take me
A bird in a cage
A bird without wings
A bird without voice
A lonely bird

Please take me

beep
boop

VROOOOM

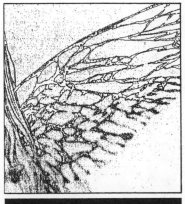

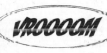

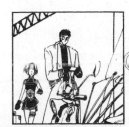

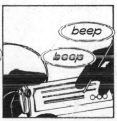

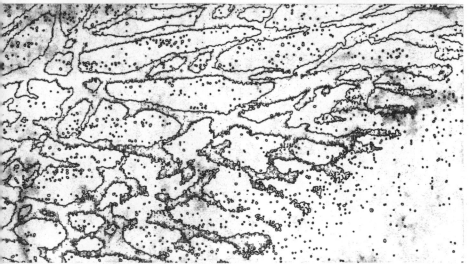

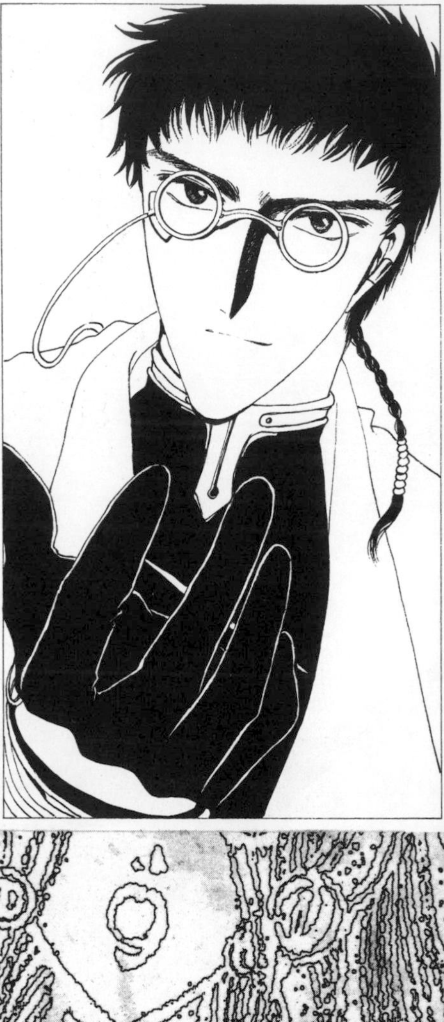
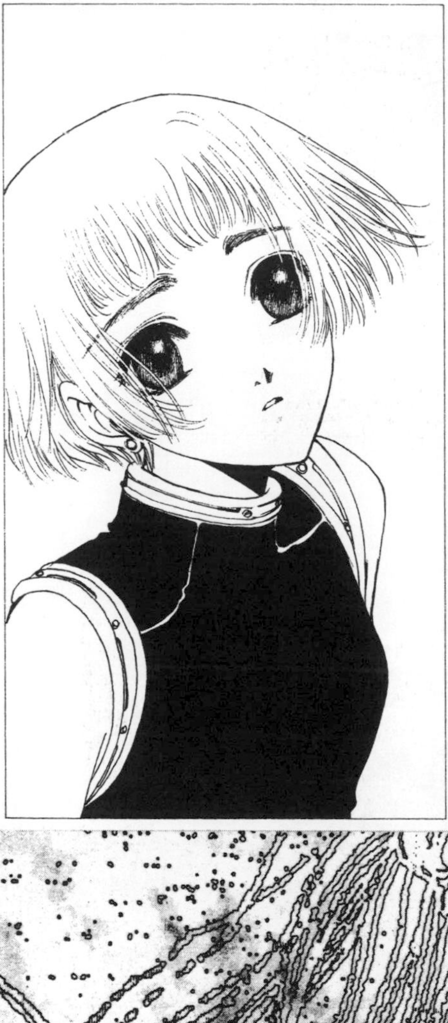
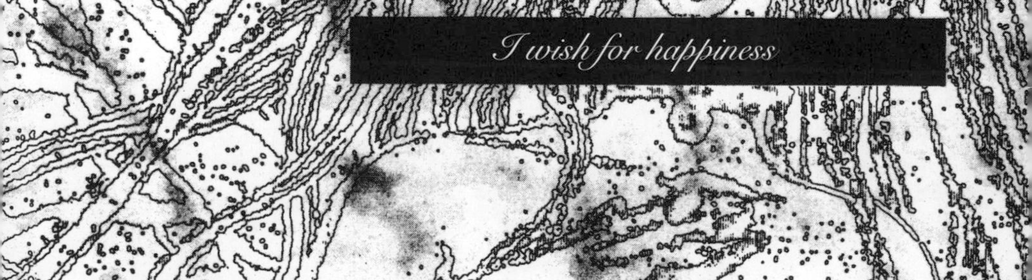
I wish for happiness

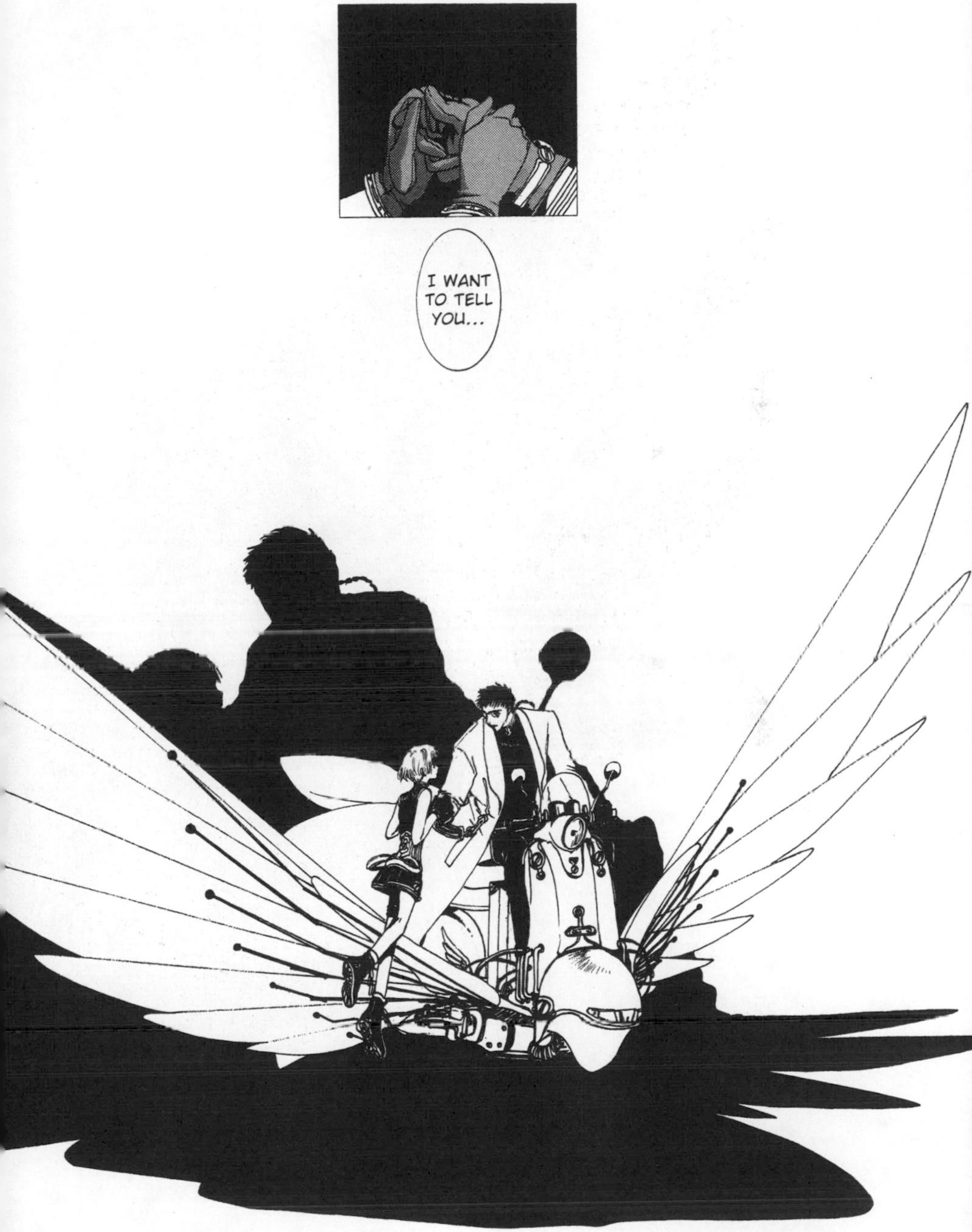
I WANT TO TELL YOU...

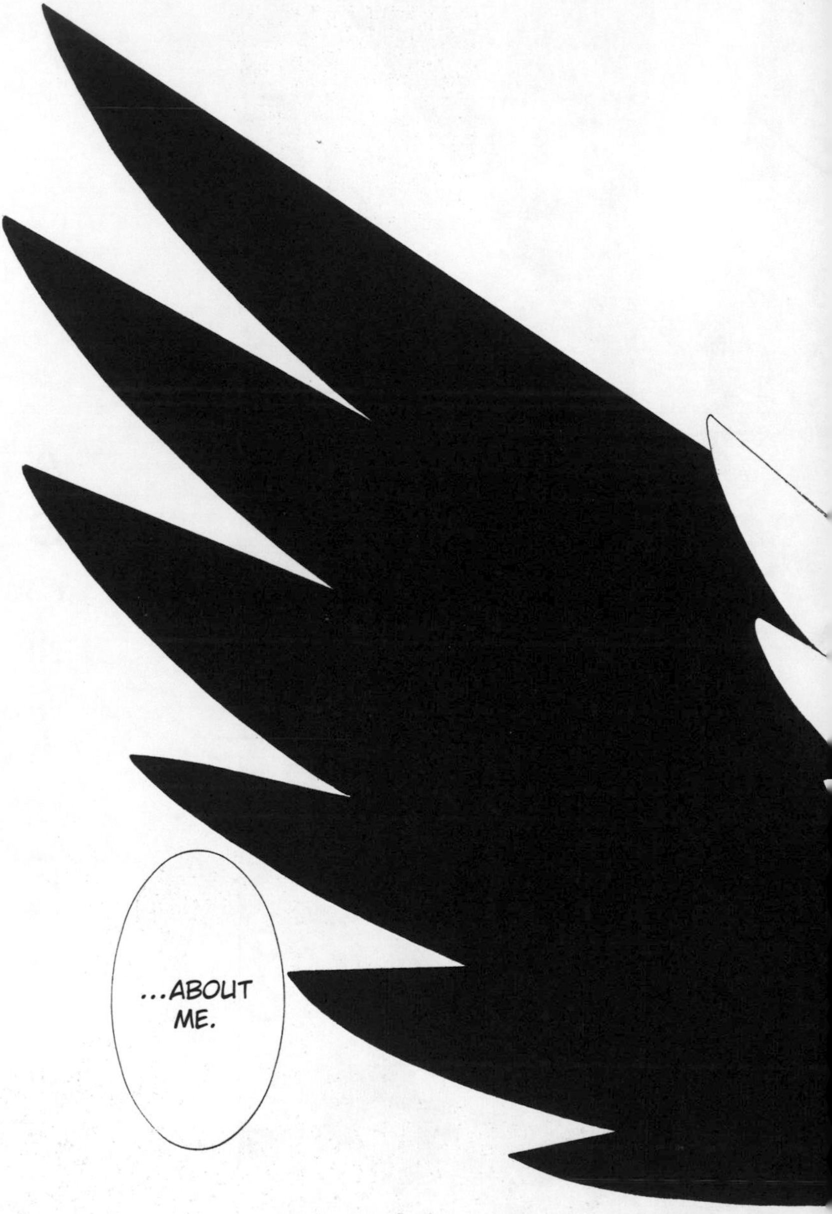
...ABOUT ME.

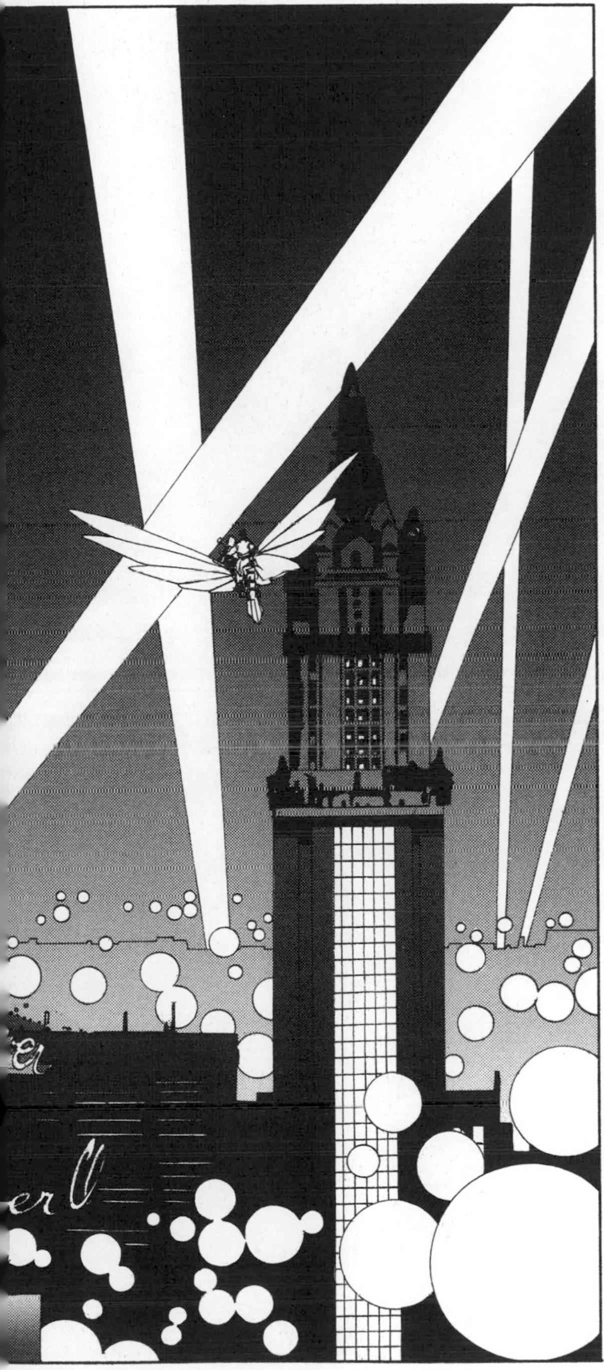

『わたしのこと』

ABOUT ME

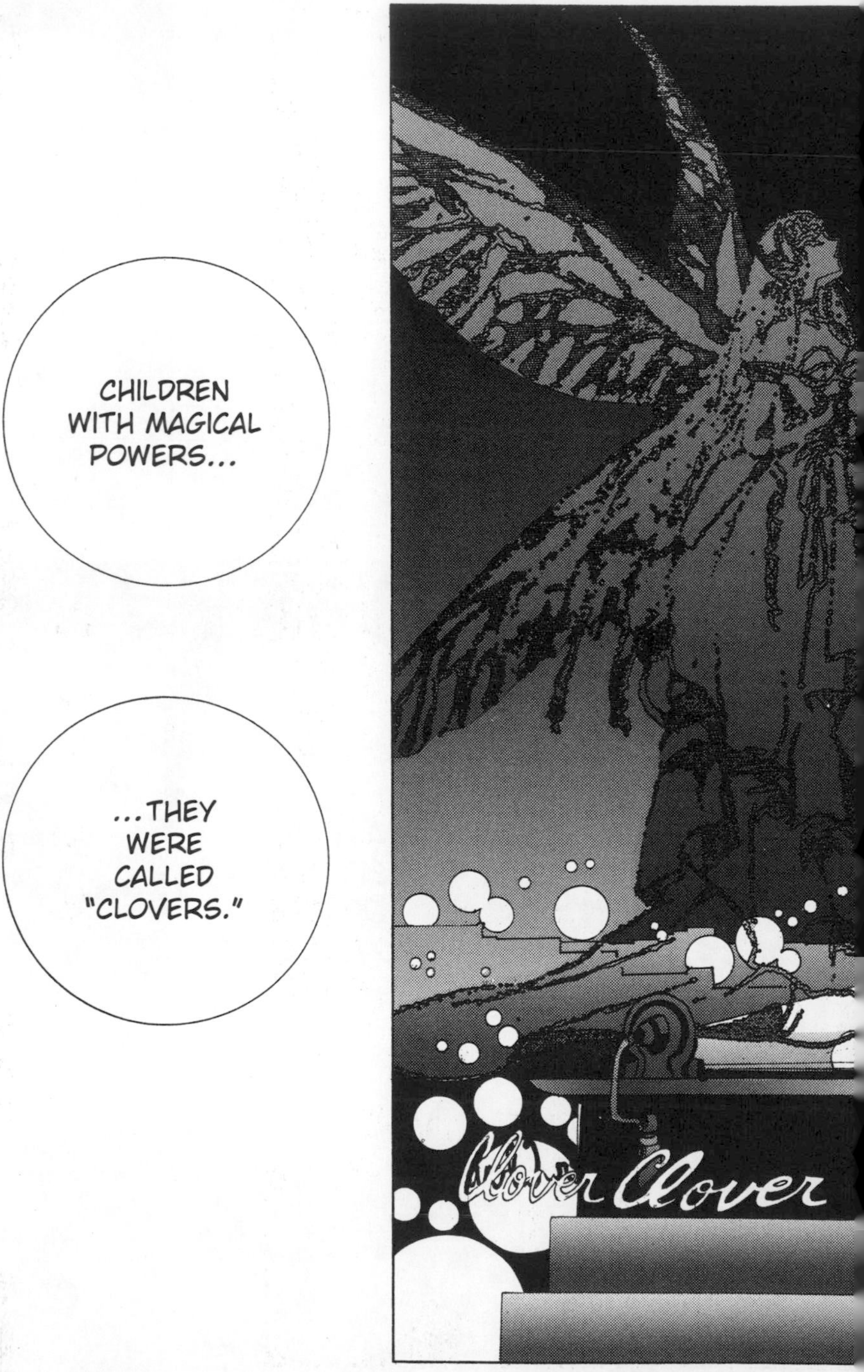
CHILDREN WITH MAGICAL POWERS...
...THEY WERE CALLED "CLOVERS."
Clover Clover

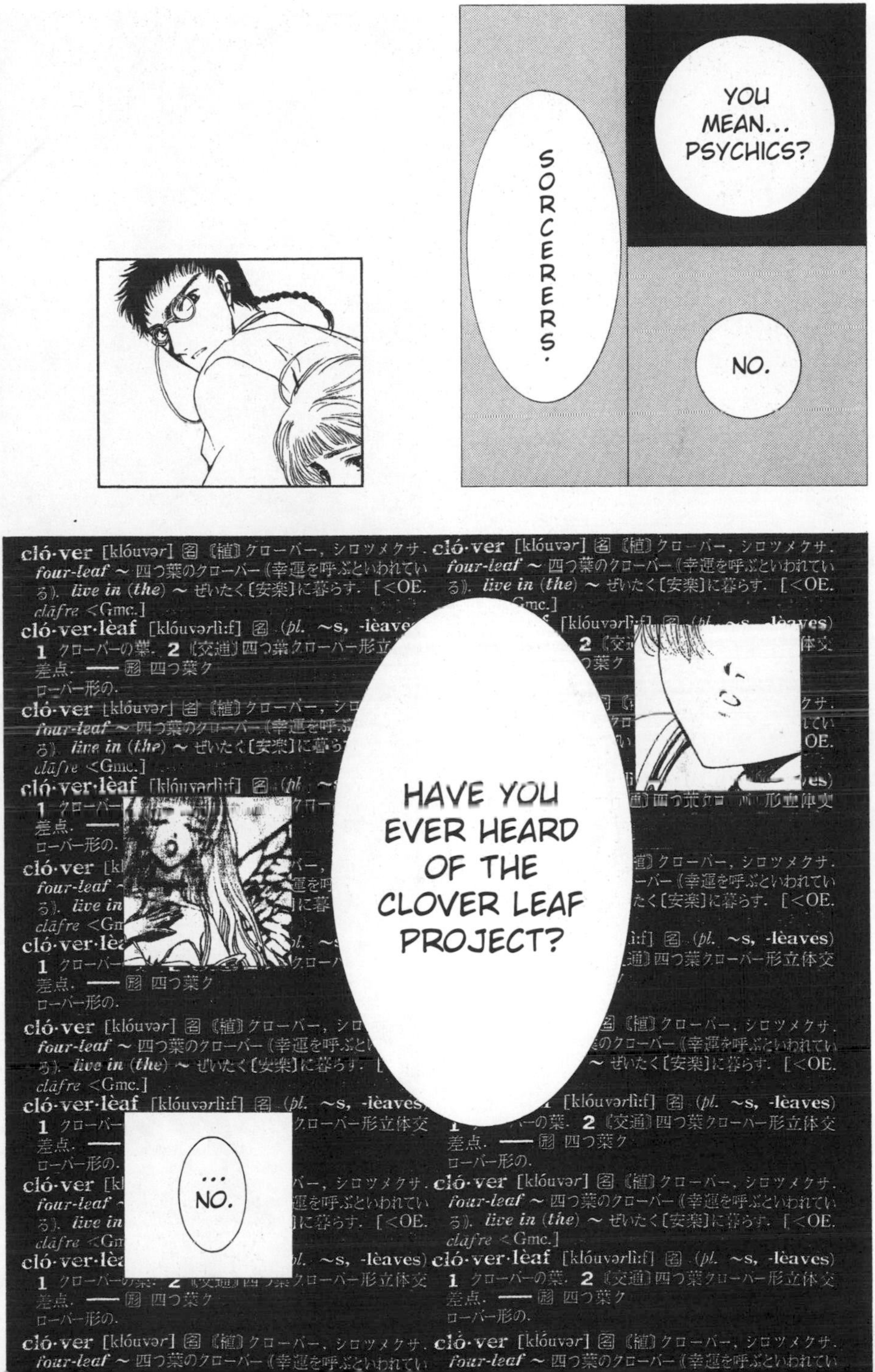
YOU MEAN... PSYCHICS?
NO.
SORCERERS.
cló·ver [klóuvər] 名〔植〕クローバー, シロツメクサ. four-leaf ～ 四つ葉のクローバー《幸運を呼ぶといわれている》. live in (the) ～ ぜいたく[安楽]に暮らす. [<OE. clāfre <Gmc.]
cló·ver·lèaf [klóuvərli:f] 名 (pl. ～s, -lèaves) 1 クローバーの葉. 2〔交通〕四つ葉クローバー形立体交差点. ── 形 四つ葉クローバー形の.
HAVE YOU EVER HEARD OF THE CLOVER LEAF PROJECT?
... NO.

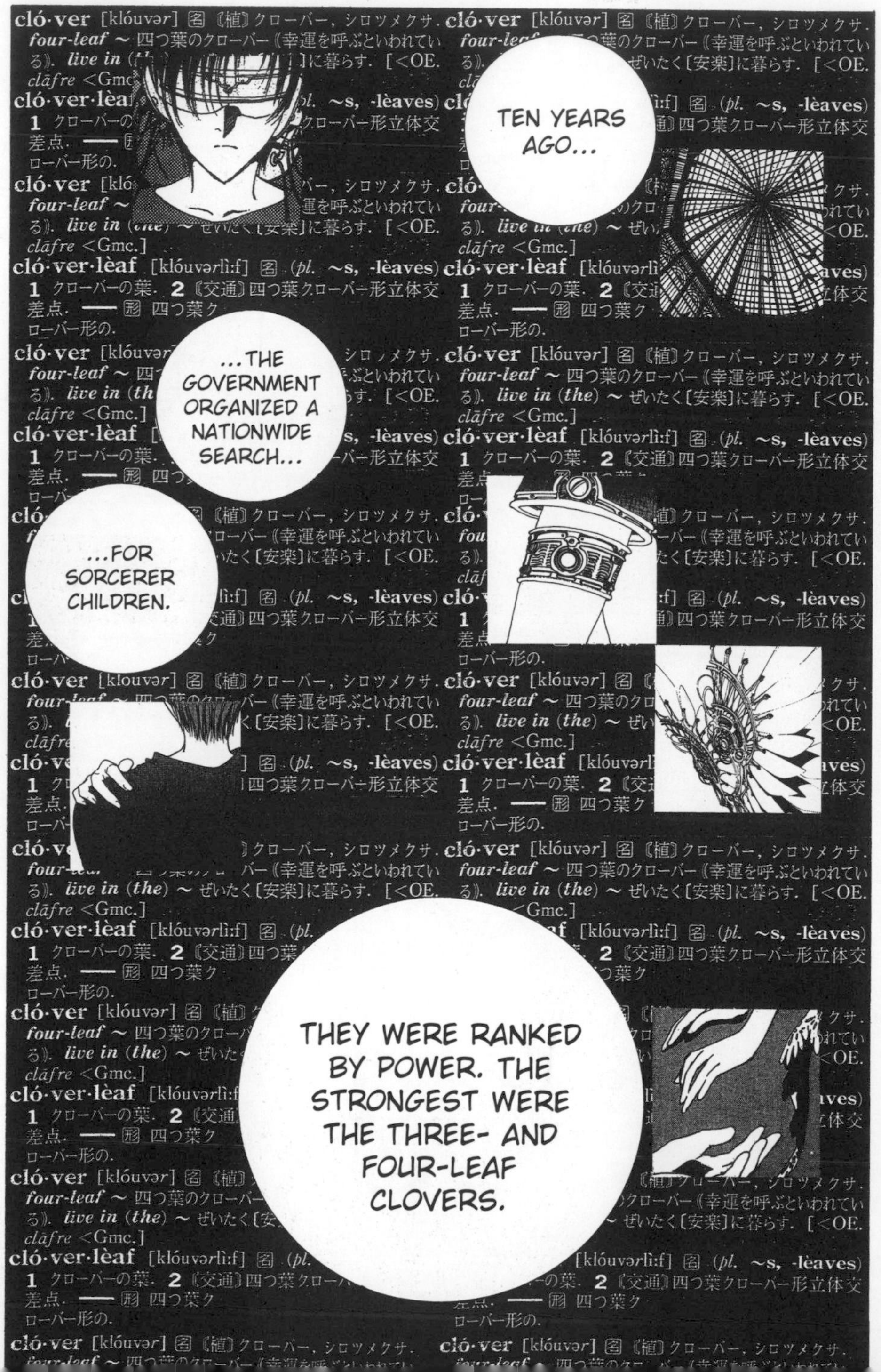
TEN YEARS AGO...
...THE GOVERNMENT ORGANIZED A NATIONWIDE SEARCH...
...FOR SORCERER CHILDREN.
THEY WERE RANKED BY POWER. THE STRONGEST WERE THE THREE- AND FOUR-LEAF CLOVERS.

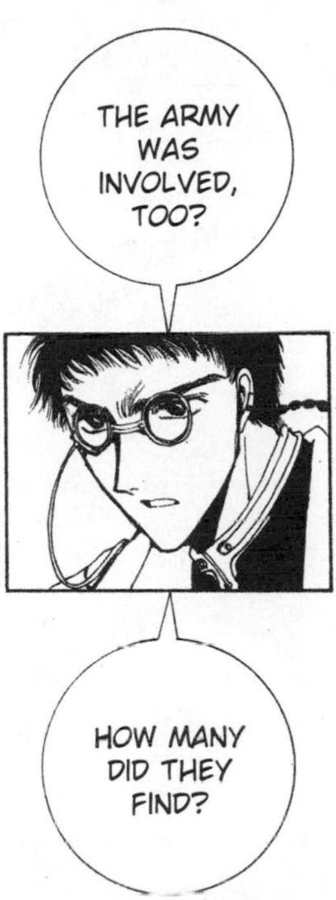
THE ARMY WAS INVOLVED, TOO?
HOW MANY DID THEY FIND?
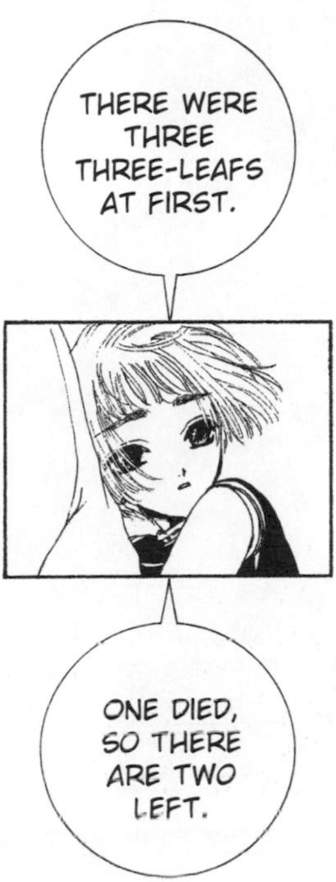
THERE WERE THREE THREE-LEAFS AT FIRST.
ONE DIED, SO THERE ARE TWO LEFT.
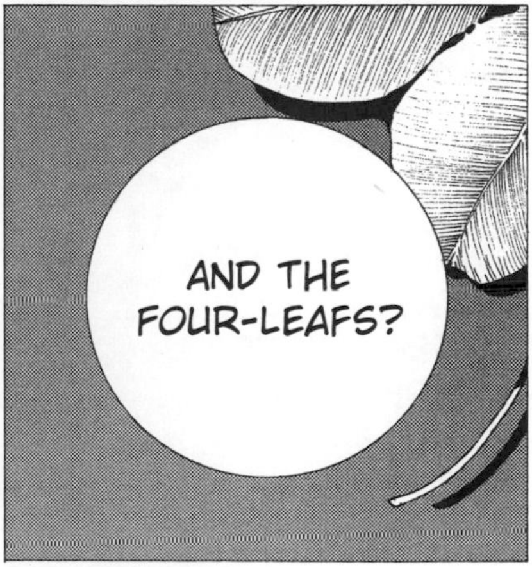
AND THE FOUR-LEAFS?

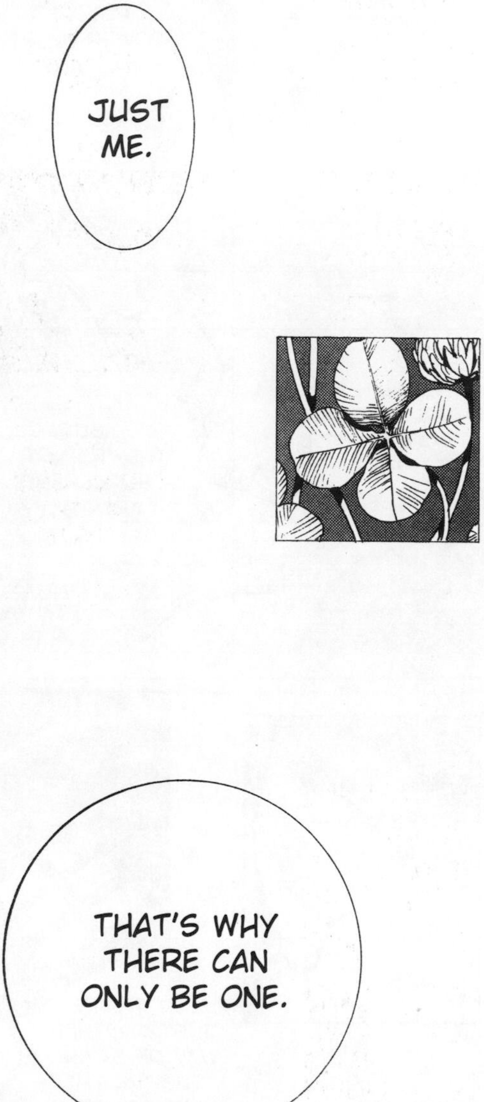

JUST ME.

THAT'S WHY THERE CAN ONLY BE ONE.

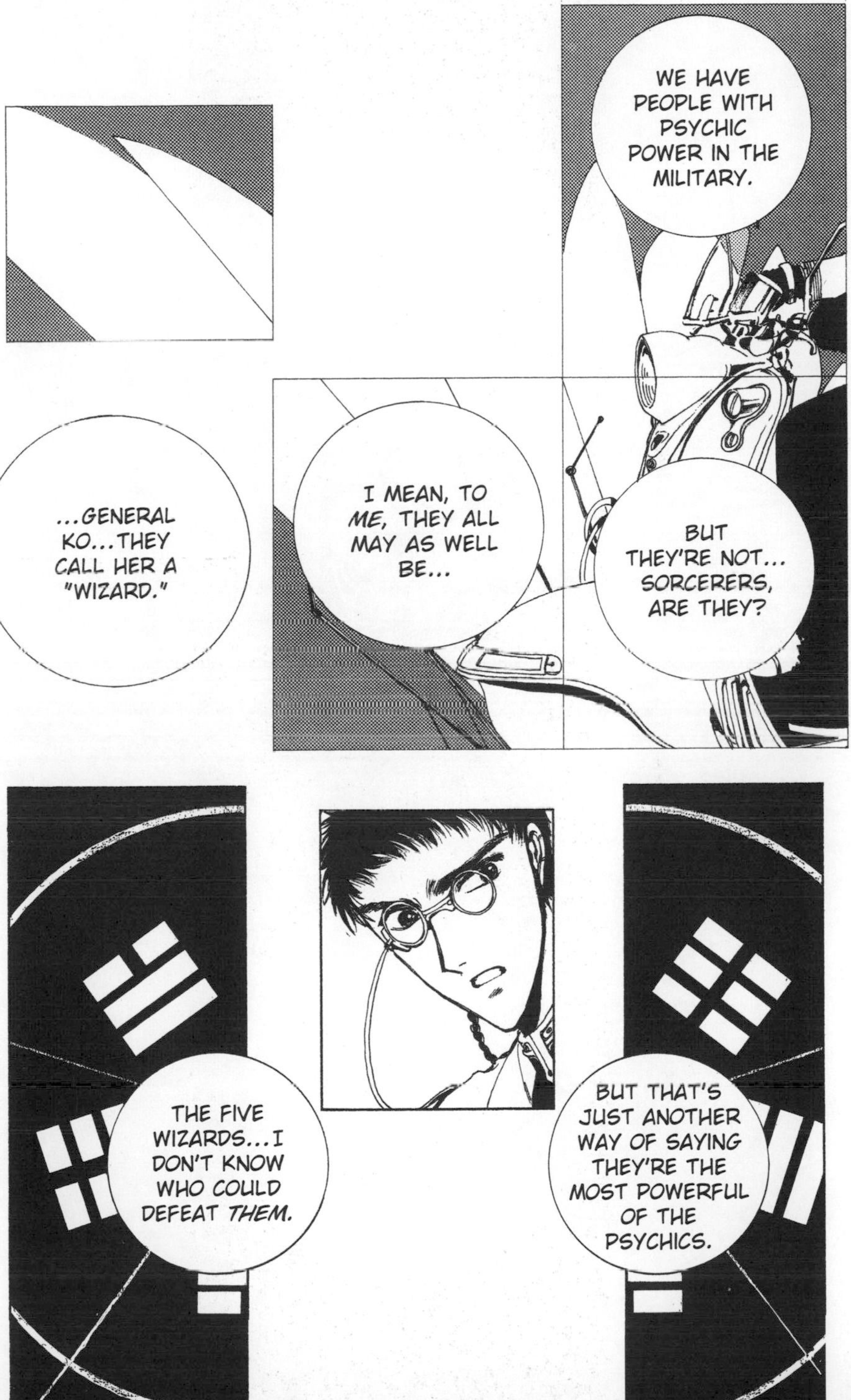
WE HAVE PEOPLE WITH PSYCHIC POWER IN THE MILITARY.
BUT THEY'RE NOT... SORCERERS, ARE THEY?
I MEAN, TO *ME*, THEY ALL MAY AS WELL BE...
...GENERAL KO...THEY CALL HER A "WIZARD."
BUT THAT'S JUST ANOTHER WAY OF SAYING THEY'RE THE MOST POWERFUL OF THE PSYCHICS.
THE FIVE WIZARDS...I DON'T KNOW WHO COULD DEFEAT *THEM*.

IT WOULD TAKE
ALL FIVE TO
EVEN HOPE TO
WIN AGAINST A
THREE-LEAF
CLOVER.

...AND A
FOUR-LEAF...?

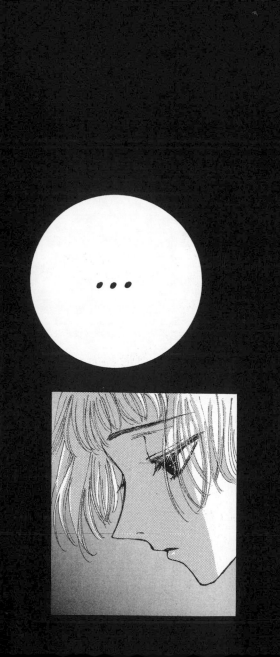

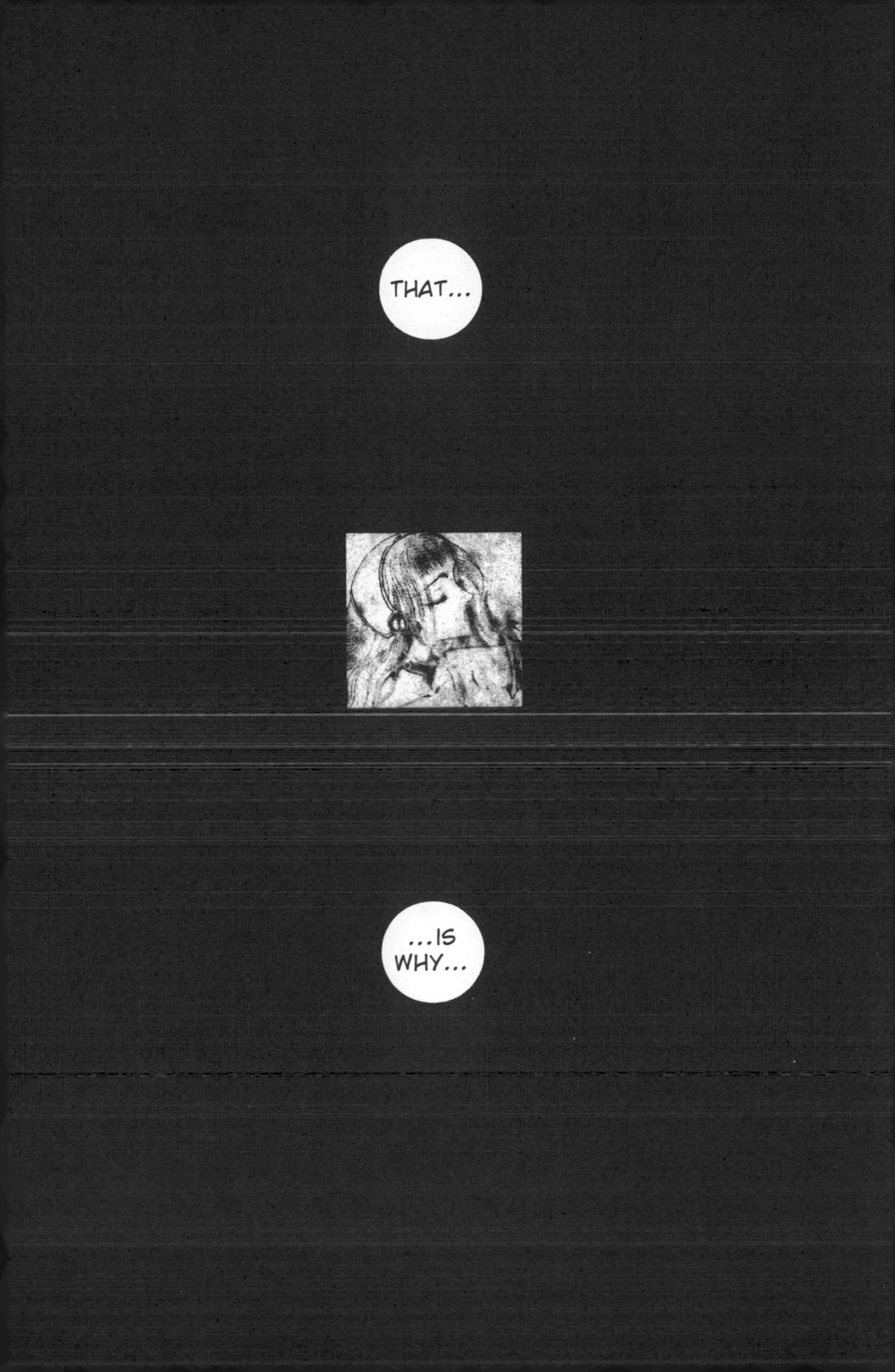
THAT...
...IS WHY...

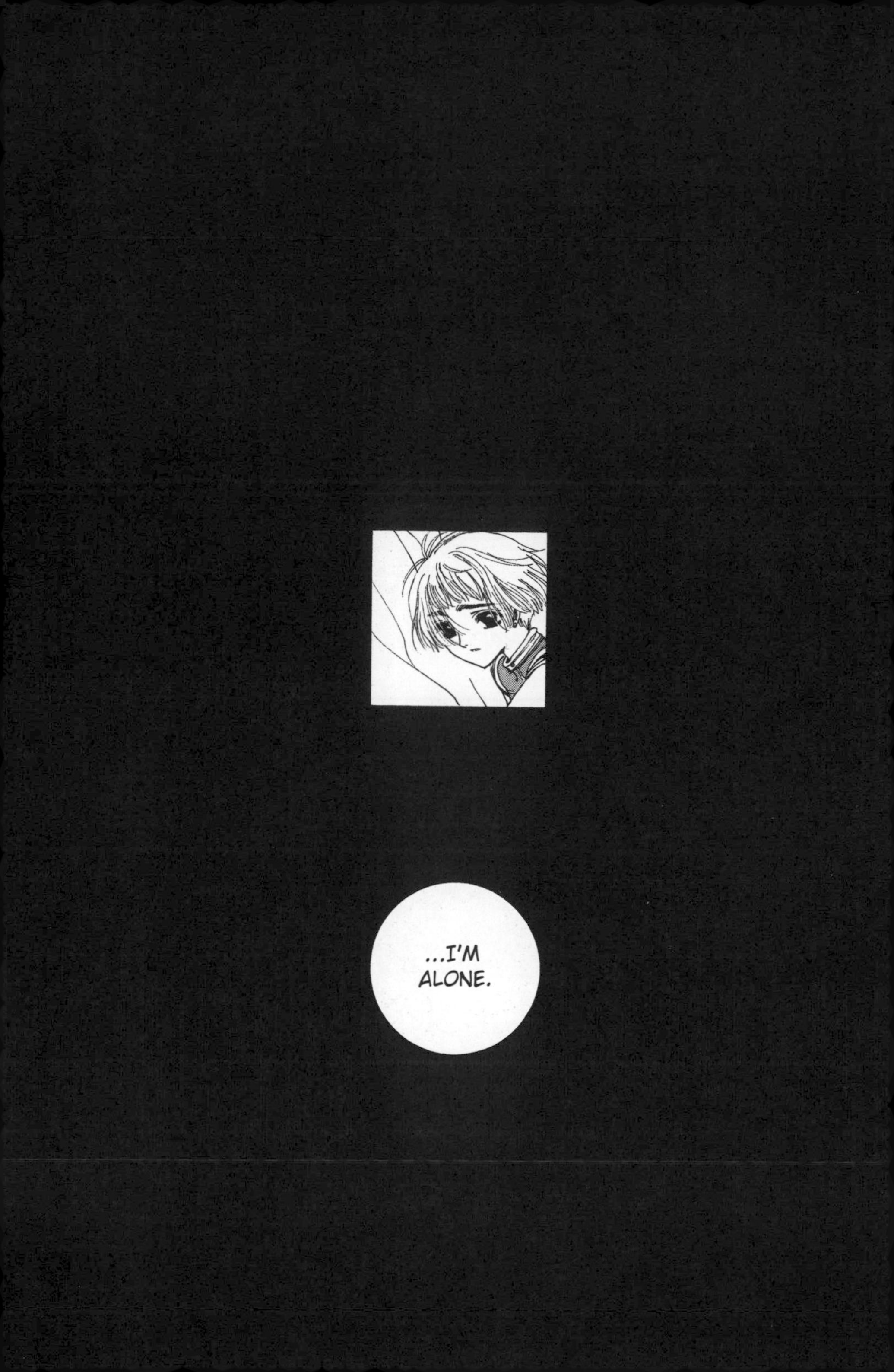
...I'M ALONE.

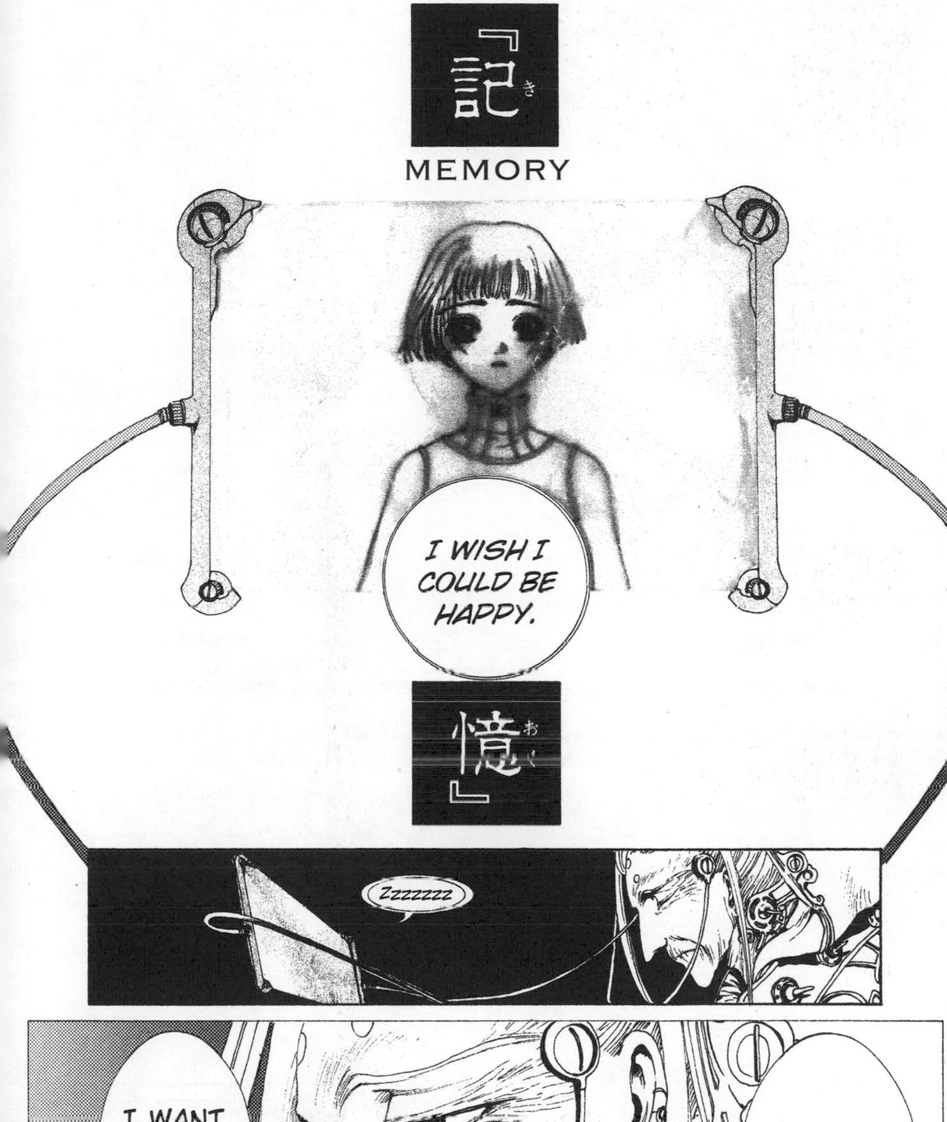
『記
MEMORY
I WISH I COULD BE HAPPY.
憶』
Zzzzzzz
IT'S HER FIRST, AND LAST WISH.
I WANT TO HELP HER FULFILL IT.

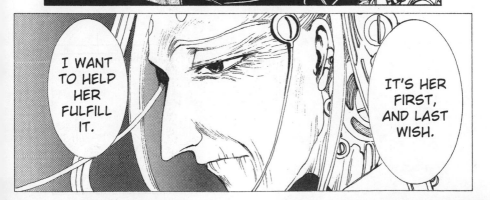

『移動の装置』

THE VEHICLE

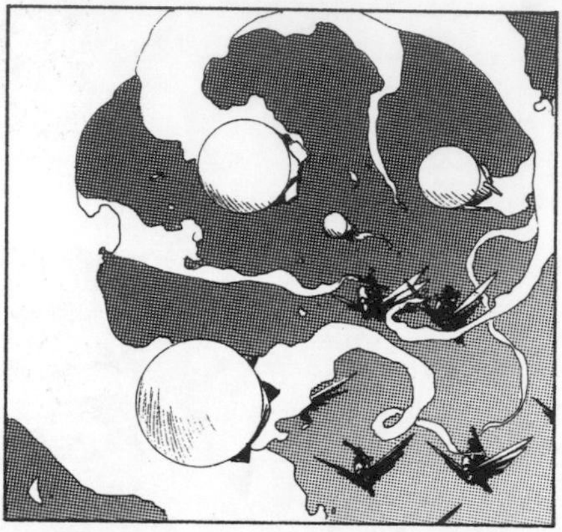

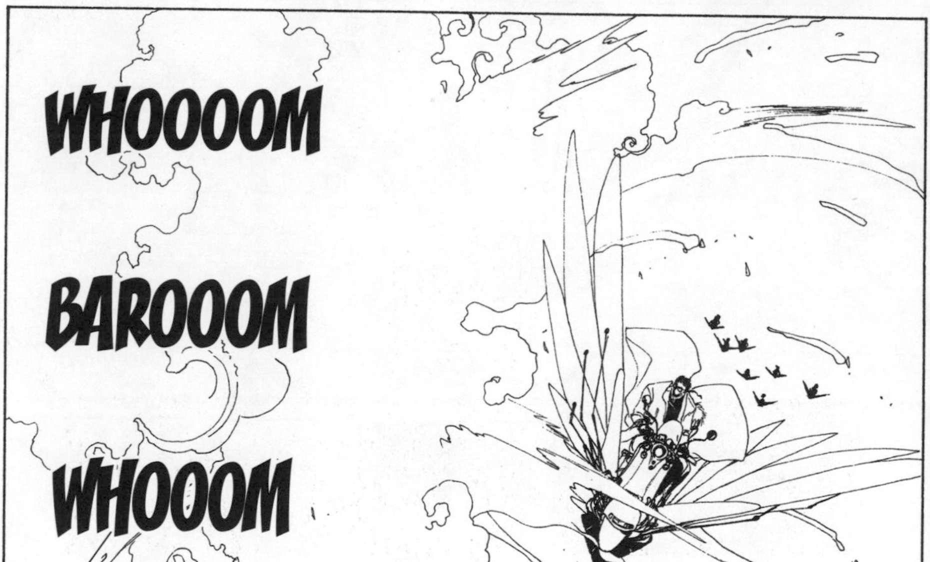
WHOOOOM
BAROOOM
WHOOOM

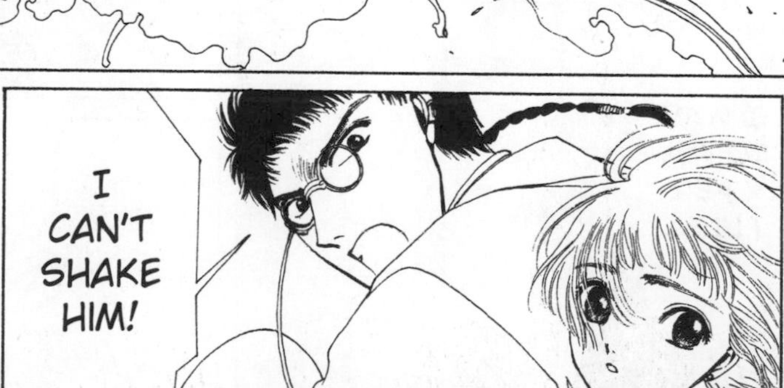
I CAN'T SHAKE HIM!

YOU CAN'T
GET RID
OF ME,
BABY...
WE BELONG
TOGETHER.

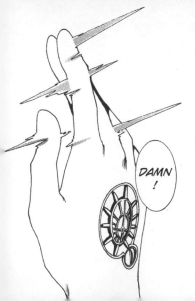

DAMN
!

bzzzt

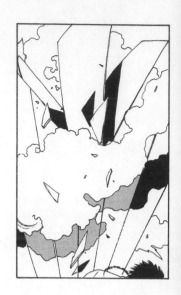

BOOOOM

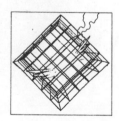

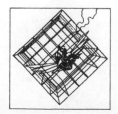

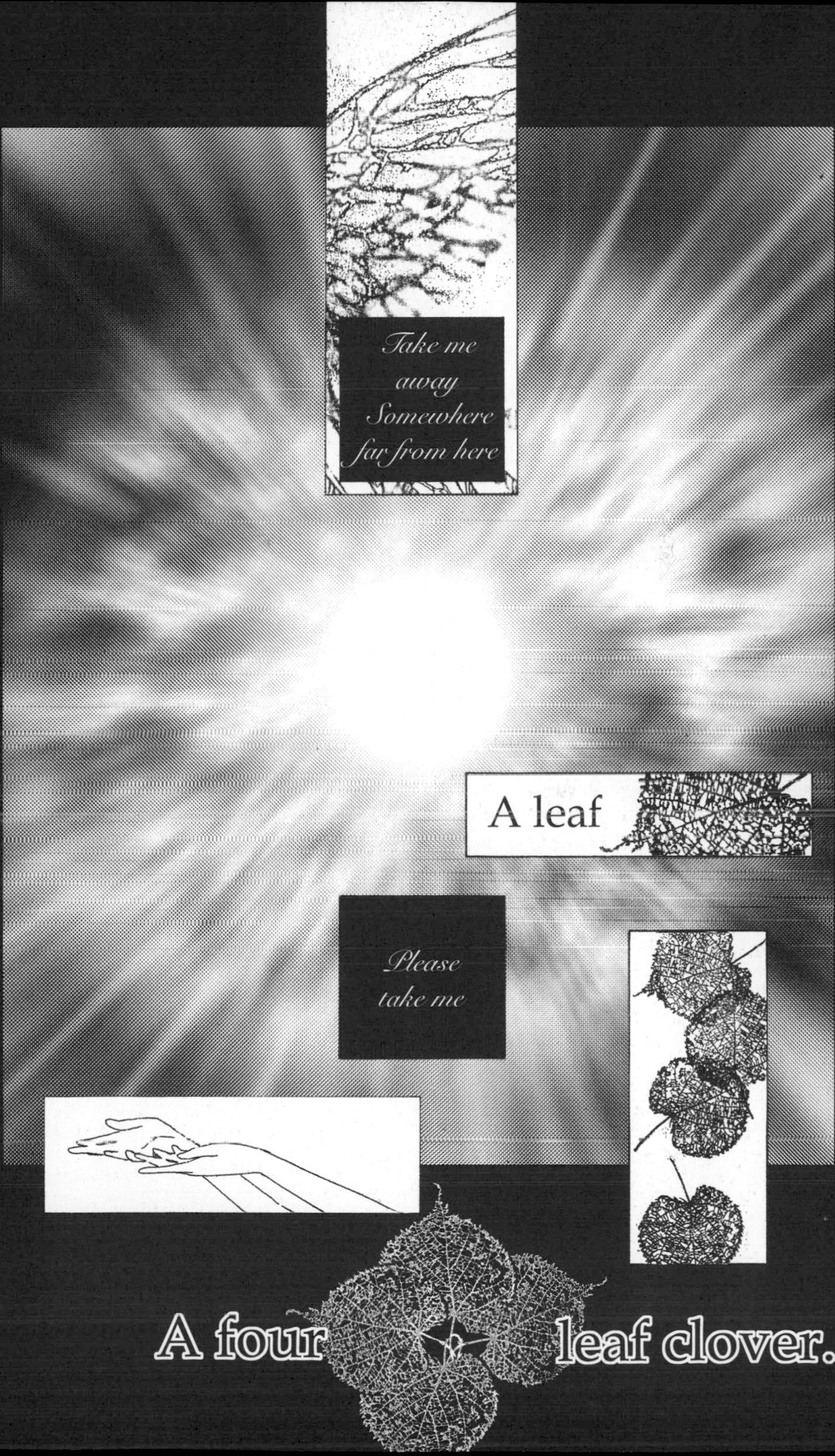

Take me away Somewhere far from here
A leaf
Please take me
A four leaf clover.

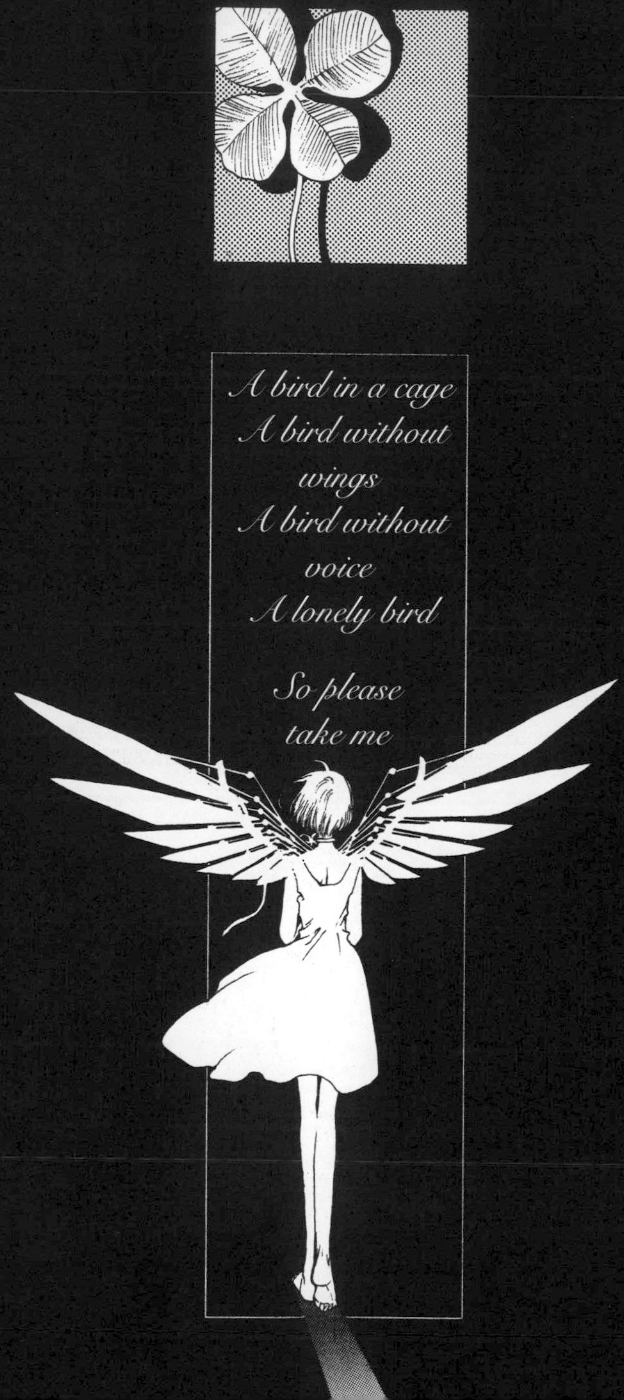
A bird in a cage
A bird without wings
A bird without voice
A lonely bird
So please take me

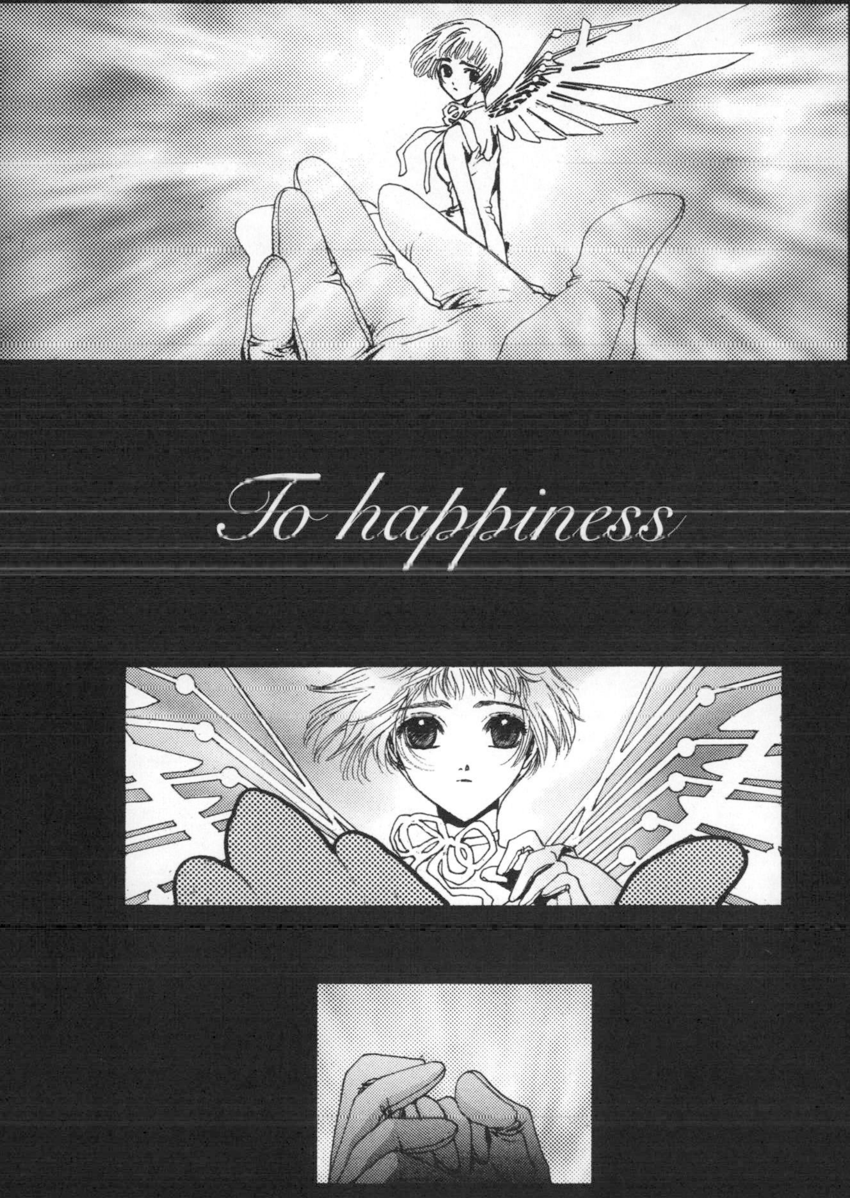
To happiness

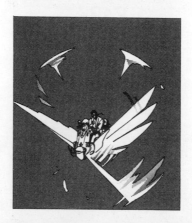

THE DESTINATION

WHAT HAPPENED ...?

RAN TRANSPORTED US.

...WHERE ARE WE?

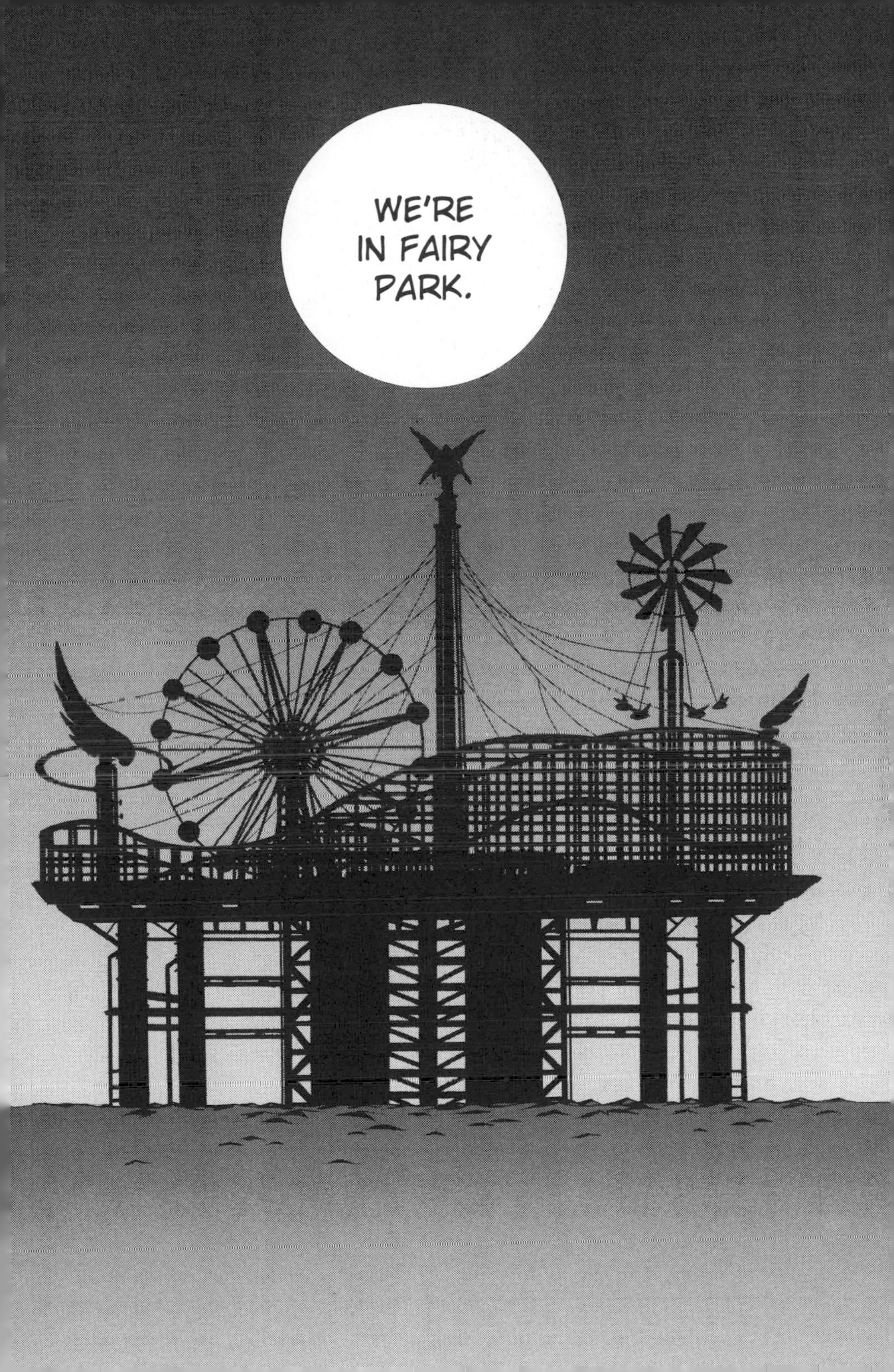
WE'RE IN FAIRY PARK.

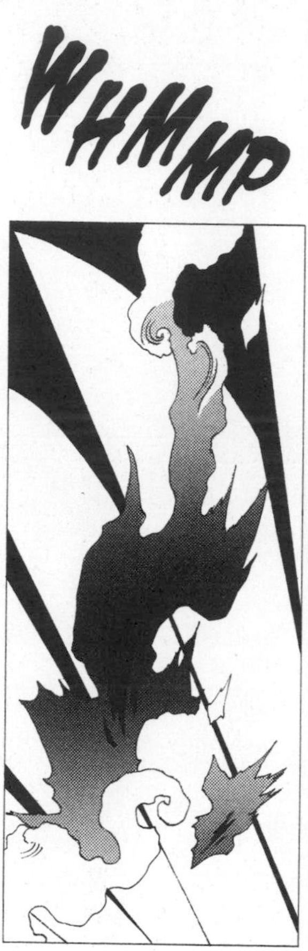
WHMMP
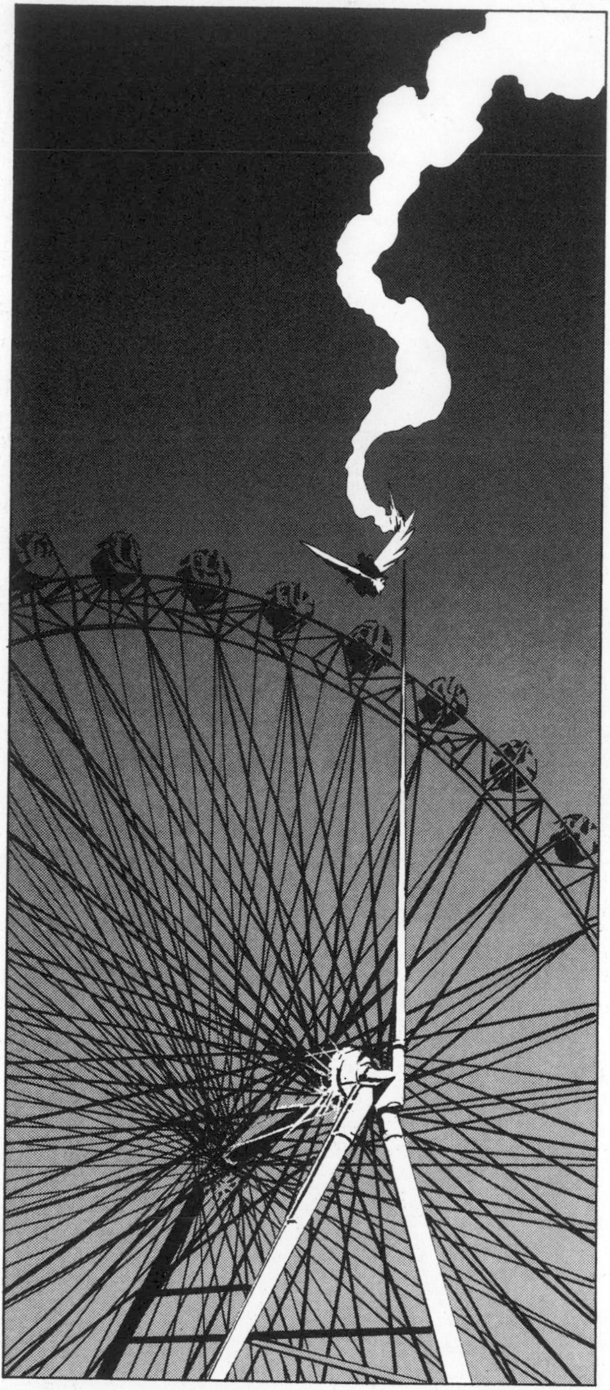

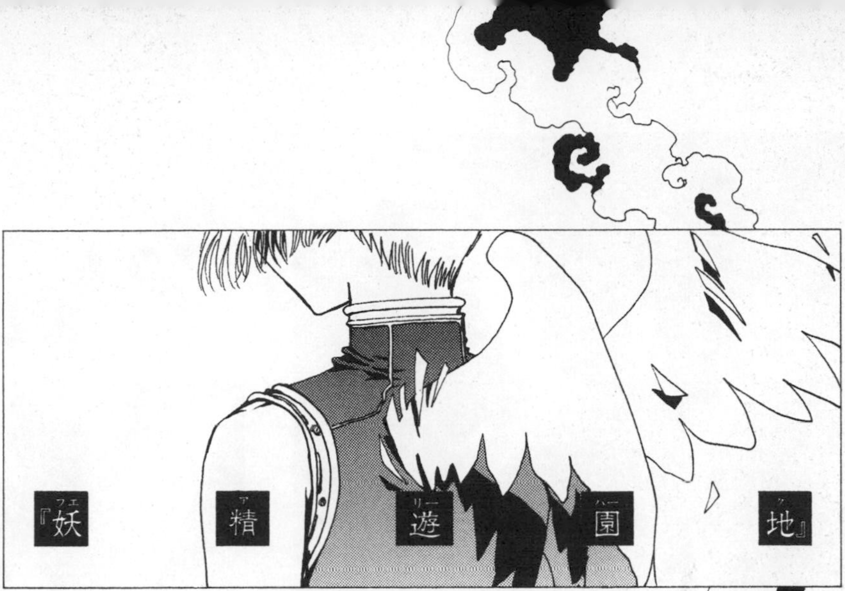
『妖精遊園地』

FAIRY PARK

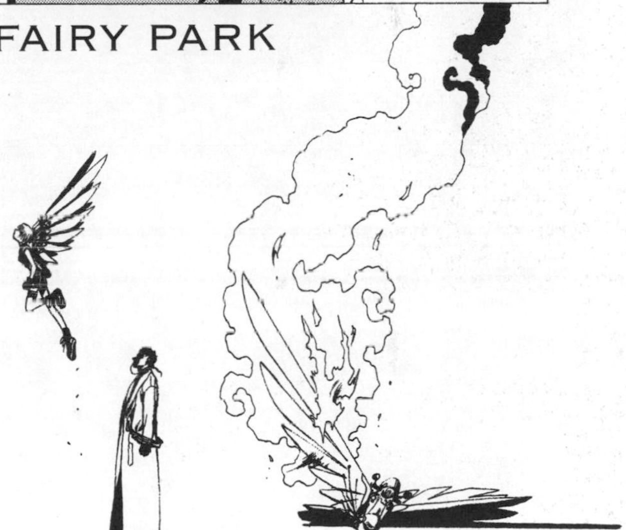

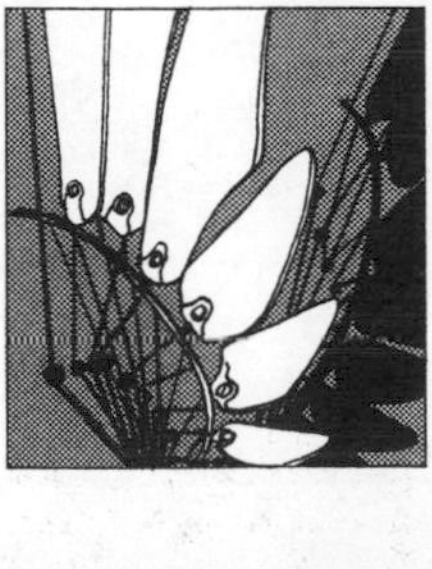

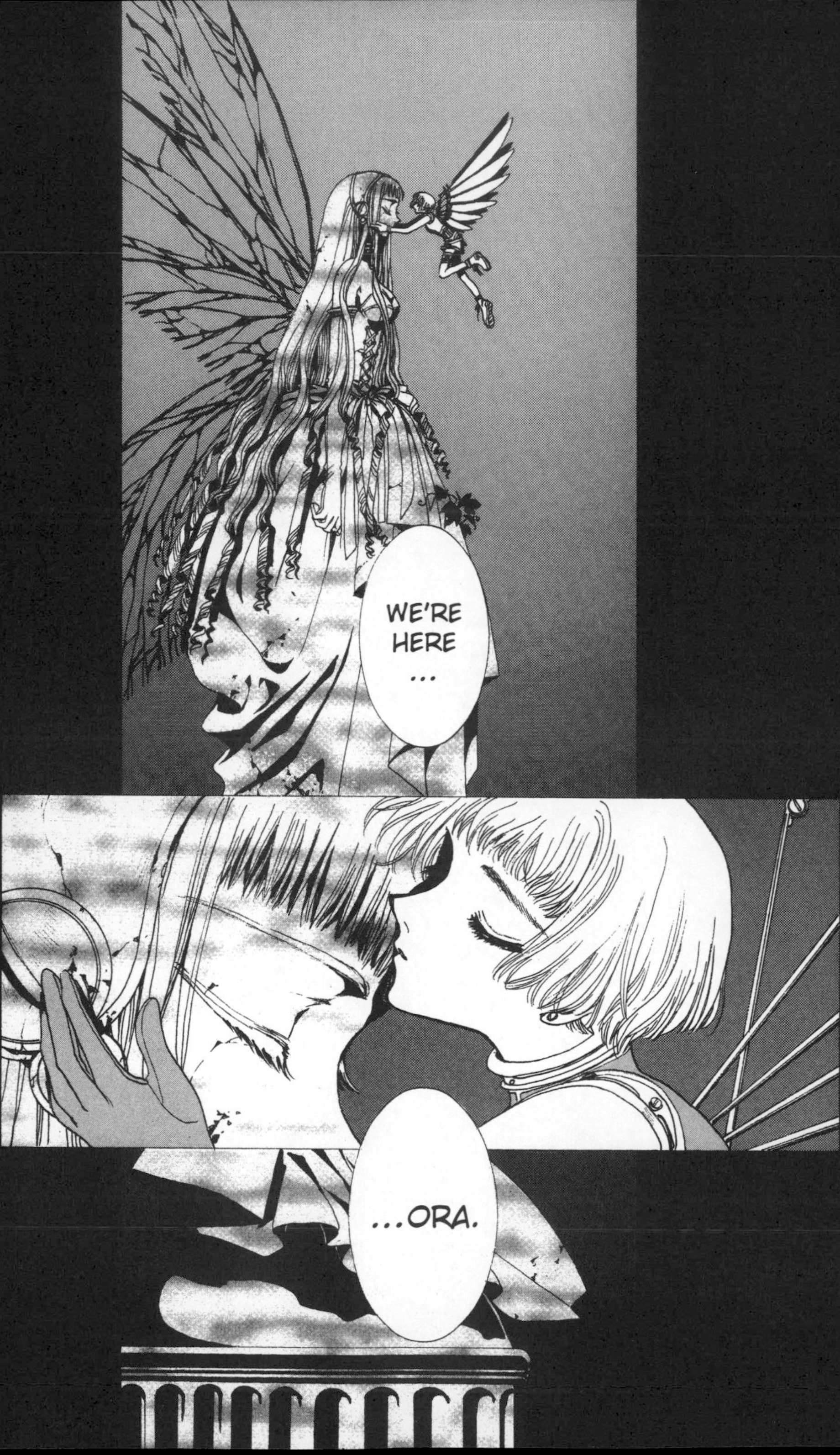
WE'RE HERE ...
...ORA.

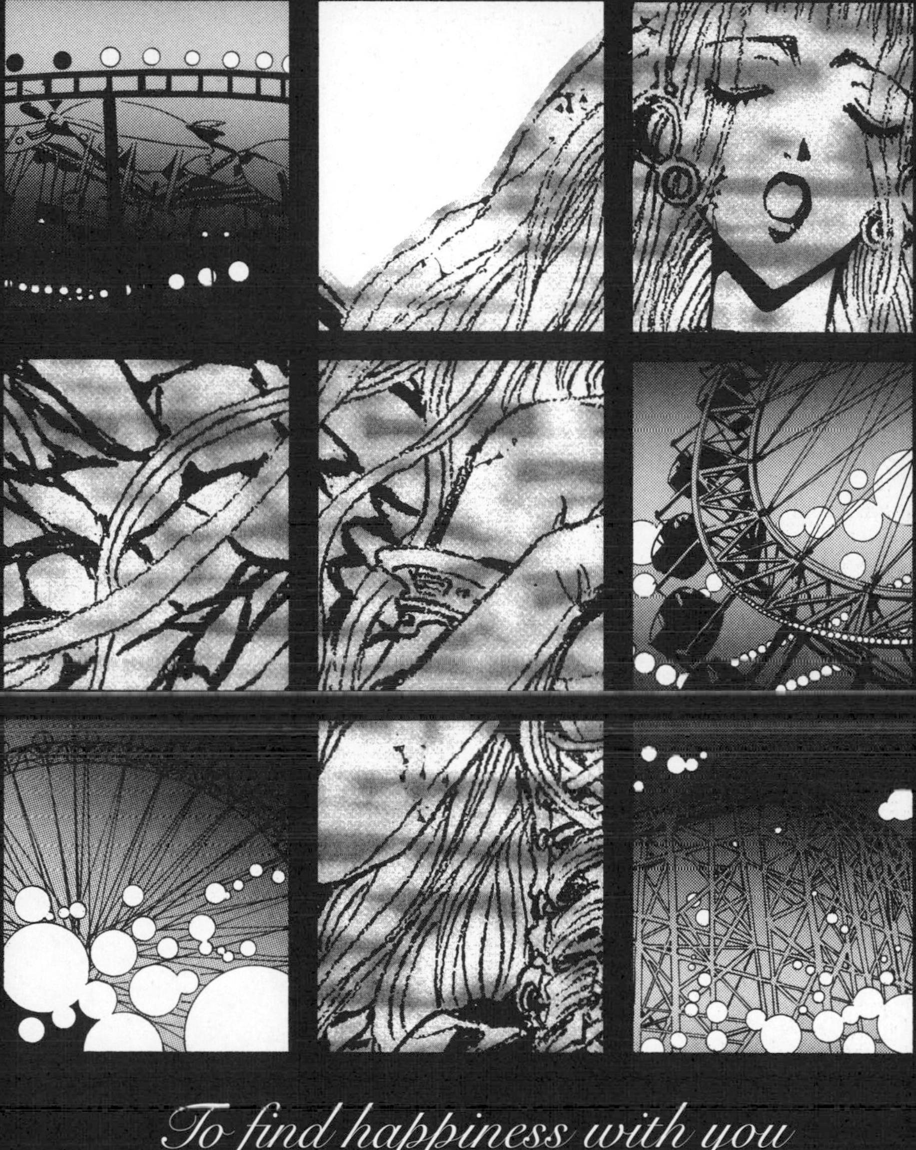

To find happiness with you

To be your happiness

I'm happy just to
be with you

Just to see
your smile

So take me

Somewhere far
from here

Take me away

To happiness

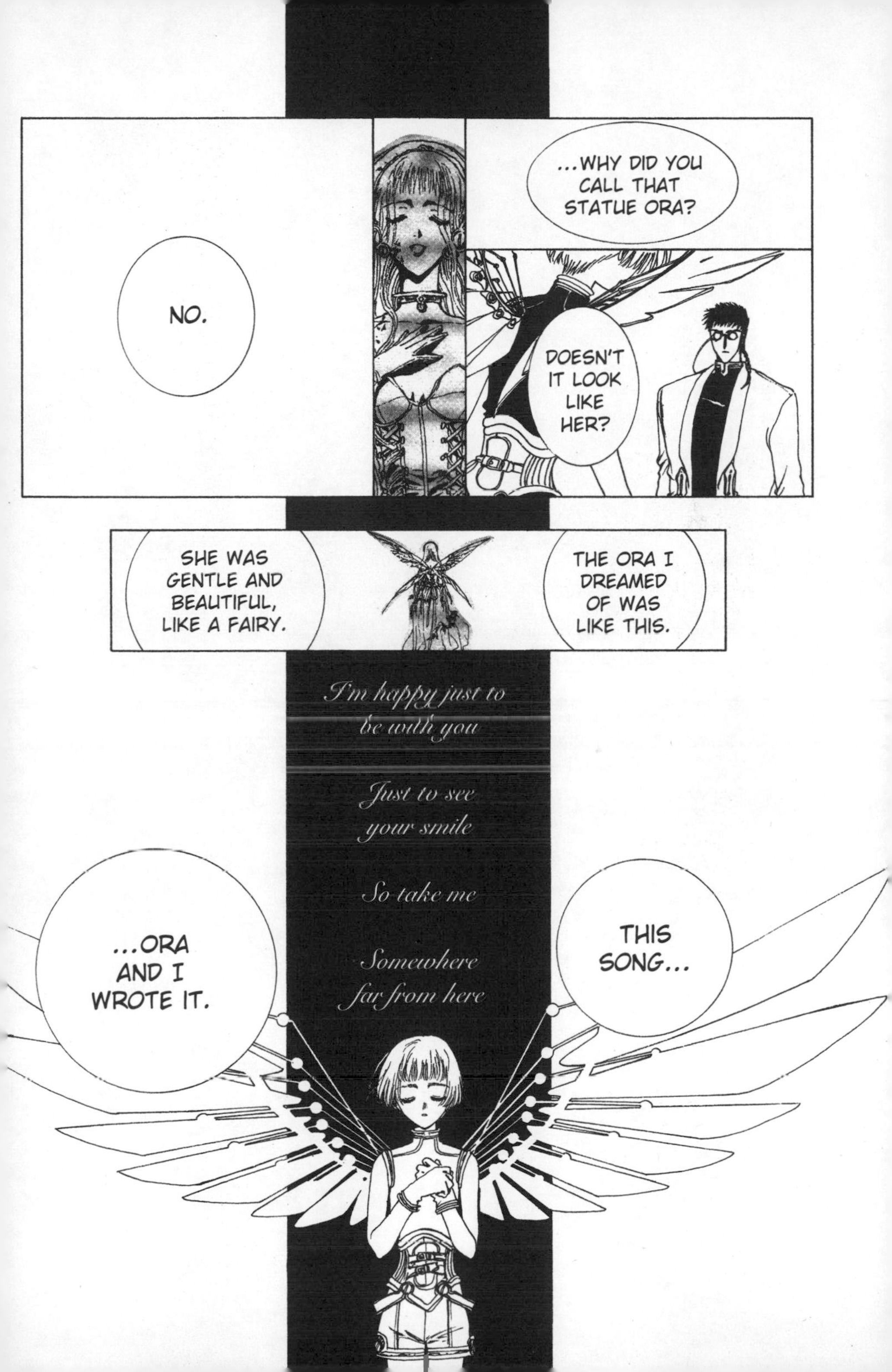
...WHY DID YOU CALL THAT STATUE ORA?
DOESN'T IT LOOK LIKE HER?
NO.
THE ORA I DREAMED OF WAS LIKE THIS.
SHE WAS GENTLE AND BEAUTIFUL, LIKE A FAIRY.
I'm happy just to be with you
Just to see your smile
So take me
Somewhere far from here
THIS SONG...
...ORA AND I WROTE IT.

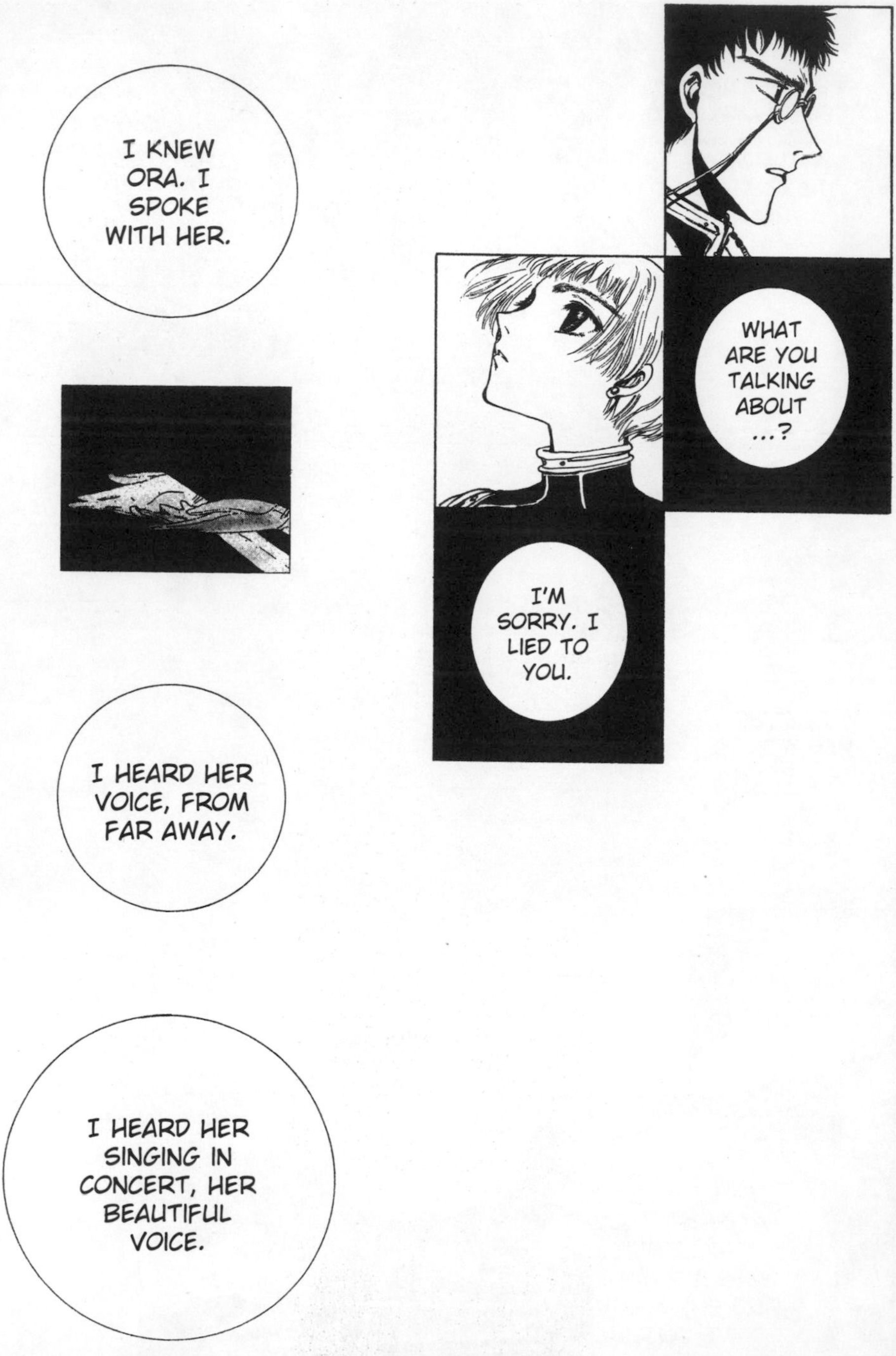
WHAT ARE YOU TALKING ABOUT ...?
I'M SORRY. I LIED TO YOU.
I KNEW ORA. I SPOKE WITH HER.
I HEARD HER VOICE, FROM FAR AWAY.
I HEARD HER SINGING IN CONCERT, HER BEAUTIFUL VOICE.

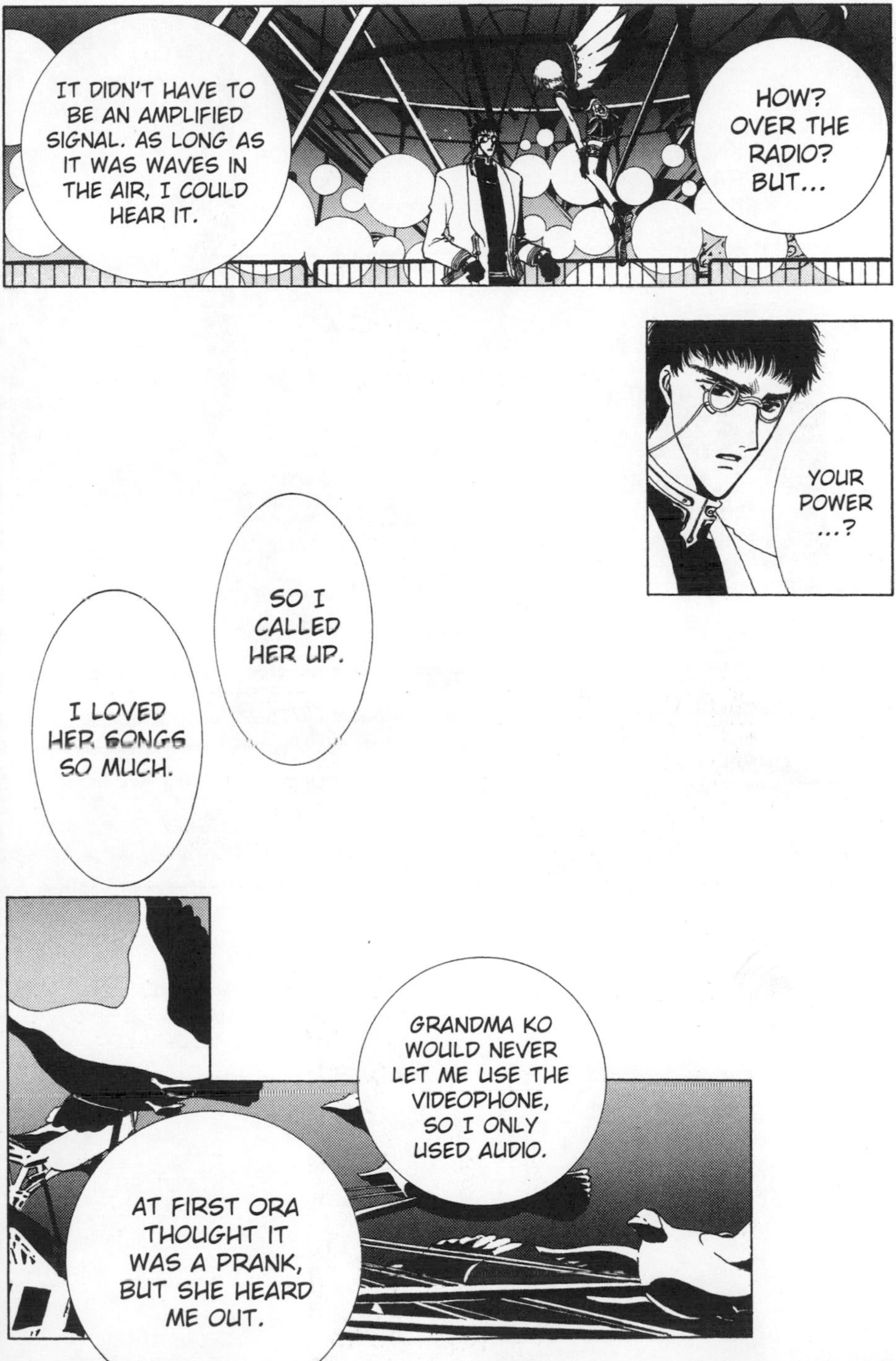
HOW? OVER THE RADIO? BUT...
IT DIDN'T HAVE TO BE AN AMPLIFIED SIGNAL. AS LONG AS IT WAS WAVES IN THE AIR, I COULD HEAR IT.
YOUR POWER ...?
SO I CALLED HER UP.
I LOVED HER SONGS SO MUCH.
GRANDMA KO WOULD NEVER LET ME USE THE VIDEOPHONE, SO I ONLY USED AUDIO.
AT FIRST ORA THOUGHT IT WAS A PRANK, BUT SHE HEARD ME OUT.

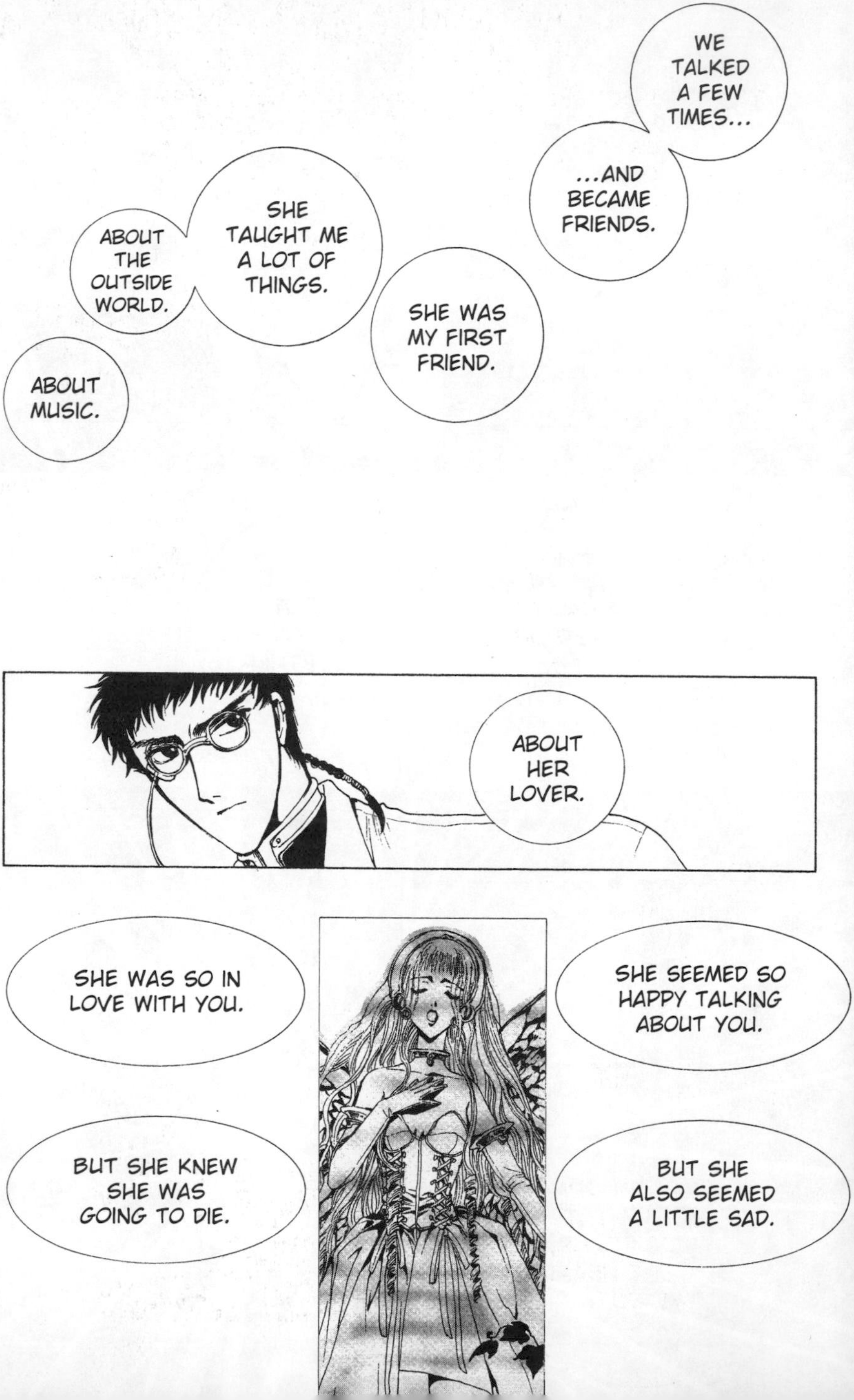
WE TALKED A FEW TIMES...
...AND BECAME FRIENDS.
SHE WAS MY FIRST FRIEND.
SHE TAUGHT ME A LOT OF THINGS.
ABOUT THE OUTSIDE WORLD.
ABOUT MUSIC.
ABOUT HER LOVER.
SHE SEEMED SO HAPPY TALKING ABOUT YOU.
BUT SHE ALSO SEEMED A LITTLE SAD.
SHE WAS SO IN LOVE WITH YOU.
BUT SHE KNEW SHE WAS GOING TO DIE.

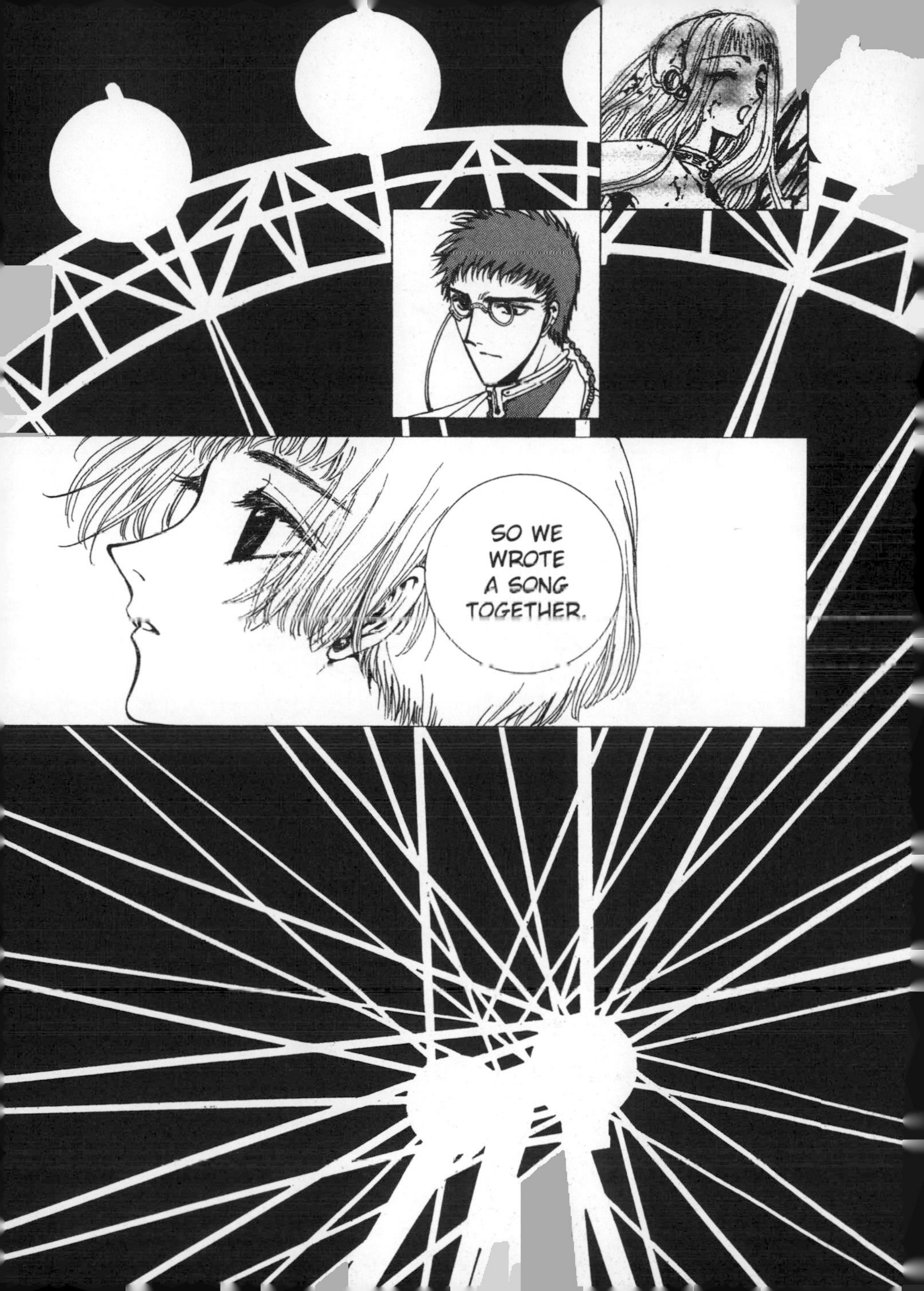
SO WE WROTE A SONG TOGETHER.

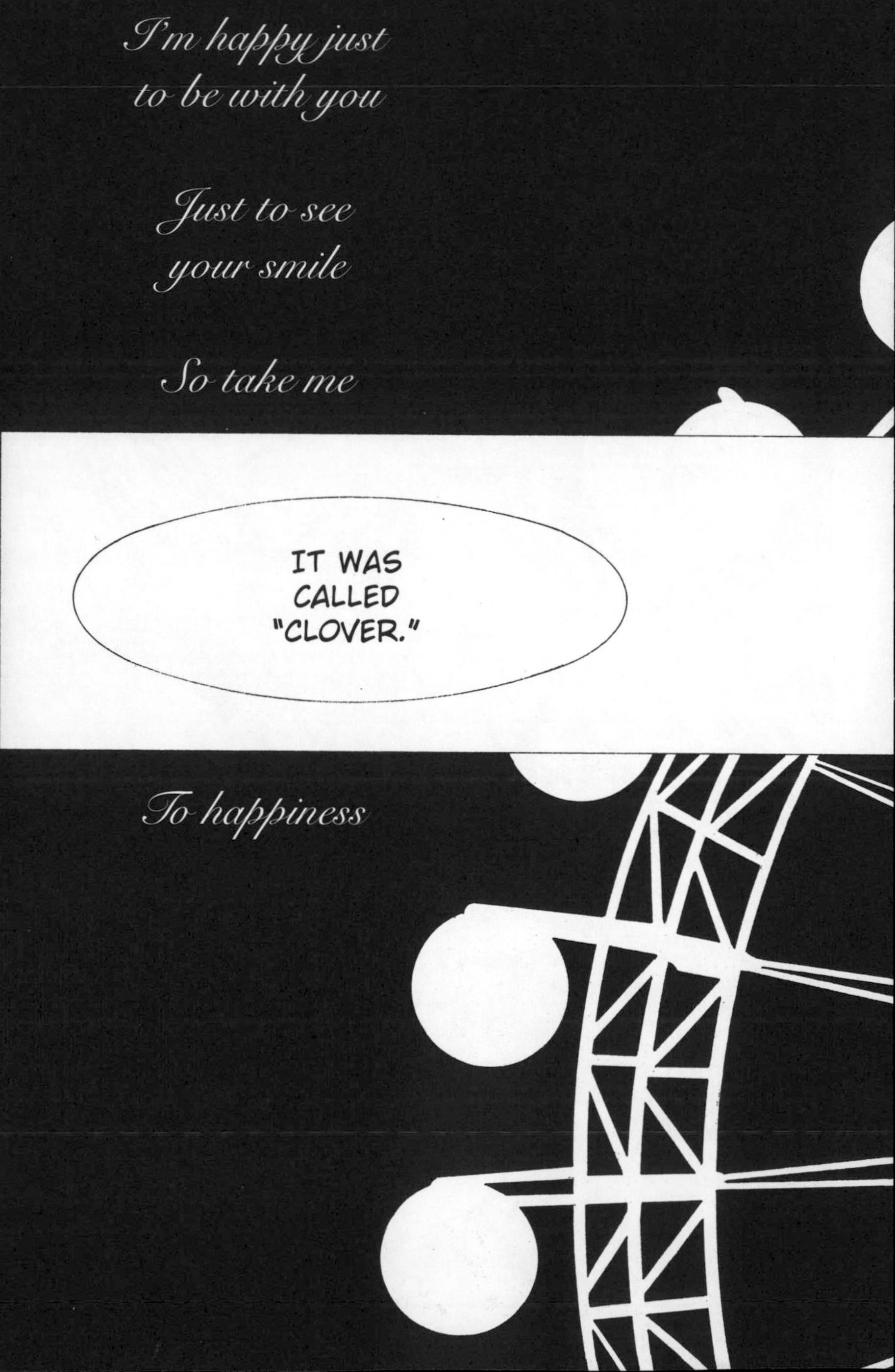
I'm happy just to be with you
Just to see your smile
So take me
IT WAS CALLED "CLOVER."
To happiness

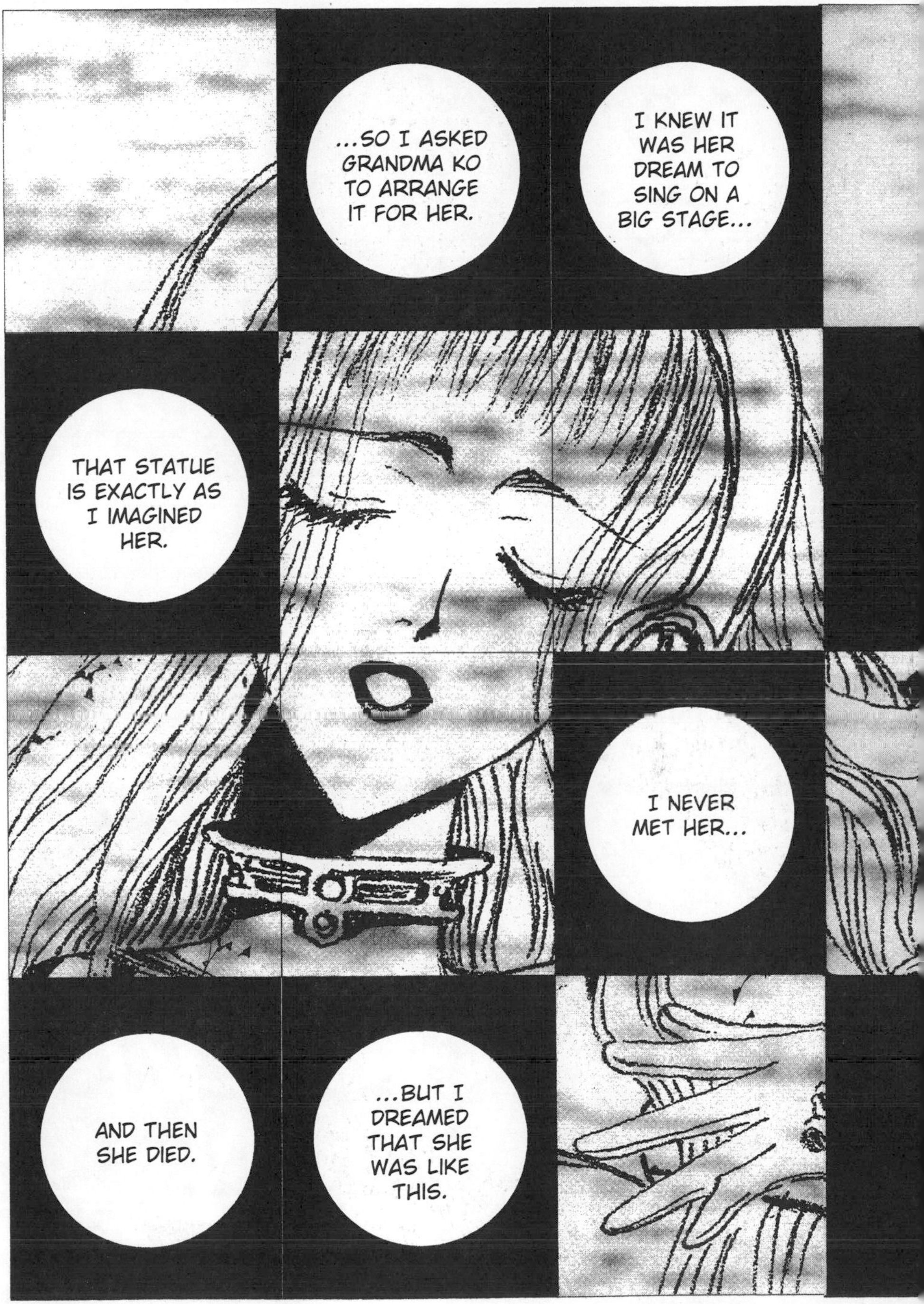
I KNEW IT WAS HER DREAM TO SING ON A BIG STAGE...
...SO I ASKED GRANDMA KO TO ARRANGE IT FOR HER.
THAT STATUE IS EXACTLY AS I IMAGINED HER.
I NEVER MET HER...
...BUT I DREAMED THAT SHE WAS LIKE THIS.
AND THEN SHE DIED.

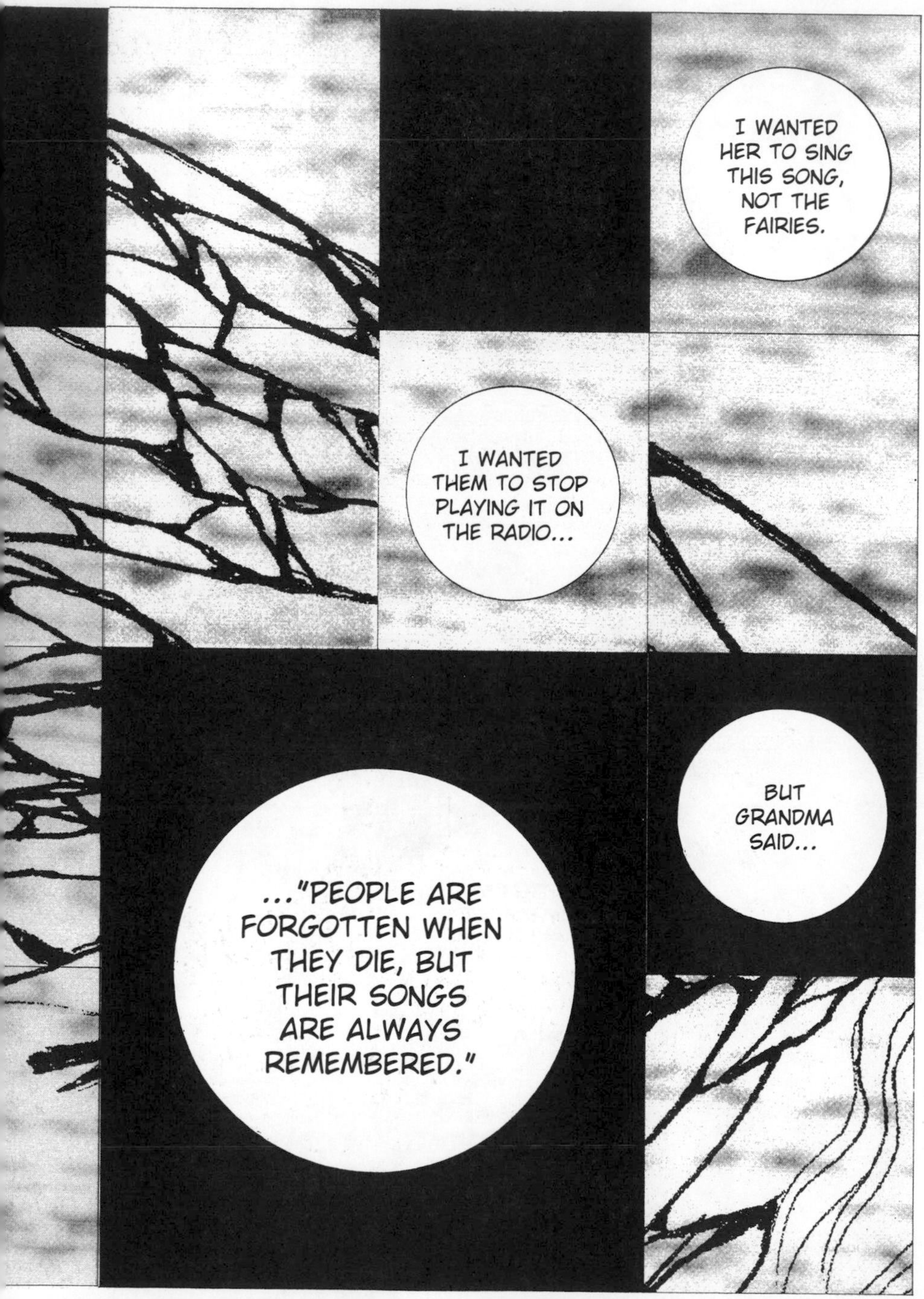
I WANTED HER TO SING THIS SONG, NOT THE FAIRIES.
I WANTED THEM TO STOP PLAYING IT ON THE RADIO...
BUT GRANDMA SAID...
..."PEOPLE ARE FORGOTTEN WHEN THEY DIE, BUT THEIR SONGS ARE ALWAYS REMEMBERED."

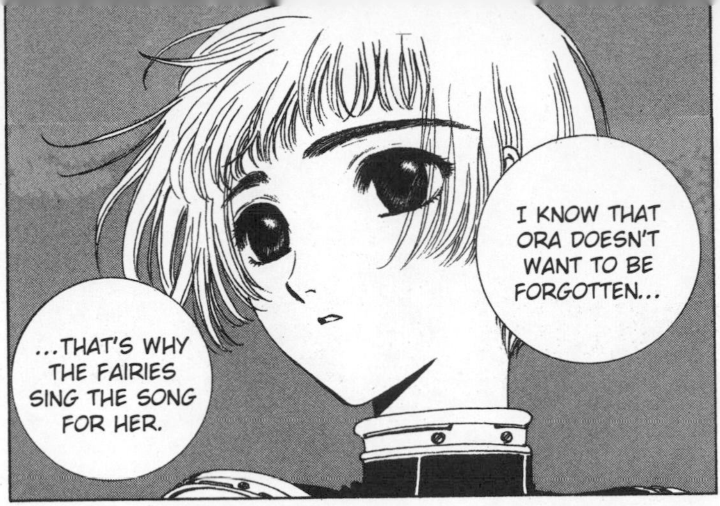
I KNOW THAT ORA DOESN'T WANT TO BE FORGOTTEN...
...THAT'S WHY THE FAIRIES SING THE SONG FOR HER.

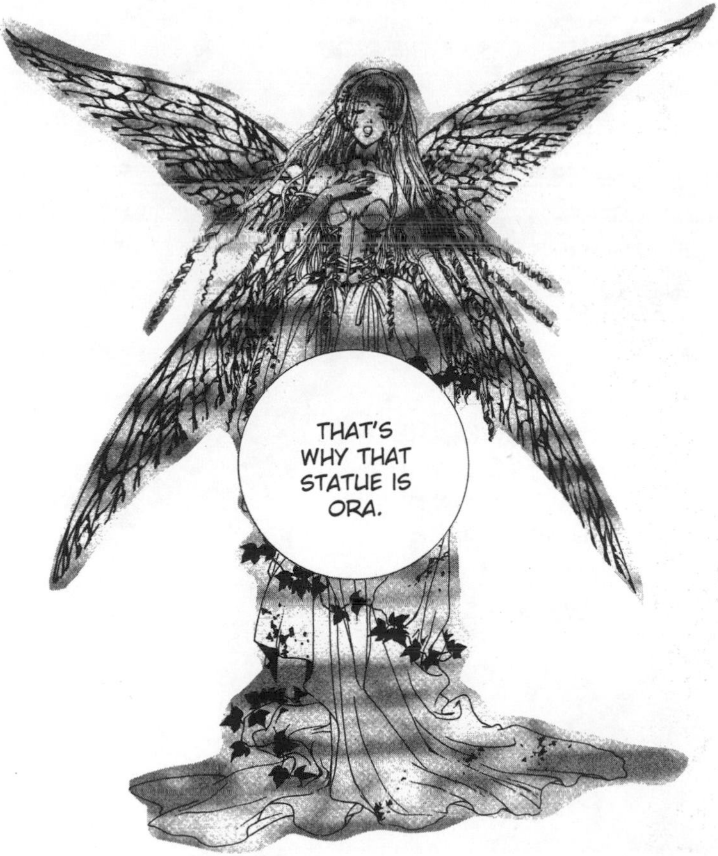
THAT'S WHY THAT STATUE IS ORA.

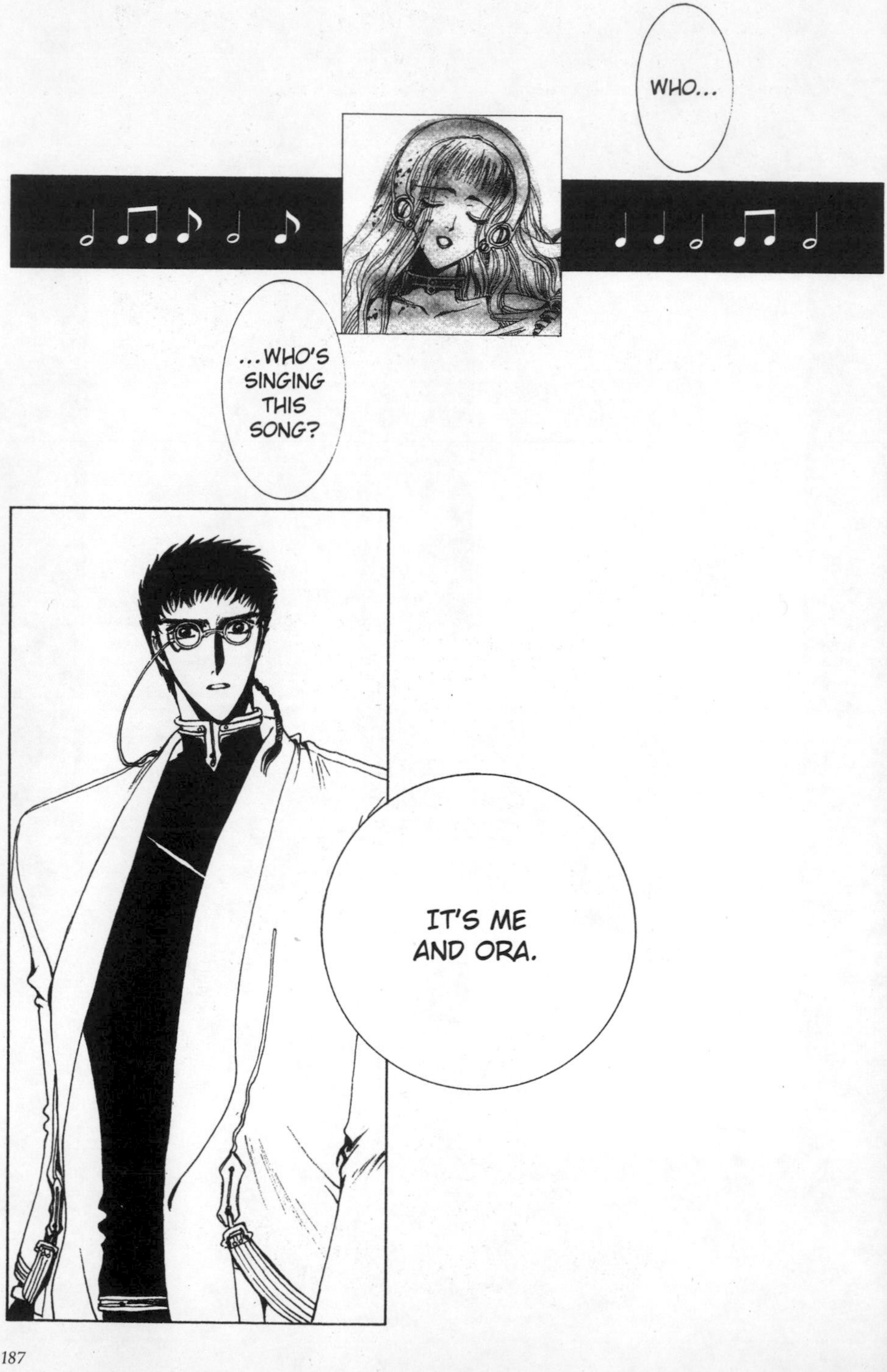
WHO...
...WHO'S SINGING THIS SONG?
IT'S ME AND ORA.

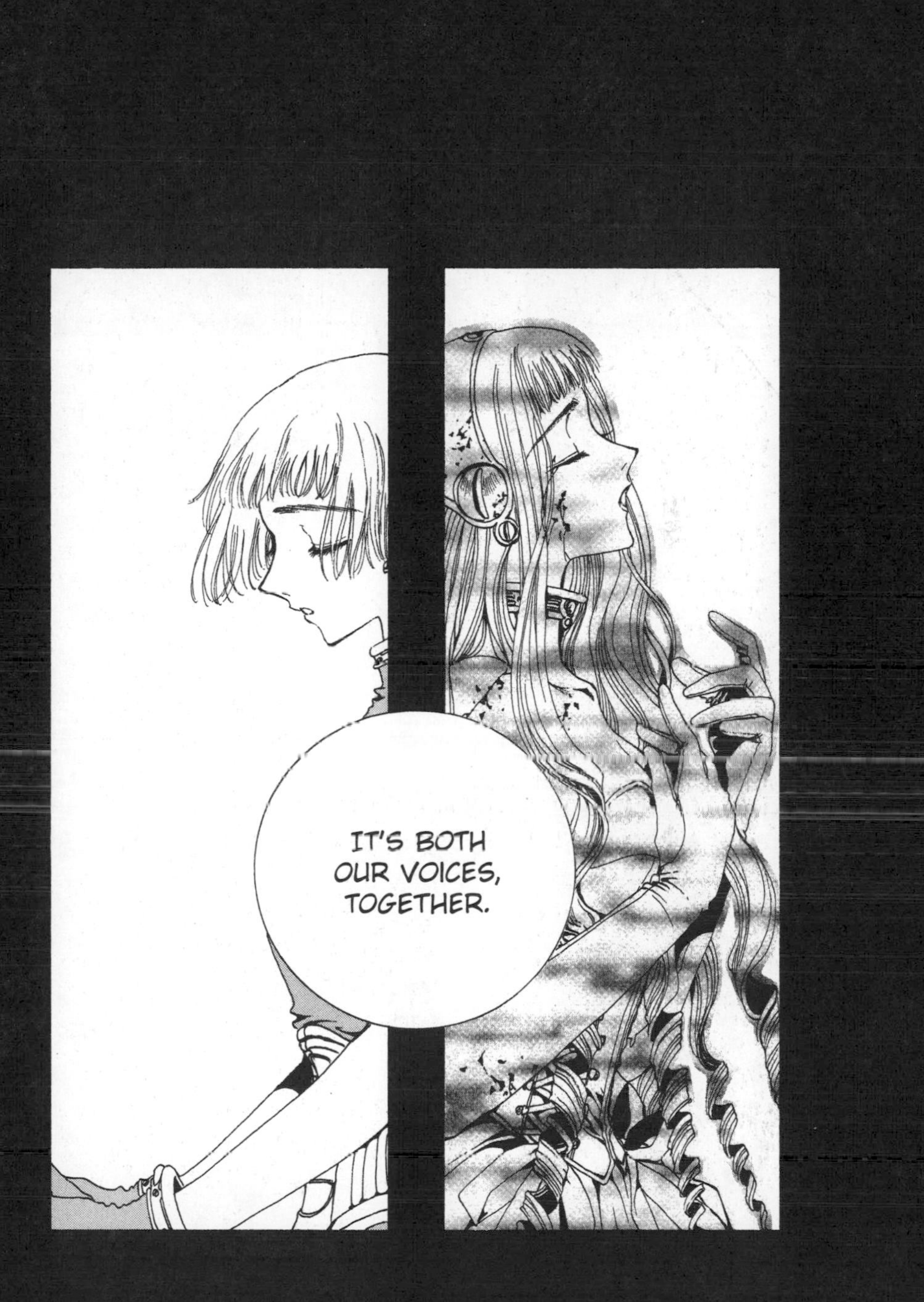
IT'S BOTH OUR VOICES, TOGETHER.

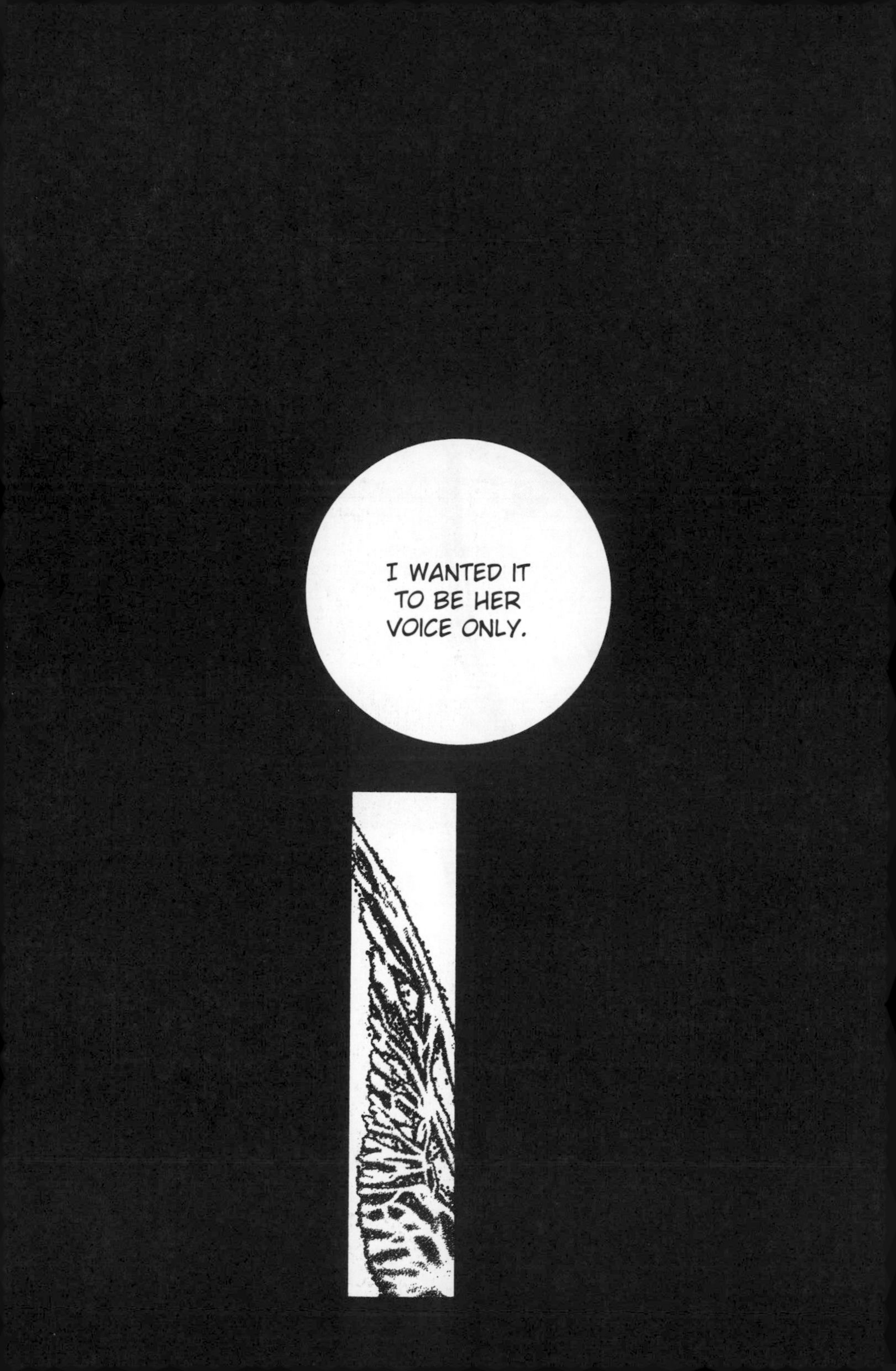
I WANTED IT TO BE HER VOICE ONLY.

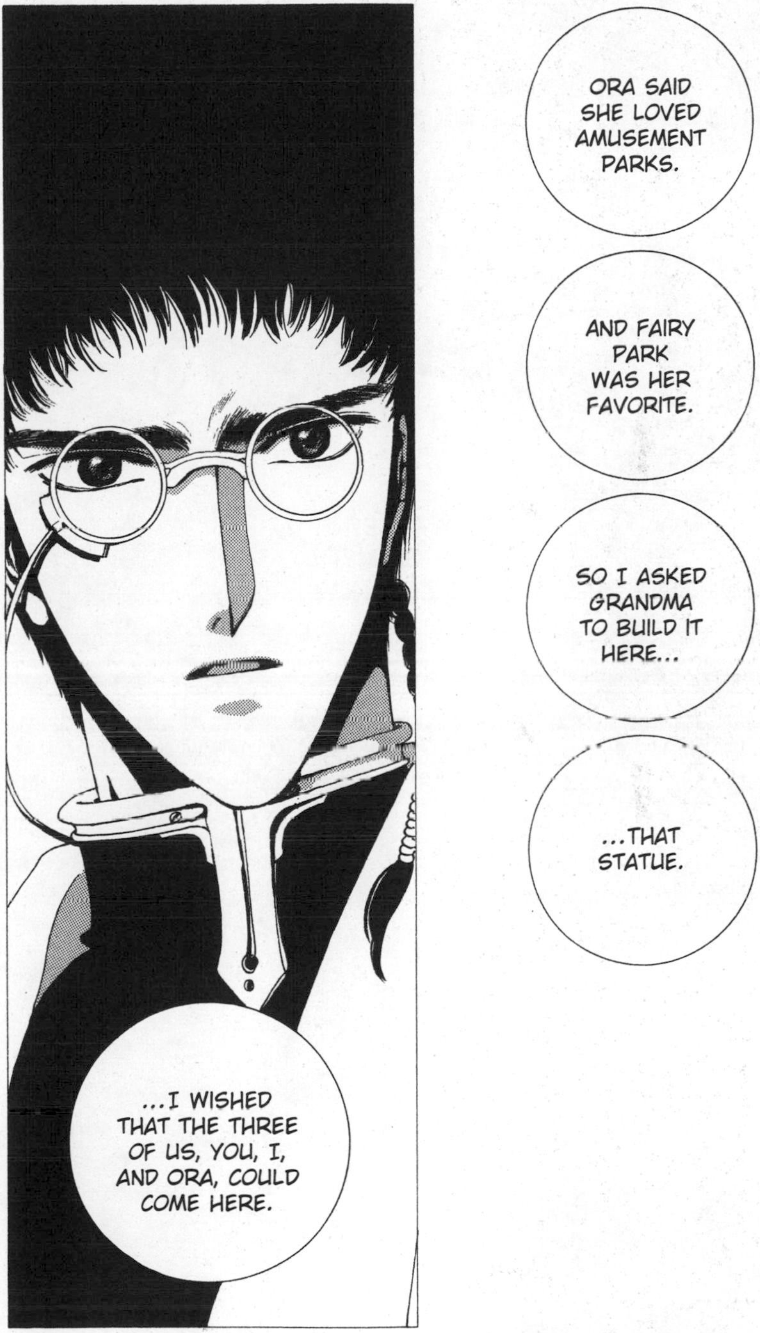
ORA SAID SHE LOVED AMUSEMENT PARKS.
AND FAIRY PARK WAS HER FAVORITE.
SO I ASKED GRANDMA TO BUILD IT HERE...
...THAT STATUE.
...I WISHED THAT THE THREE OF US, YOU, I, AND ORA, COULD COME HERE.

*I'm just happy just
to be with you*

*Just to see
your smile*

*So take me
Somewhere
far from here*

*I wish
for happiness*

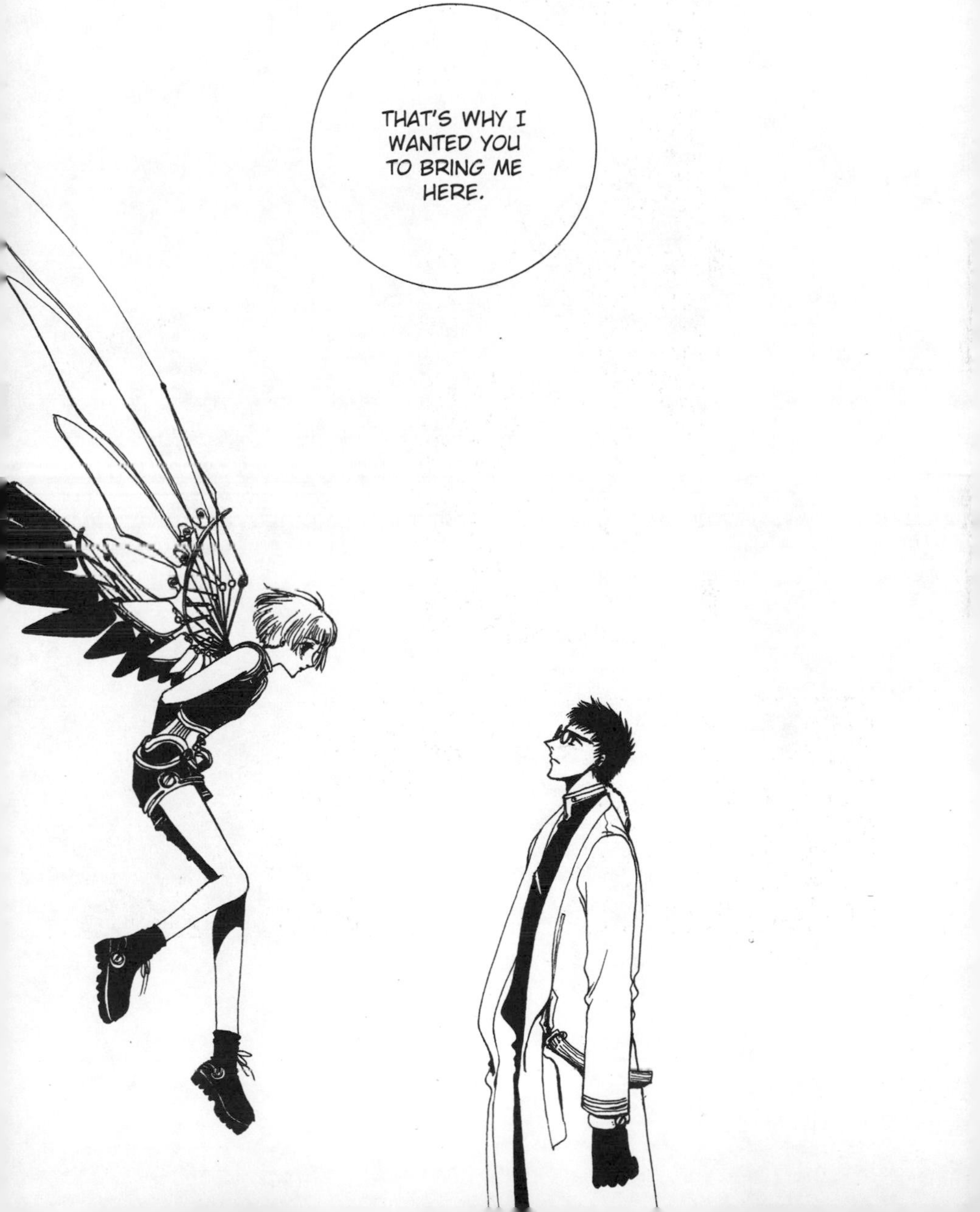
THAT'S WHY I WANTED YOU TO BRING ME HERE.

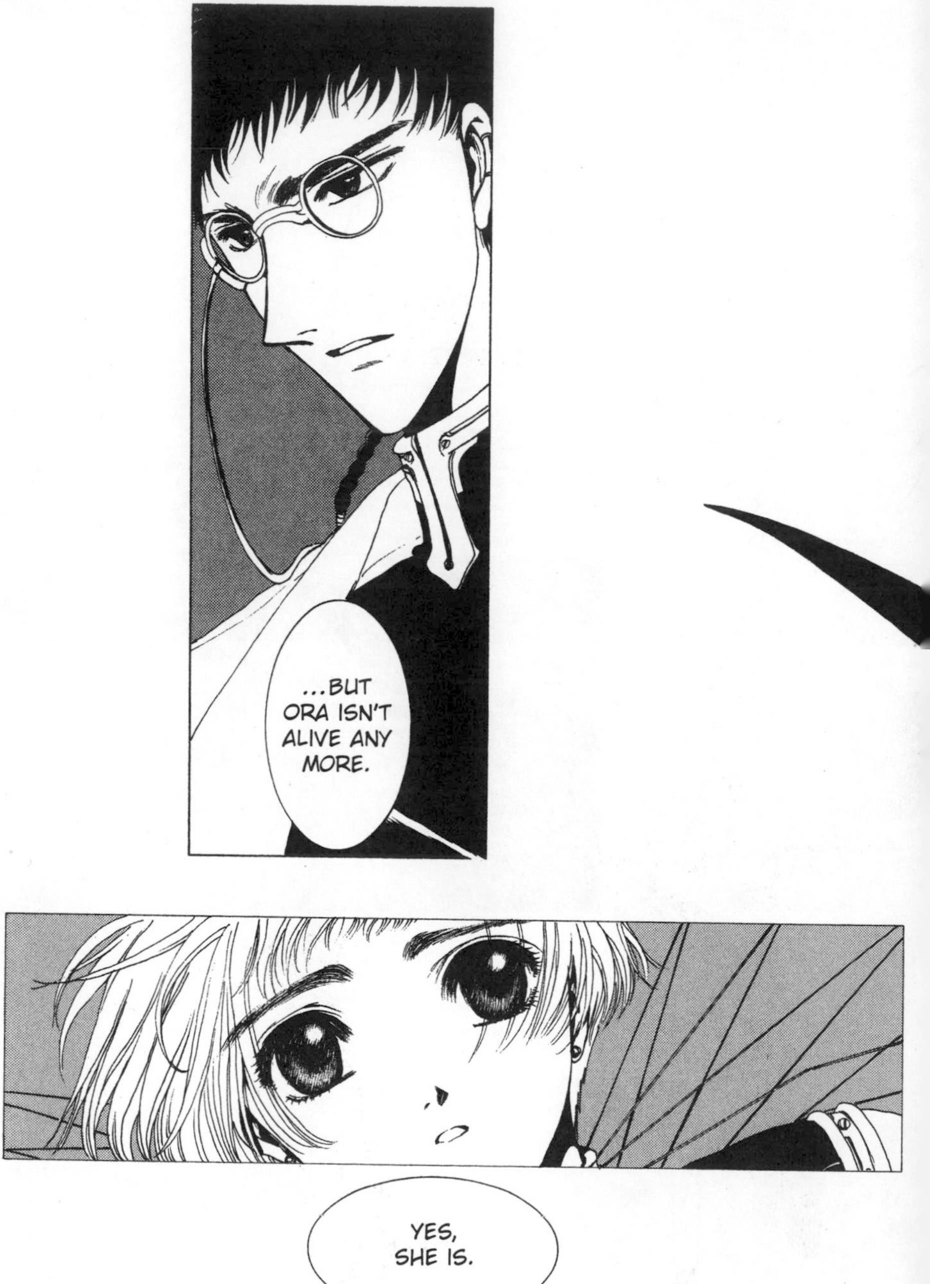
...BUT ORA ISN'T ALIVE ANY MORE.
YES, SHE IS.

HERE.

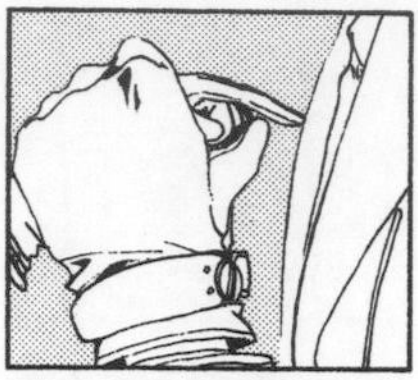
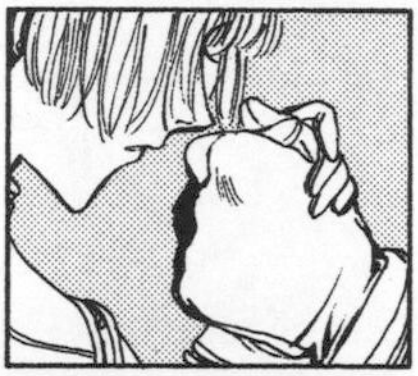
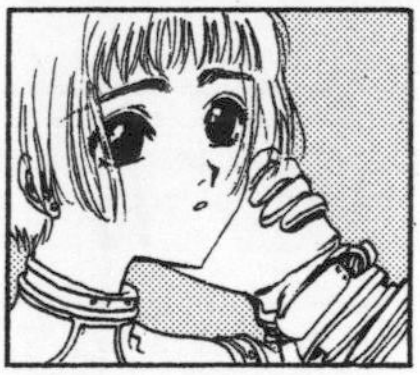
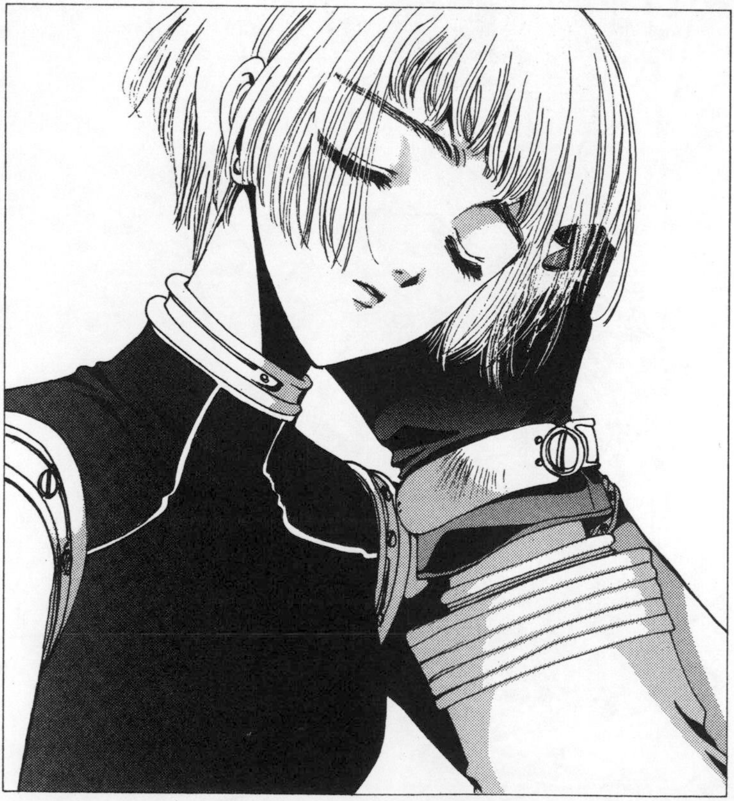

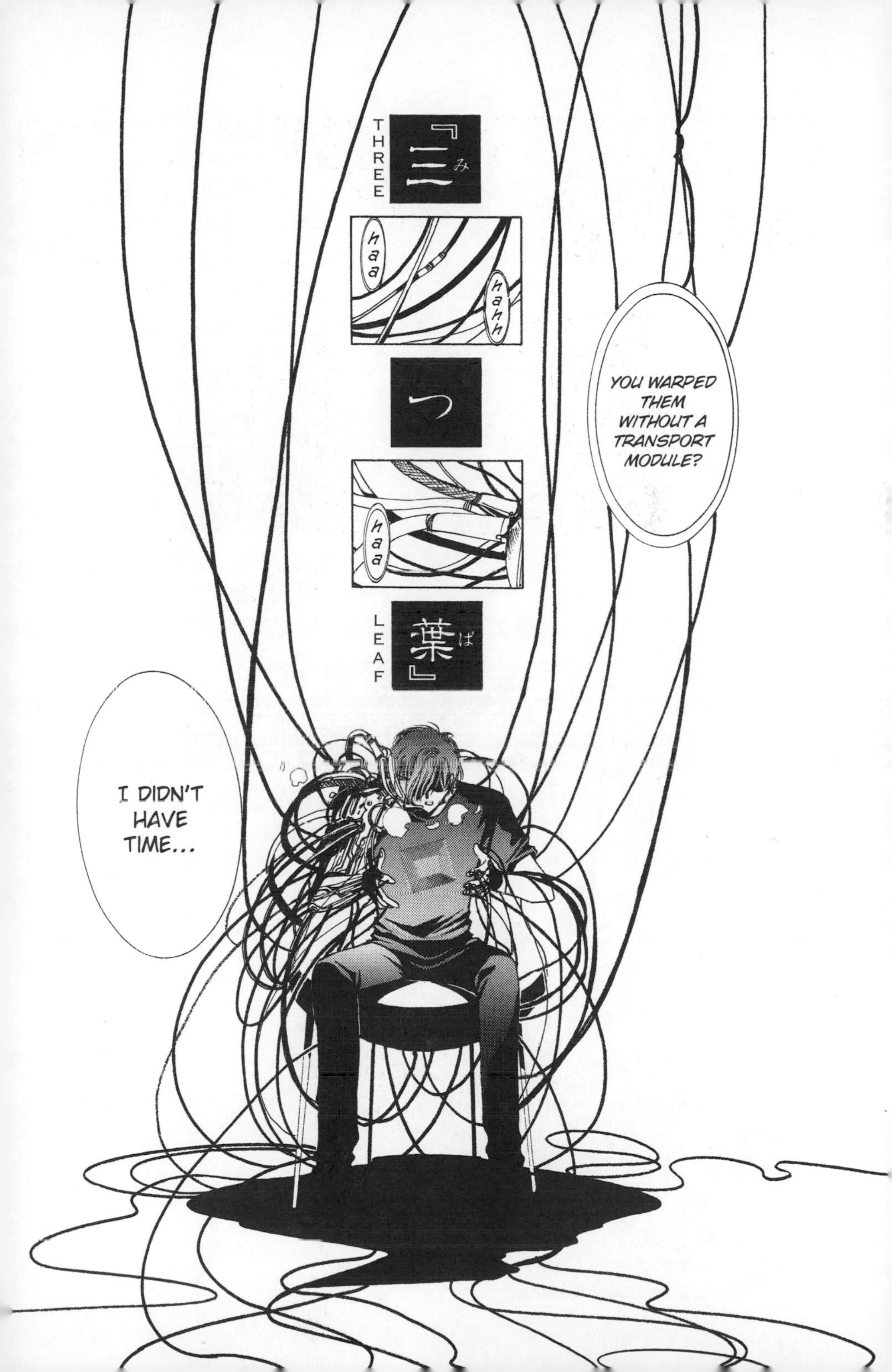

THREE
『三み
haa
hahh
つ
haa
LEAF
葉ば』
YOU WARPED THEM WITHOUT A TRANSPORT MODULE?
I DIDN'T HAVE TIME...

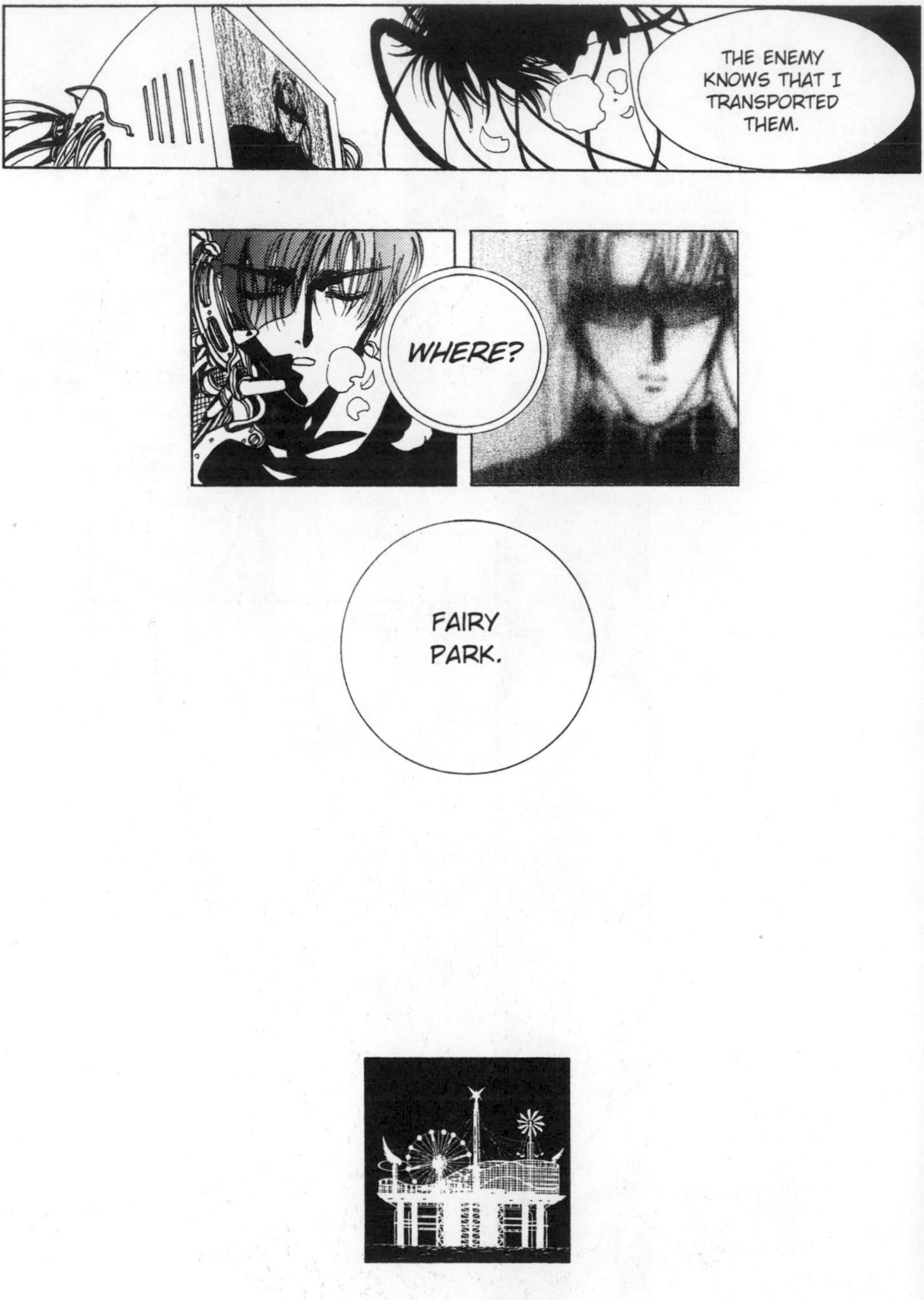
THE ENEMY KNOWS THAT I TRANSPORTED THEM.
WHERE?
FAIRY PARK.

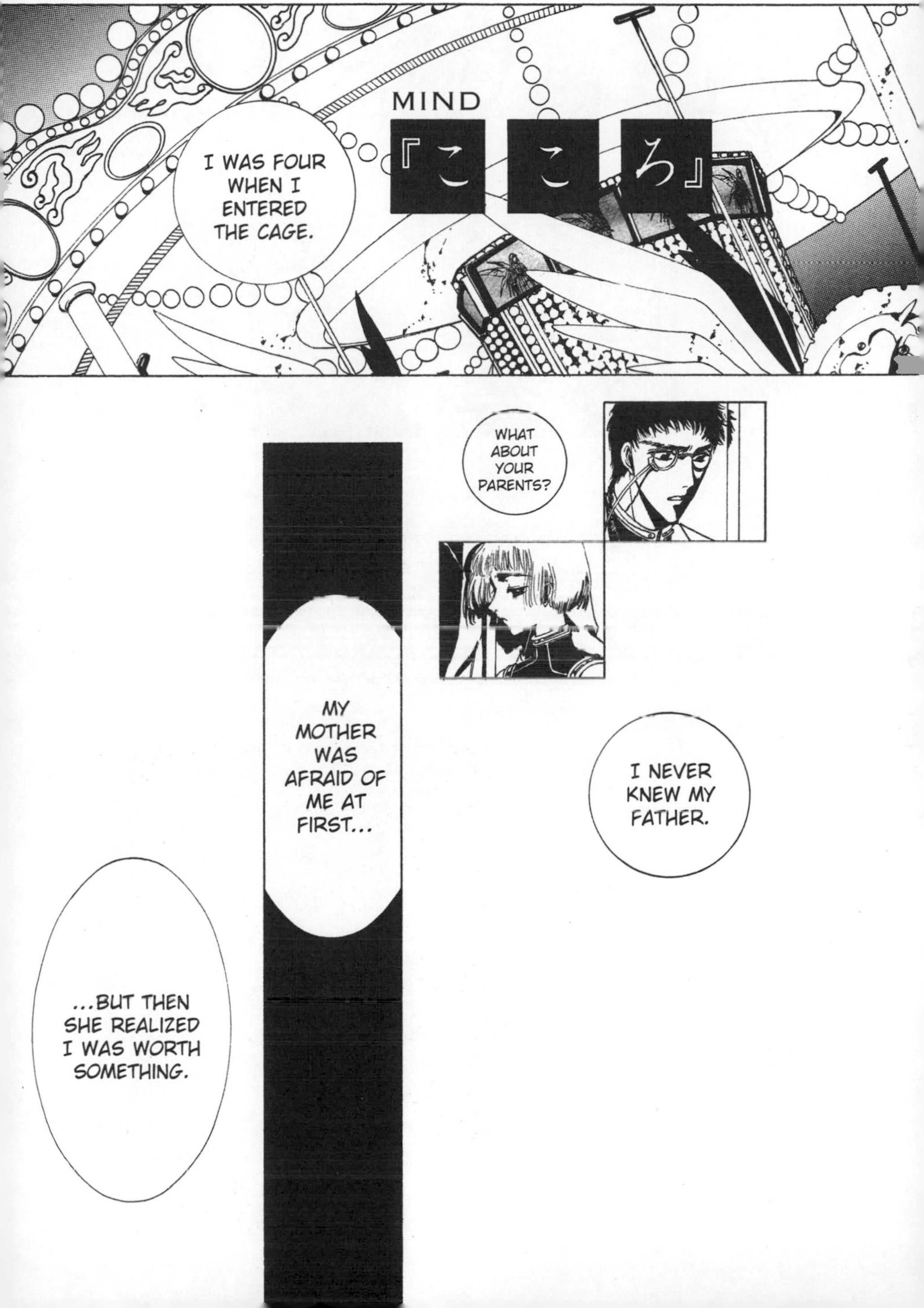
MIND
『こころ』
I WAS FOUR WHEN I ENTERED THE CAGE.
WHAT ABOUT YOUR PARENTS?
I NEVER KNEW MY FATHER.
MY MOTHER WAS AFRAID OF ME AT FIRST...
...BUT THEN SHE REALIZED I WAS WORTH SOMETHING.

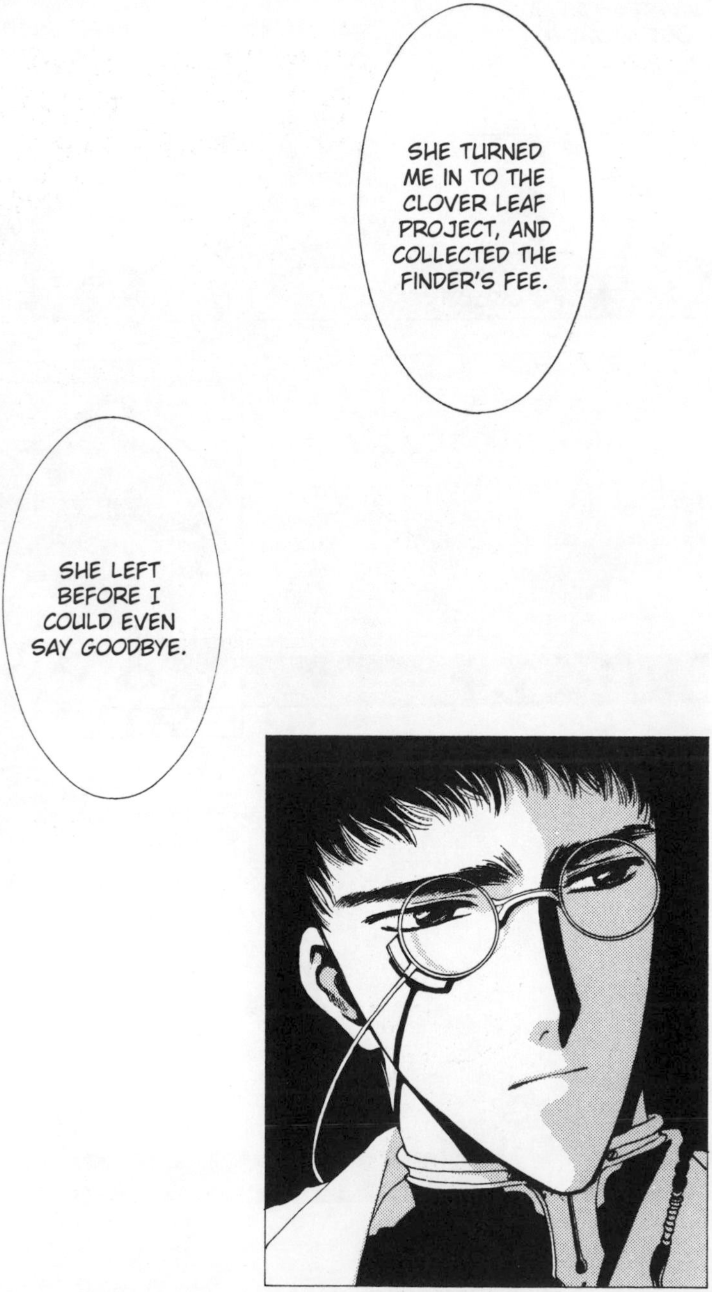
SHE TURNED ME IN TO THE CLOVER LEAF PROJECT, AND COLLECTED THE FINDER'S FEE.
SHE LEFT BEFORE I COULD EVEN SAY GOODBYE.

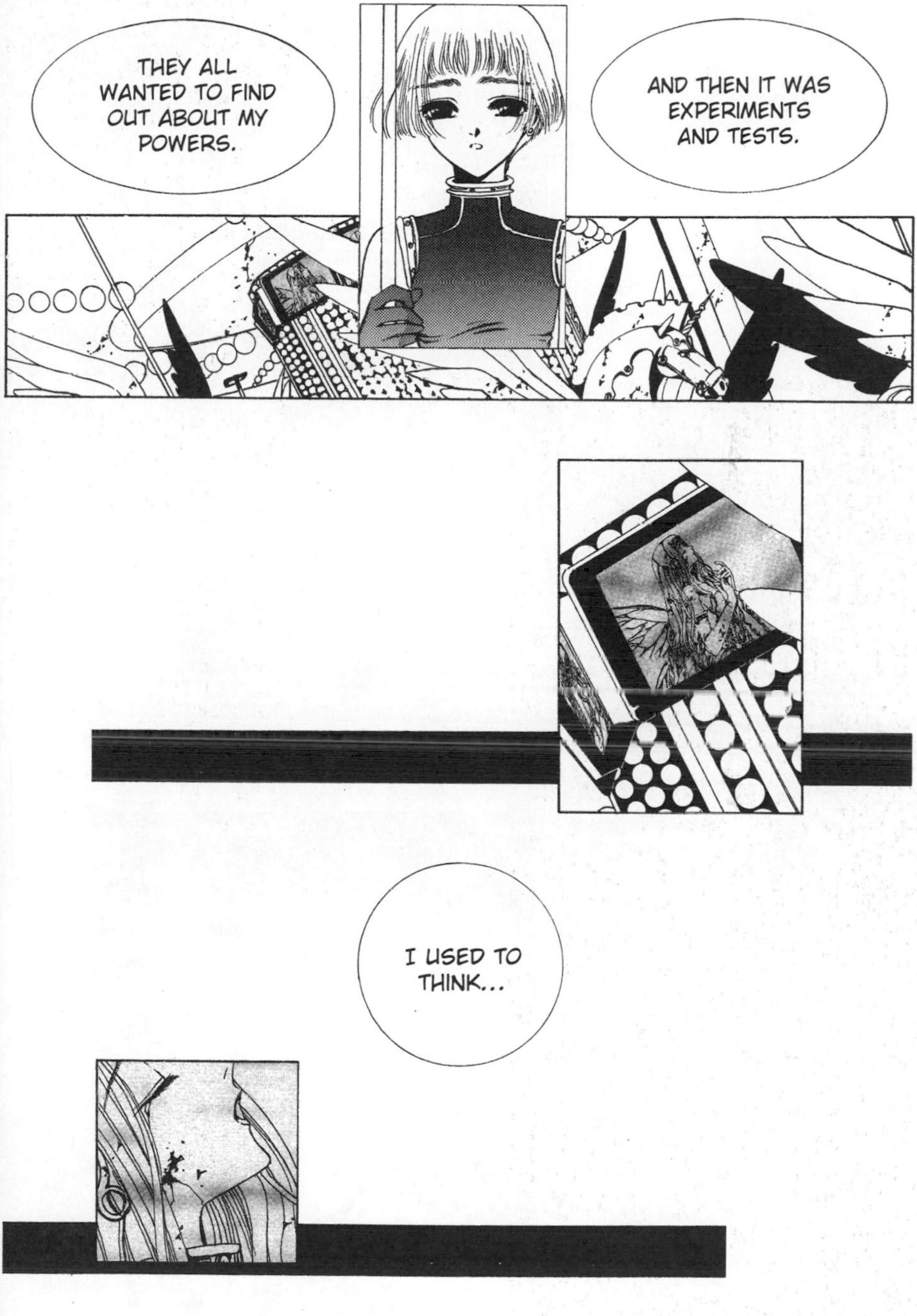
THEY ALL WANTED TO FIND OUT ABOUT MY POWERS.
AND THEN IT WAS EXPERIMENTS AND TESTS.
I USED TO THINK...

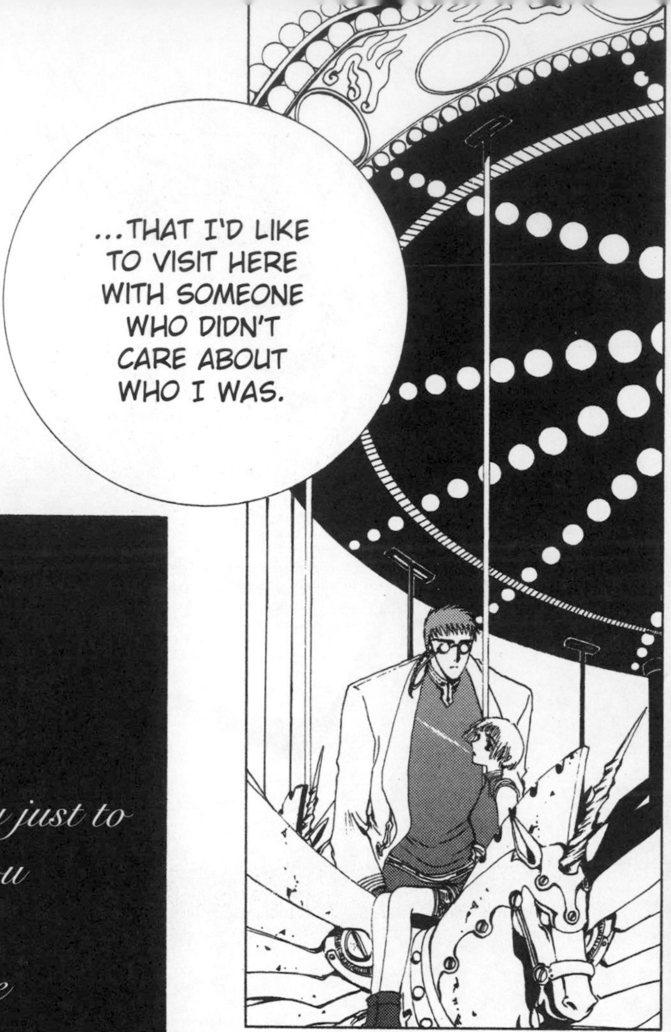
...THAT I'D LIKE TO VISIT HERE WITH SOMEONE WHO DIDN'T CARE ABOUT WHO I WAS.

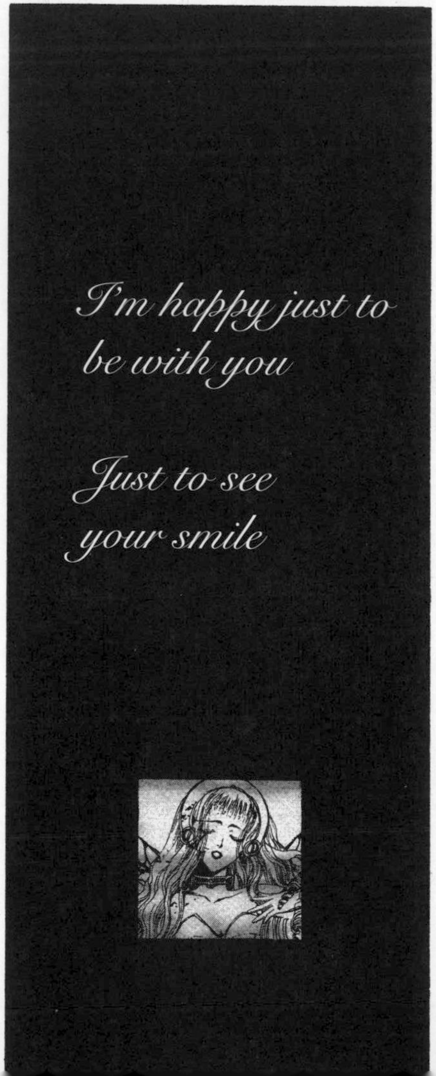
I'm happy just to be with you
Just to see your smile

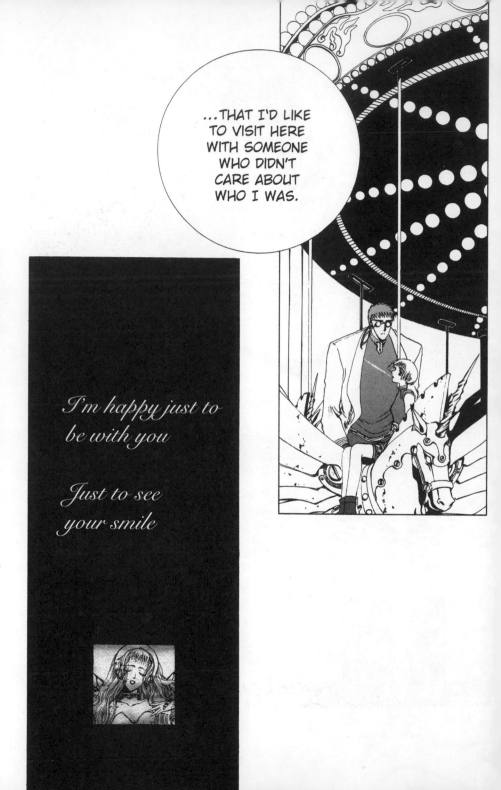

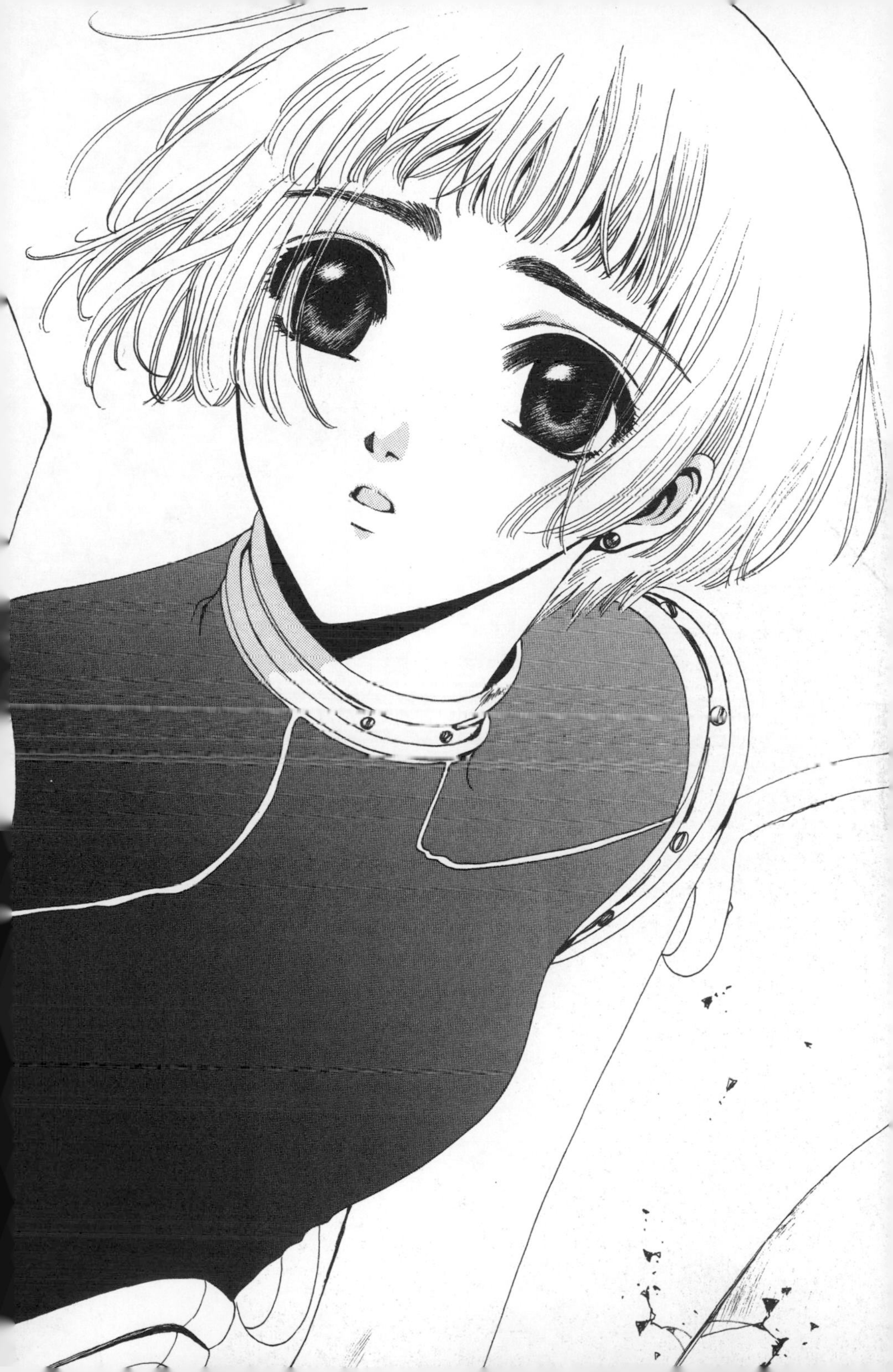

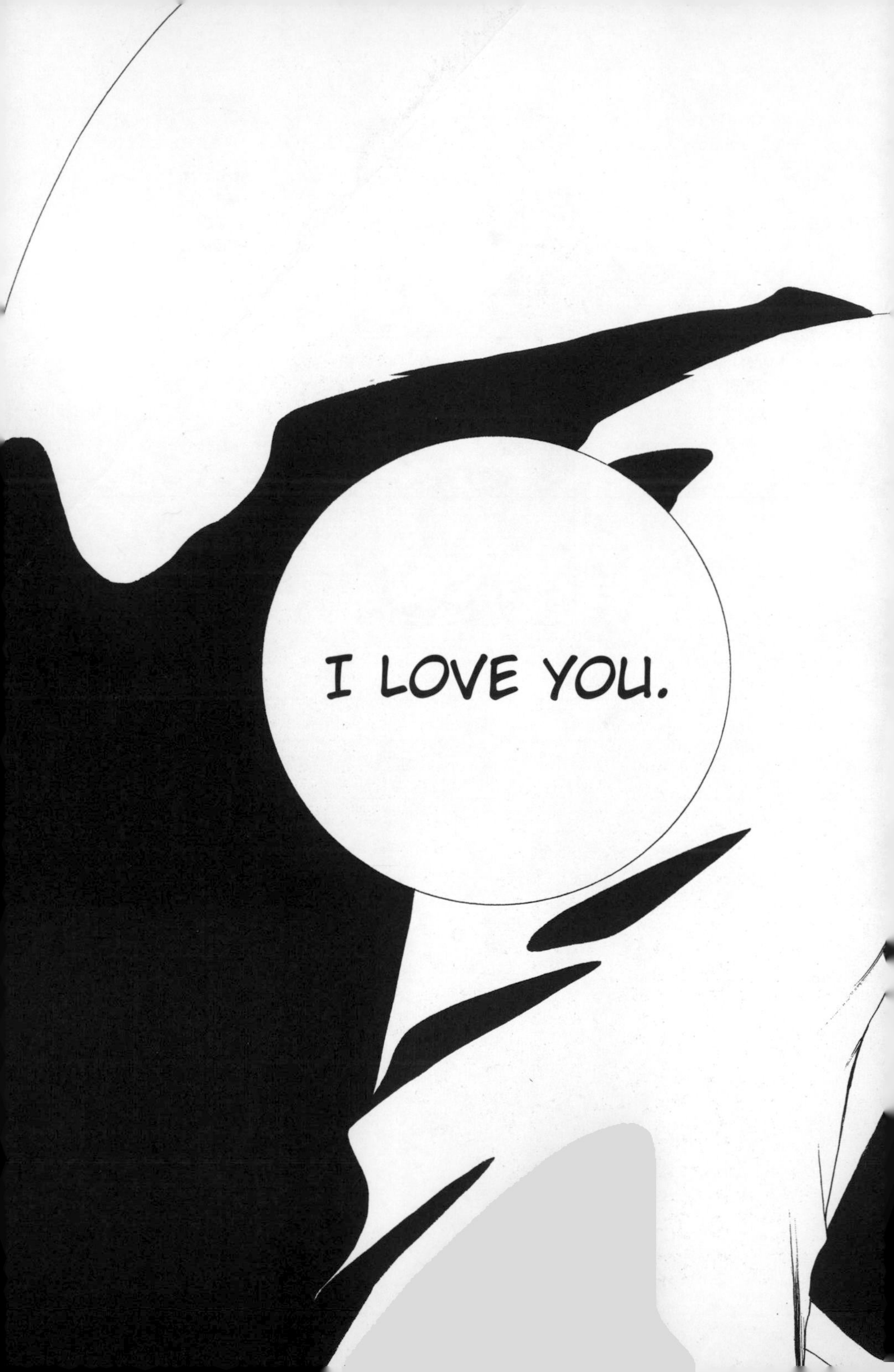
I LOVE YOU.

ORA TOLD ME ALL ABOUT YOU...
...I ALWAYS WANTED TO MEET YOU.

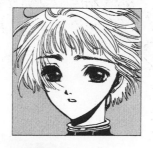

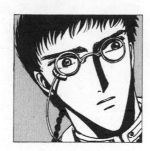

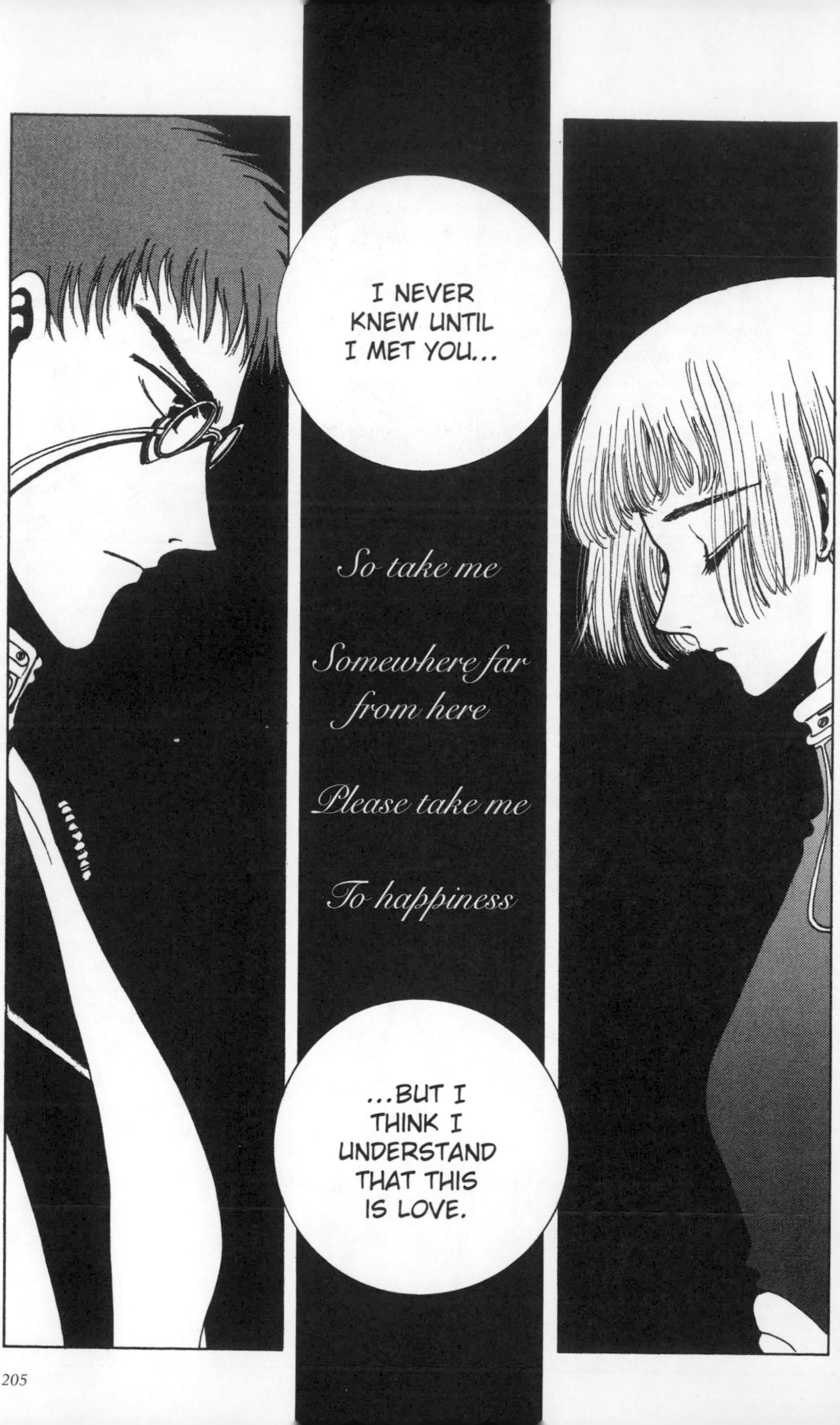
I NEVER KNEW UNTIL I MET YOU...
So take me
Somewhere far from here
Please take me
To happiness
...BUT I THINK I UNDERSTAND THAT THIS IS LOVE.

RRRMMMMBBBLL

PEGASUS

『天馬』

KRAKK

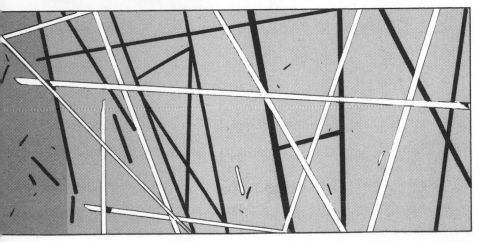

BAROOOM

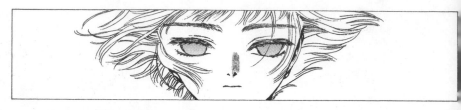

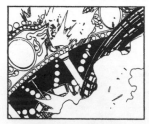

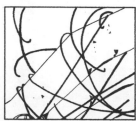

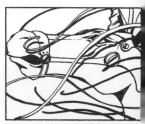

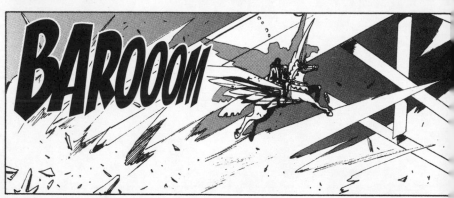

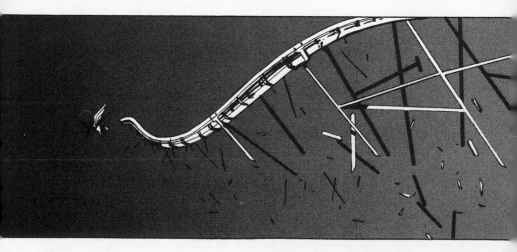

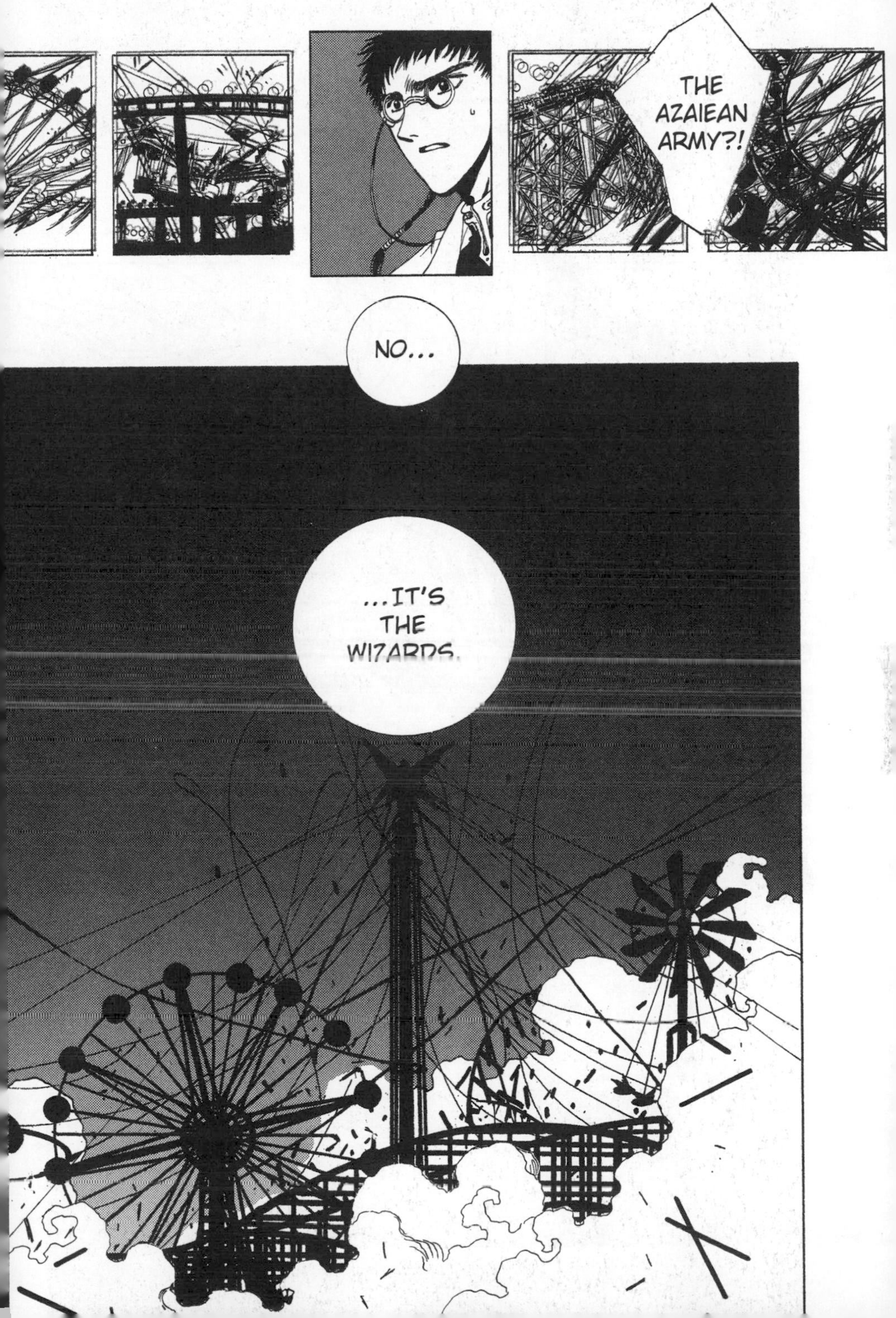
THE AZAIEAN ARMY?!
NO...
...IT'S THE WIZARDS.

I wish for happiness
I seek happiness

To find happiness
with you

To be your happiness

So take me
Somewhere far from here

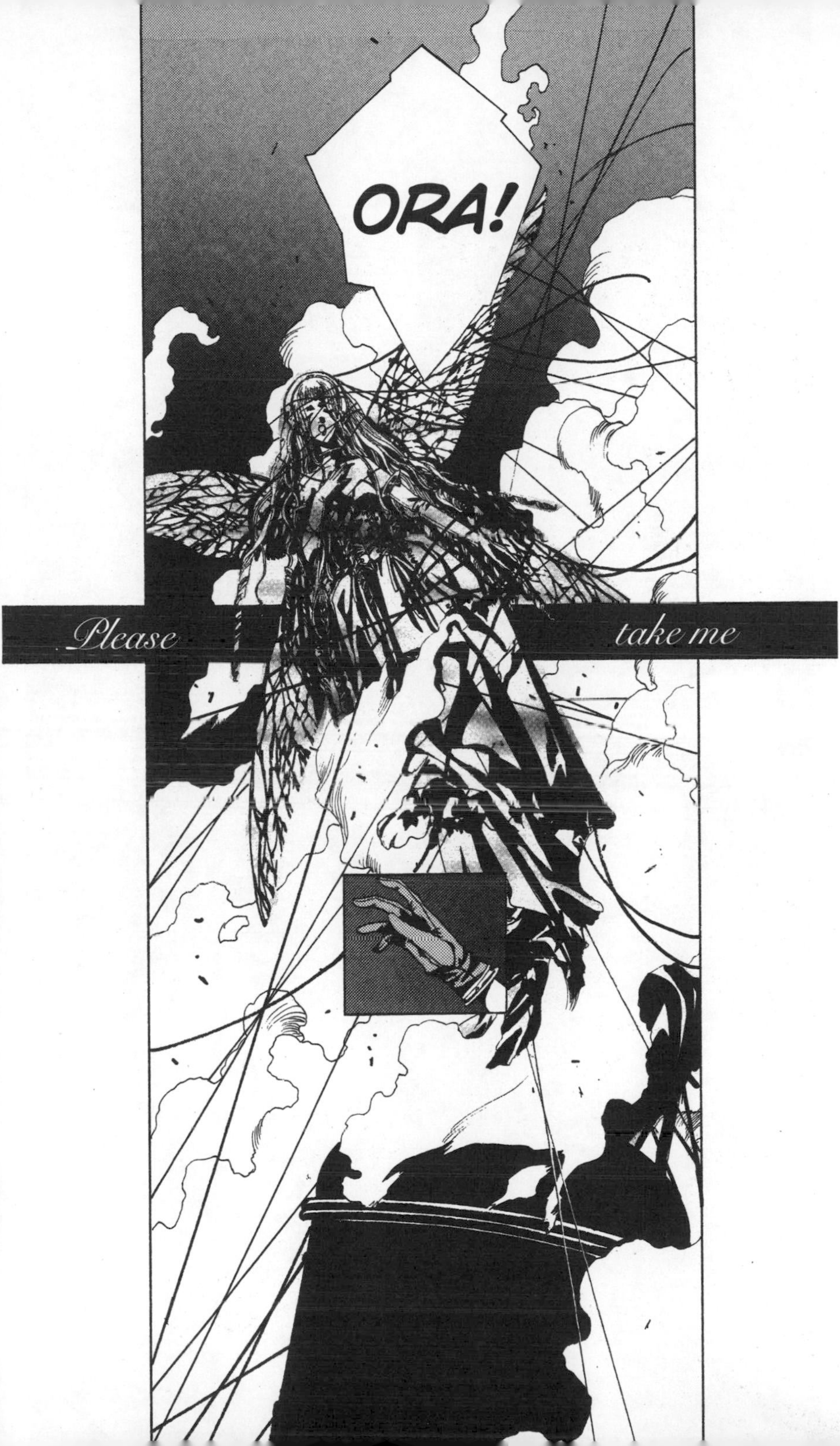
ORA!
Please
take me

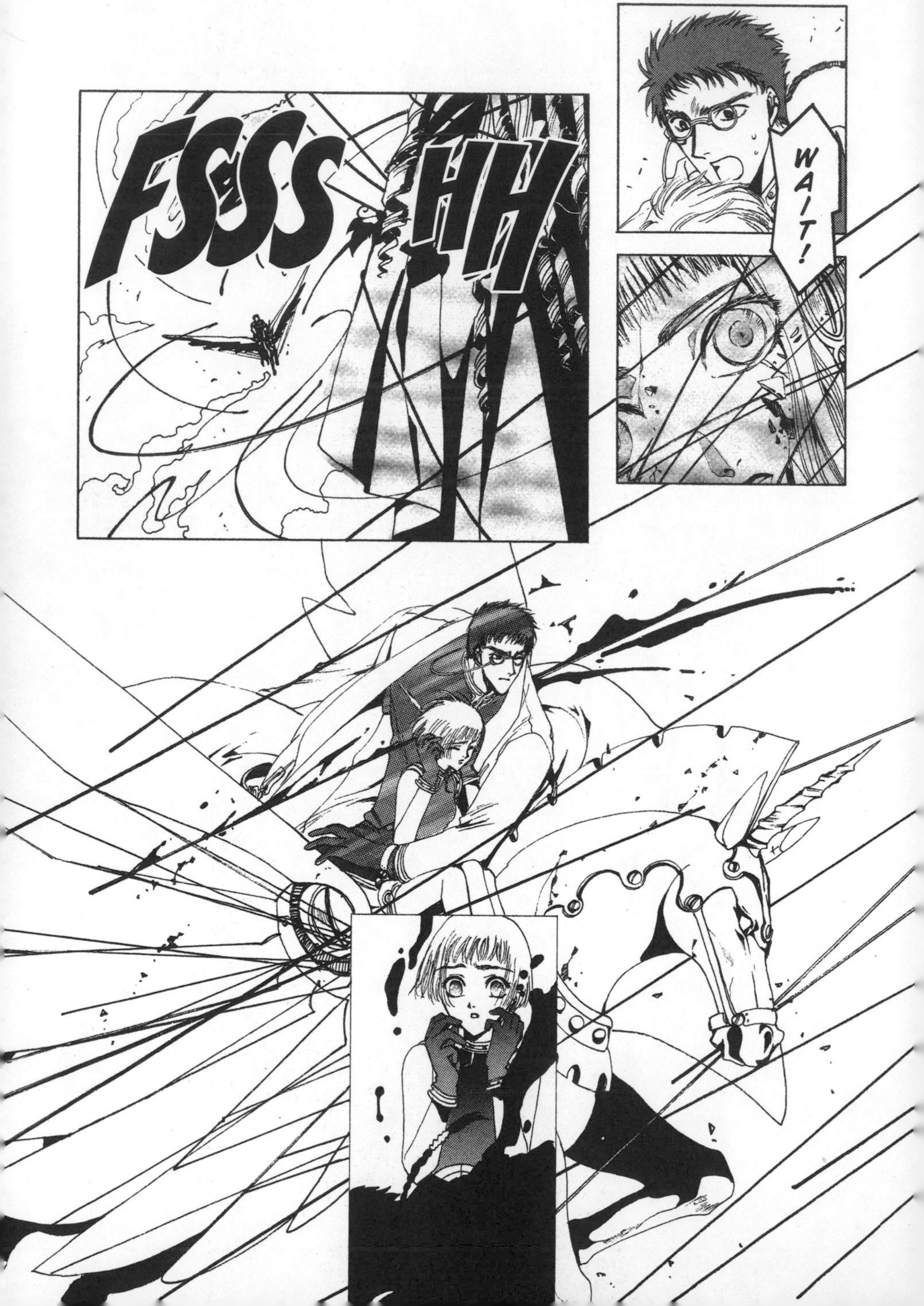
WAIT!
FSSSHH

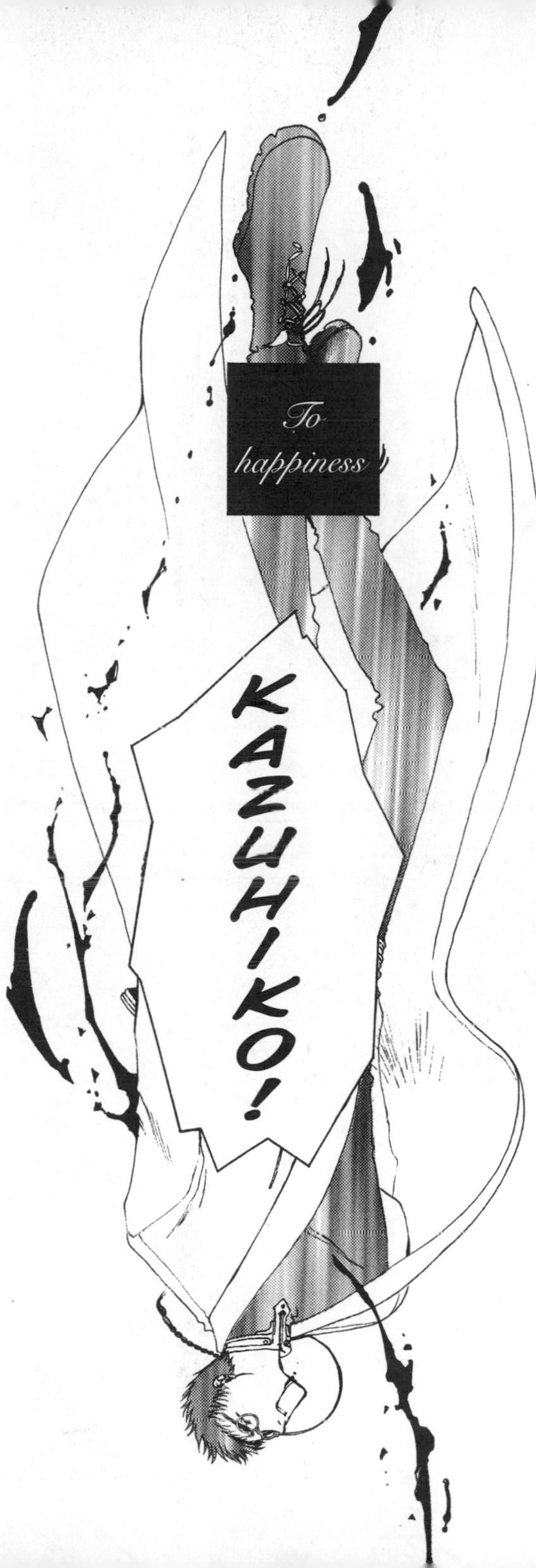
To happiness
KAZUHIKO!

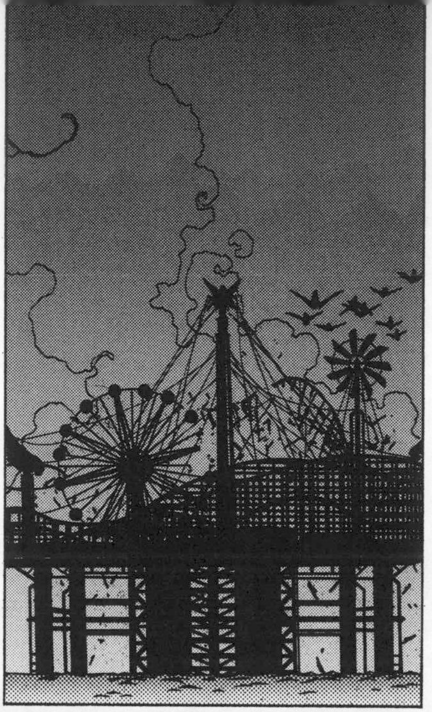

『影絵』
かげ え

SHADOW PLAY

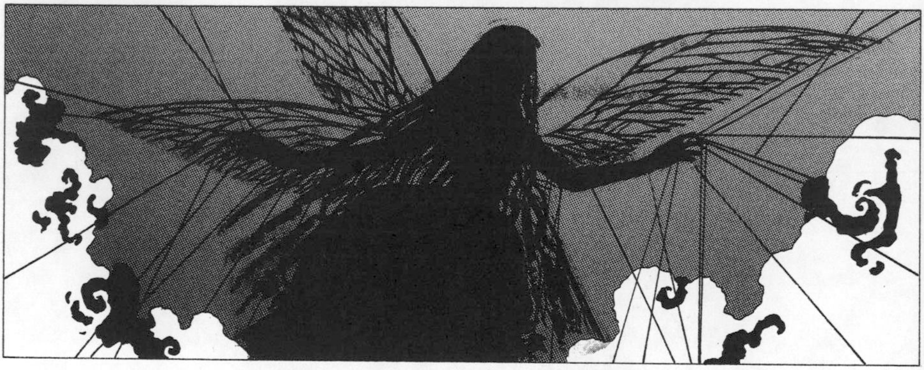

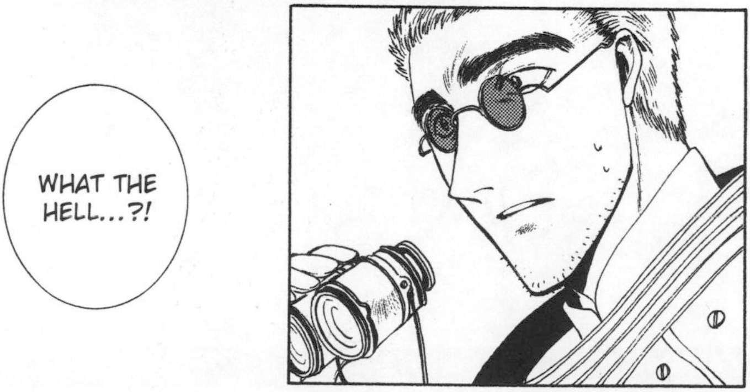
WHAT THE HELL...?!

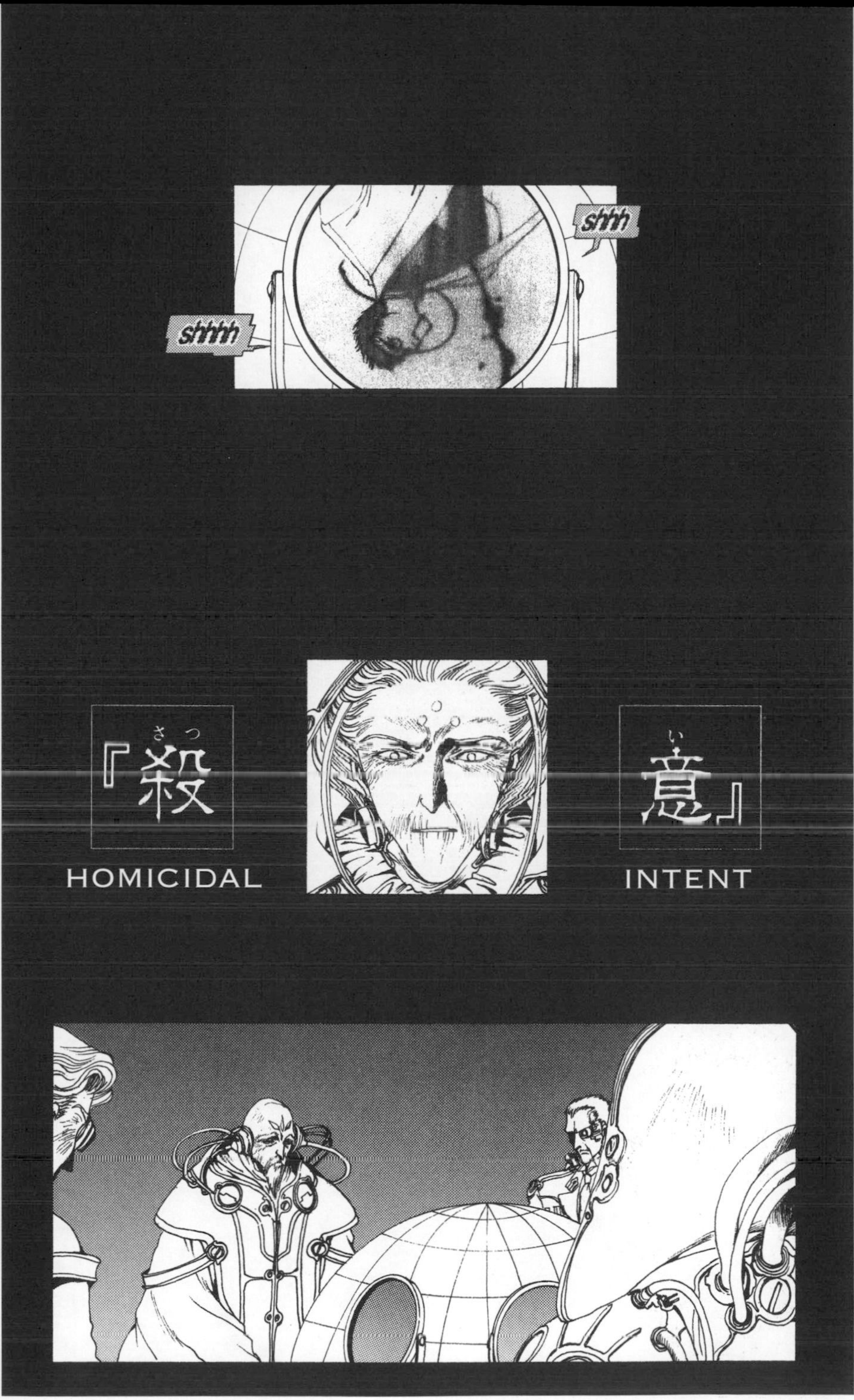
shhh
shhhh
『殺意』
HOMICIDAL INTENT

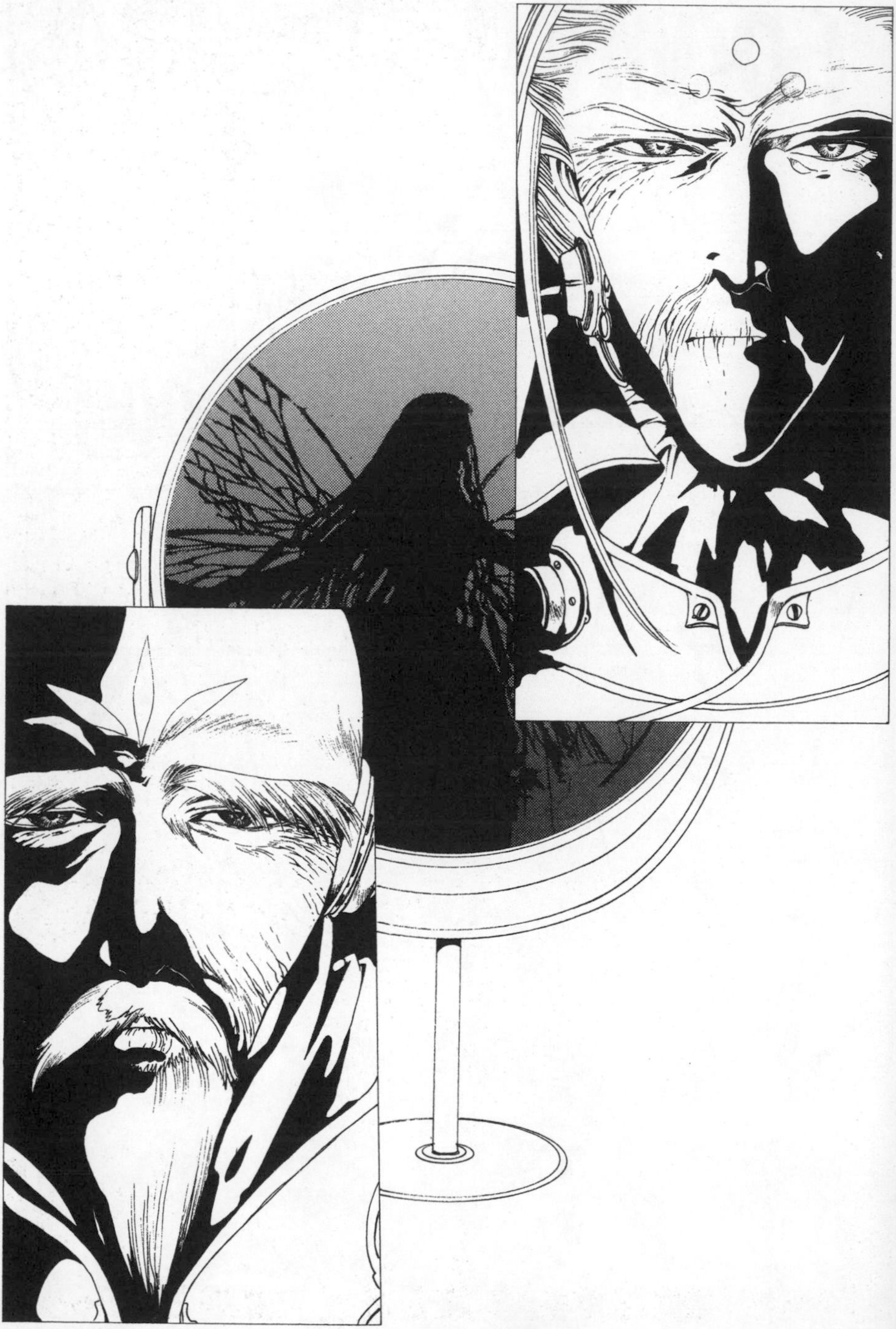

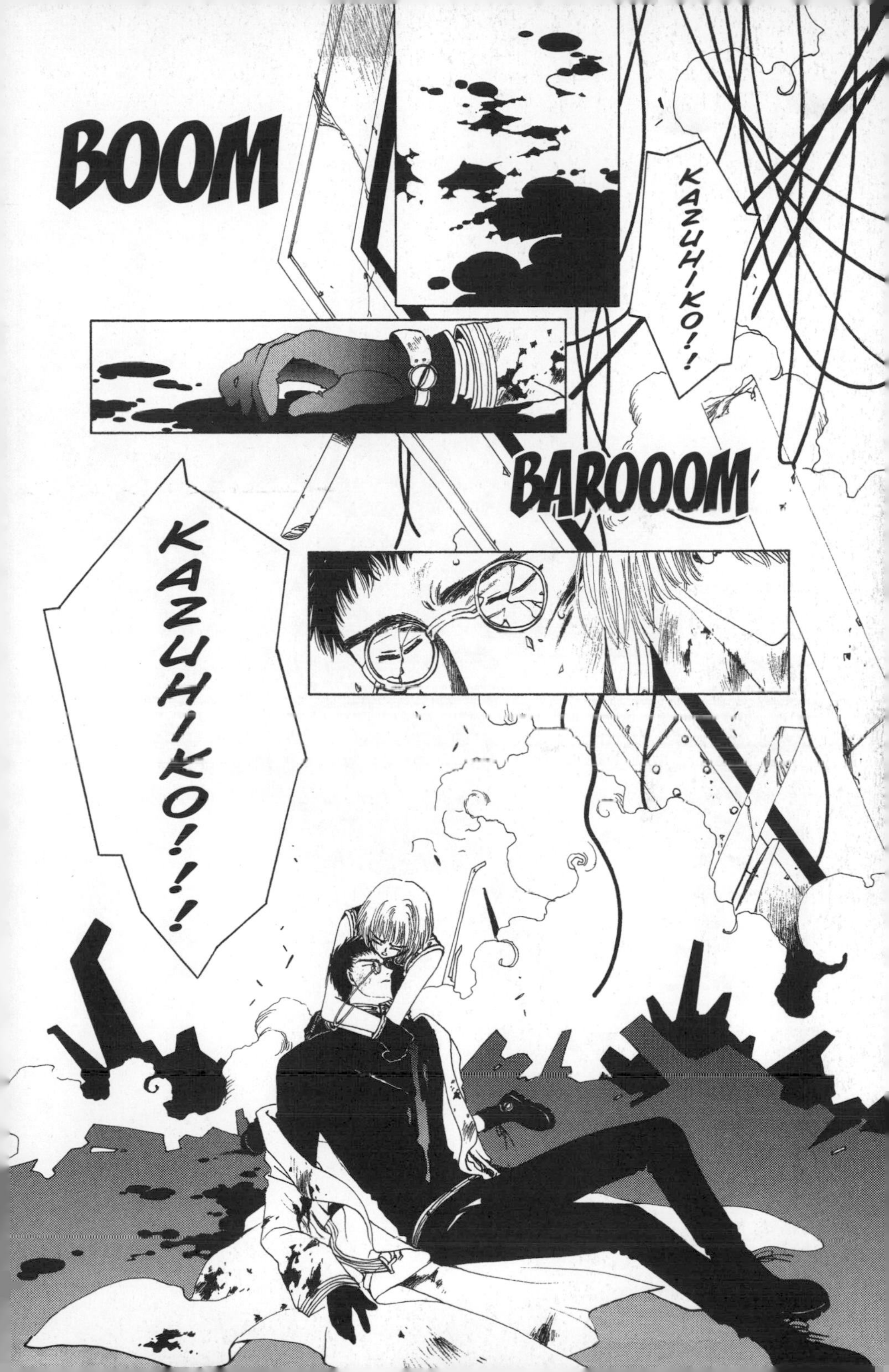
BOOM
KAZUHIKO!!
BAROOOM
KAZUHIKO!!!

I wish for happiness
I seek happiness

To find happiness with you
To be your happiness

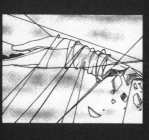

So take me

Somewhere
far from here

RRMMM

MMMMM

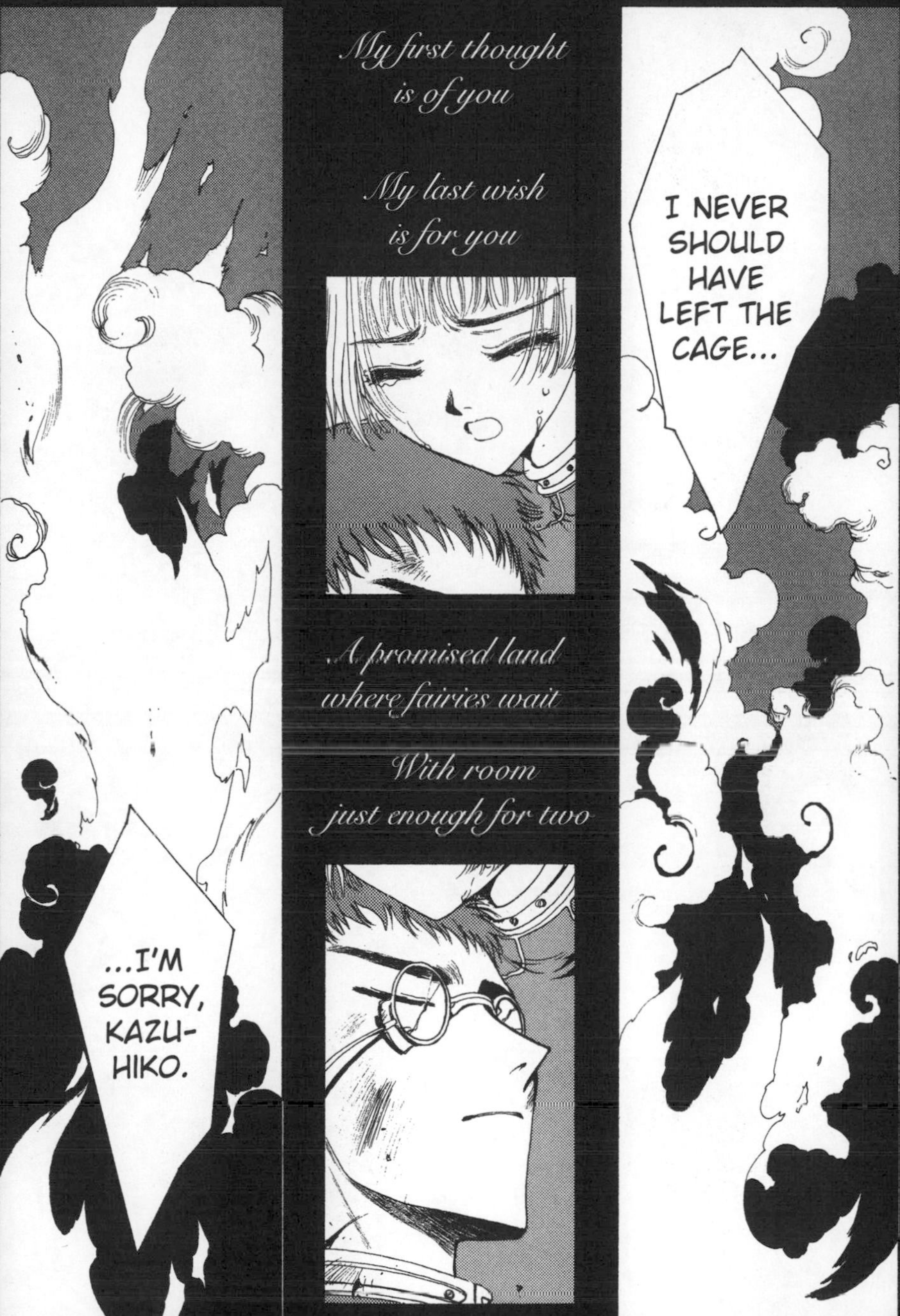
I NEVER SHOULD HAVE LEFT THE CAGE...
My first thought is of you
My last wish is for you
A promised land where fairies wait
With room just enough for two
...I'M SORRY, KAZUHIKO.

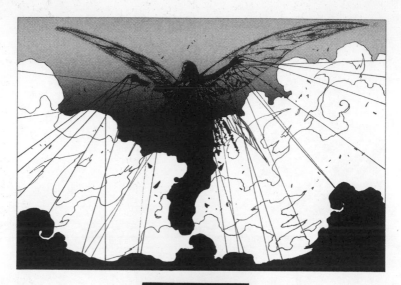

Please
take me

BOOOMMM

krack

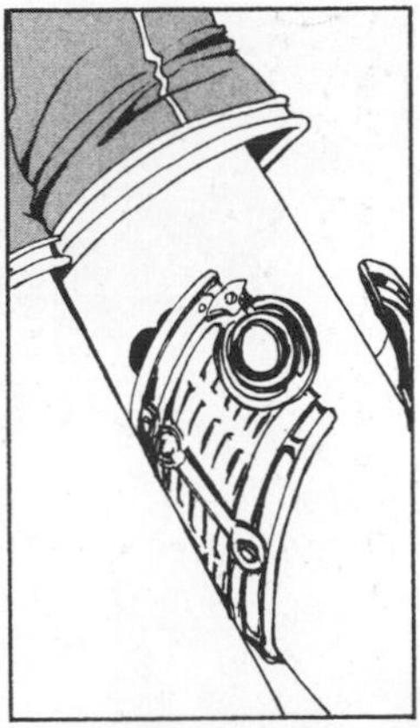
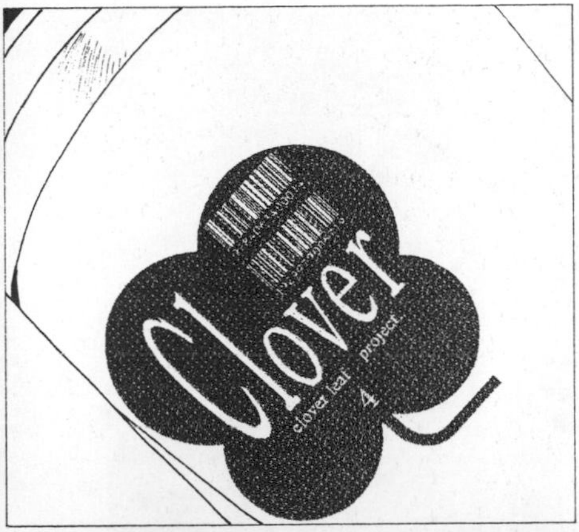
Clover
clover leaf project
4
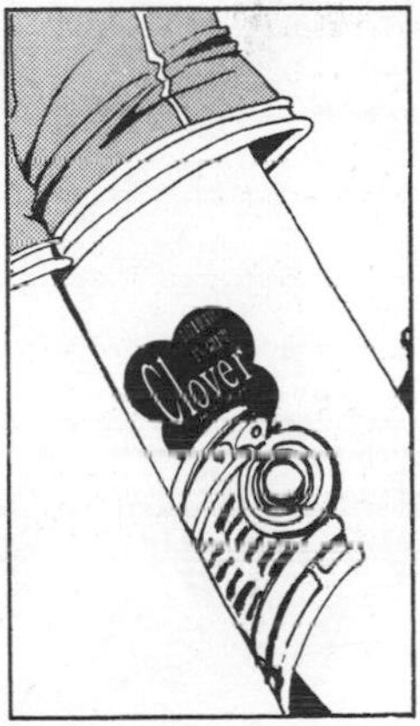
Clover
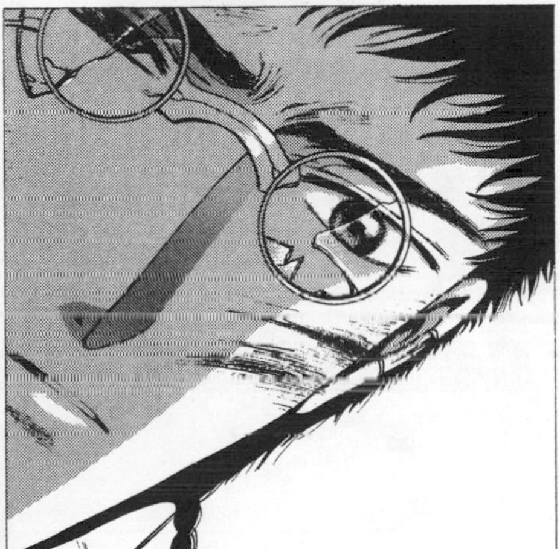
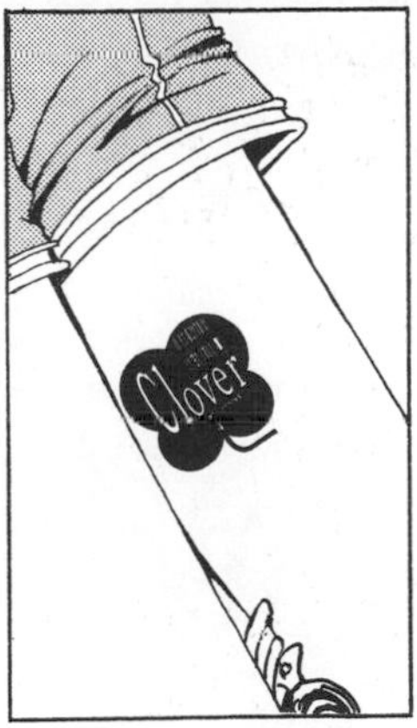
Clover
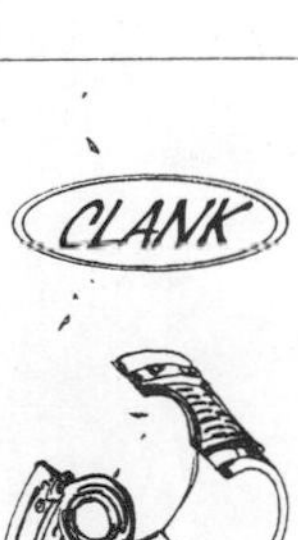
CLANK

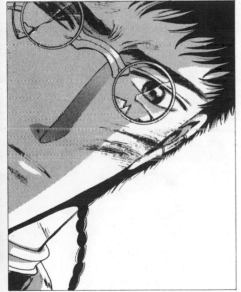

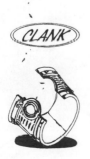

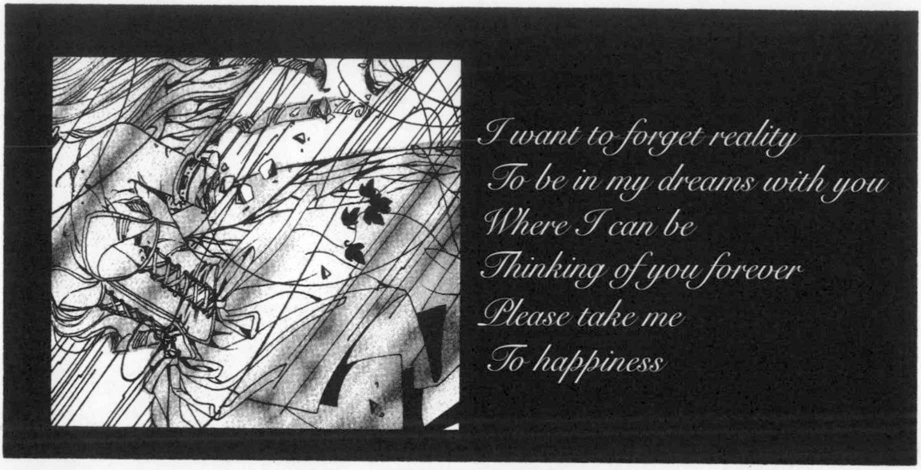
I want to forget reality
To be in my dreams with you
Where I can be
Thinking of you forever
Please take me
To happiness

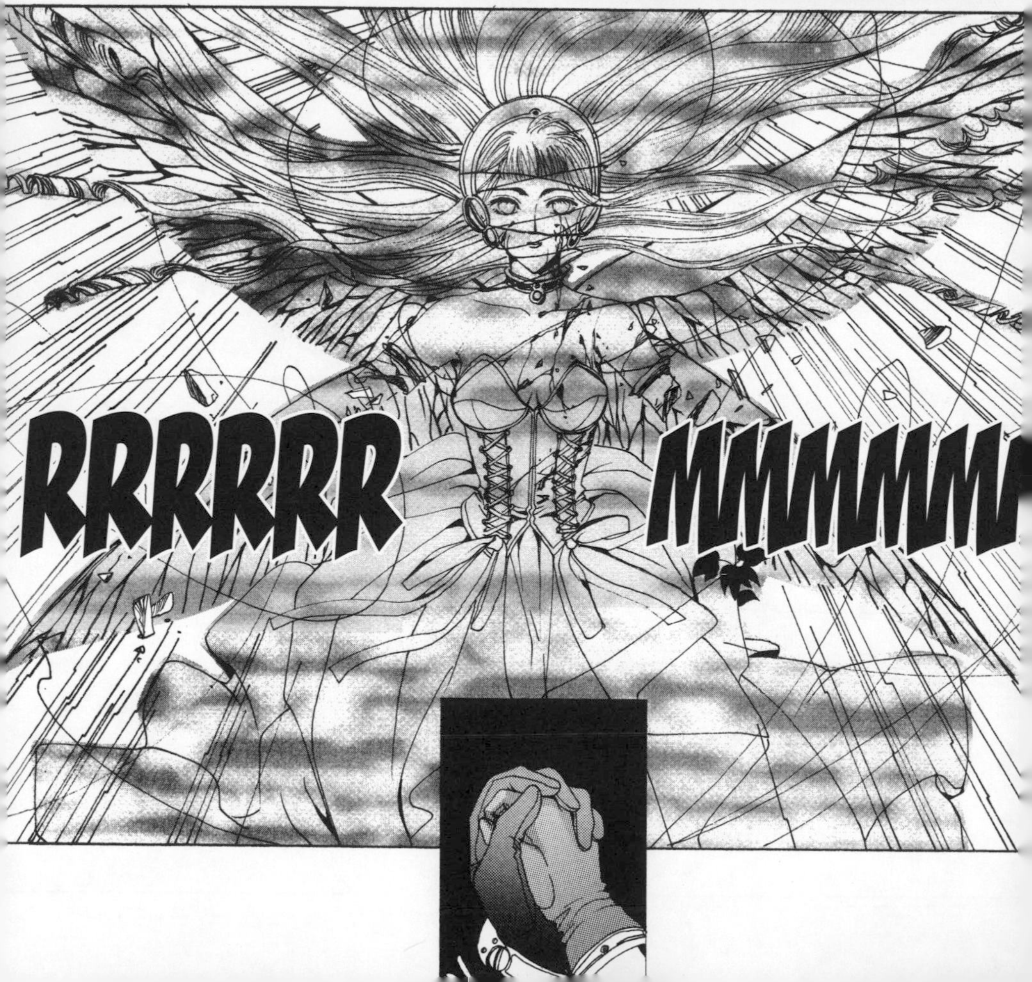
RRRRRR
MMMMMM

...HELP ...ME FINISH THIS.

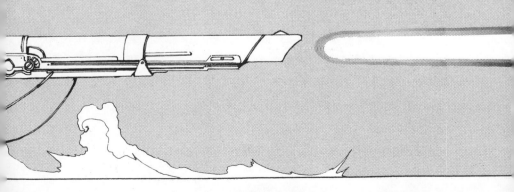

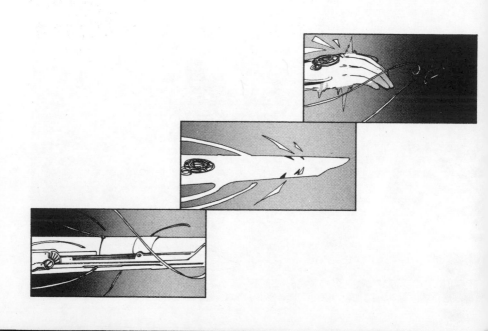
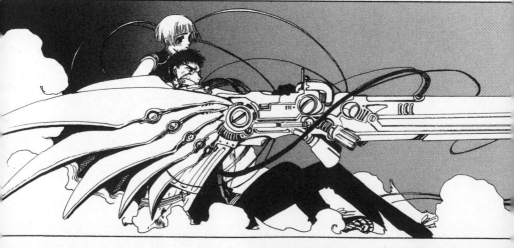

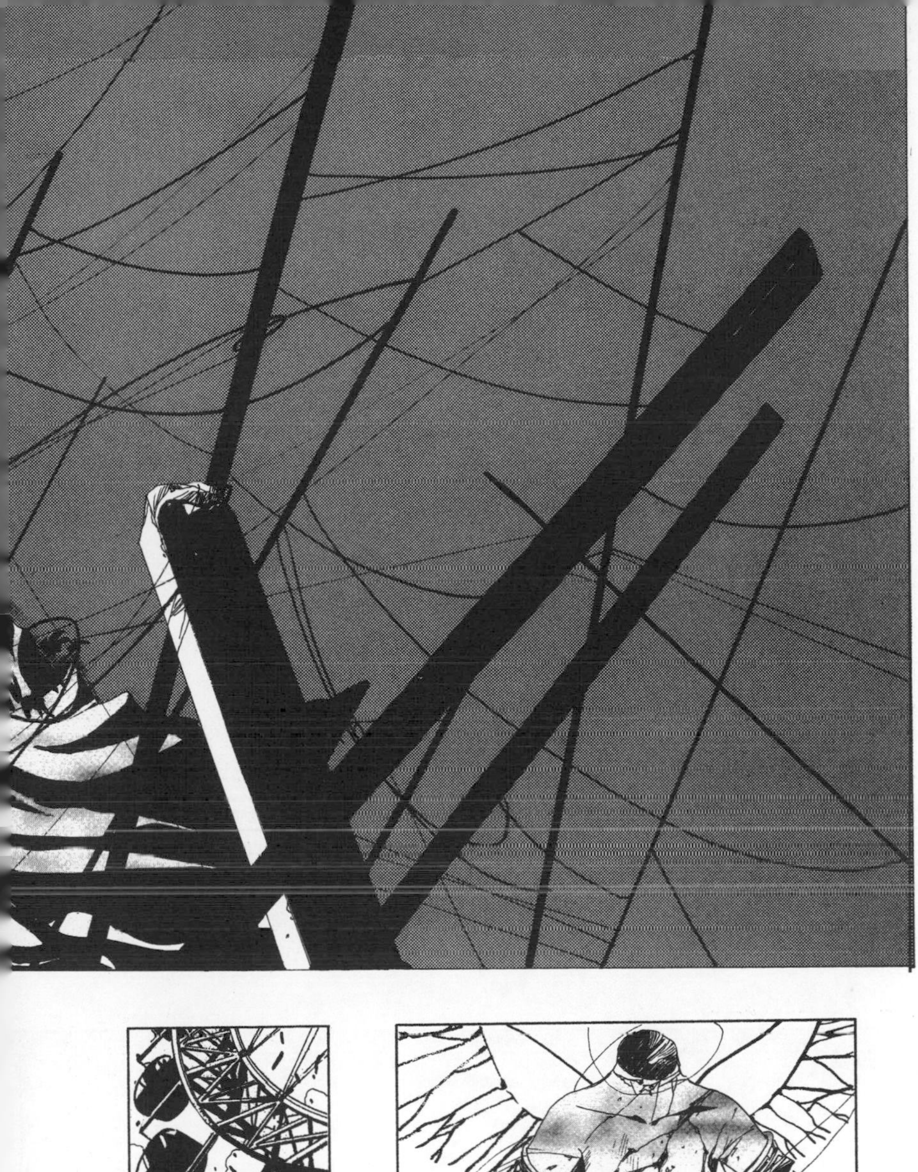
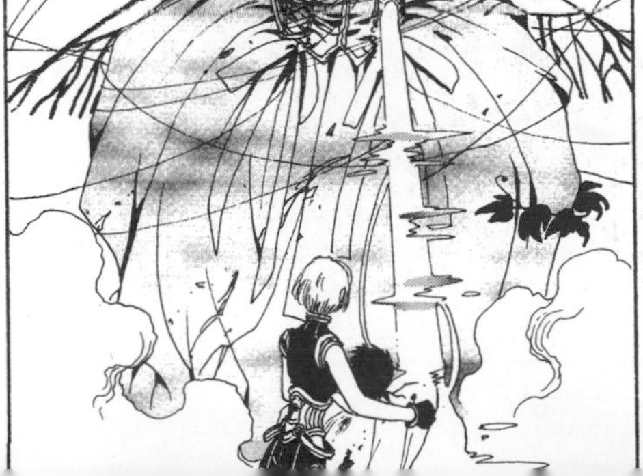

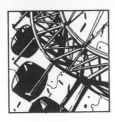

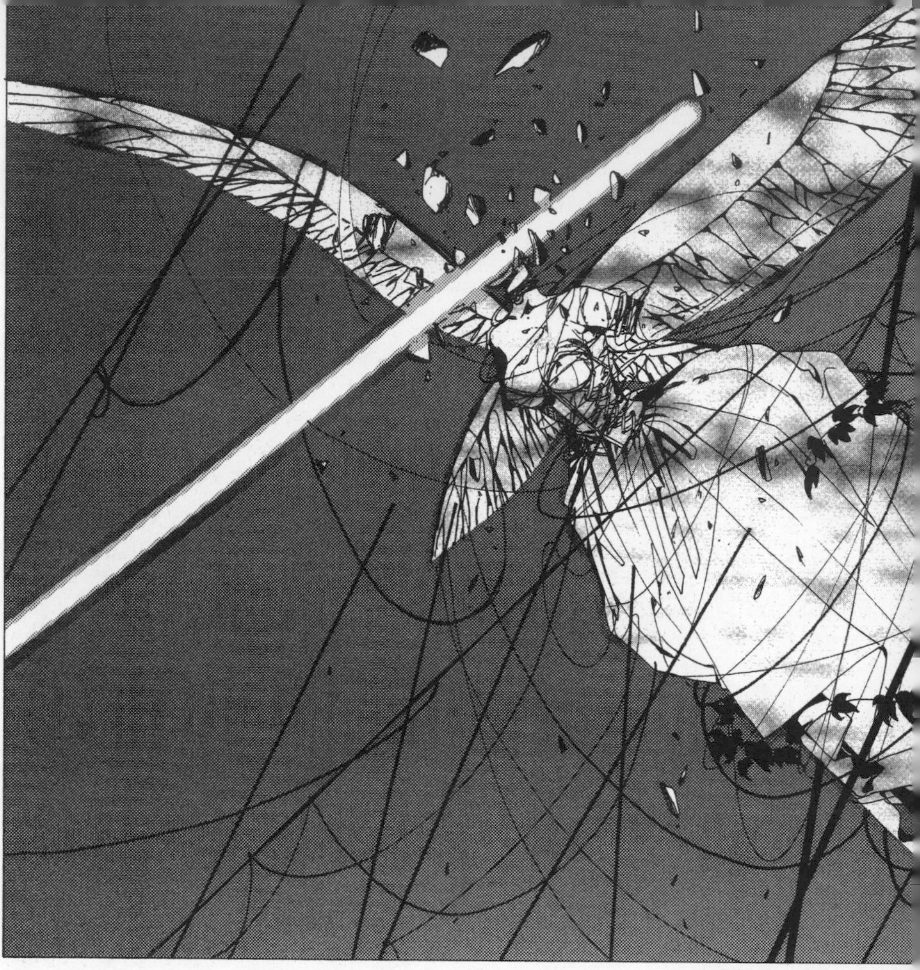
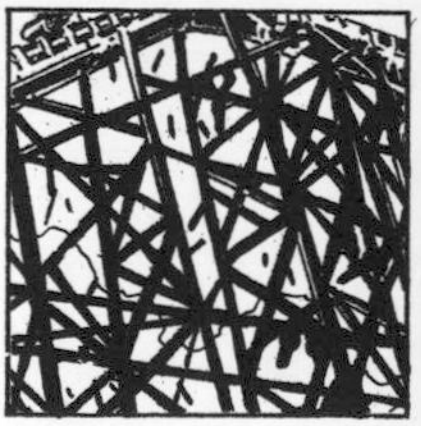
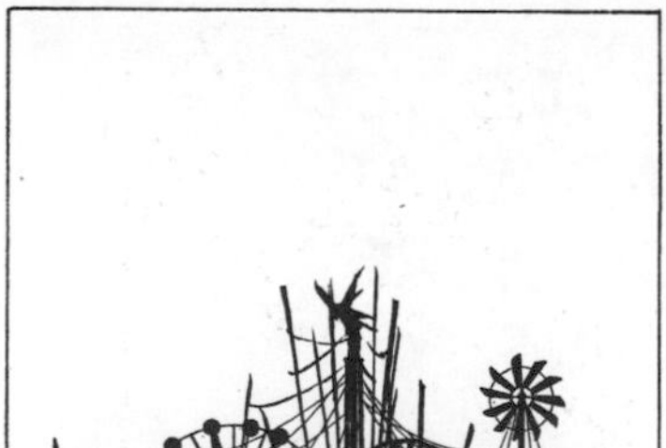

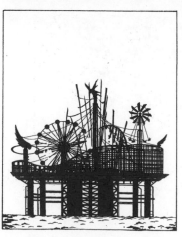

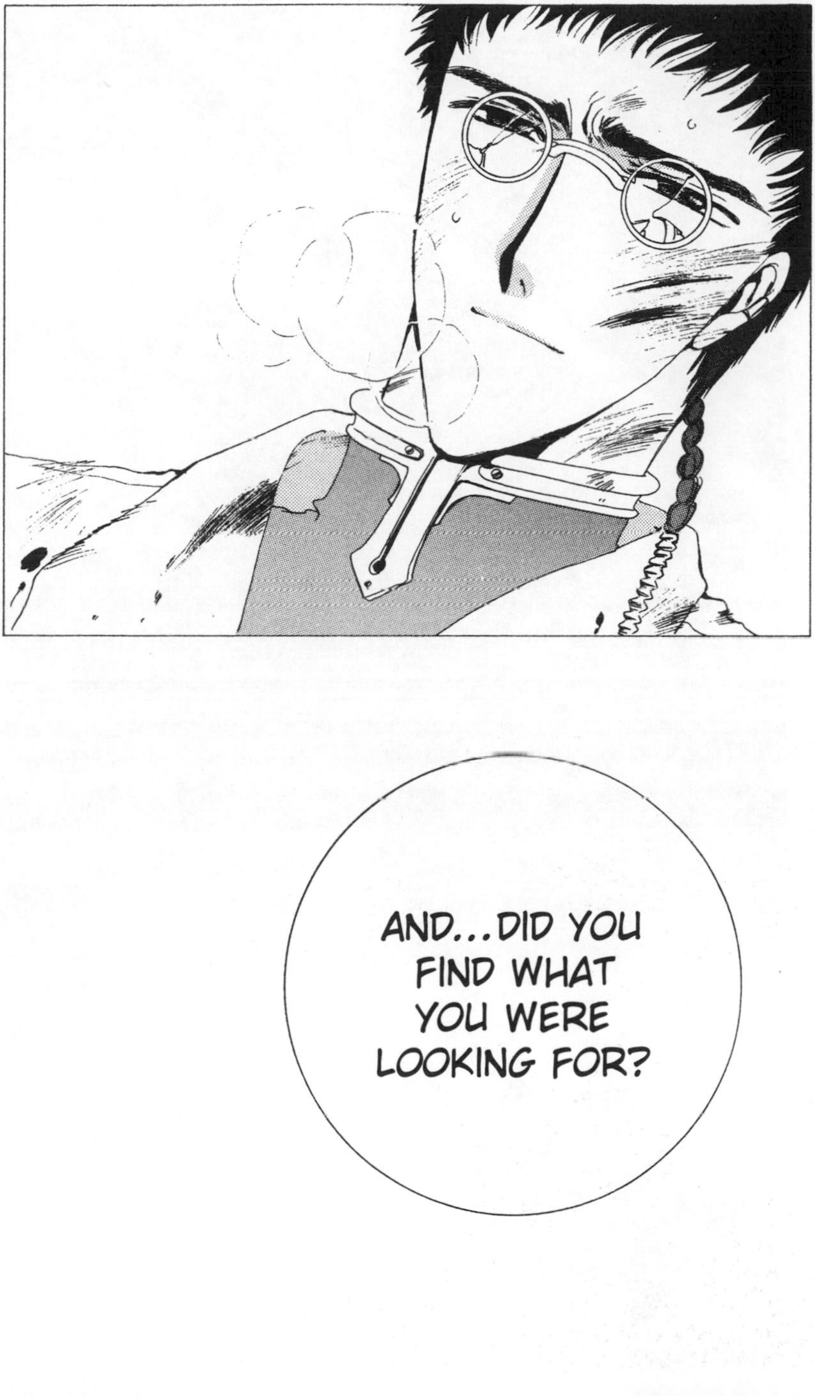
AND...DID YOU FIND WHAT YOU WERE LOOKING FOR?

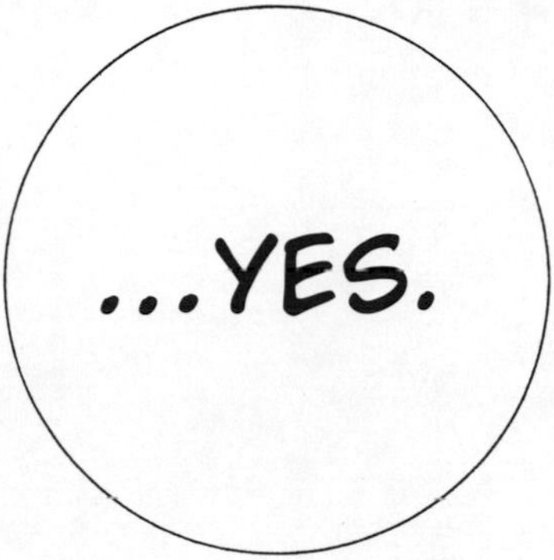
...YES.

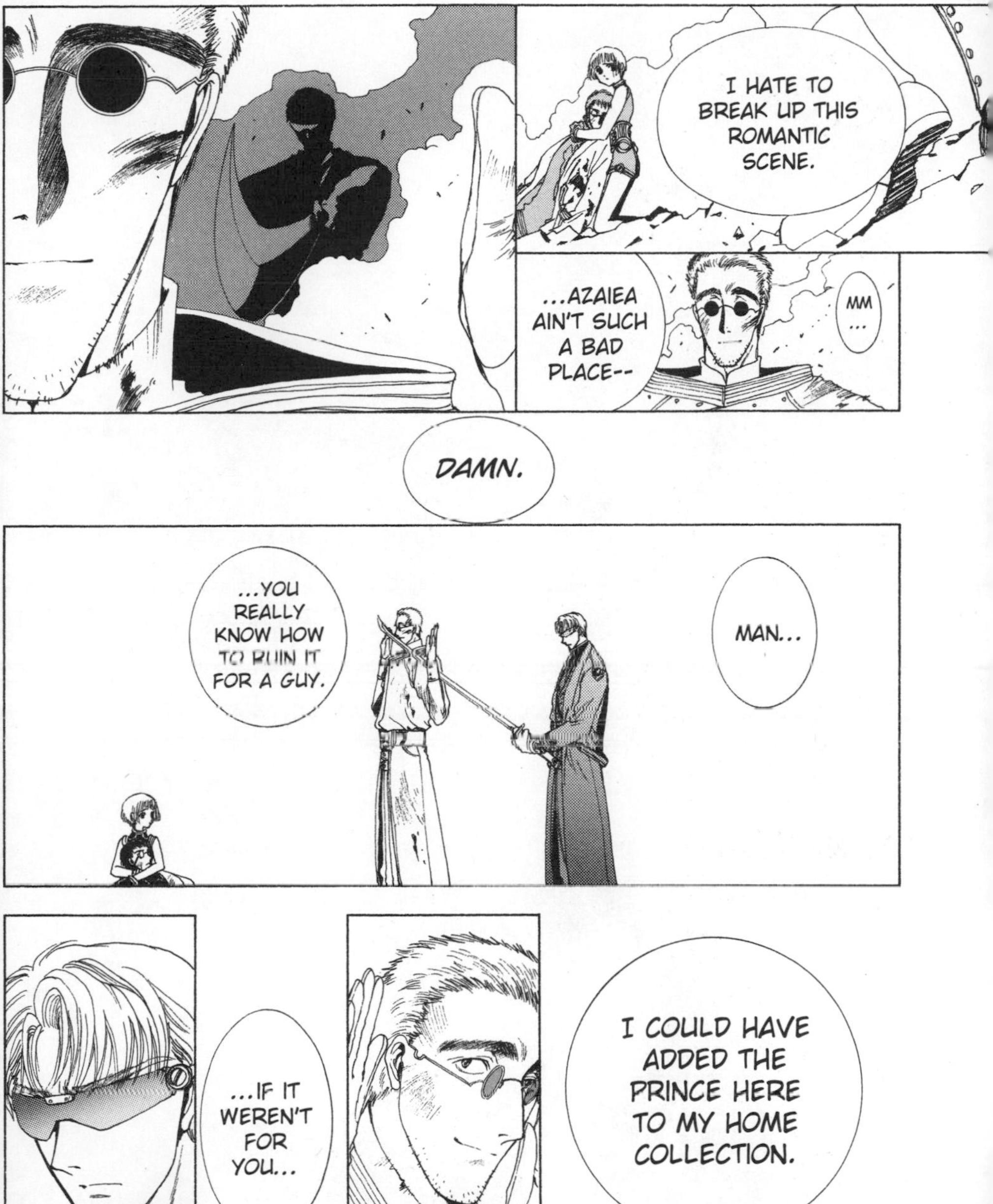
I HATE TO BREAK UP THIS ROMANTIC SCENE.
MM...
...AZAIEA AIN'T SUCH A BAD PLACE--
DAMN.
MAN...
...YOU REALLY KNOW HOW TO RUIN IT FOR A GUY.
I COULD HAVE ADDED THE PRINCE HERE TO MY HOME COLLECTION.
...IF IT WEREN'T FOR YOU...

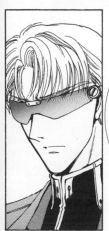

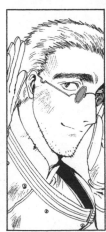

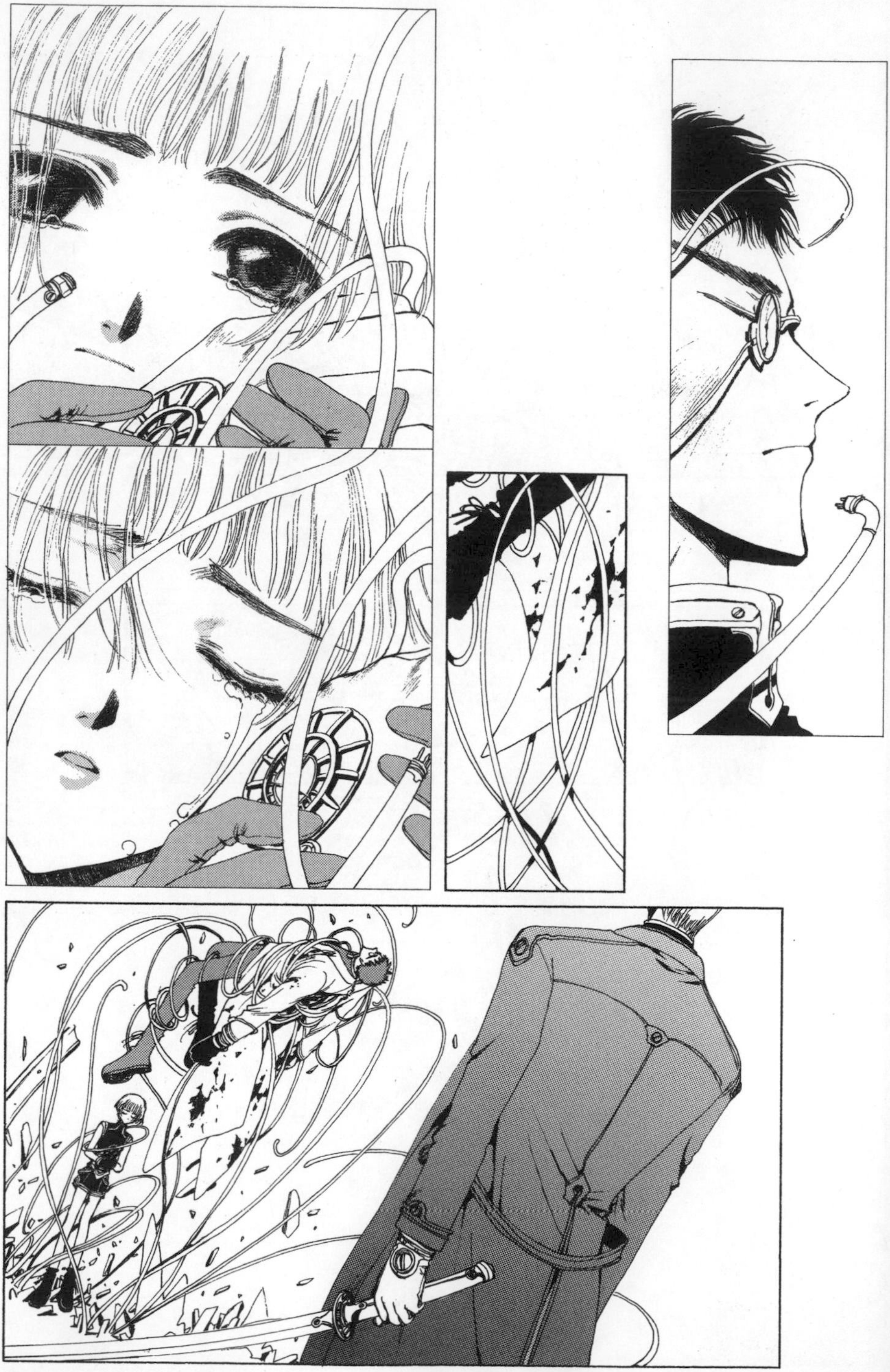

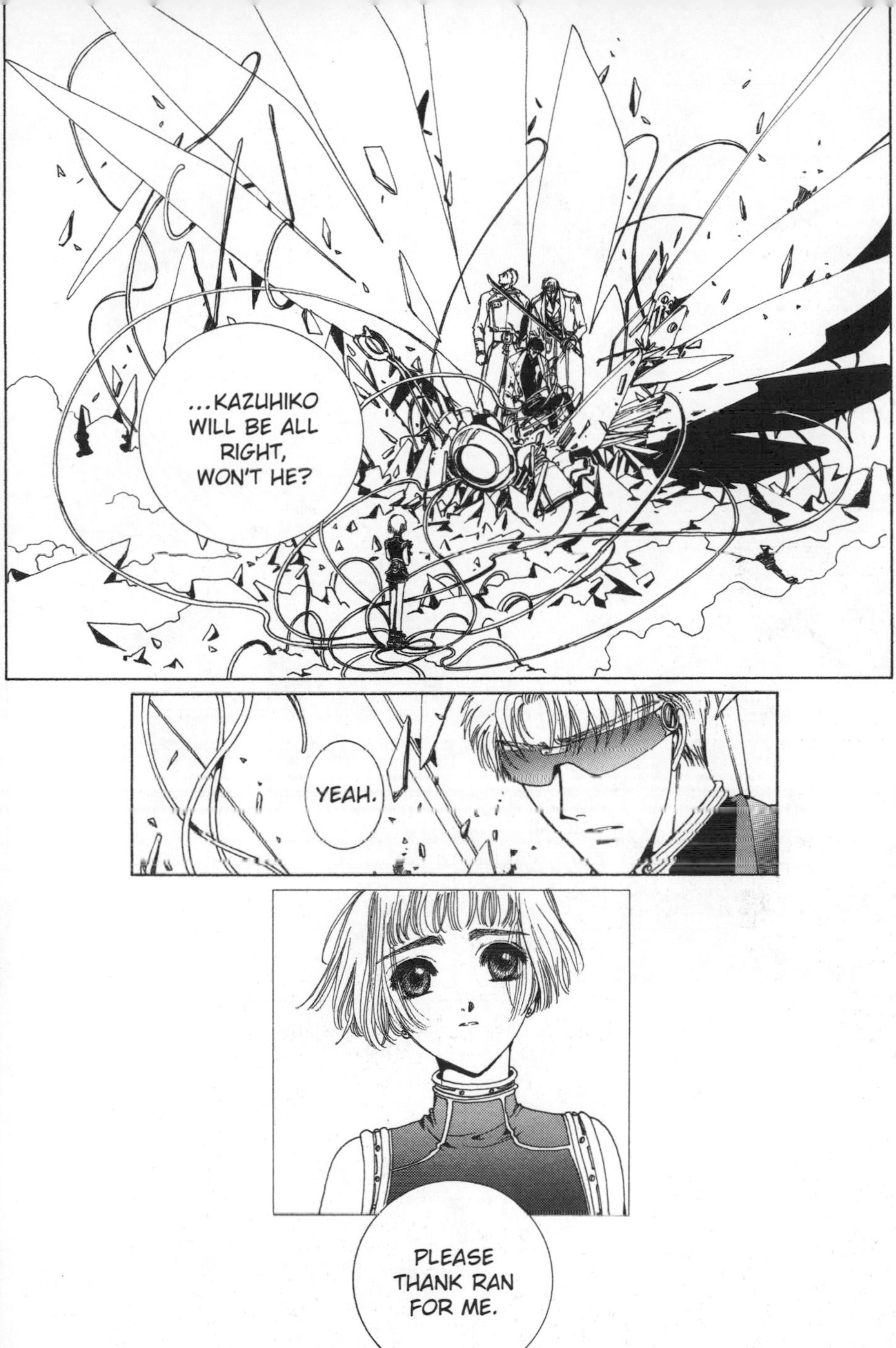
...KAZUHIKO WILL BE ALL RIGHT, WON'T HE?
YEAH.
PLEASE THANK RAN FOR ME.

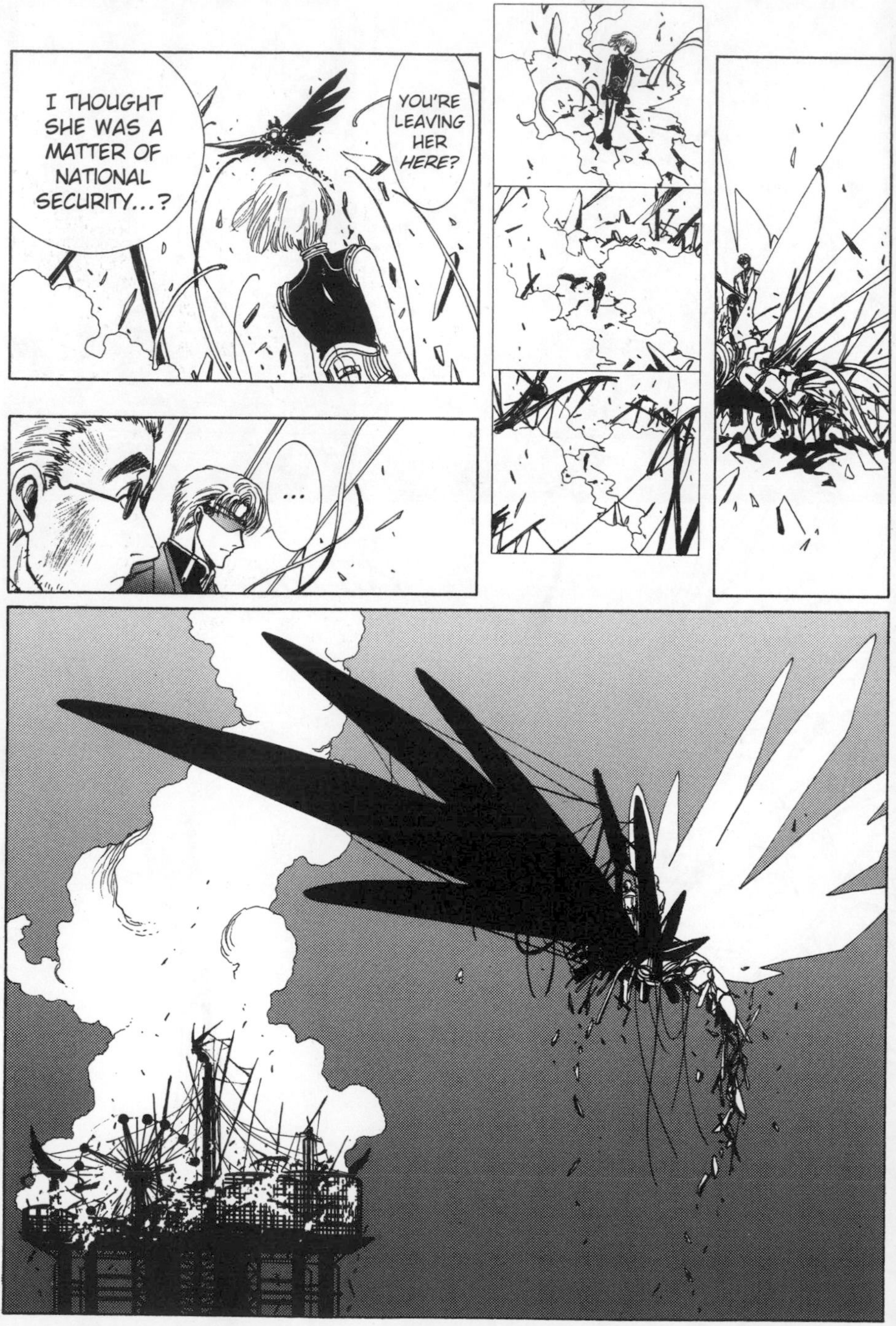
YOU'RE LEAVING HER *HERE?*
I THOUGHT SHE WAS A MATTER OF NATIONAL SECURITY...?
...

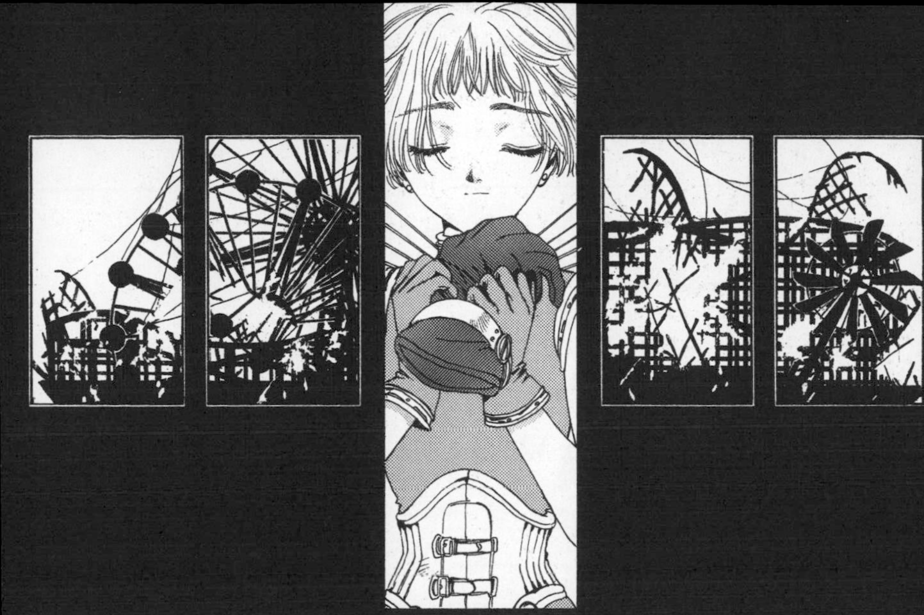

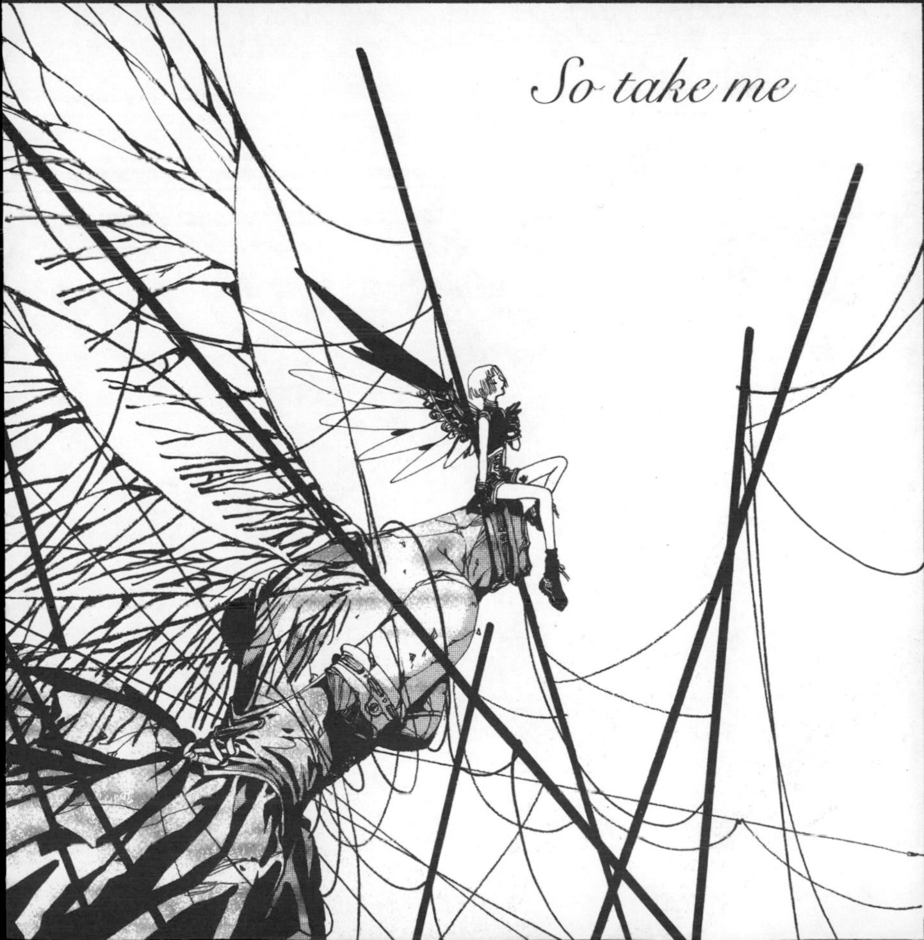
So take me

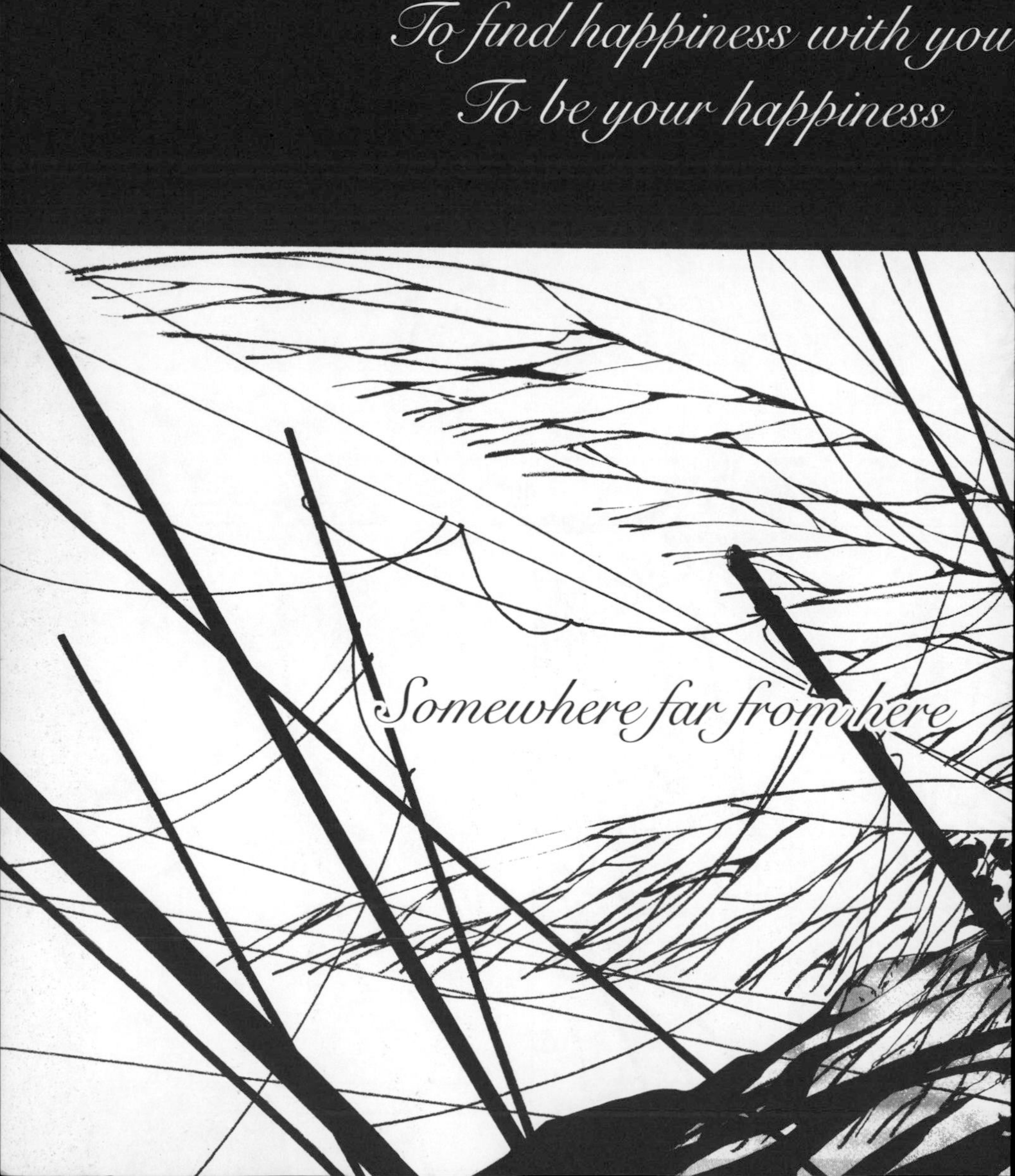
To find happiness with you
To be your happiness
Somewhere far from here

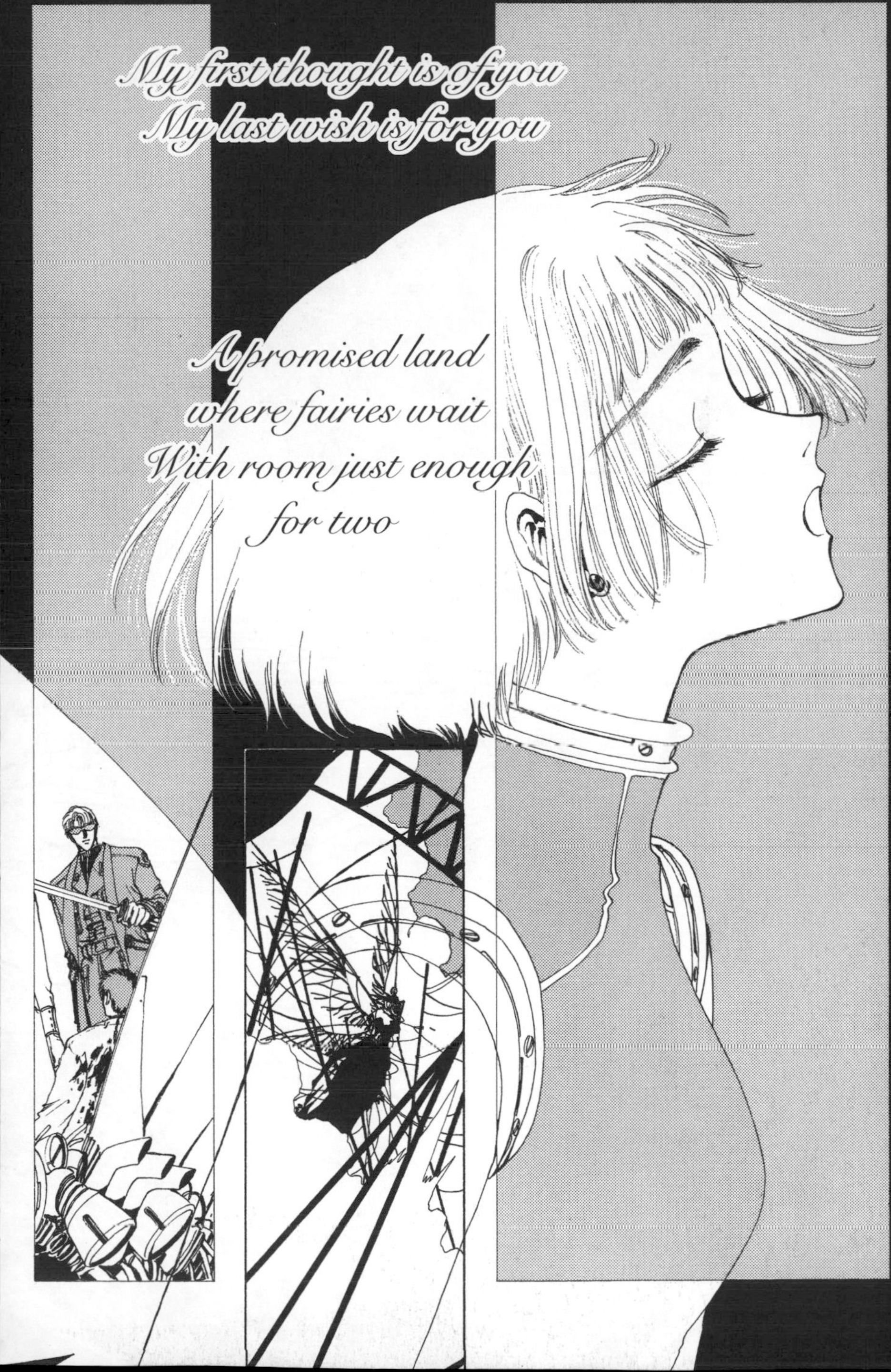
My first thought is of you
My last wish is for you
A promised land
where fairies wait
With room just enough
for two

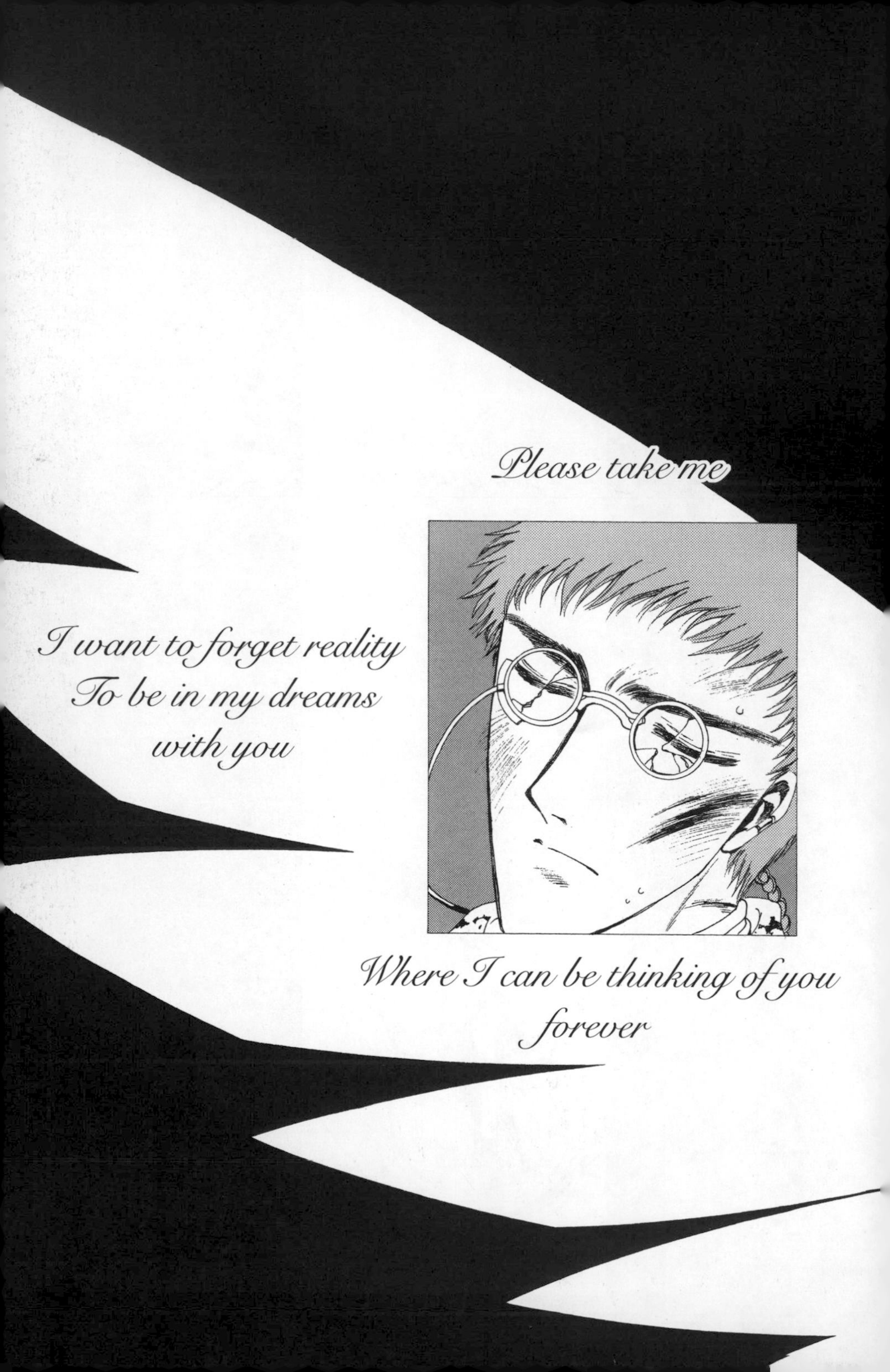
Please take me
Where I can be thinking of you forever
I want to forget reality
To be in my dreams
with you

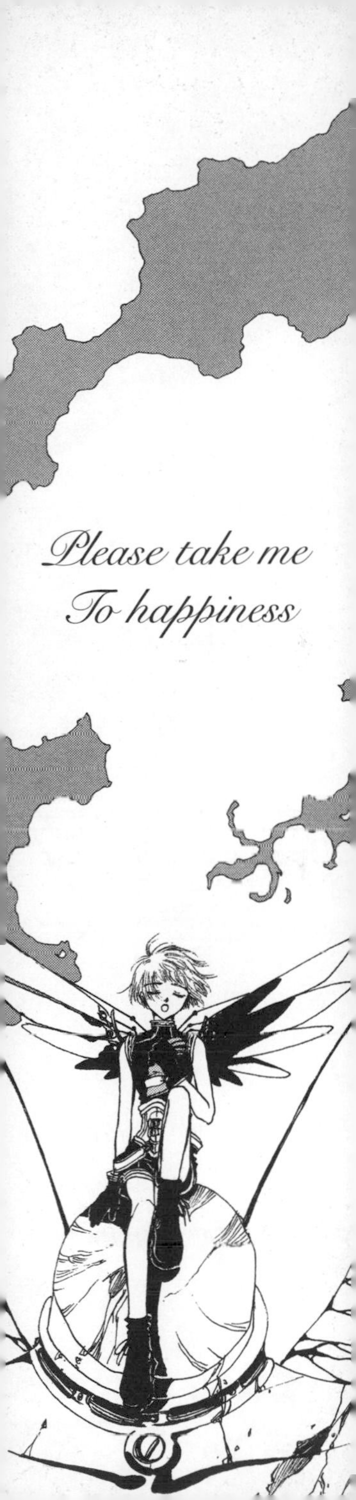
Please take me
To happiness

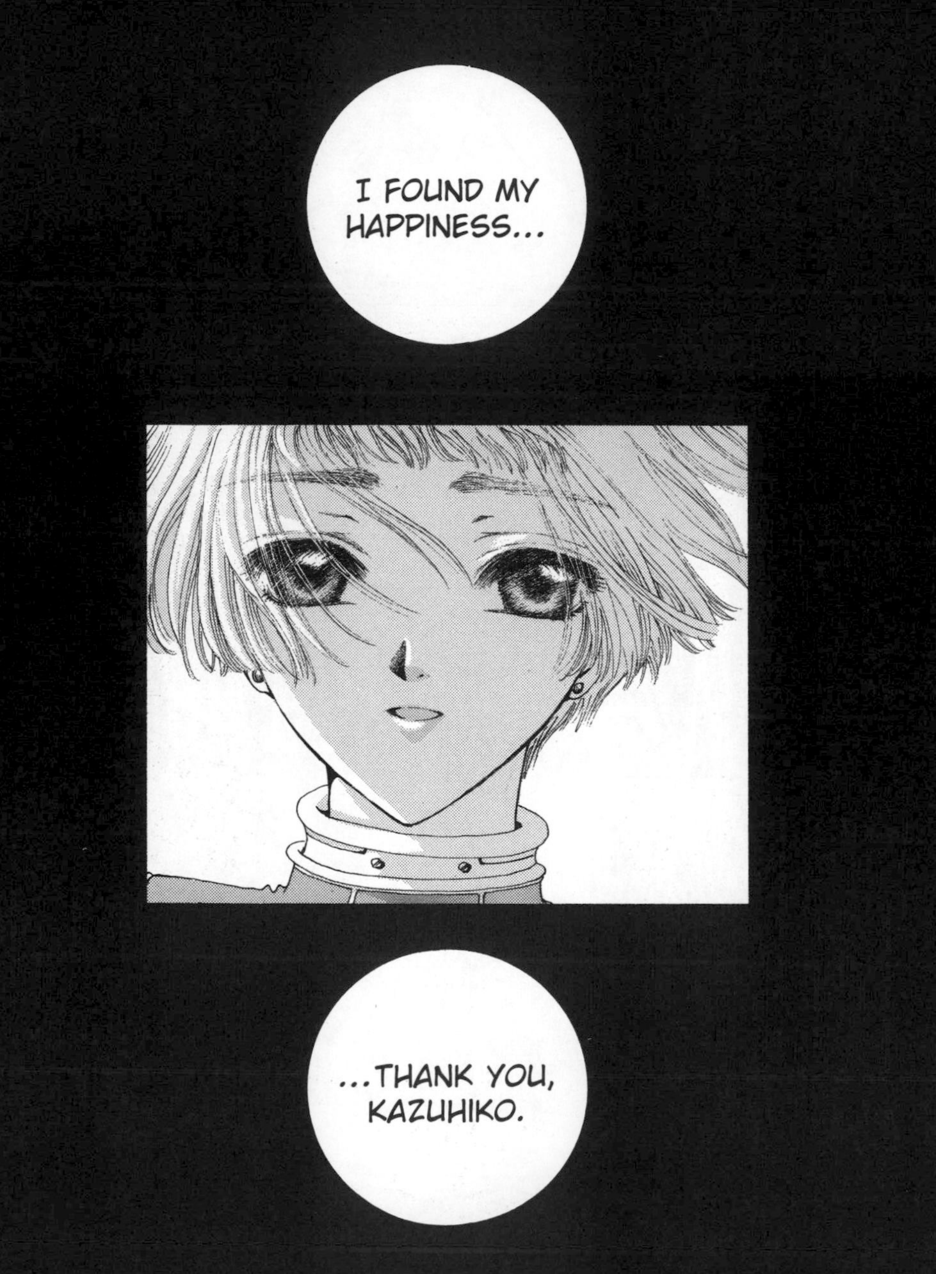
I FOUND MY HAPPINESS...
...THANK YOU, KAZUHIKO.

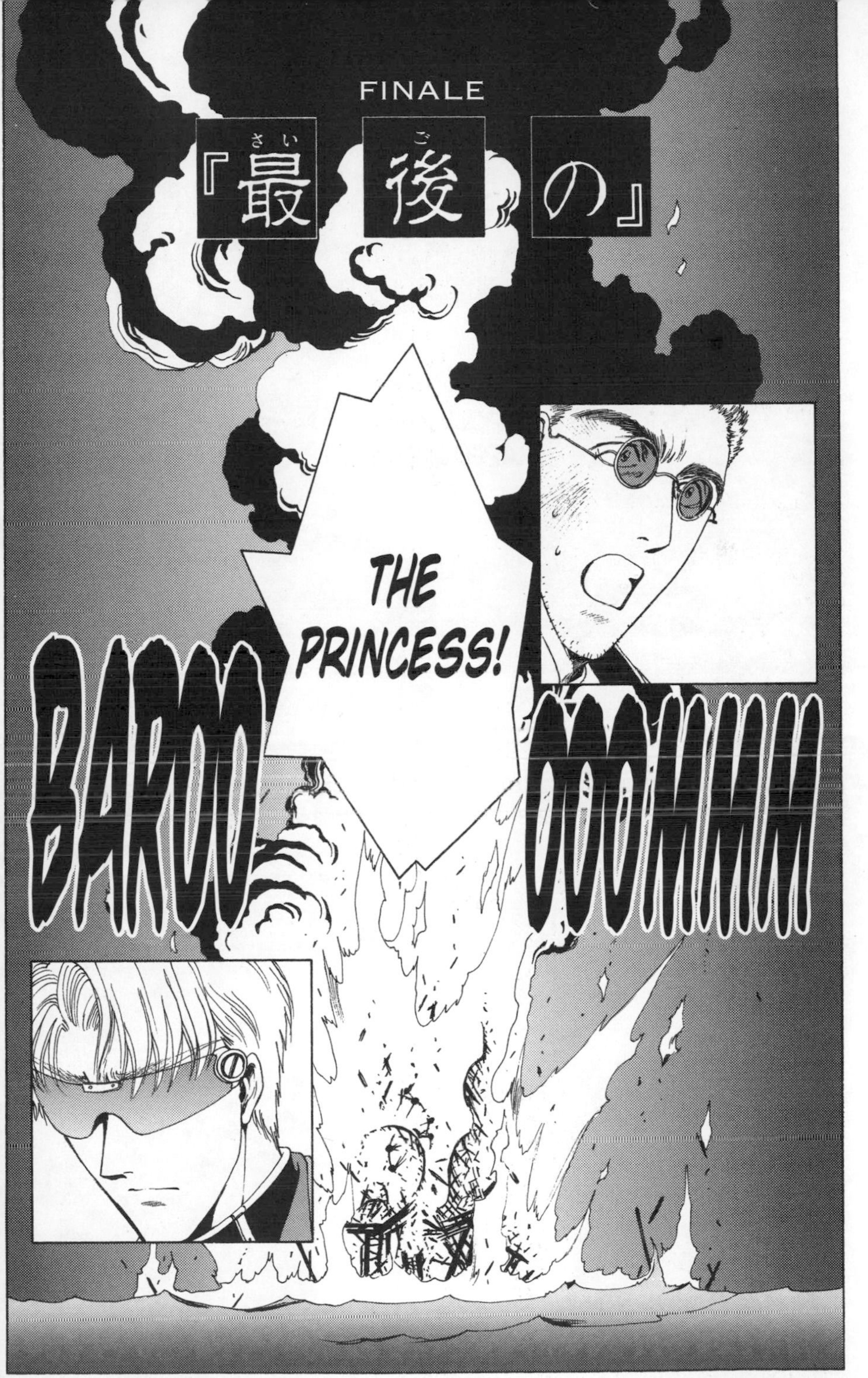
FINALE
『最後の』
THE PRINCESS!
BAROOOOOOMMMM

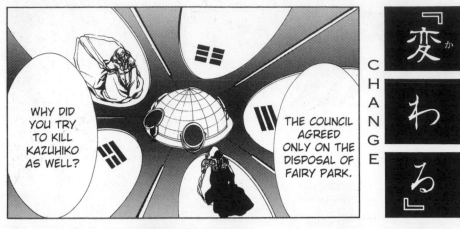

『変(か)わる』

CHANGE

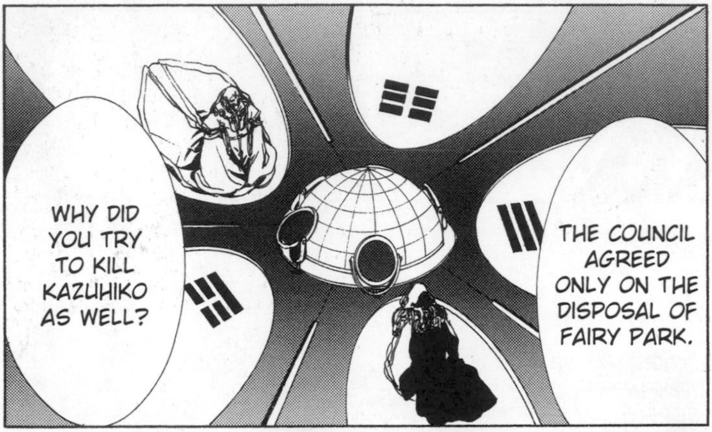
THE COUNCIL AGREED ONLY ON THE DISPOSAL OF FAIRY PARK.
WHY DID YOU TRY TO KILL KAZUHIKO AS WELL?

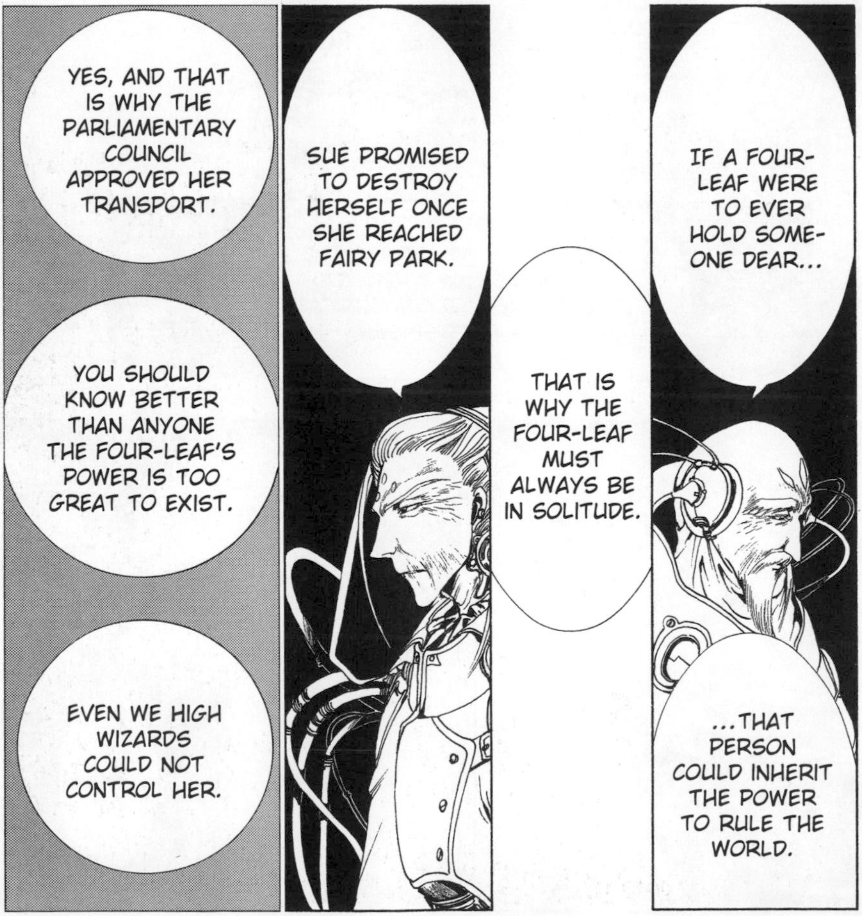
IF A FOUR-LEAF WERE TO EVER HOLD SOME-ONE DEAR...
...THAT PERSON COULD INHERIT THE POWER TO RULE THE WORLD.
THAT IS WHY THE FOUR-LEAF MUST ALWAYS BE IN SOLITUDE.
SUE PROMISED TO DESTROY HERSELF ONCE SHE REACHED FAIRY PARK.
YES, AND THAT IS WHY THE PARLIAMENTARY COUNCIL APPROVED HER TRANSPORT.
YOU SHOULD KNOW BETTER THAN ANYONE THE FOUR-LEAF'S POWER IS TOO GREAT TO EXIST.
EVEN WE HIGH WIZARDS COULD NOT CONTROL HER.

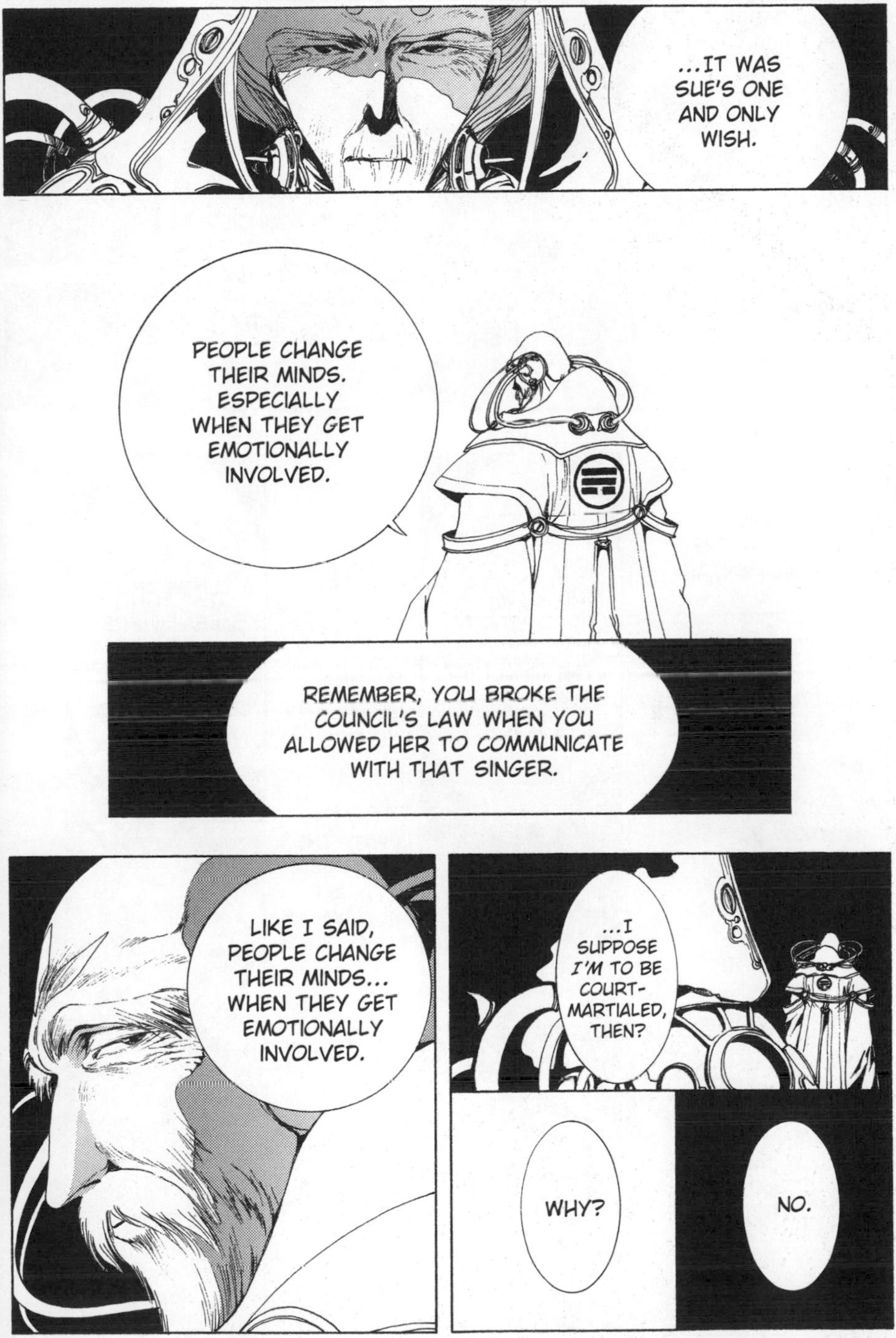
...IT WAS SUE'S ONE AND ONLY WISH.
PEOPLE CHANGE THEIR MINDS. ESPECIALLY WHEN THEY GET EMOTIONALLY INVOLVED.
REMEMBER, YOU BROKE THE COUNCIL'S LAW WHEN YOU ALLOWED HER TO COMMUNICATE WITH THAT SINGER.
...I SUPPOSE *I'M* TO BE COURT-MARTIALED, THEN?
NO.
WHY?
LIKE I SAID, PEOPLE CHANGE THEIR MINDS... WHEN THEY GET EMOTIONALLY INVOLVED.

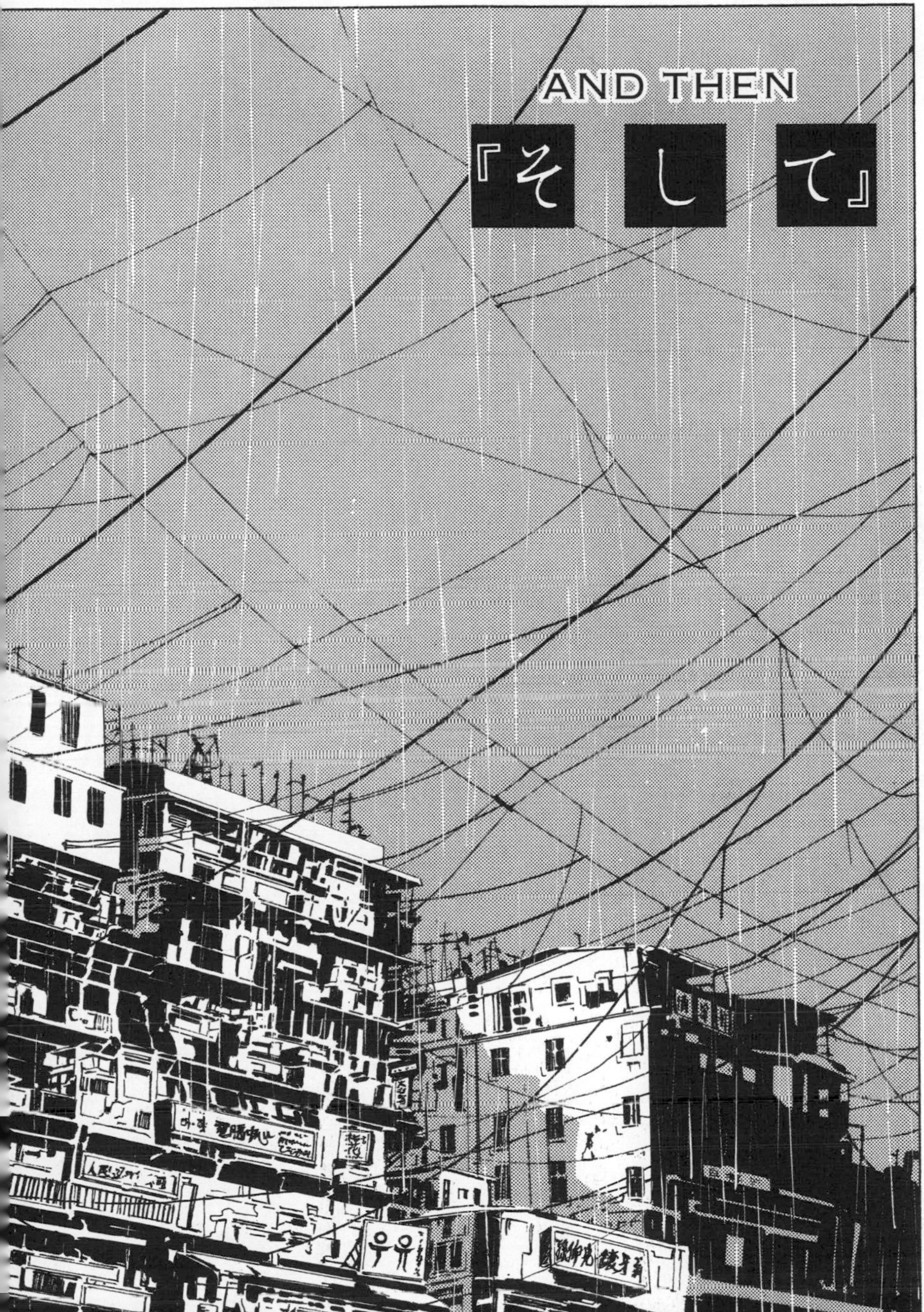
AND THEN
『そして』

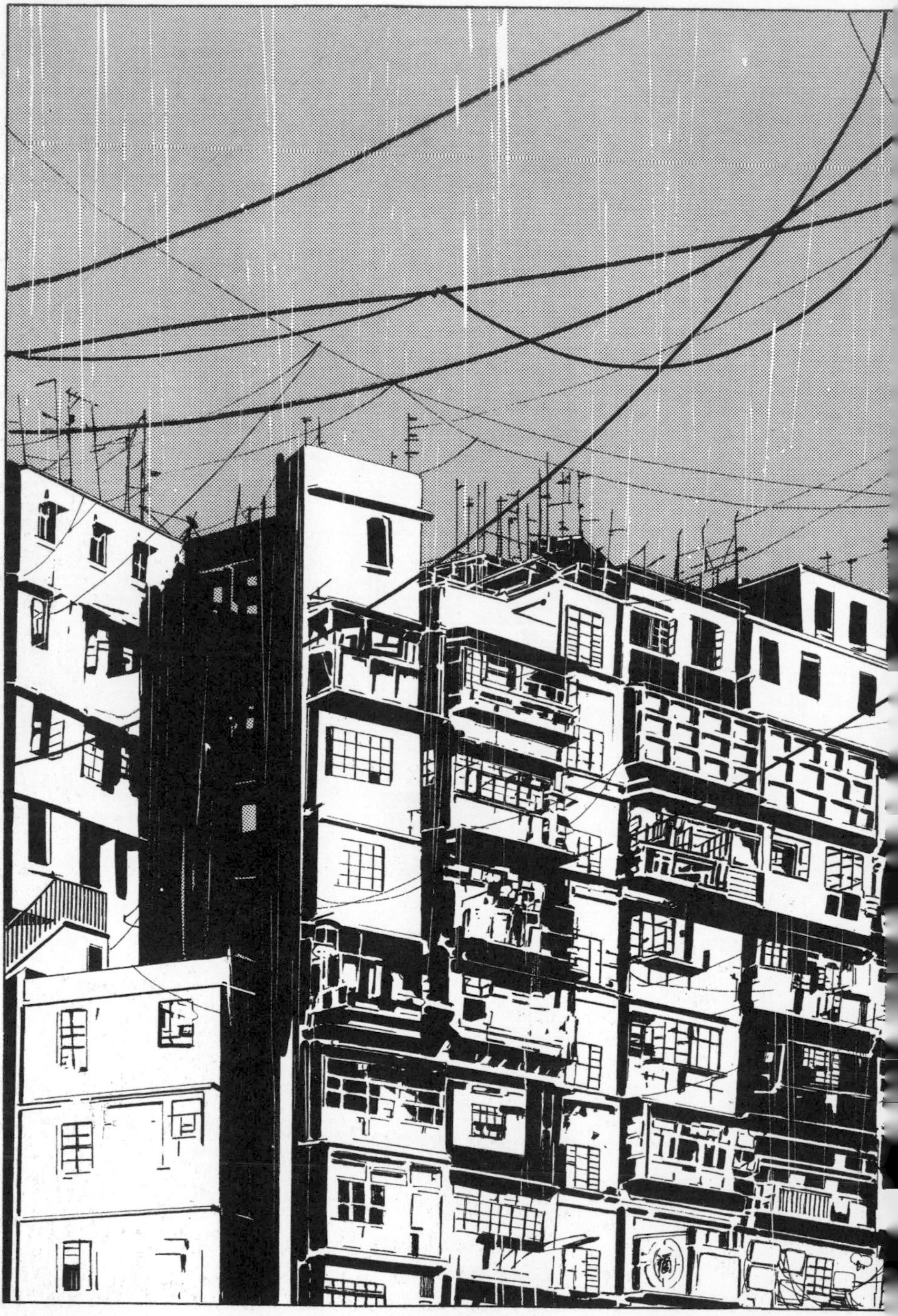

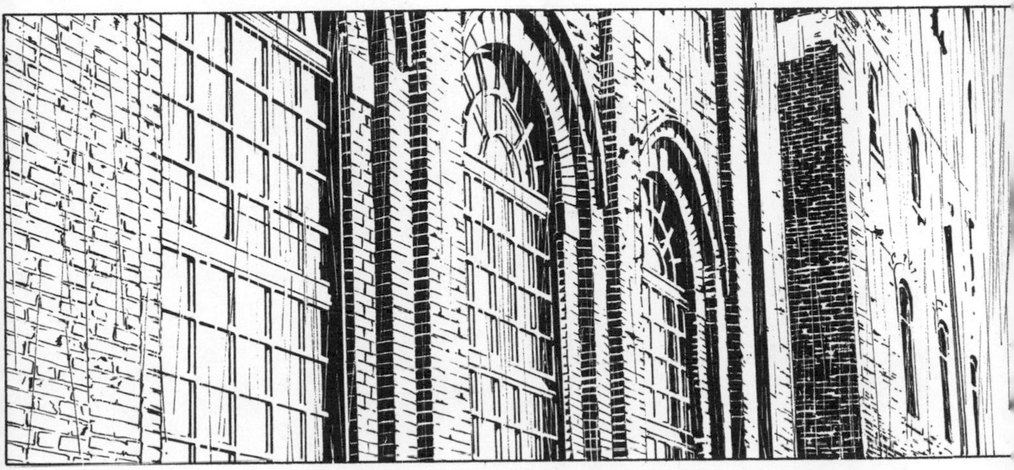

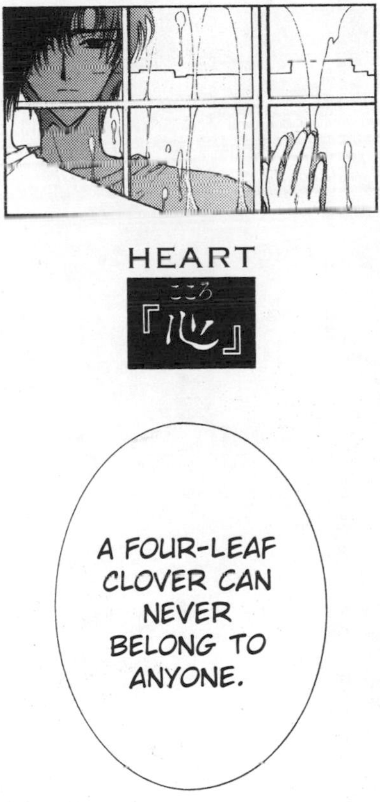

HEART

こころ

『心』

A FOUR-LEAF
CLOVER CAN
NEVER
BELONG TO
ANYONE.

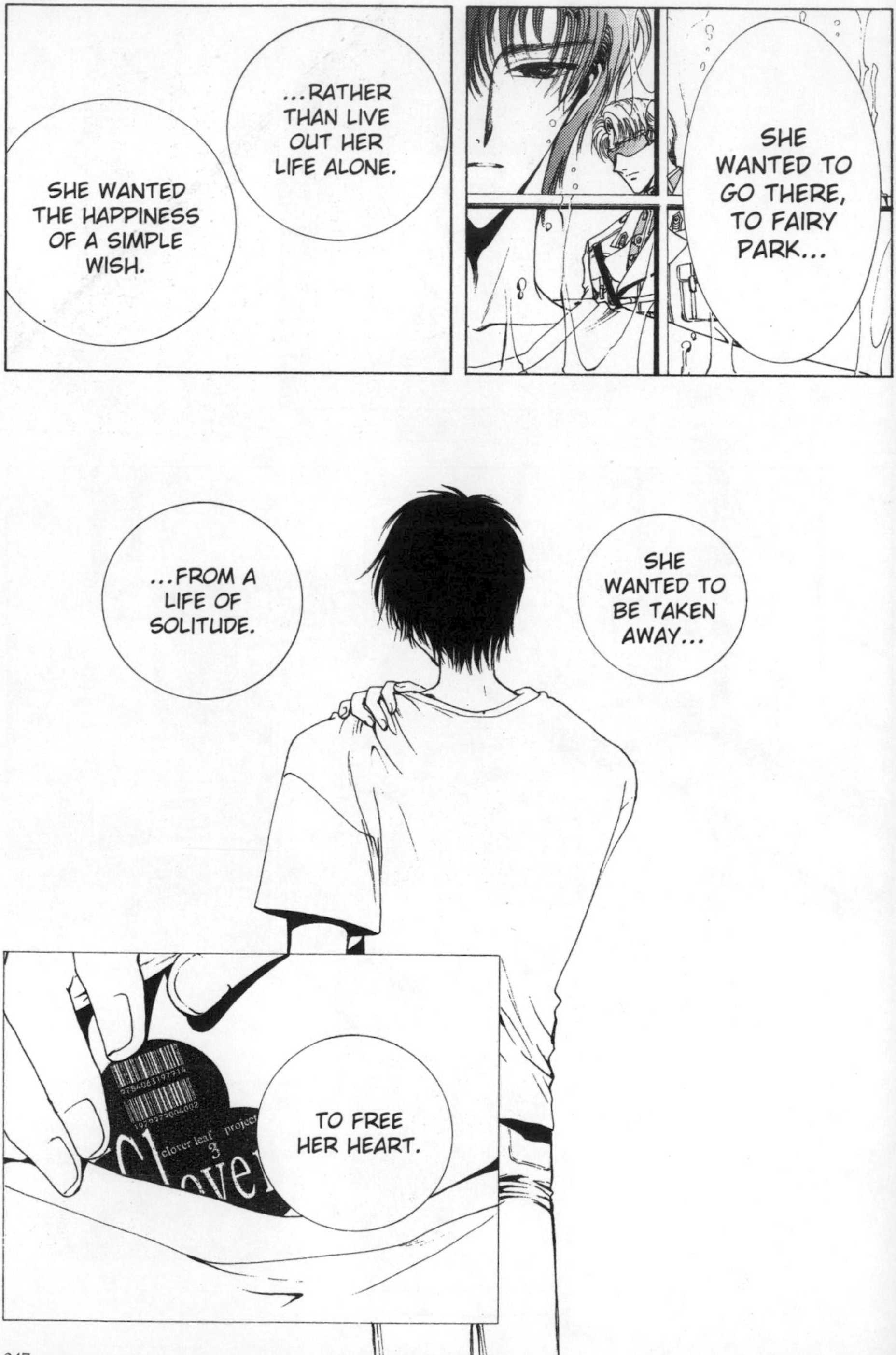
SHE WANTED TO GO THERE, TO FAIRY PARK...
SHE WANTED THE HAPPINESS OF A SIMPLE WISH.
...RATHER THAN LIVE OUT HER LIFE ALONE.
SHE WANTED TO BE TAKEN AWAY...
...FROM A LIFE OF SOLITUDE.
TO FREE HER HEART.
clover leaf project
3
Clover

THE LEAF

『葉』

*I wish for
happiness*

*I seek
happiness*

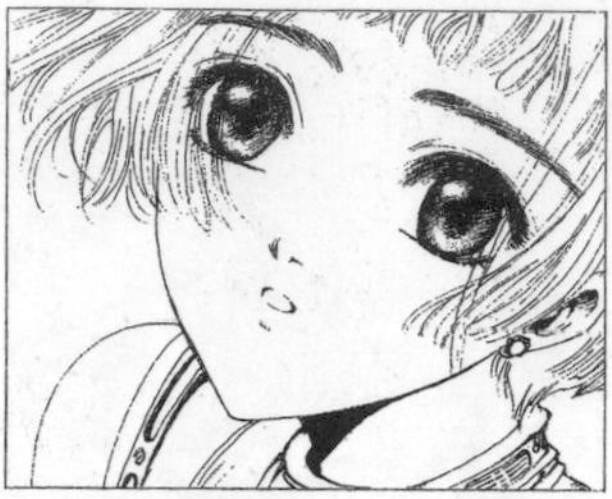

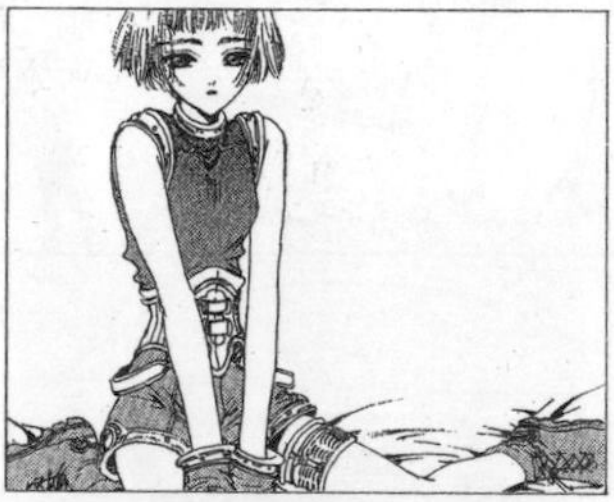

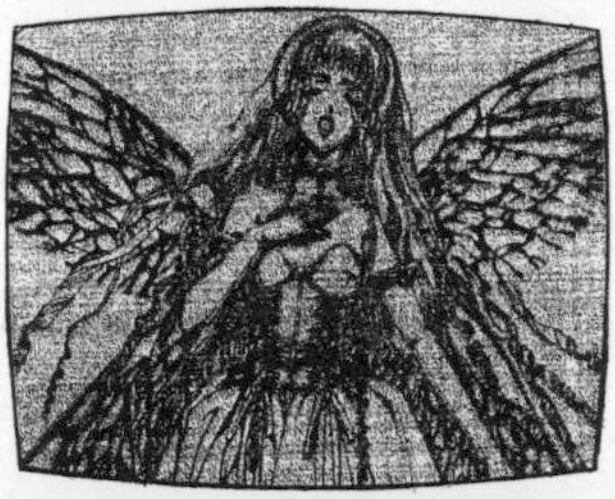

Please take me

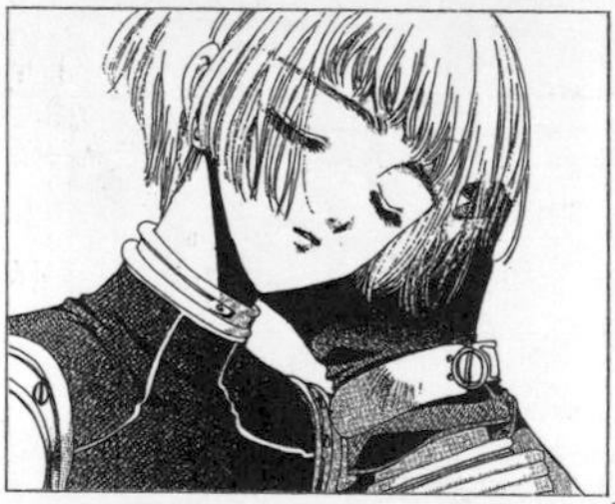

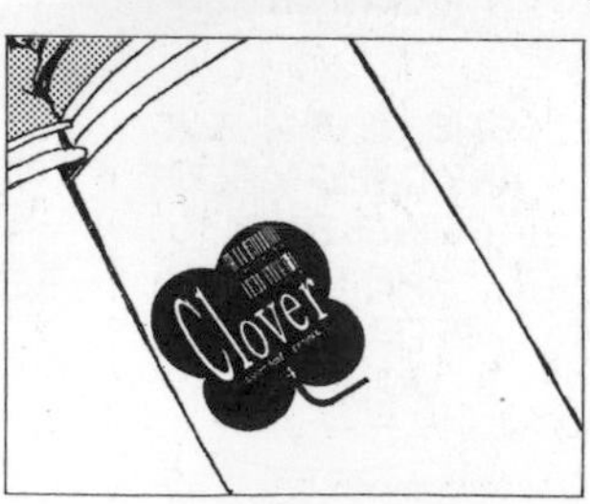
Clover

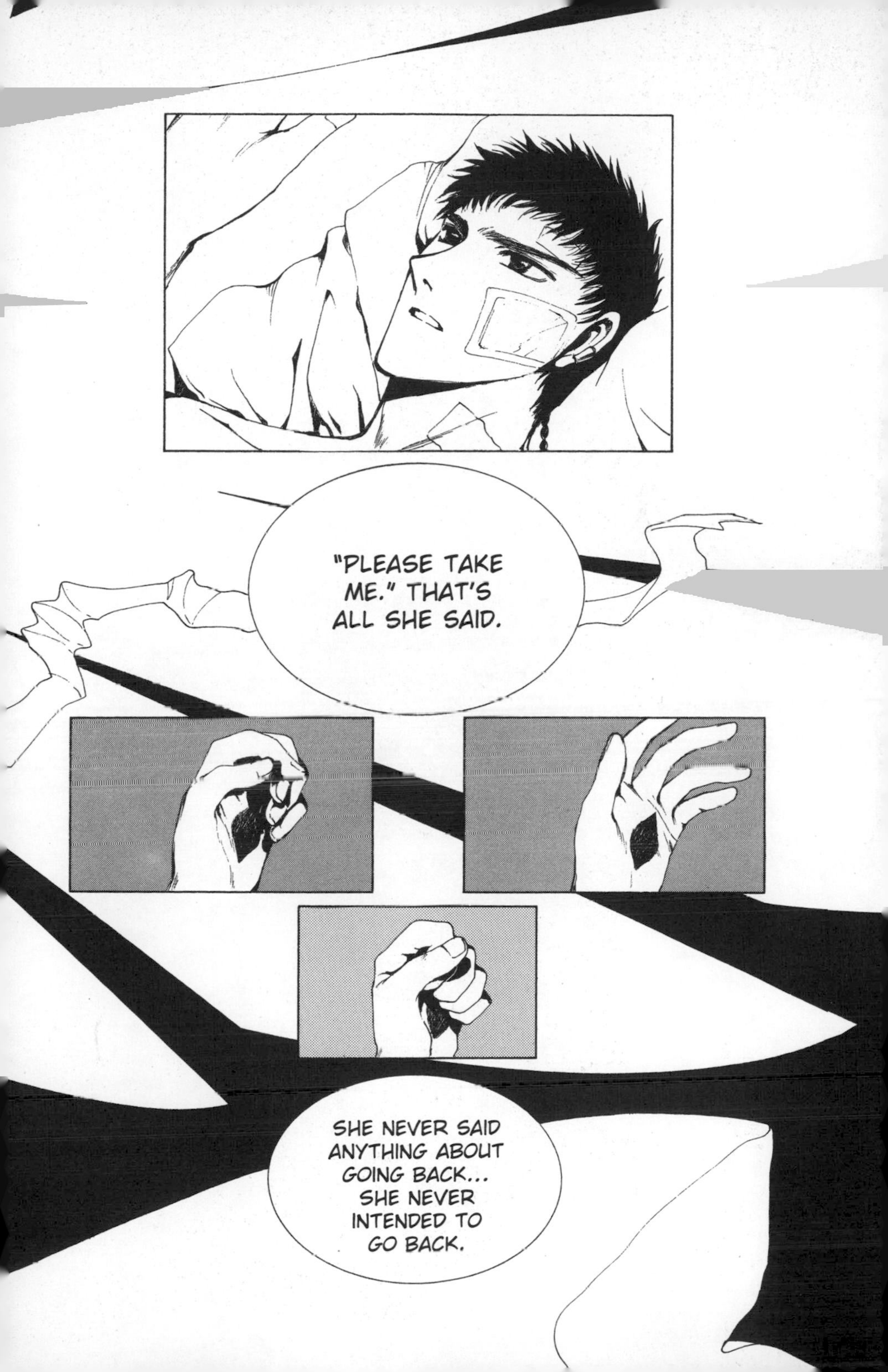
"PLEASE TAKE ME." THAT'S ALL SHE SAID.
SHE NEVER SAID ANYTHING ABOUT GOING BACK... SHE NEVER INTENDED TO GO BACK.

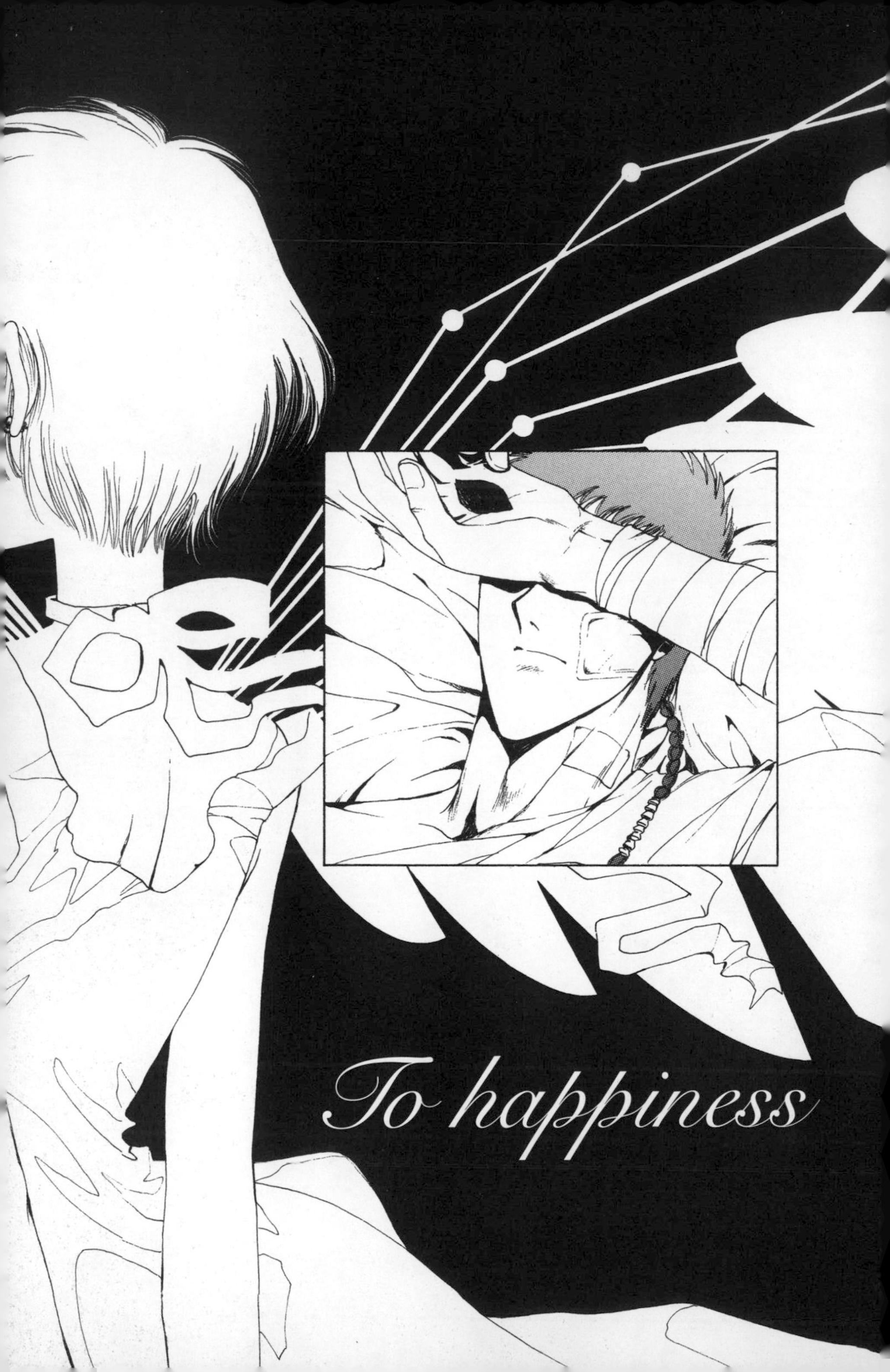
To happiness

If you find a four-leaf
clover
It will bring you
happiness

But
Don't tell anyone

Where the clovers
Bloom white flowers

Or how many leaves
from its stem extend

A four-leaf clover

I only want your happiness
But I cannot be yours to share it

They say
A four-leaf clover
brings happiness

But
Don't tell anyone

Where you found
The four-leaf clover

Or how many leaves
From its stem extend

A four-leaf clover

How I wish to make you happy
But I won't be there to see

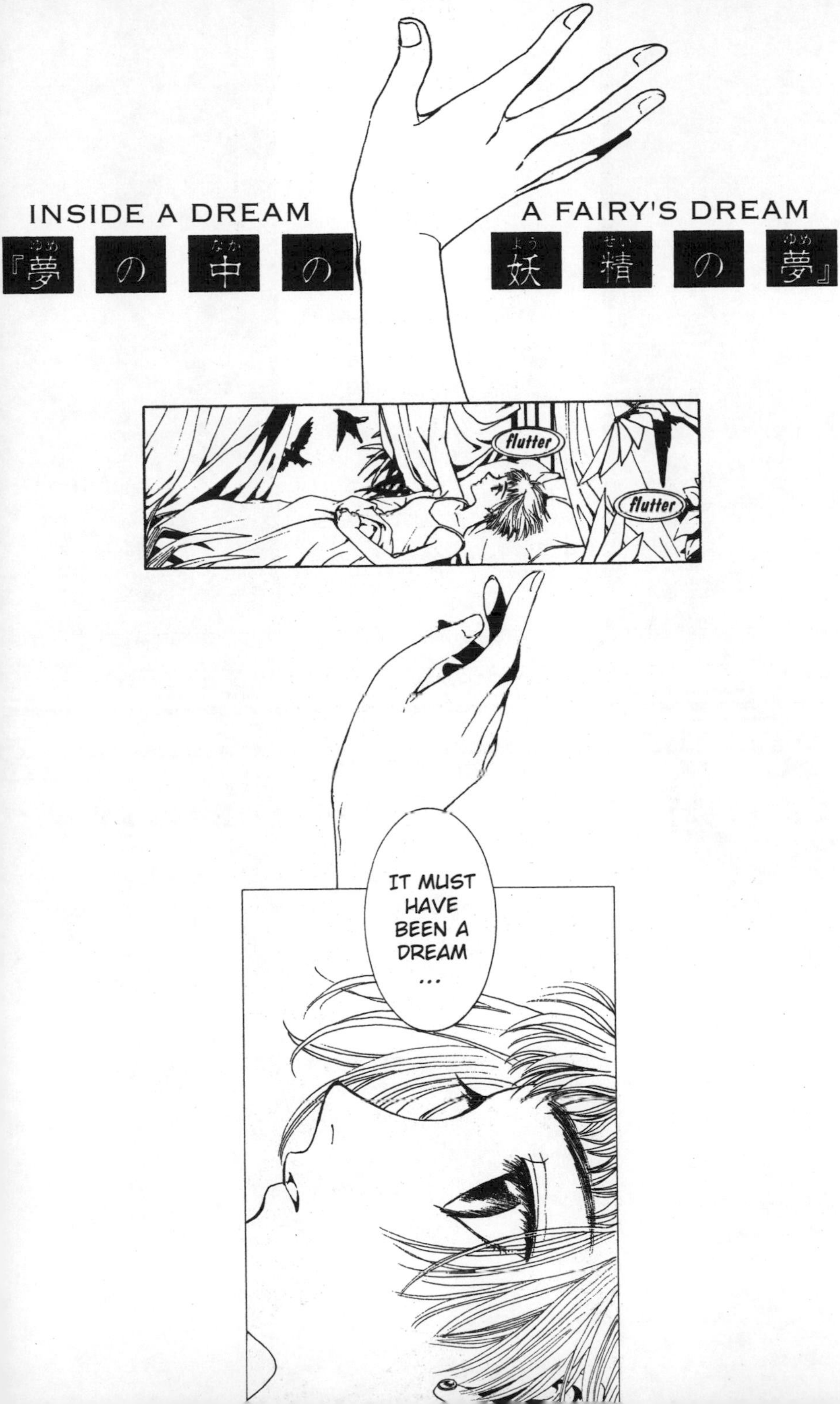
INSIDE A DREAM A FAIRY'S DREAM
『夢の中の妖精の夢』
flutter
flutter
IT MUST HAVE BEEN A DREAM ...

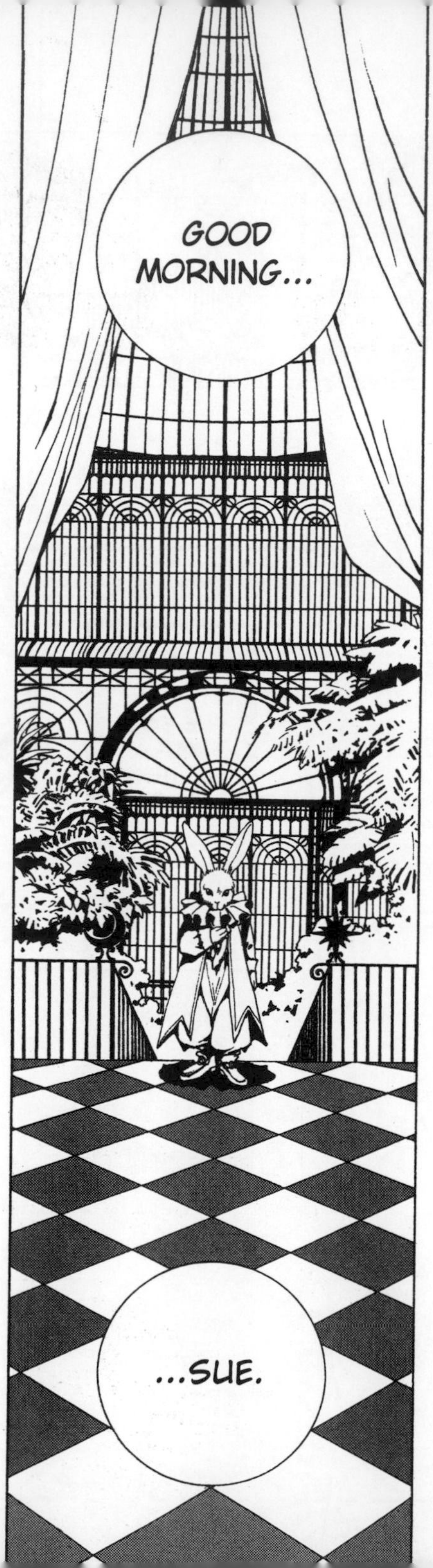
GOOD MORNING...
...SUE.

I JUST HAD A DREAM.

A DREAM ABOUT A FAIRY.

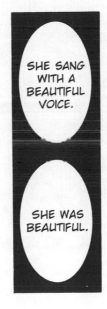

SHE SANG WITH A BEAUTIFUL VOICE.

SHE WAS BEAUTIFUL.

AND I SAW WHAT SHE WAS DREAMING.

WHO IS
SHE?

It's my dream

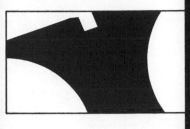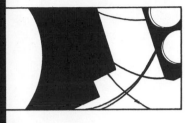

 ORA

『織 ORA 葉』

A beautiful dream

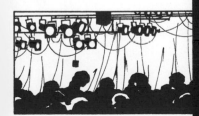

Never before seen

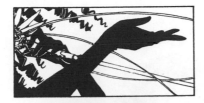

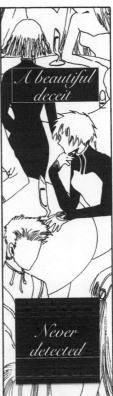

A beautiful deceit
Never detected

A beautiful love

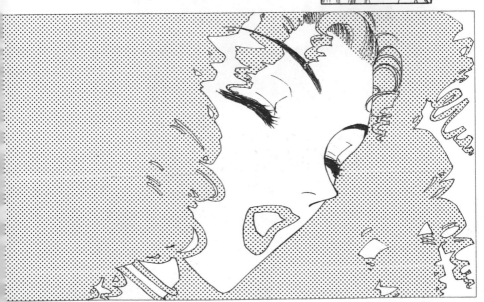

That no one can break

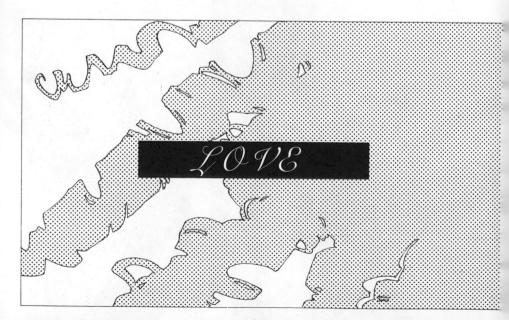

LOVE

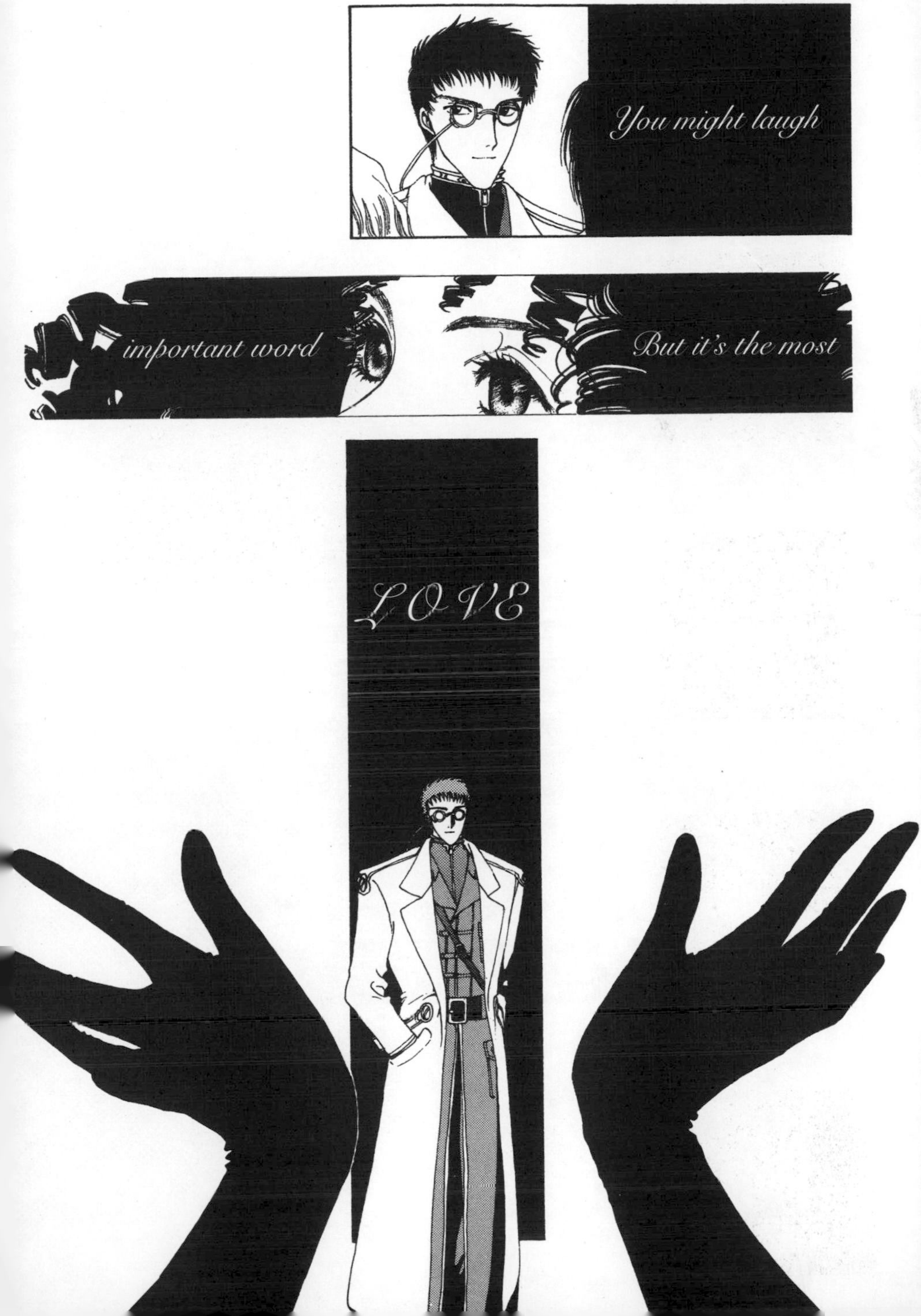
You might laugh
But it's the most
important word
LOVE

*You might laugh
But it's the most
important word*

I...

Love...

You.

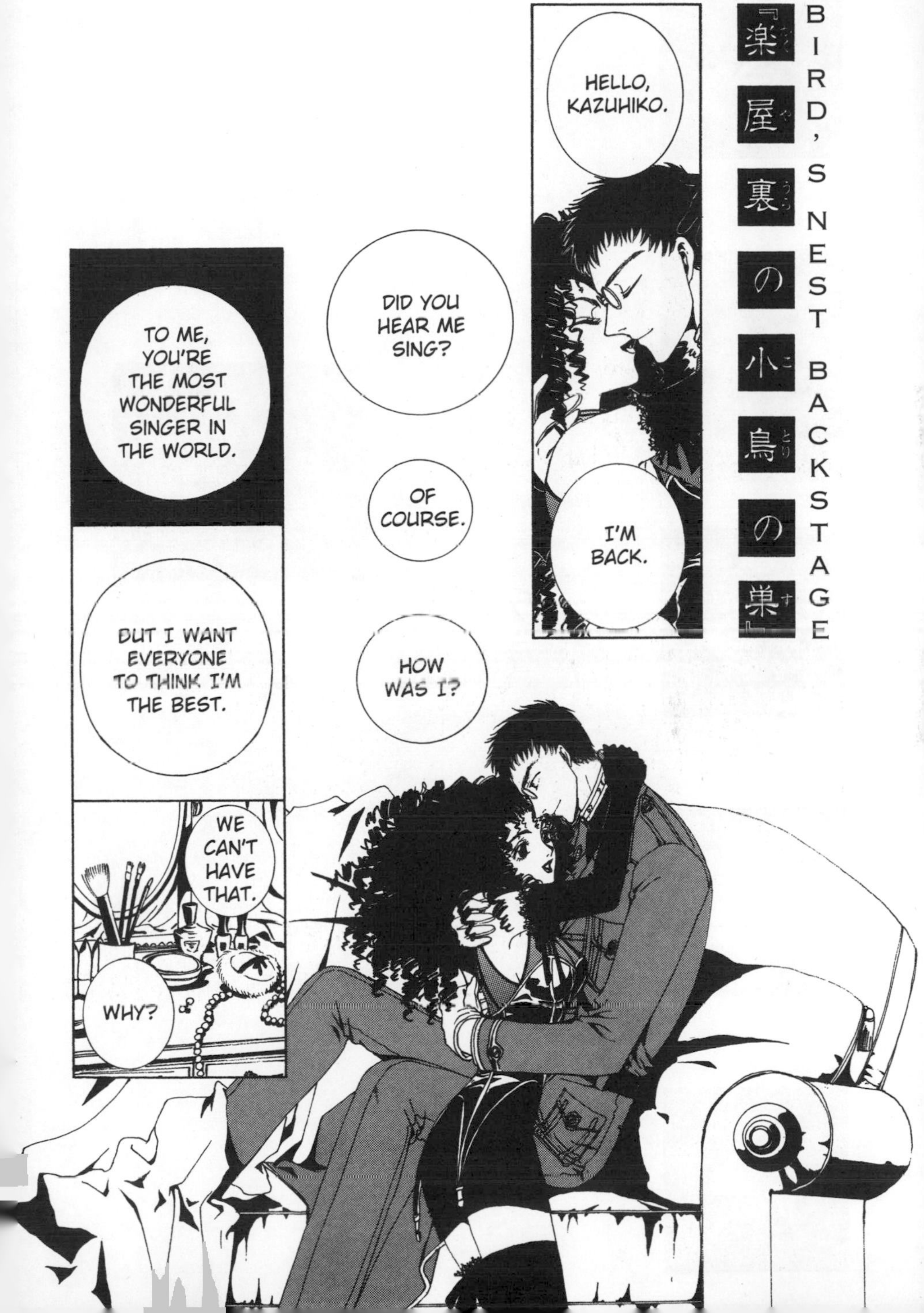
『楽屋裏の小鳥の巣』
BIRD'S NEST BACKSTAGE
HELLO, KAZUHIKO.
I'M BACK.
DID YOU HEAR ME SING?
OF COURSE.
HOW WAS I?
TO ME, YOU'RE THE MOST WONDERFUL SINGER IN THE WORLD.
BUT I WANT EVERYONE TO THINK I'M THE BEST.
WE CAN'T HAVE THAT.
WHY?

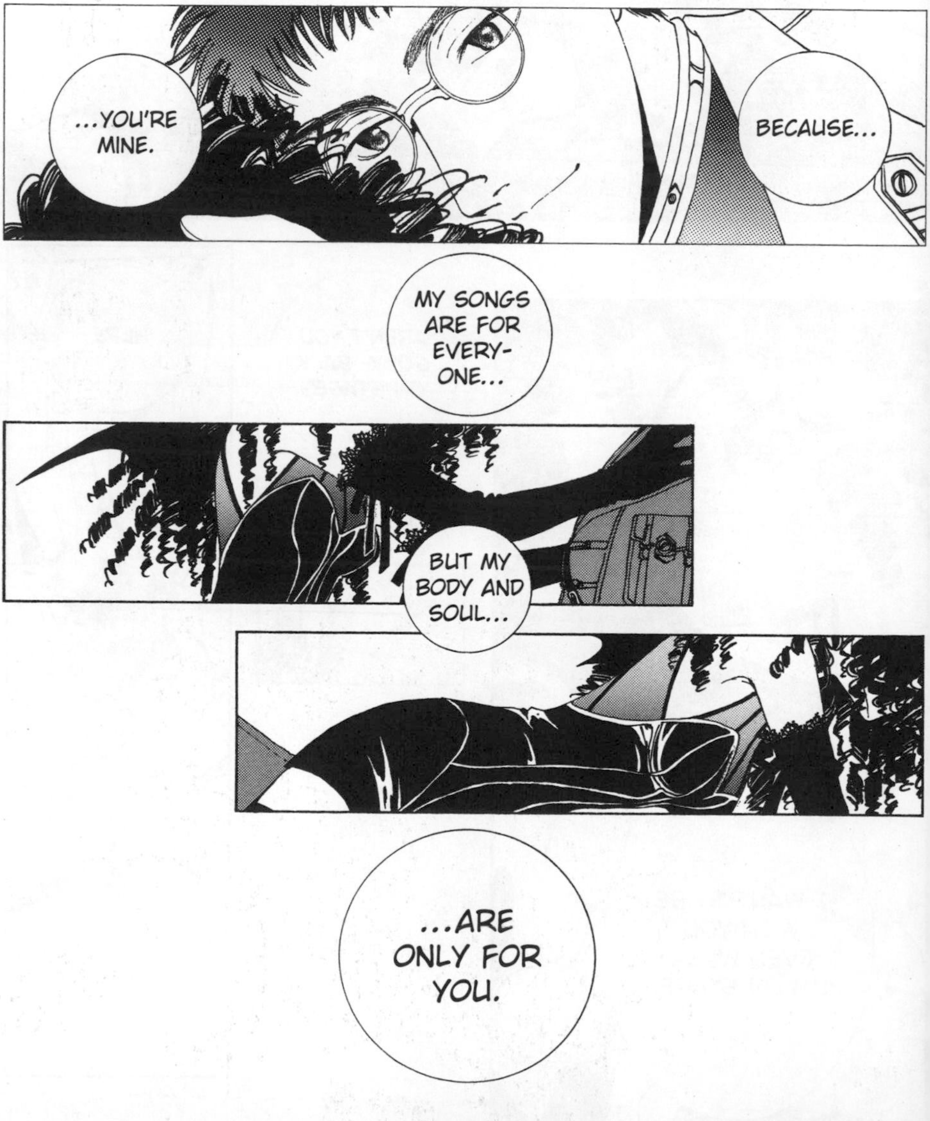
BECAUSE...
...YOU'RE MINE.
MY SONGS ARE FOR EVERY-ONE...
BUT MY BODY AND SOUL...
...ARE ONLY FOR YOU.

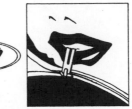

ziiiipp

LET'S DO IT.

AREN'T YOU GOING BACK ON STAGE?

HERE?

I WANT TO BE WITH YOU EVEN WHEN I'M ON STAGE.

HERE.

PLEASE.

BIRD'S NEST IN A GILDED CAGE

『籠の中の小鳥の巣』

Now

*Come close
to me*

*I'll sing
an endless song*

God, please show me

*The deepest red
The truest love*

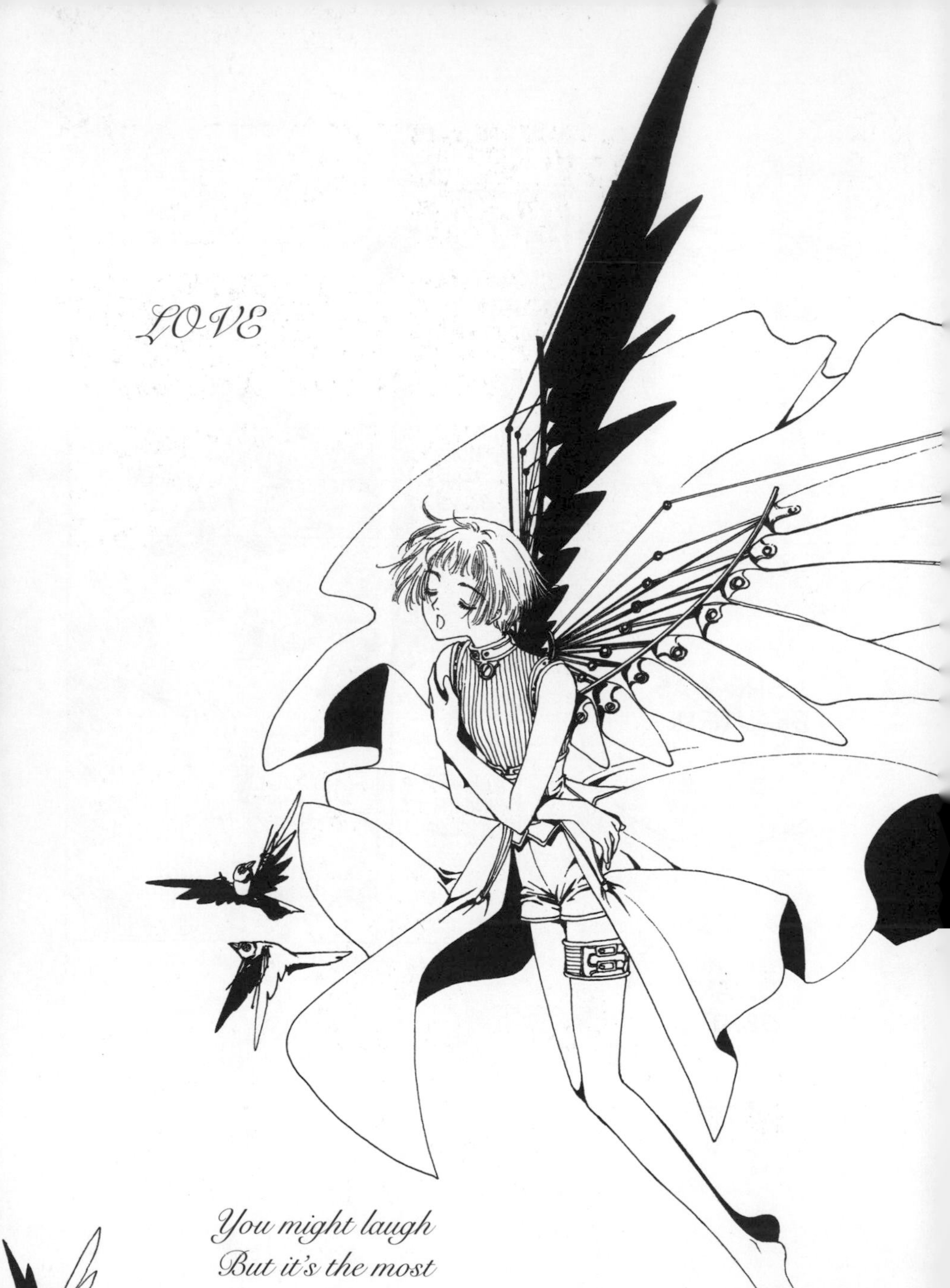
LOVE
You might laugh
But it's the most
beautiful word

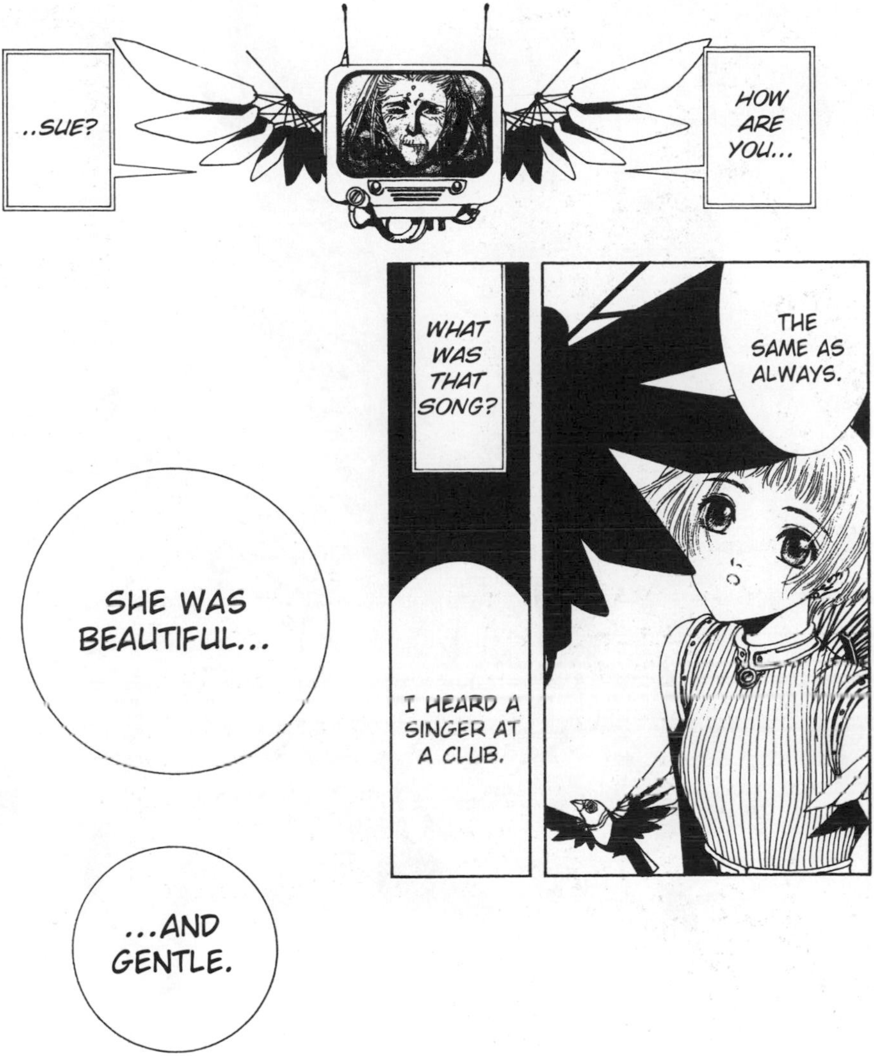
HOW ARE YOU...
..SUE?
THE SAME AS ALWAYS.
WHAT WAS THAT SONG?
I HEARD A SINGER AT A CLUB.
SHE WAS BEAUTIFUL...
...AND GENTLE.

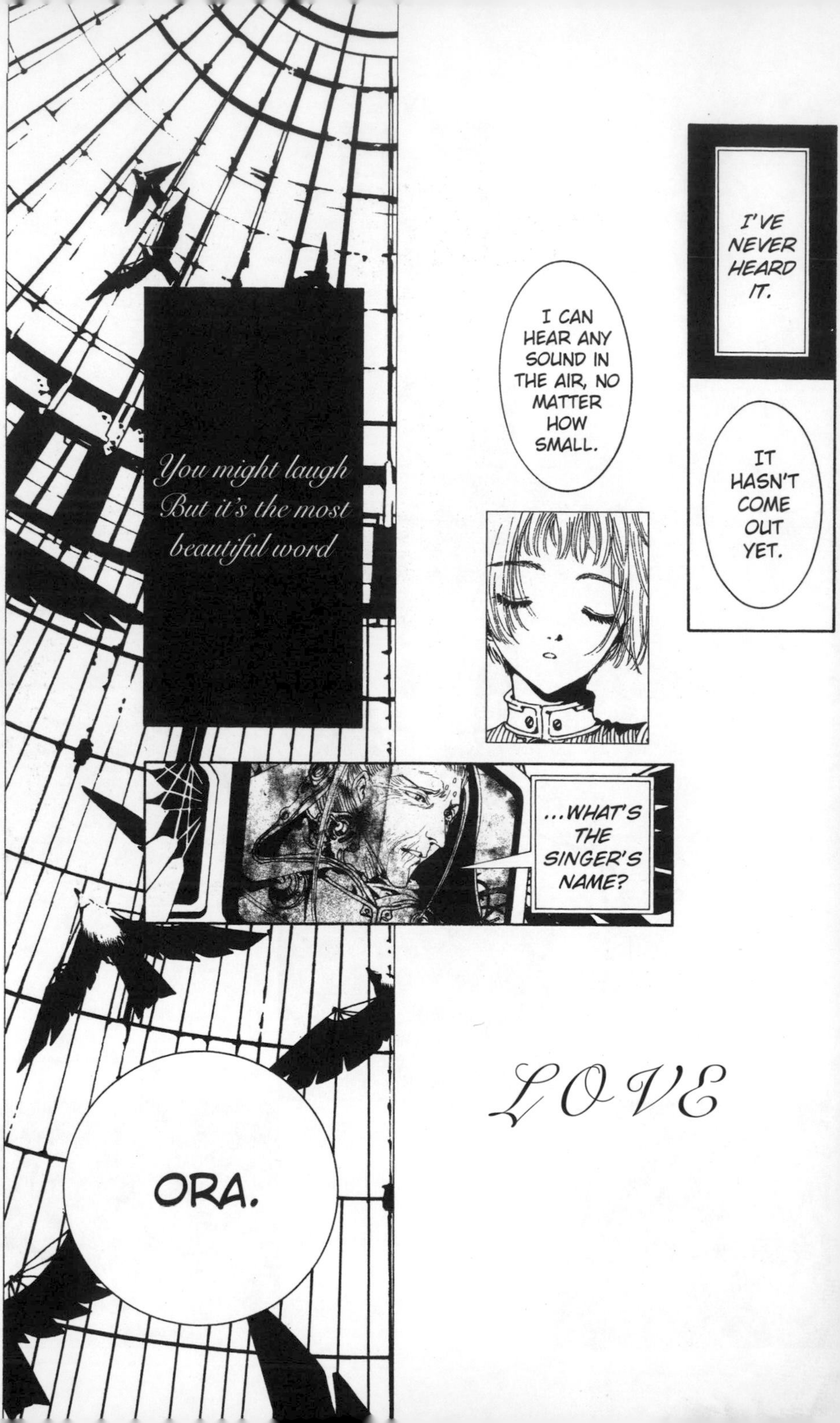

I'VE NEVER HEARD IT.
IT HASN'T COME OUT YET.
I CAN HEAR ANY SOUND IN THE AIR, NO MATTER HOW SMALL.
...WHAT'S THE SINGER'S NAME?
ORA.
You might laugh
But it's the most
beautiful word
LOVE

FLOWER 『再会の花』 OF REUNION

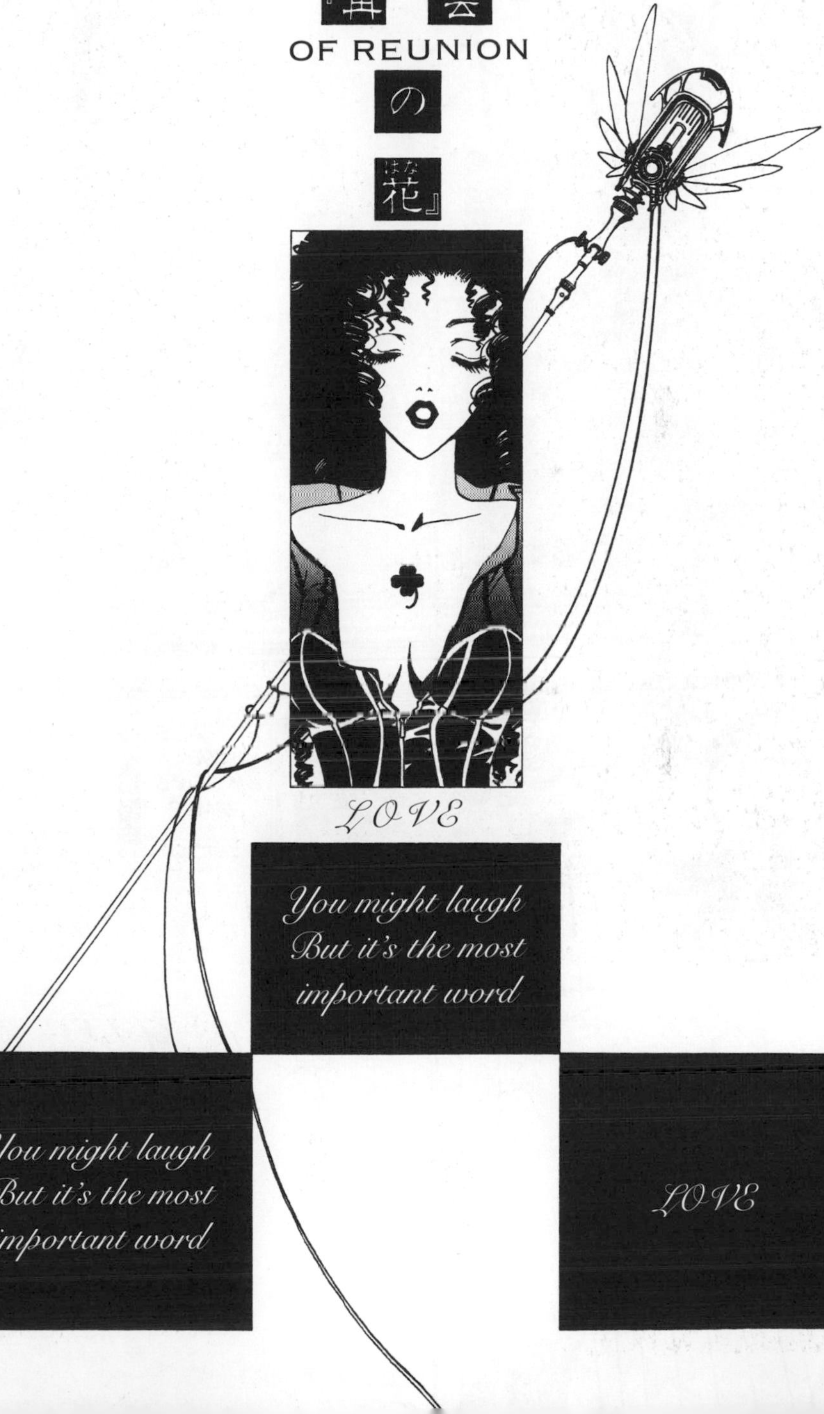

LOVE

You might laugh
But it's the most
important word

You might laugh
But it's the most
important word

LOVE

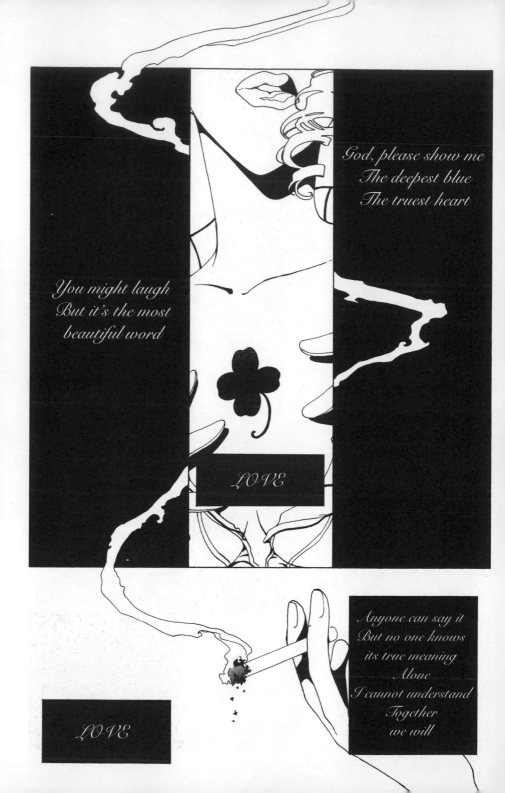

God, please show me
The deepest blue
The truest heart

You might laugh
But it's the most
beautiful word

LOVE

Anyone can say it
But no one knows
its true meaning
Alone
I cannot understand
Together
we will

LOVE

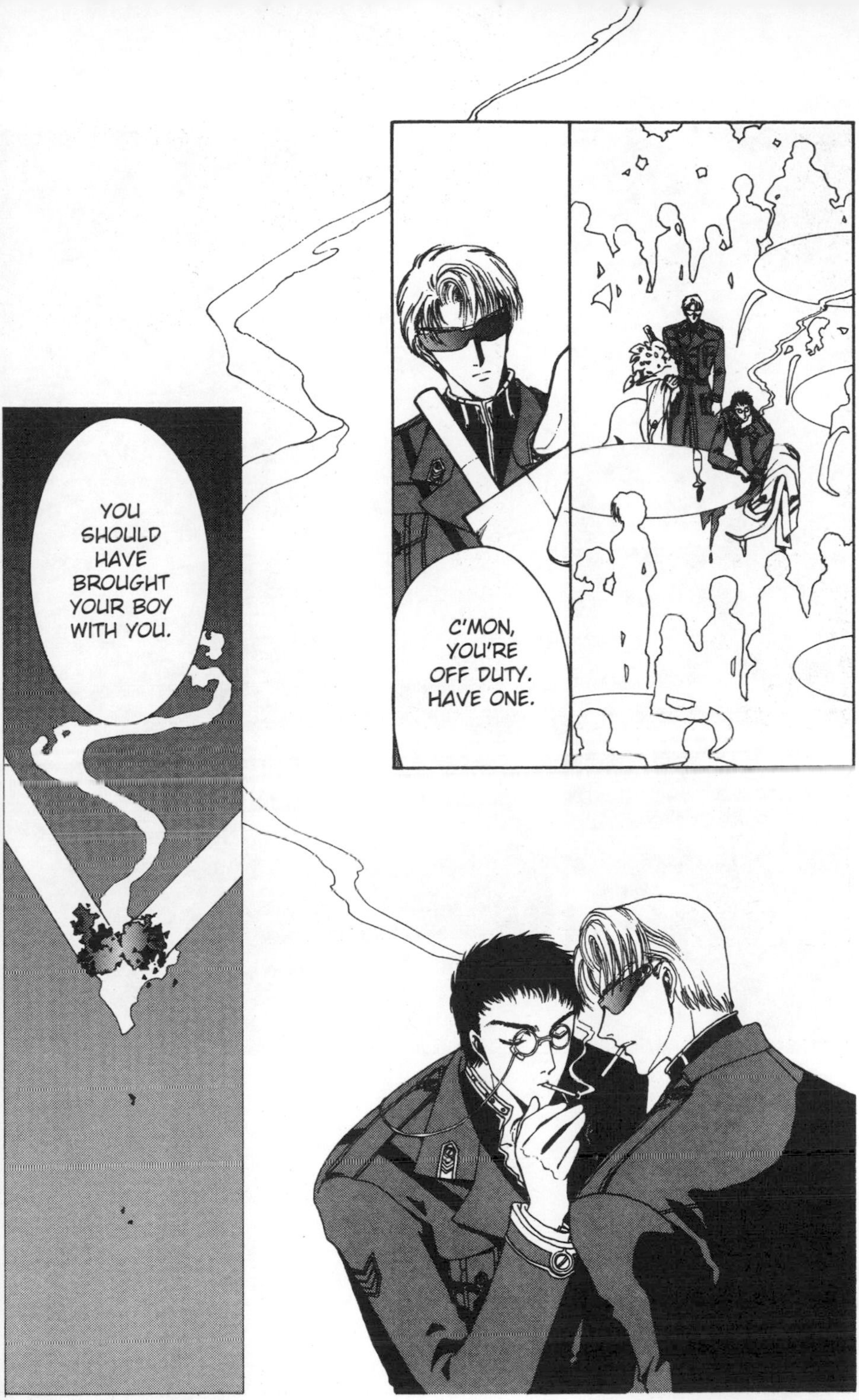
C'MON, YOU'RE OFF DUTY. HAVE ONE.
YOU SHOULD HAVE BROUGHT YOUR BOY WITH YOU.

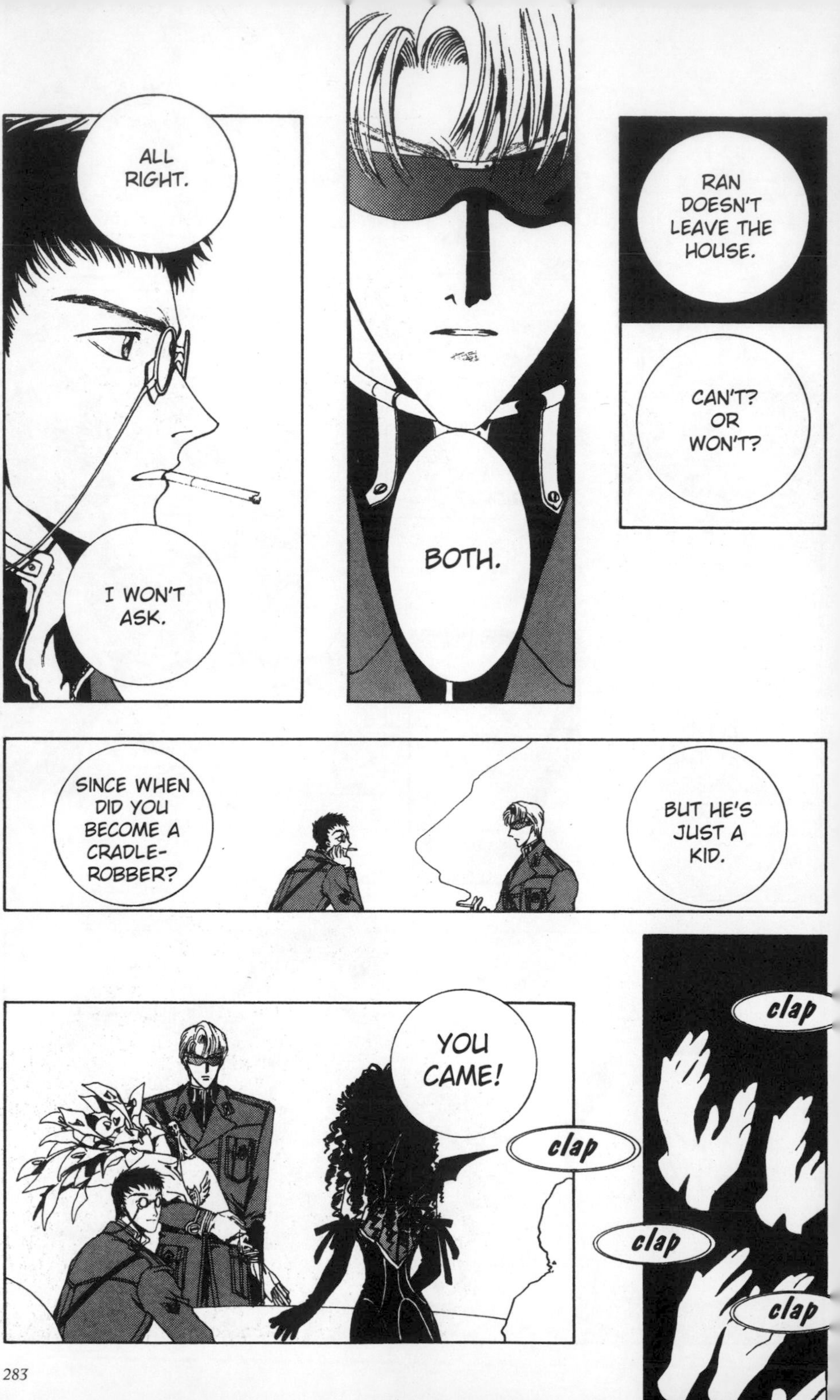
RAN DOESN'T LEAVE THE HOUSE.
CAN'T? OR WON'T?
BOTH.
ALL RIGHT.
I WON'T ASK.
BUT HE'S JUST A KID.
SINCE WHEN DID YOU BECOME A CRADLE-ROBBER?
clap
clap
clap
YOU CAME!
clap

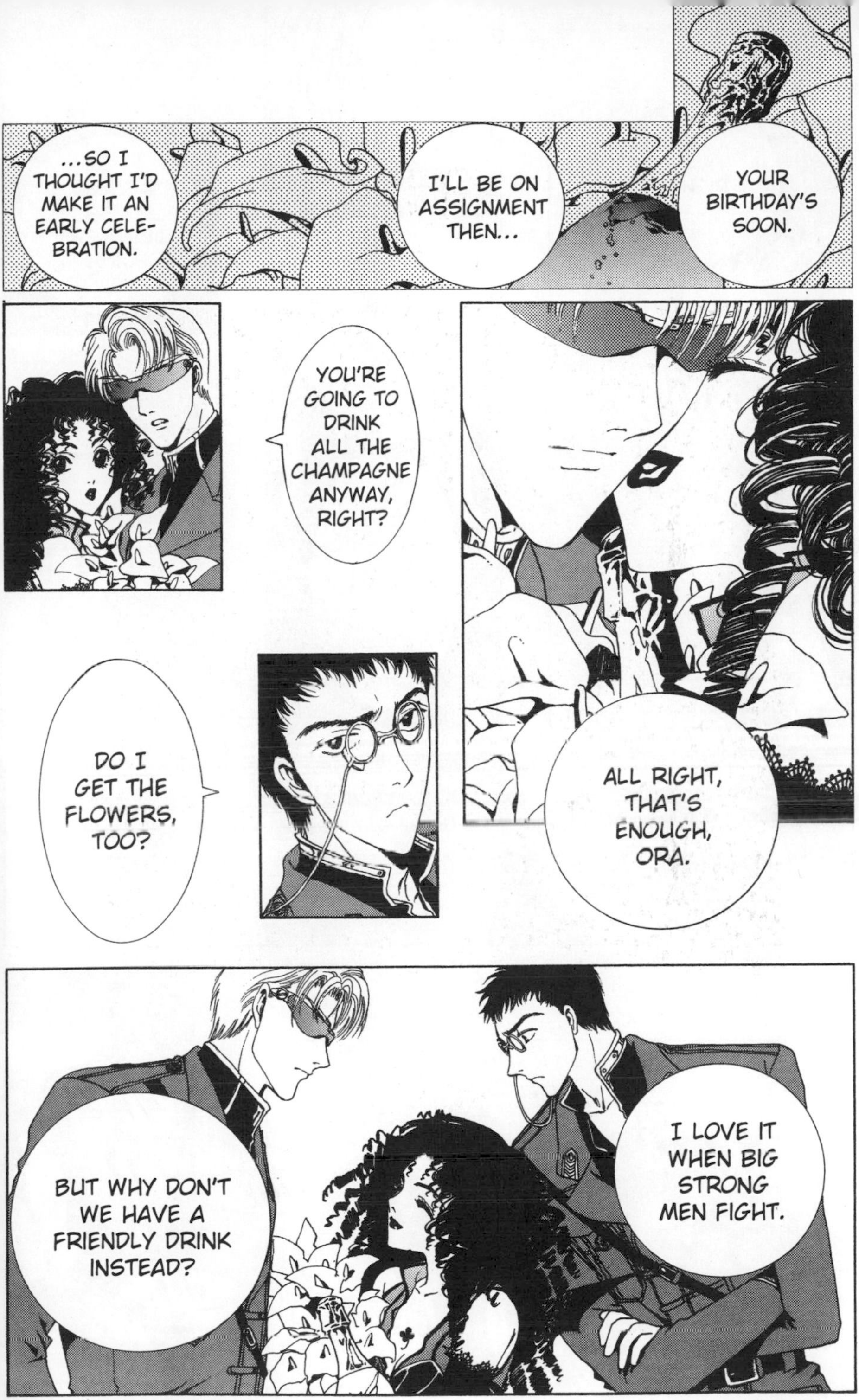
YOUR BIRTHDAY'S SOON.
I'LL BE ON ASSIGNMENT THEN...
...SO I THOUGHT I'D MAKE IT AN EARLY CELE-BRATION.
YOU'RE GOING TO DRINK ALL THE CHAMPAGNE ANYWAY, RIGHT?
ALL RIGHT, THAT'S ENOUGH, ORA.
DO I GET THE FLOWERS, TOO?
I LOVE IT WHEN BIG STRONG MEN FIGHT.
BUT WHY DON'T WE HAVE A FRIENDLY DRINK INSTEAD?

『虫(むし)

BUG

の

EYE

目(め)』

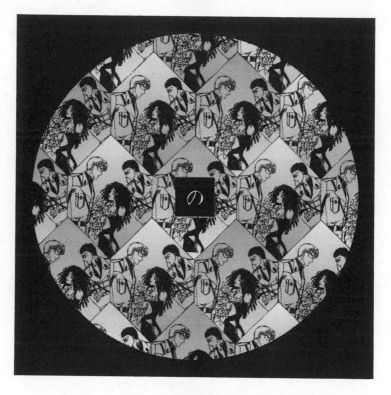

ALONE

「ひとり」

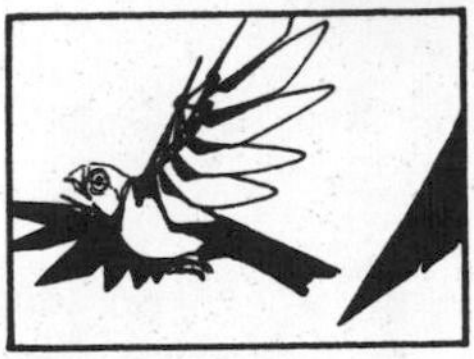

ONE BIRD.

ONE DOG, ONE CAT.

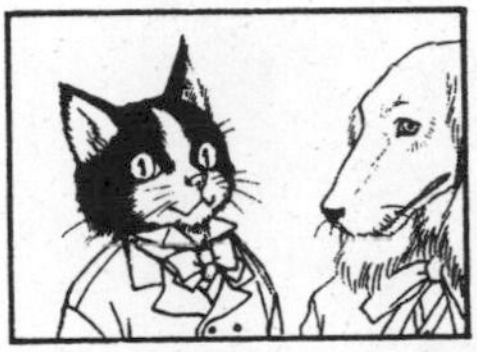

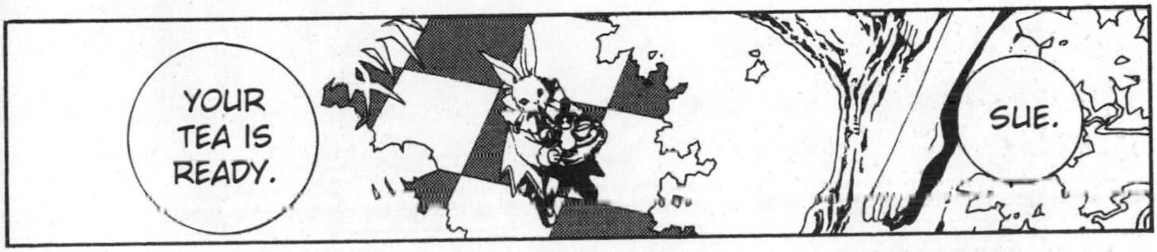
SUE.
YOUR TEA IS READY.

ONE RABBIT.

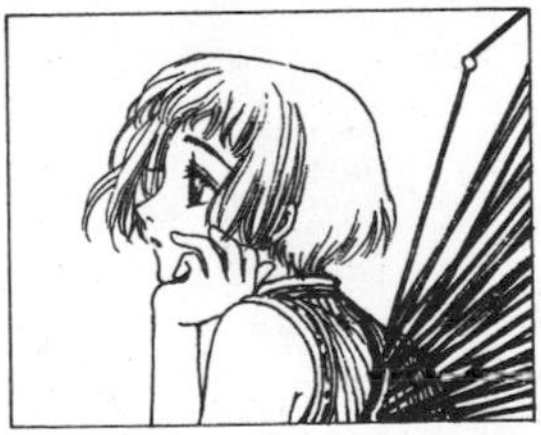

AND I'M ALONE TOO.

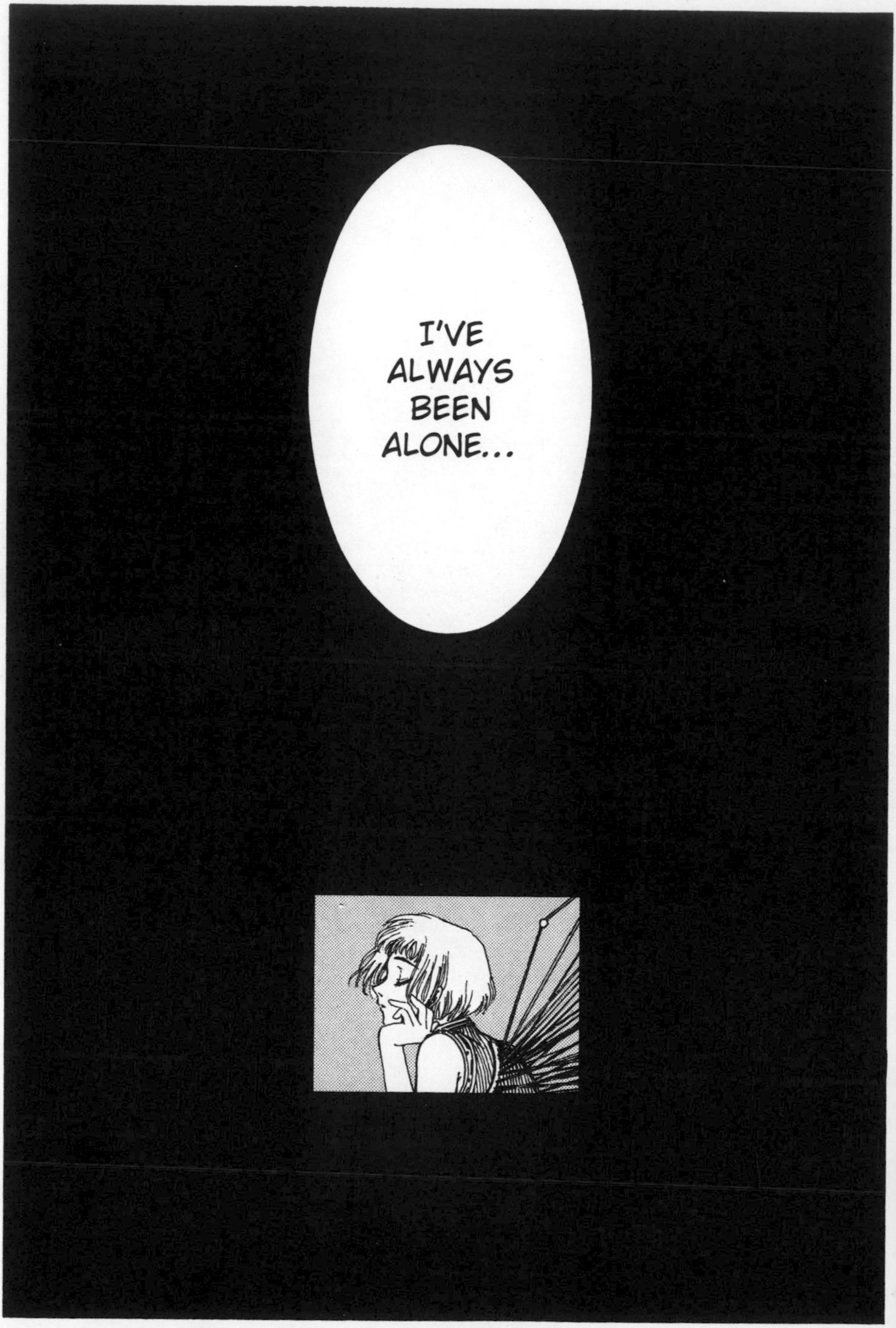
I'VE ALWAYS BEEN ALONE...

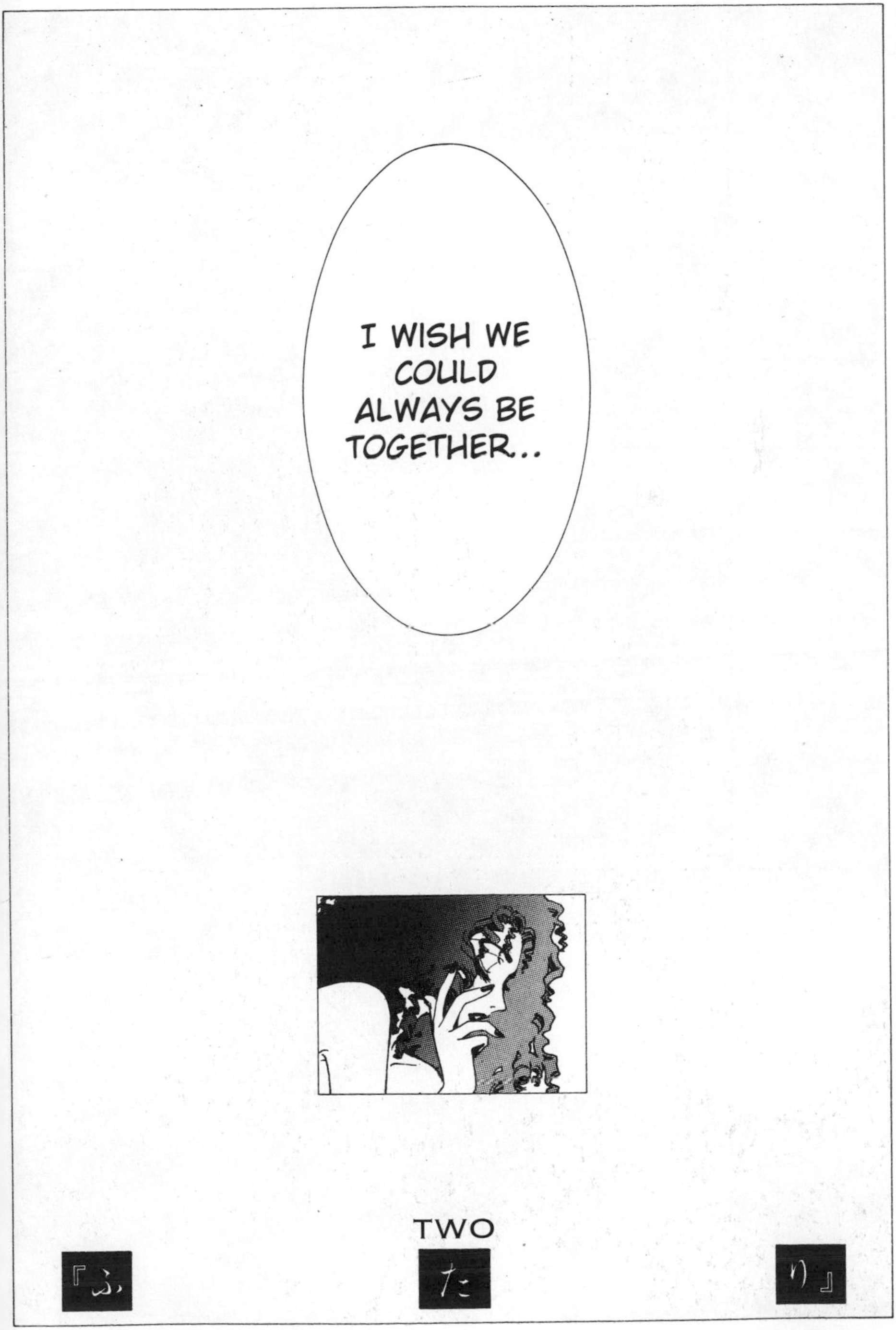
I WISH WE COULD ALWAYS BE TOGETHER...
TWO
『ふたり』

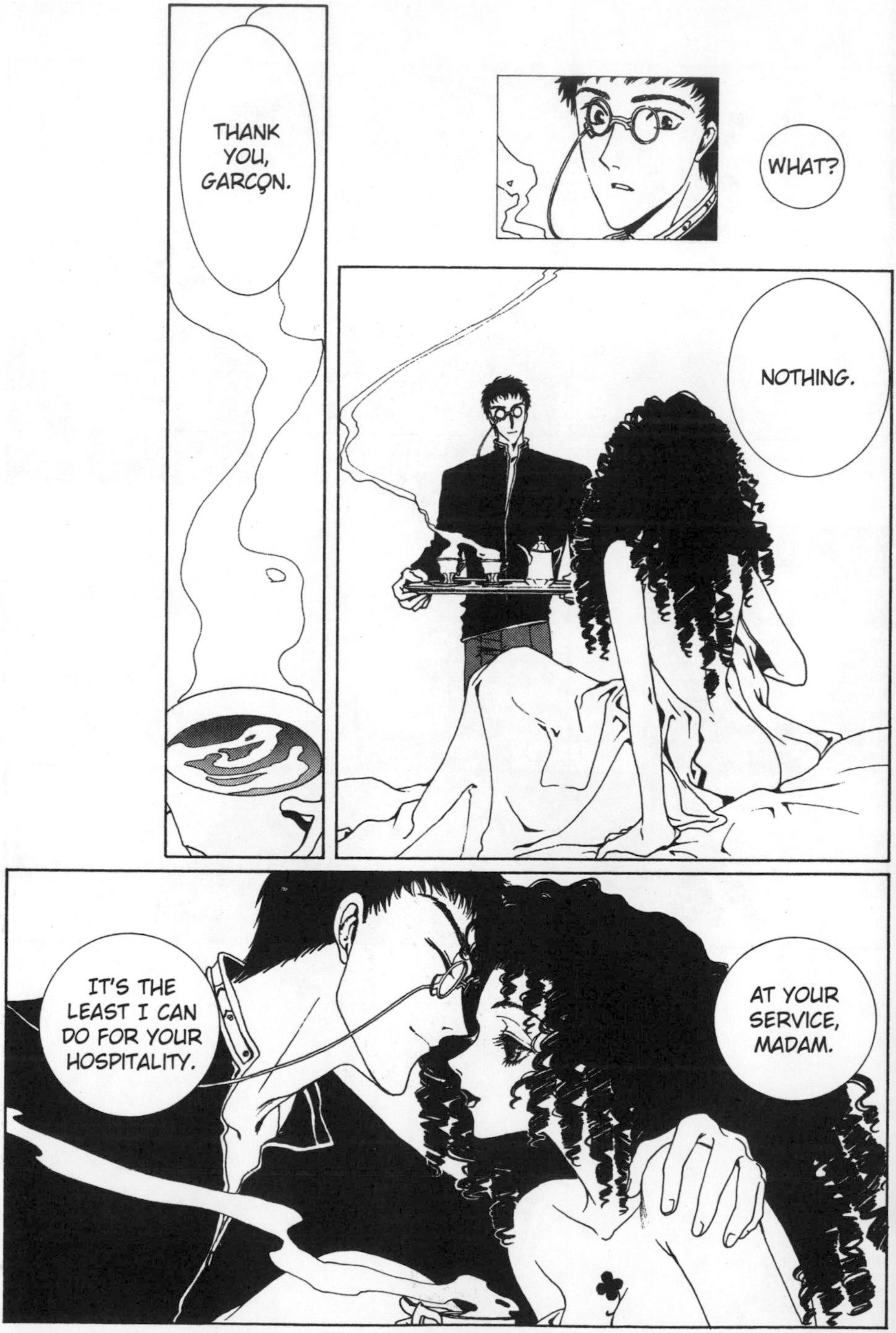
THANK YOU, GARÇON.
WHAT?
NOTHING.
IT'S THE LEAST I CAN DO FOR YOUR HOSPITALITY.
AT YOUR SERVICE, MADAM.

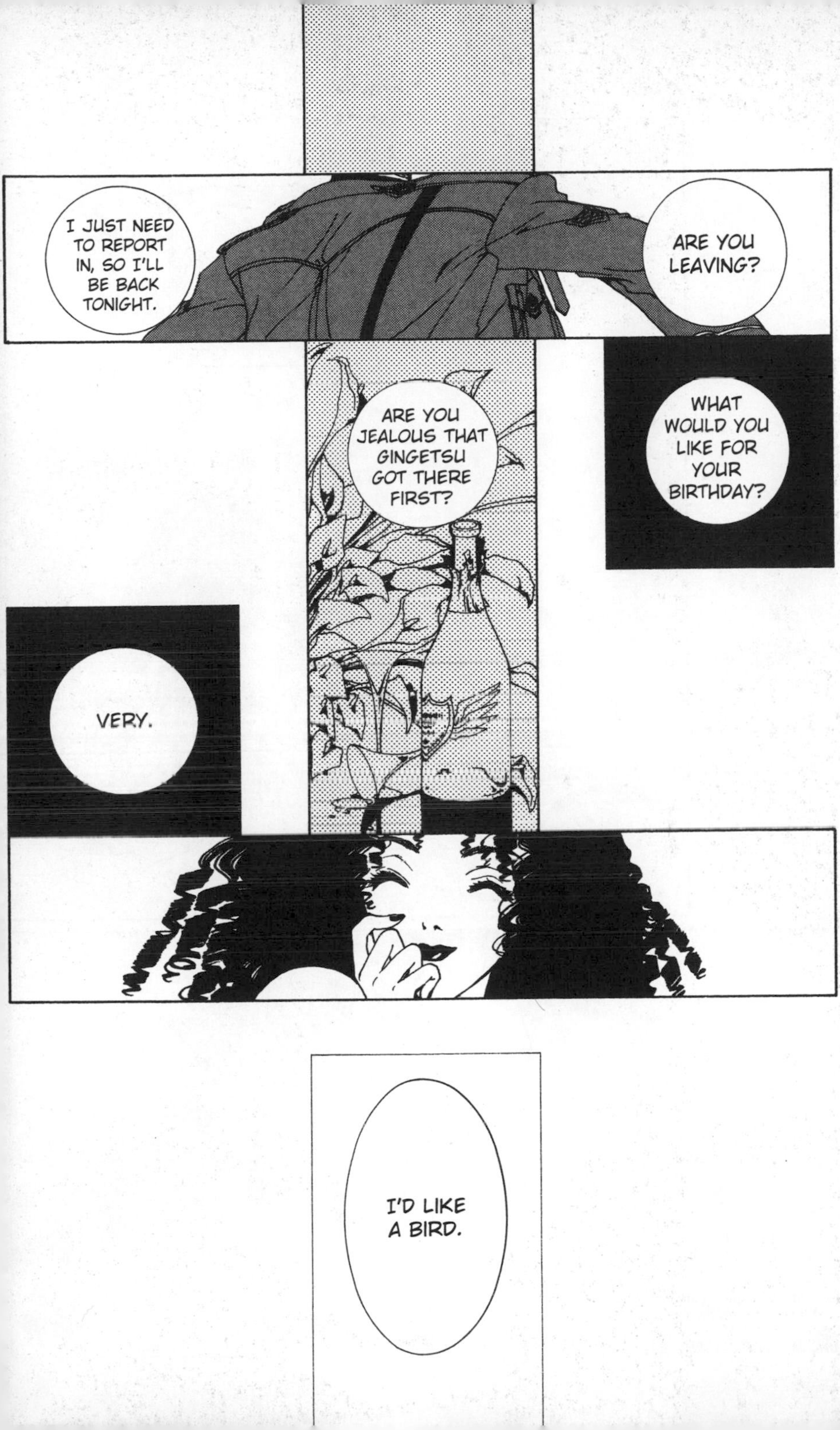
ARE YOU LEAVING?
I JUST NEED TO REPORT IN, SO I'LL BE BACK TONIGHT.
ARE YOU JEALOUS THAT GINGETSU GOT THERE FIRST?
VERY.
WHAT WOULD YOU LIKE FOR YOUR BIRTHDAY?
I'D LIKE A BIRD.

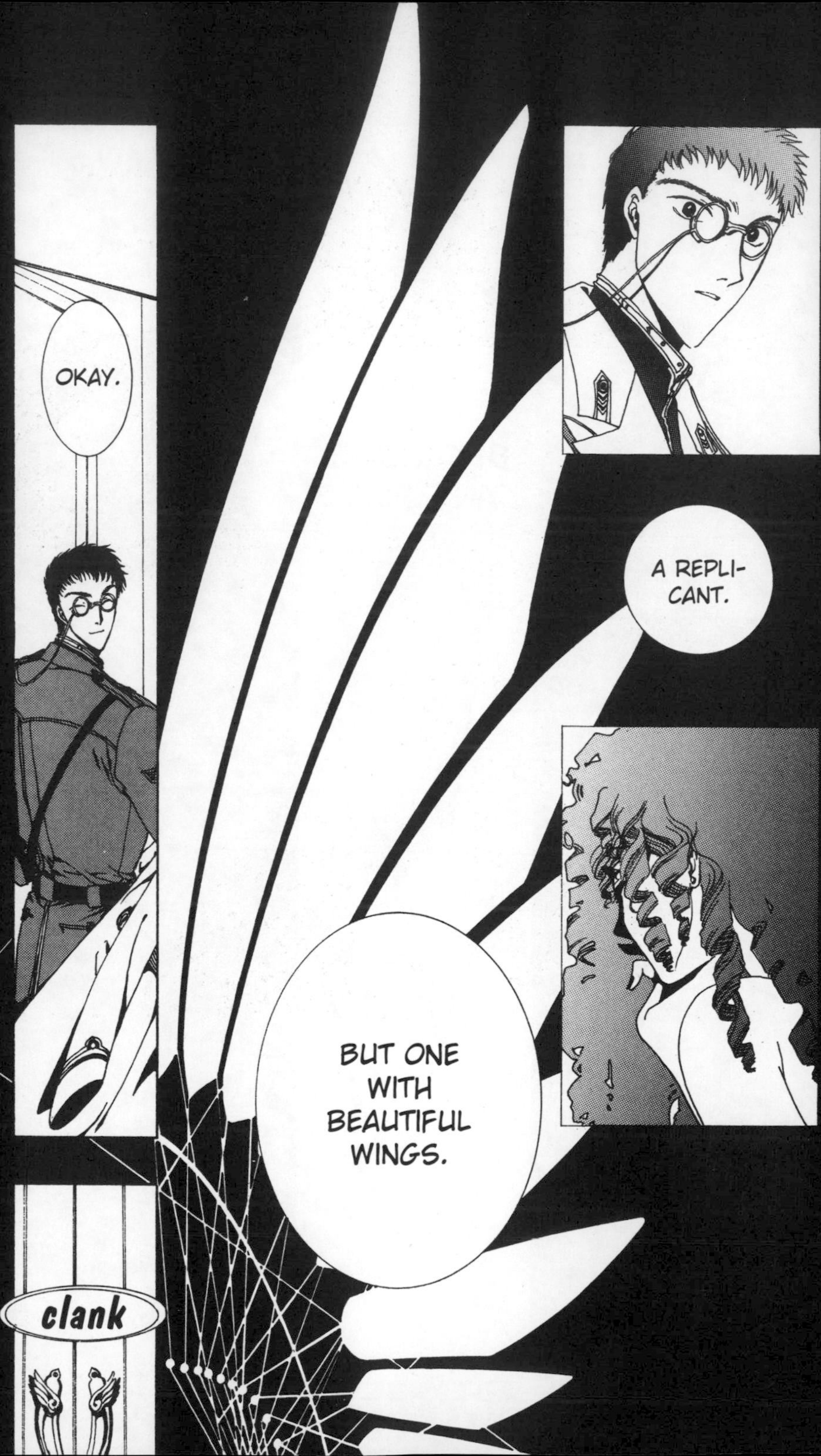
A REPLI-
CANT.
BUT ONE WITH BEAUTIFUL WINGS.
OKAY.
clank

BECAUSE I CAN'T FLY...

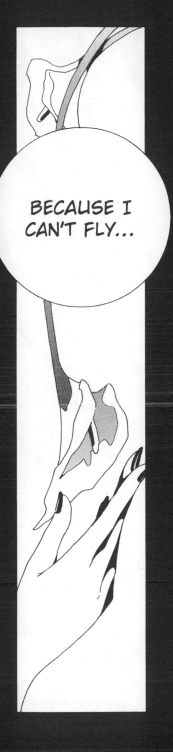

『きこえる』

I CAN HEAR

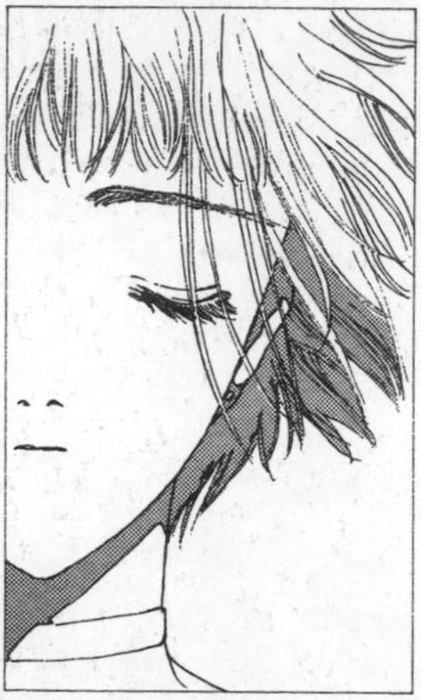

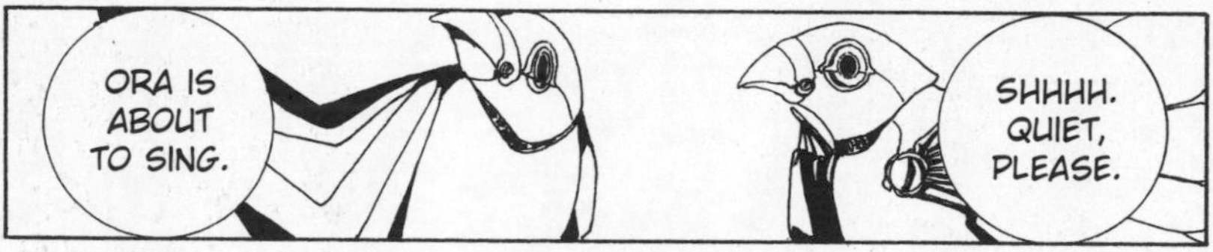
SHHHH. QUIET, PLEASE.
ORA IS ABOUT TO SING.

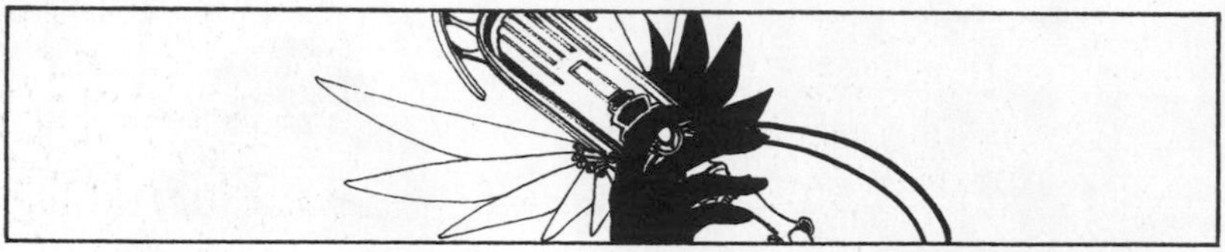

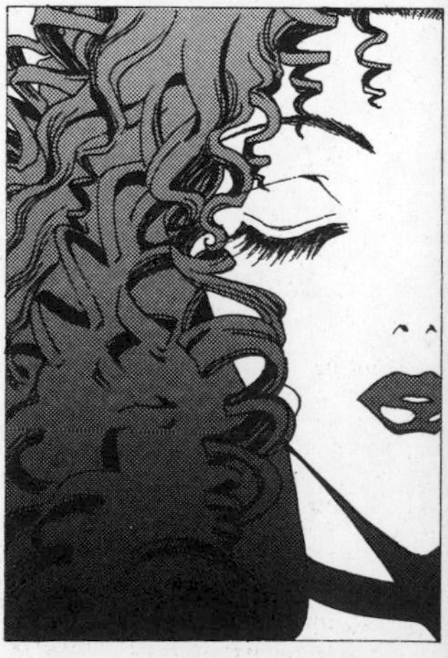

『はじまる』

THE BEGINNING

LOVE
It's my dream

A beautiful dream
Never before seen

A beautiful deceit
Never caught

A beautiful love
That no one can break

LOVE

You might laugh
But it's the most
beautiful word

『誰(だれ)

も

知(し)

ら

DUET

な

NO ONE

い

KNOWS

二(デュ)

重(エッ)

唱(ト)』

God, please
show me
The deepest red
The truest love

Now
come close
to me
I'll sing
an endless
song

LOVE

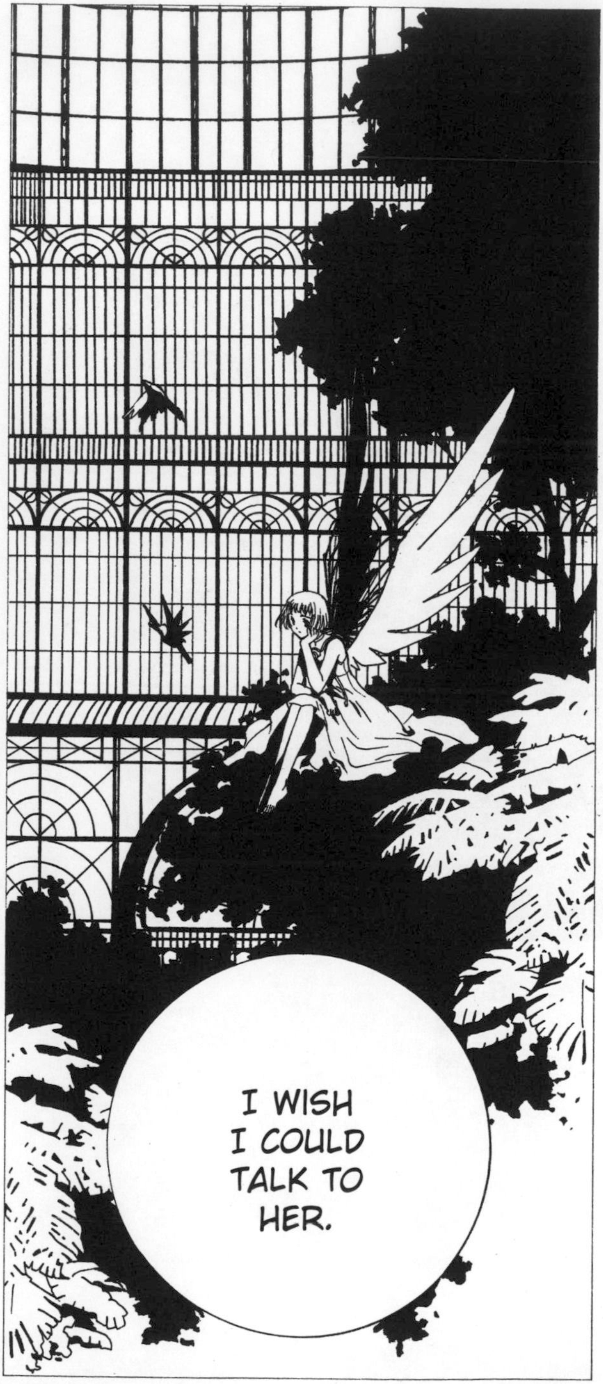
I WISH I COULD TALK TO HER.

『魚(さかな)

FISH

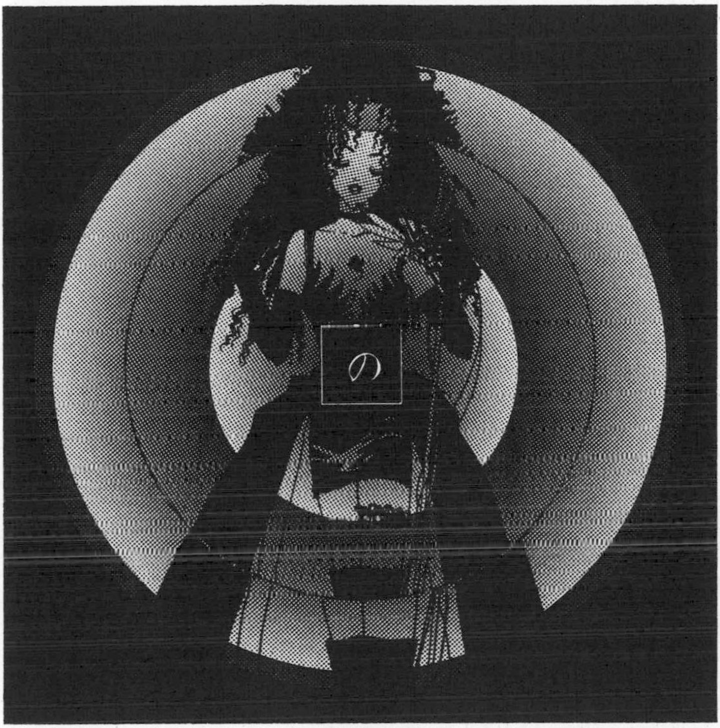
の

EYE

目(め)』

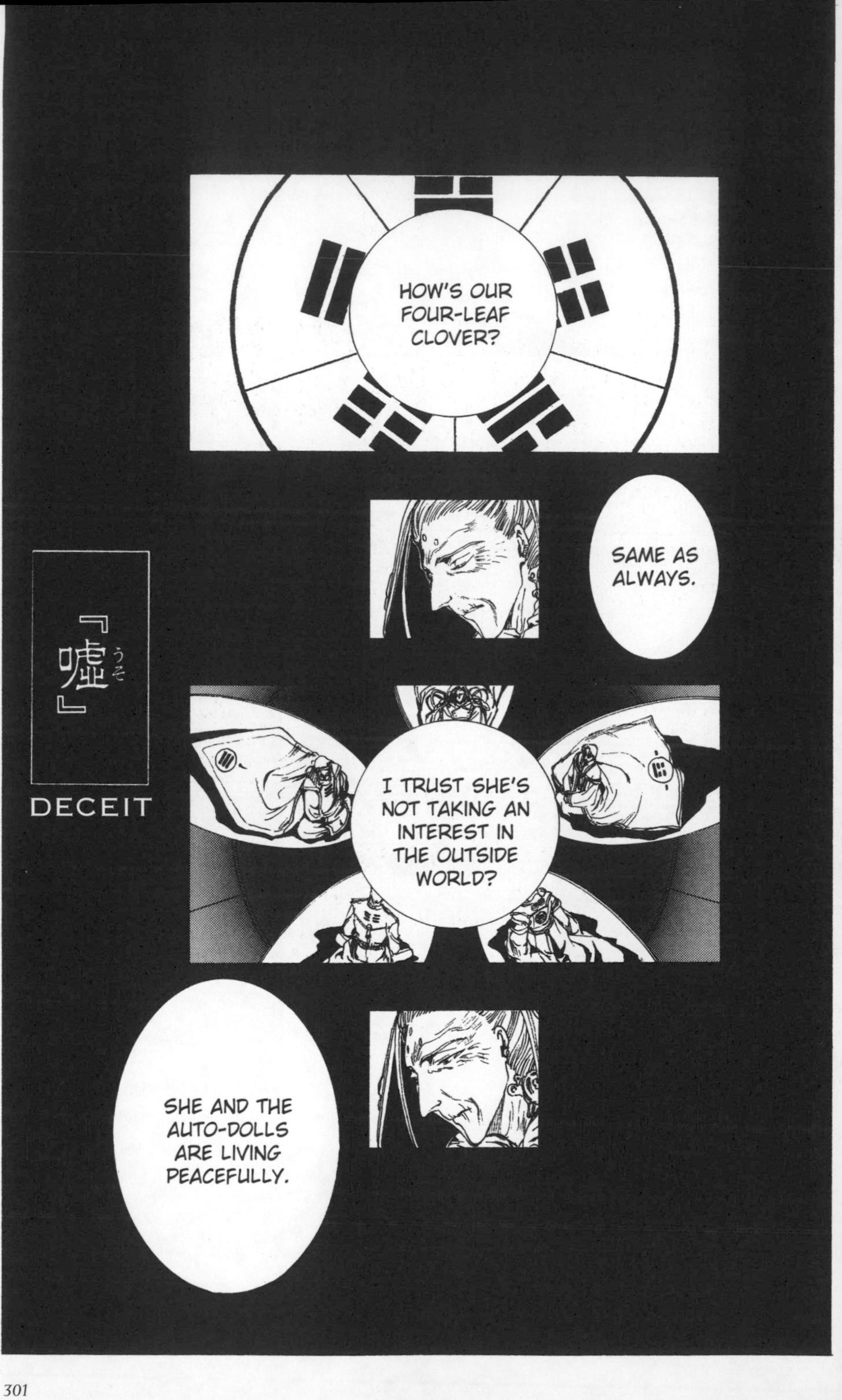
『嘘うそ』
DECEIT
HOW'S OUR FOUR-LEAF CLOVER?
SAME AS ALWAYS.
I TRUST SHE'S NOT TAKING AN INTEREST IN THE OUTSIDE WORLD?
SHE AND THE AUTO-DOLLS ARE LIVING PEACEFULLY.

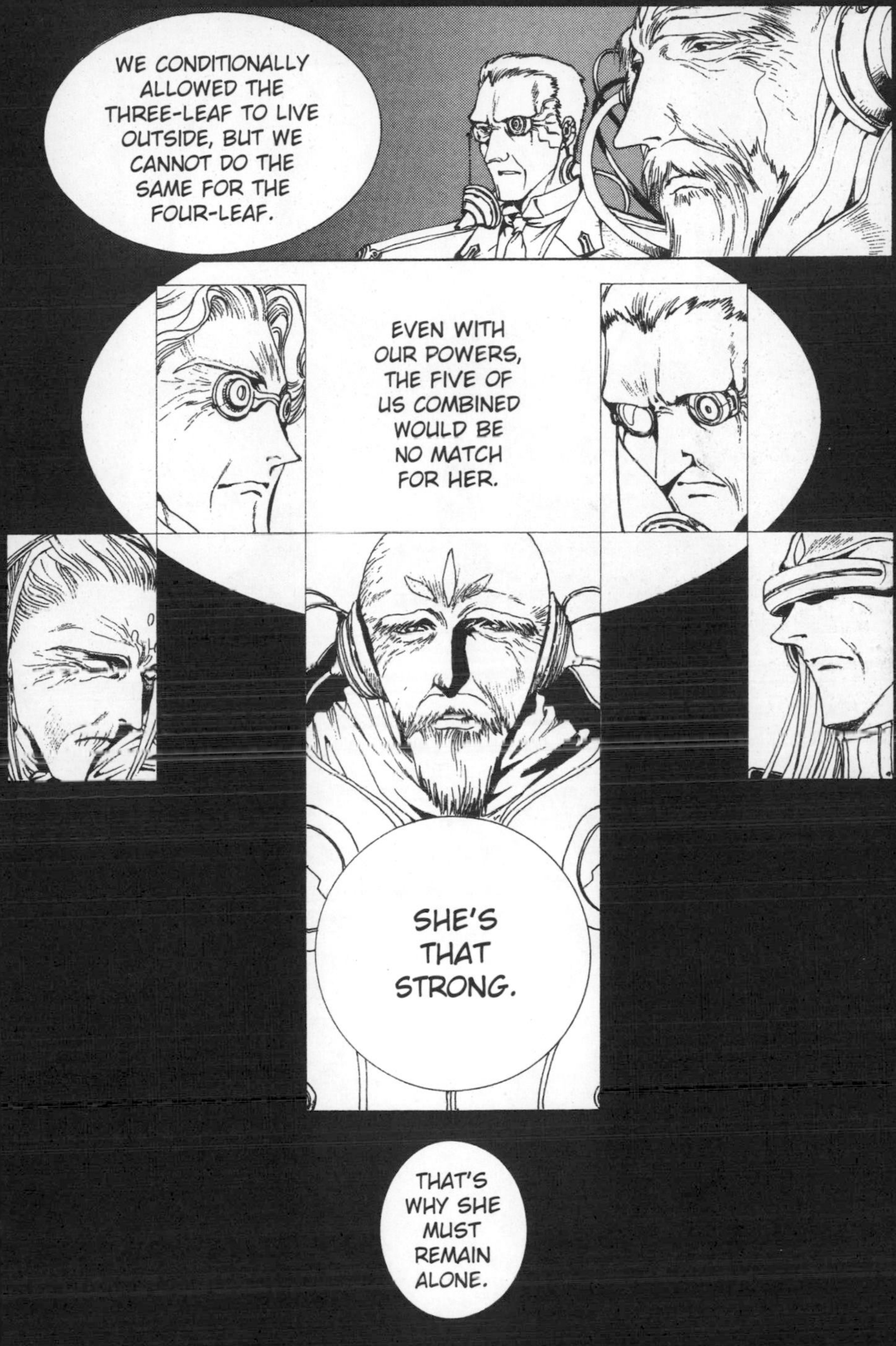
WE CONDITIONALLY ALLOWED THE THREE-LEAF TO LIVE OUTSIDE, BUT WE CANNOT DO THE SAME FOR THE FOUR-LEAF.
EVEN WITH OUR POWERS, THE FIVE OF US COMBINED WOULD BE NO MATCH FOR HER.
SHE'S THAT STRONG.
THAT'S WHY SHE MUST REMAIN ALONE.

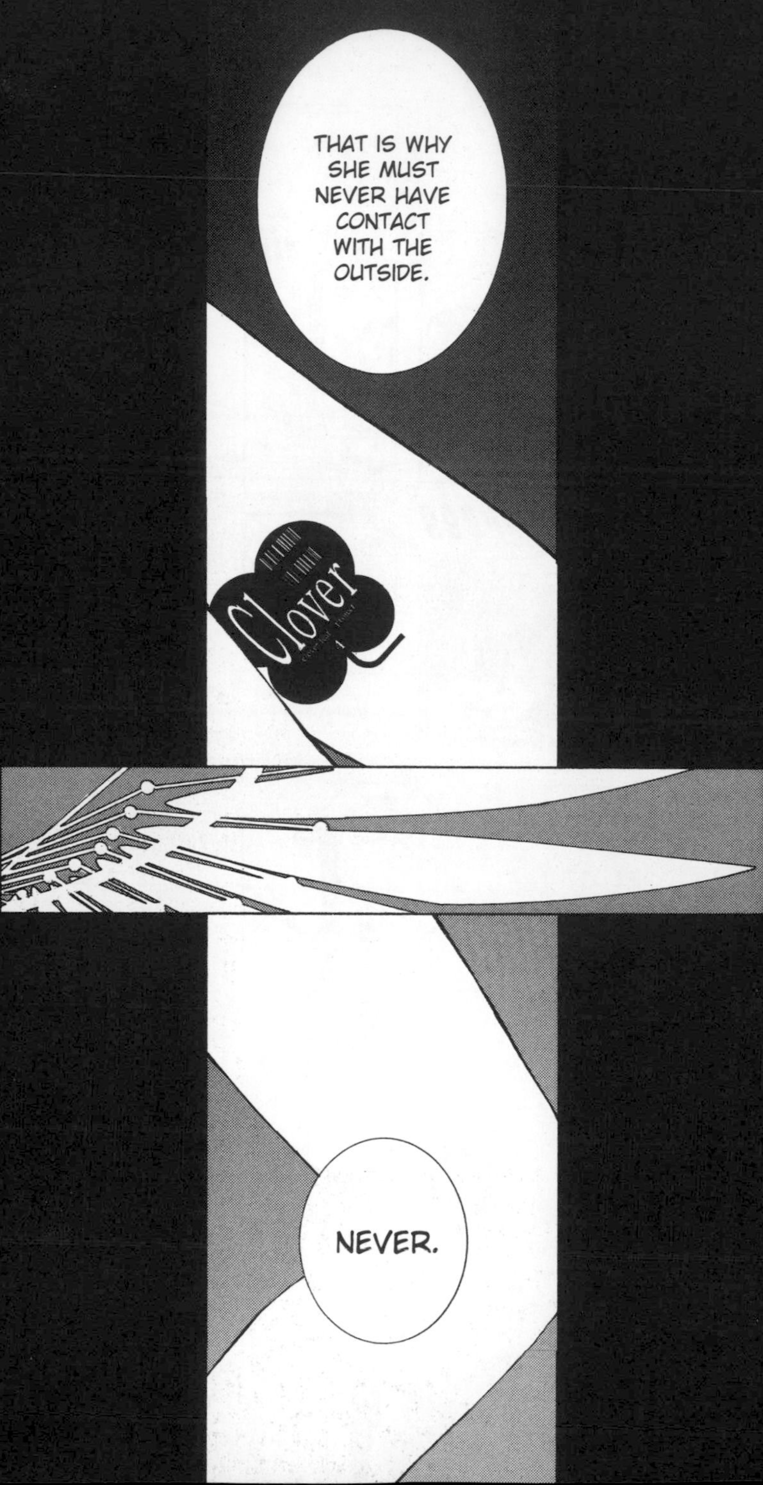
THAT IS WHY SHE MUST NEVER HAVE CONTACT WITH THE OUTSIDE.
Clover
NEVER.

『小鳥から小鳥への電話』

CALL FROM BIRD TO BIRD

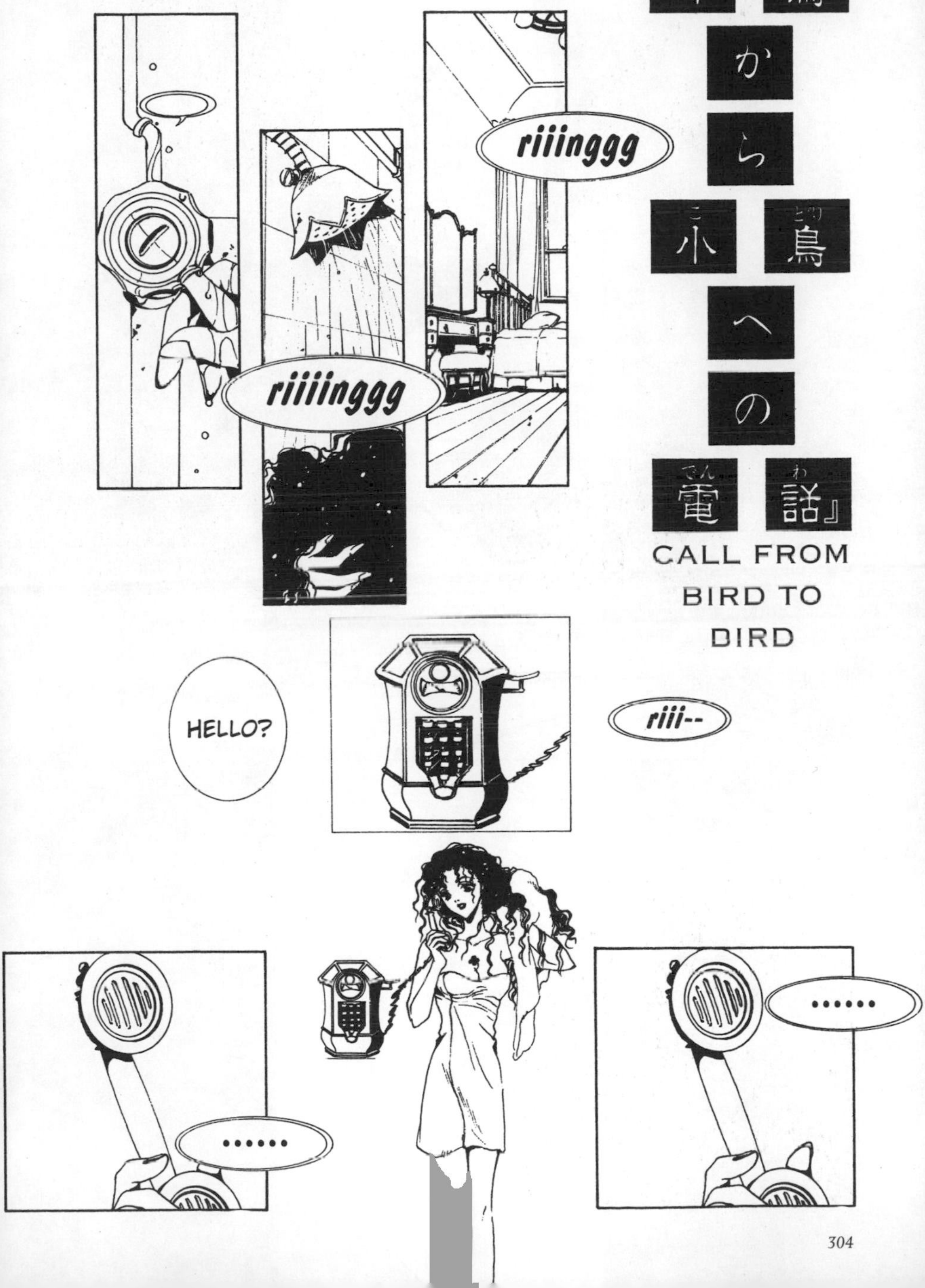
riiinggg
riiiinggg
riii--
HELLO?
......
......

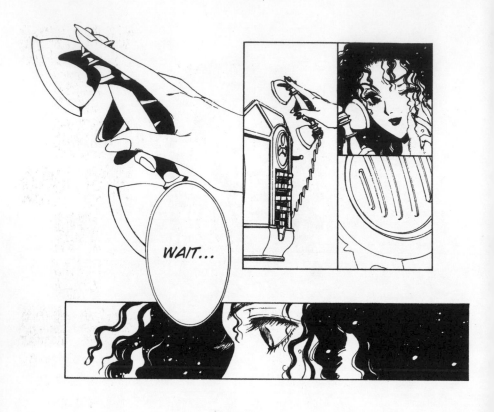

WAIT...

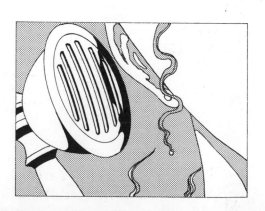

...I'M A BIG FAN OF YOURS.

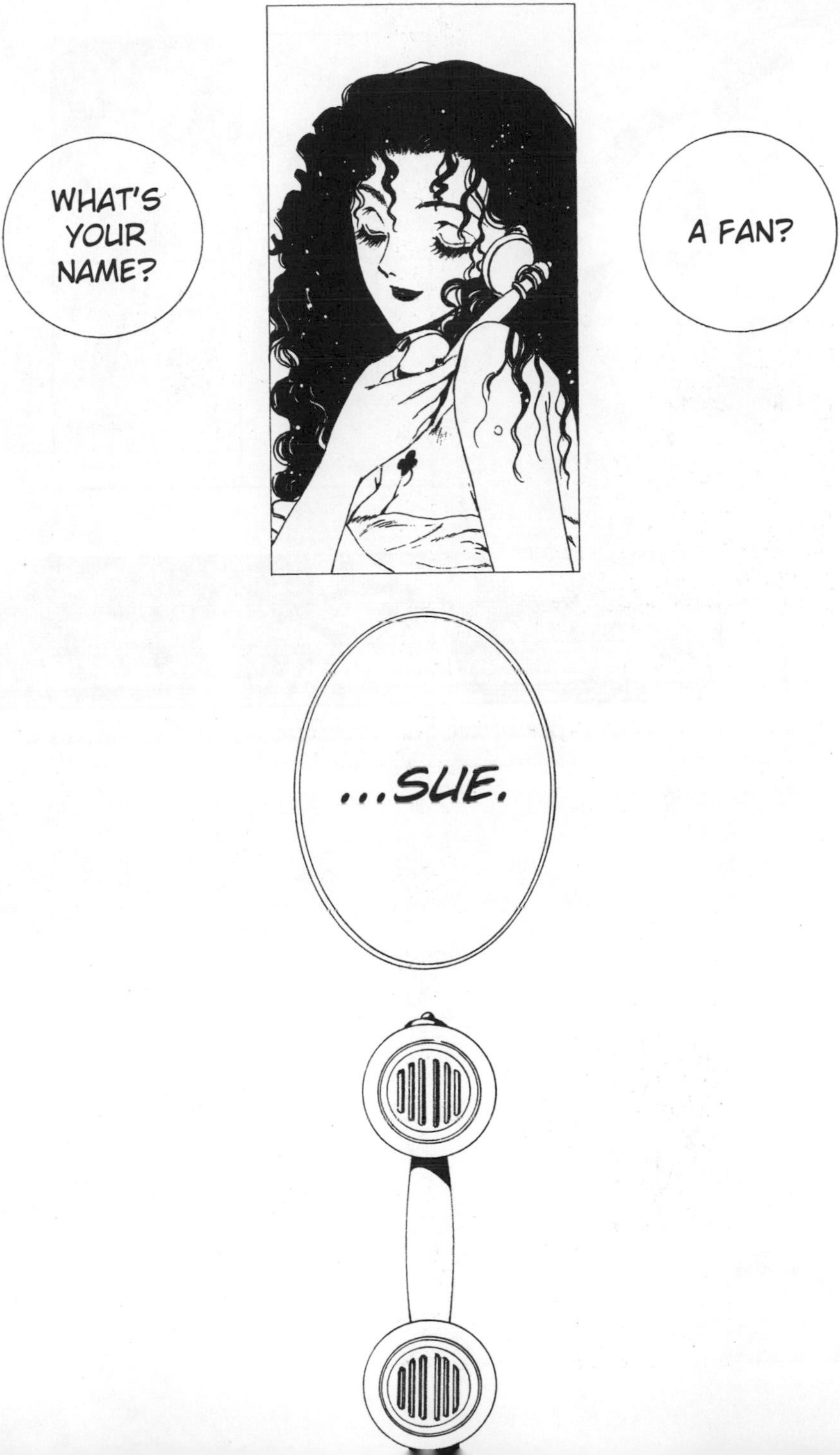
A FAN?
WHAT'S YOUR NAME?
...SUE.

『小鳥に贈られる小鳥』

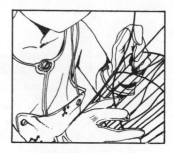

GIFT FROM

BIRD TO

BIRD

YOU'RE
VERY
GOOD AT
THAT.

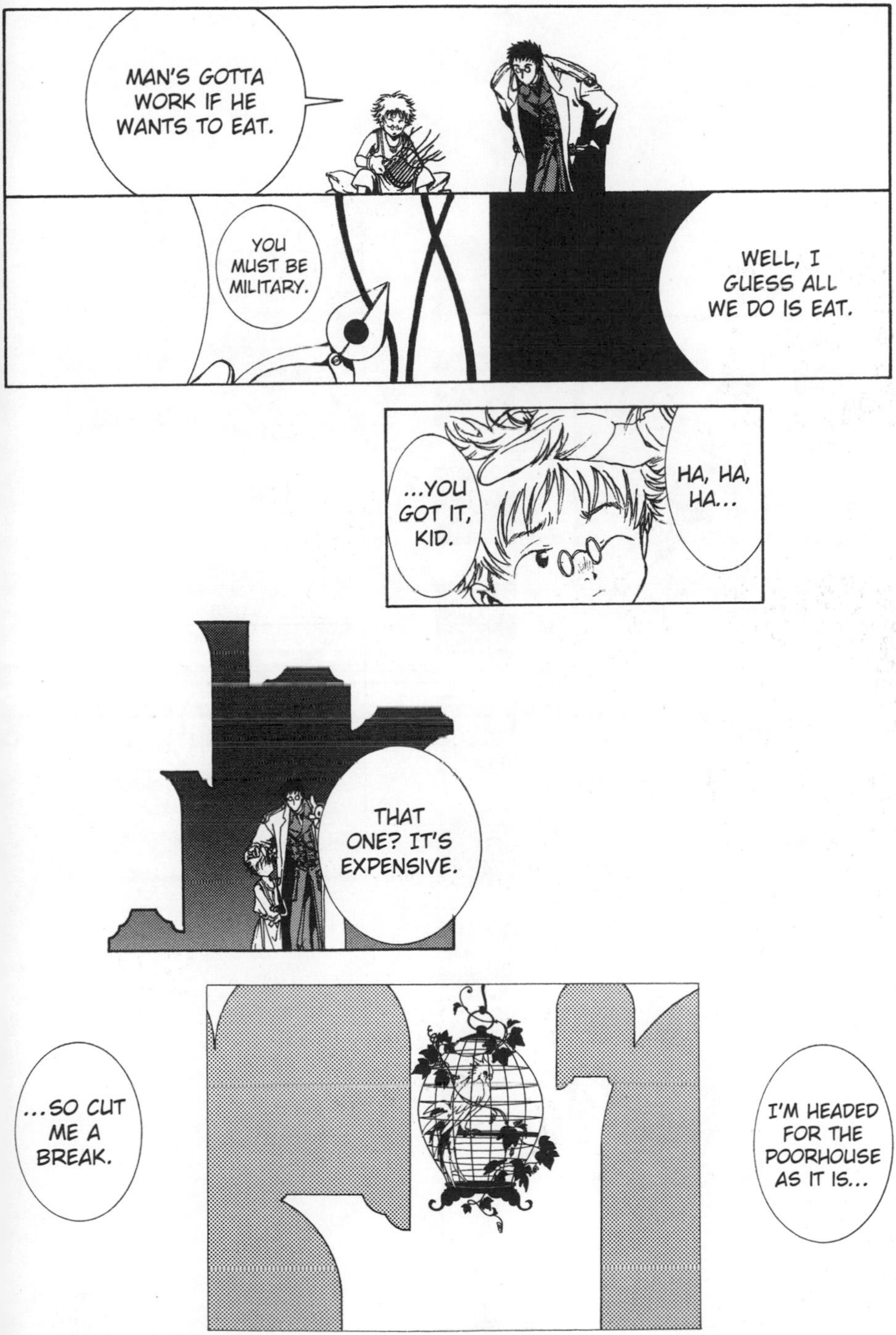
MAN'S GOTTA WORK IF HE WANTS TO EAT.
WELL, I GUESS ALL WE DO IS EAT.
YOU MUST BE MILITARY.
HA, HA, HA...
...YOU GOT IT, KID.
THAT ONE? IT'S EXPENSIVE.
I'M HEADED FOR THE POORHOUSE AS IT IS...
...SO CUT ME A BREAK.

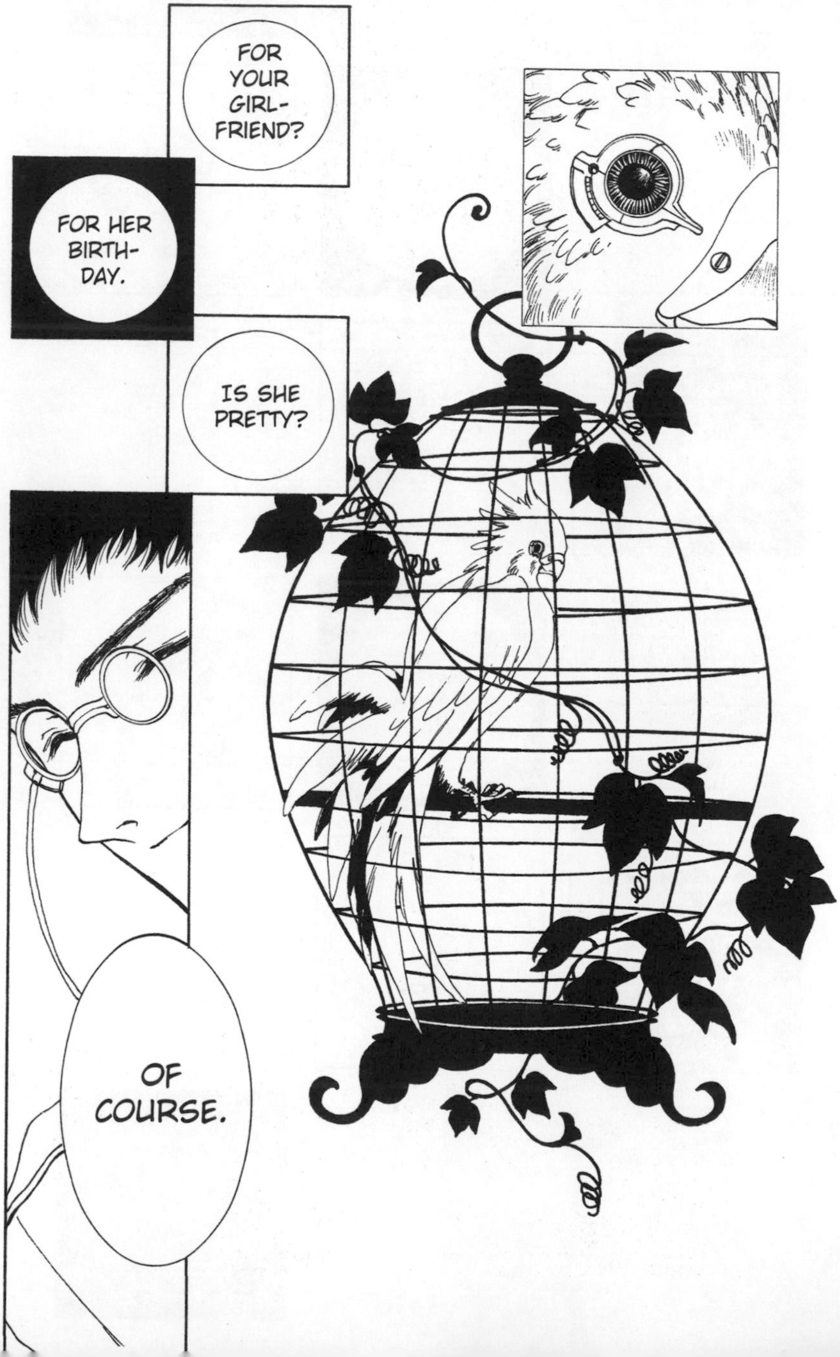
FOR YOUR GIRL-FRIEND?
FOR HER BIRTH-DAY.
IS SHE PRETTY?
OF COURSE.

CONTACT

 I'M SORRY TO CALL YOU AT HOME.

 HOW DID YOU GET THIS NUMBER?

 ARE YOU MAD AT ME?

 I APPRECIATE MY FEMALE FANS.

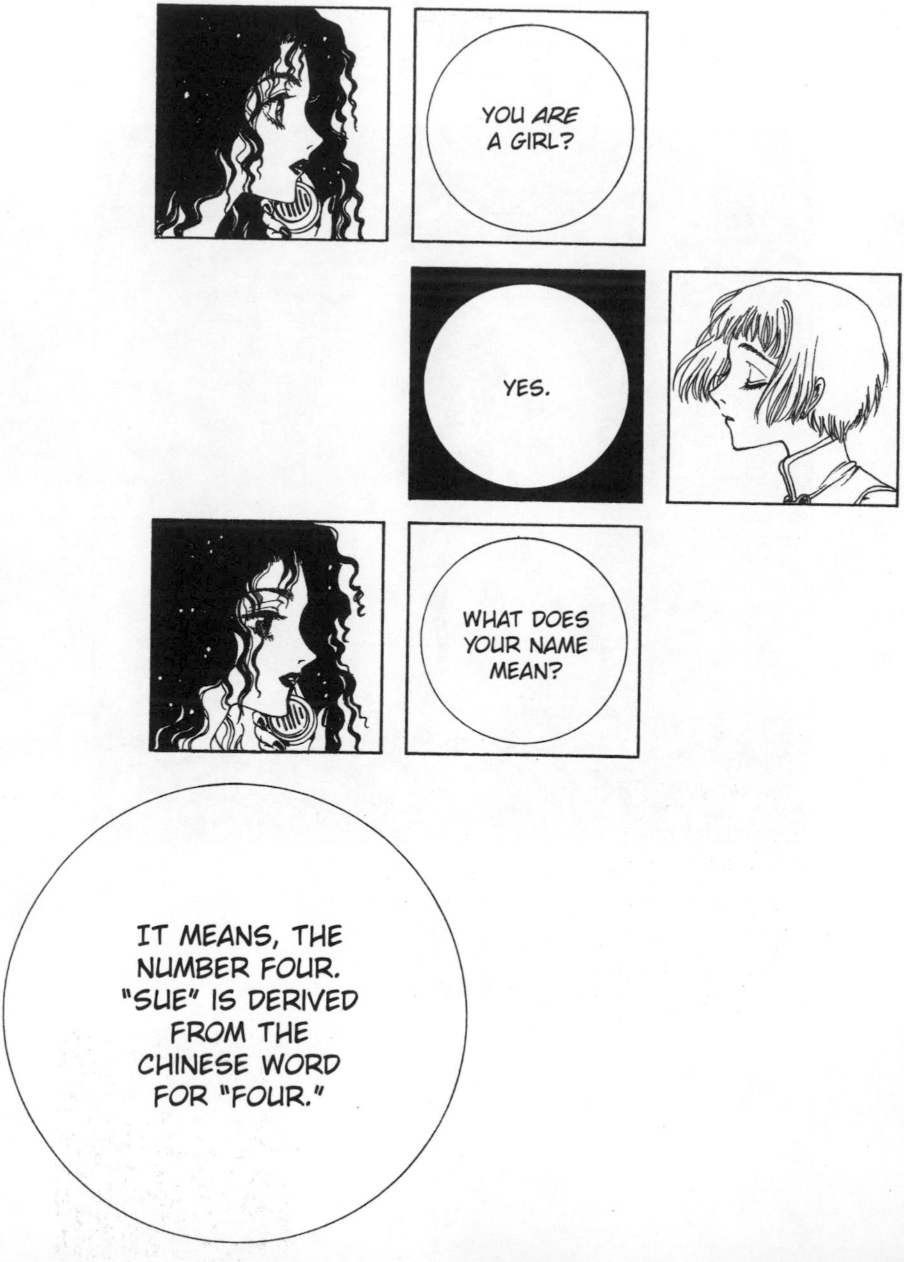
YOU ARE A GIRL?
YES.
WHAT DOES YOUR NAME MEAN?
IT MEANS, THE NUMBER FOUR. "SUE" IS DERIVED FROM THE CHINESE WORD FOR "FOUR."

『猫
CAT'S

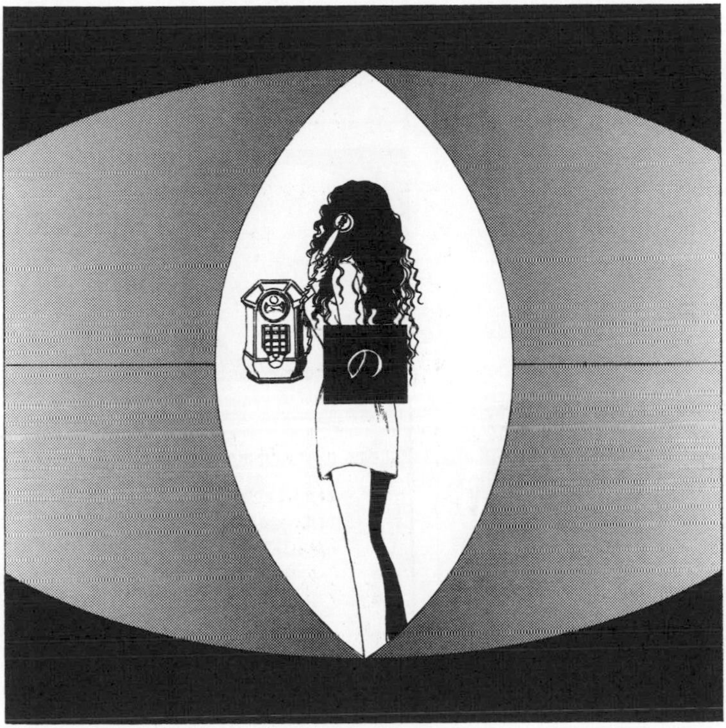
の

EYE
目』

『約束』

PROMISE

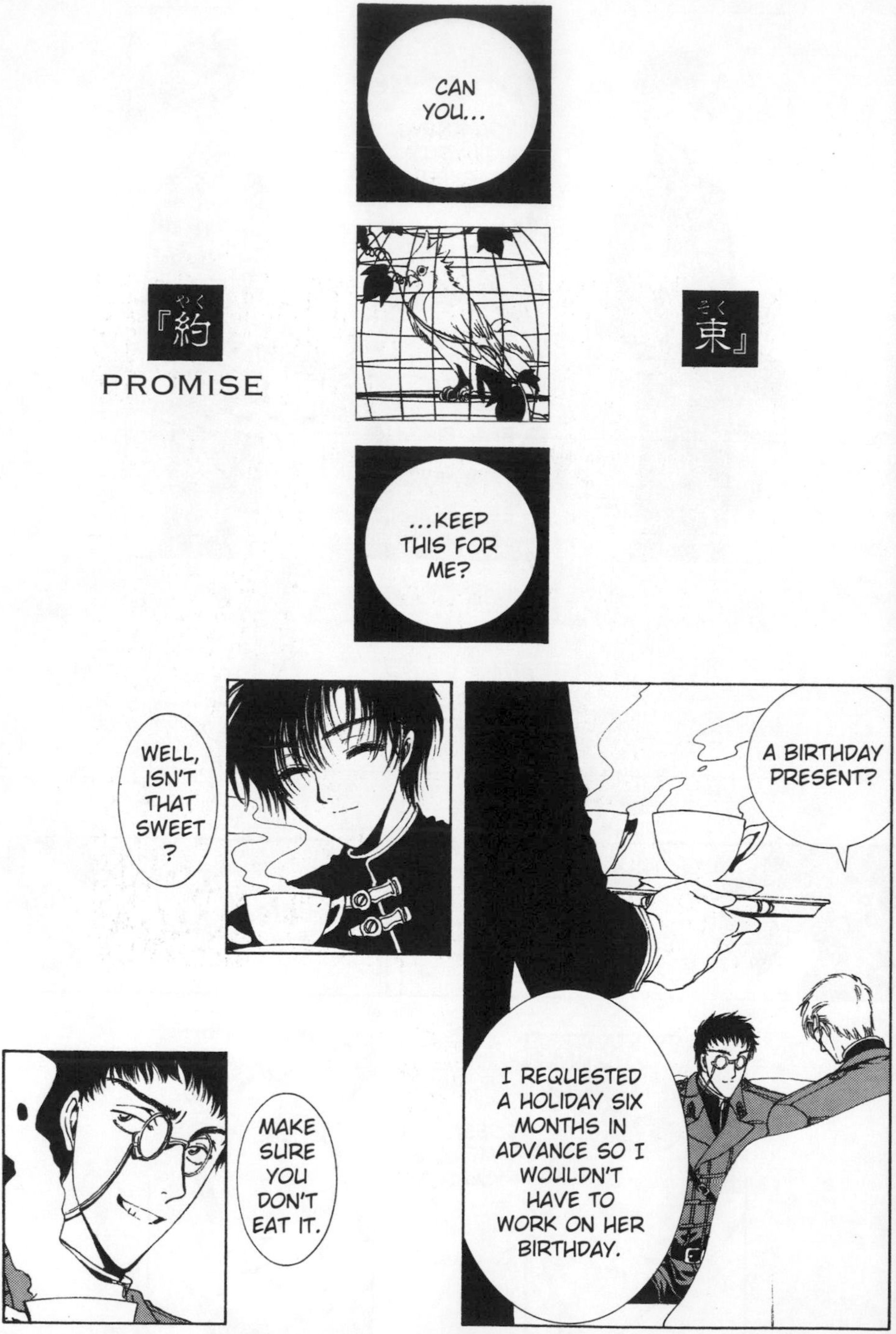

CAN YOU...
...KEEP THIS FOR ME?
A BIRTHDAY PRESENT?
WELL, ISN'T THAT SWEET?
I REQUESTED A HOLIDAY SIX MONTHS IN ADVANCE SO I WOULDN'T HAVE TO WORK ON HER BIRTHDAY.
MAKE SURE YOU DON'T EAT IT.

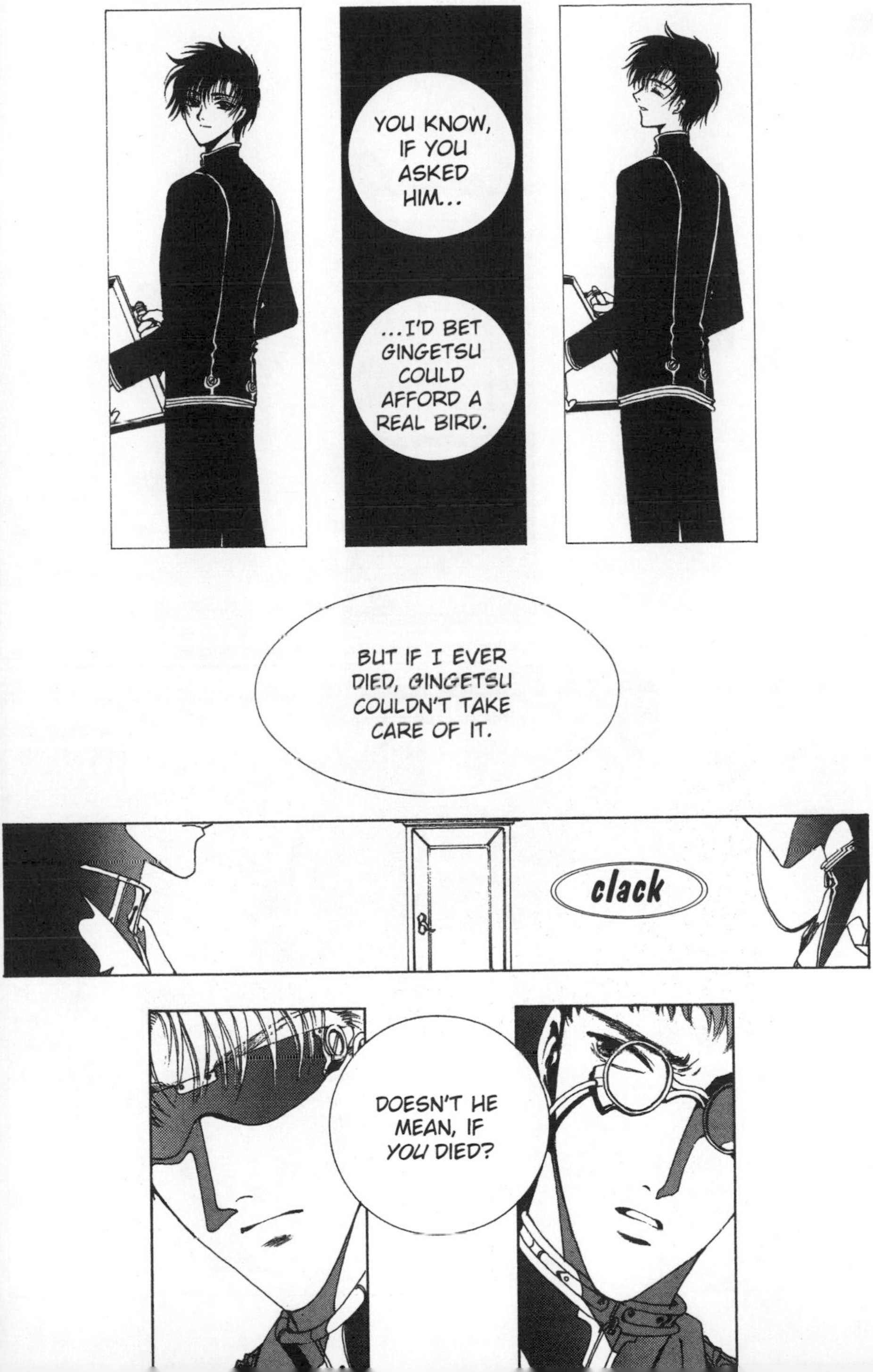
YOU KNOW, IF YOU ASKED HIM...
...I'D BET GINGETSU COULD AFFORD A REAL BIRD.
BUT IF I EVER DIED, GINGETSU COULDN'T TAKE CARE OF IT.
clack
DOESN'T HE MEAN, IF *YOU* DIED?

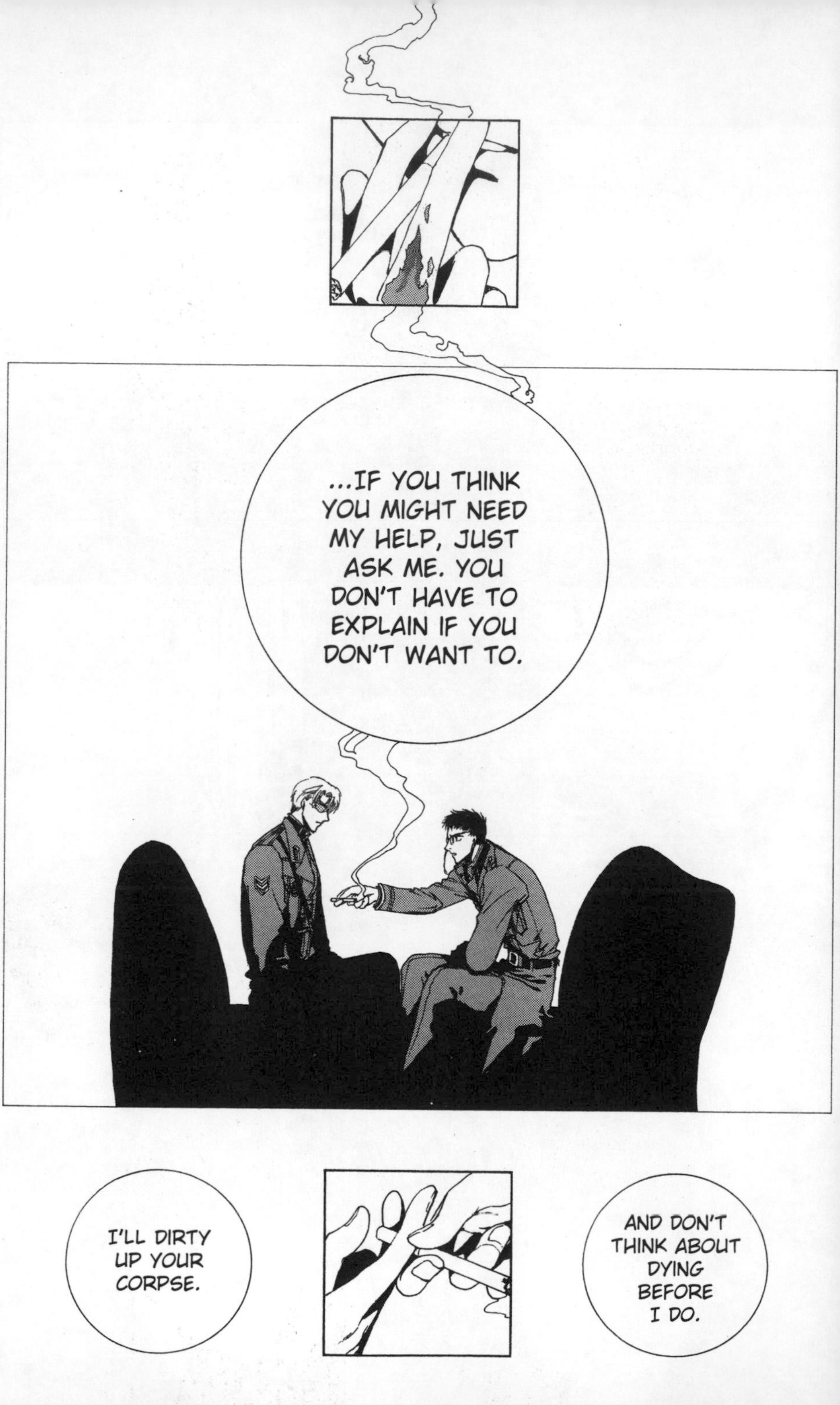
...IF YOU THINK YOU MIGHT NEED MY HELP, JUST ASK ME. YOU DON'T HAVE TO EXPLAIN IF YOU DON'T WANT TO.
AND DON'T THINK ABOUT DYING BEFORE I DO.
I'LL DIRTY UP YOUR CORPSE.

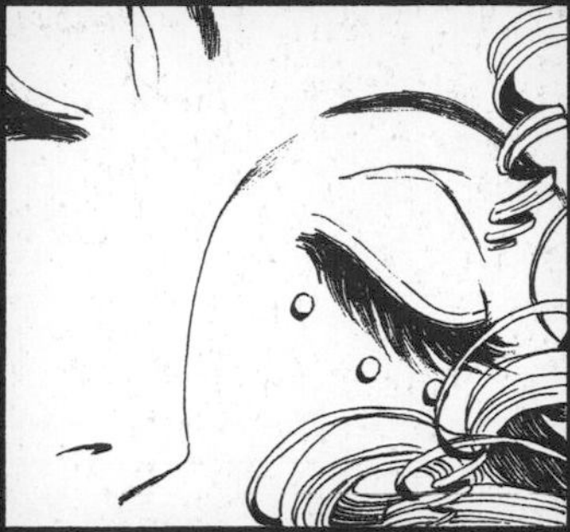
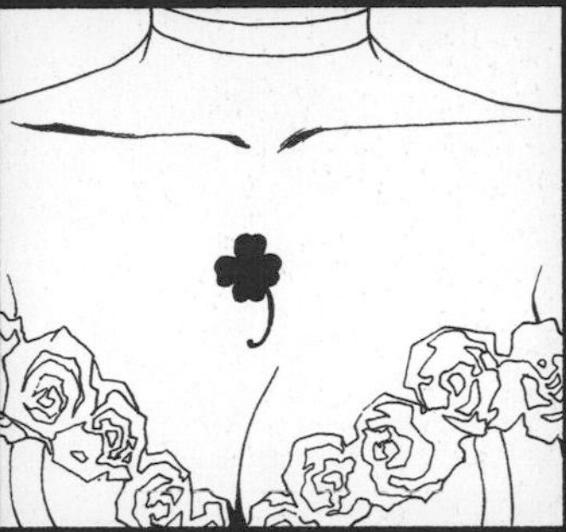

It's my dream

ONSTAGE

『舞台（ステージ）』

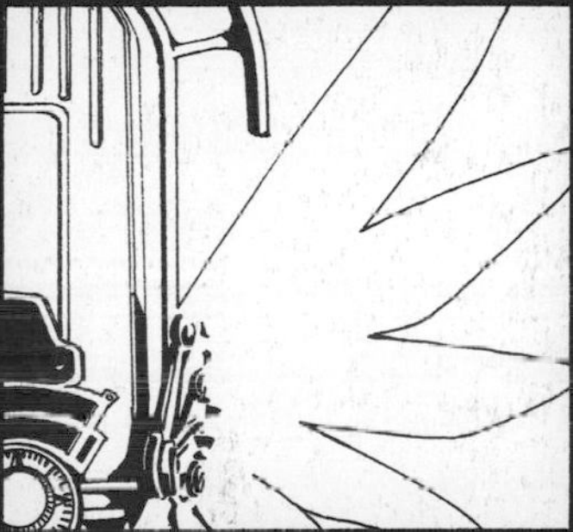
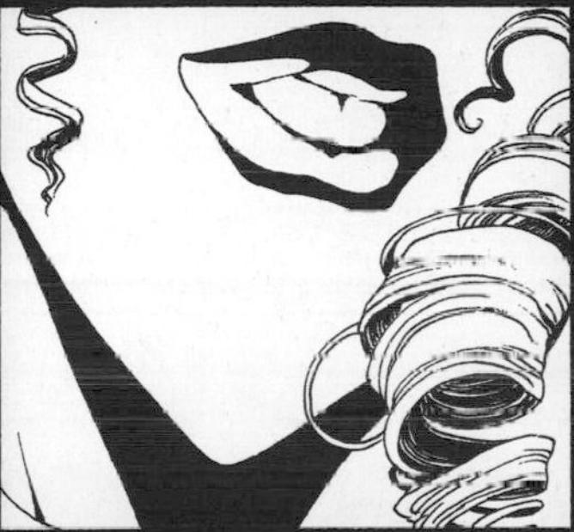

A wonderful soul
Whom everyone admires

A wonderful moment
Which everyone desires

A wonderful romance
What everyone dreams of

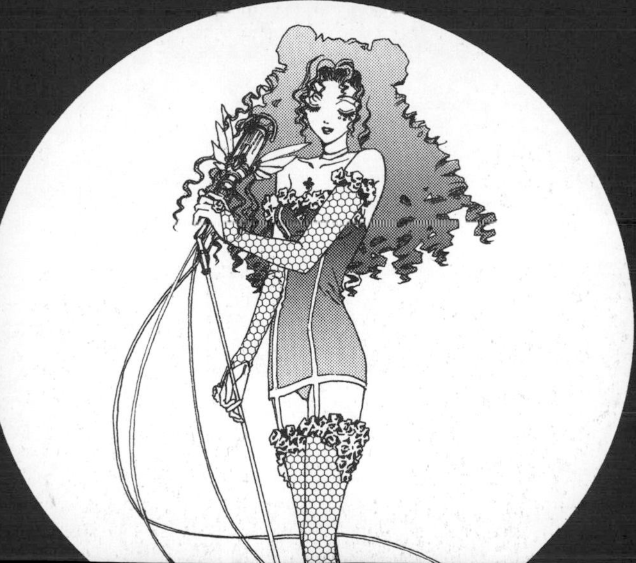

LOVE

True love is unmatched

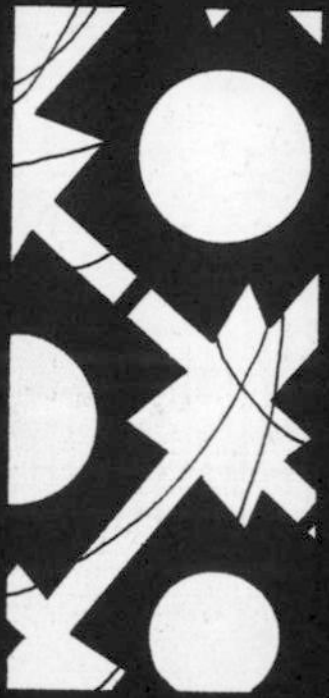

LOVE

You might laugh

But once lost, it never returns

LOVE

You might laugh

But to us, the most

important word

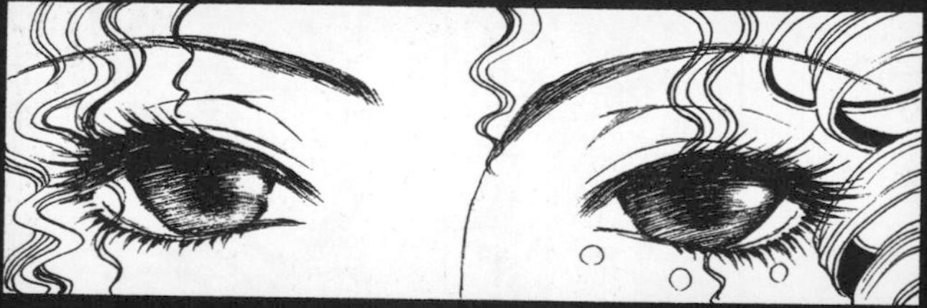

LOVE

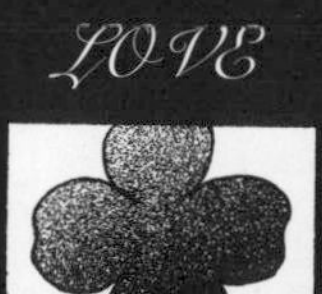

『小鳥の内緒話』

A BIRD'S SECRET

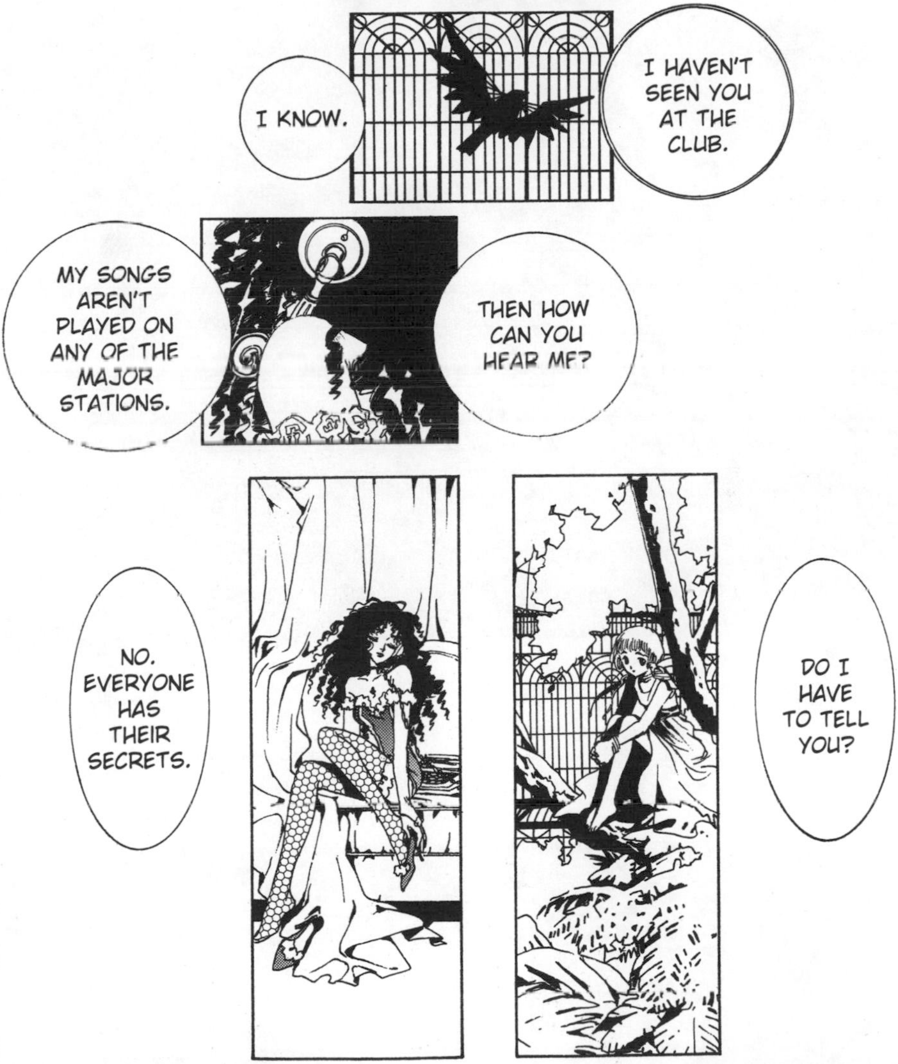
I HAVEN'T SEEN YOU AT THE CLUB.
I KNOW.
MY SONGS AREN'T PLAYED ON ANY OF THE MAJOR STATIONS.
THEN HOW CAN YOU HEAR ME?
DO I HAVE TO TELL YOU?
NO. EVERYONE HAS THEIR SECRETS.

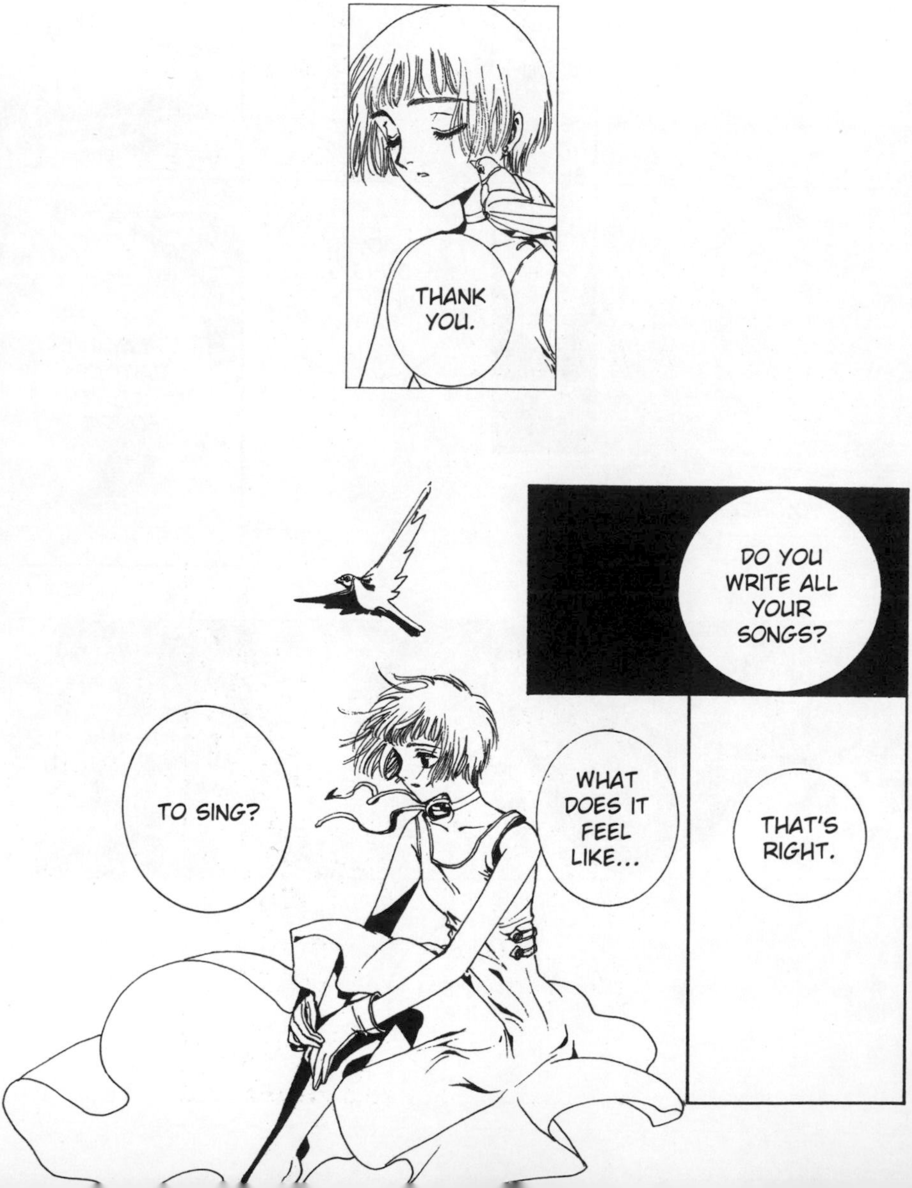
THANK YOU.
DO YOU WRITE ALL YOUR SONGS?
THAT'S RIGHT.
WHAT DOES IT FEEL LIKE...
TO SING?

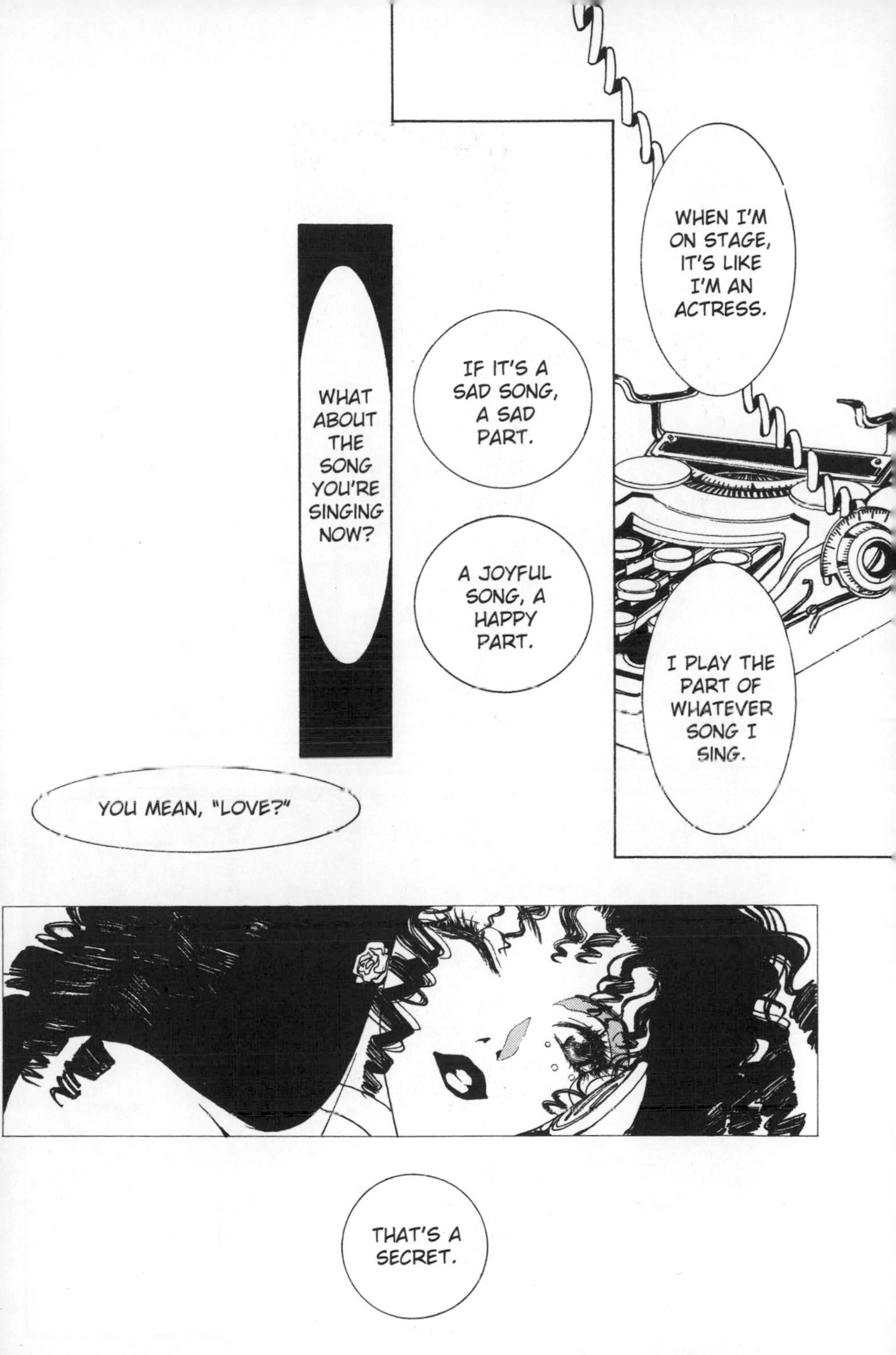
WHEN I'M ON STAGE, IT'S LIKE I'M AN ACTRESS.
I PLAY THE PART OF WHATEVER SONG I SING.
IF IT'S A SAD SONG, A SAD PART.
A JOYFUL SONG, A HAPPY PART.
WHAT ABOUT THE SONG YOU'RE SINGING NOW?
YOU MEAN, "LOVE?"
THAT'S A SECRET.

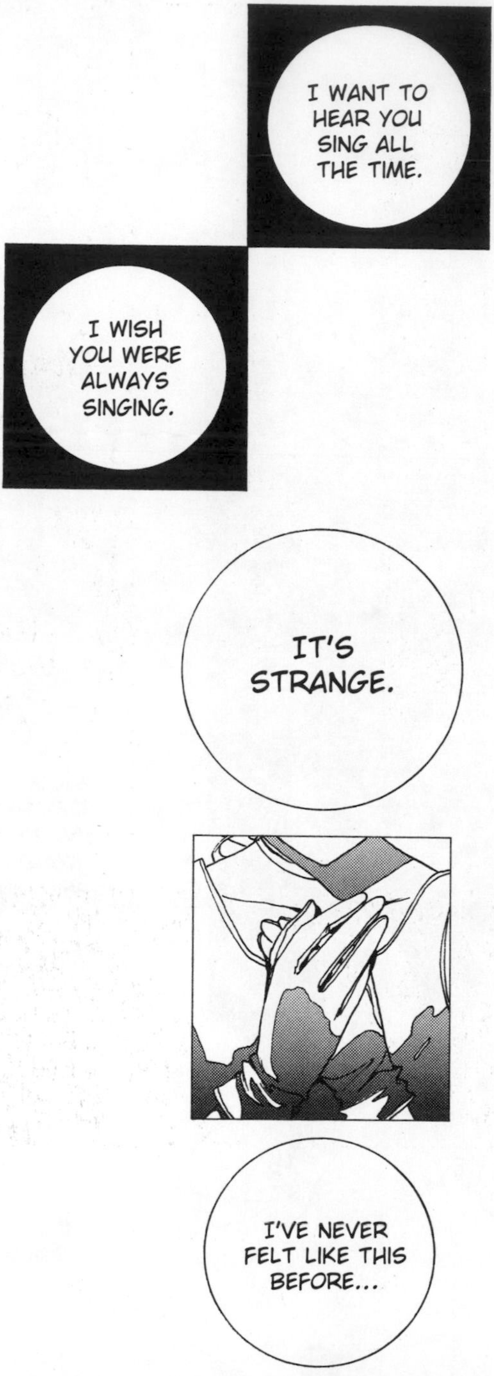

I WANT TO HEAR YOU SING ALL THE TIME.

I WISH YOU WERE ALWAYS SINGING.

IT'S STRANGE.

I'VE NEVER FELT LIKE THIS BEFORE...

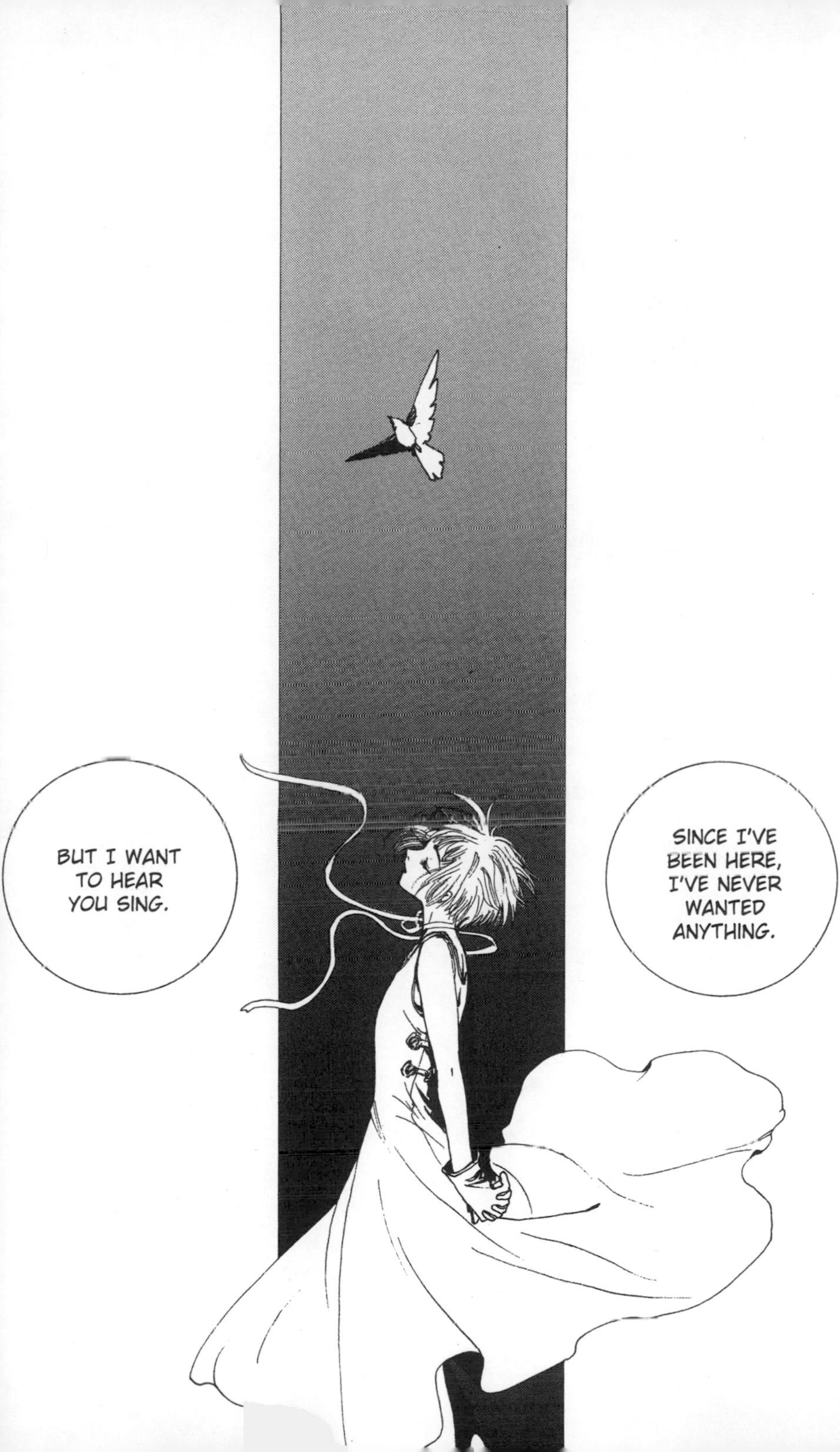
SINCE I'VE BEEN HERE, I'VE NEVER WANTED ANYTHING.
BUT I WANT TO HEAR YOU SING.

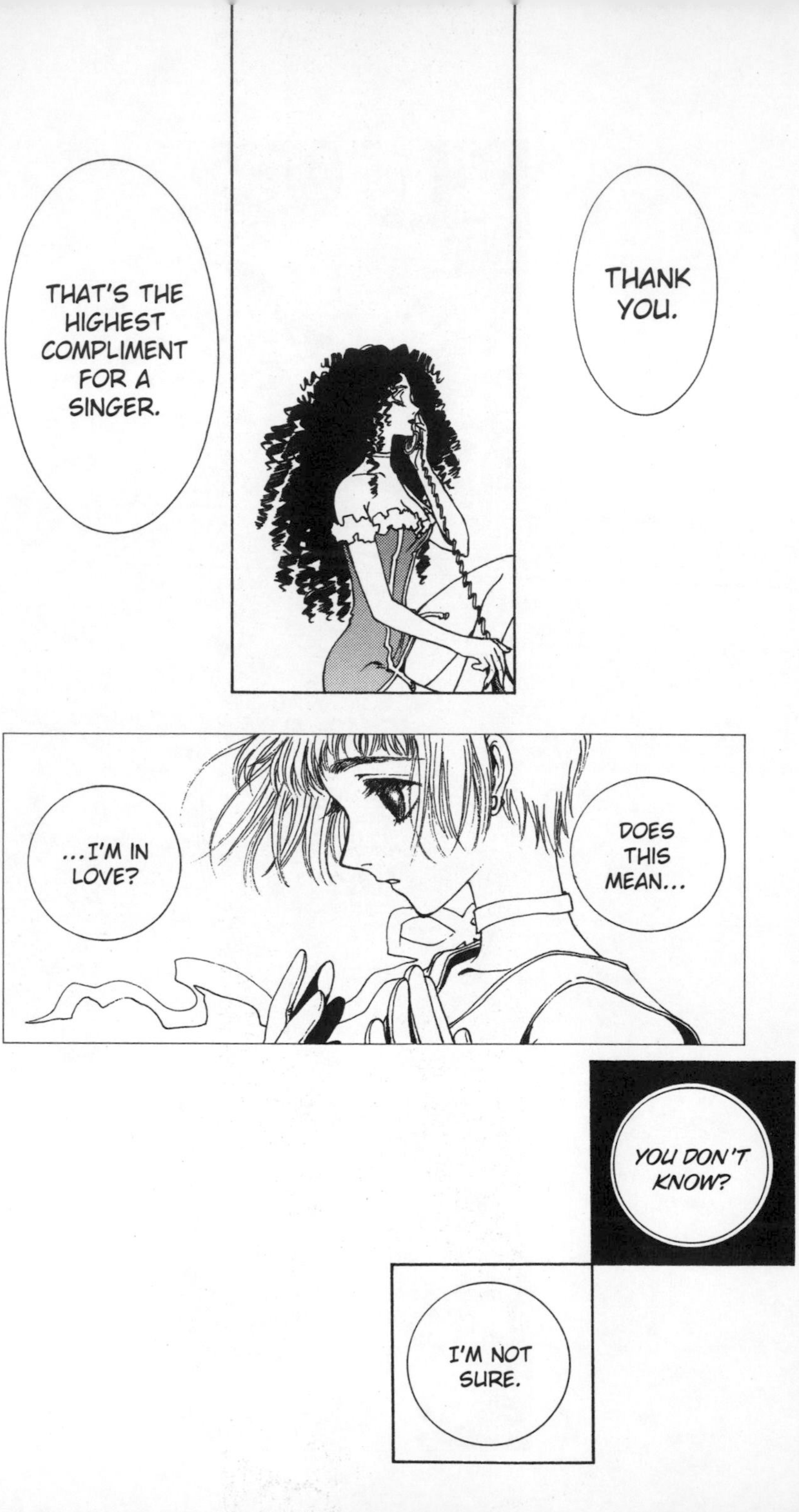
THANK YOU.
THAT'S THE HIGHEST COMPLIMENT FOR A SINGER.
DOES THIS MEAN...
...I'M IN LOVE?
YOU DON'T KNOW?
I'M NOT SURE.

IF YOUR
HEART SAYS
YES, THEN
YOU'RE IN
LOVE.

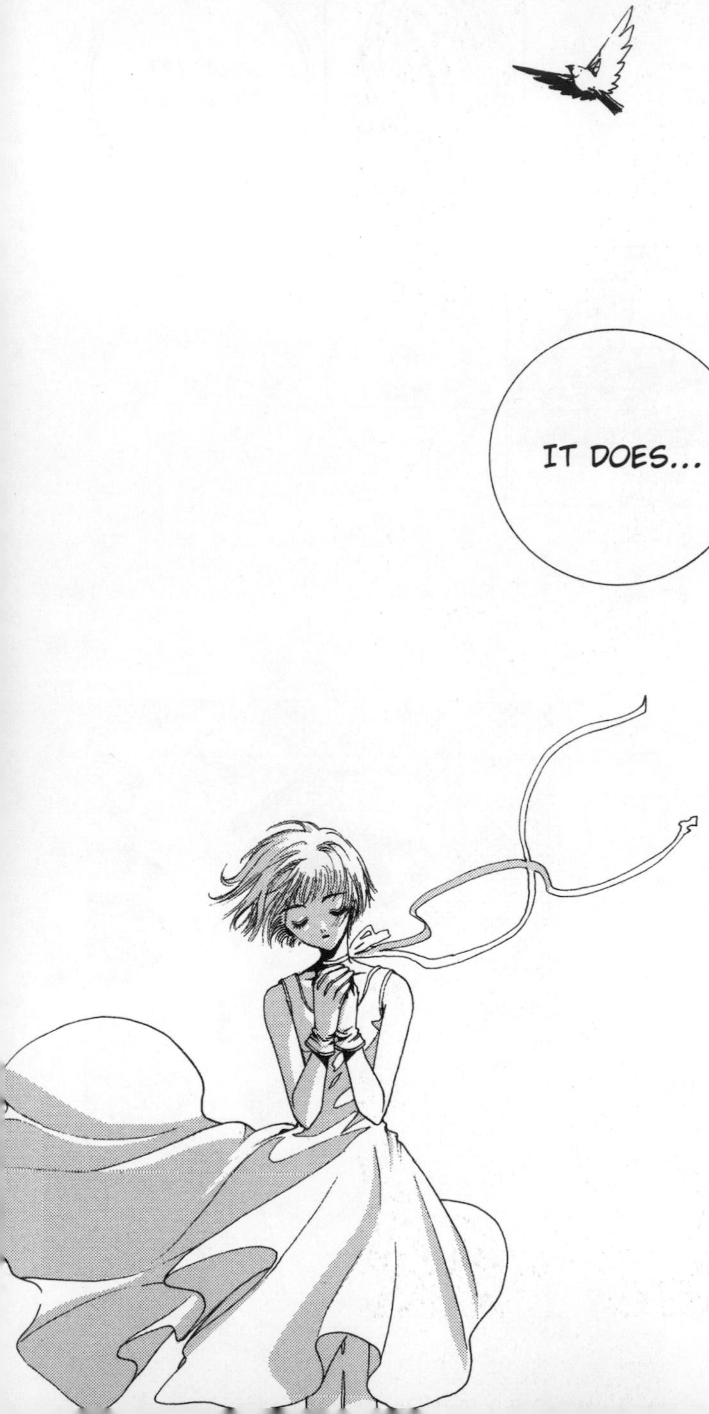
IT DOES...

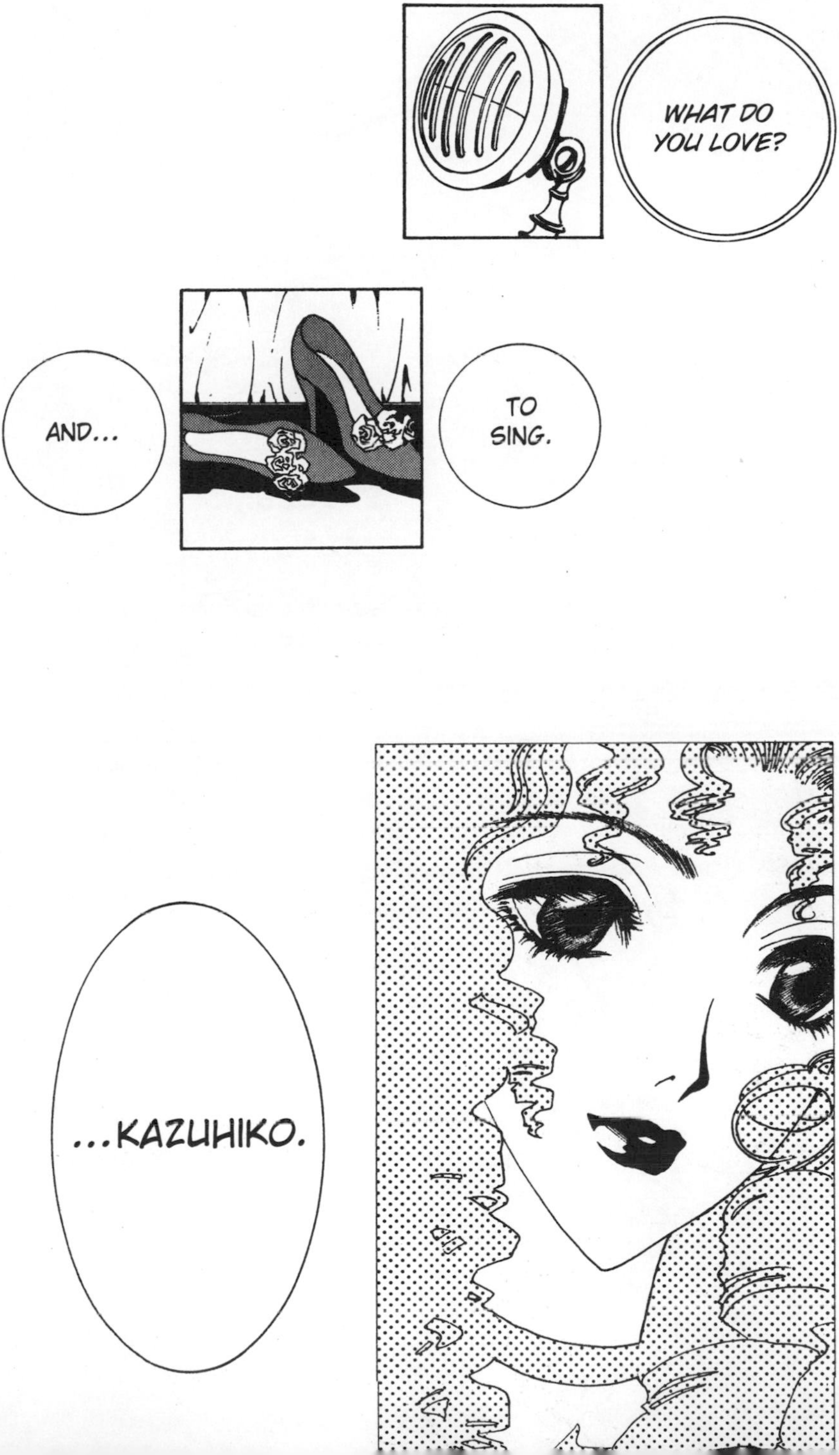
WHAT DO YOU LOVE?
TO SING.
AND...
...KAZUHIKO.

KAZUHIKO?

RAIN

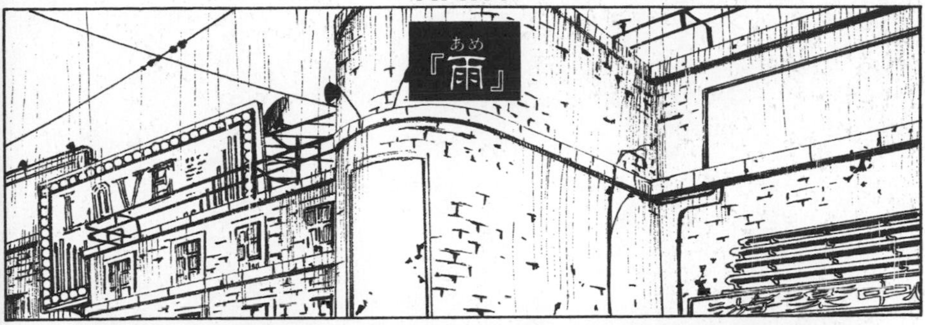
あめ
『雨』
LOVE

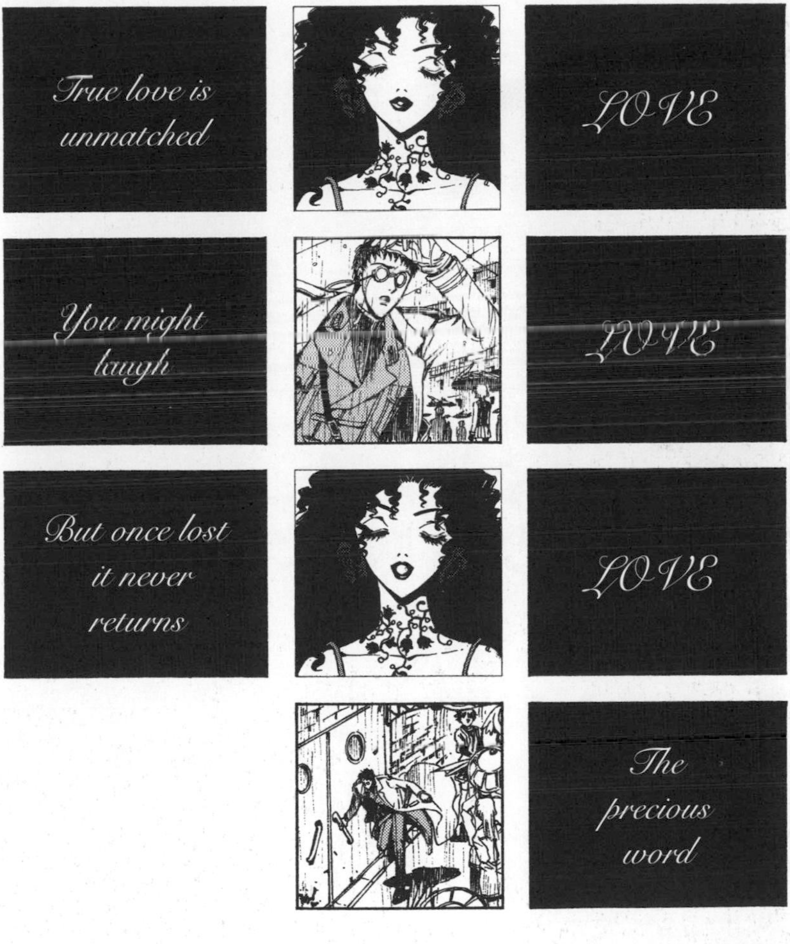
LOVE
True love is unmatched
LOVE
You might laugh
LOVE
But once lost it never returns
The precious word

LOVE

Hear the whisper of the heart

Hear its true voice
Listen carefully

Where lies true love?

To whom shall you give true love?

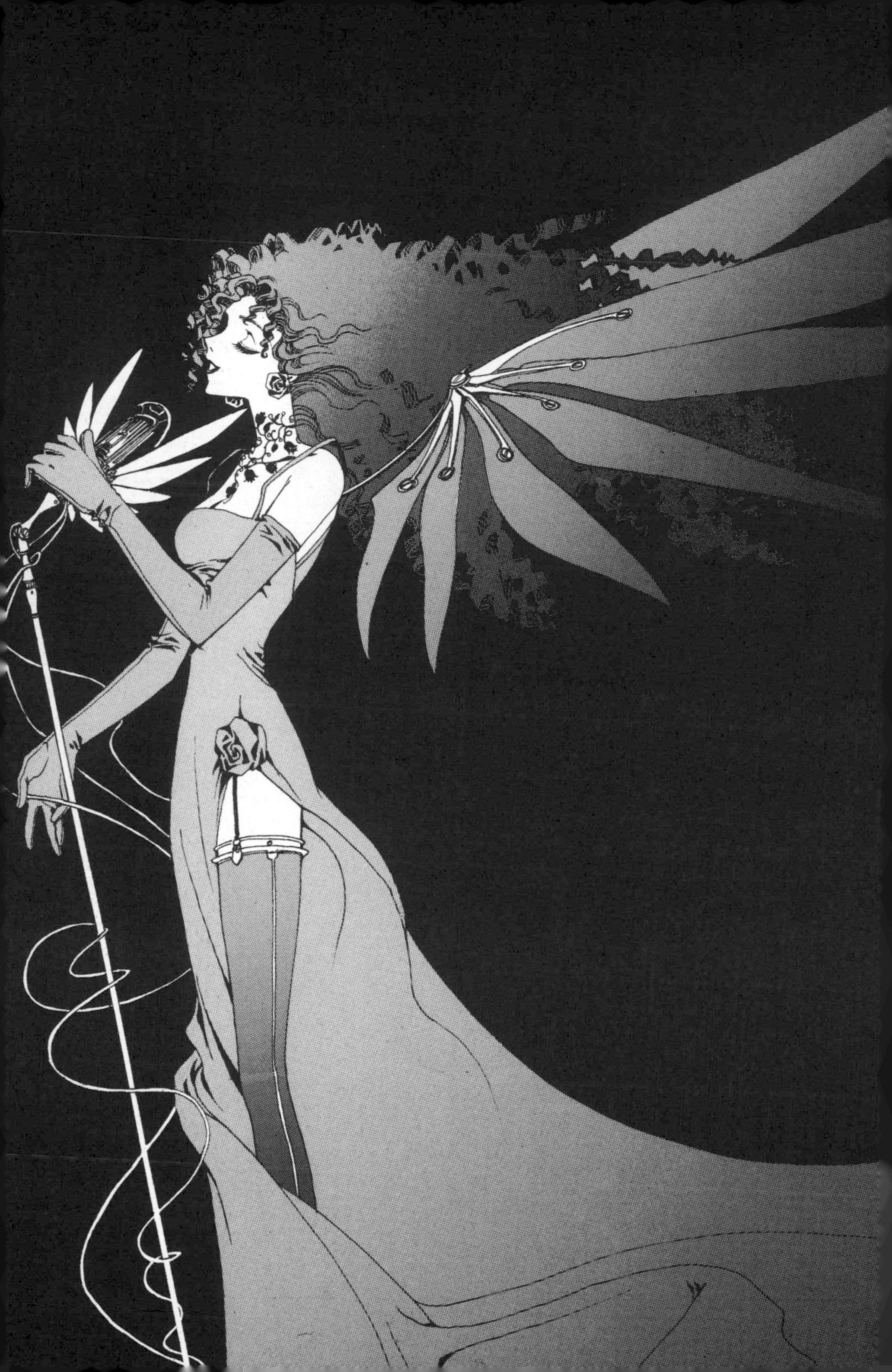

LOVE
You might laugh
But it's the most
important word

『たった一人のために
うたう歌』
A SONG FOR ONE

DID YOU
CHANGE
THE LYRICS
TODAY?

Hear the whisper
of the heart
Hear its true voice

Listen carefully
Where lies true love?
To whom shall
you give true love?

THAT'S THE PART I CHANGED.

THERE.

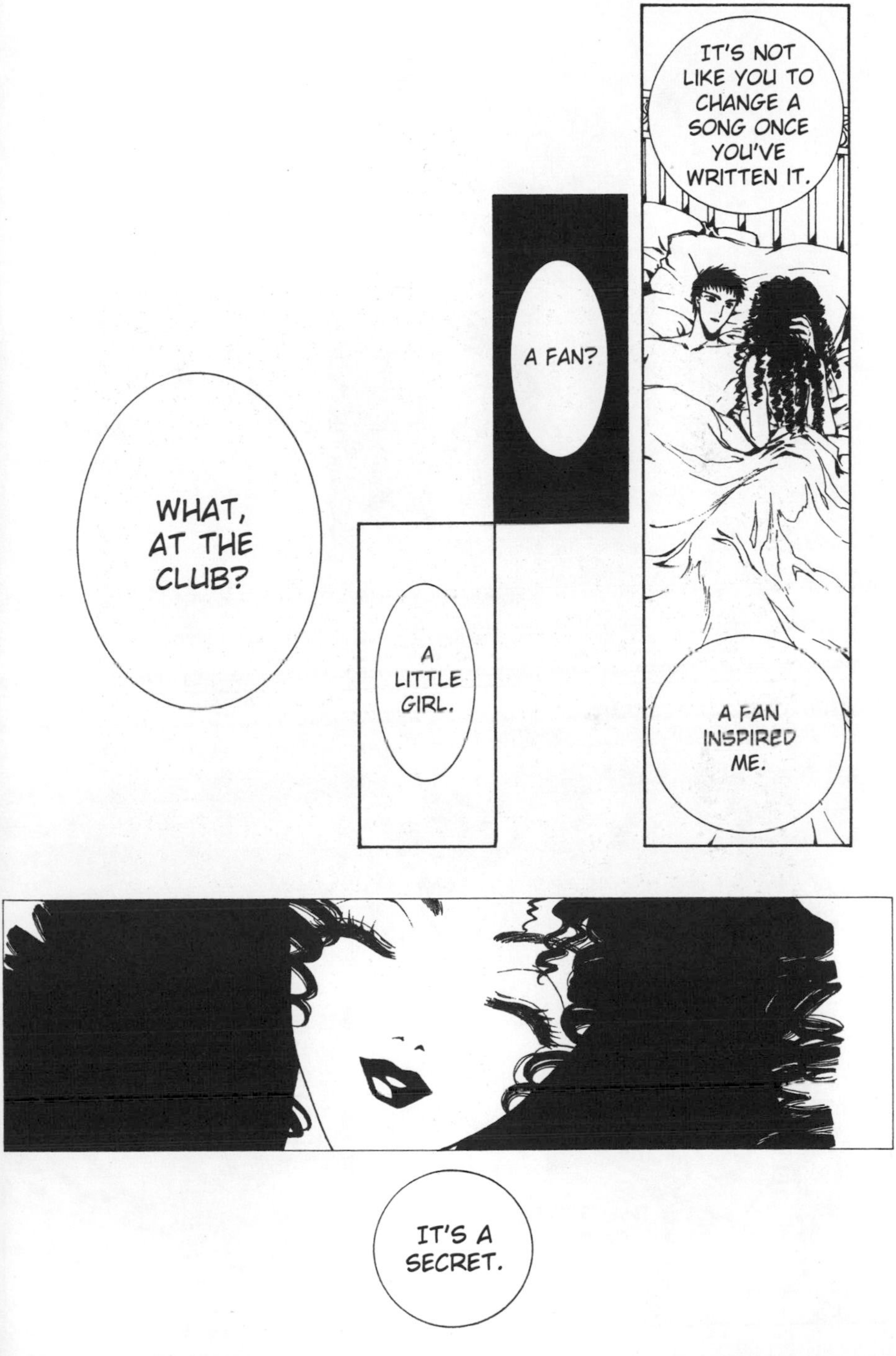
IT'S NOT LIKE YOU TO CHANGE A SONG ONCE YOU'VE WRITTEN IT.
A FAN INSPIRED ME.
A FAN?
A LITTLE GIRL.
WHAT, AT THE CLUB?
IT'S A SECRET.

『鳥(とり)

BIRD'S

の

EYE

目(め)』

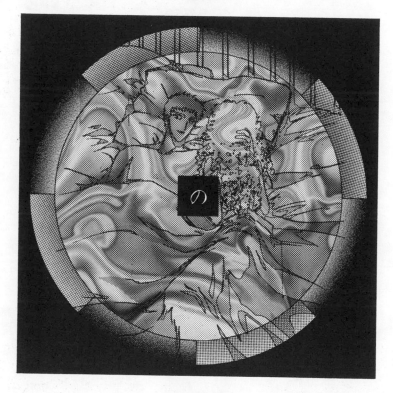

『小鳥の心の小鳥』

BIRD IN THE HEART OF A BIRD

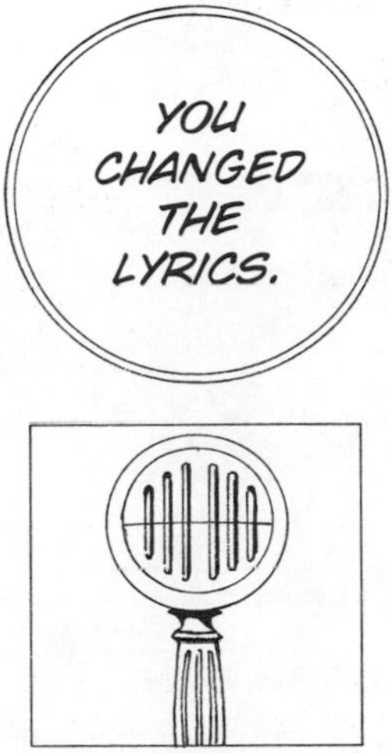
YOU CHANGED THE LYRICS.

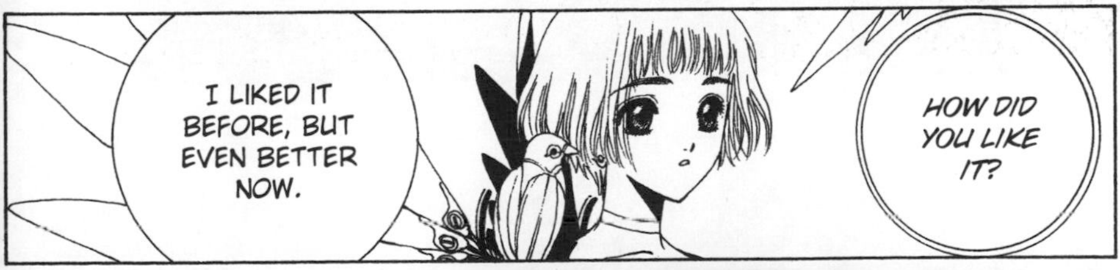
HOW DID YOU LIKE IT?
I LIKED IT BEFORE, BUT EVEN BETTER NOW.

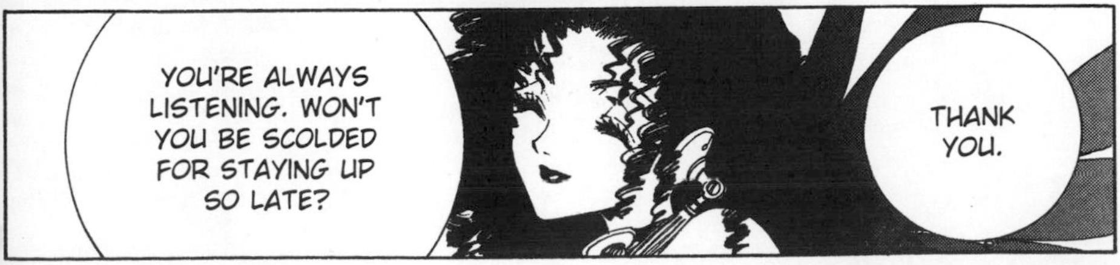
THANK YOU.
YOU'RE ALWAYS LISTENING. WON'T YOU BE SCOLDED FOR STAYING UP SO LATE?

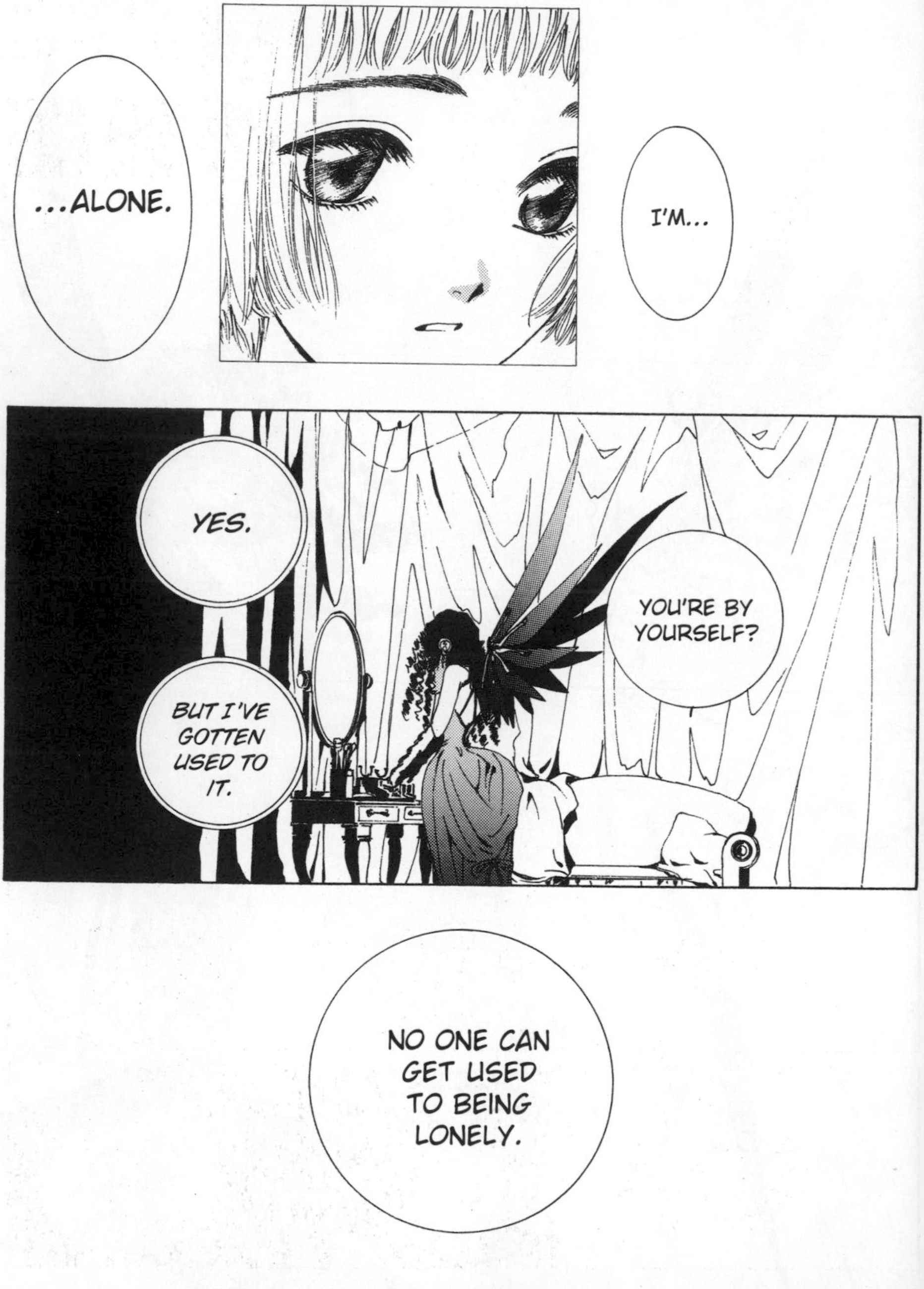
I'M...
...ALONE.
YOU'RE BY YOURSELF?
YES.
BUT I'VE GOTTEN USED TO IT.
NO ONE CAN GET USED TO BEING LONELY.

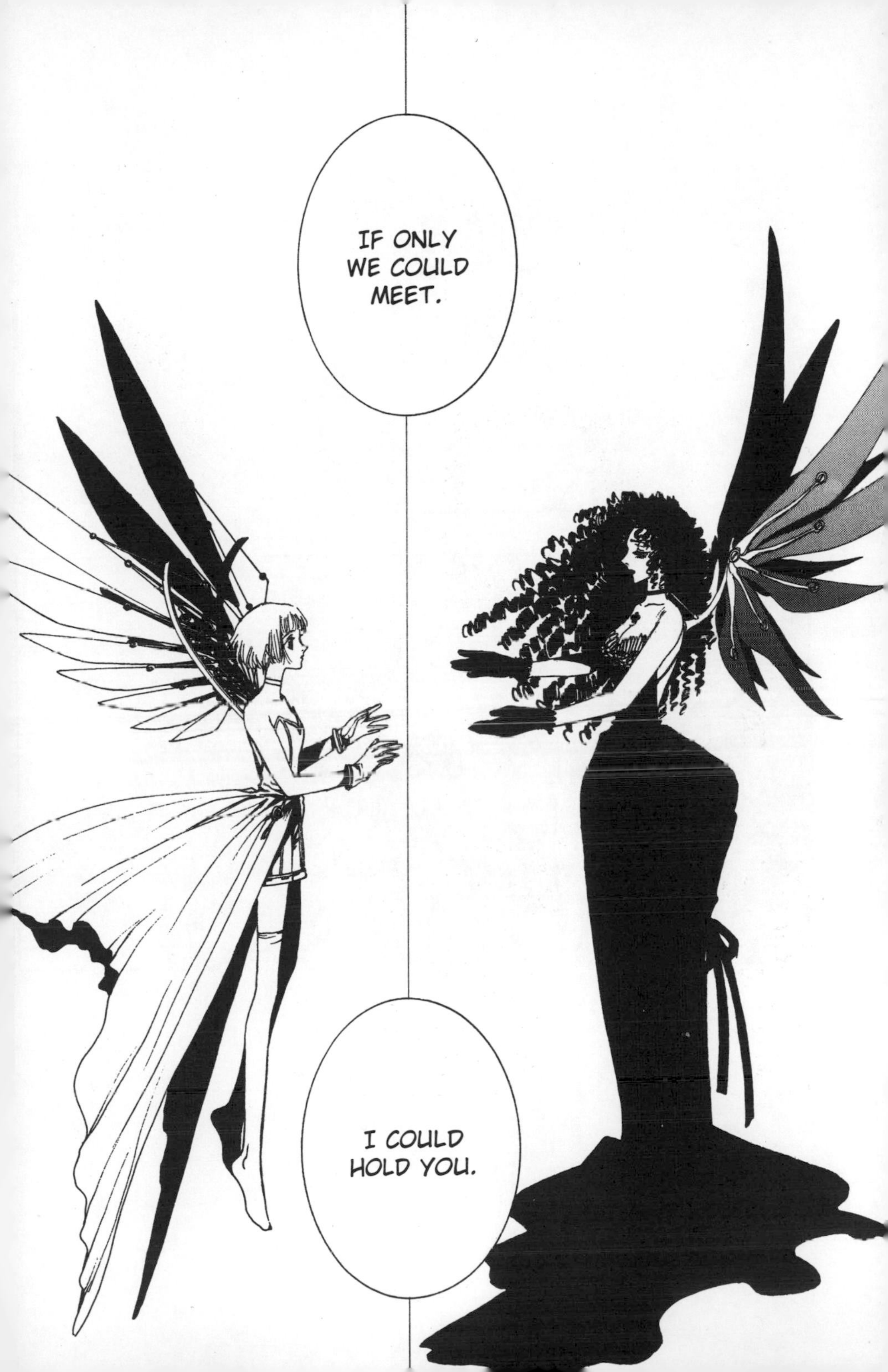
IF ONLY WE COULD MEET.
I COULD HOLD YOU.

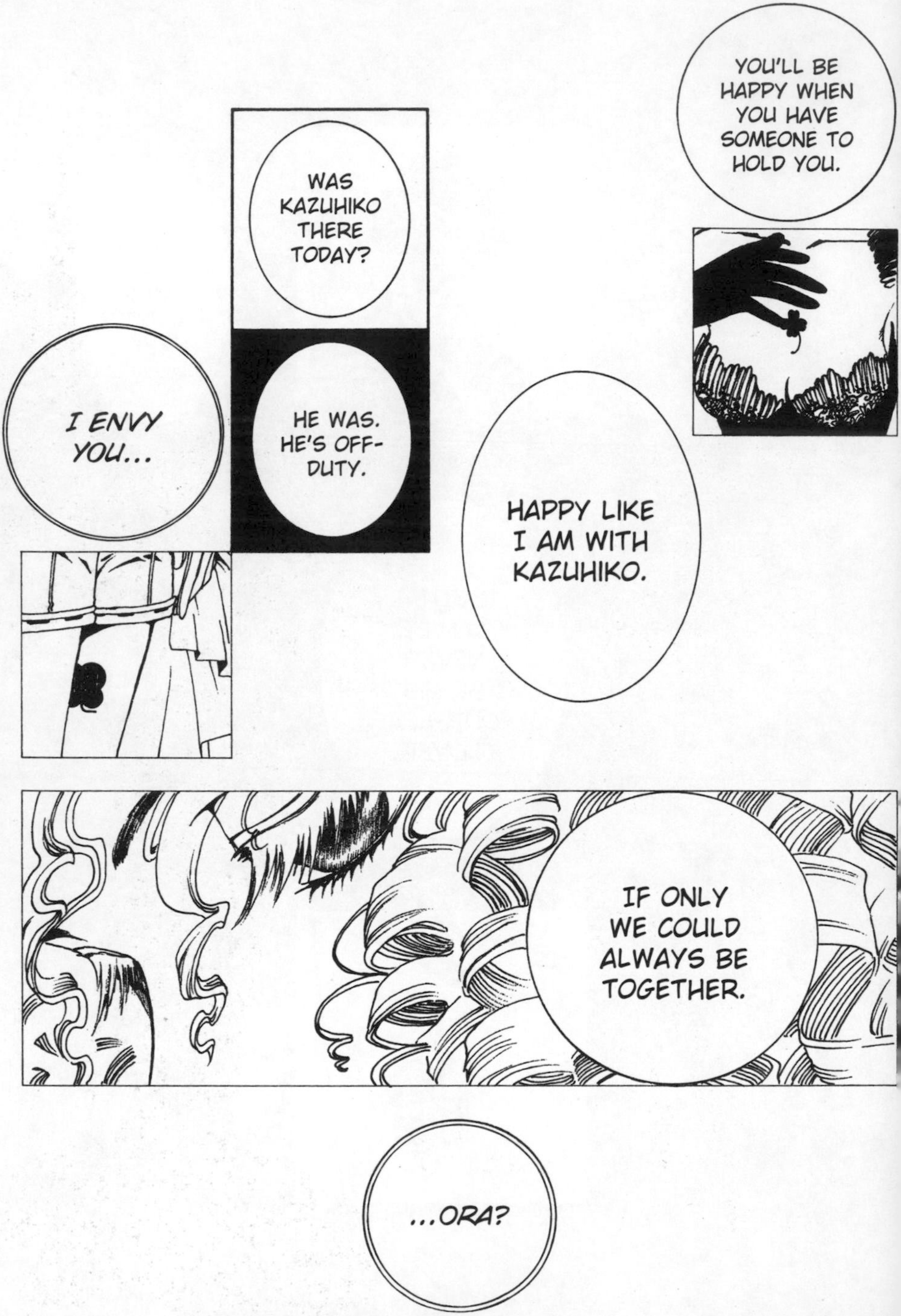
YOU'LL BE HAPPY WHEN YOU HAVE SOMEONE TO HOLD YOU.
HAPPY LIKE I AM WITH KAZUHIKO.
WAS KAZUHIKO THERE TODAY?
HE WAS. HE'S OFF-DUTY.
I ENVY YOU...
IF ONLY WE COULD ALWAYS BE TOGETHER.
...ORA?

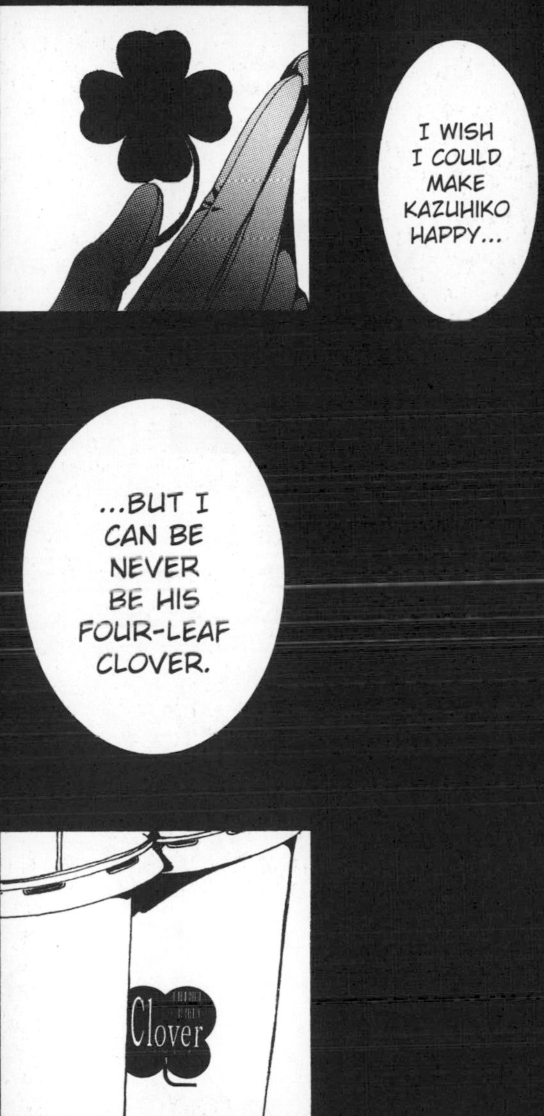
I WISH I COULD MAKE KAZUHIKO HAPPY...
...BUT I CAN BE NEVER BE HIS FOUR-LEAF CLOVER.
Clover

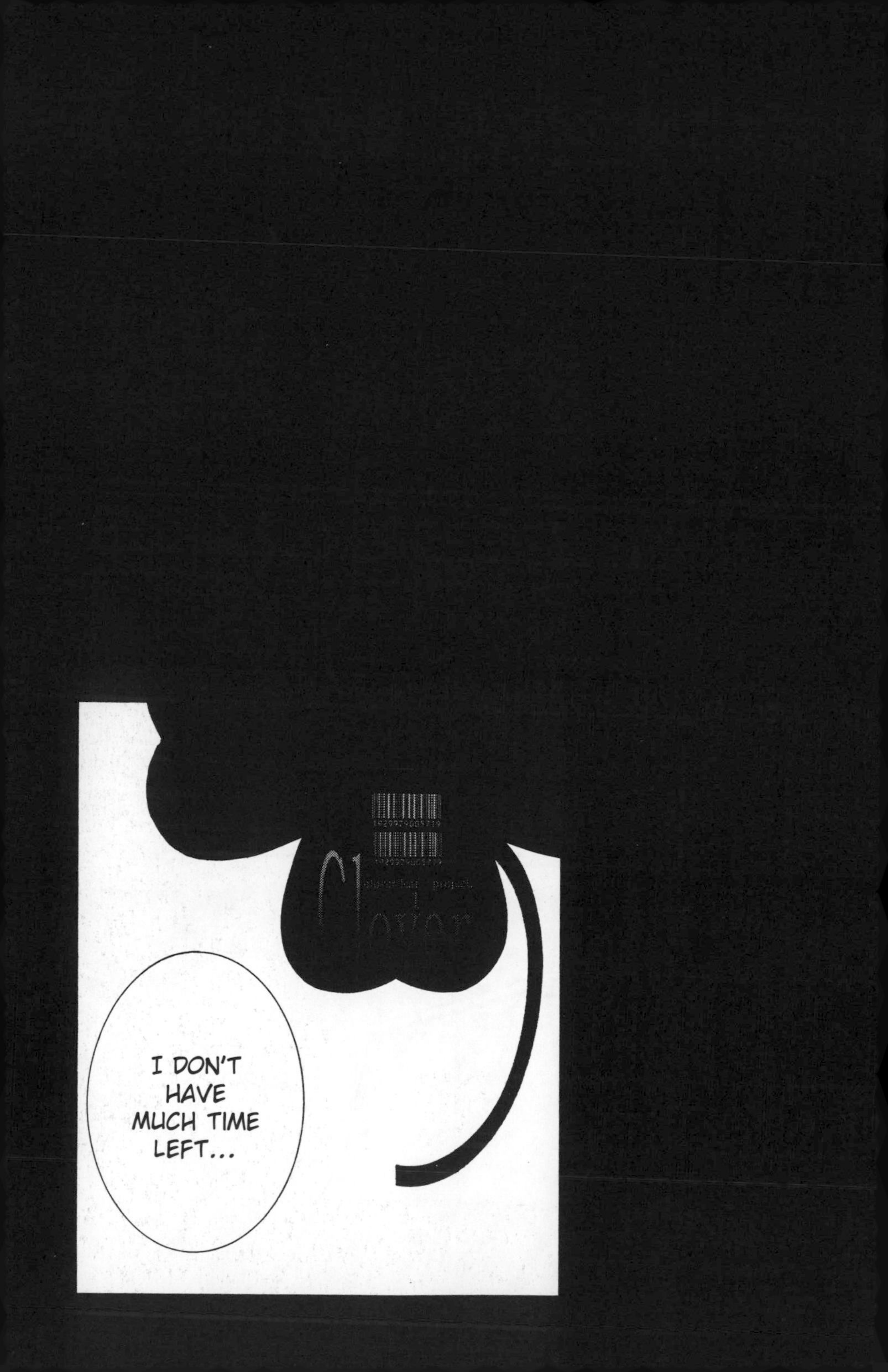
I DON'T HAVE MUCH TIME LEFT...

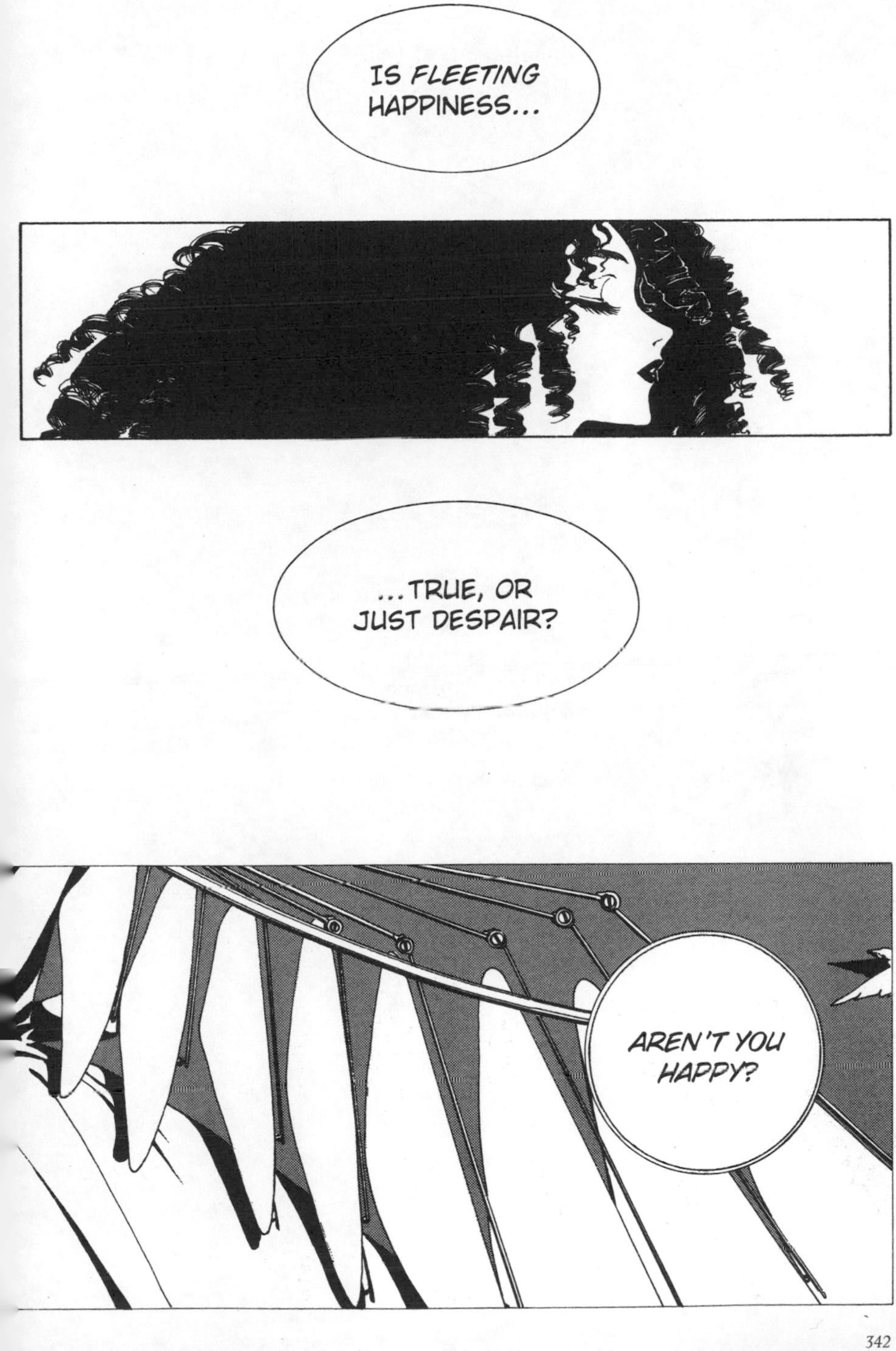
IS FLEETING HAPPINESS...
...TRUE, OR JUST DESPAIR?
AREN'T YOU HAPPY?

EVEN IF I KNOW IT'S GOING TO END...

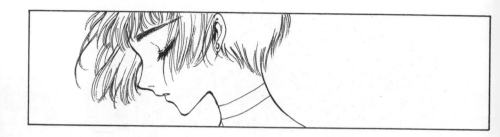

...I WANT TO BE HAPPY.

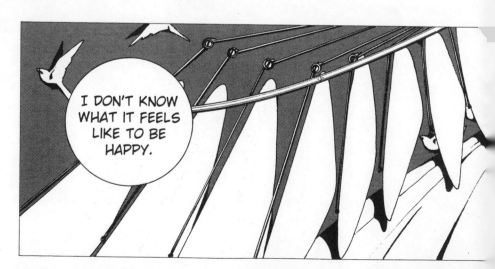

I DON'T KNOW WHAT IT FEELS LIKE TO BE HAPPY.

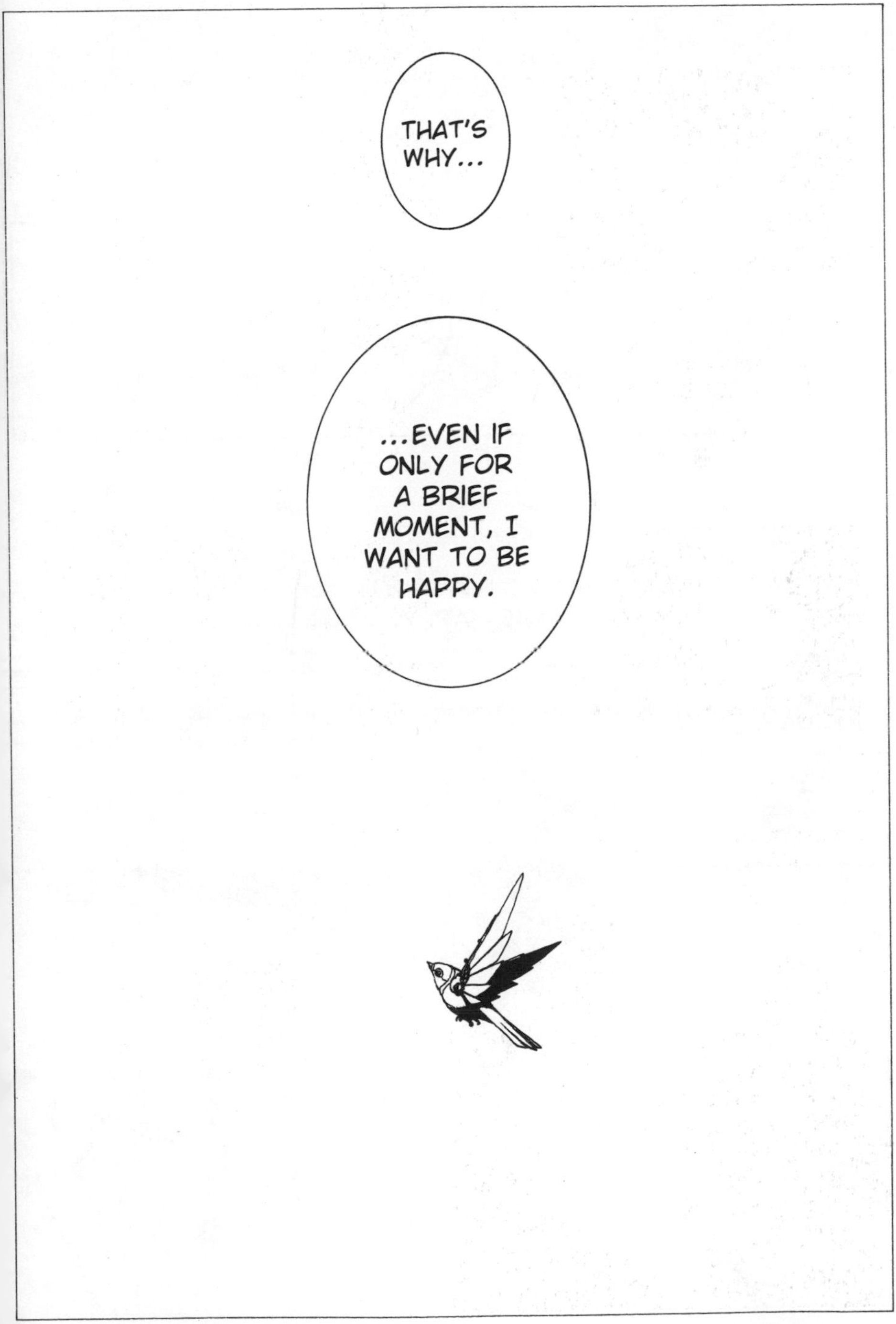
THAT'S WHY...
...EVEN IF ONLY FOR A BRIEF MOMENT, I WANT TO BE HAPPY.

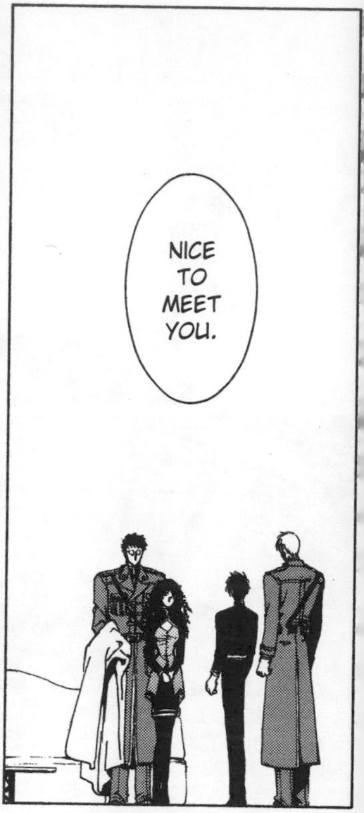
NICE TO MEET YOU.

『はじめまして』

HOW DO YOU DO?

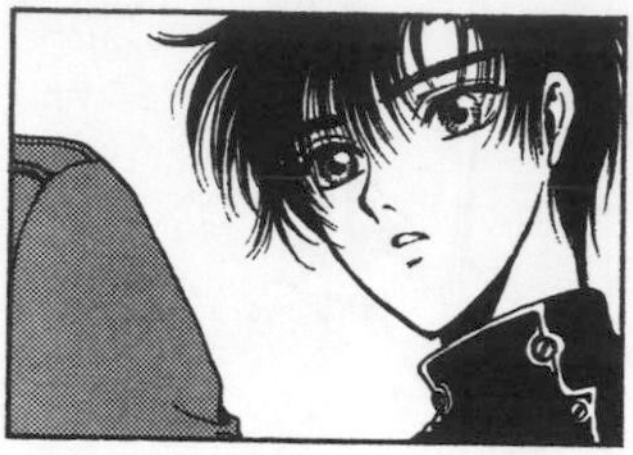

IS THERE SOMETHING ON MY FACE?

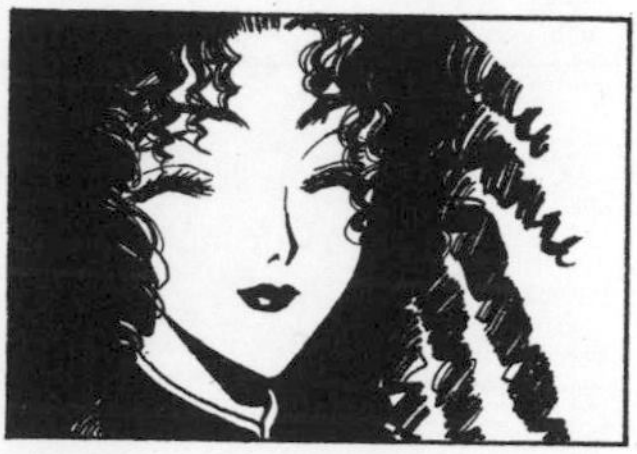

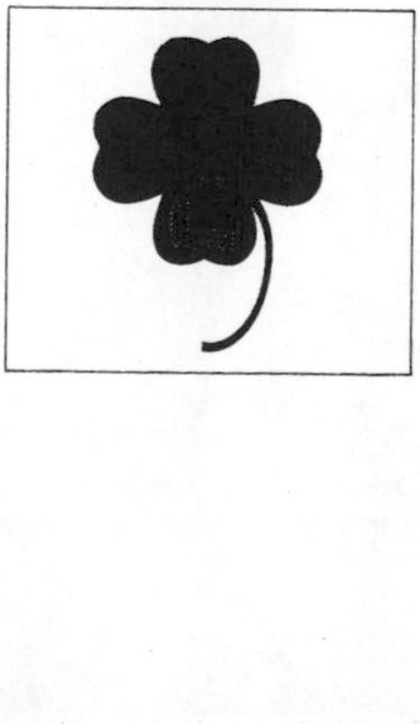

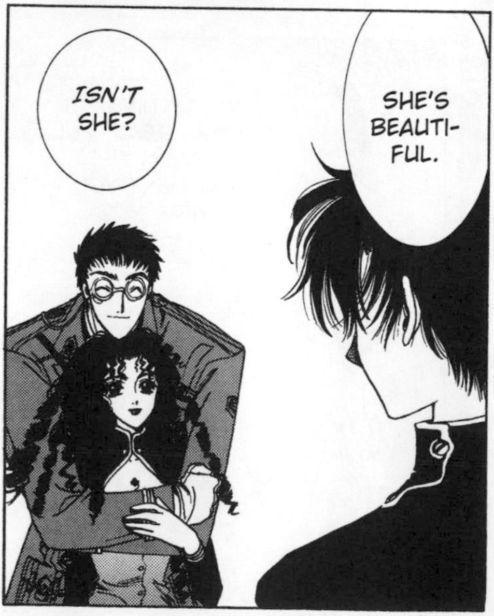
SHE'S BEAUTI-FUL.
ISN'T SHE?

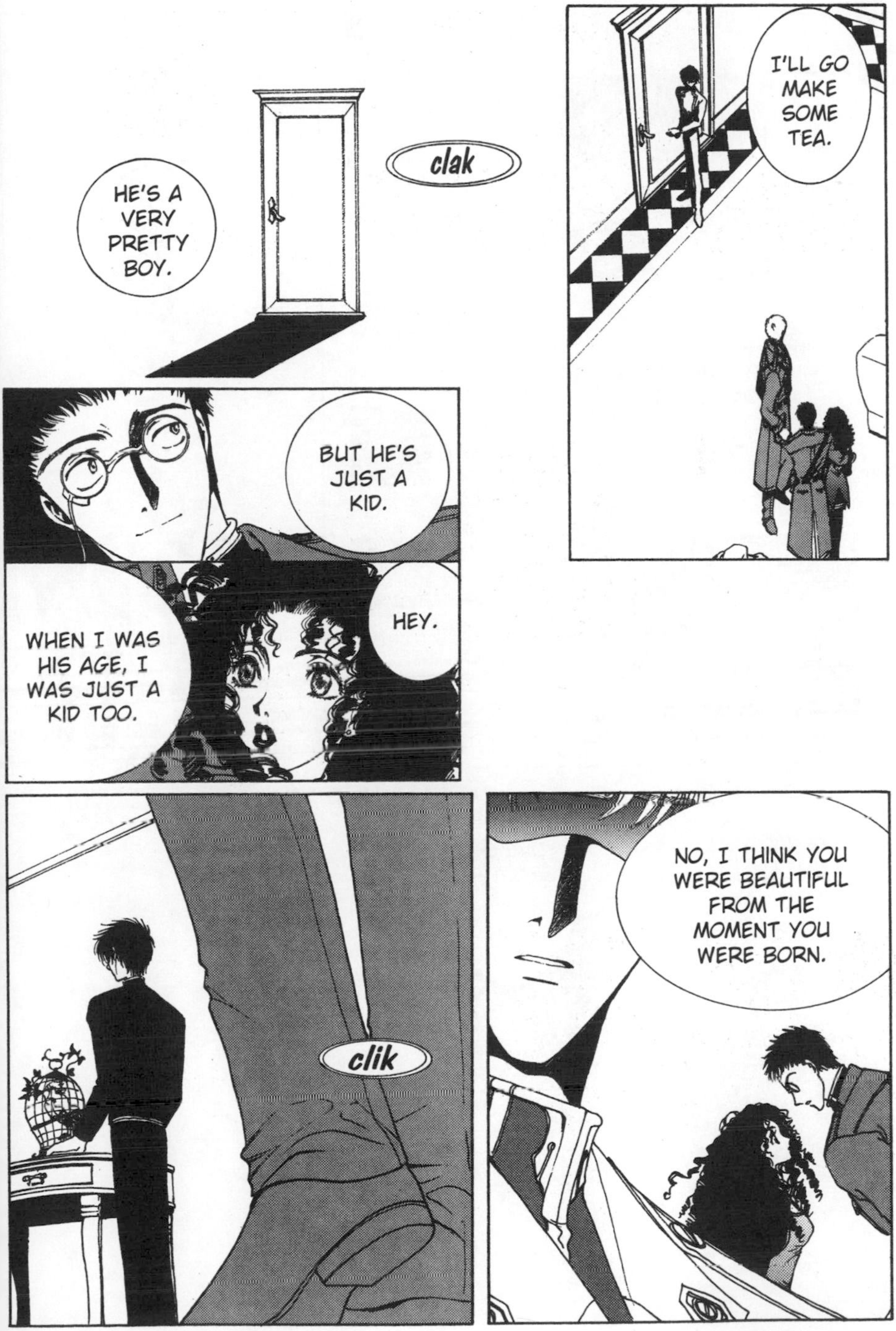
I'LL GO MAKE SOME TEA.
clak
HE'S A VERY PRETTY BOY.
BUT HE'S JUST A KID.
HEY.
WHEN I WAS HIS AGE, I WAS JUST A KID TOO.
NO, I THINK YOU WERE BEAUTIFUL FROM THE MOMENT YOU WERE BORN.
clik

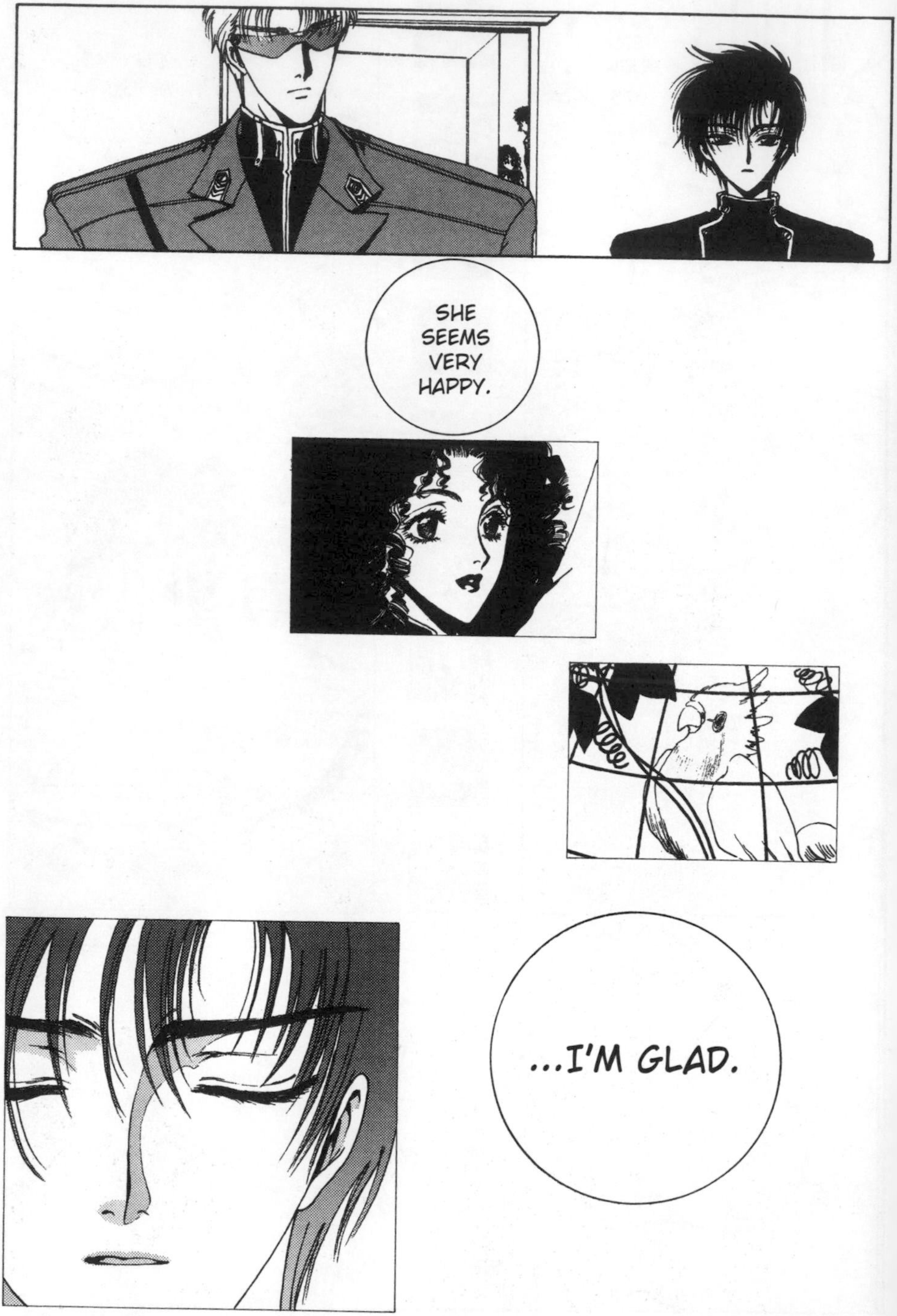
SHE SEEMS VERY HAPPY.
...I'M GLAD.

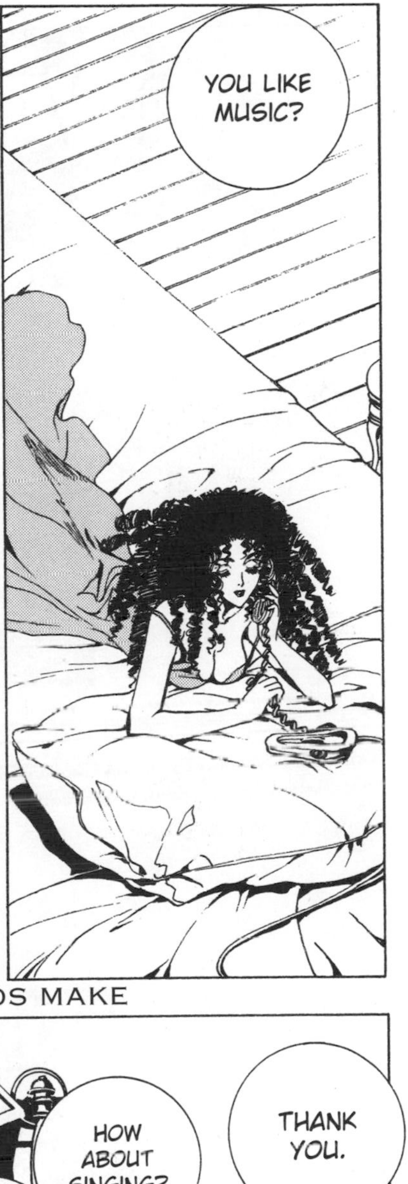
YOU LIKE MUSIC?

『小鳥と小鳥が創る歌』

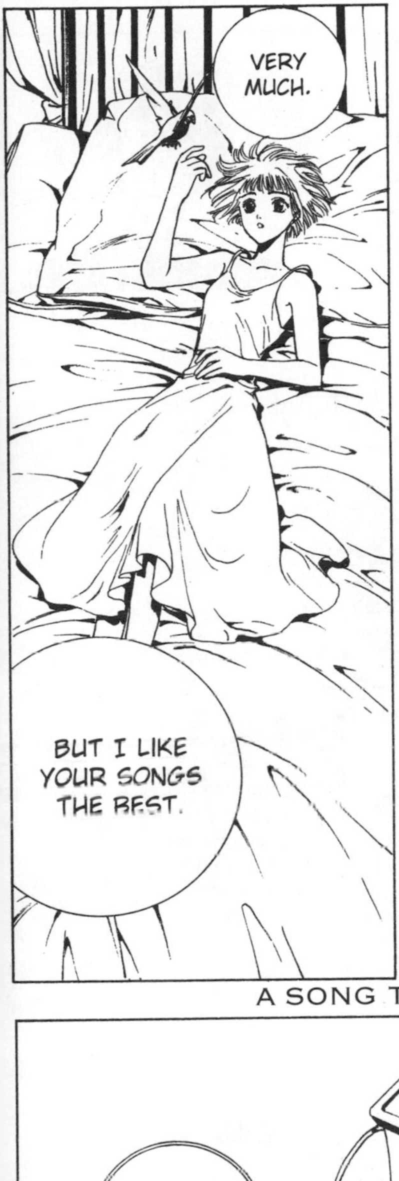
VERY MUCH.
BUT I LIKE YOUR SONGS THE BEST.

A SONG TWO BIRDS MAKE

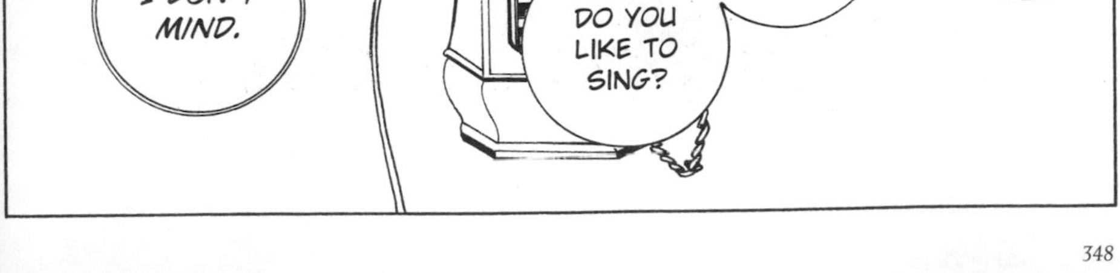
THANK YOU.
HOW ABOUT SINGING?
DO YOU LIKE TO SING?
I DON'T MIND.

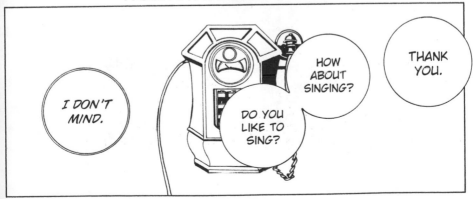

I'M SORRY.

SUE...

WHEN I SING, I'M NOT ALONE.

I DON'T WANT TO INCONVE-NIENCE YOU.

...IF YOU CAN'T LEAVE THERE, CAN I VISIT YOU?

SINCE I'M HERE BY MYSELF, I CAN ONLY TALK TO MYSELF.

SUE...

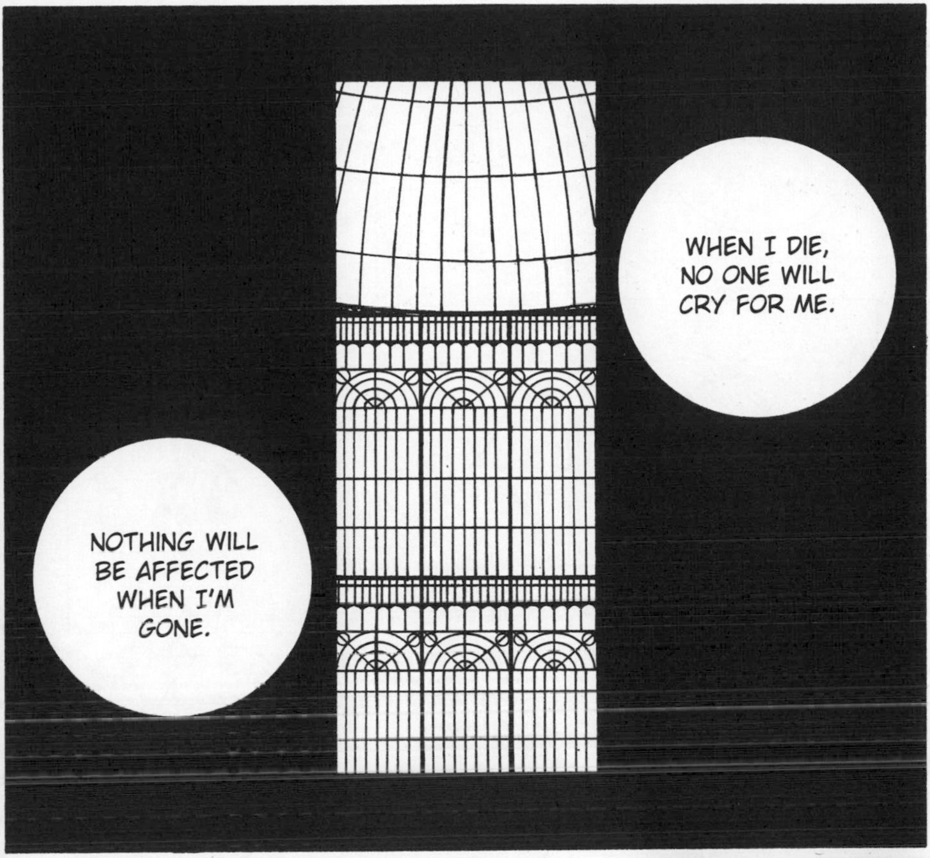
WHEN I DIE, NO ONE WILL CRY FOR ME.
NOTHING WILL BE AFFECTED WHEN I'M GONE.
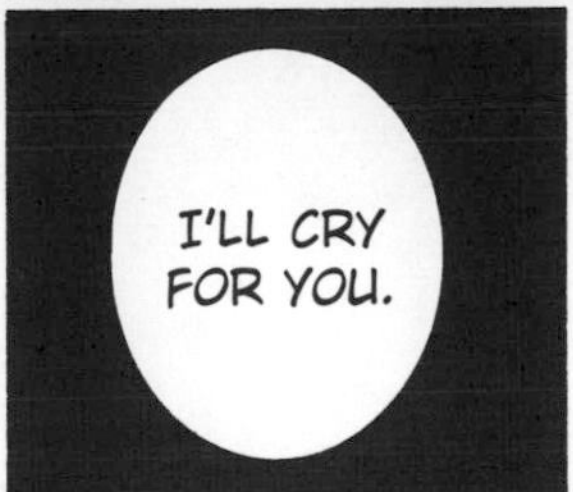
I'LL CRY FOR YOU.
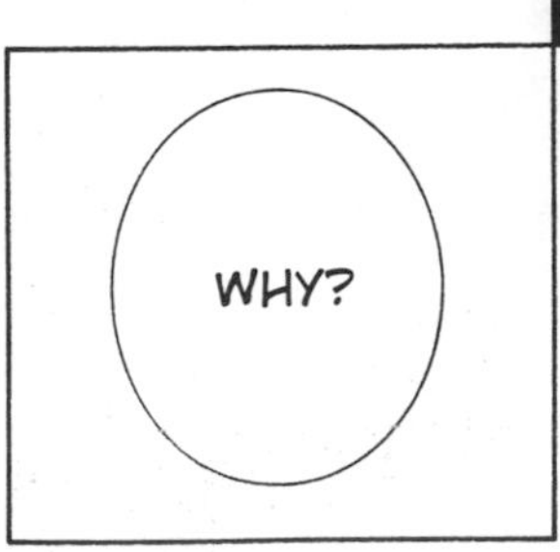
WHY?

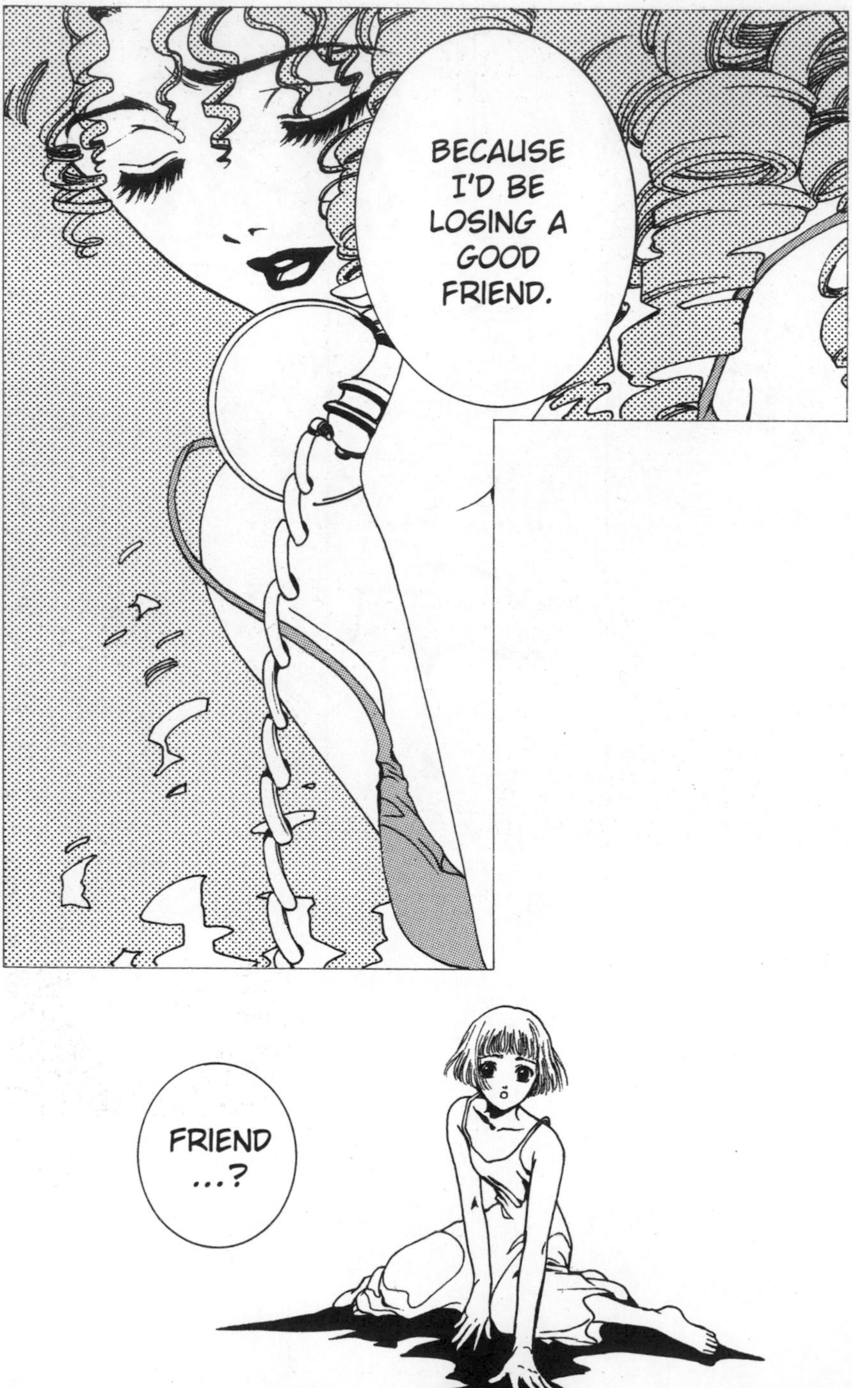
BECAUSE I'D BE LOSING A GOOD FRIEND.
FRIEND ...?

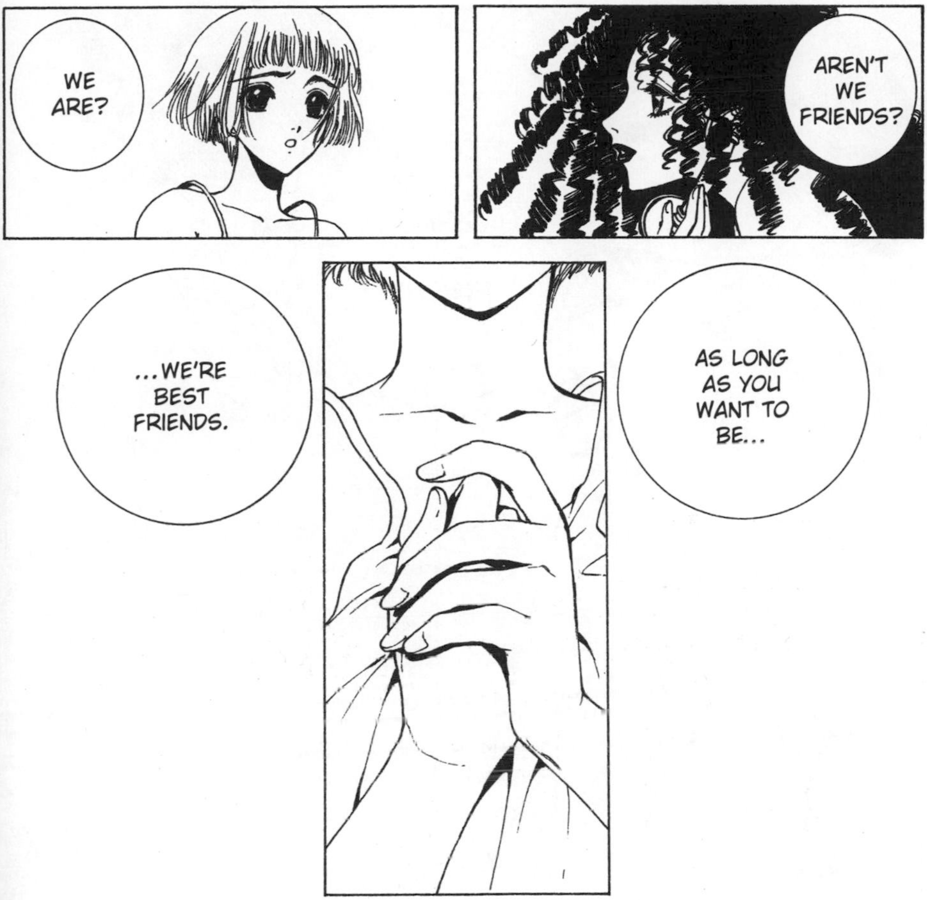
AREN'T WE FRIENDS?
WE ARE?
AS LONG AS YOU WANT TO BE...
...WE'RE BEST FRIENDS.

...THANK
YOU.

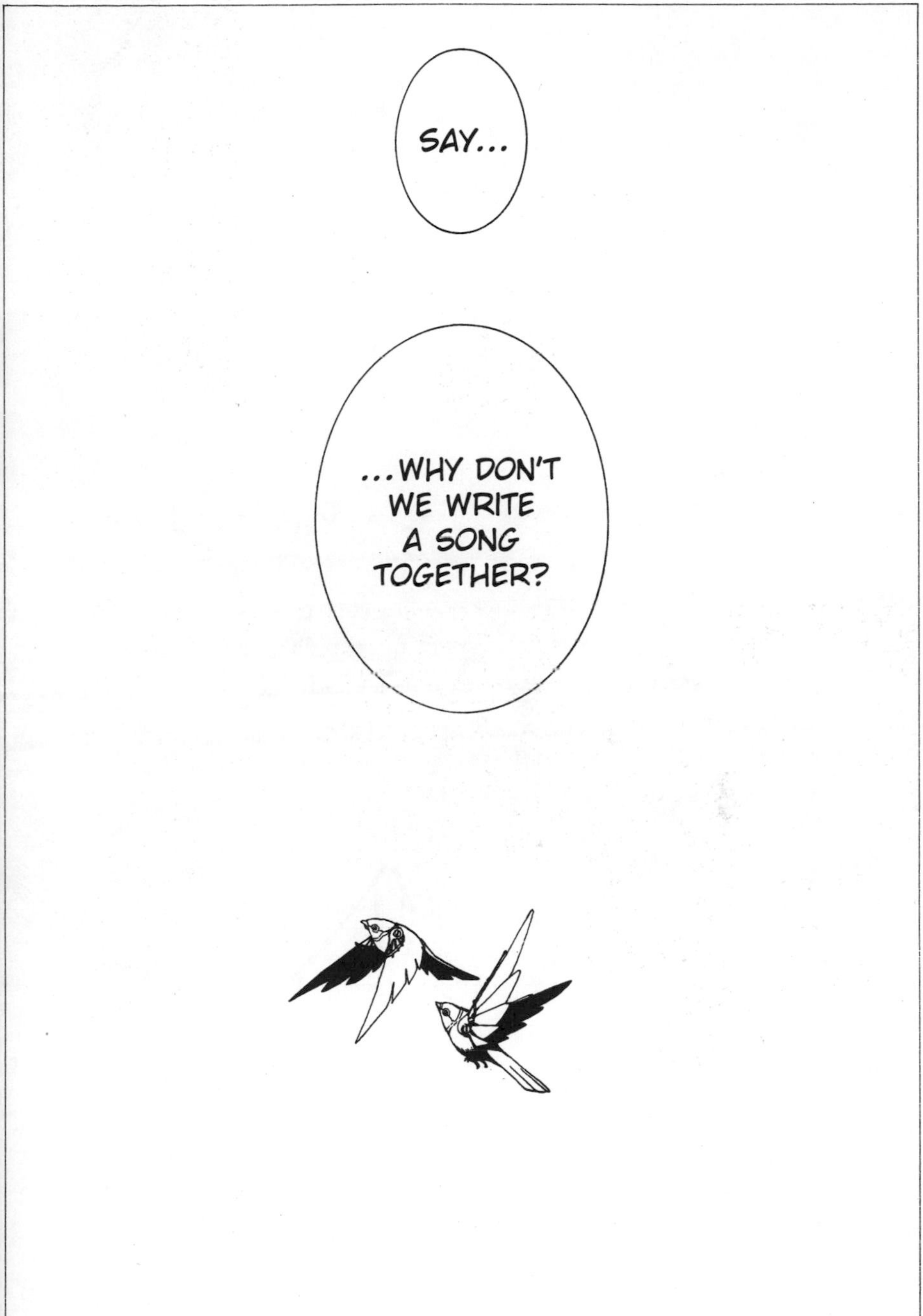
SAY...
...WHY DON'T WE WRITE A SONG TOGETHER?

『小鳥たちの内緒の歌』

THE SECRET BIRD SONG

...I seek happiness
To find happiness with you

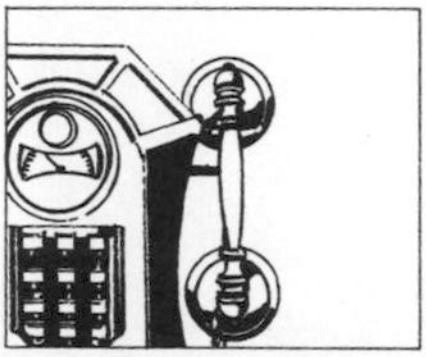

So take me
Someplace far away
Far from here

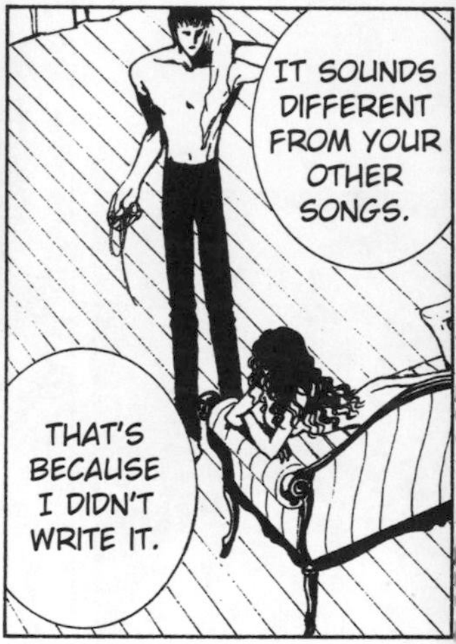
IT SOUNDS DIFFERENT FROM YOUR OTHER SONGS.
THAT'S BECAUSE I DIDN'T WRITE IT.

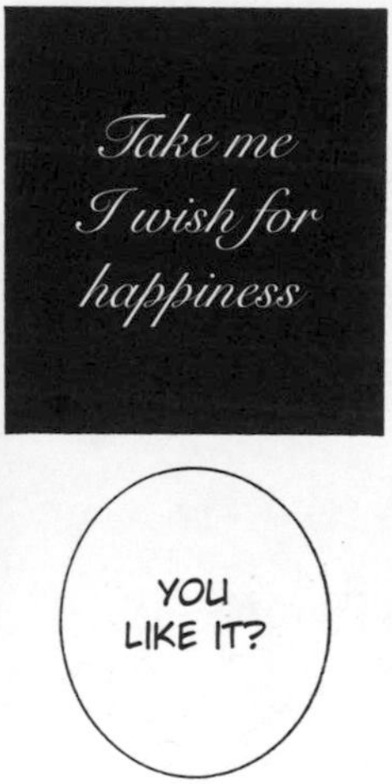
Take me I wish for happiness
YOU LIKE IT?

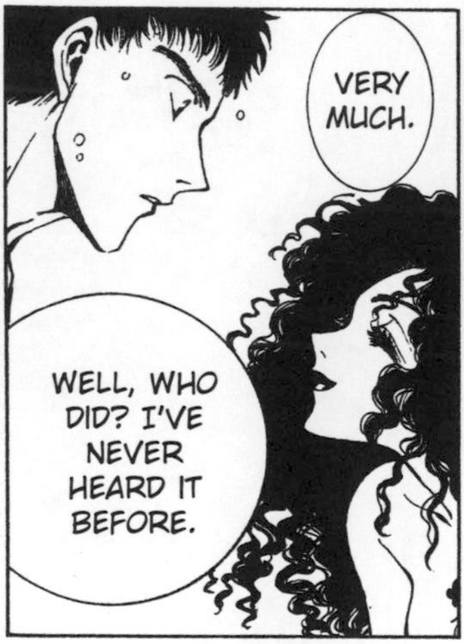
VERY MUCH.
WELL, WHO DID? I'VE NEVER HEARD IT BEFORE.

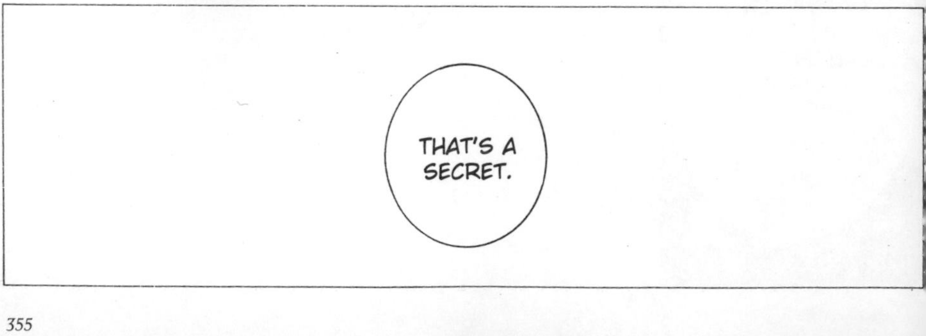
THAT'S A SECRET.

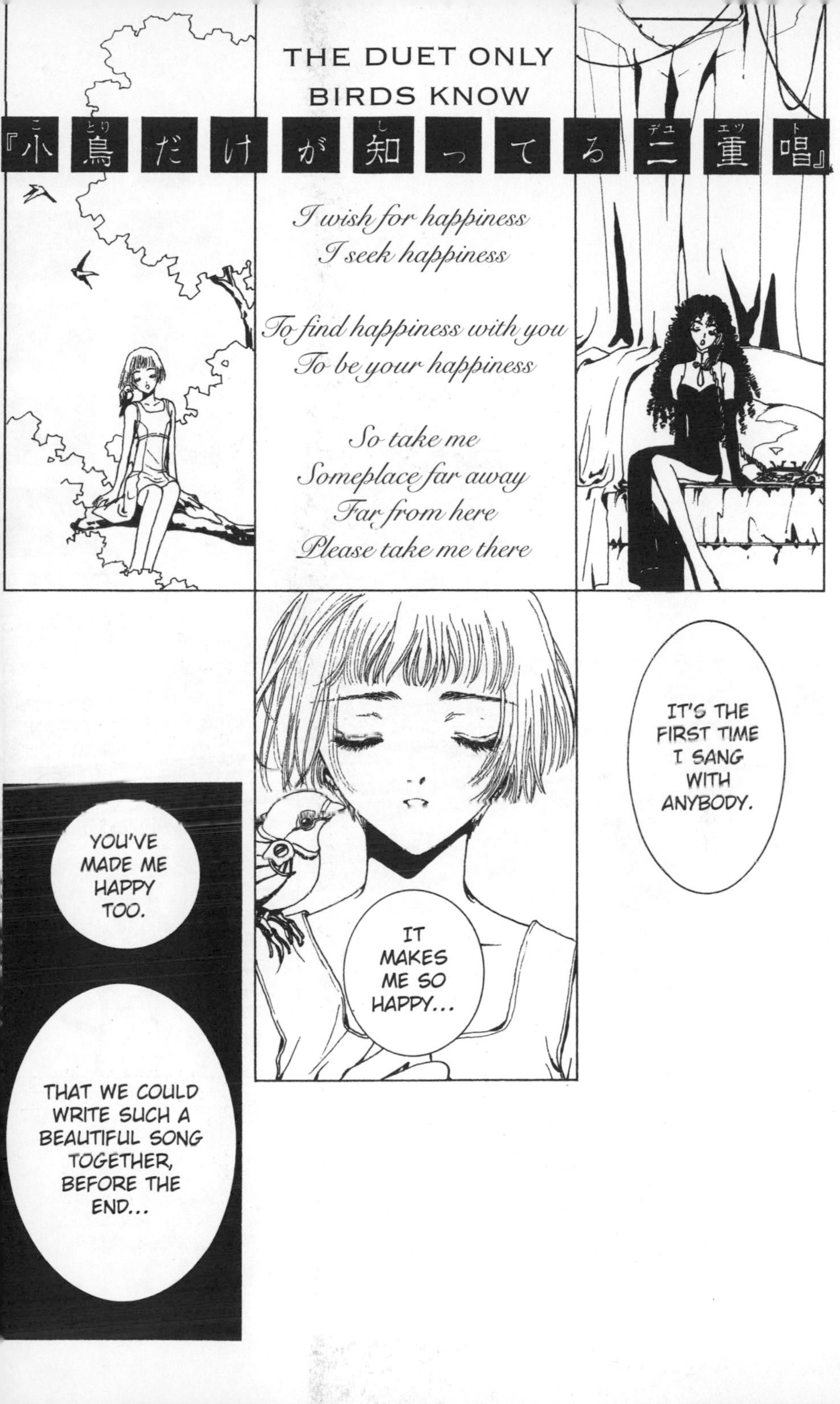
THE DUET ONLY BIRDS KNOW
『小鳥だけが知ってる二重唱』
I wish for happiness
I seek happiness
To find happiness with you
To be your happiness
So take me
Someplace far away
Far from here
Please take me there
IT'S THE FIRST TIME I SANG WITH ANYBODY.
IT MAKES ME SO HAPPY...
YOU'VE MADE ME HAPPY TOO.
THAT WE COULD WRITE SUCH A BEAUTIFUL SONG TOGETHER, BEFORE THE END...

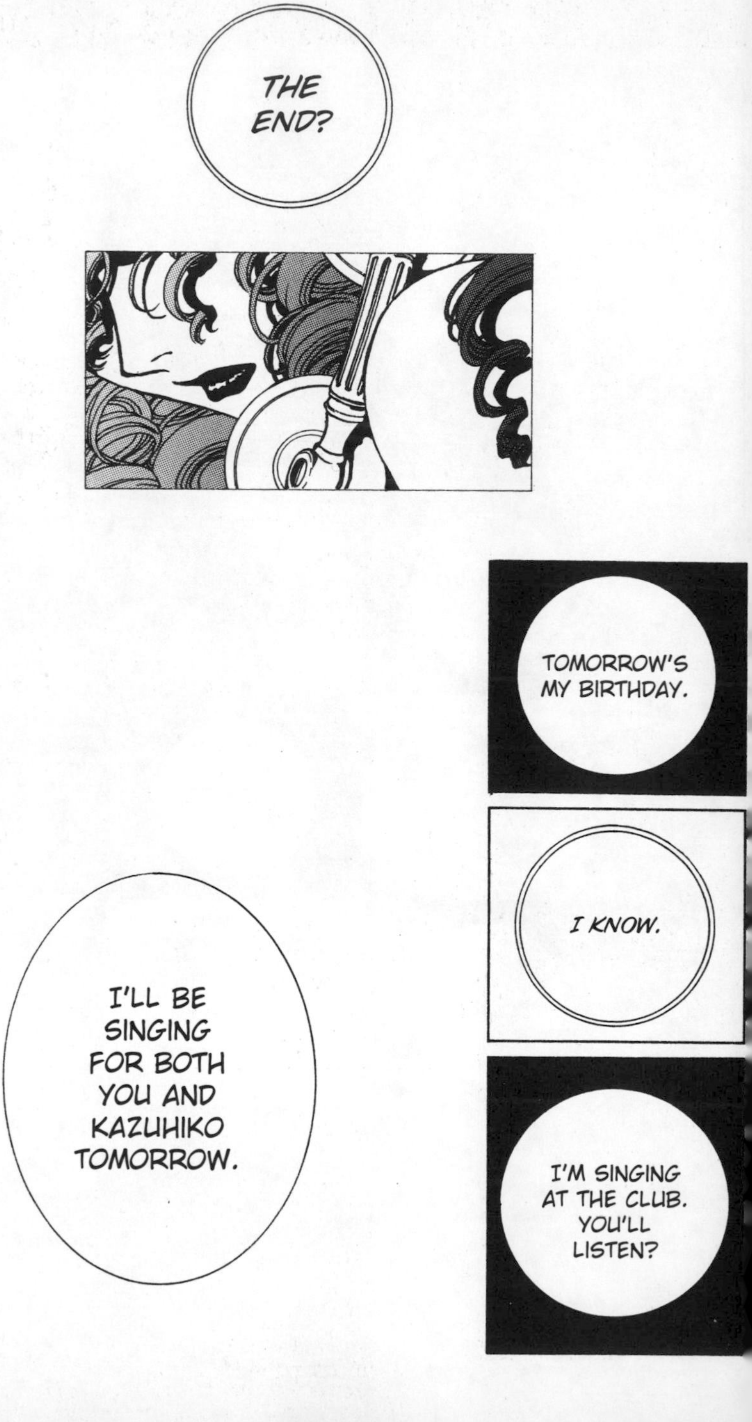
THE END?
TOMORROW'S MY BIRTHDAY.
I KNOW.
I'M SINGING AT THE CLUB. YOU'LL LISTEN?
I'LL BE SINGING FOR BOTH YOU AND KAZUHIKO TOMORROW.

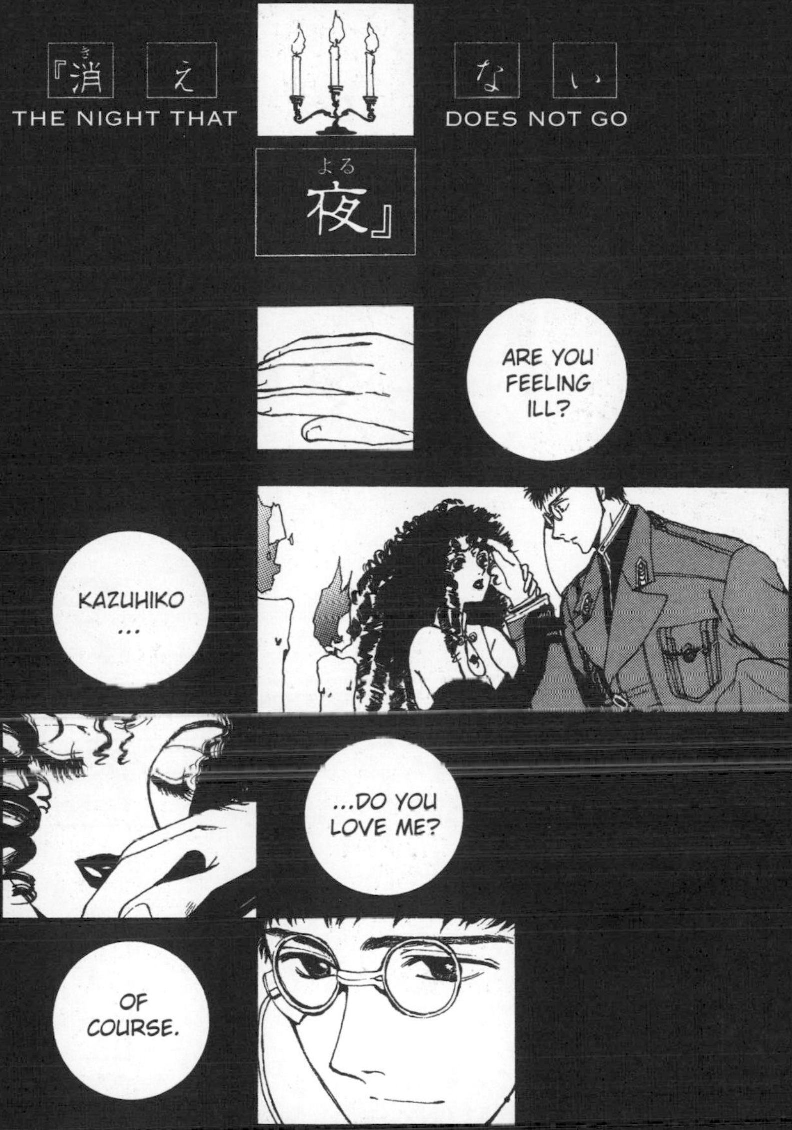
『消えない夜』
THE NIGHT THAT DOES NOT GO
ARE YOU FEELING ILL?
KAZUHIKO ...
...DO YOU LOVE ME?
OF COURSE.

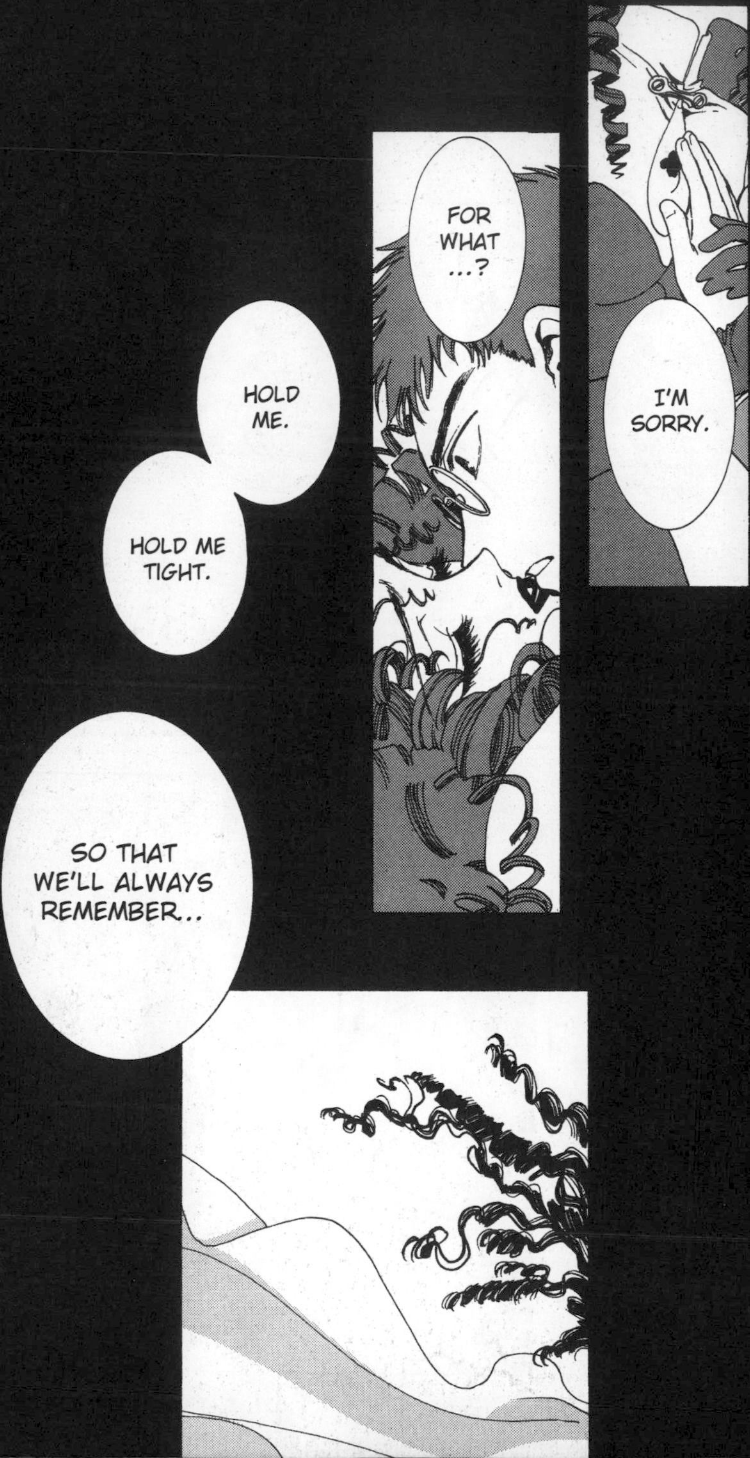
I'M SORRY.
FOR WHAT ...?
HOLD ME.
HOLD ME TIGHT.
SO THAT WE'LL ALWAYS REMEMBER...

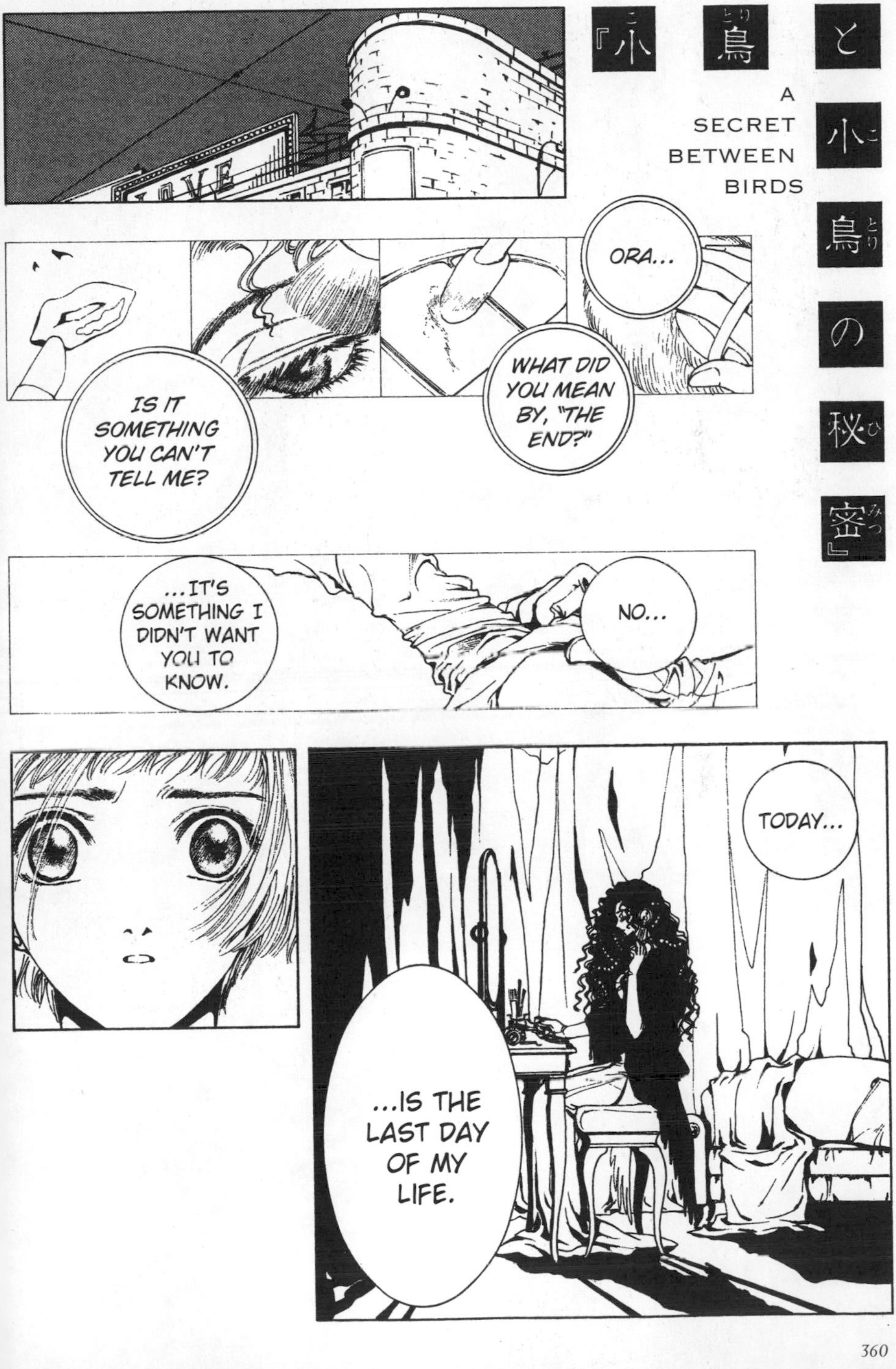
『小鳥と小鳥の秘密』
A SECRET BETWEEN BIRDS
ORA...
WHAT DID YOU MEAN BY, "THE END?"
IS IT SOMETHING YOU CAN'T TELL ME?
NO...
...IT'S SOMETHING I DIDN'T WANT YOU TO KNOW.
TODAY...
...IS THE LAST DAY OF MY LIFE.

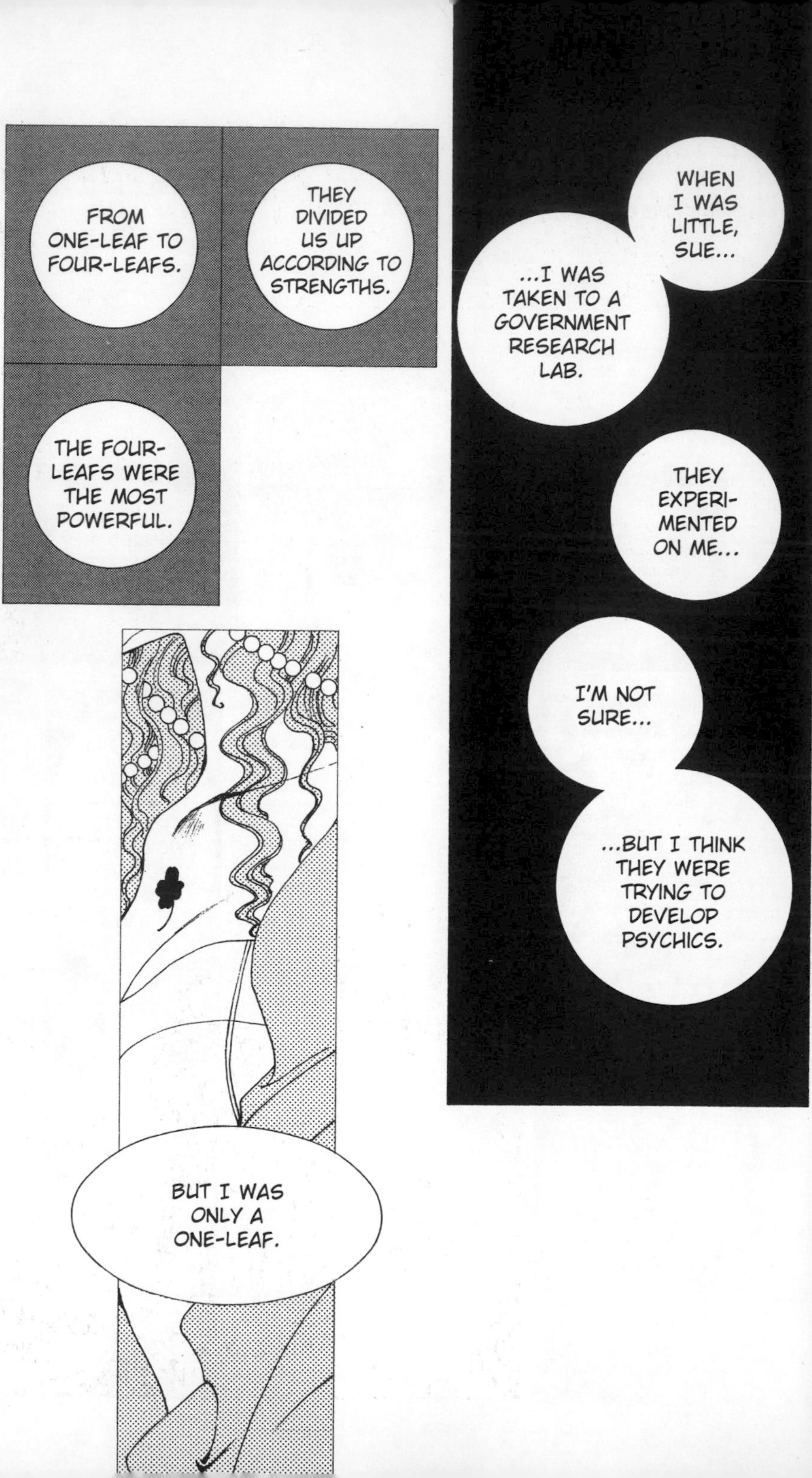
WHEN I WAS LITTLE, SUE...
...I WAS TAKEN TO A GOVERNMENT RESEARCH LAB.
THEY EXPERIMENTED ON ME...
I'M NOT SURE...
...BUT I THINK THEY WERE TRYING TO DEVELOP PSYCHICS.
THEY DIVIDED US UP ACCORDING TO STRENGTHS.
FROM ONE-LEAF TO FOUR-LEAFS.
THE FOUR-LEAFS WERE THE MOST POWERFUL.
BUT I WAS ONLY A ONE-LEAF.

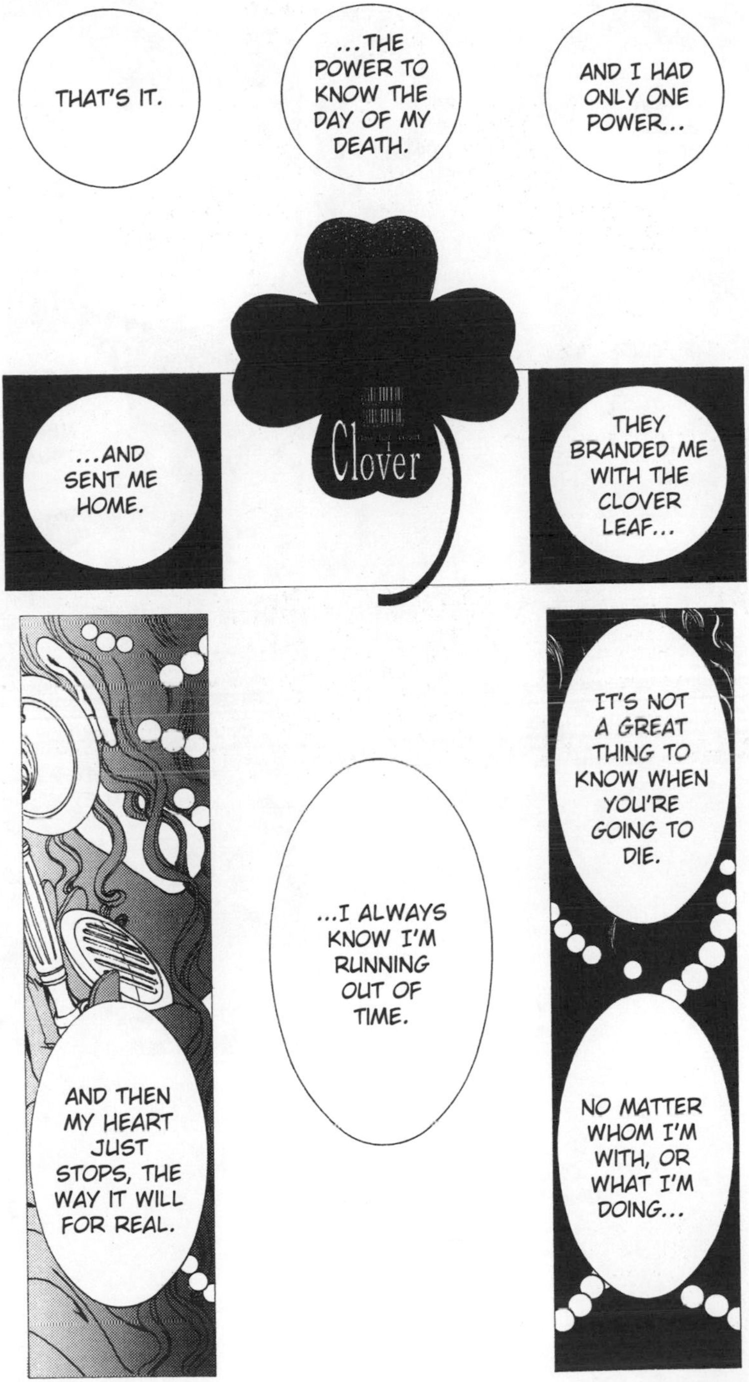
AND I HAD ONLY ONE POWER...
...THE POWER TO KNOW THE DAY OF MY DEATH.
THAT'S IT.
THEY BRANDED ME WITH THE CLOVER LEAF...
Clover
...AND SENT ME HOME.
IT'S NOT A GREAT THING TO KNOW WHEN YOU'RE GOING TO DIE.
NO MATTER WHOM I'M WITH, OR WHAT I'M DOING...
...I ALWAYS KNOW I'M RUNNING OUT OF TIME.
AND THEN MY HEART JUST STOPS, THE WAY IT WILL FOR REAL.

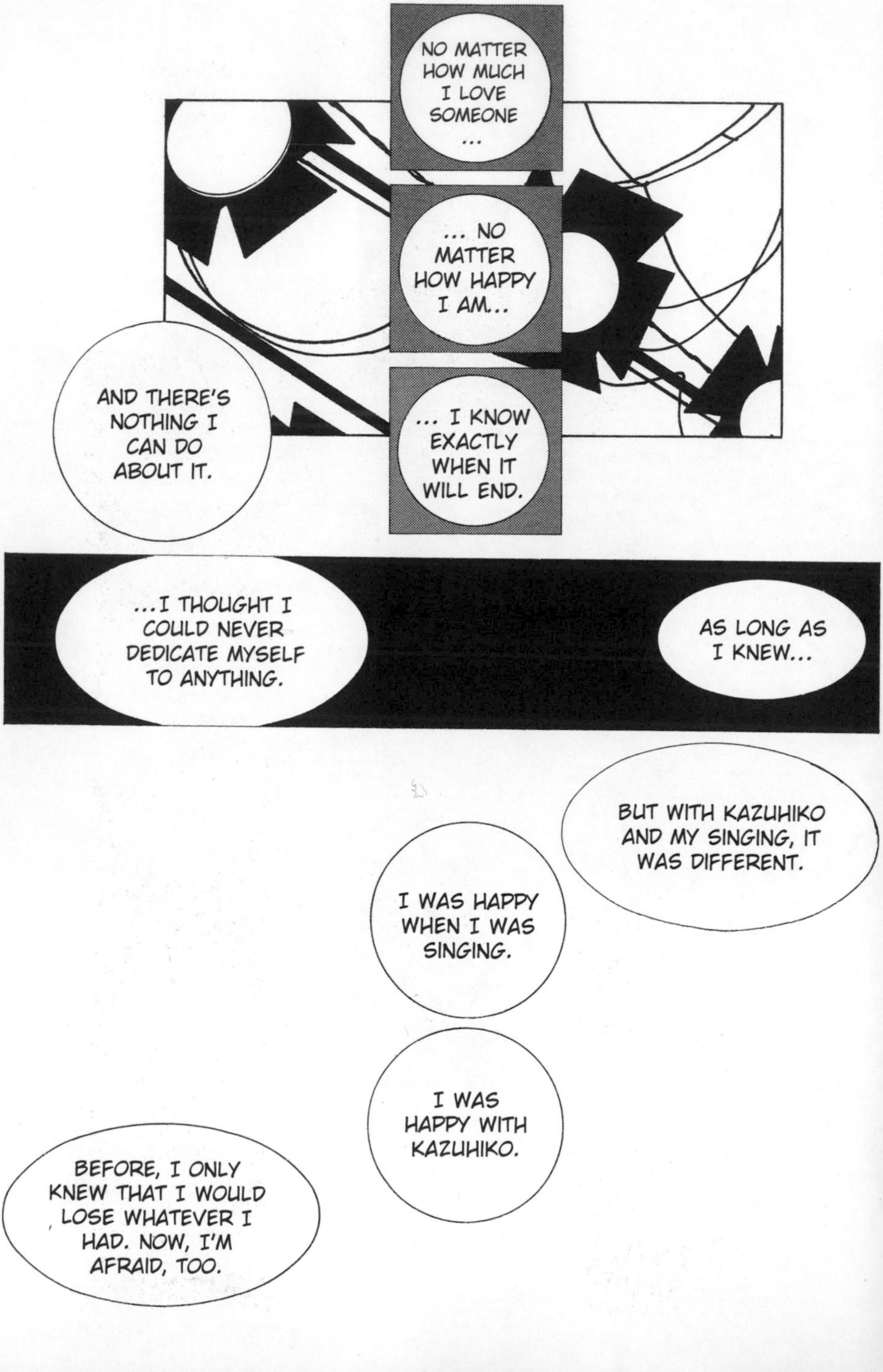
NO MATTER HOW MUCH I LOVE SOMEONE ...
... NO MATTER HOW HAPPY I AM...
... I KNOW EXACTLY WHEN IT WILL END.
AND THERE'S NOTHING I CAN DO ABOUT IT.
AS LONG AS I KNEW...
...I THOUGHT I COULD NEVER DEDICATE MYSELF TO ANYTHING.
BUT WITH KAZUHIKO AND MY SINGING, IT WAS DIFFERENT.
I WAS HAPPY WHEN I WAS SINGING.
I WAS HAPPY WITH KAZUHIKO.
BEFORE, I ONLY KNEW THAT I WOULD LOSE WHATEVER I HAD. NOW, I'M AFRAID, TOO.

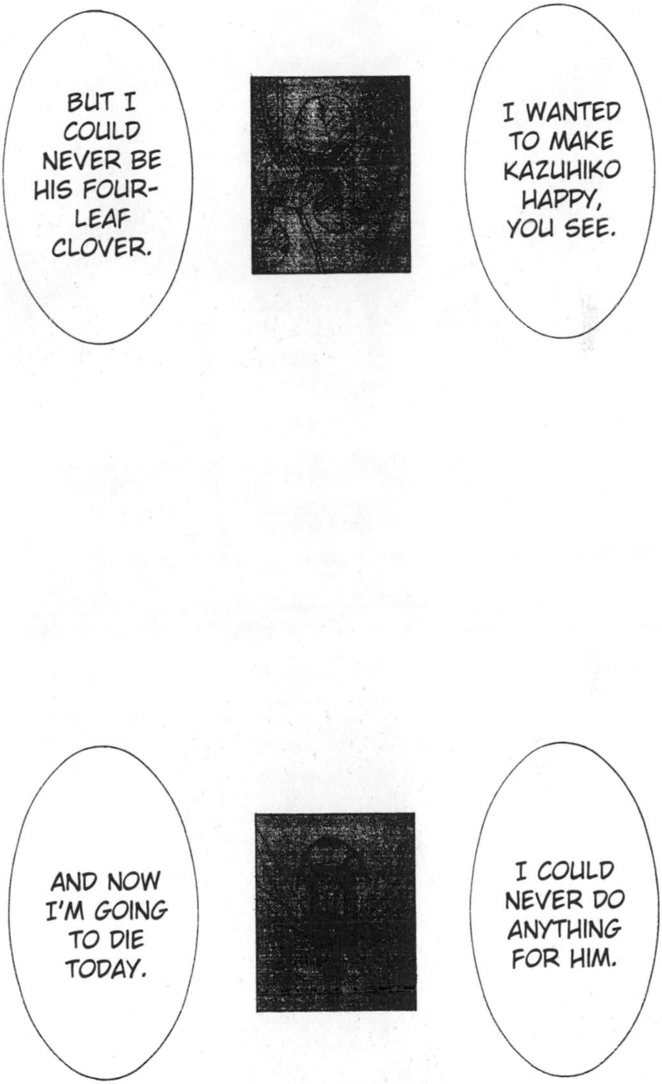

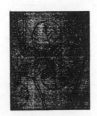

I WANTED TO MAKE KAZUHIKO HAPPY, YOU SEE.
BUT I COULD NEVER BE HIS FOUR-LEAF CLOVER.
I COULD NEVER DO ANYTHING FOR HIM.
AND NOW I'M GOING TO DIE TODAY.

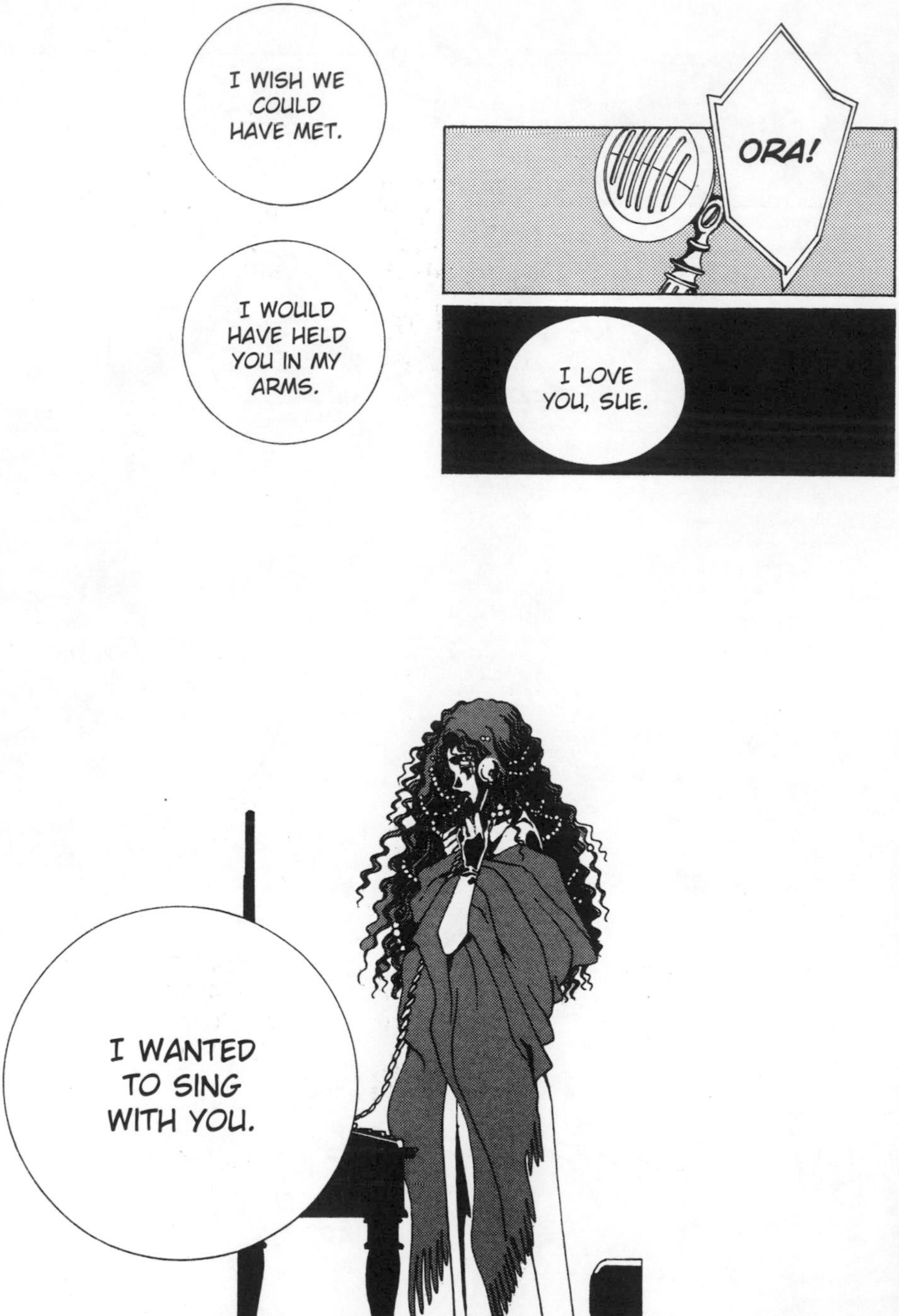
ORA!
I LOVE YOU, SUE.
I WISH WE COULD HAVE MET.
I WOULD HAVE HELD YOU IN MY ARMS.
I WANTED TO SING WITH YOU.

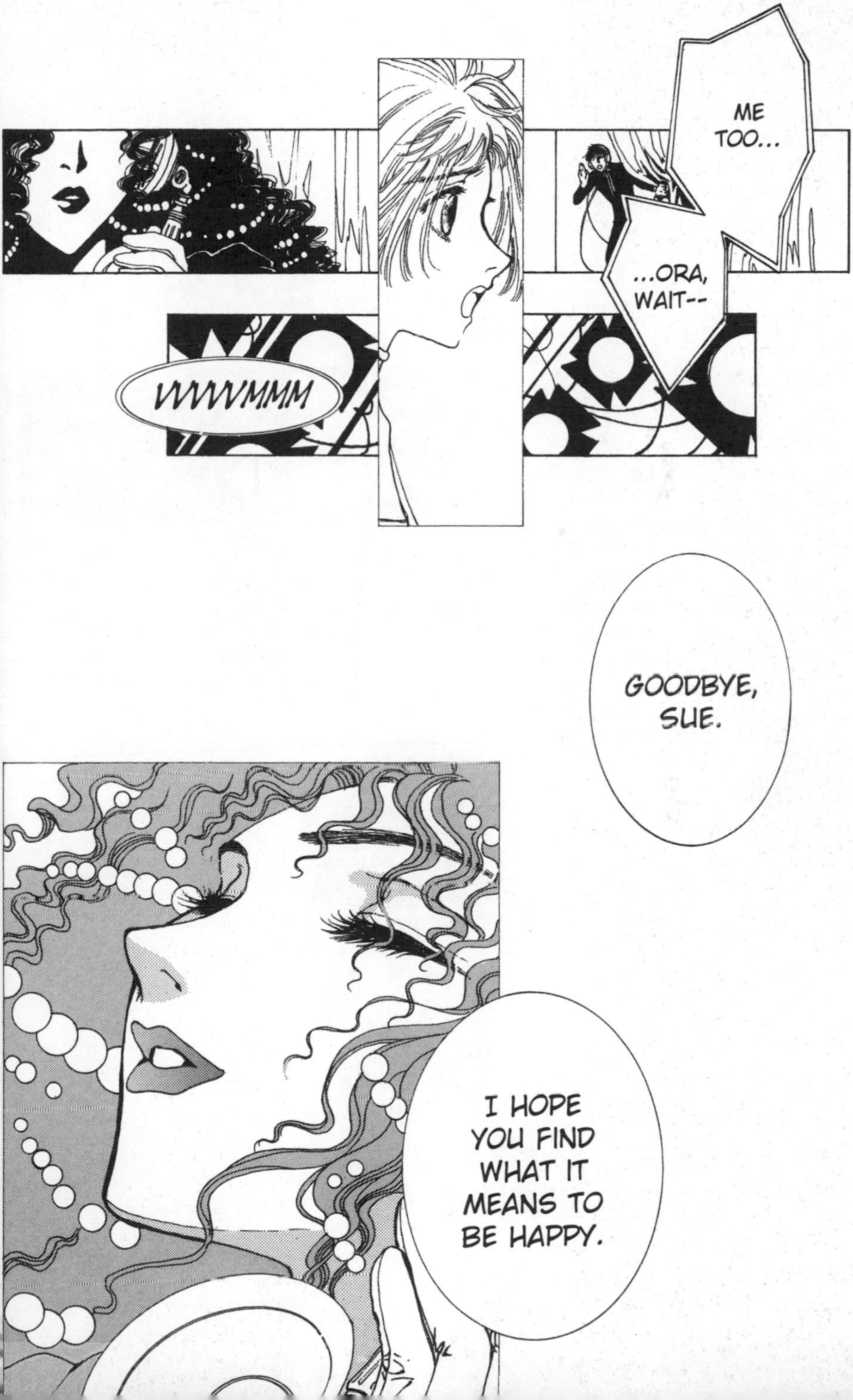
ME TOO...
...ORA, WAIT--
VVVVMMM
GOODBYE, SUE.
I HOPE YOU FIND WHAT IT MEANS TO BE HAPPY.

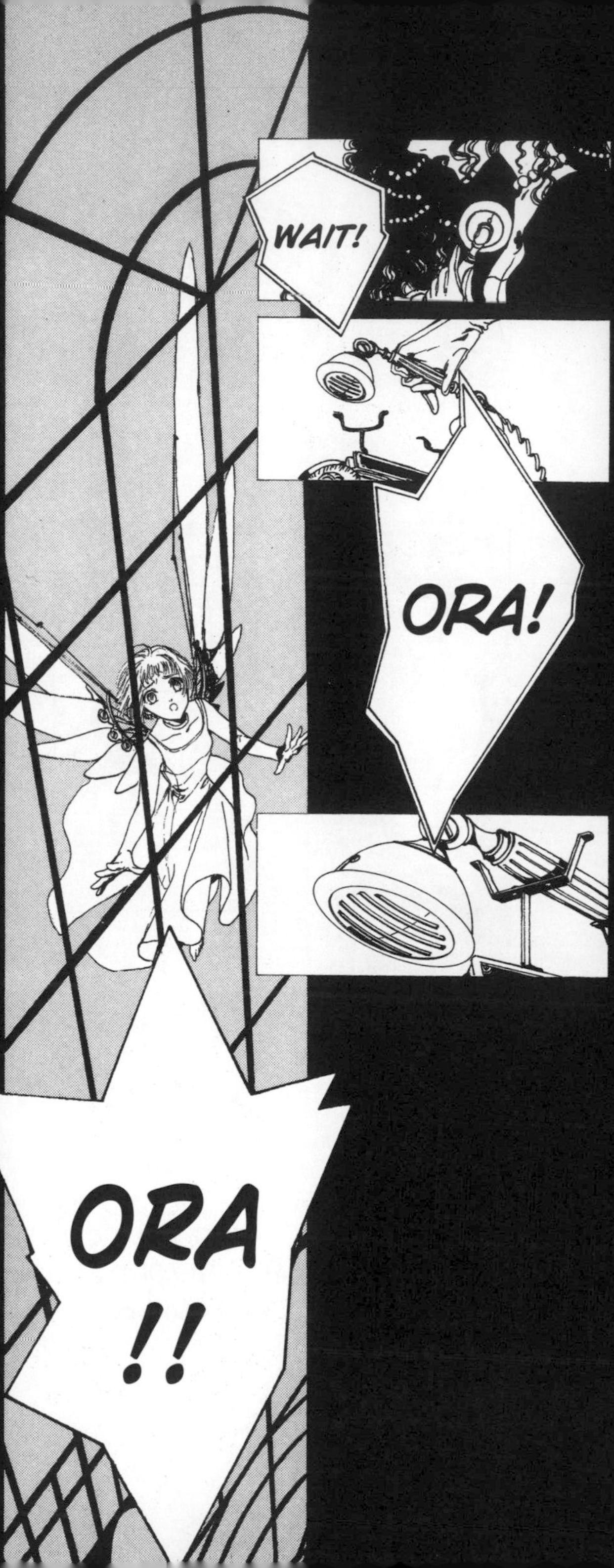
WAIT!
ORA!
ORA !!

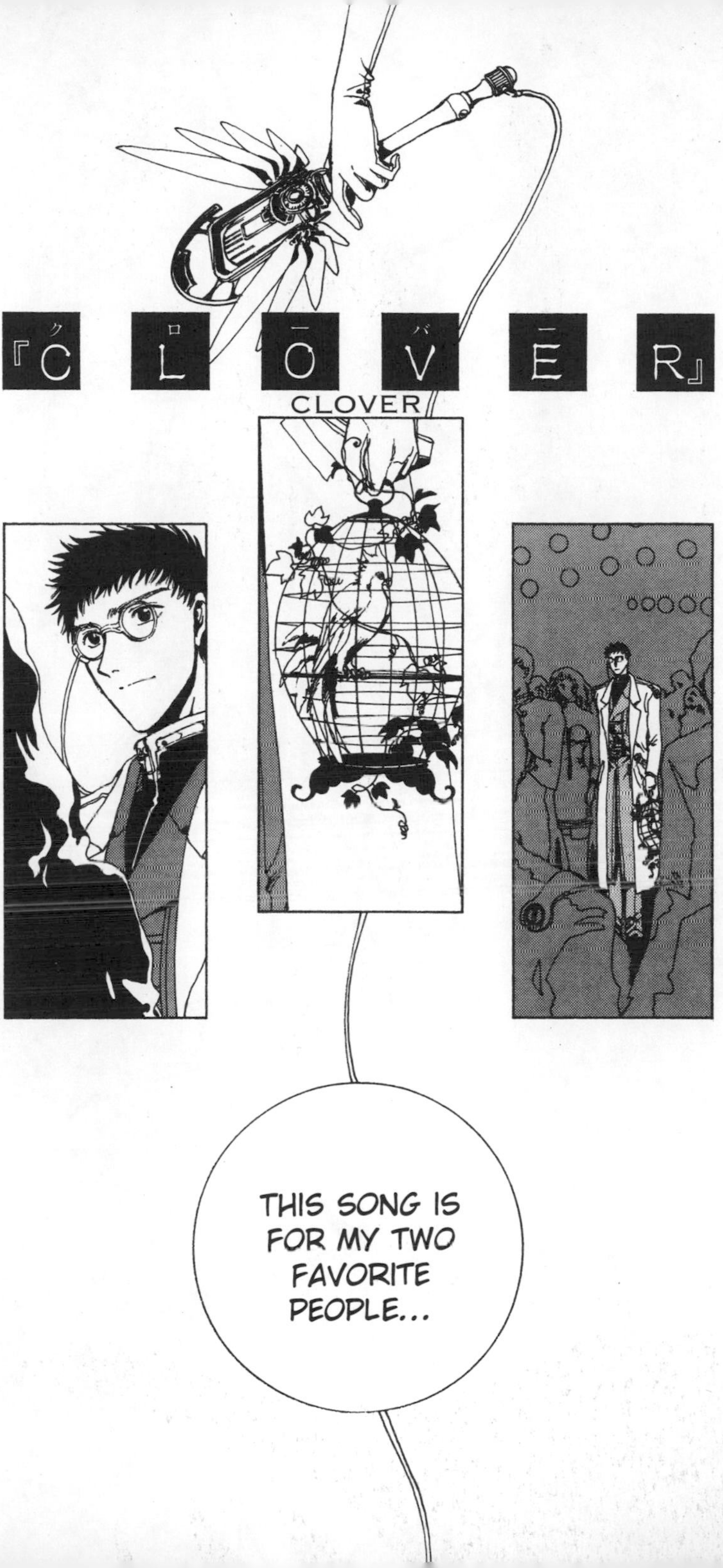
『CLOVER』
クローバー
CLOVER
THIS SONG IS FOR MY TWO FAVORITE PEOPLE...

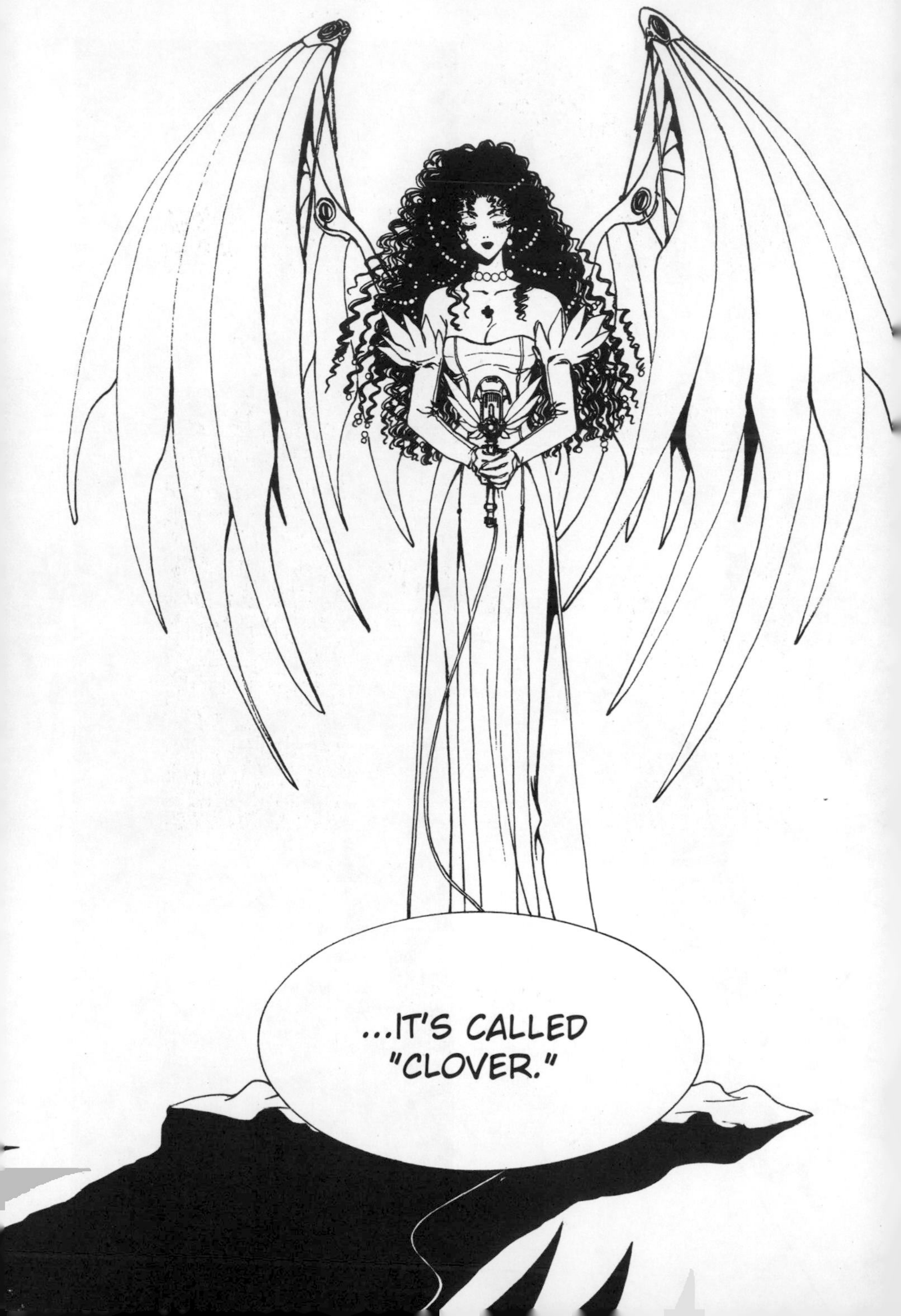
...IT'S CALLED "CLOVER."

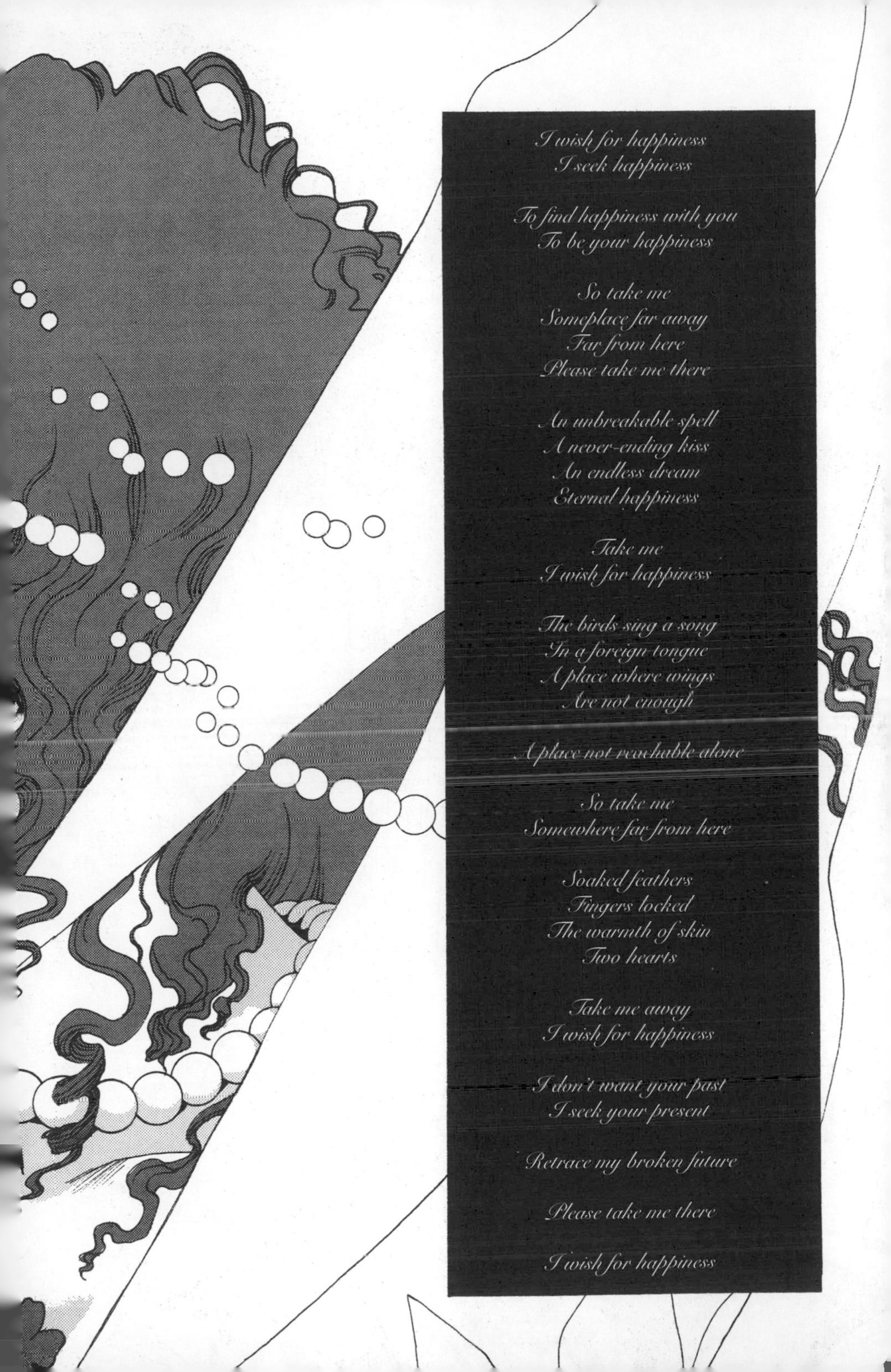
I wish for happiness
I seek happiness

To find happiness with you
To be your happiness

So take me
Someplace far away
Far from here
Please take me there

An unbreakable spell
A never-ending kiss
An endless dream
Eternal happiness

Take me
I wish for happiness

The birds sing a song
In a foreign tongue
A place where wings
Are not enough

A place not reachable alone

So take me
Somewhere far from here

Soaked feathers
Fingers locked
The warmth of skin
Two hearts

Take me away
I wish for happiness

I don't want your past
I seek your present

Retrace my broken future

Please take me there

I wish for happiness

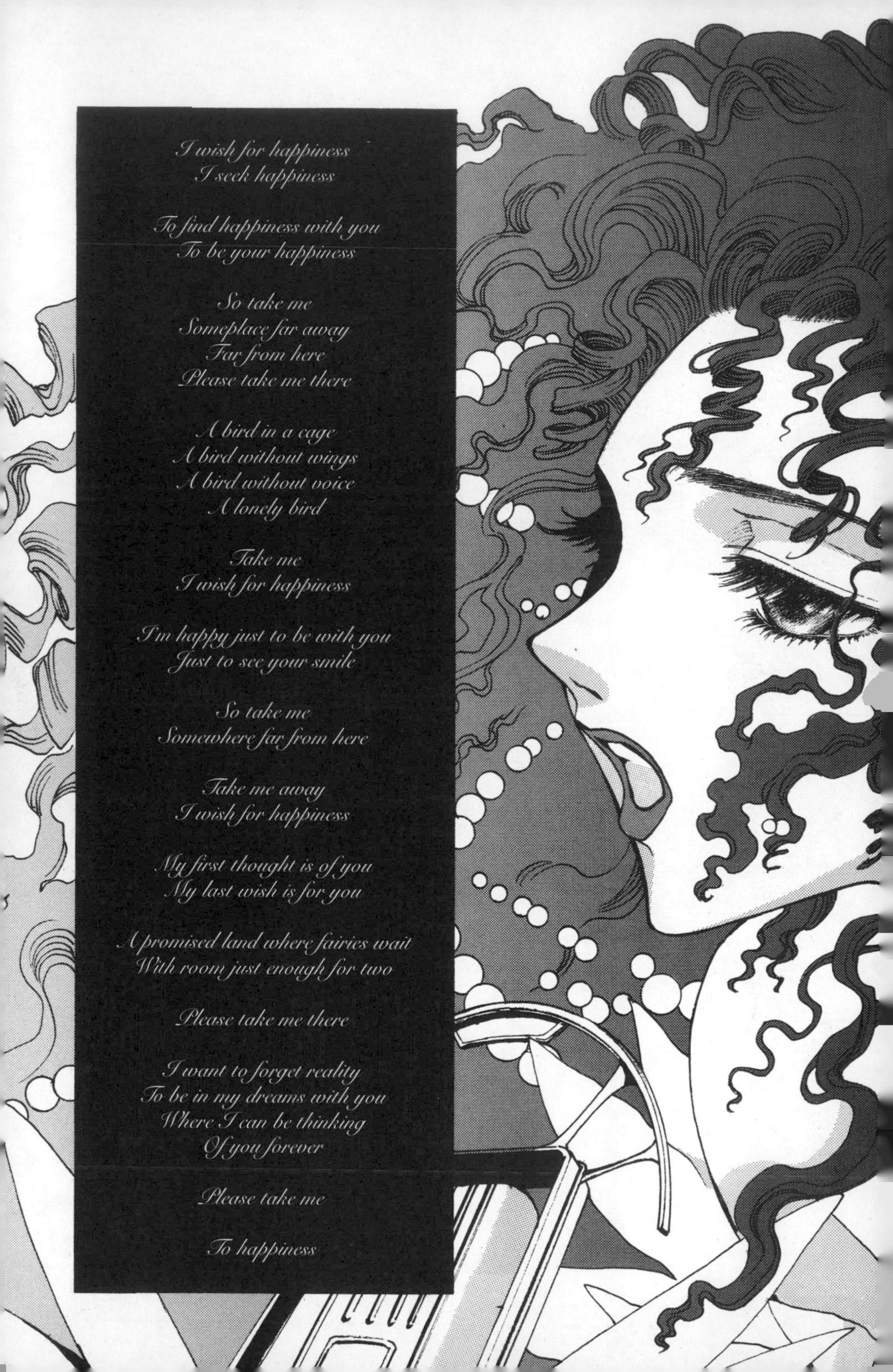
I wish for happiness
I seek happiness

To find happiness with you
To be your happiness

So take me
Someplace far away
Far from here
Please take me there

A bird in a cage
A bird without wings
A bird without voice
A lonely bird

Take me
I wish for happiness

I'm happy just to be with you
Just to see your smile

So take me
Somewhere far from here

Take me away
I wish for happiness

My first thought is of you
My last wish is for you

A promised land where fairies wait
With room just enough for two

Please take me there

I want to forget reality
To be in my dreams with you
Where I can be thinking
Of you forever

Please take me

To happiness

MAN'S

『人』

の

『目』

EYE

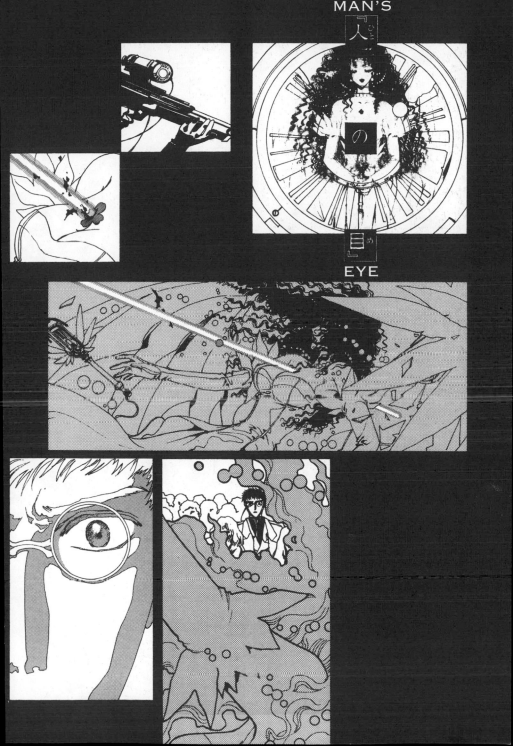

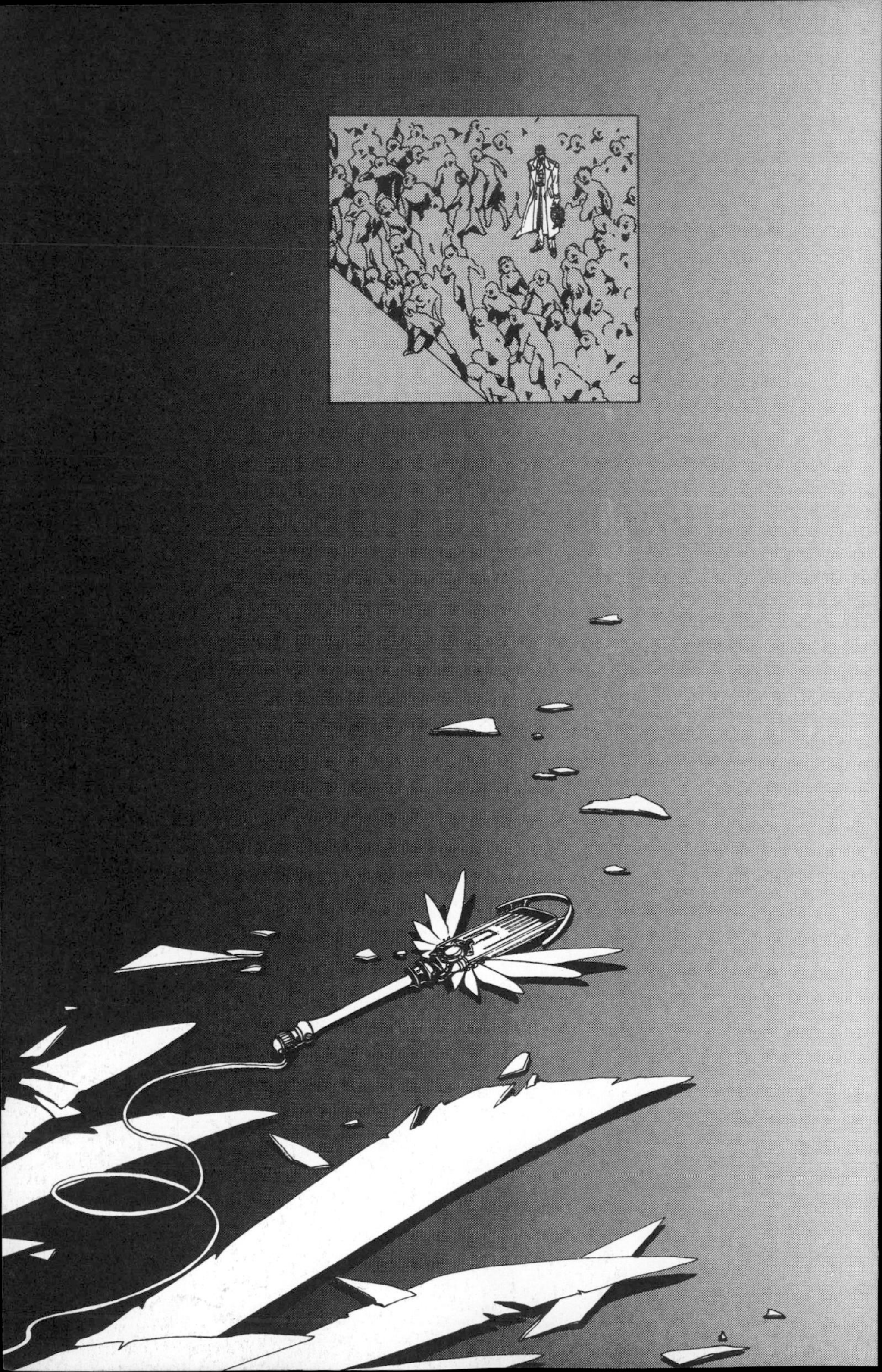

『小鳥の涙』
BIRD'S TEAR

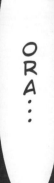

ORA...

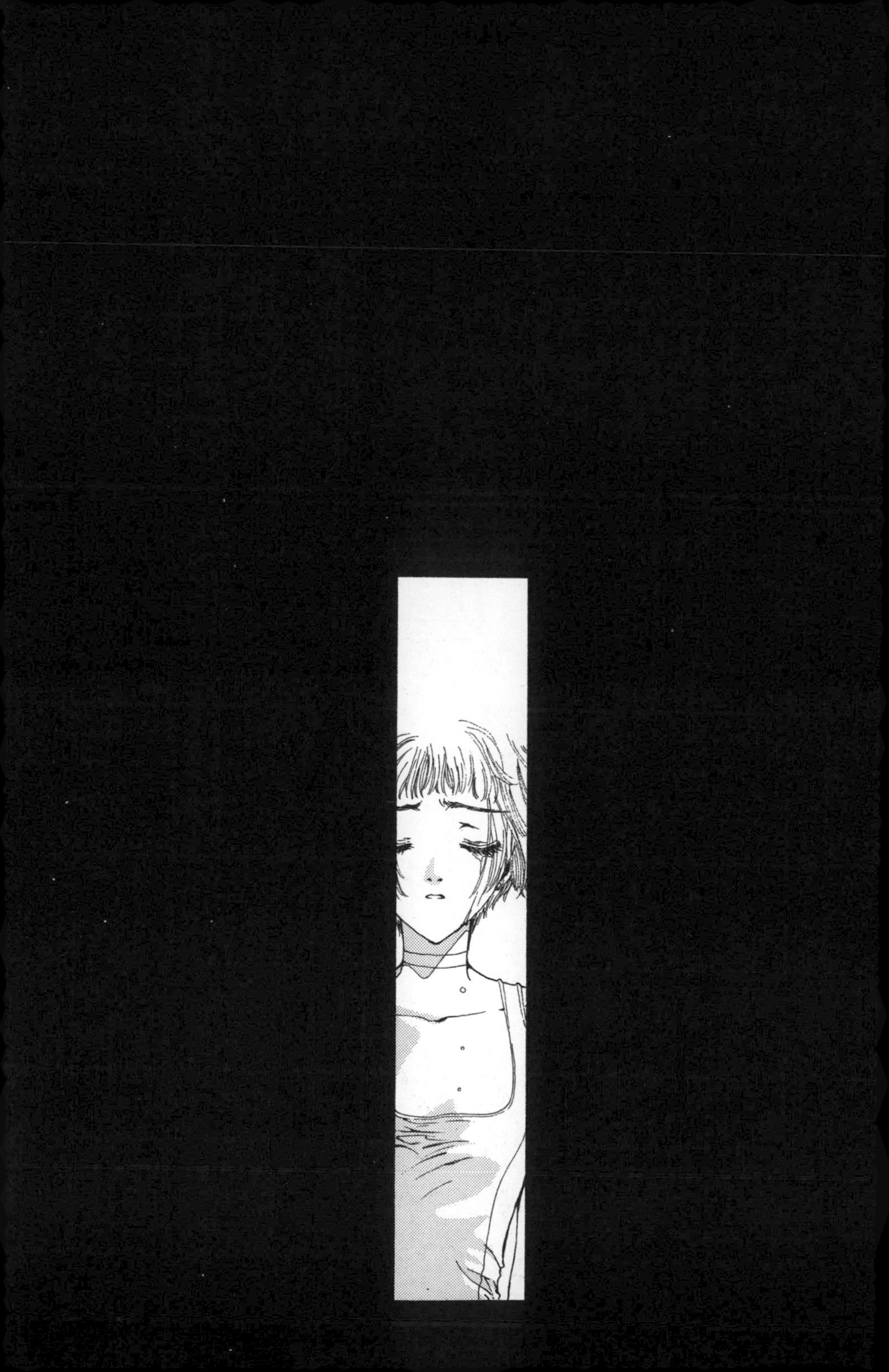

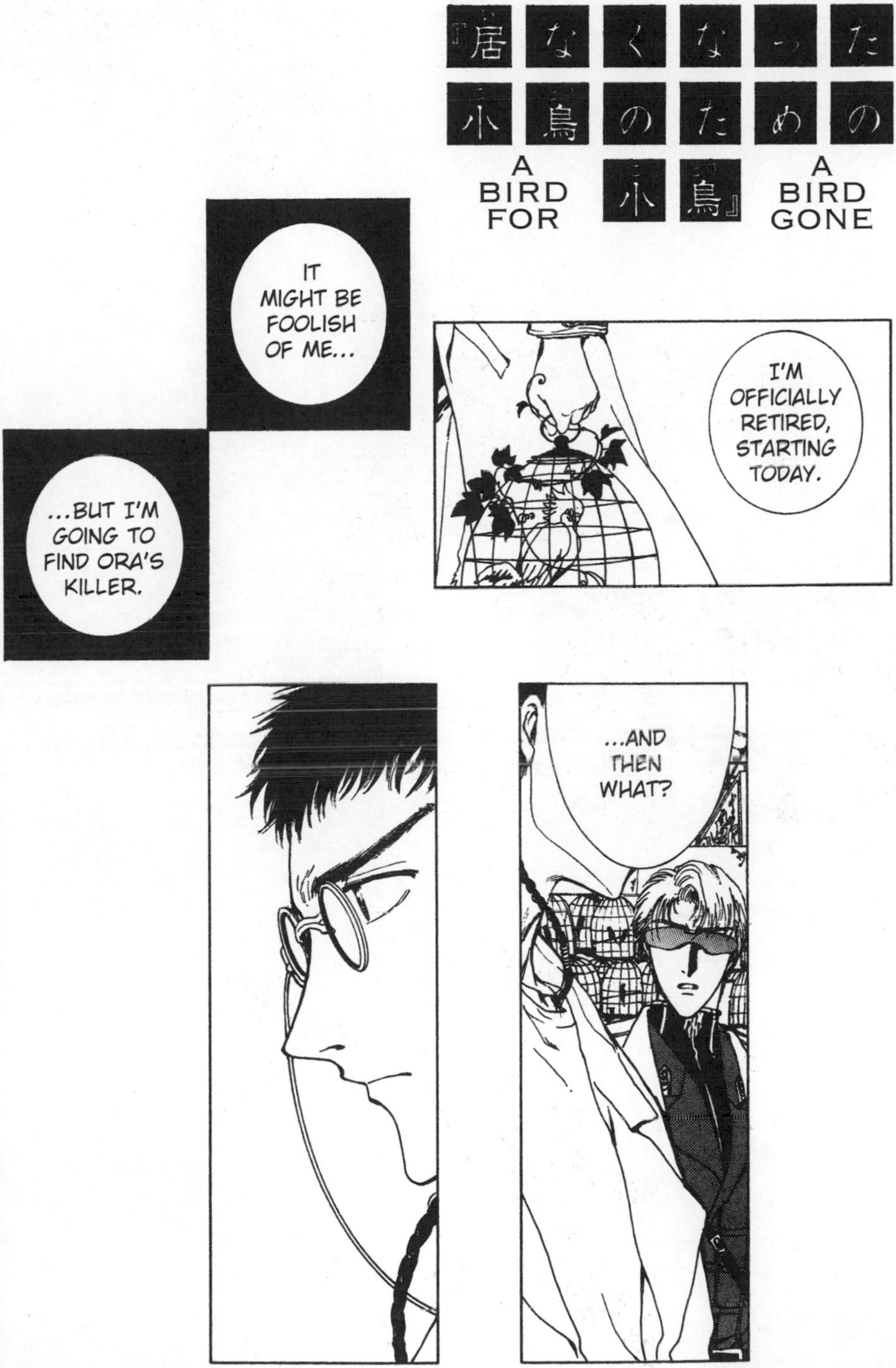
『居なくなった小鳥のための小鳥』
A BIRD FOR A BIRD GONE
I'M OFFICIALLY RETIRED, STARTING TODAY.
IT MIGHT BE FOOLISH OF ME...
...BUT I'M GOING TO FIND ORA'S KILLER.
...AND THEN WHAT?

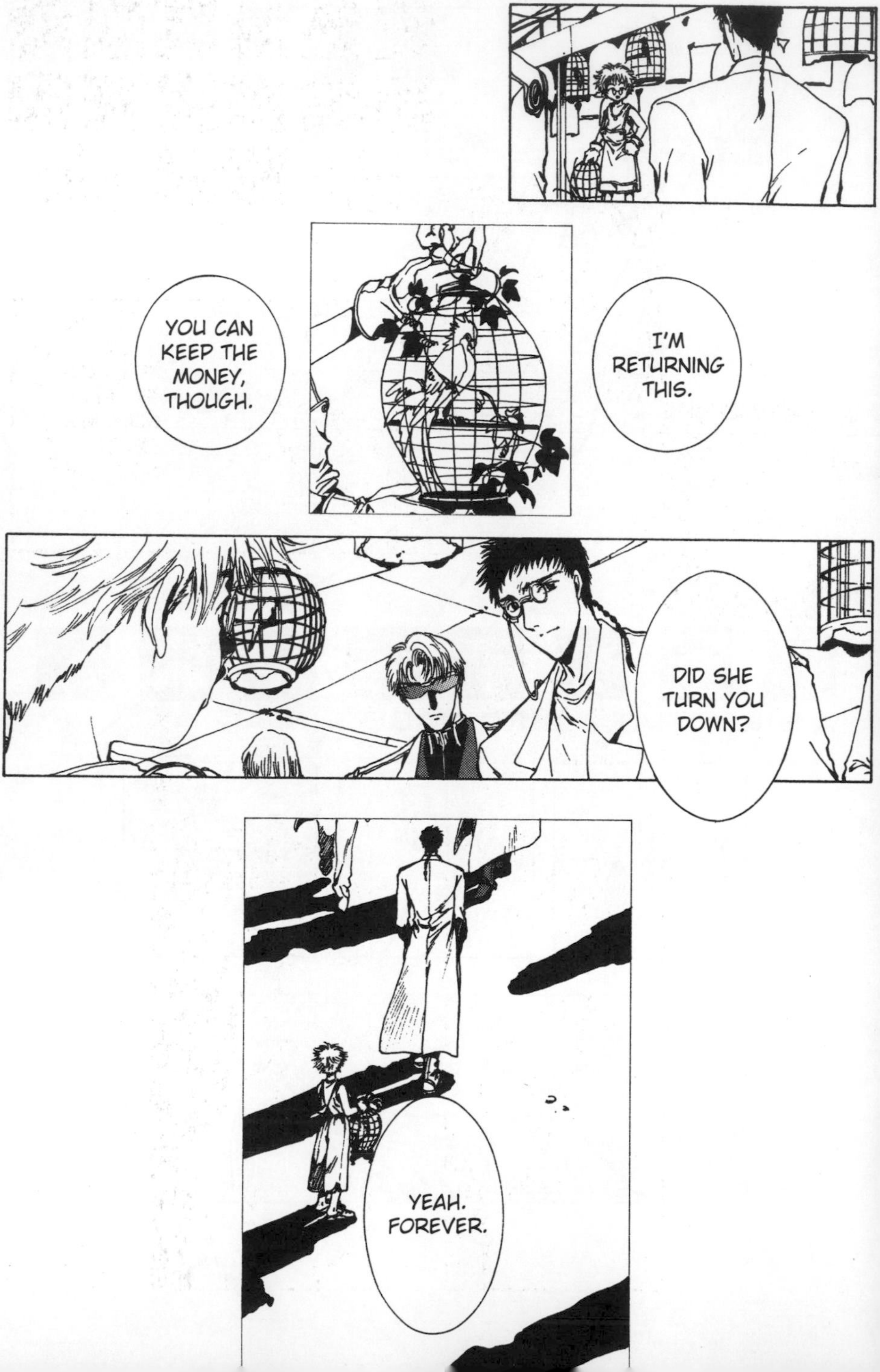
I'M RETURNING THIS.
YOU CAN KEEP THE MONEY, THOUGH.
DID SHE TURN YOU DOWN?
YEAH. FOREVER.

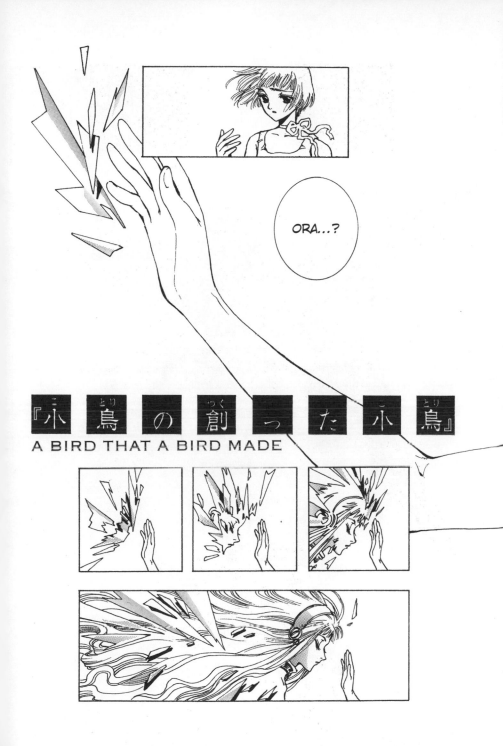

ORA...?

『小鳥の創った小鳥』
A BIRD THAT A BIRD MADE

They say
A four-leaf clover
brings happiness

But please
keep it a secret

Don't tell anyone
where you found it

Or how many leaves it has

A four-leaf clover.

How I wish to make you happy
But I won't be there to see

*If you find a
four-leaf clover
You will
discover happiness*

*But it can
Never be found*

*Happiness lies inside
A secret cage*

*No one can possess
The four-leaf clover*

*But then,
What of the three-leaf clover?*

FOUR-LEAF CLOVER 『四つ葉のクローバー』

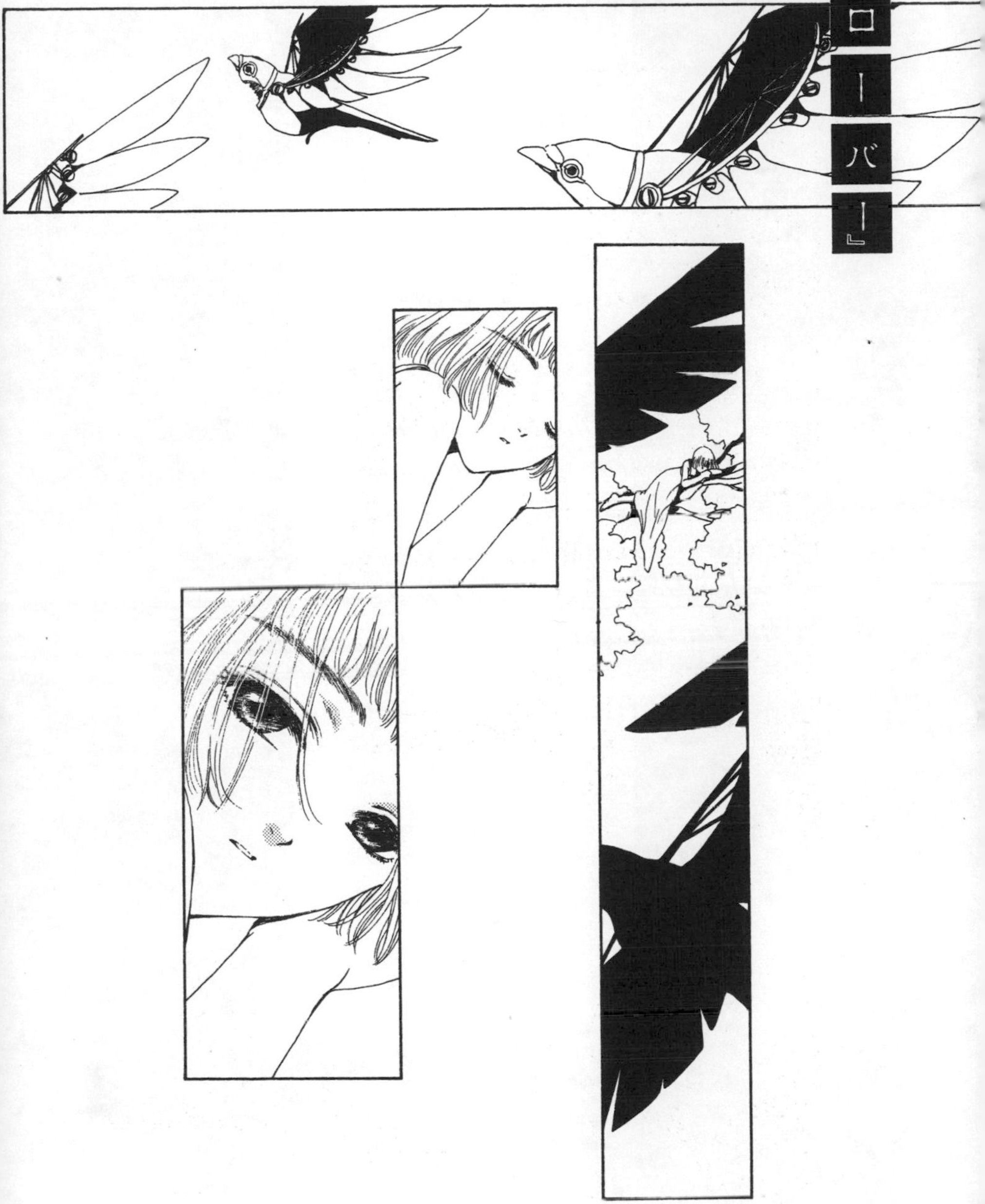

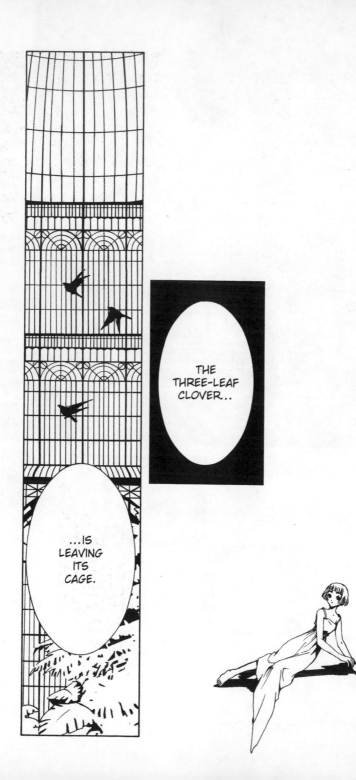

THE
THREE-LEAF
CLOVER...

...IS
LEAVING
ITS
CAGE.

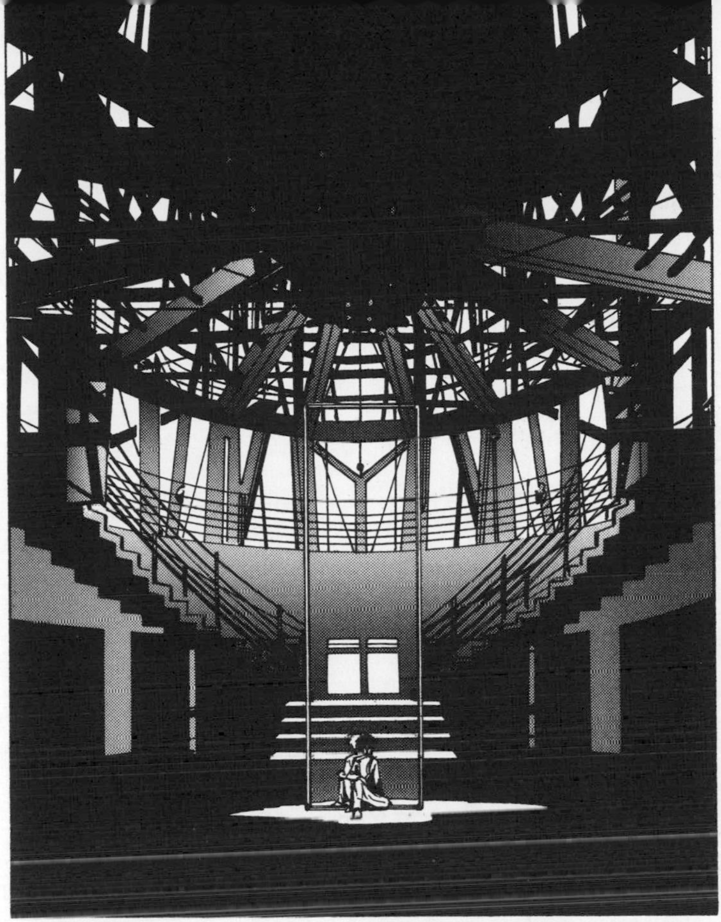

『三つ葉のクローバー』
THREE-LEAF CLOVER

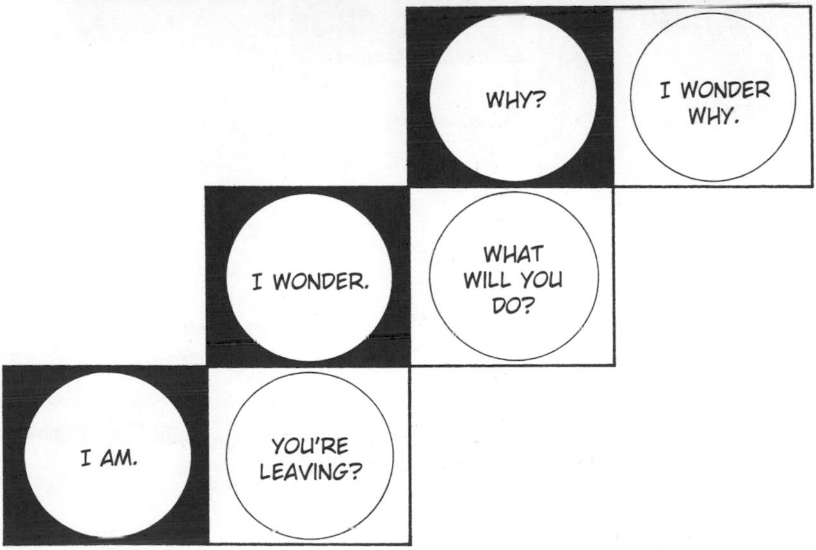
I WONDER WHY.
WHY?
WHAT WILL YOU DO?
I WONDER.
YOU'RE LEAVING?
I AM.

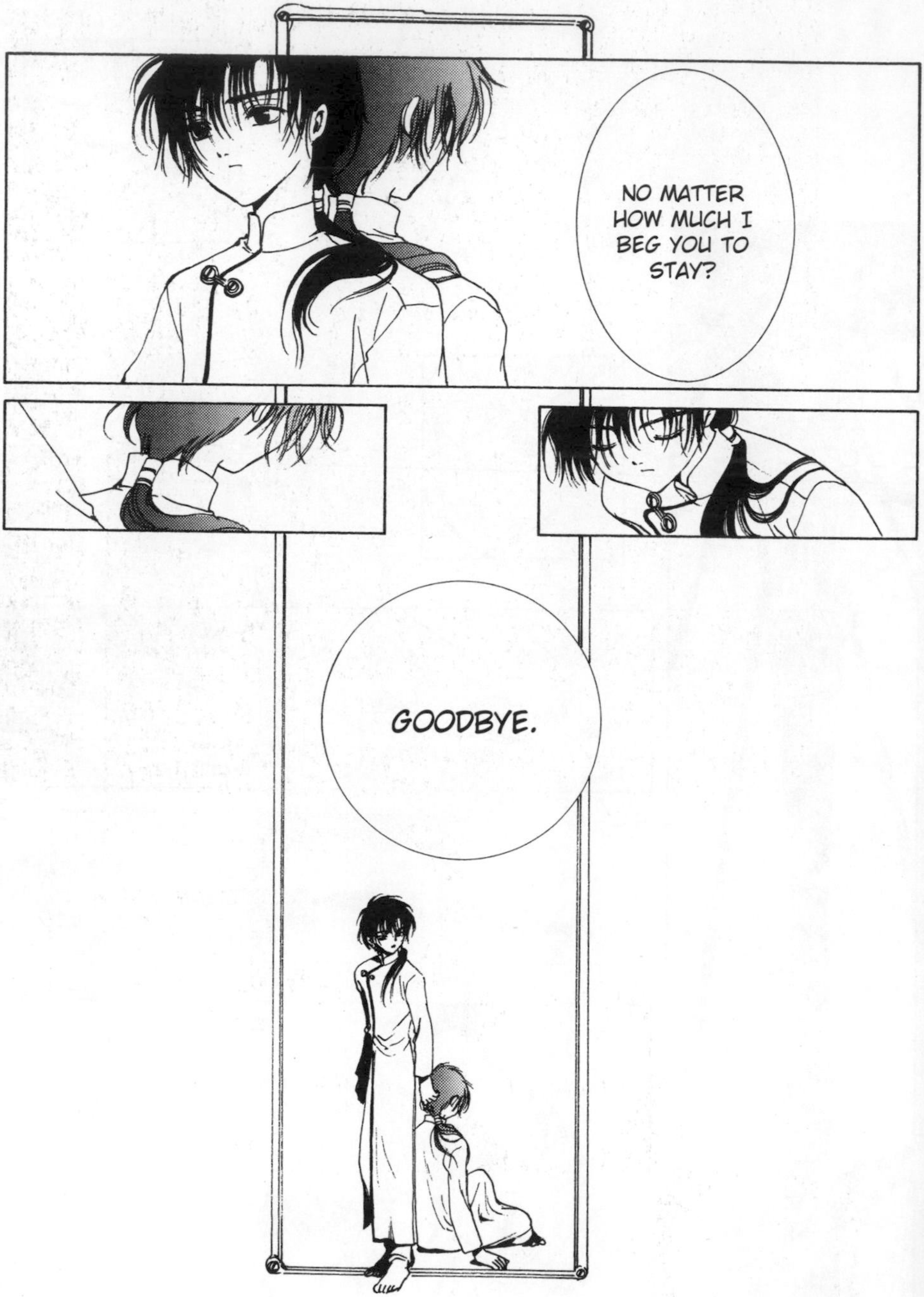
NO MATTER HOW MUCH I BEG YOU TO STAY?
GOODBYE.

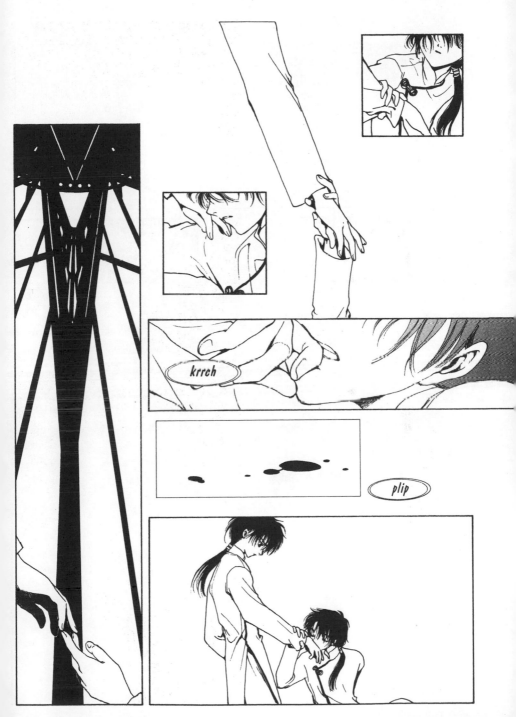

krrch

plip

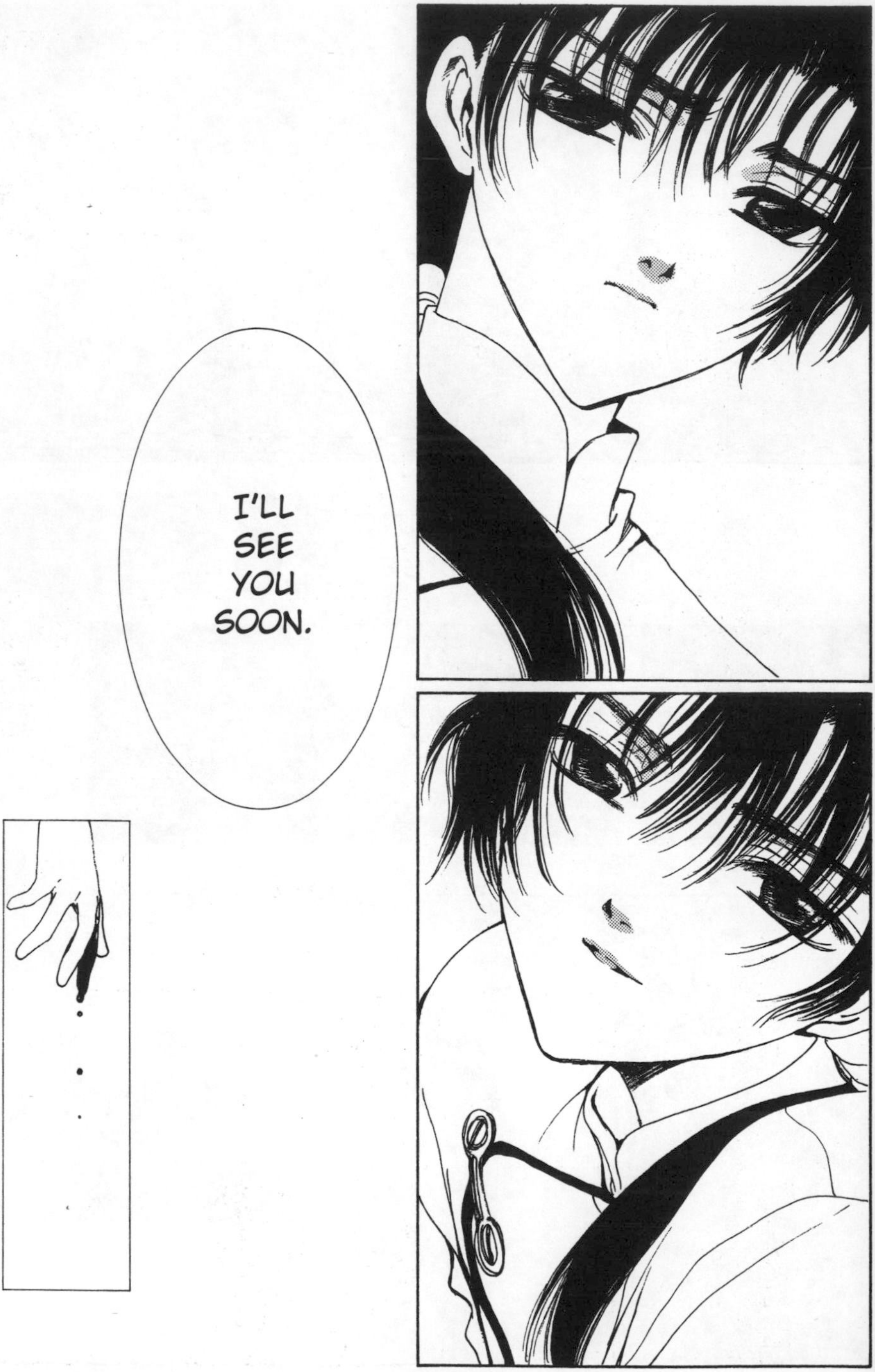
I'LL SEE YOU SOON.

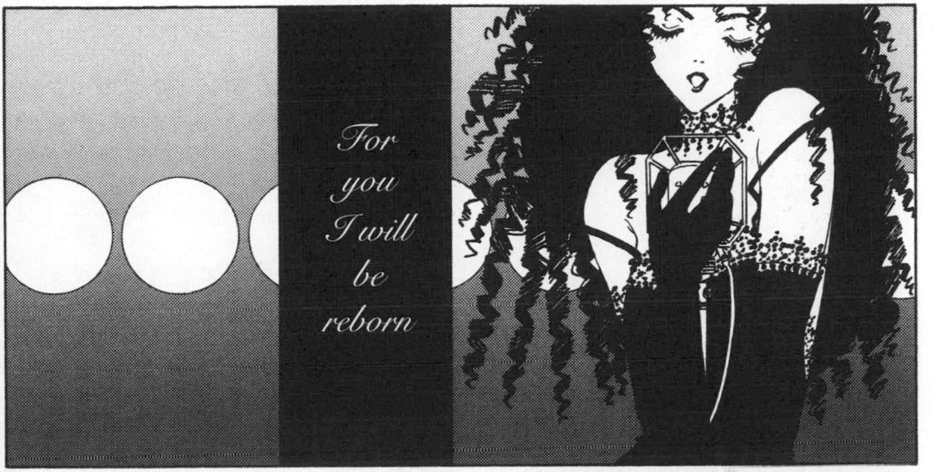
For you I will be reborn

SINGING VOICE 『歌う声』

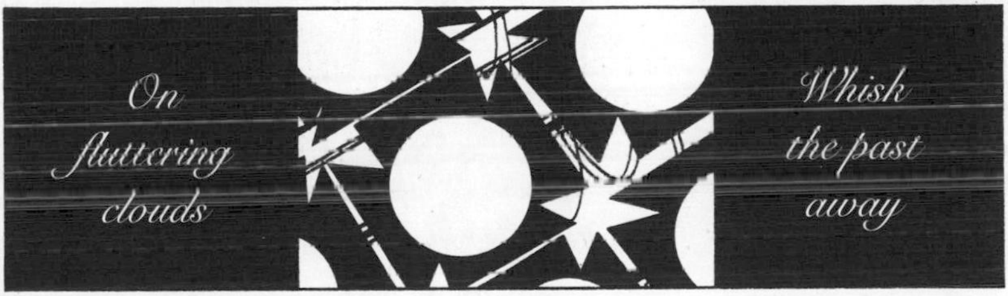
On fluttering clouds
Whisk the past away

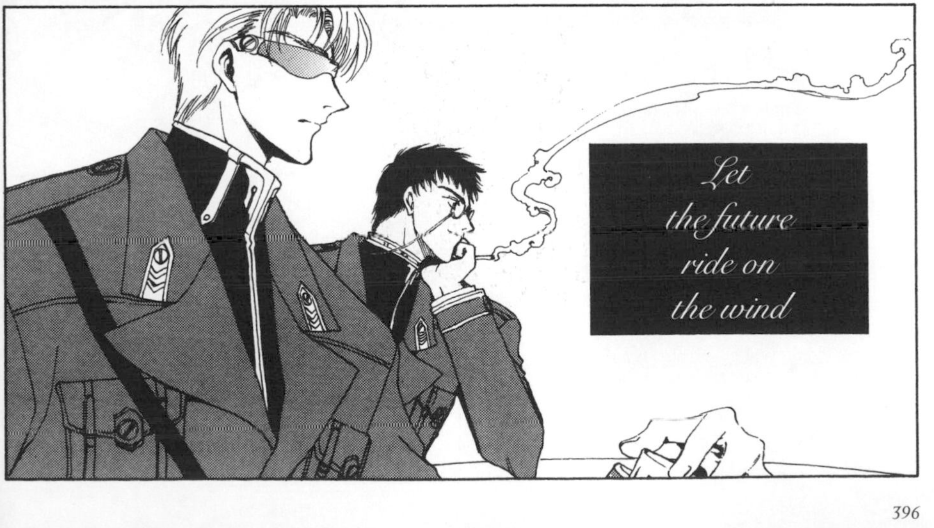
Let the future ride on the wind

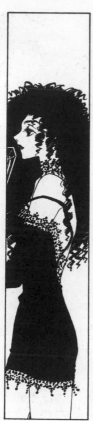

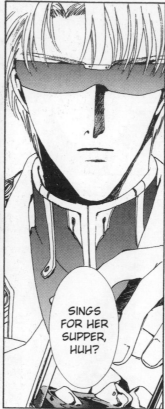

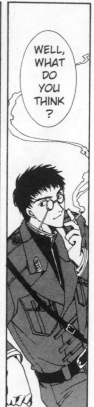

WELL, WHAT DO YOU THINK?
SINGS FOR HER SUPPER, HUH?

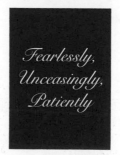

Fearlessly, Unceasingly, Patiently

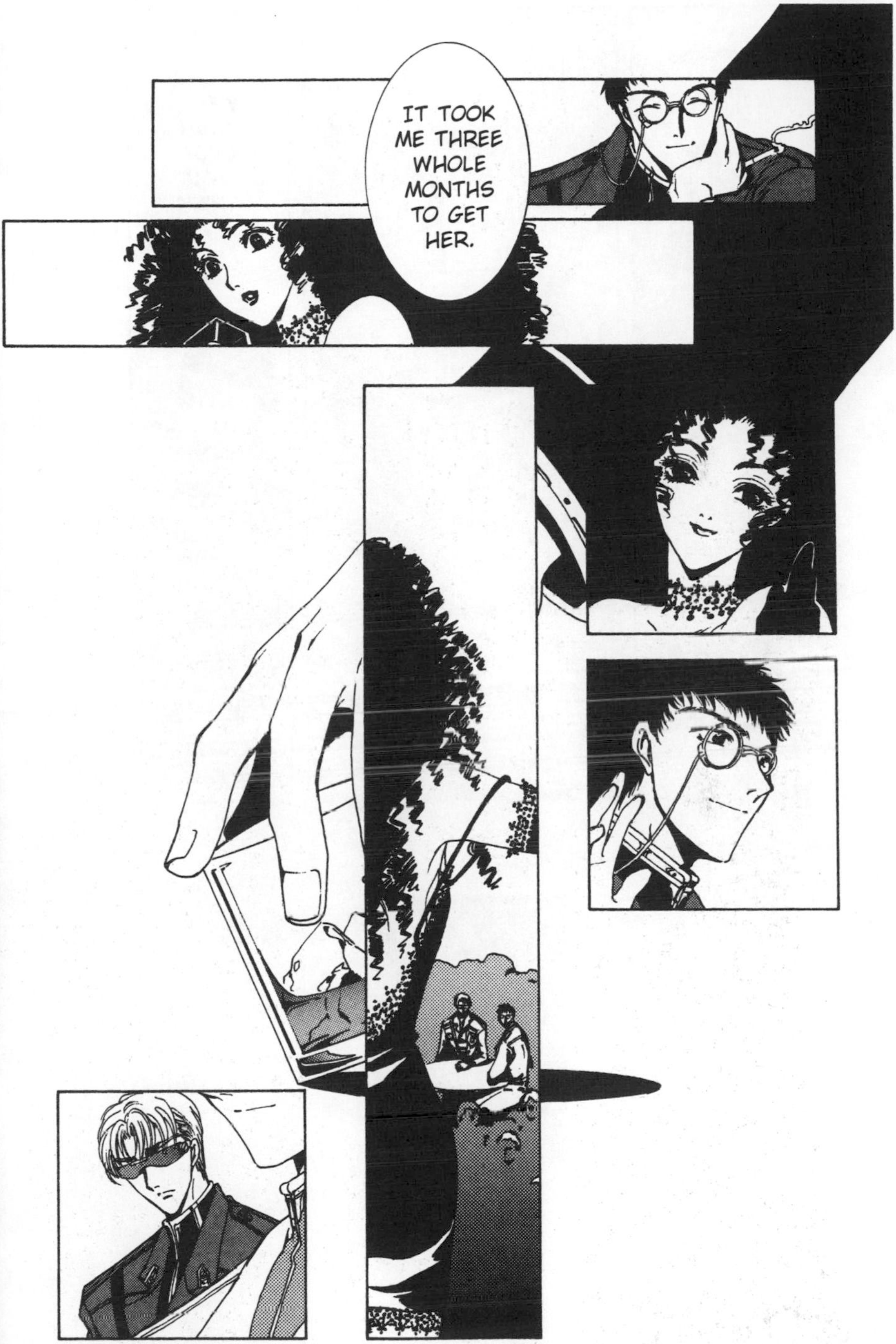
IT TOOK ME THREE WHOLE MONTHS TO GET HER.

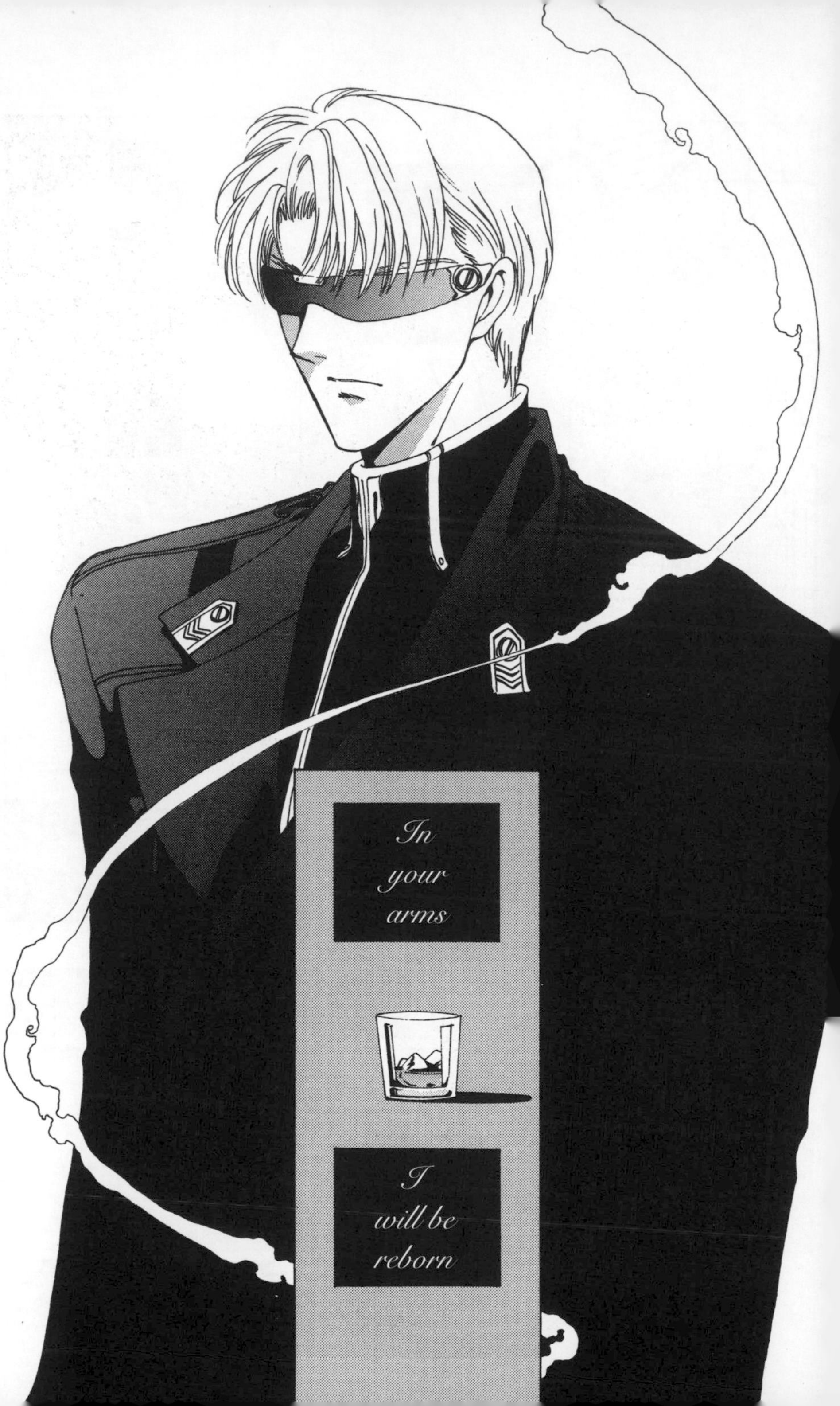
In your arms
I will be reborn

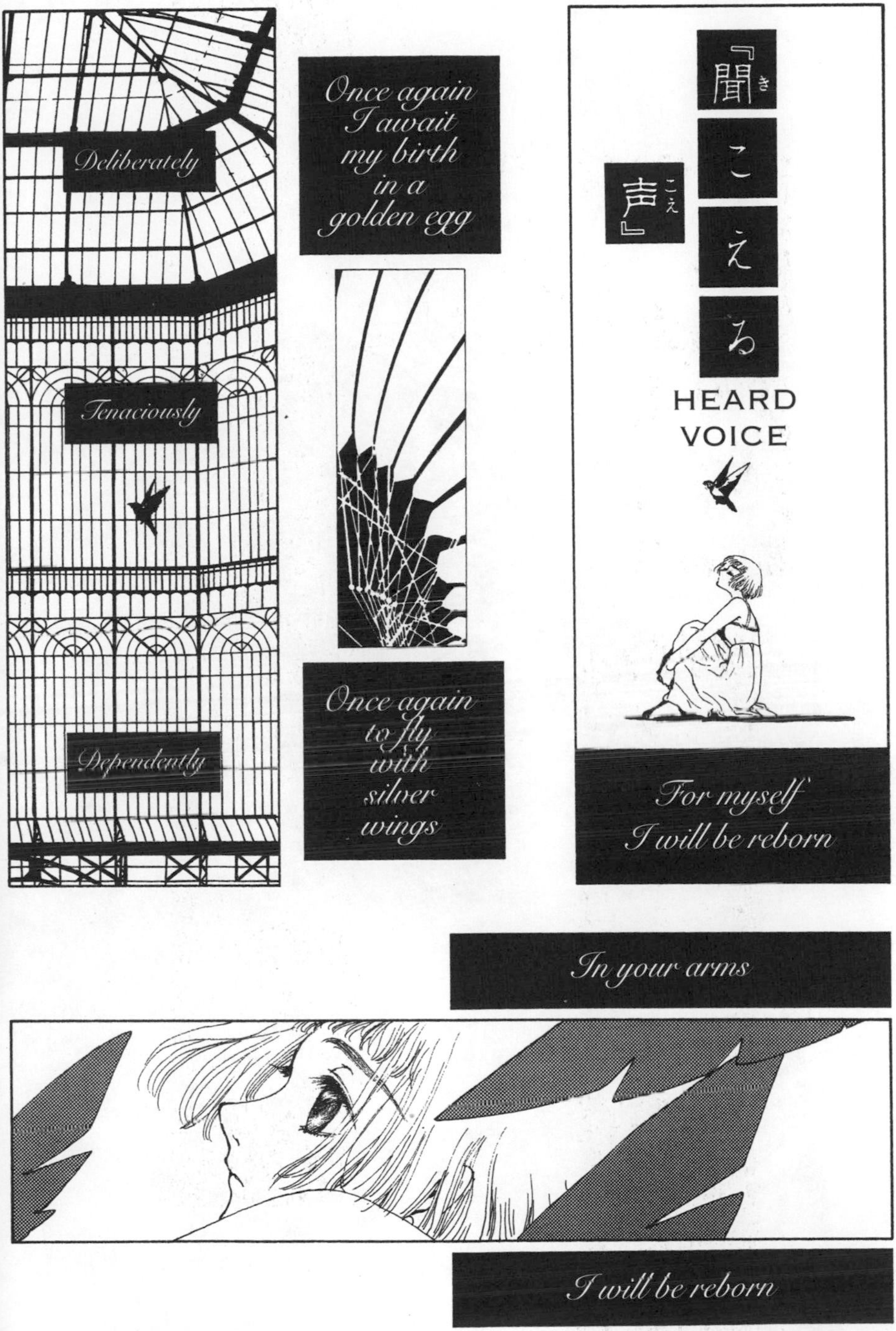
『聞(き)こえる声(こえ)』
HEARD VOICE
For myself I will be reborn
Once again I await my birth in a golden egg
Once again to fly with silver wings
Deliberately
Tenaciously
Dependently
In your arms
I will be reborn

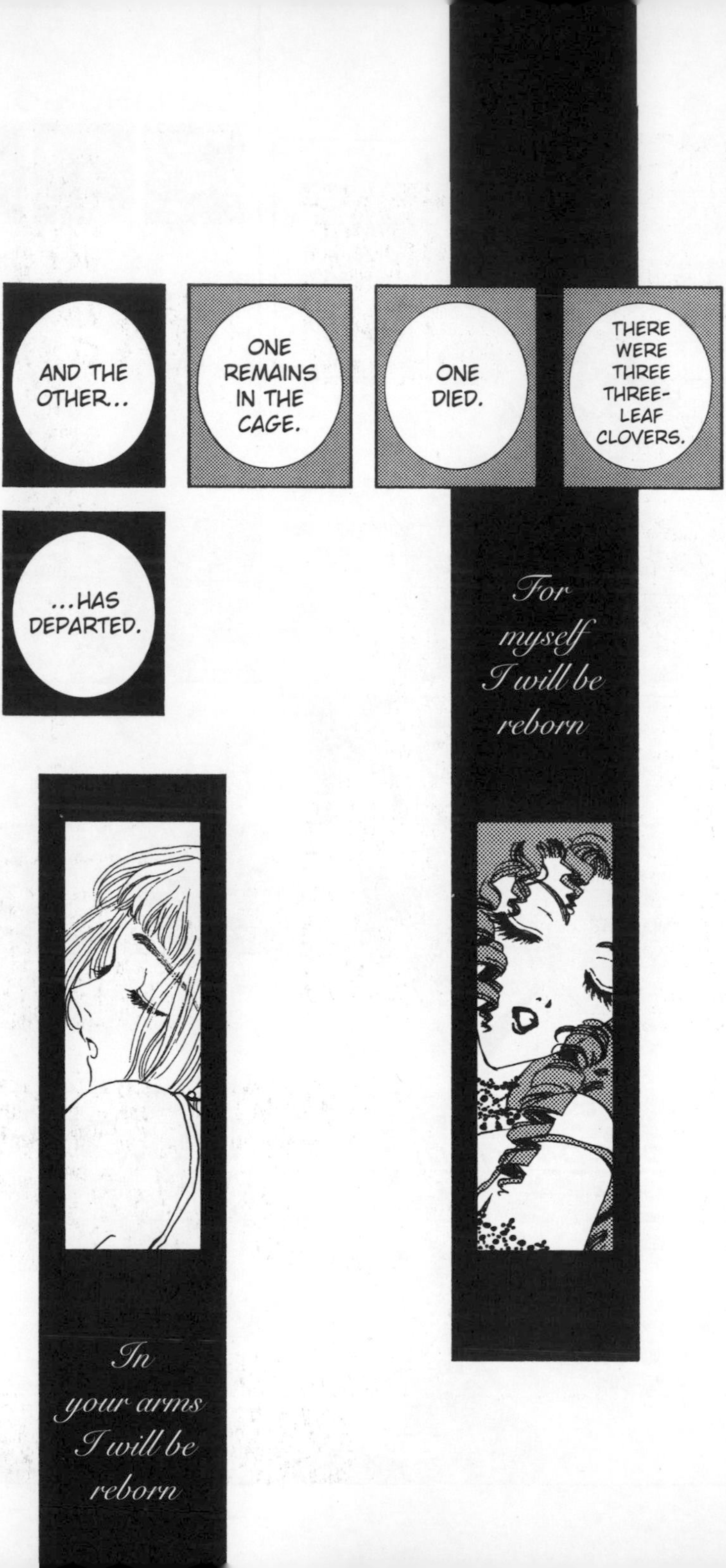
THERE WERE THREE THREE-LEAF CLOVERS.
ONE DIED.
ONE REMAINS IN THE CAGE.
AND THE OTHER...
...HAS DEPARTED.
For myself I will be reborn
In your arms I will be reborn

CALLING SOUND

『呼ぶ音』

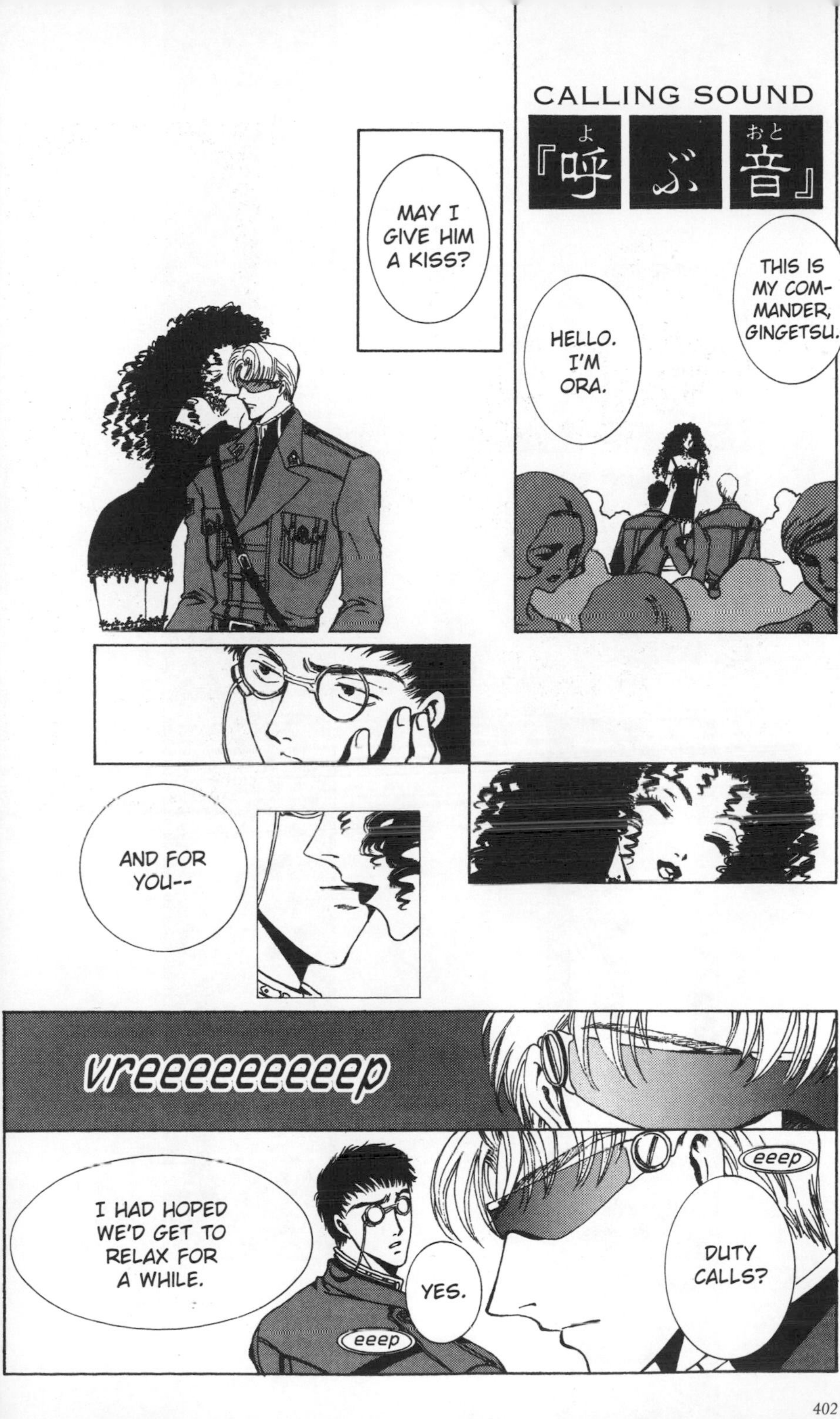
THIS IS MY COMMANDER, GINGETSU.
HELLO. I'M ORA.
MAY I GIVE HIM A KISS?
AND FOR YOU--
vreeeeeeeeeep
eeep
DUTY CALLS?
YES.
eeep
I HAD HOPED WE'D GET TO RELAX FOR A WHILE.

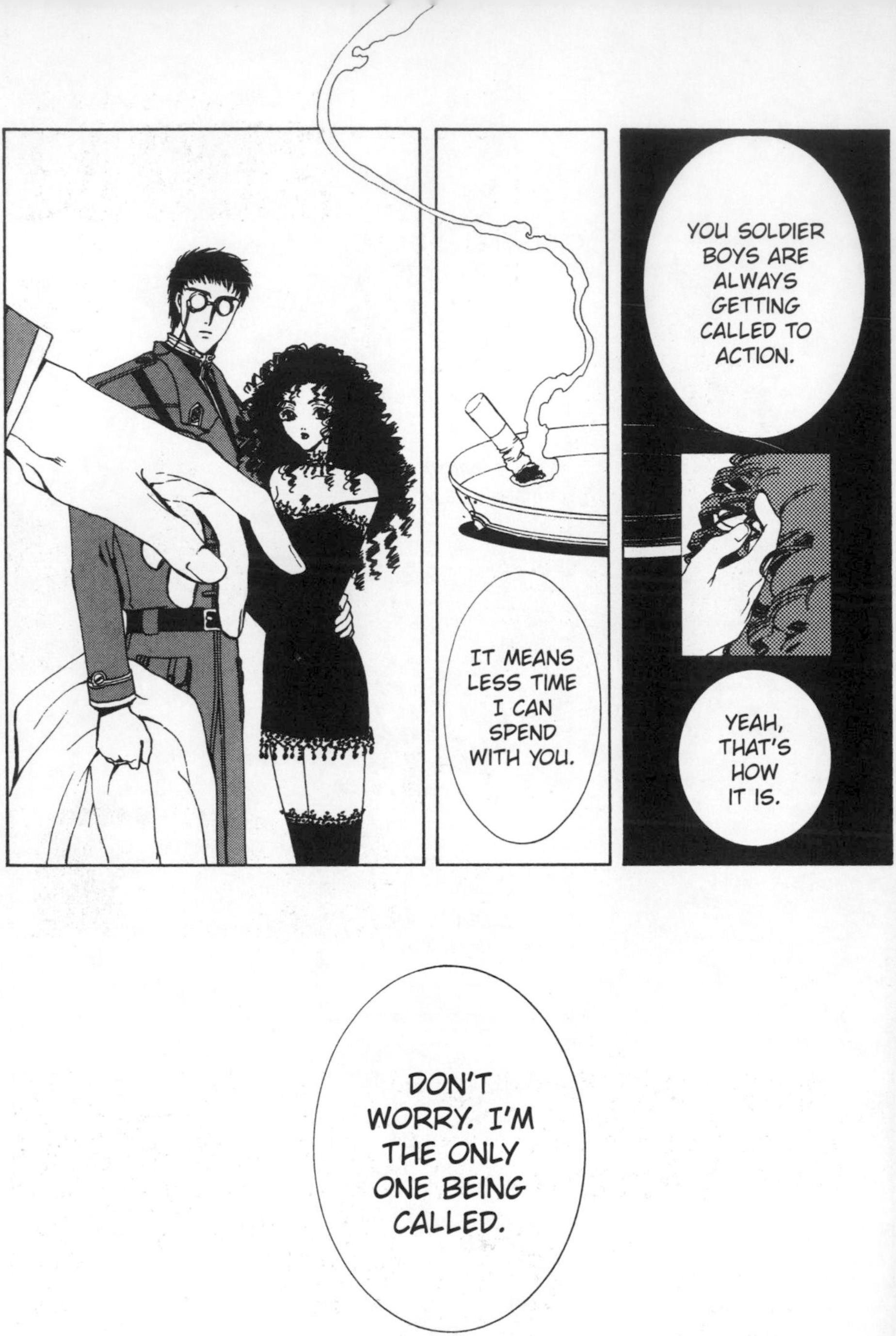
YOU SOLDIER BOYS ARE ALWAYS GETTING CALLED TO ACTION.
YEAH, THAT'S HOW IT IS.
IT MEANS LESS TIME I CAN SPEND WITH YOU.
DON'T WORRY. I'M THE ONLY ONE BEING CALLED.

COMMUNICATION

『通 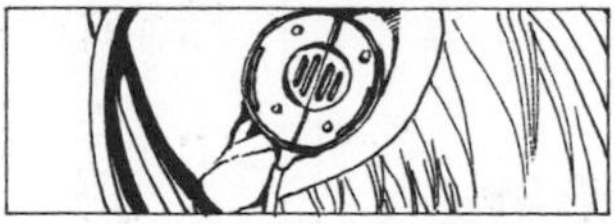 信』

THE THREE-LEAF HAS ESCAPED.

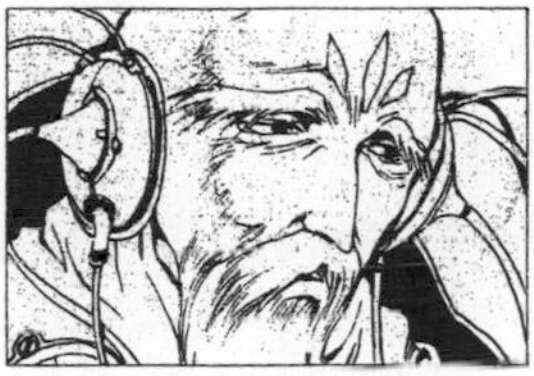
ONE OF THEM HAS LEFT THE CAGE.
AT LEAST THEY DIDN'T BOTH LEAVE.

AZAIEA HASN'T FOUND OUT YET...

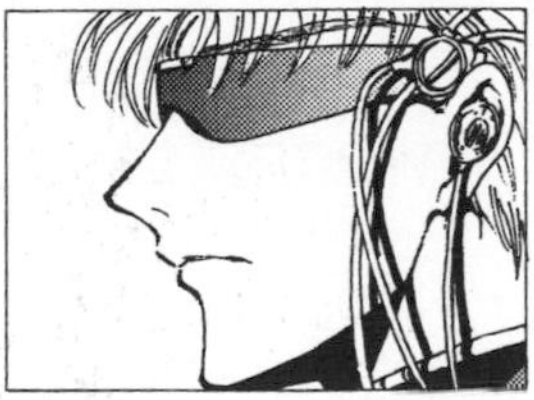

...BUT THE REAL PROBLEM IS THE COUNCIL.

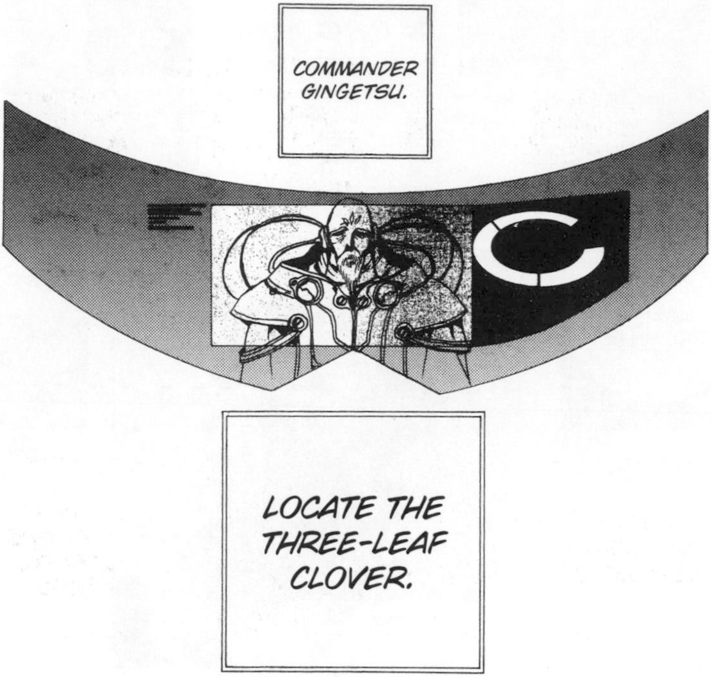
COMMANDER GINGETSU.
LOCATE THE THREE-LEAF CLOVER.

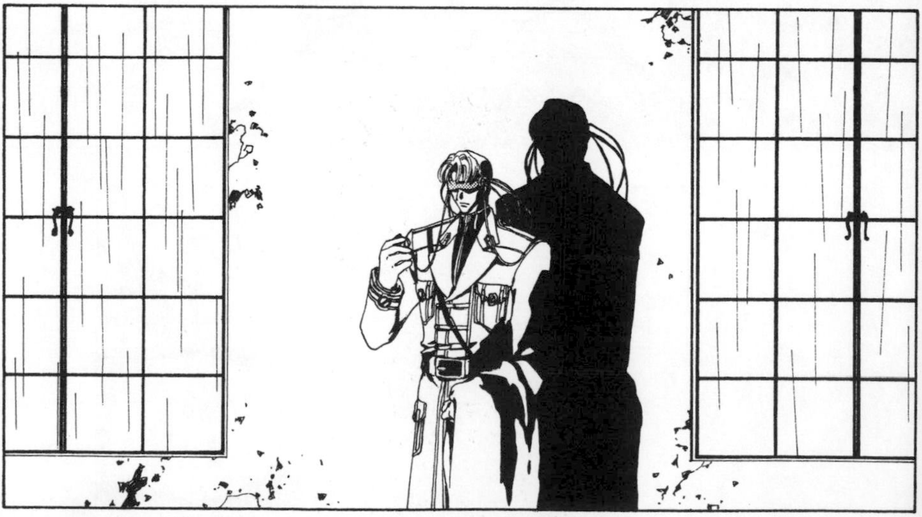

『約 A PROMISE 束』

...YOU DON'T HAVE TO GO?

ARE YOU SURE...

HE AND I HAVE A PROMISE.

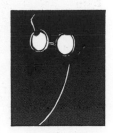

WHAT KIND OF PROMISE?

THAT HE WON'T DIE BEFORE I DO.

TO NOT DIE IS THE GREATEST GIFT YOU CAN GIVE SOMEONE YOU LOVE.

...WHAT IS IT?

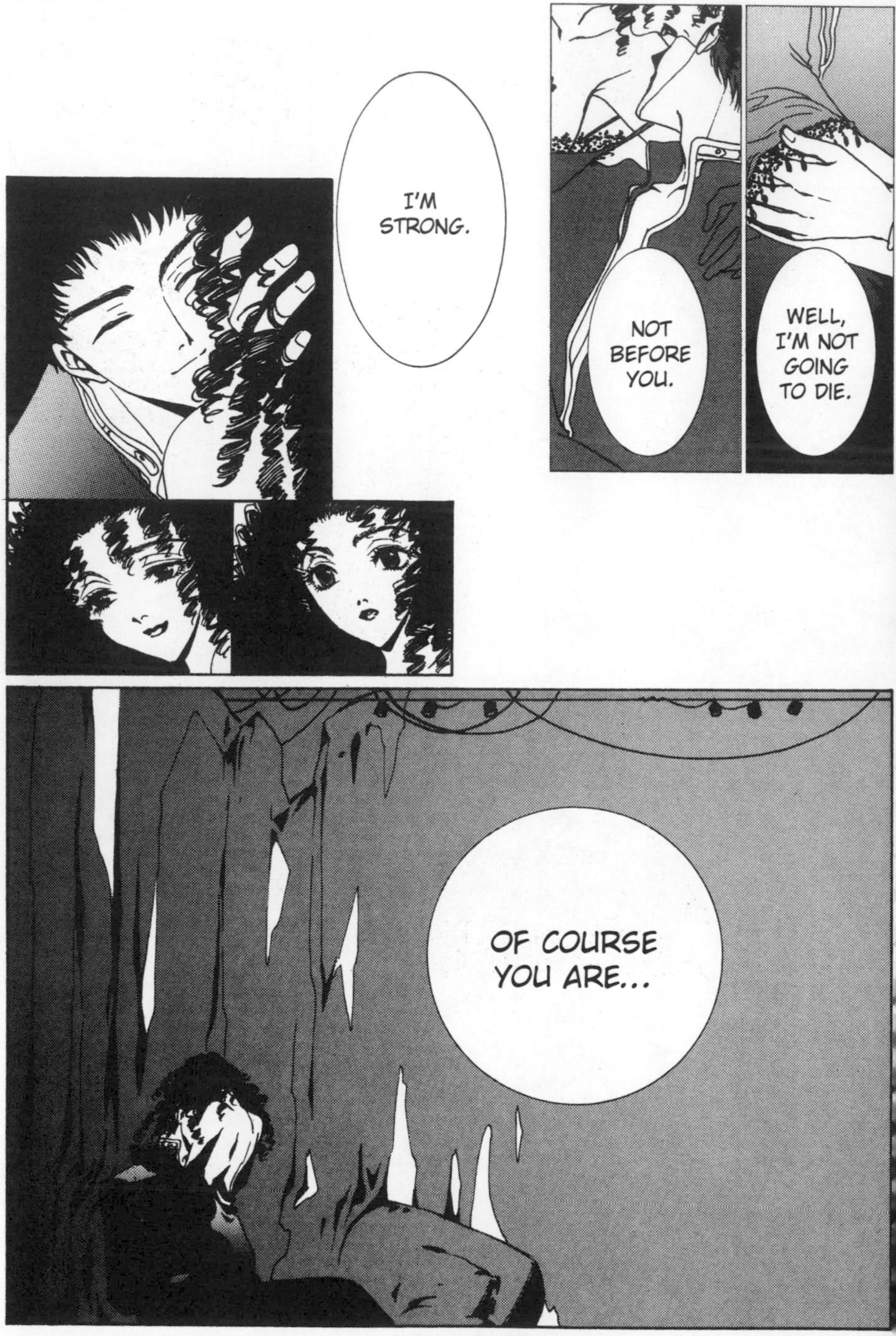
WELL, I'M NOT GOING TO DIE.
NOT BEFORE YOU.
I'M STRONG.
OF COURSE YOU ARE...

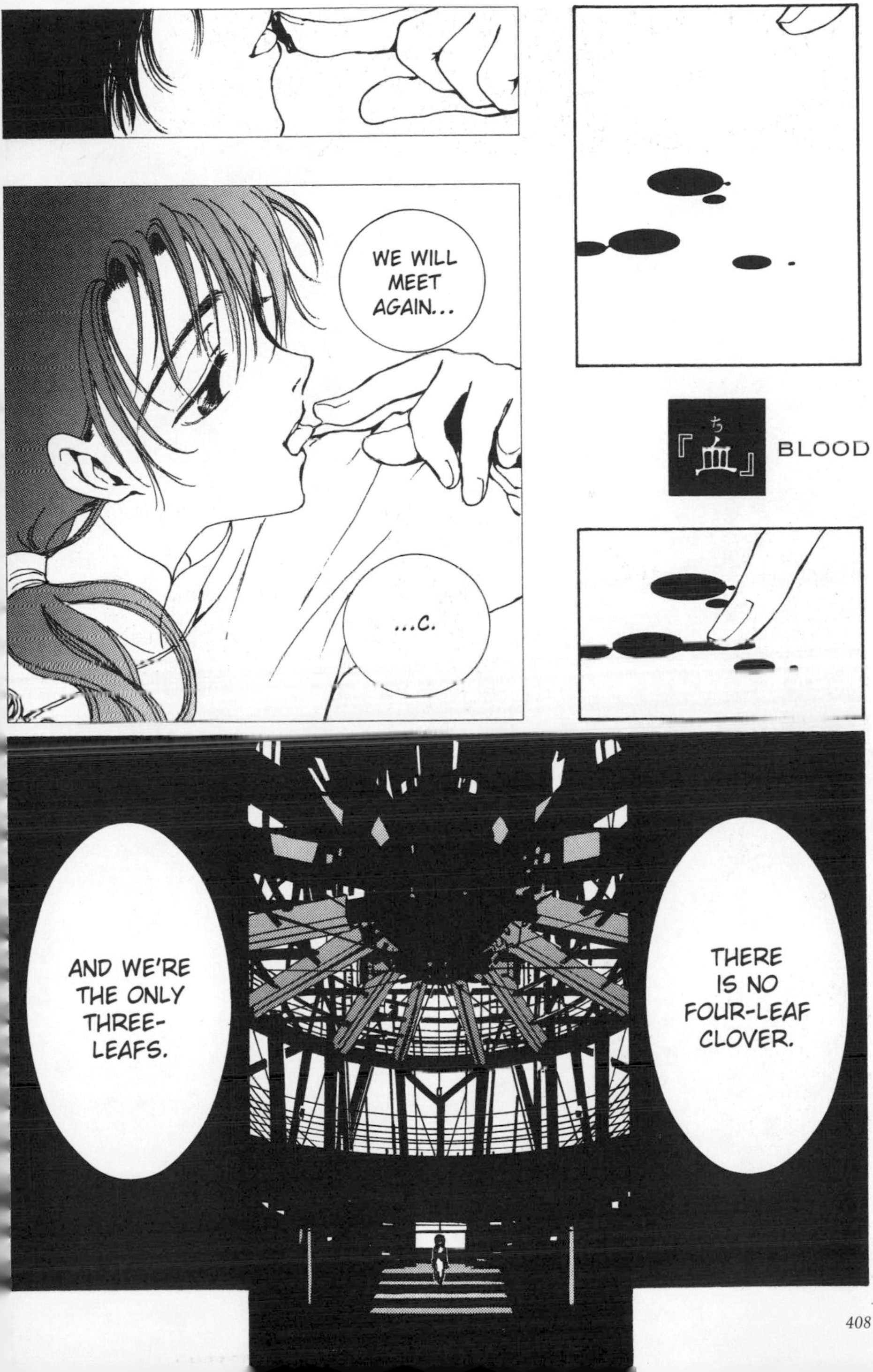
『血』 BLOOD
WE WILL MEET AGAIN...
...C.
THERE IS NO FOUR-LEAF CLOVER.
AND WE'RE THE ONLY THREE-LEAFS.

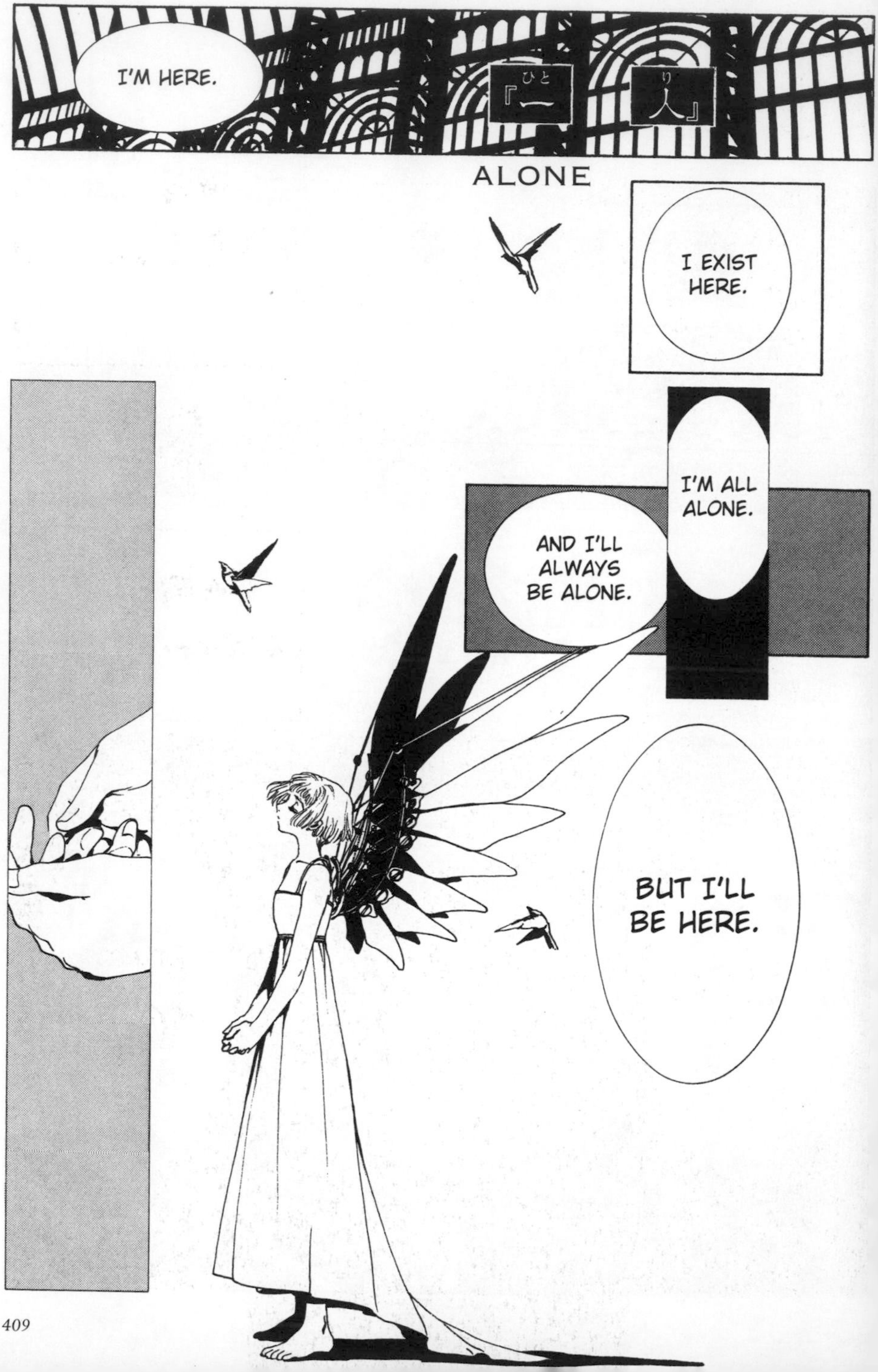
I'M HERE.
『一人』
ALONE
I EXIST HERE.
I'M ALL ALONE.
AND I'LL ALWAYS BE ALONE.
BUT I'LL BE HERE.

THE HUNTED

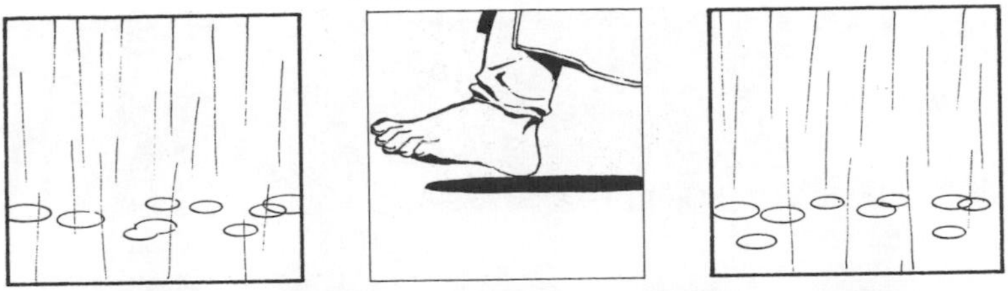

『追われる者』

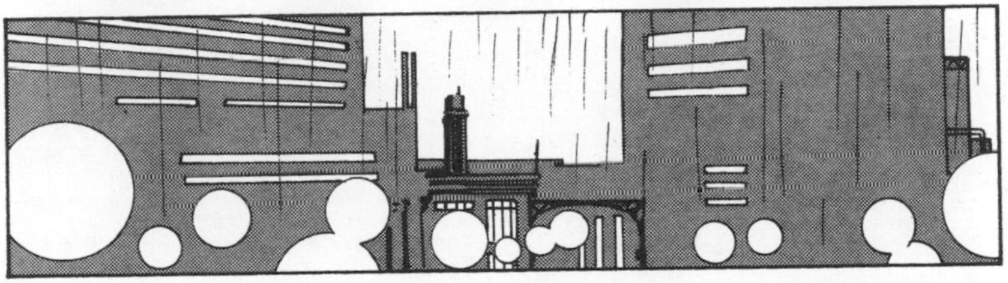

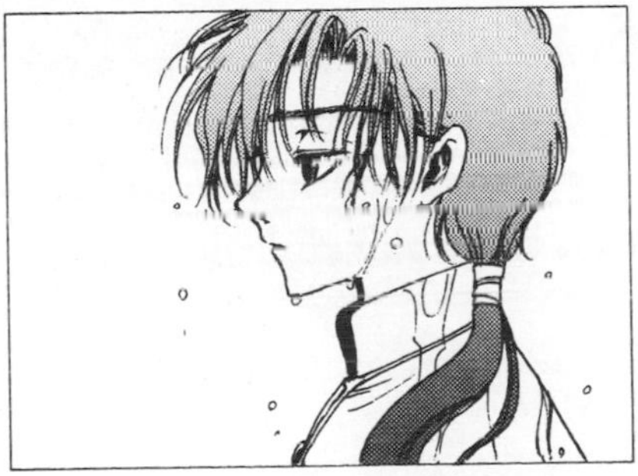

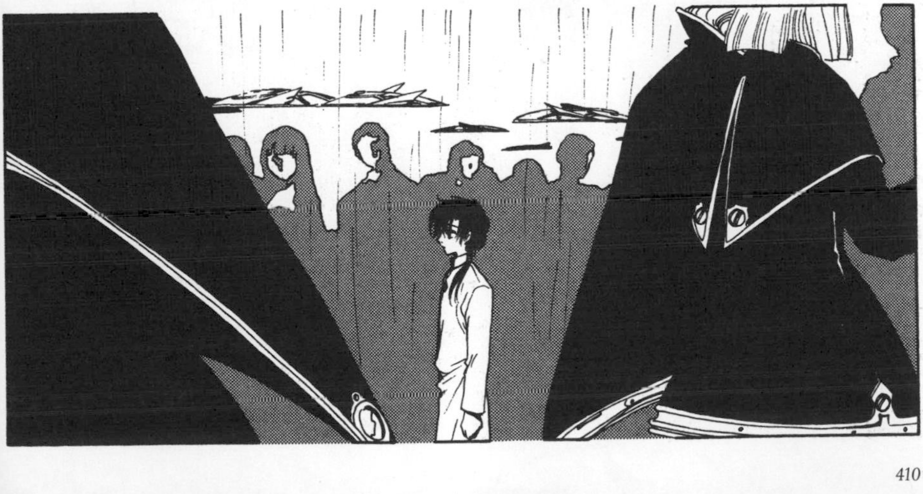

THE HUNTER

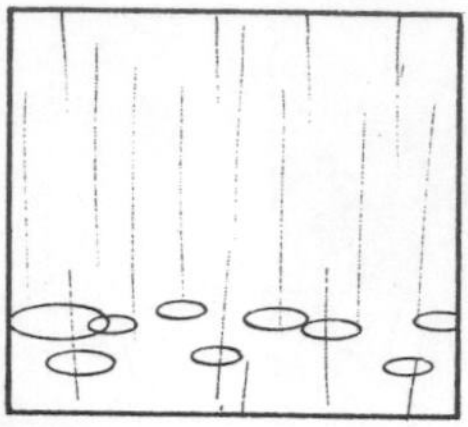
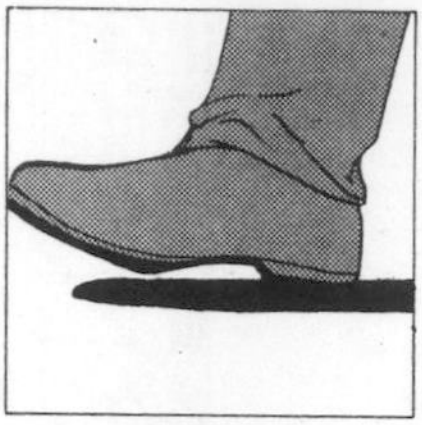
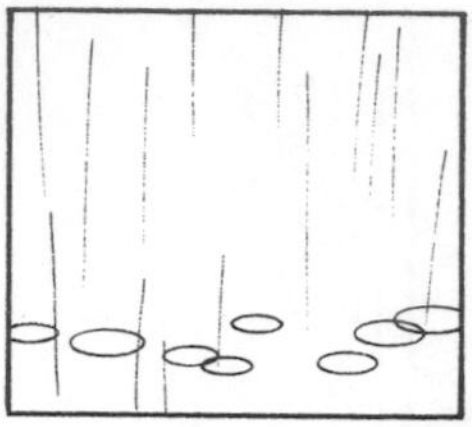

『追(お)う者(もの)』

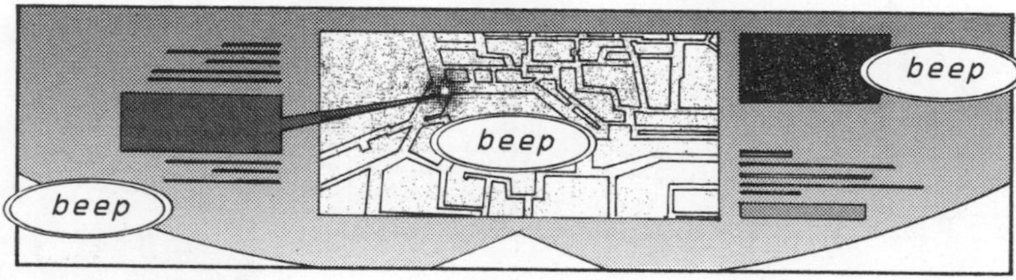
beep
beep
beep

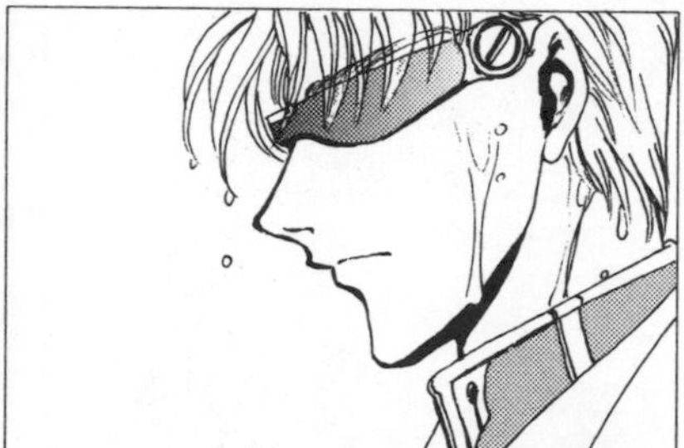

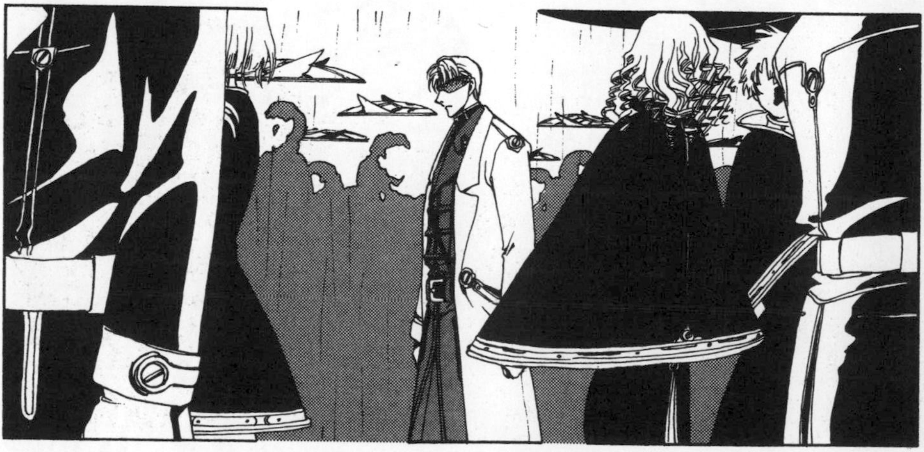

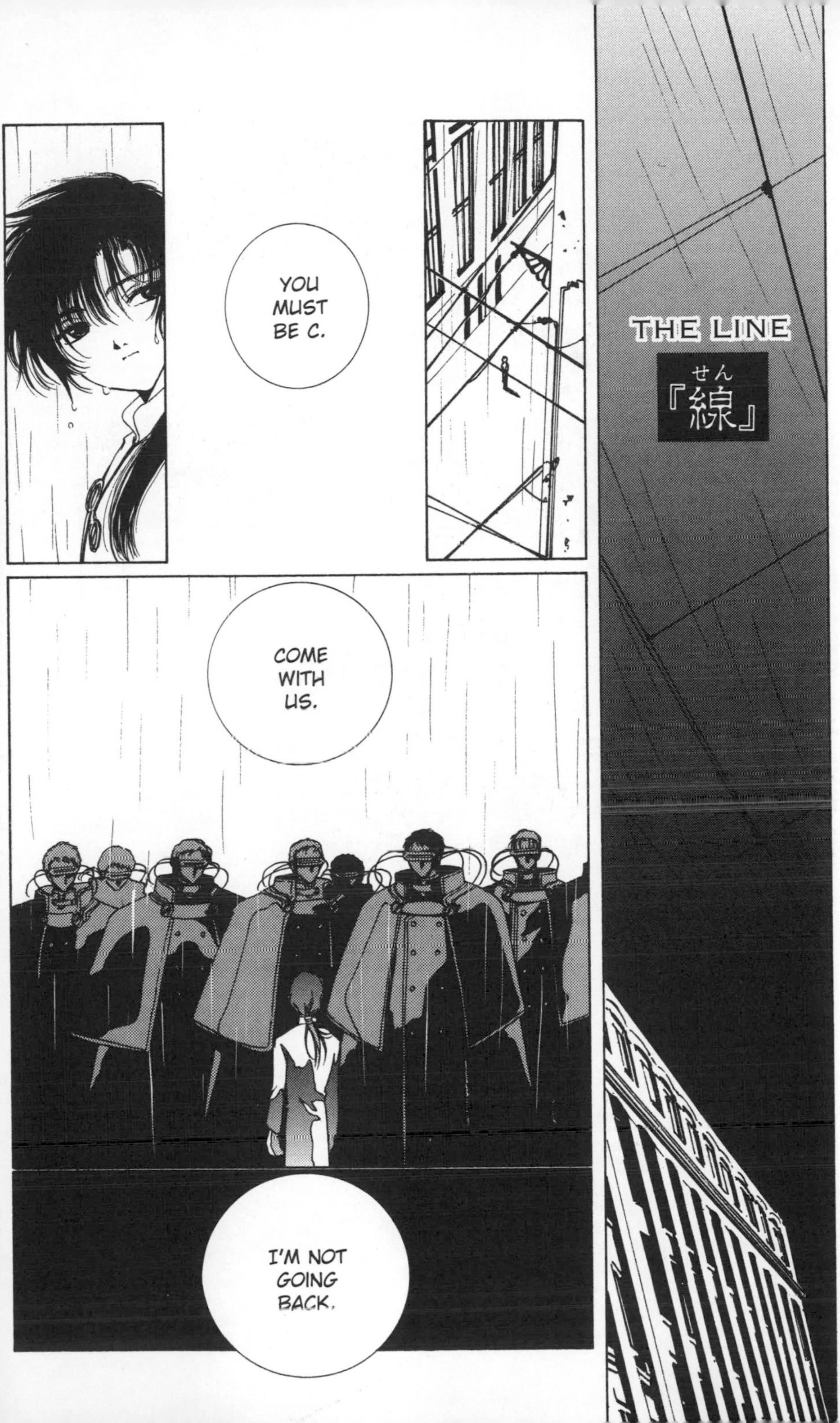
THE LINE
せん
『線』
YOU MUST BE C.
COME WITH US.
I'M NOT GOING BACK.

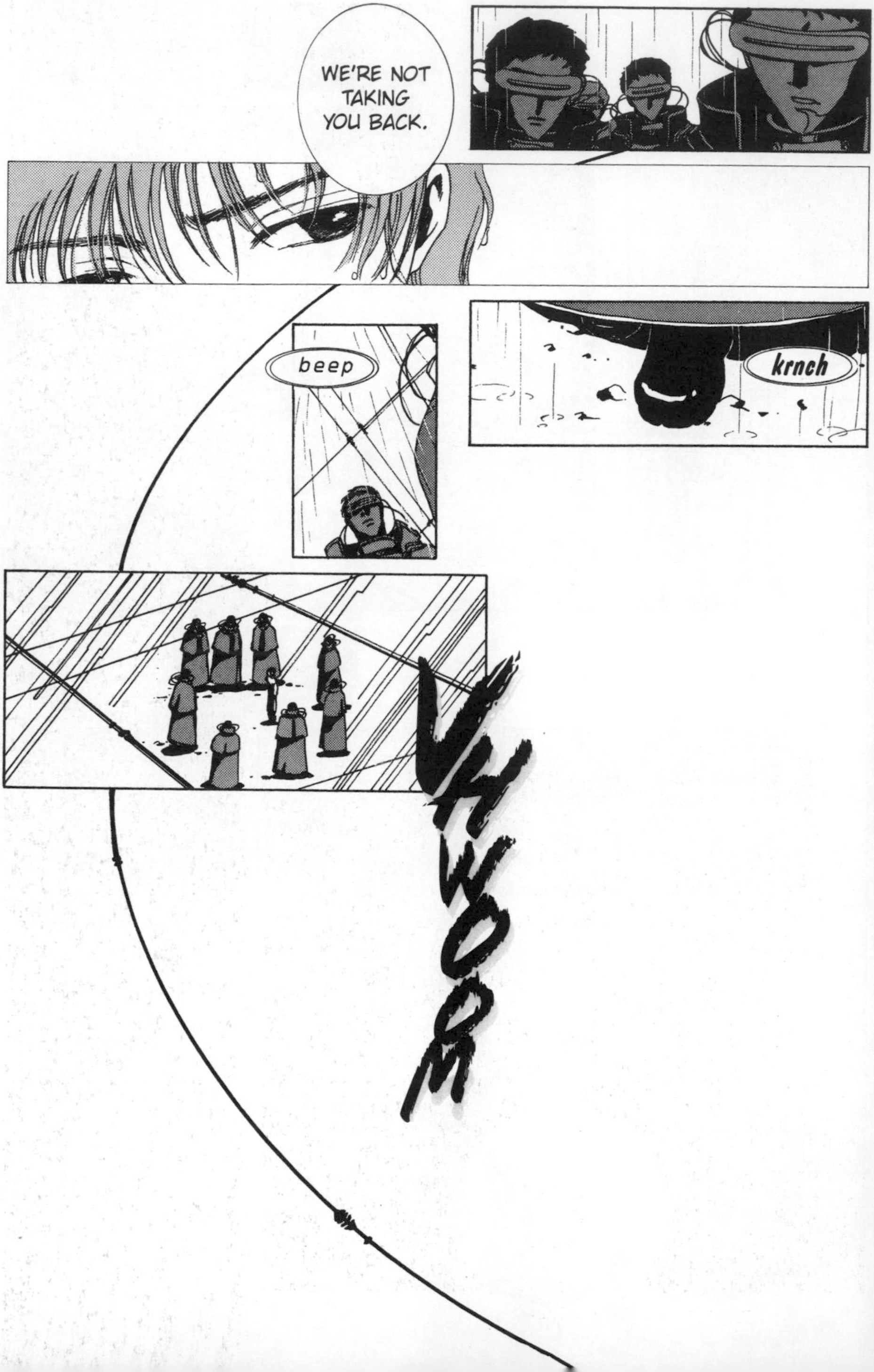
WE'RE NOT TAKING YOU BACK.
krnch
beep
WHOOM

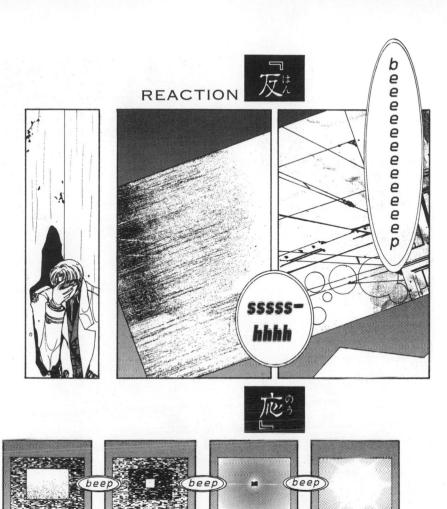

REACTION 『反』

beeeeeeeeeeep

sssss-hhhh

『応』

beep beep beep

I MUST BE CLOSE.

beeep

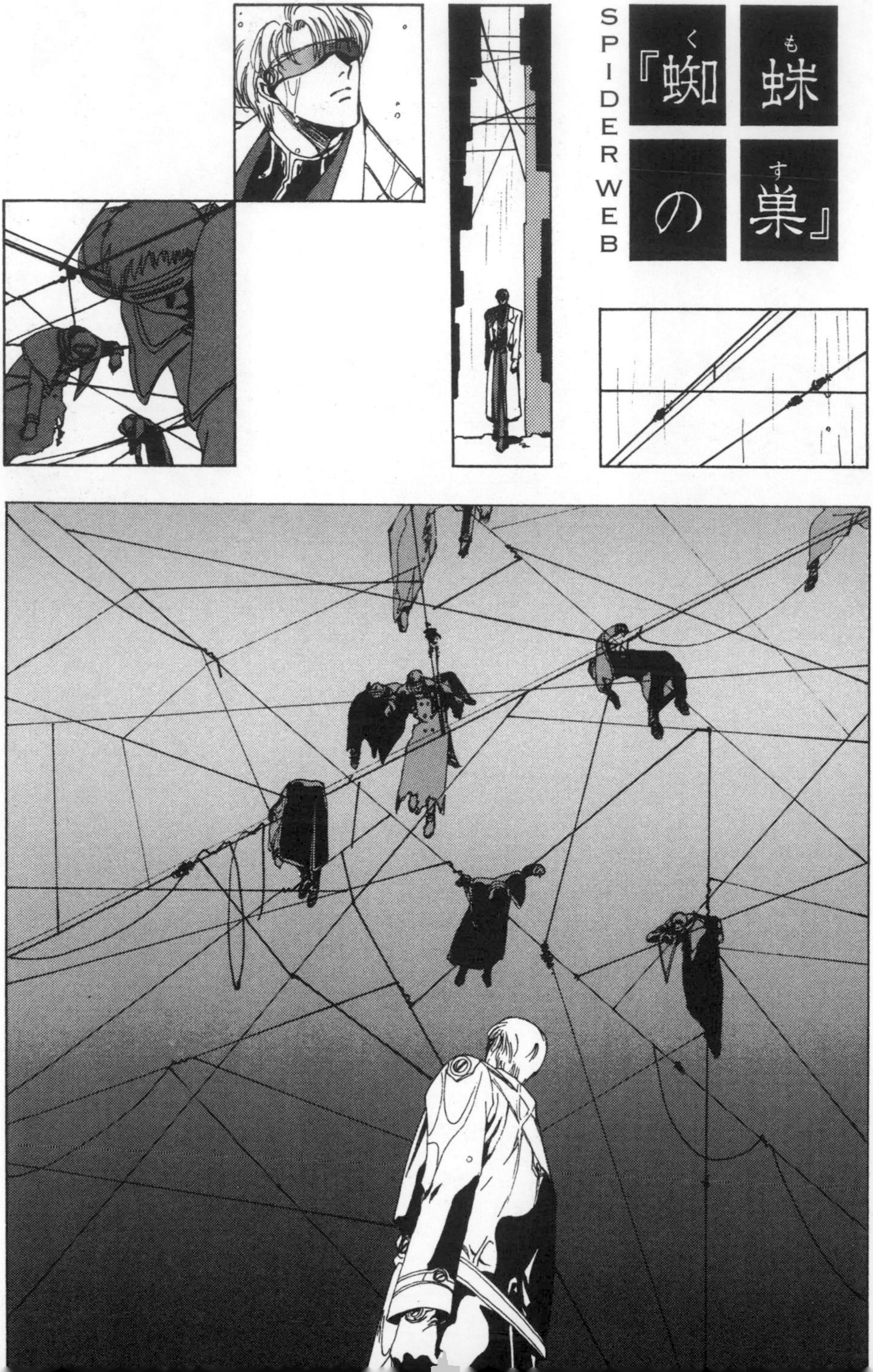
『蜘蛛の巣』
SPIDER WEB

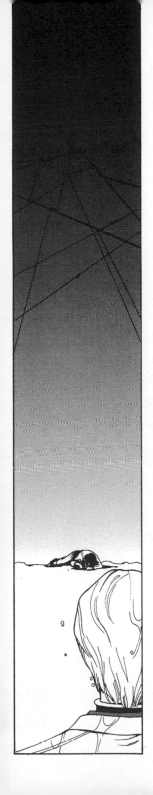

...I'M
NOT
GOING
BACK.

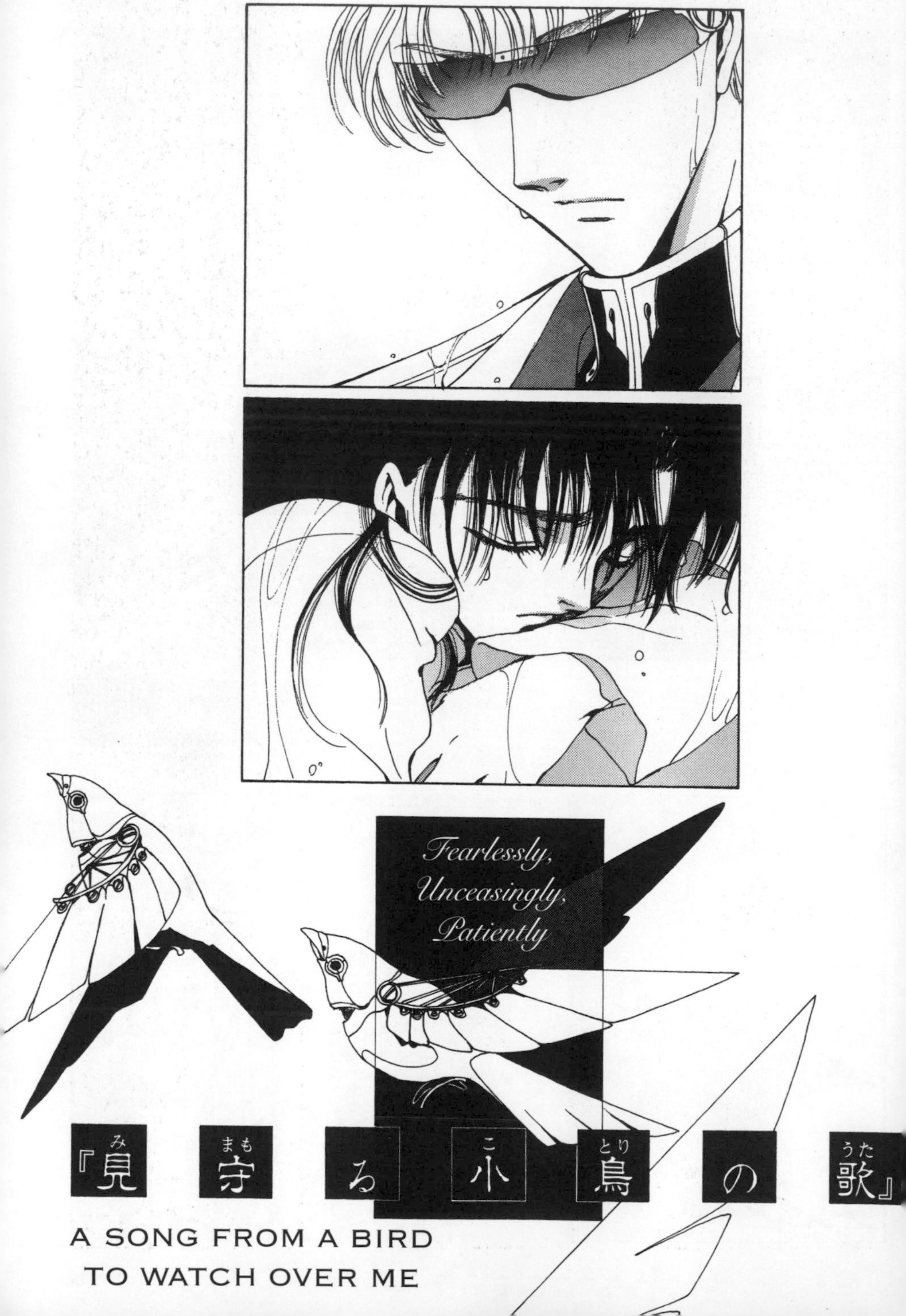
Fearlessly,
Unceasingly,
Patiently

『見守る小鳥の歌』

A SONG FROM A BIRD TO WATCH OVER ME

In your arms
I will be reborn
THE THREE-LEAF CLOVER...
...THEY FOUND HIM.
A PLACE TO RETURN TO
『帰る場所』
I'VE SECURED HIM.
SHALL I RETURN HIM TO THE LAB?

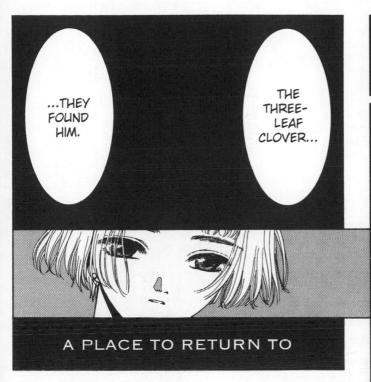

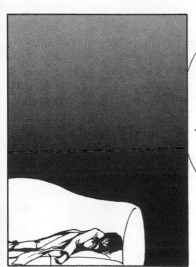

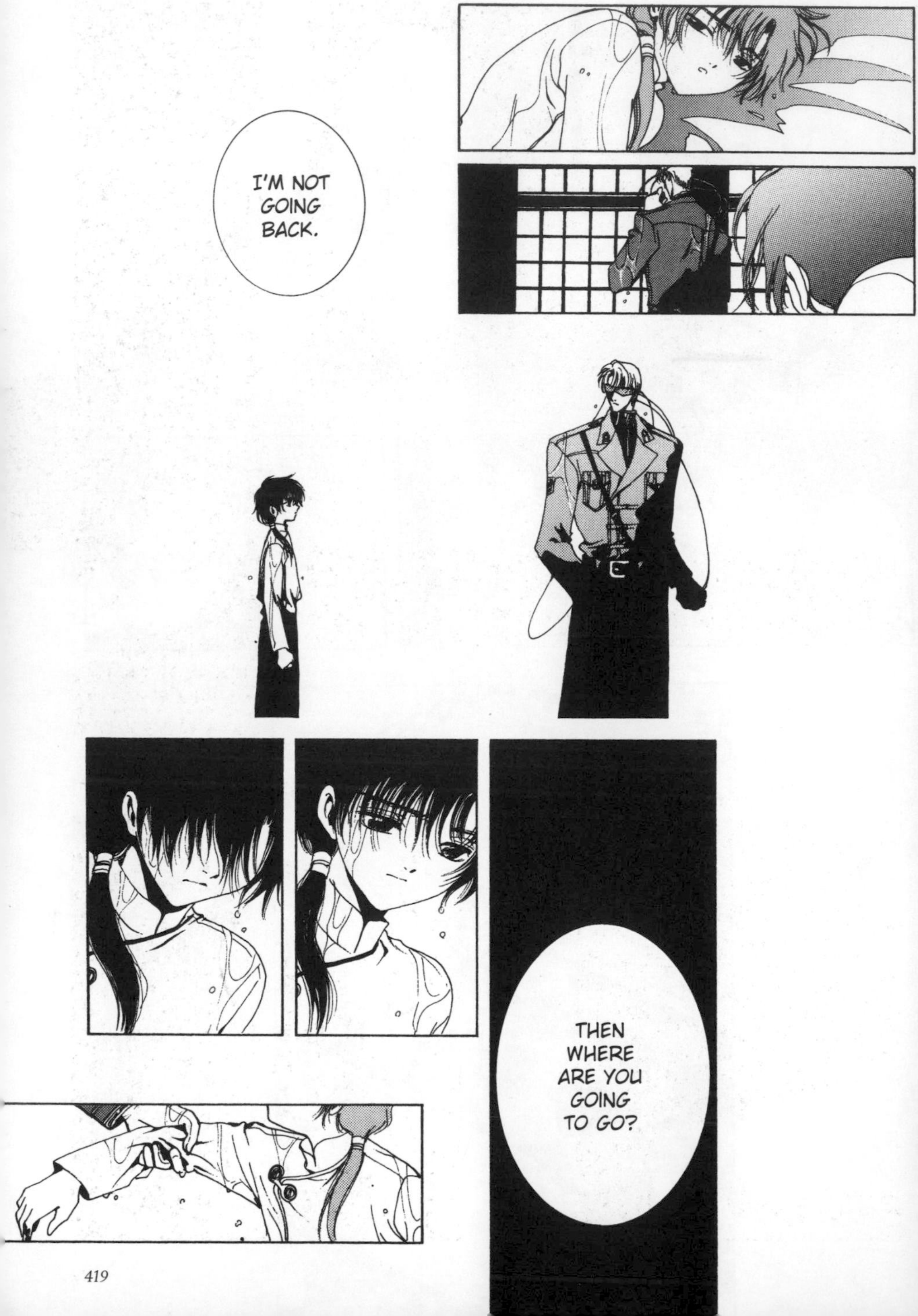
I'M NOT GOING BACK.
THEN WHERE ARE YOU GOING TO GO?

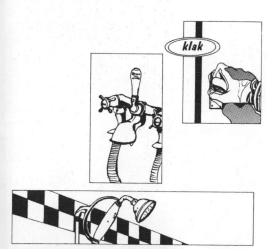

klak

...NO...

YOU DON'T WANT TO CATCH A COLD, DO YOU?

chak

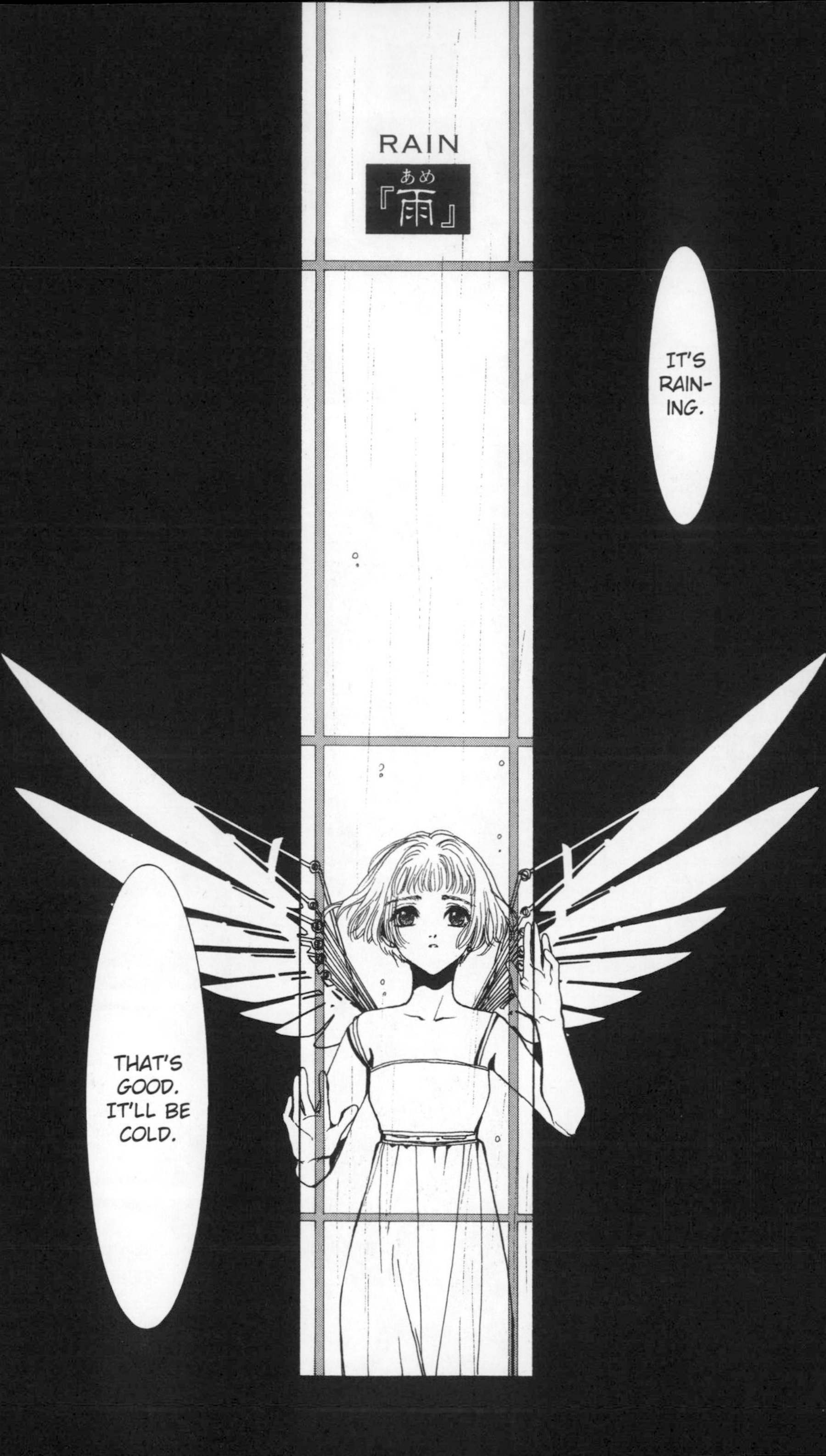
RAIN
あめ
『雨』
IT'S RAIN-ING.
THAT'S GOOD. IT'LL BE COLD.

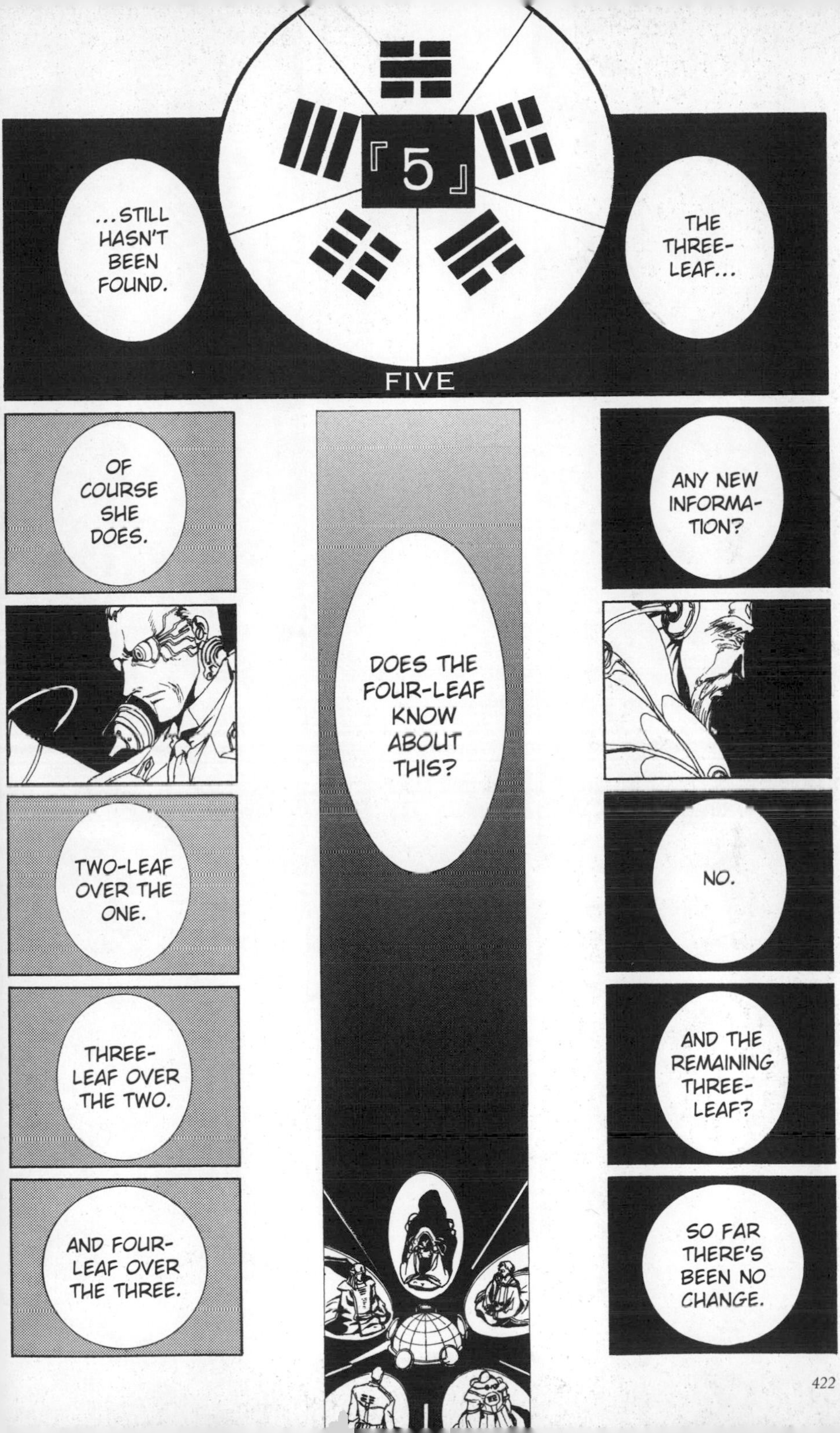
『5』
FIVE
THE THREE-LEAF...
...STILL HASN'T BEEN FOUND.
ANY NEW INFORMATION?
NO.
AND THE REMAINING THREE-LEAF?
SO FAR THERE'S BEEN NO CHANGE.
DOES THE FOUR-LEAF KNOW ABOUT THIS?
OF COURSE SHE DOES.
TWO-LEAF OVER THE ONE.
THREE-LEAF OVER THE TWO.
AND FOUR-LEAF OVER THE THREE.

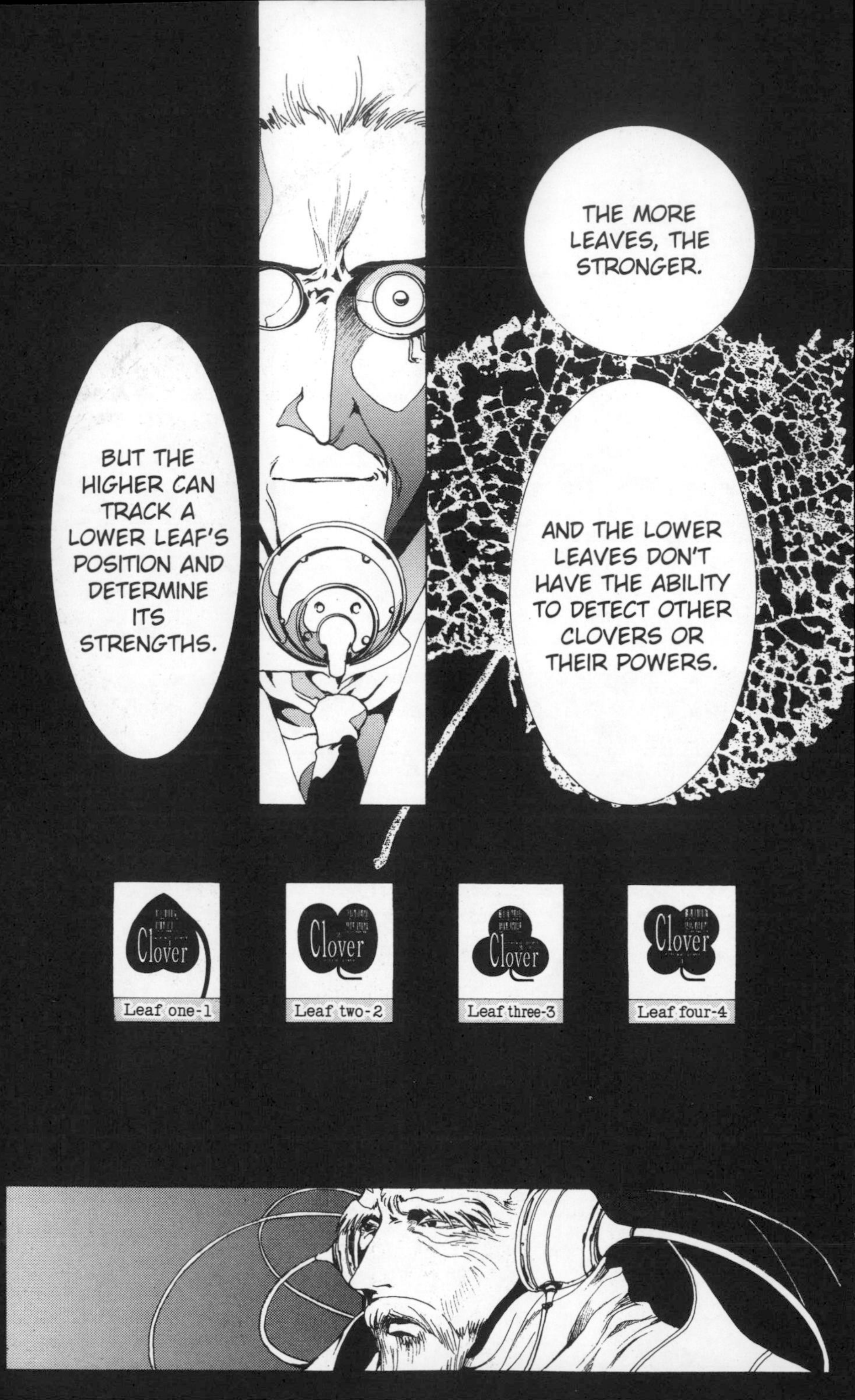
THE MORE LEAVES, THE STRONGER.
AND THE LOWER LEAVES DON'T HAVE THE ABILITY TO DETECT OTHER CLOVERS OR THEIR POWERS.
BUT THE HIGHER CAN TRACK A LOWER LEAF'S POSITION AND DETERMINE ITS STRENGTHS.
Clover
Leaf four-4
Clover
Leaf three-3
Clover
Leaf two-2
Clover
Leaf one-1

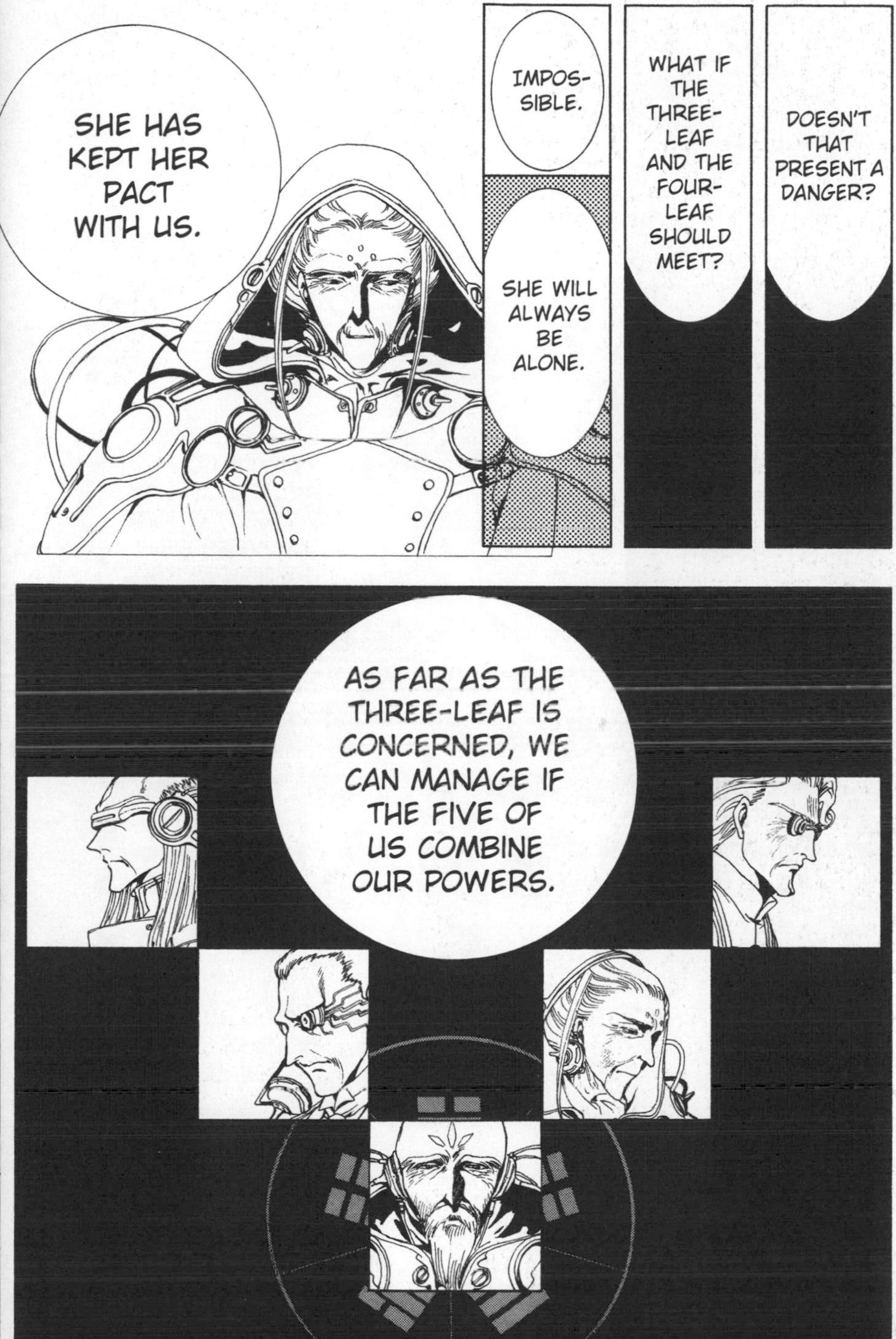
DOESN'T THAT PRESENT A DANGER?
WHAT IF THE THREE-LEAF AND THE FOUR-LEAF SHOULD MEET?
IMPOSSIBLE.
SHE WILL ALWAYS BE ALONE.
SHE HAS KEPT HER PACT WITH US.
AS FAR AS THE THREE-LEAF IS CONCERNED, WE CAN MANAGE IF THE FIVE OF US COMBINE OUR POWERS.

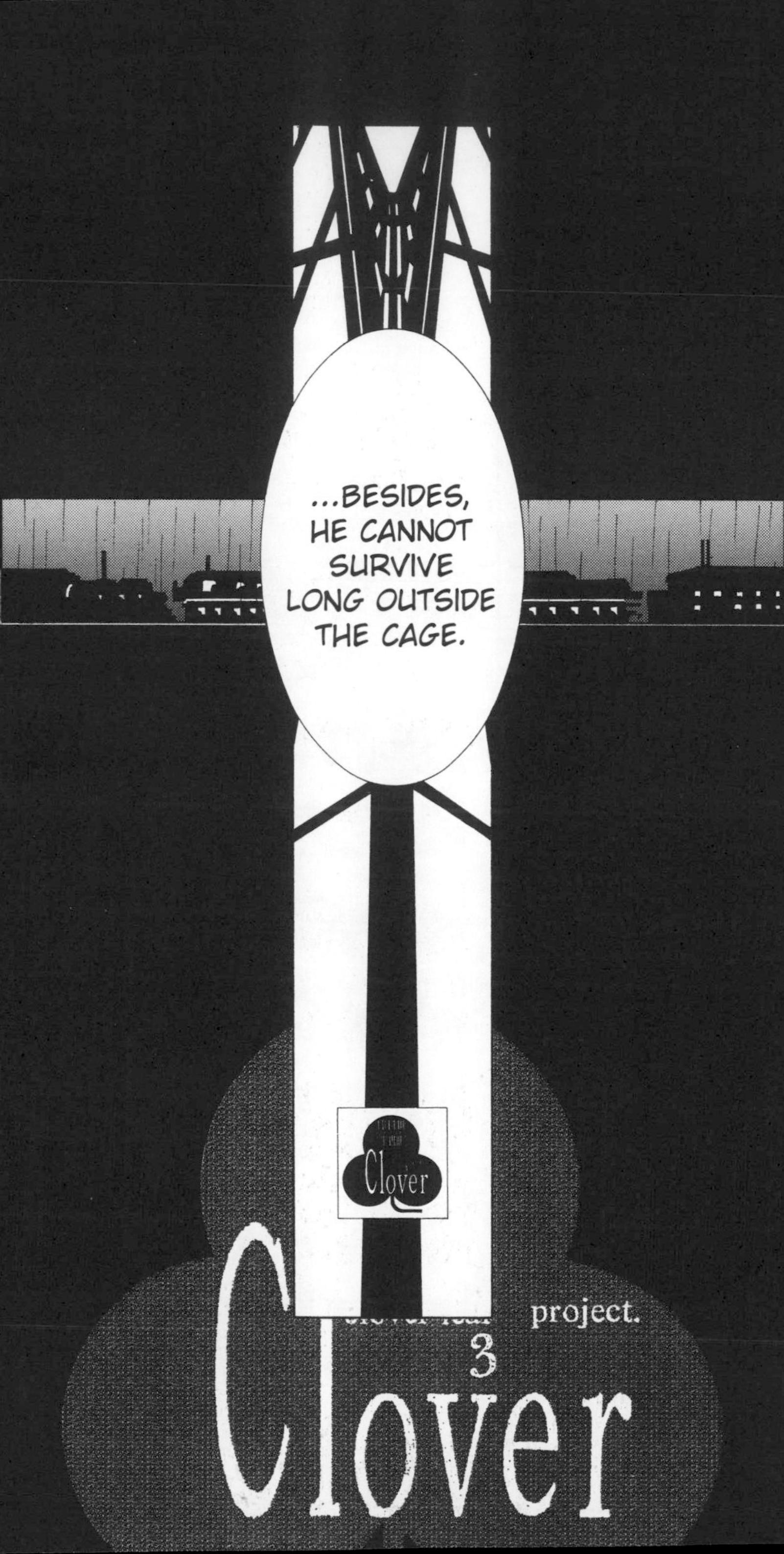
...BESIDES, HE CANNOT SURVIVE LONG OUTSIDE THE CAGE.
Clover
project.
3
Clover

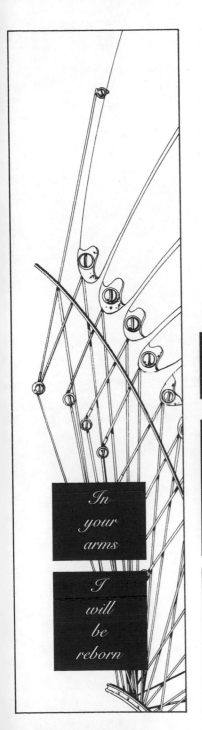

For
you

I will be
reborn

The bliss
of our meeting
Is a gentle light

Our eventual
parting
a pouring rain

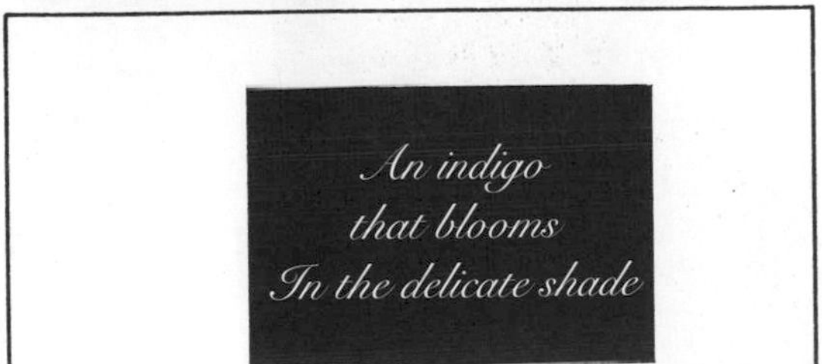

In
your
arms

I
will
be
reborn

An indigo
that blooms
In the delicate shade

Clover

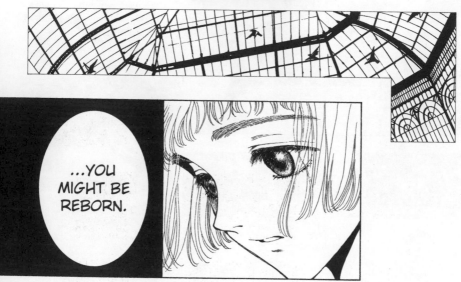

...YOU MIGHT BE REBORN.

WHAT'S THIS?

THREE
『3』

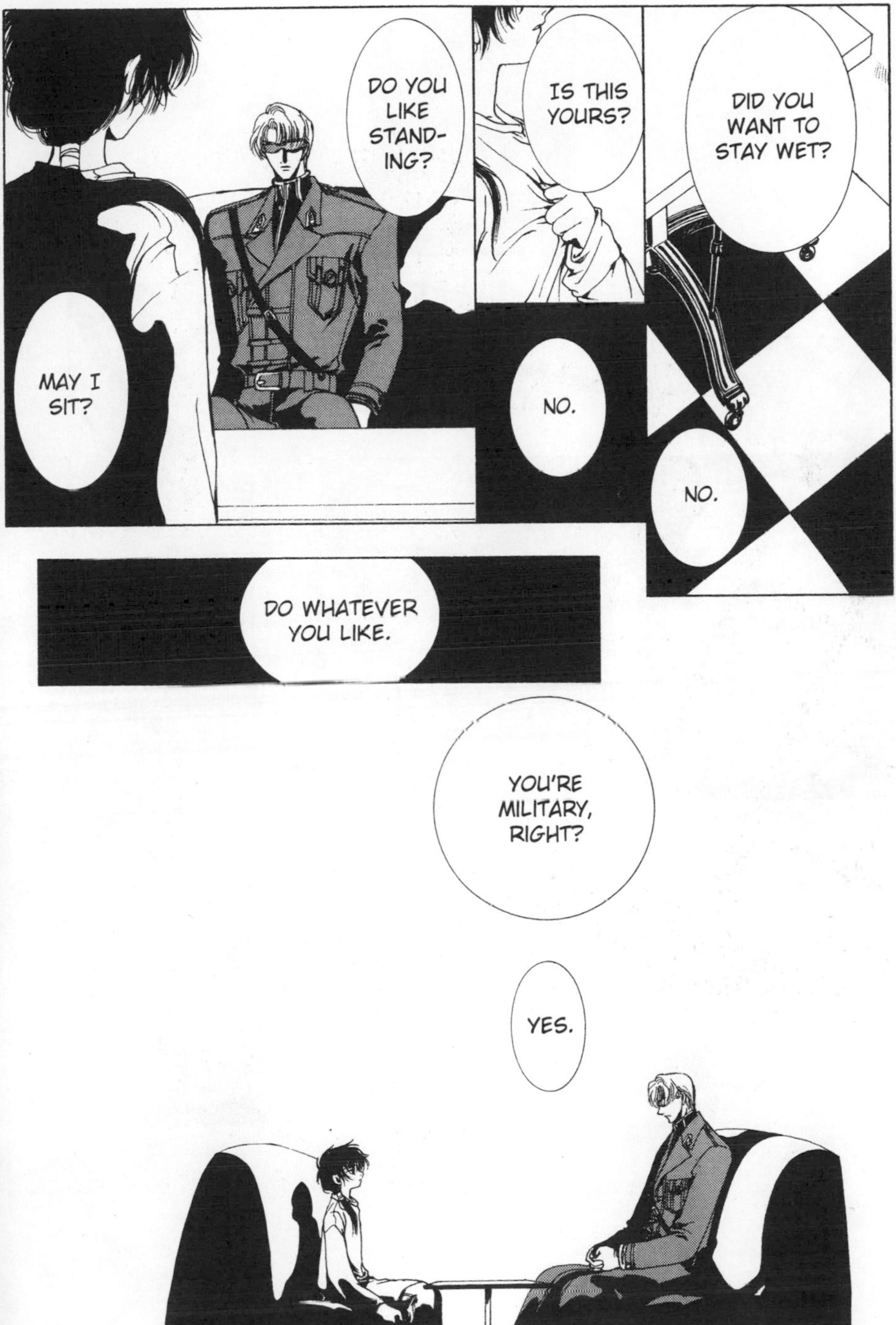
DID YOU WANT TO STAY WET?
NO.
IS THIS YOURS?
NO.
DO YOU LIKE STAND-ING?
MAY I SIT?
DO WHATEVER YOU LIKE.
YOU'RE MILITARY, RIGHT?
YES.

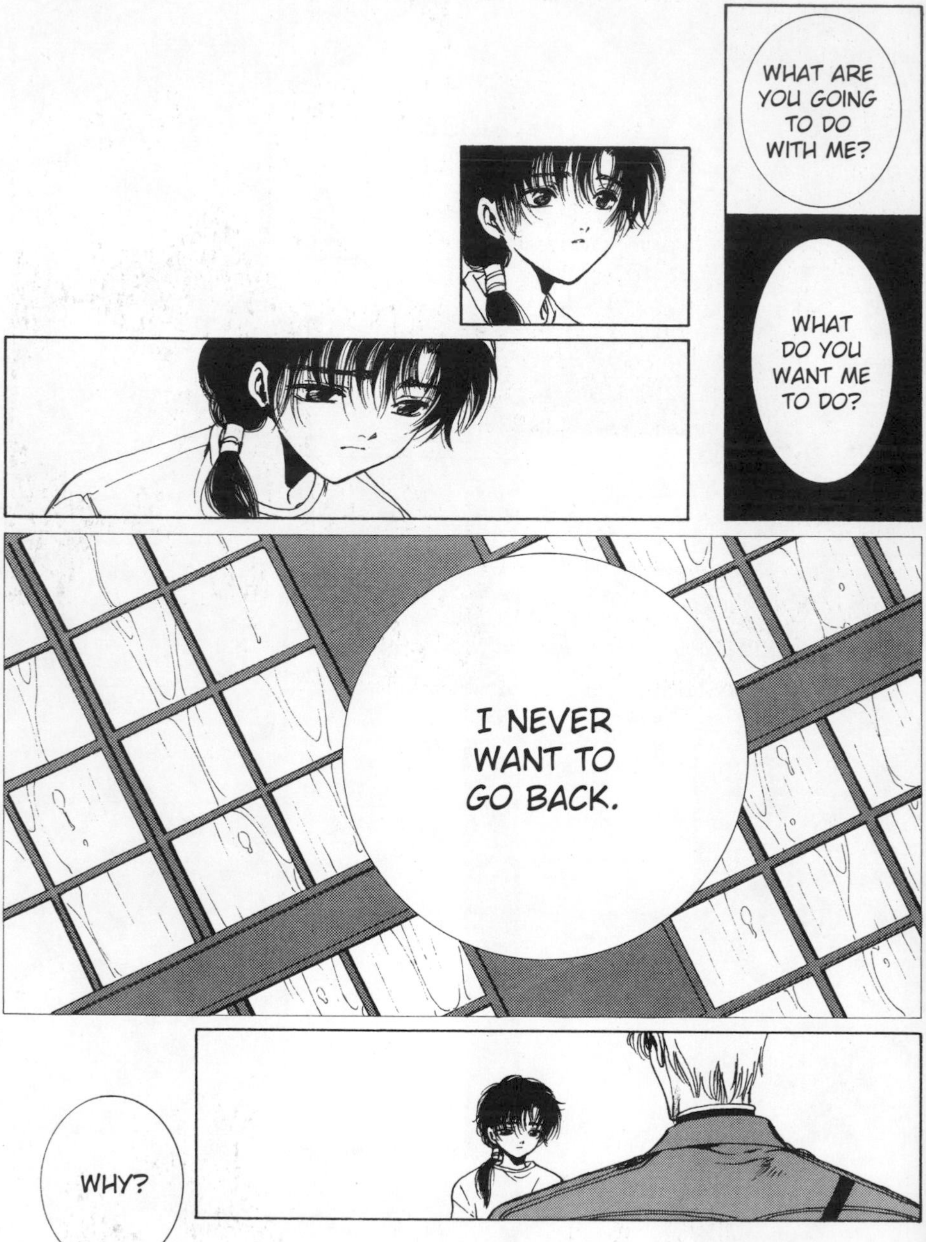
WHAT ARE YOU GOING TO DO WITH ME?
WHAT DO YOU WANT ME TO DO?
I NEVER WANT TO GO BACK.
WHY?

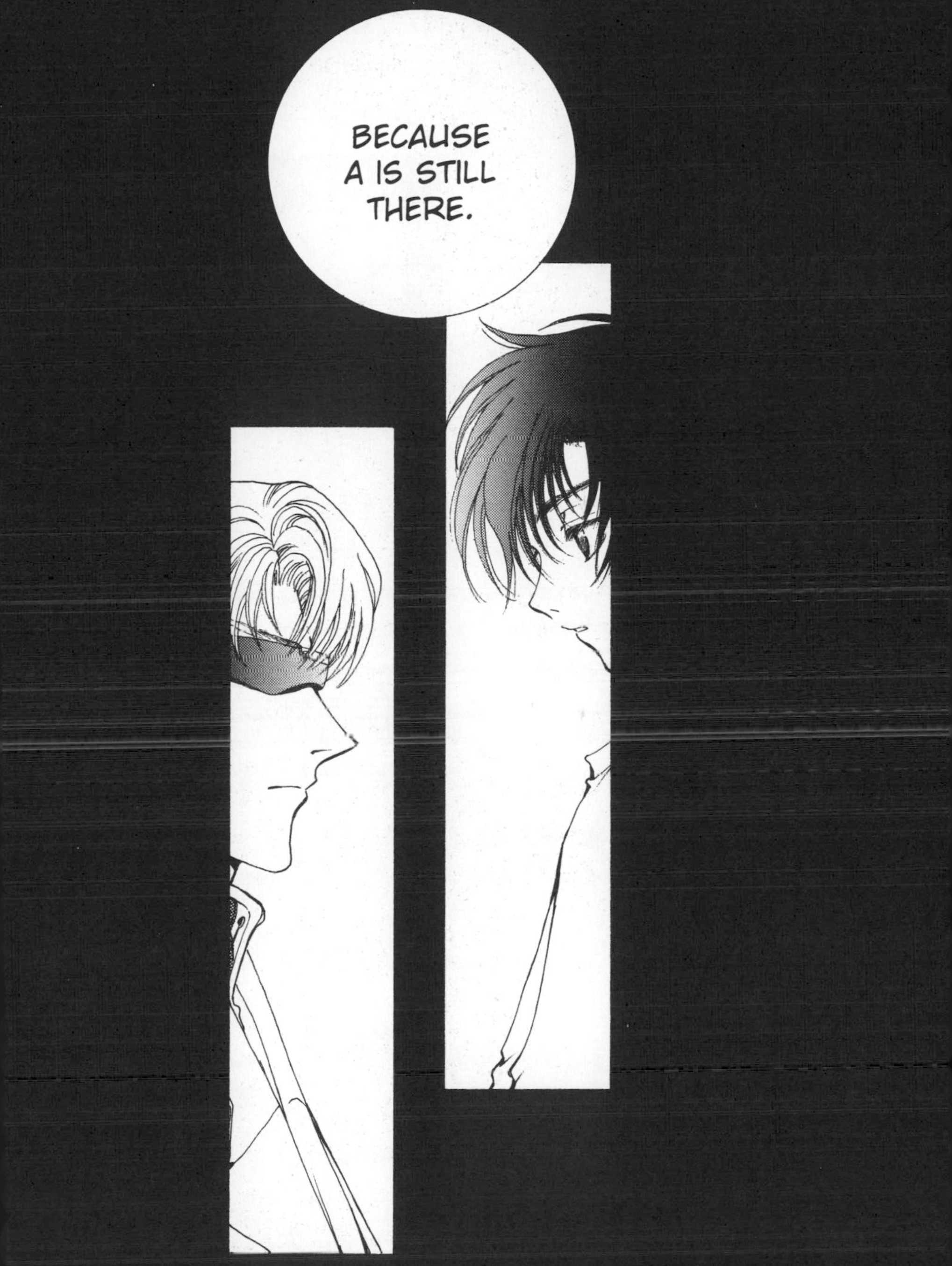
BECAUSE A IS STILL THERE.

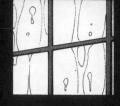

...I'D LIKE
TO SPEAK
TO THE
WIZARDS.

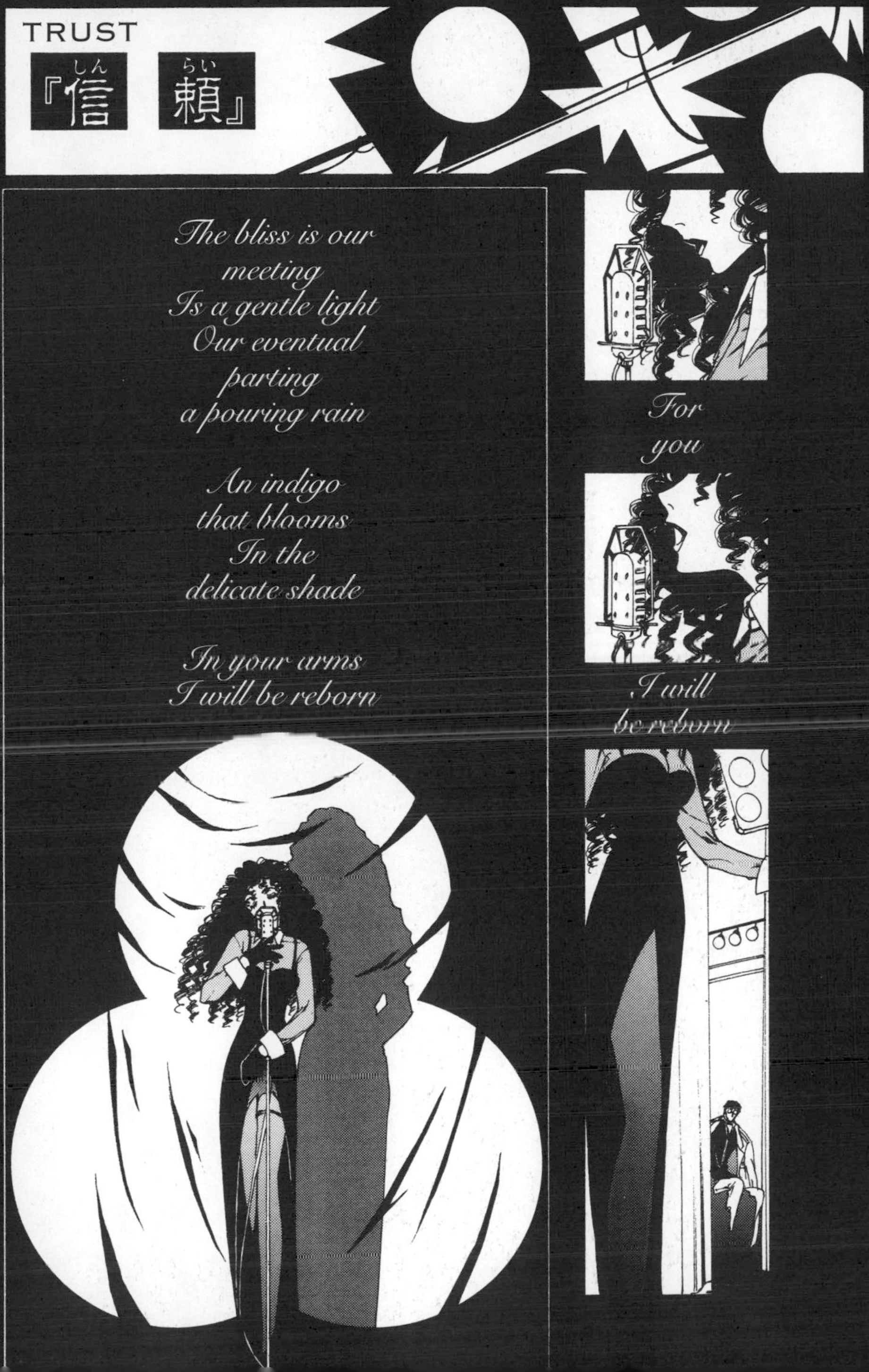

TRUST
『信頼』
しん らい
The bliss is our meeting
Is a gentle light
Our eventual parting
a pouring rain
An indigo that blooms
In the delicate shade
In your arms
I will be reborn
For you
I will be reborn

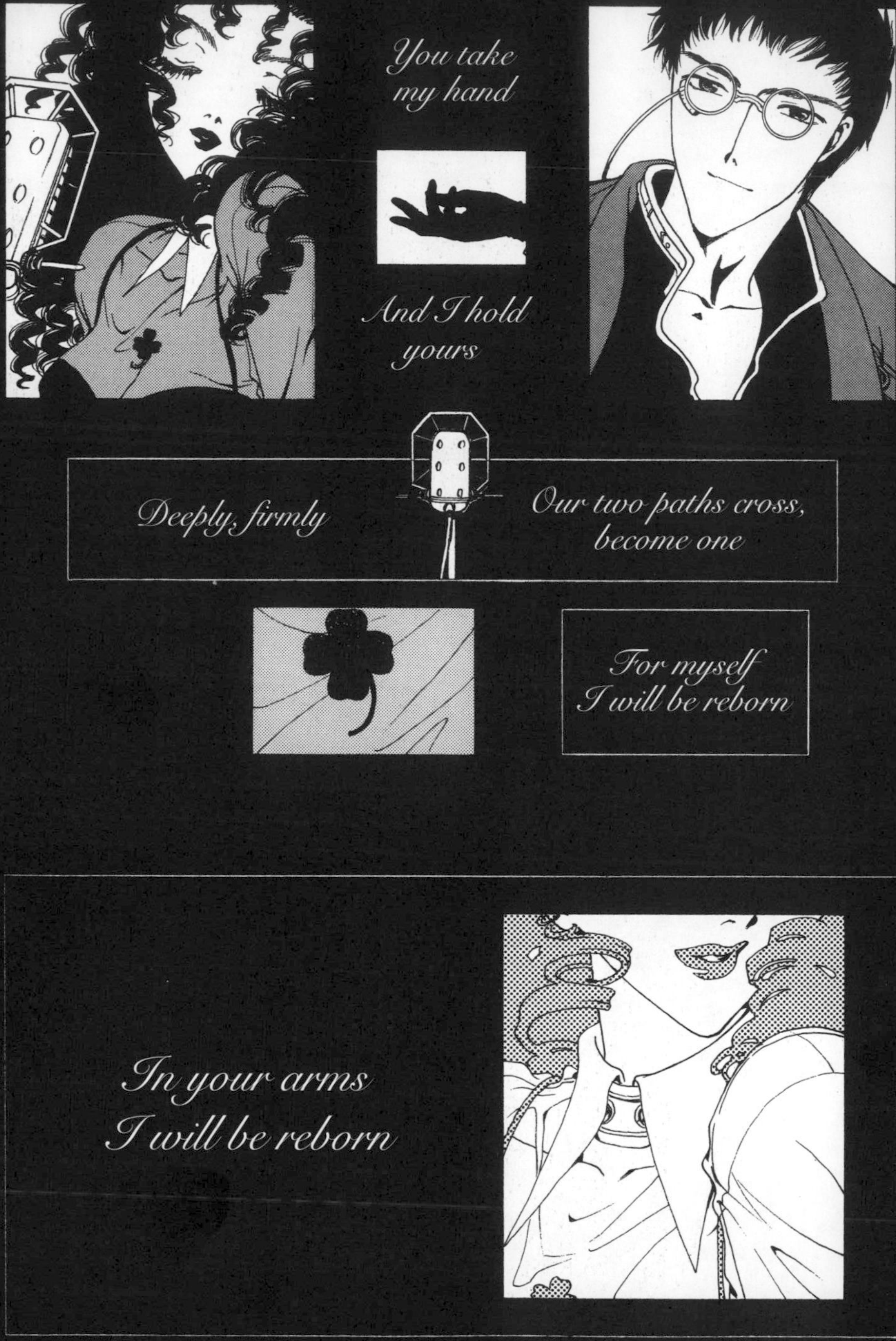
You take my hand
And I hold yours
Deeply, firmly
Our two paths cross, become one
For myself I will be reborn
In your arms I will be reborn

NO TRANSMISSIONS...

beep

beep

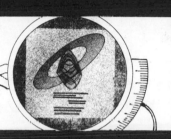

...SO I *ASSUME* THAT EVERYTHING'S ALL RIGHT...

...
GINGETSU.

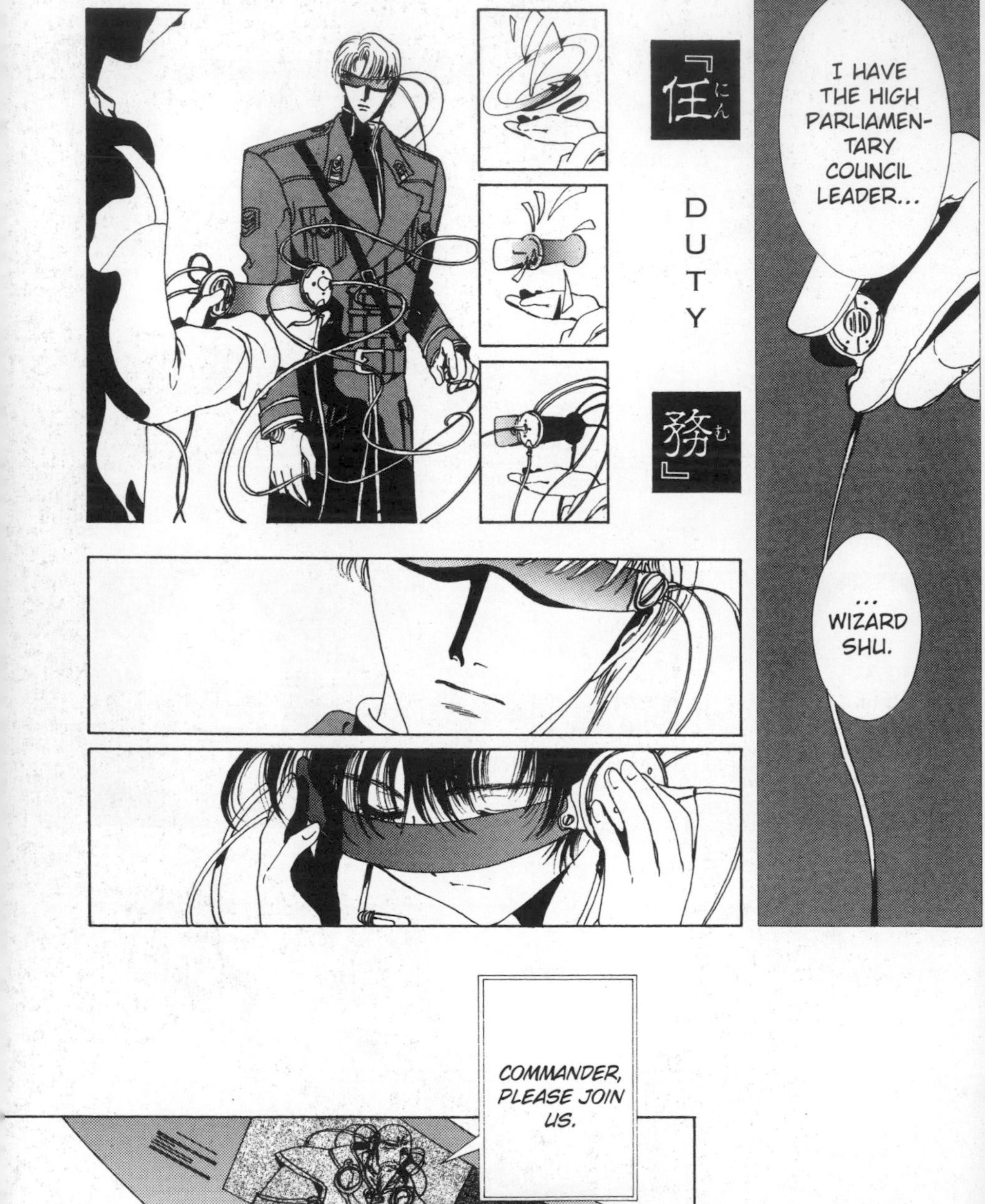
I HAVE THE HIGH PARLIAMENTARY COUNCIL LEADER...
...WIZARD SHU.
『任務』
DUTY
COMMANDER, PLEASE JOIN US.

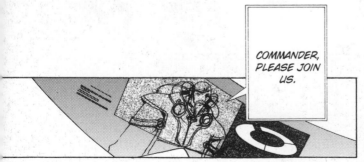

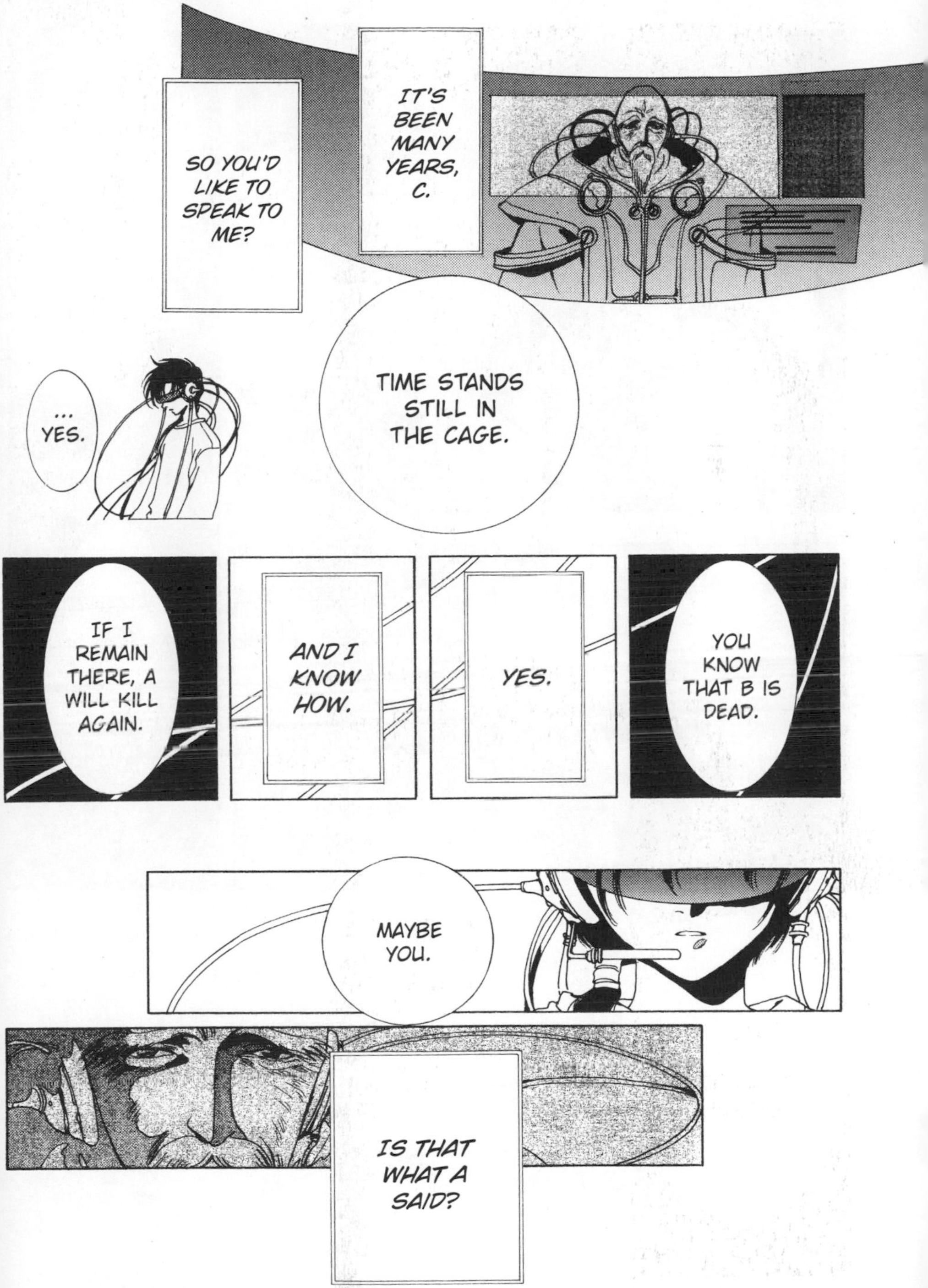
IT'S BEEN MANY YEARS, C.
SO YOU'D LIKE TO SPEAK TO ME?
TIME STANDS STILL IN THE CAGE.
... YES.
YOU KNOW THAT B IS DEAD.
YES.
AND I KNOW HOW.
IF I REMAIN THERE, A WILL KILL AGAIN.
MAYBE YOU.
IS THAT WHAT A SAID?

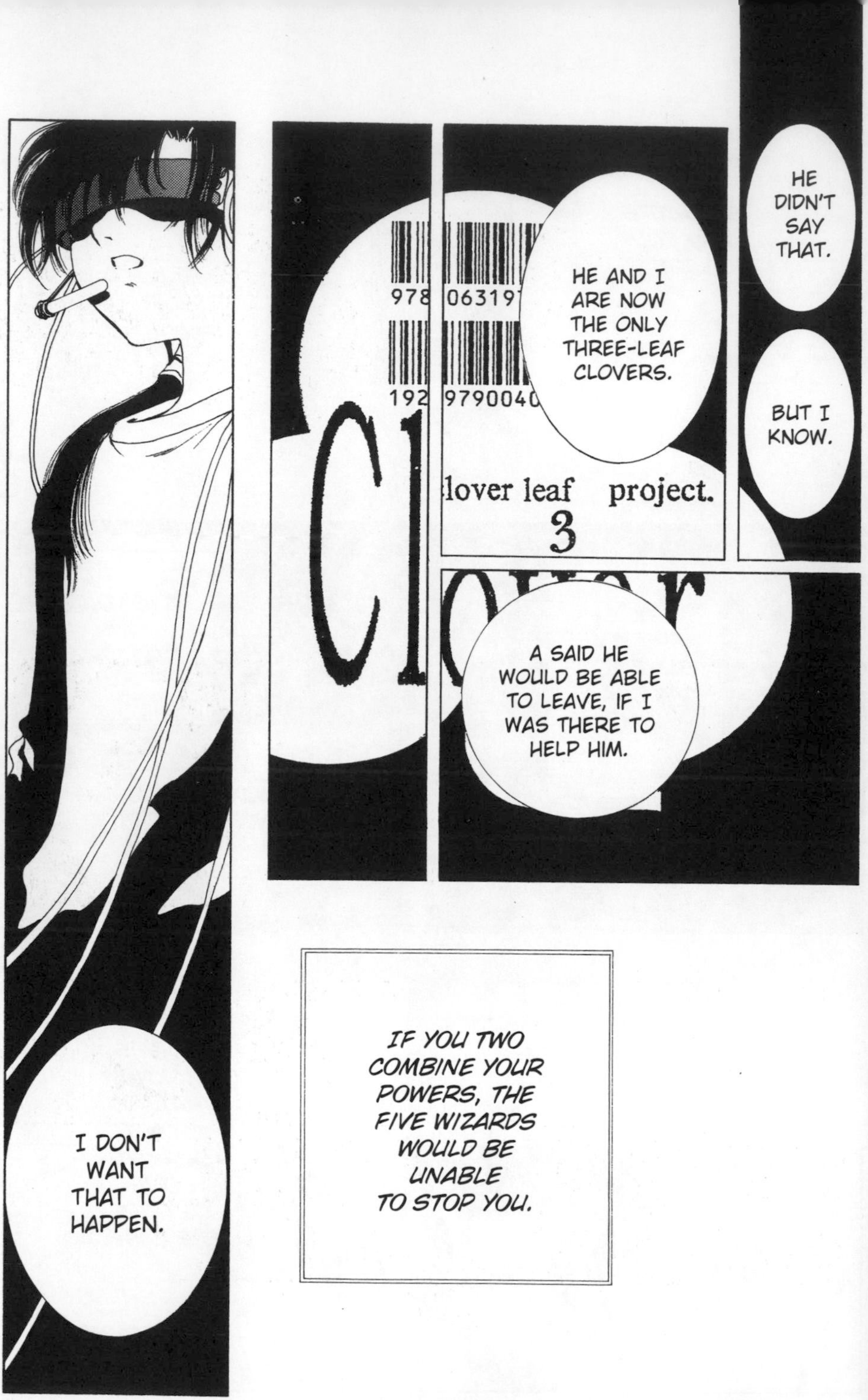
HE DIDN'T SAY THAT.
BUT I KNOW.
HE AND I ARE NOW THE ONLY THREE-LEAF CLOVERS.
lover leaf project.
3
A SAID HE WOULD BE ABLE TO LEAVE, IF I WAS THERE TO HELP HIM.
IF YOU TWO COMBINE YOUR POWERS, THE FIVE WIZARDS WOULD BE UNABLE TO STOP YOU.
I DON'T WANT THAT TO HAPPEN.

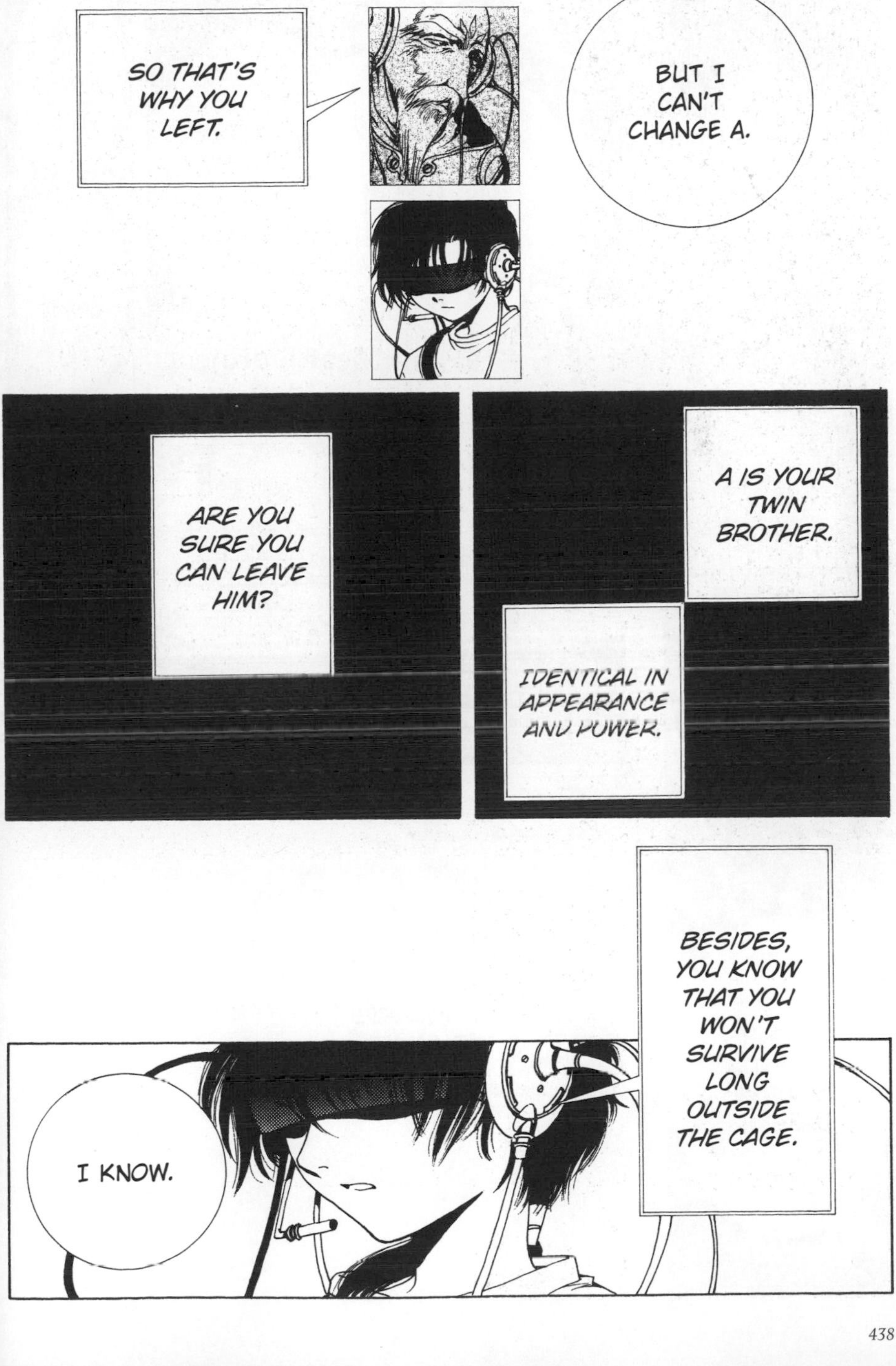
BUT I CAN'T CHANGE A.
SO THAT'S WHY YOU LEFT.
A IS YOUR TWIN BROTHER.
IDENTICAL IN APPEARANCE AND POWER.
ARE YOU SURE YOU CAN LEAVE HIM?
BESIDES, YOU KNOW THAT YOU WON'T SURVIVE LONG OUTSIDE THE CAGE.
I KNOW.

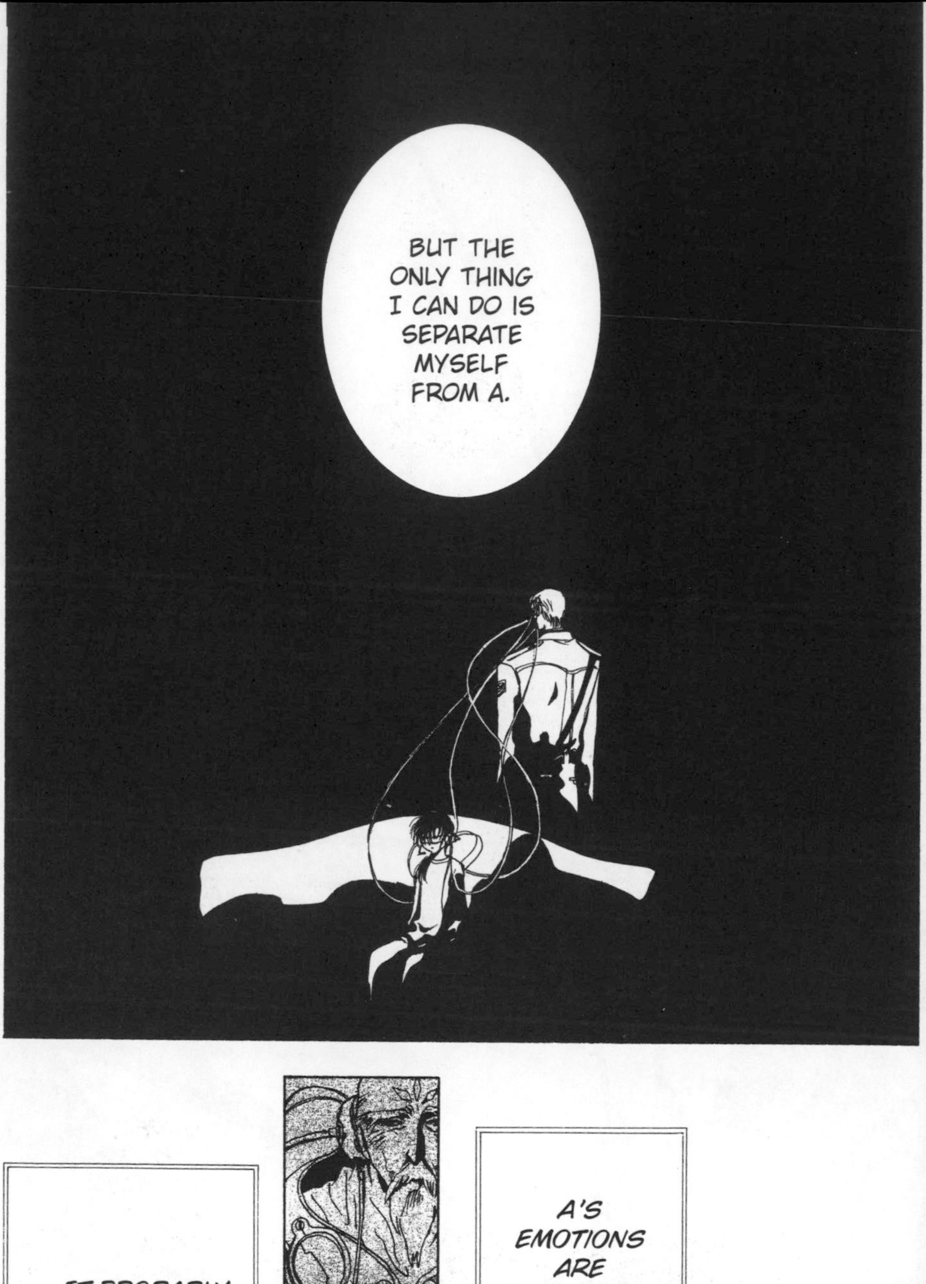
BUT THE ONLY THING I CAN DO IS SEPARATE MYSELF FROM A.
A'S EMOTIONS ARE UNSTABLE...
...IT PROBABLY IS DANGEROUS TO KEEP YOU TWO TOGETHER.

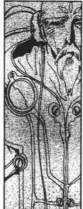

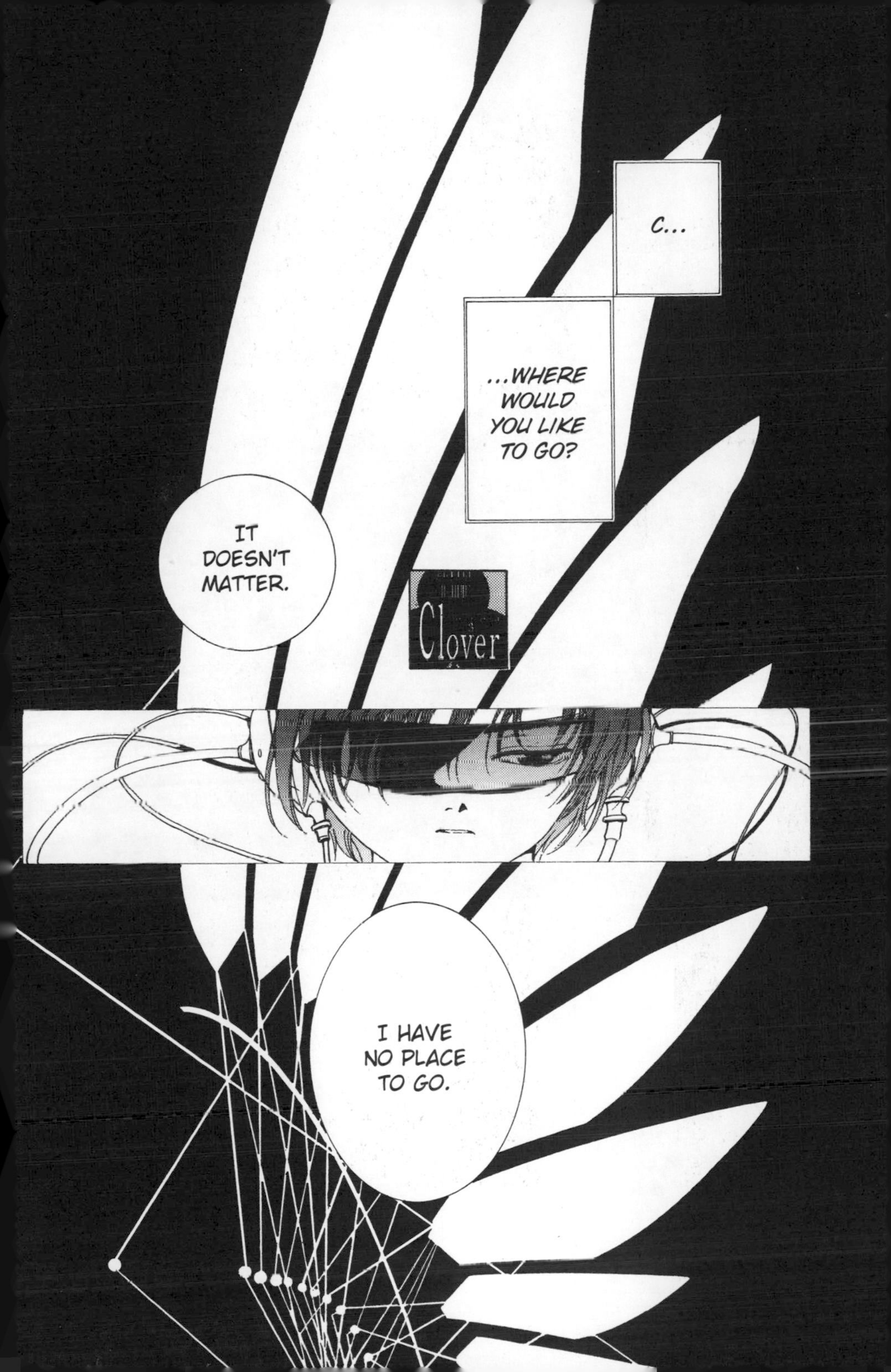
C...
...WHERE WOULD YOU LIKE TO GO?
IT DOESN'T MATTER.
Clover
I HAVE NO PLACE TO GO.

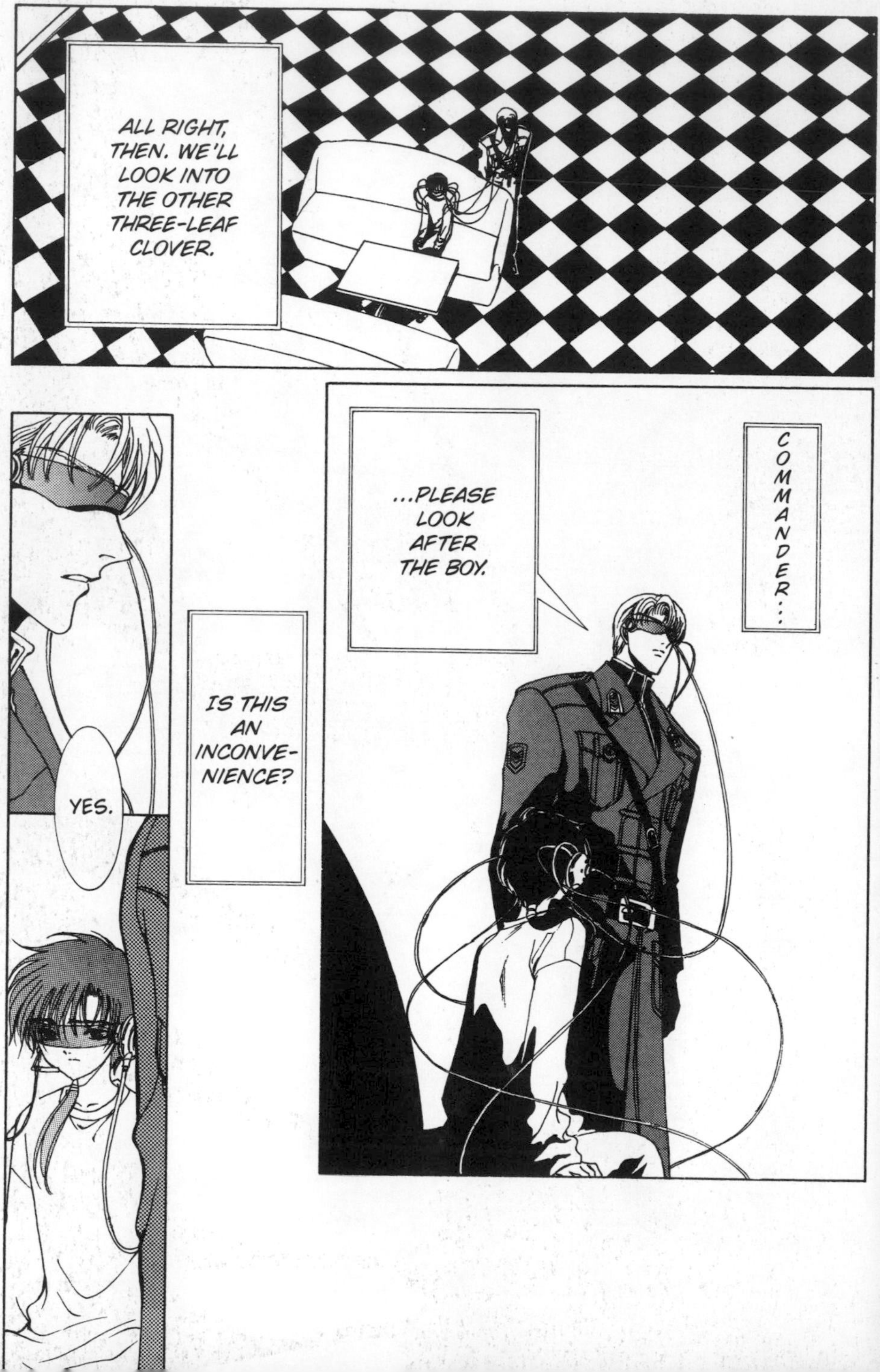
ALL RIGHT, THEN. WE'LL LOOK INTO THE OTHER THREE-LEAF CLOVER.
COMMANDER...
...PLEASE LOOK AFTER THE BOY.
IS THIS AN INCONVENIENCE?
YES.

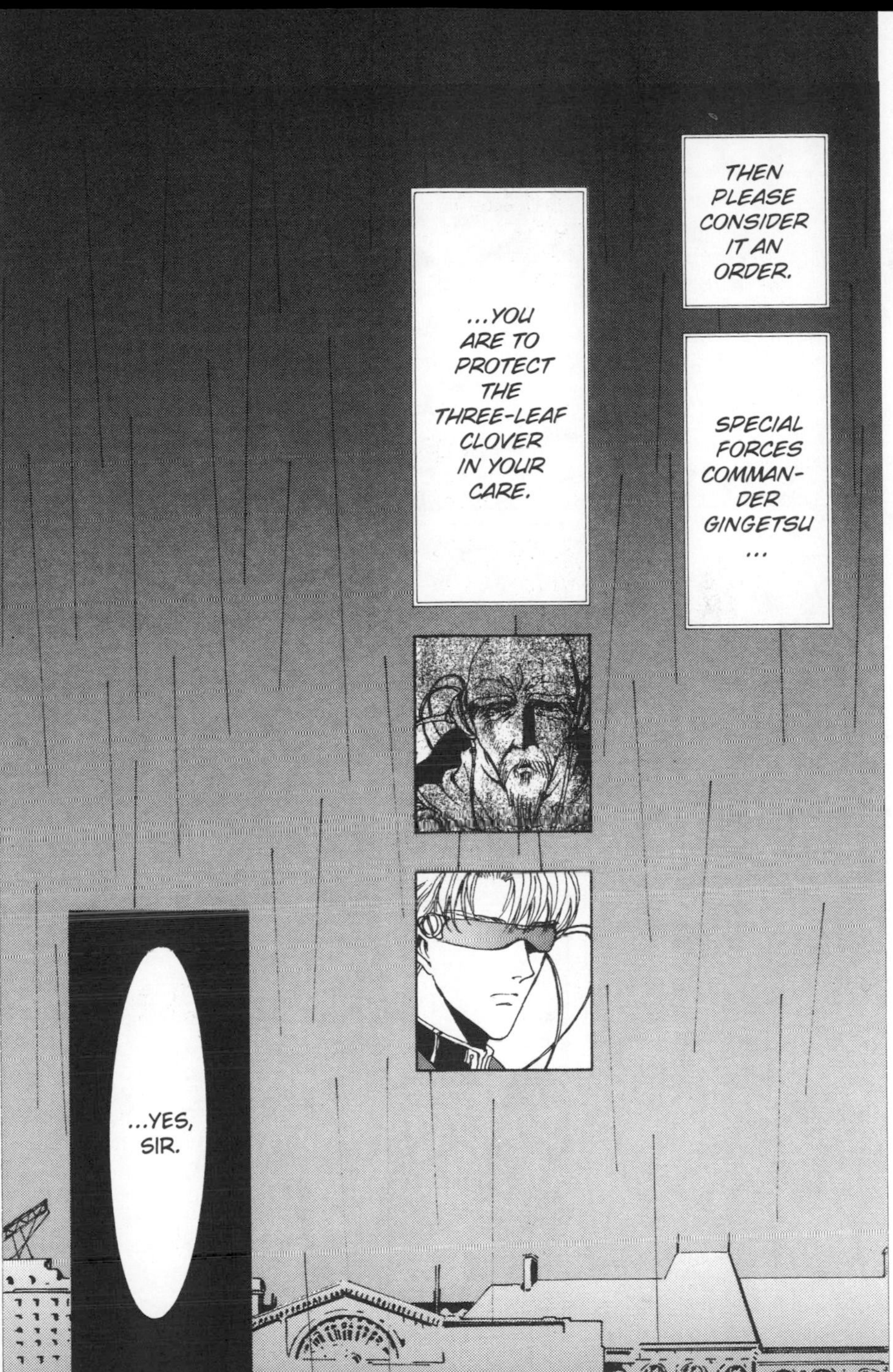
THEN PLEASE CONSIDER IT AN ORDER.
SPECIAL FORCES COMMANDER GINGETSU...
...YOU ARE TO PROTECT THE THREE-LEAF CLOVER IN YOUR CARE.
...YES, SIR.

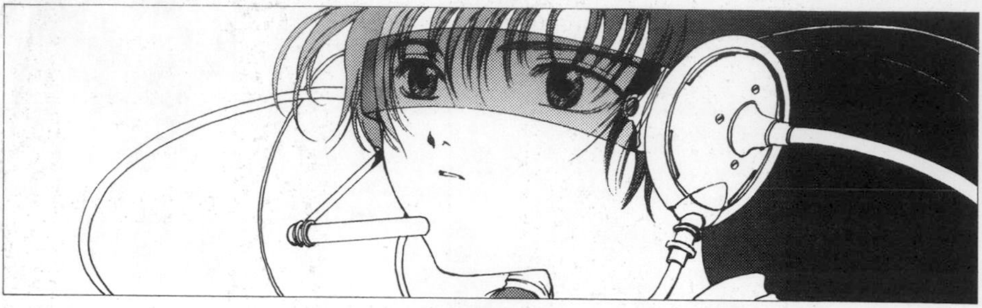

『印』 SEAL

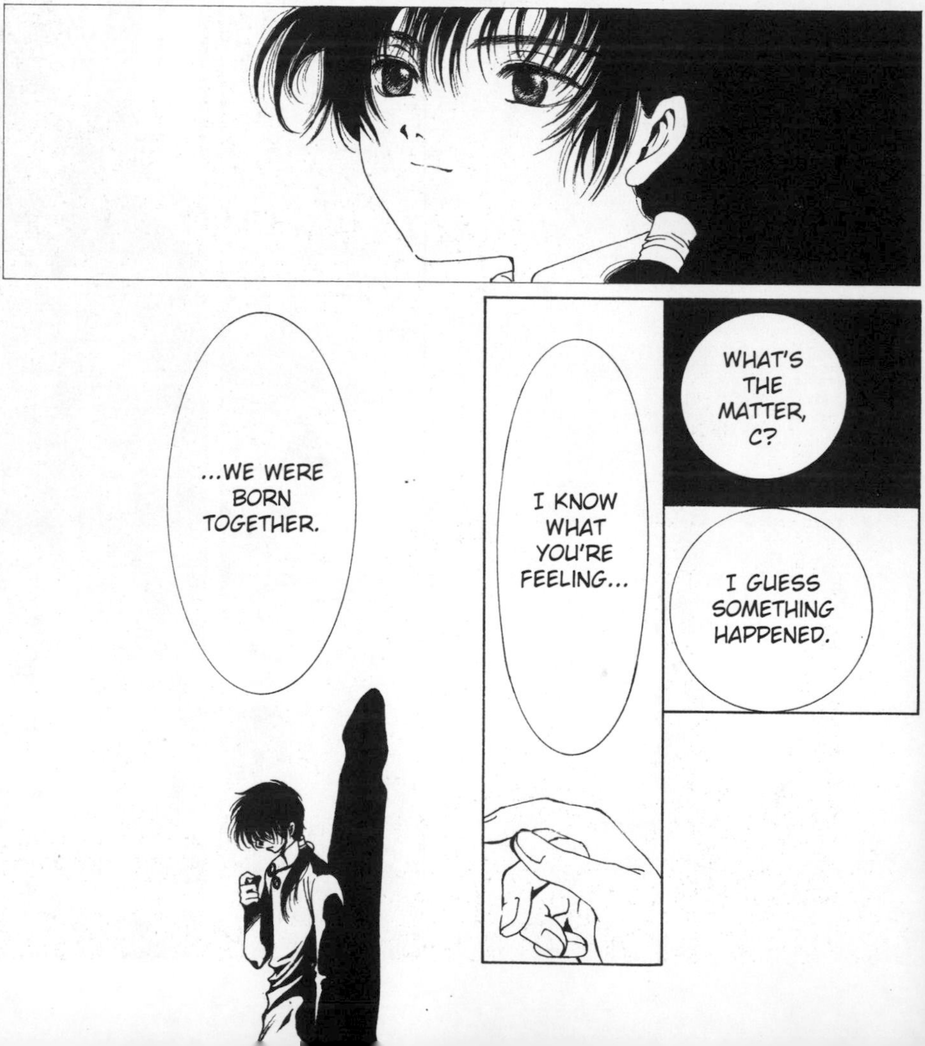
WHAT'S THE MATTER, C?
I GUESS SOMETHING HAPPENED.
I KNOW WHAT YOU'RE FEELING...
...WE WERE BORN TOGETHER.

AND
WE WILL
ALWAYS BE
TOGETHER.

Clover
ALWAYS...
FOREVER.

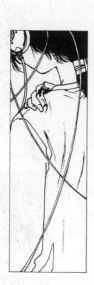

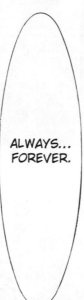

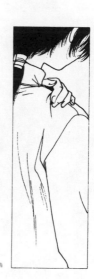

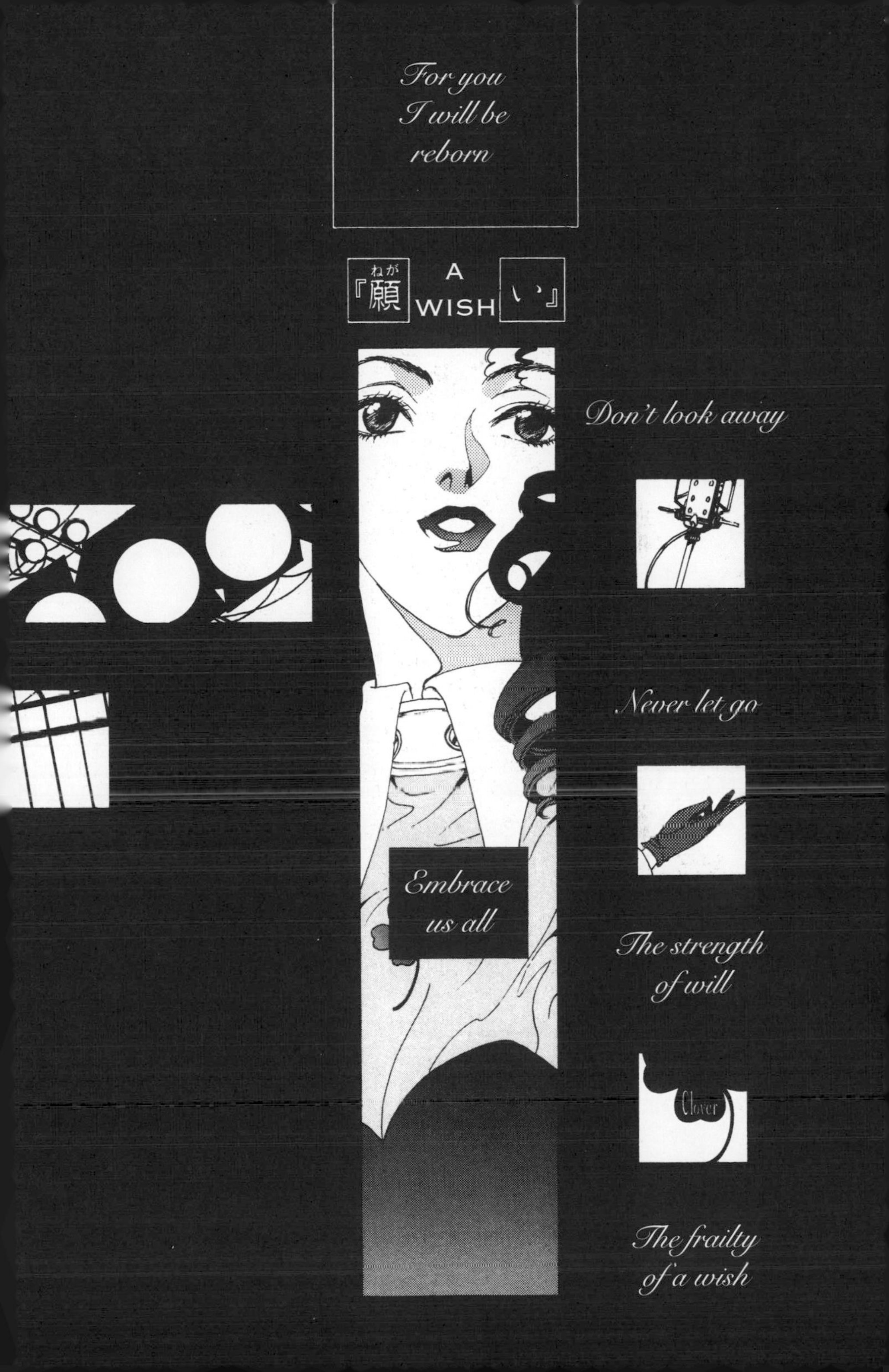
For you
I will be
reborn
『願い』 A WISH
Don't look away
Never let go
Embrace us all
The strength
of will
Clover
The frailty
of a wish

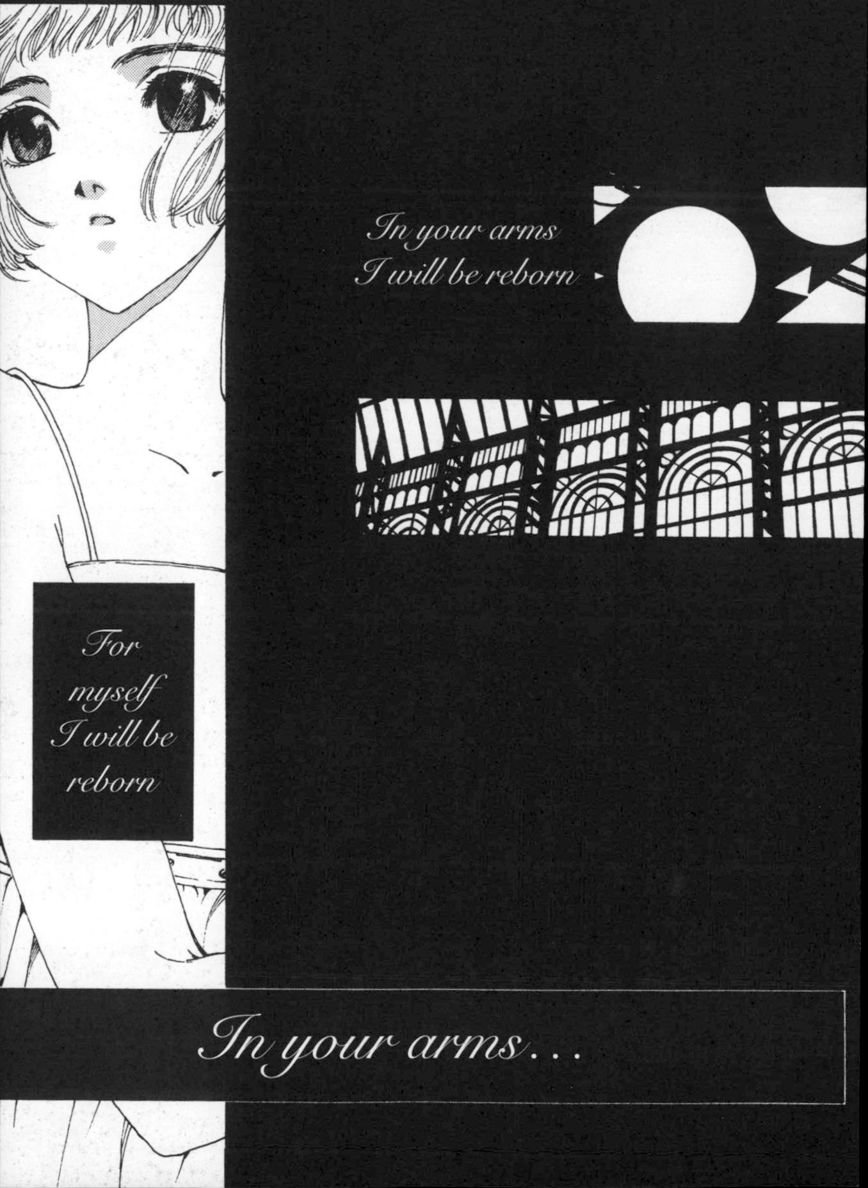
In your arms
I will be reborn
For myself I will be reborn
In your arms...

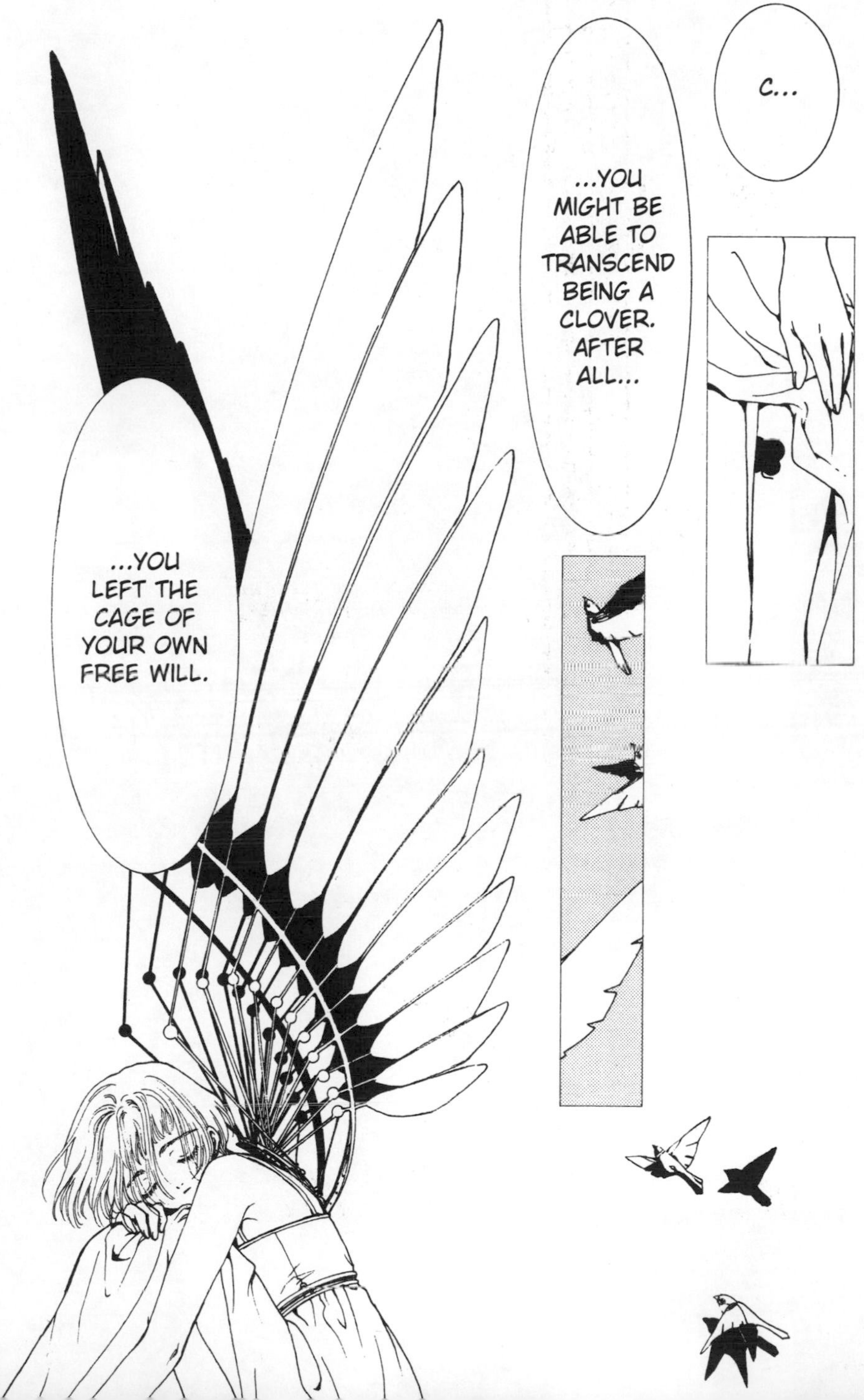
C...
...YOU MIGHT BE ABLE TO TRANSCEND BEING A CLOVER. AFTER ALL...
...YOU LEFT THE CAGE OF YOUR OWN FREE WILL.

THE BLISS OF CLOVER

『クローバーのしあわせ』

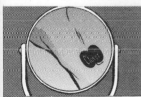  

 THESE ARE THE BRANDS OF THE CLOVER LEAF PROJECT.

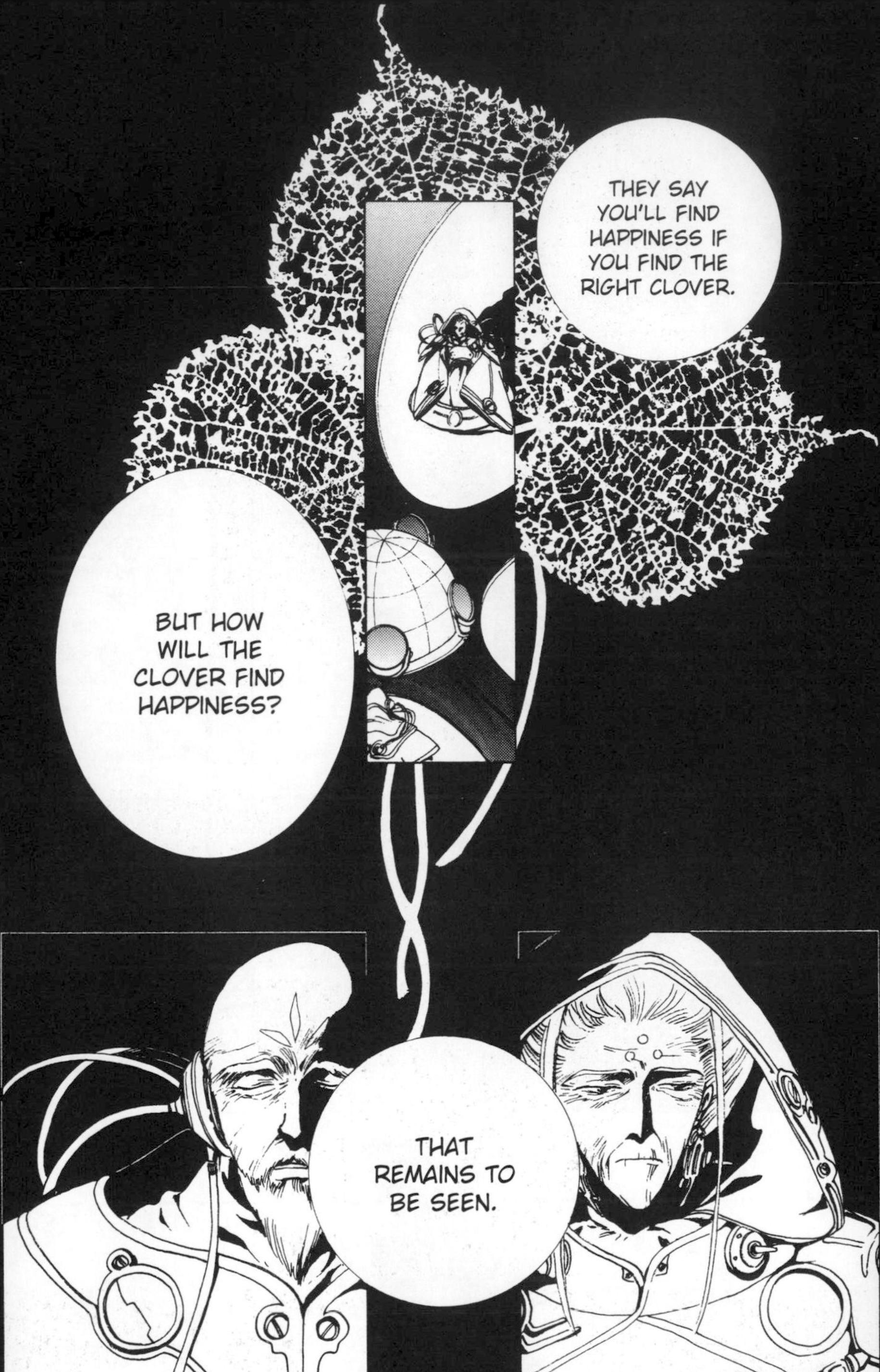
THEY SAY YOU'LL FIND HAPPINESS IF YOU FIND THE RIGHT CLOVER.
BUT HOW WILL THE CLOVER FIND HAPPINESS?
THAT REMAINS TO BE SEEN.

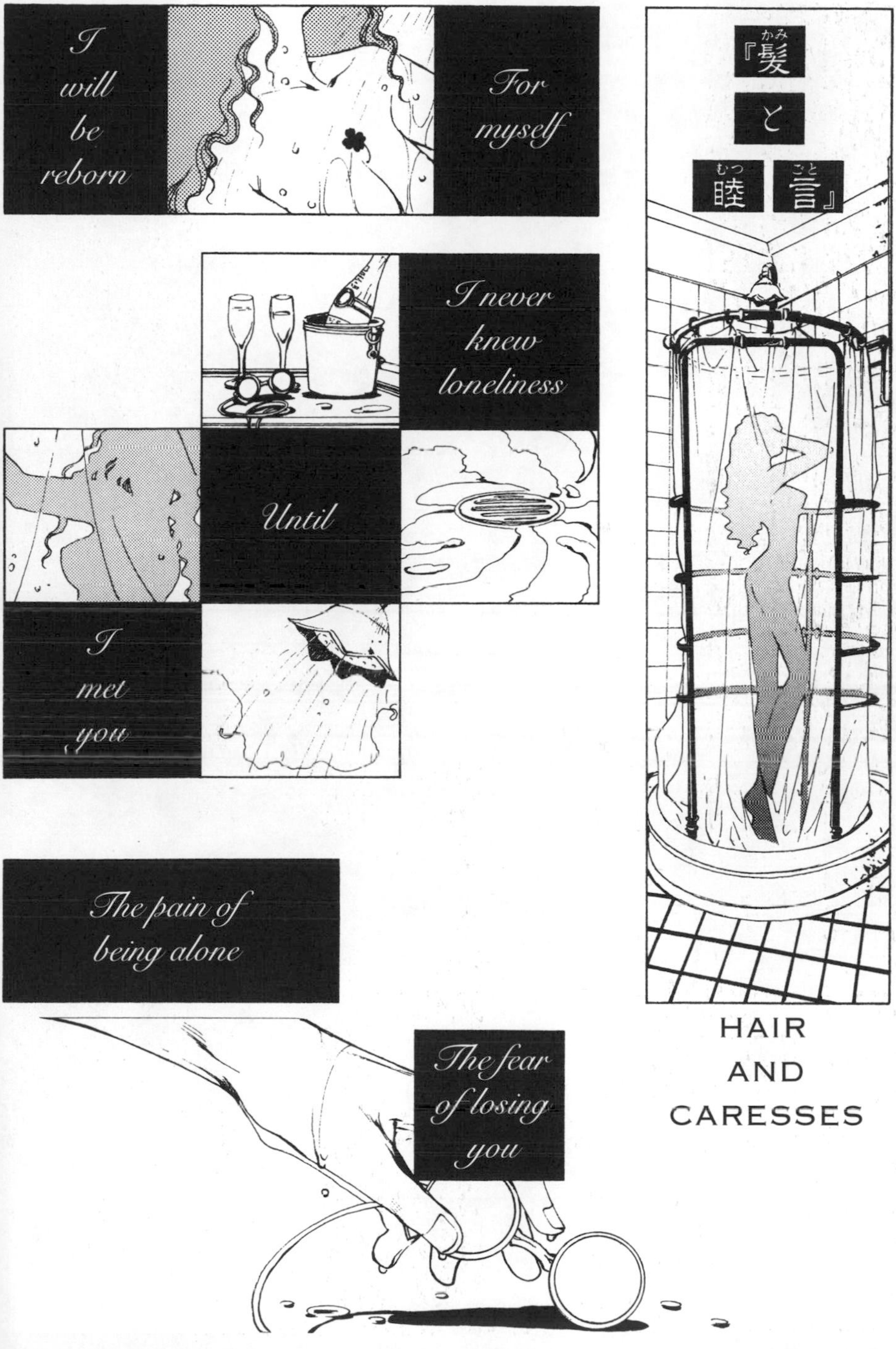
『髪と睦言』
HAIR AND CARESSES
For myself
I will be reborn
I never knew loneliness
Until
I met you
The pain of being alone
The fear of losing you

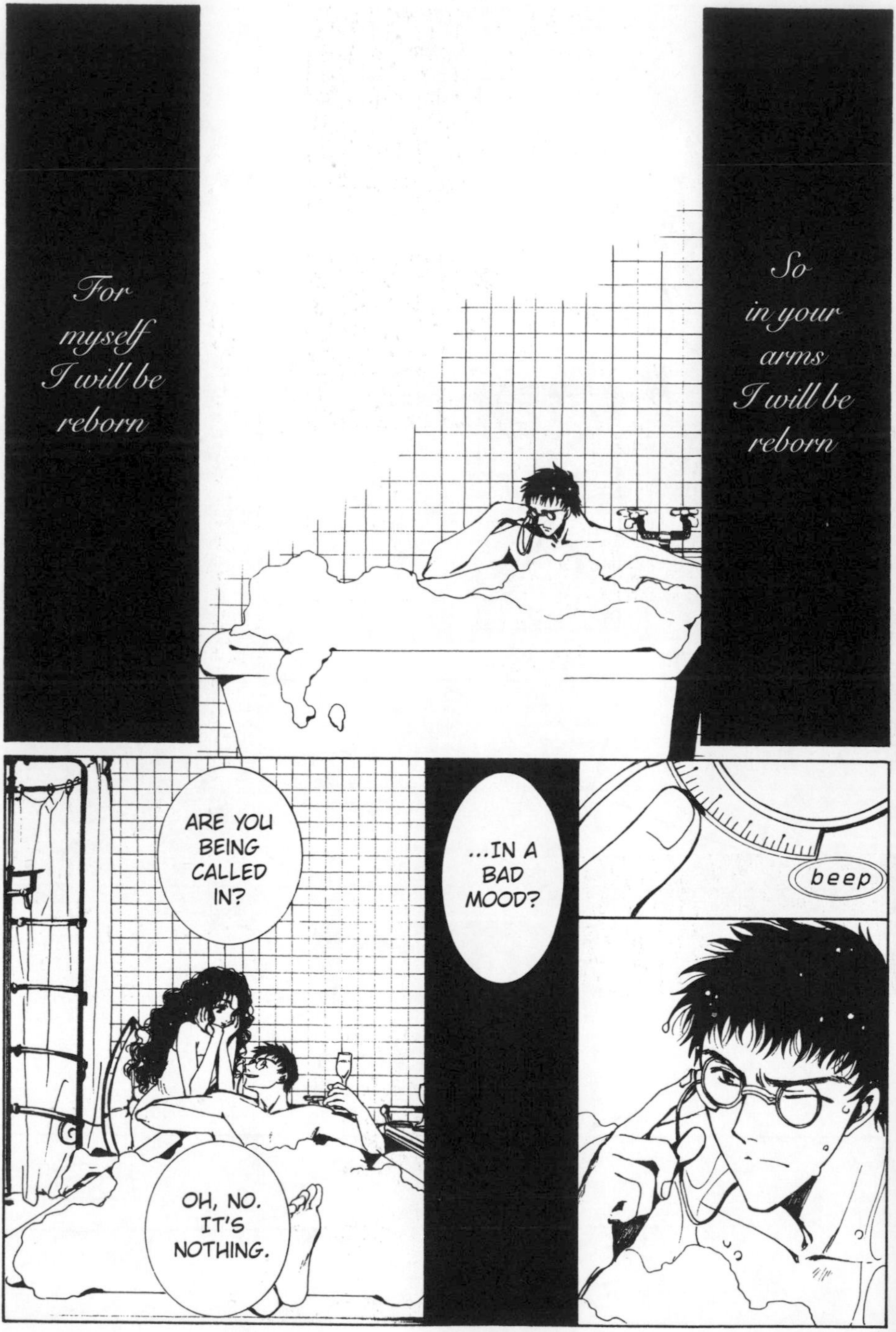
So in your arms I will be reborn
For myself I will be reborn
beep
...IN A BAD MOOD?
ARE YOU BEING CALLED IN?
OH, NO. IT'S NOTHING.

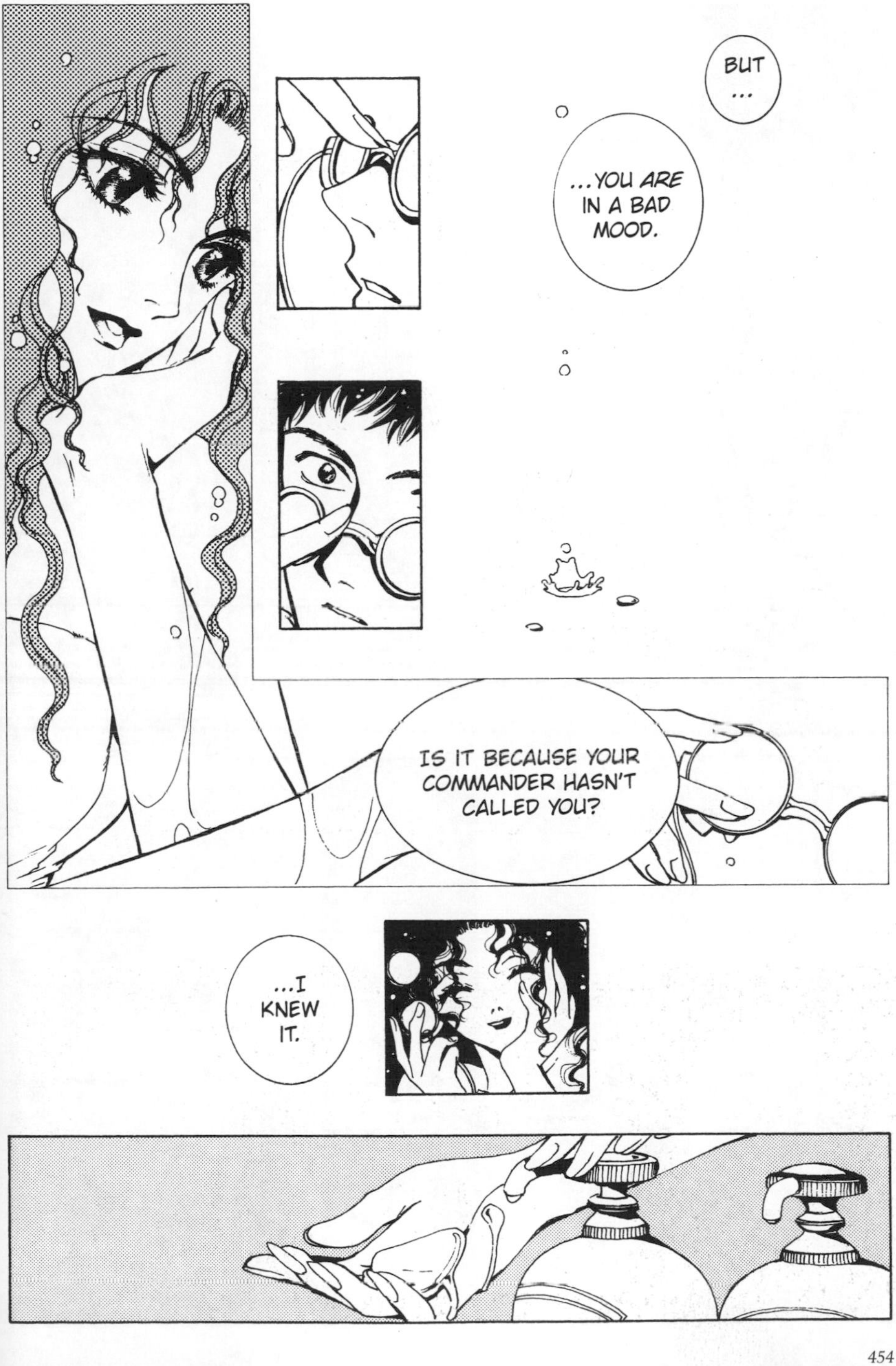
BUT ...
...YOU ARE IN A BAD MOOD.
IS IT BECAUSE YOUR COMMANDER HASN'T CALLED YOU?
...I KNEW IT.

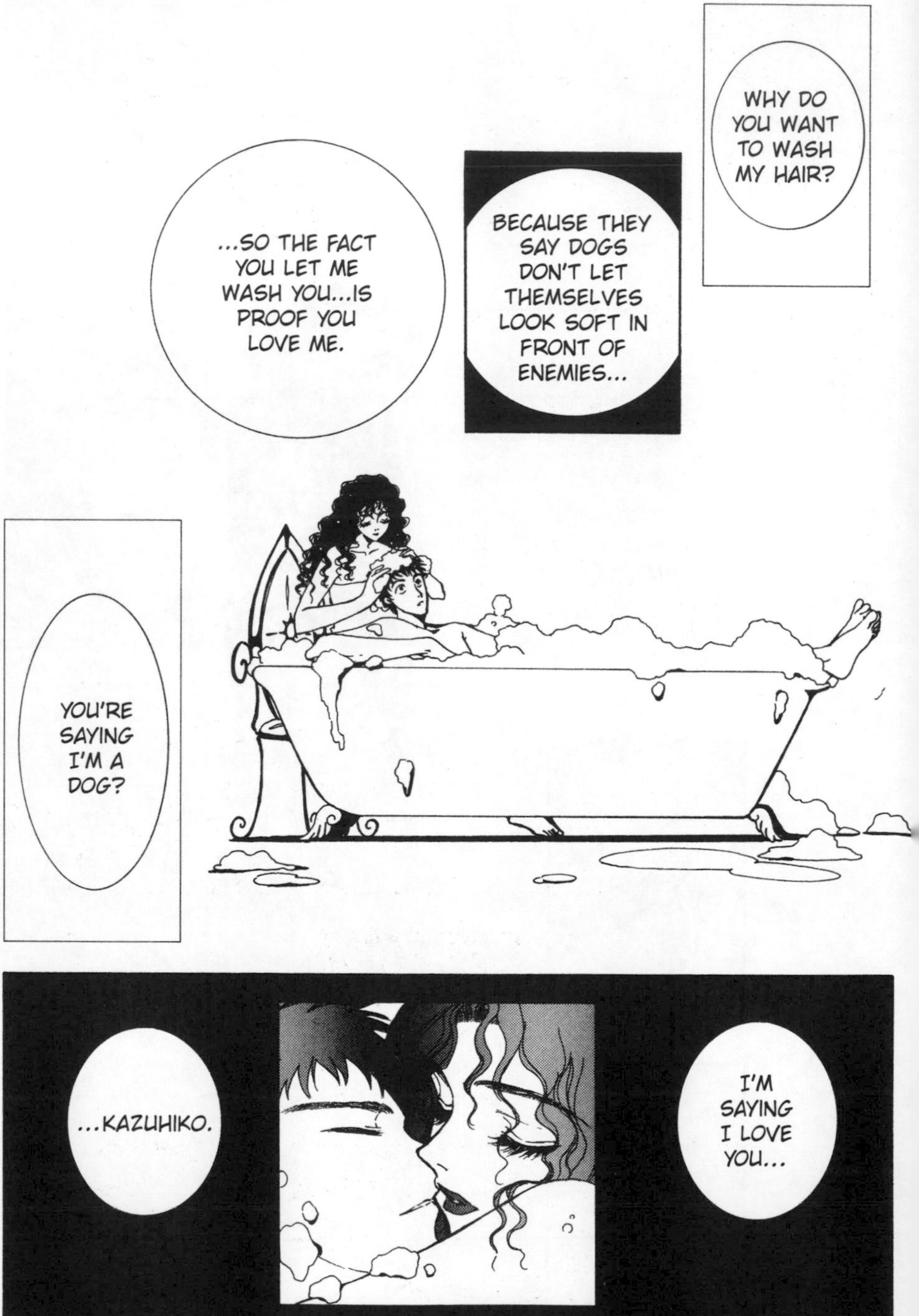
WHY DO YOU WANT TO WASH MY HAIR?
BECAUSE THEY SAY DOGS DON'T LET THEMSELVES LOOK SOFT IN FRONT OF ENEMIES...
...SO THE FACT YOU LET ME WASH YOU...IS PROOF YOU LOVE ME.
YOU'RE SAYING I'M A DOG?
I'M SAYING I LOVE YOU...
...KAZUHIKO.

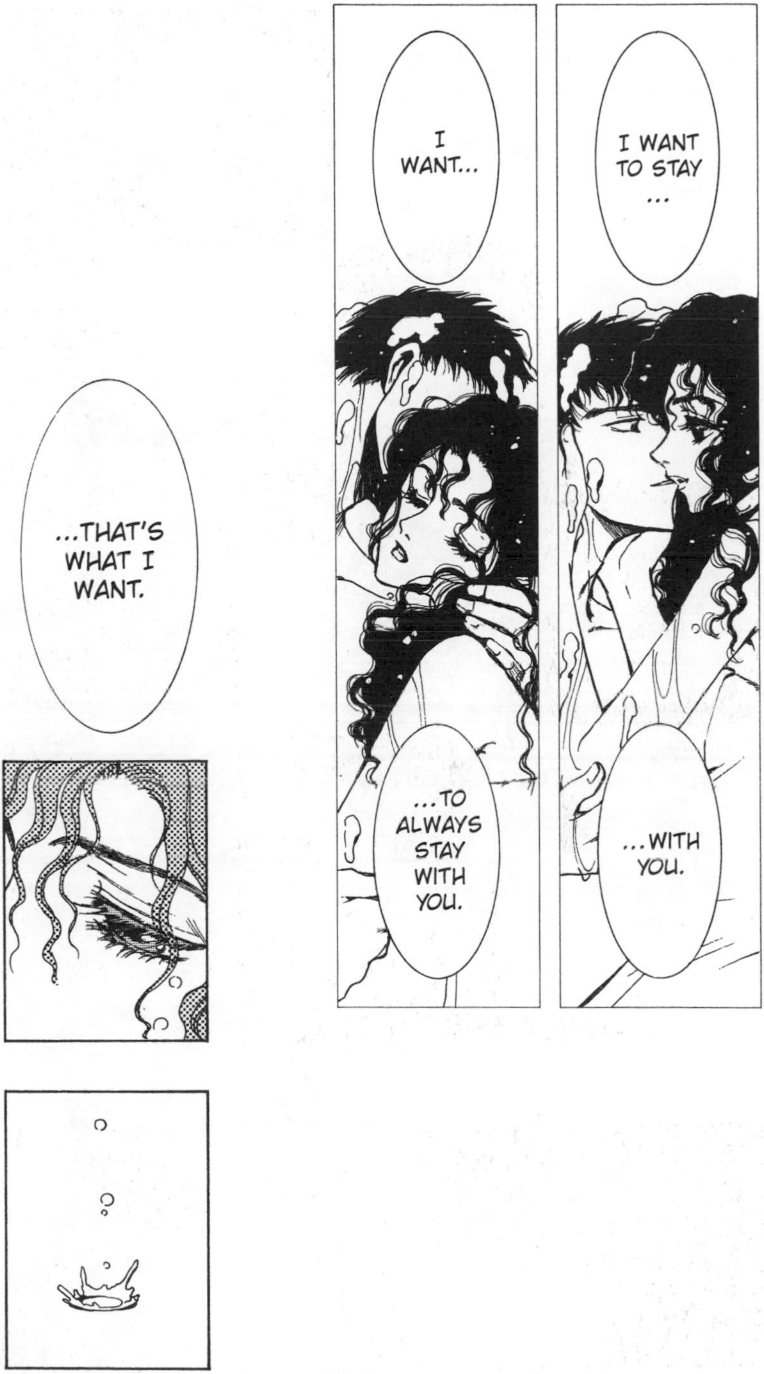
I WANT TO STAY ...
...WITH YOU.
I WANT...
...TO ALWAYS STAY WITH YOU.
...THAT'S WHAT I WANT.

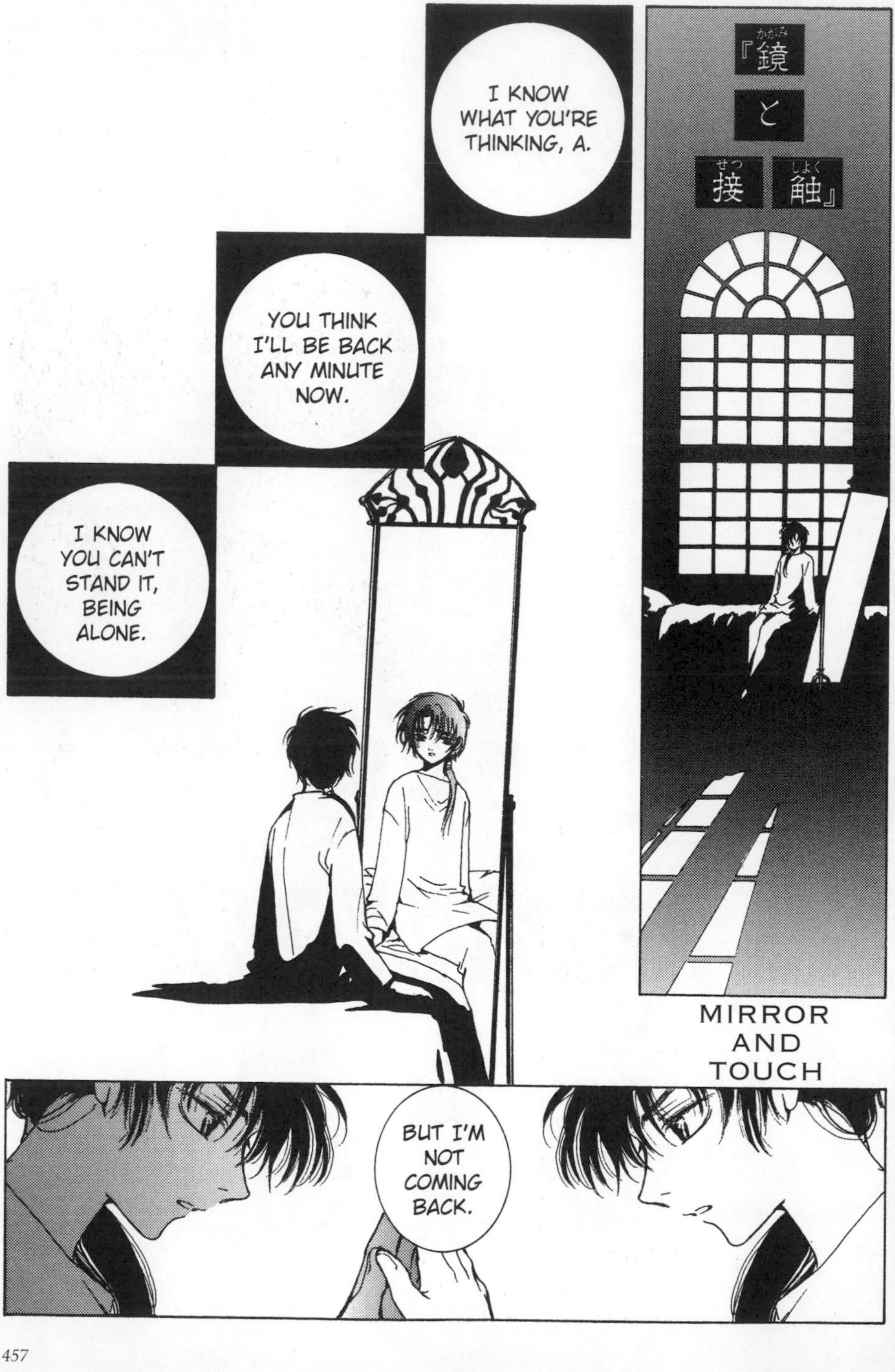
『鏡と接触』
MIRROR AND TOUCH
I KNOW WHAT YOU'RE THINKING, A.
YOU THINK I'LL BE BACK ANY MINUTE NOW.
I KNOW YOU CAN'T STAND IT, BEING ALONE.
BUT I'M NOT COMING BACK.

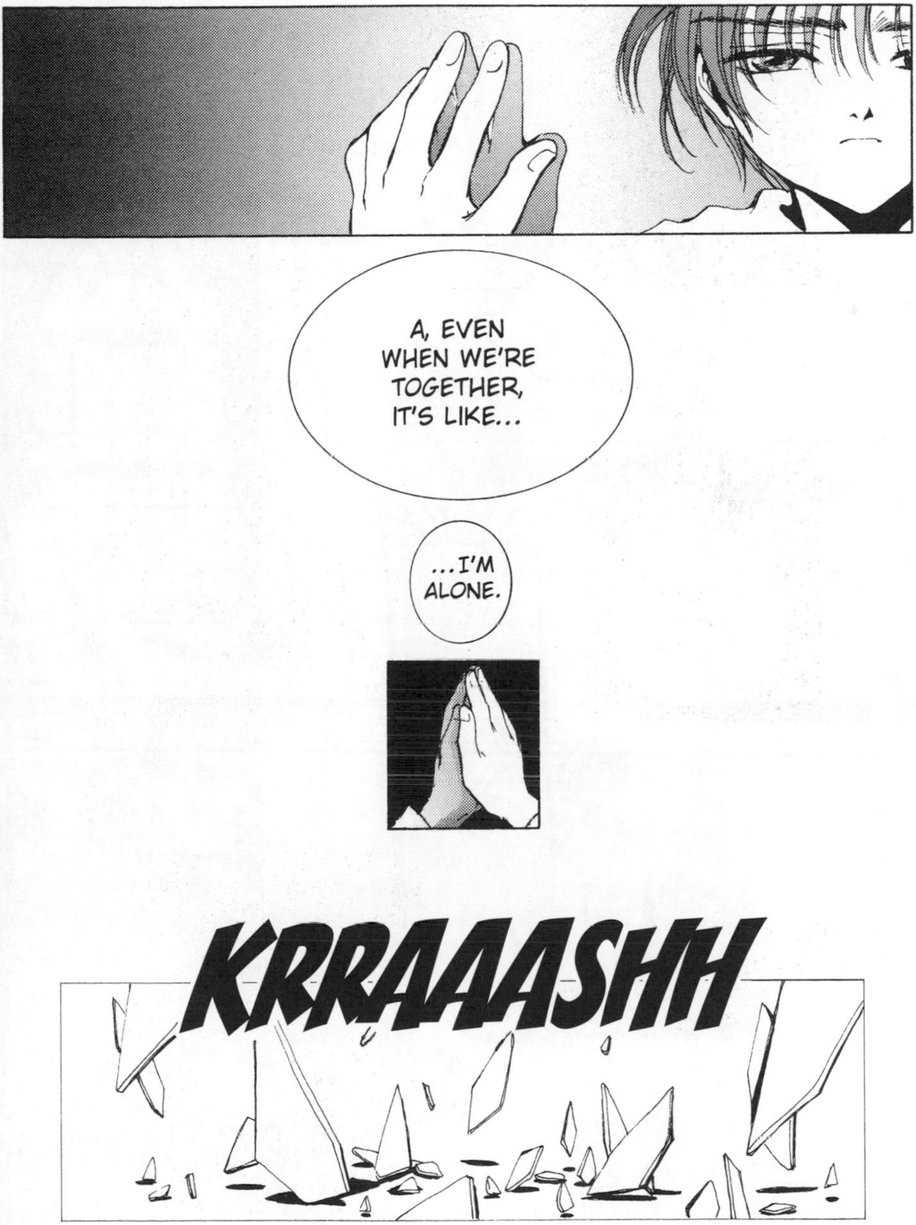
A, EVEN WHEN WE'RE TOGETHER, IT'S LIKE...
...I'M ALONE.
KRRAAASHH

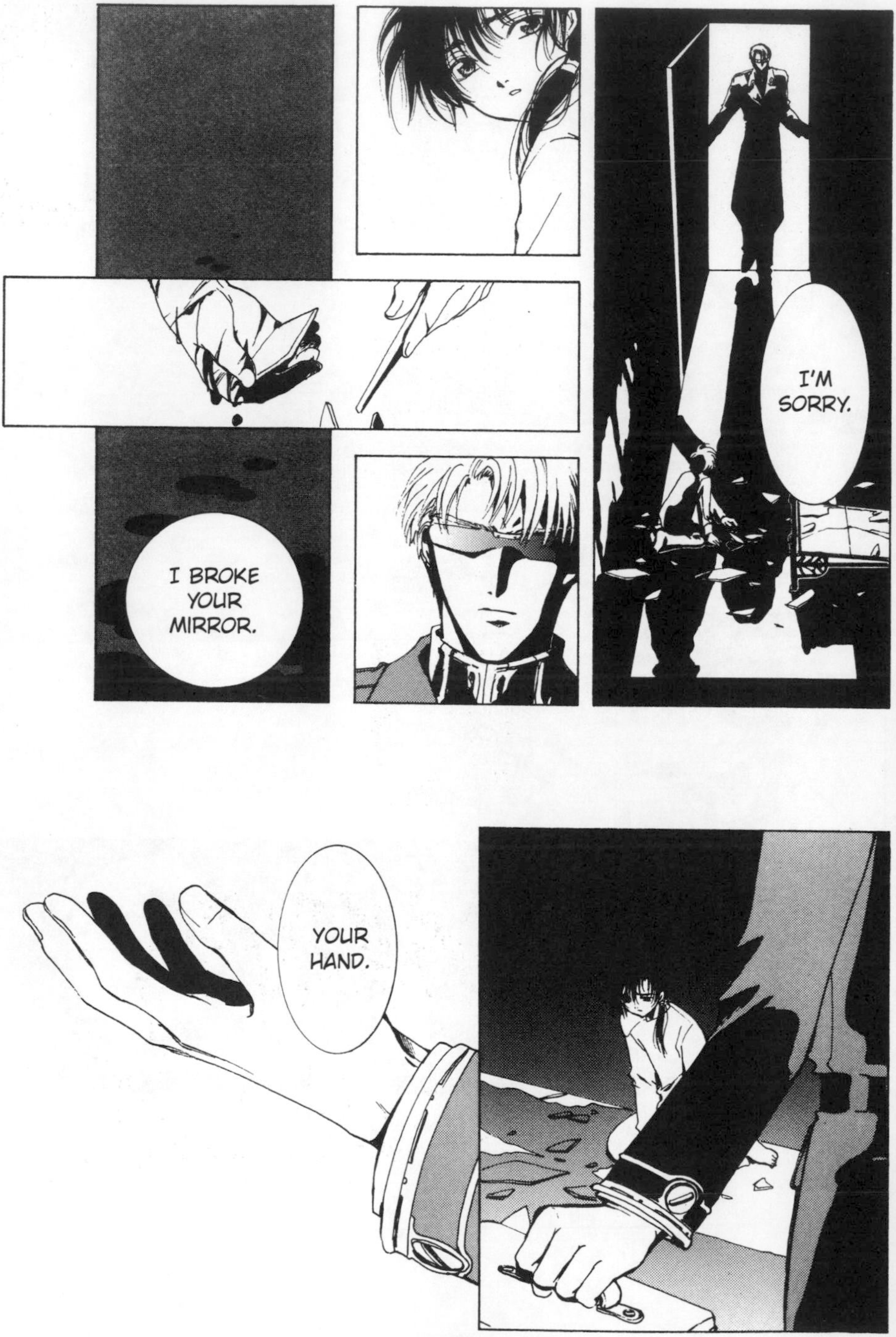
I'M SORRY.
I BROKE YOUR MIRROR.
YOUR HAND.

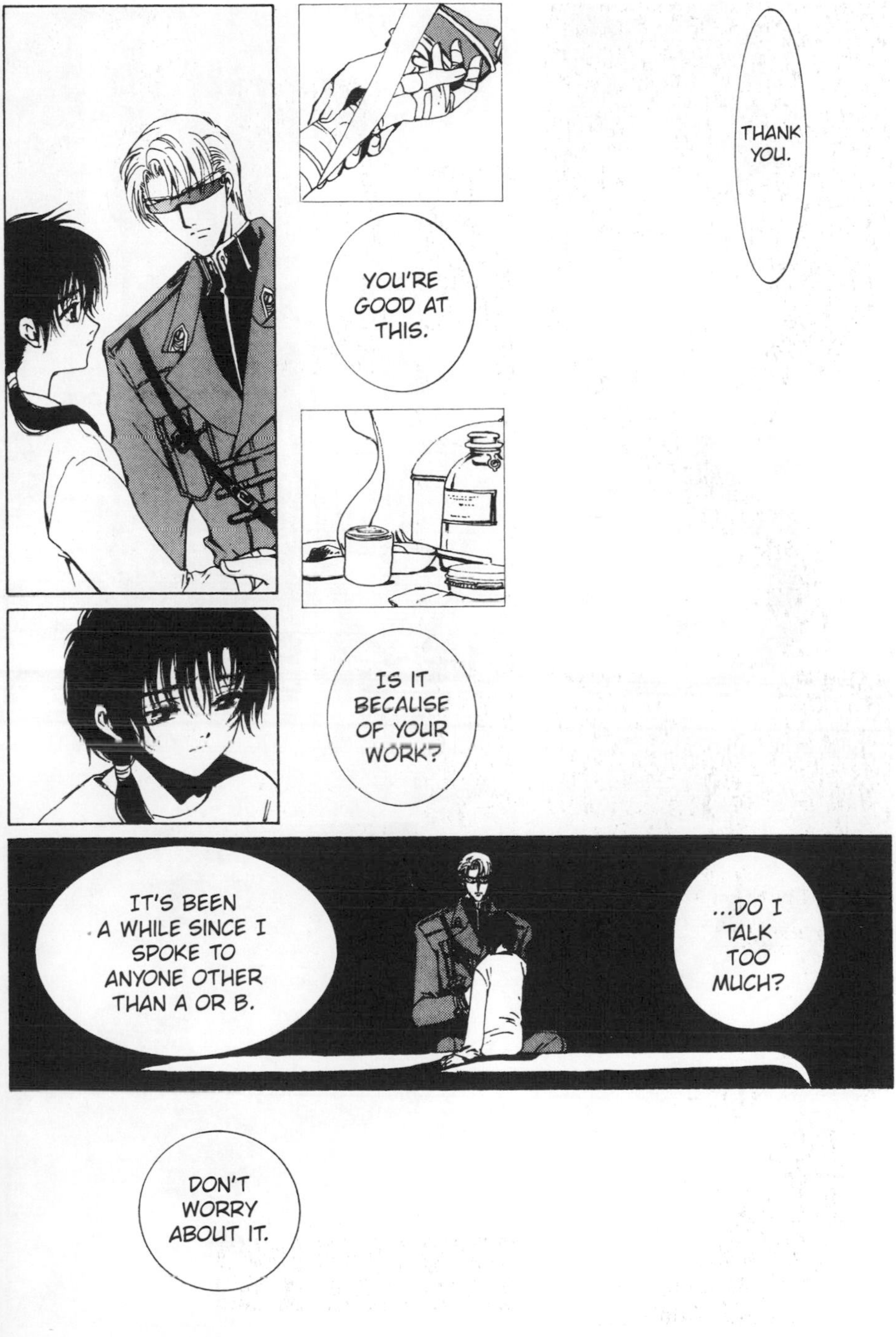
THANK YOU.
YOU'RE GOOD AT THIS.
IS IT BECAUSE OF YOUR WORK?
...DO I TALK TOO MUCH?
IT'S BEEN A WHILE SINCE I SPOKE TO ANYONE OTHER THAN A OR B.
DON'T WORRY ABOUT IT.

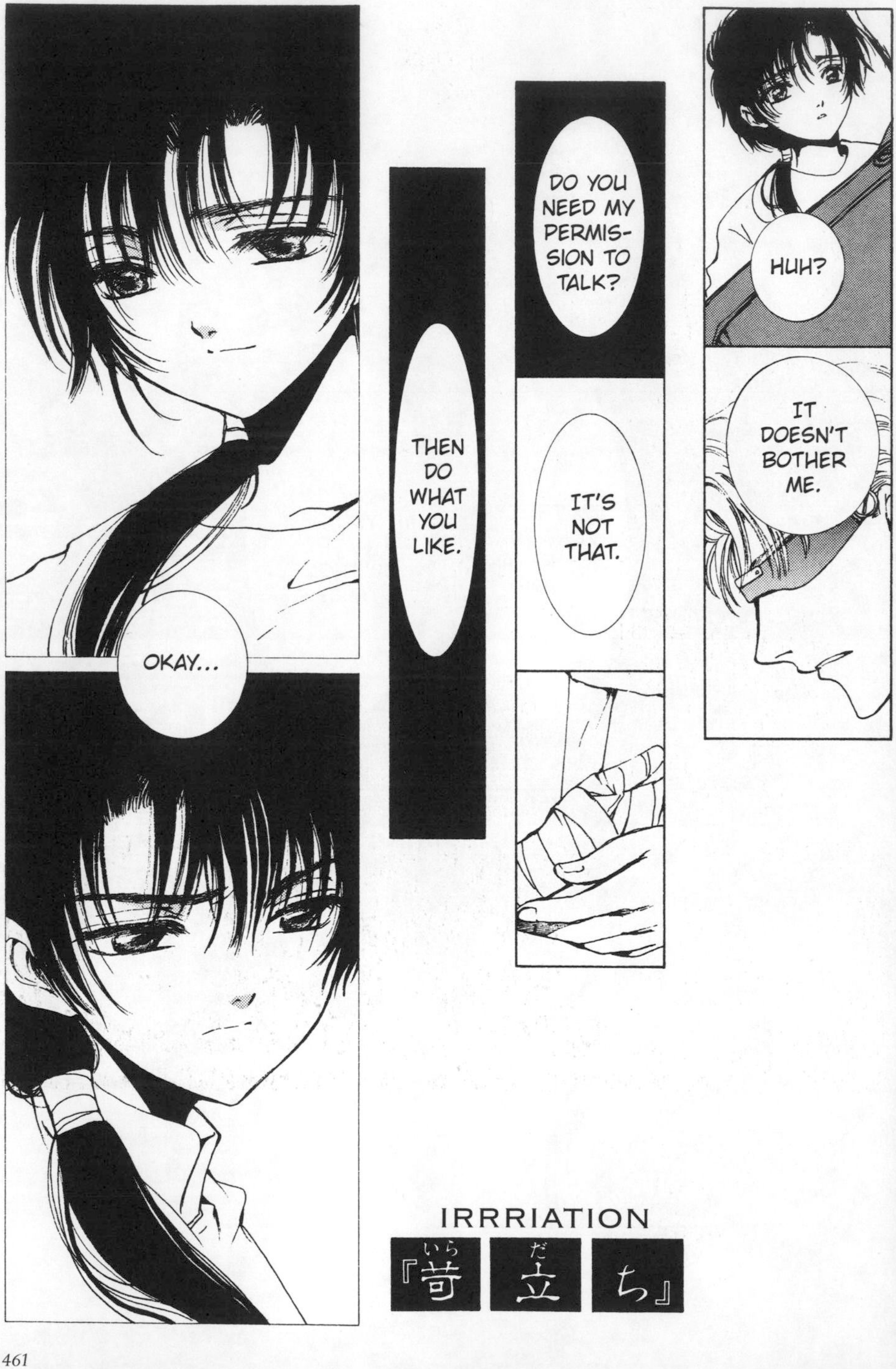
HUH?
IT DOESN'T BOTHER ME.
DO YOU NEED MY PERMISSION TO TALK?
IT'S NOT THAT.
THEN DO WHAT YOU LIKE.
OKAY...
IRRRIATION
『苛立ち』

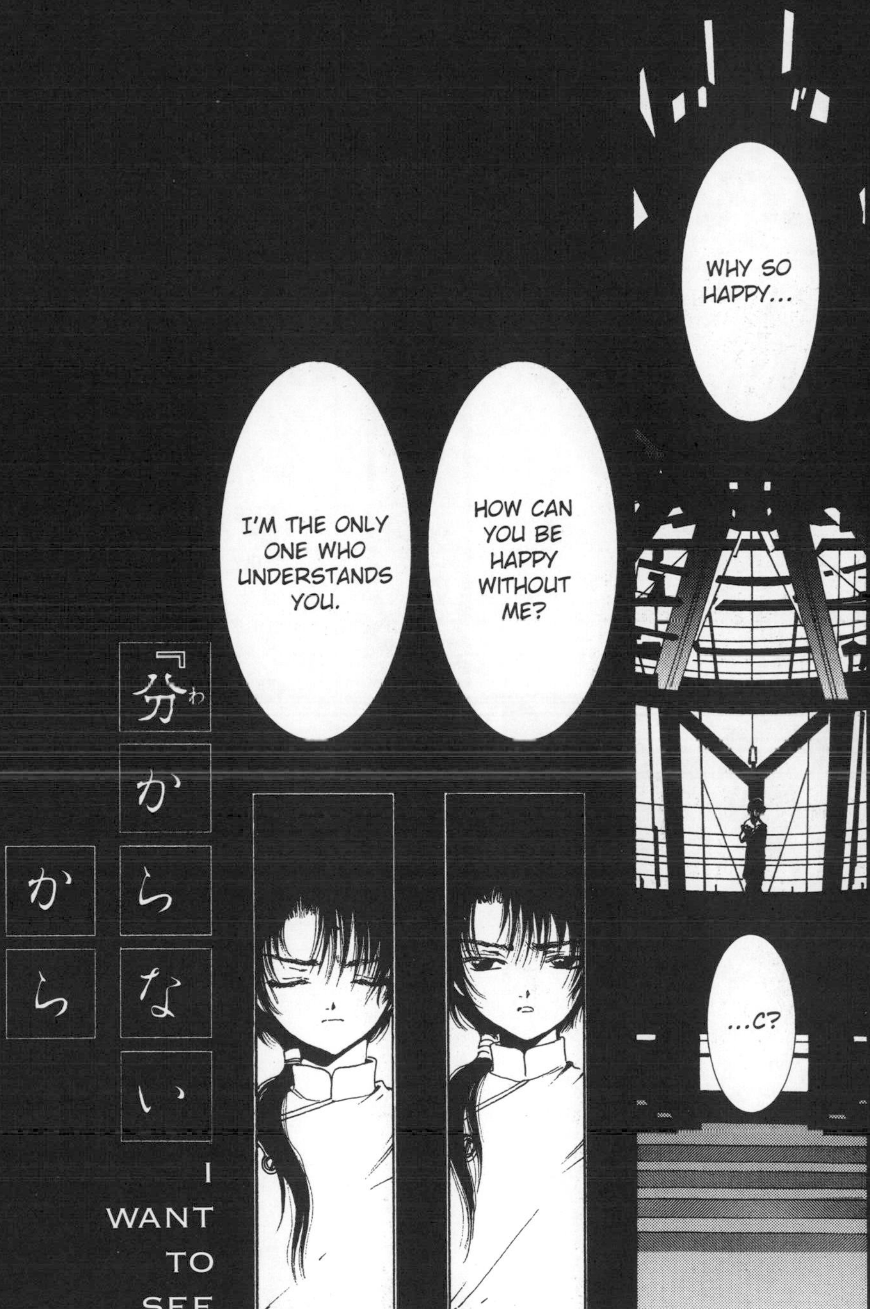
WHY SO HAPPY...
HOW CAN YOU BE HAPPY WITHOUT ME?
I'M THE ONLY ONE WHO UNDERSTANDS YOU.
...C?
『分からないから
I WANT TO SEE

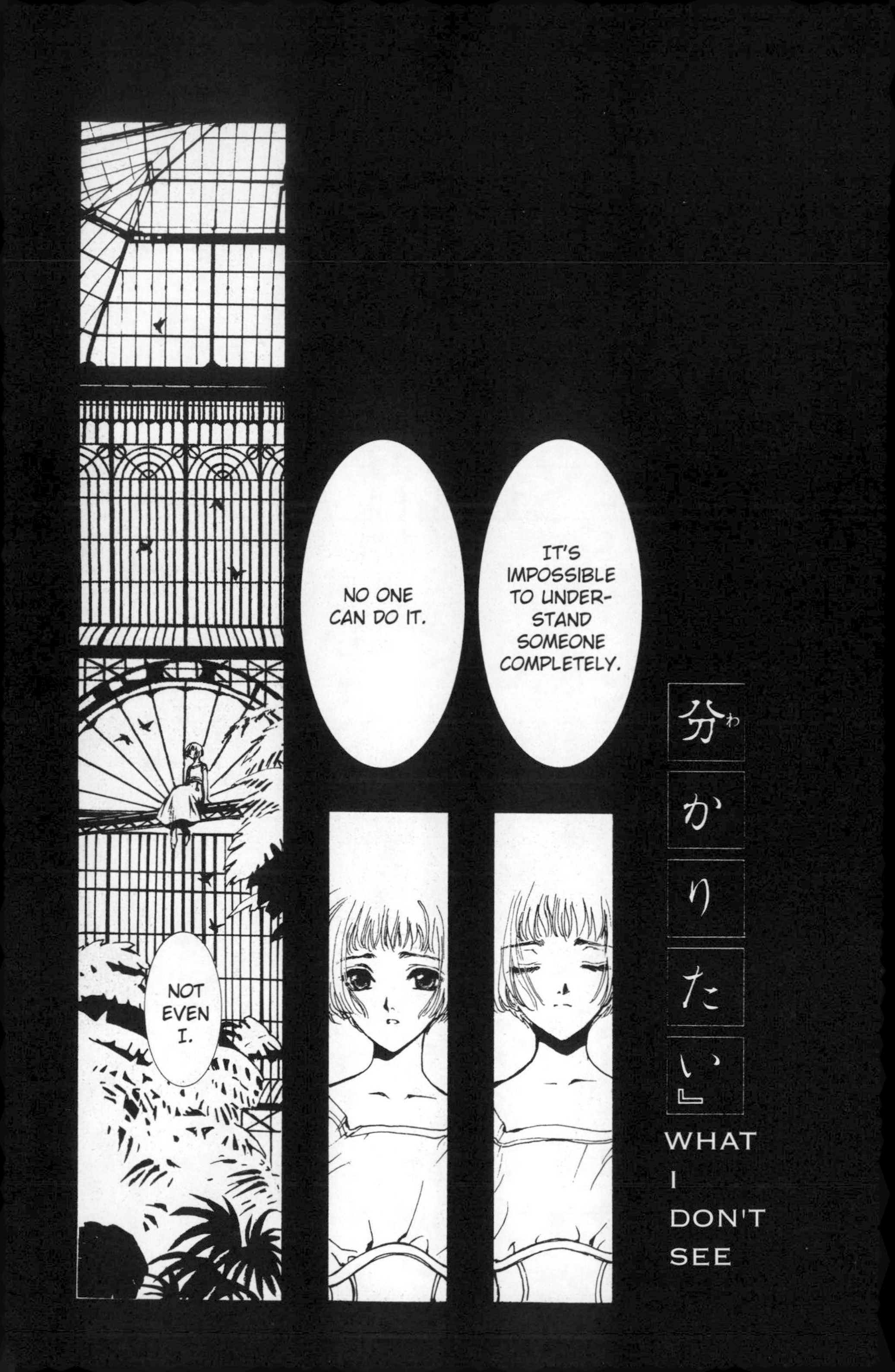
分かりたい』
WHAT I DON'T SEE
IT'S IMPOSSIBLE TO UNDER-STAND SOMEONE COMPLETELY.
NO ONE CAN DO IT.
NOT EVEN I.

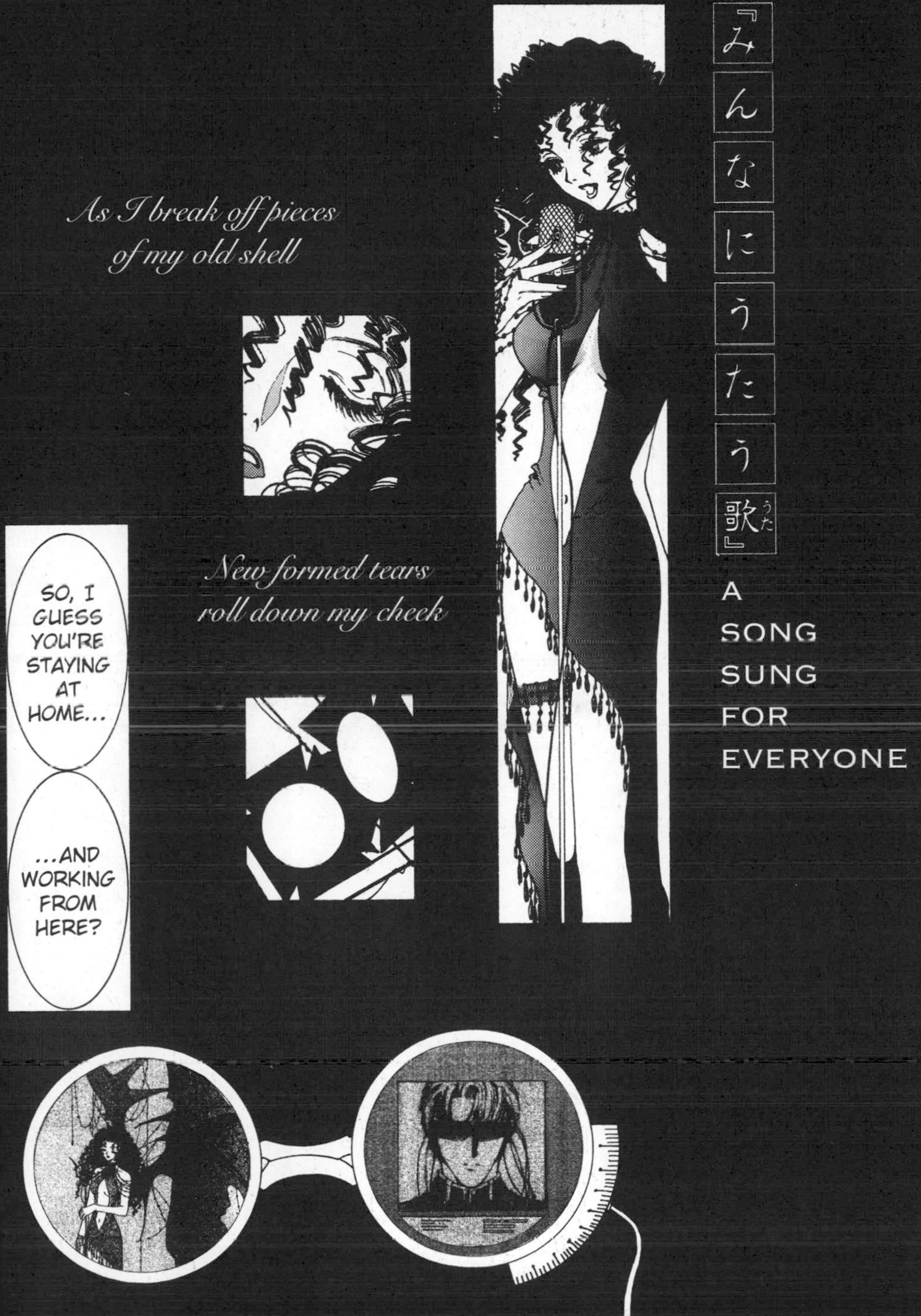
『みんなにうたう歌』
A SONG SUNG FOR EVERYONE
As I break off pieces of my old shell
New formed tears roll down my cheek
SO, I GUESS YOU'RE STAYING AT HOME...
...AND WORKING FROM HERE?

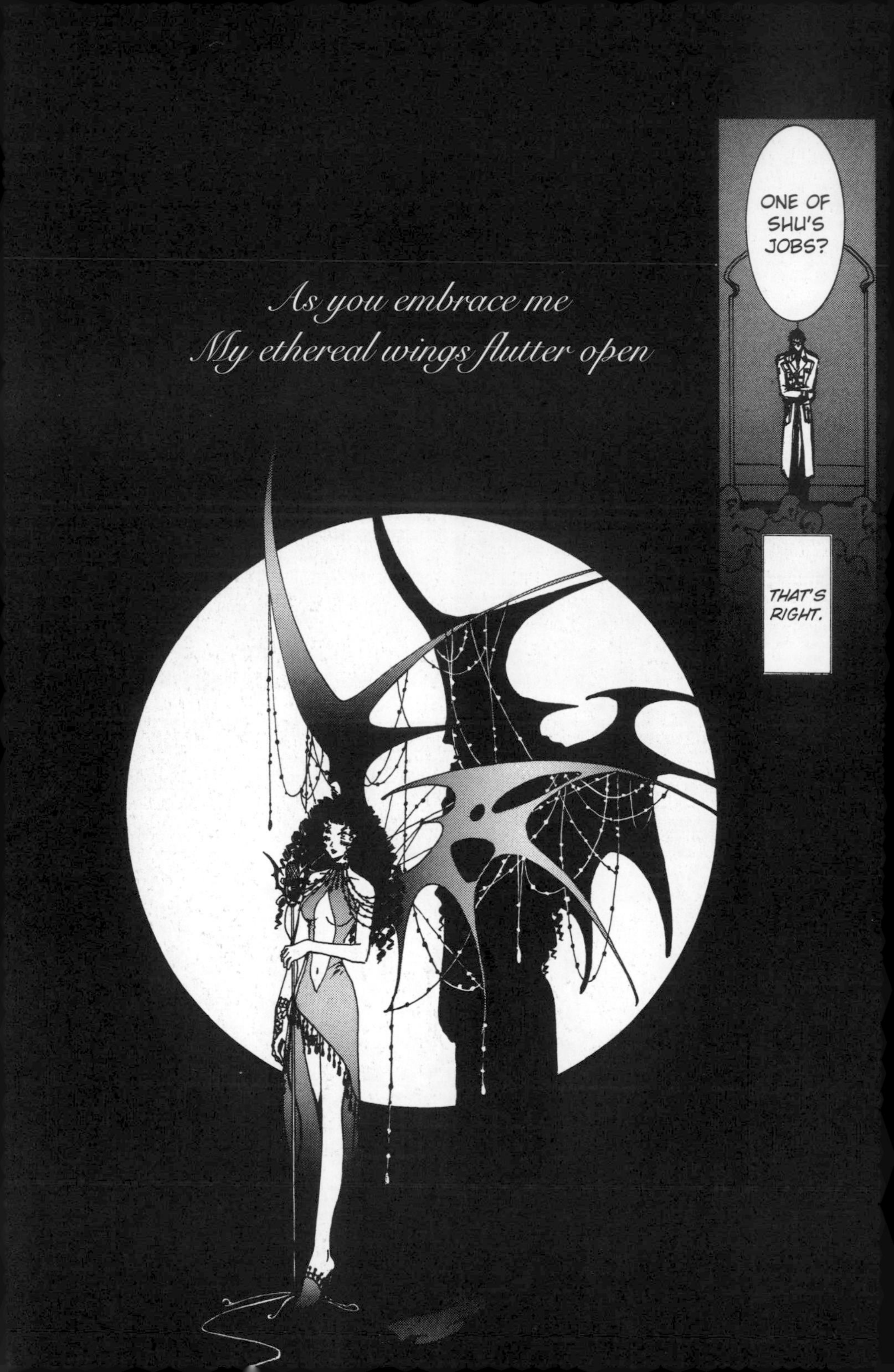
ONE OF SHU'S JOBS?
THAT'S RIGHT.
As you embrace me
My ethereal wings flutter open

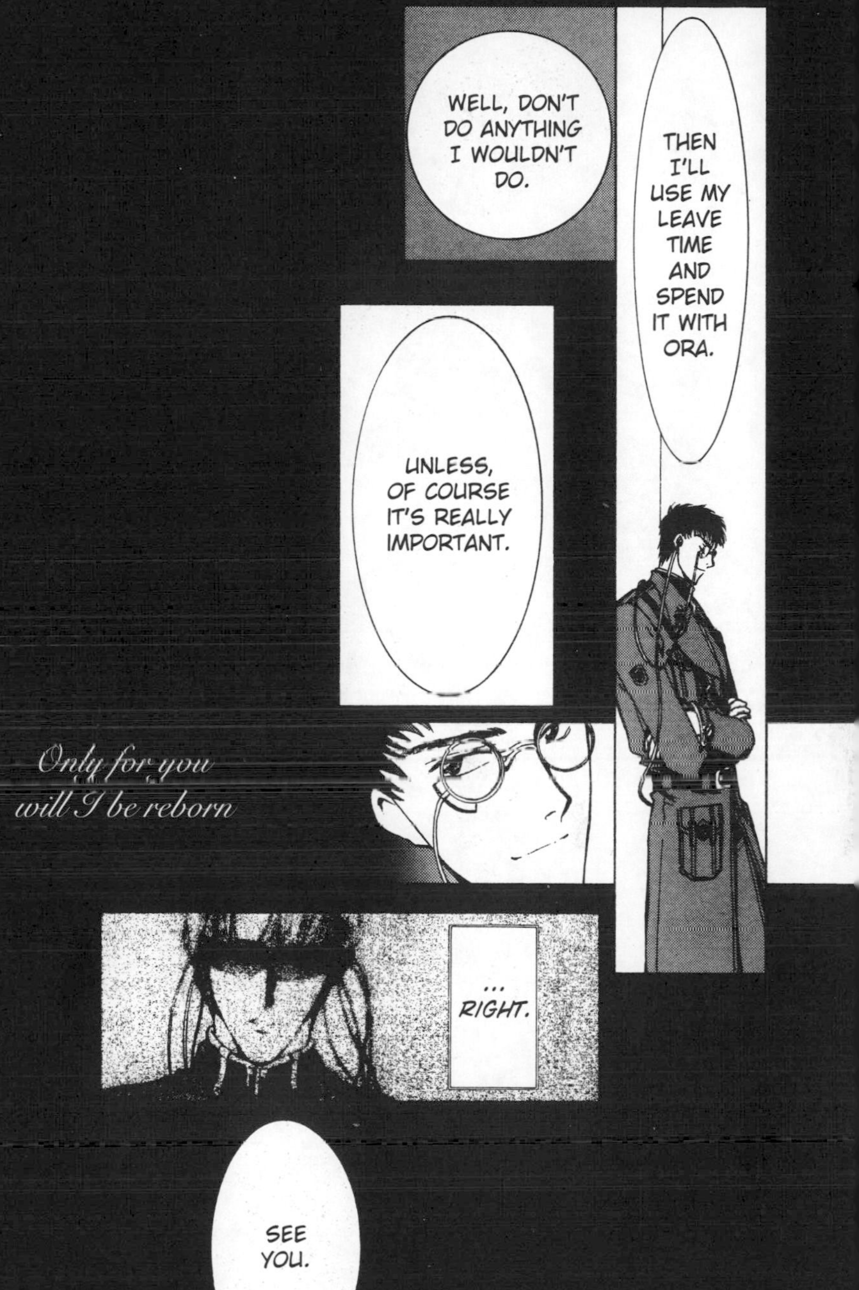
THEN I'LL USE MY LEAVE TIME AND SPEND IT WITH ORA.
WELL, DON'T DO ANYTHING I WOULDN'T DO.
UNLESS, OF COURSE IT'S REALLY IMPORTANT.
...RIGHT.
Only for you will I be reborn
SEE YOU.

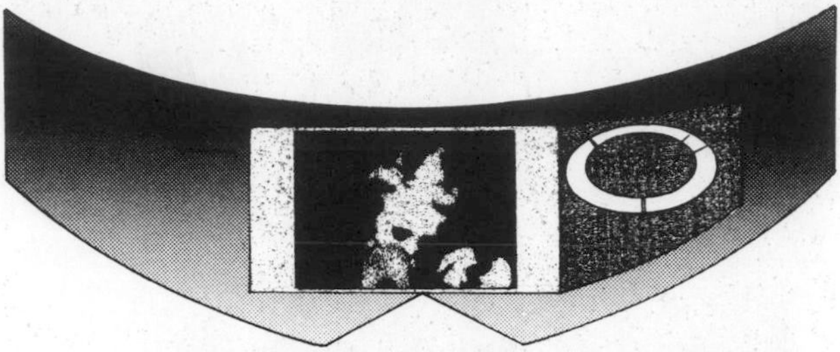

A SONG FOR A COUPLE

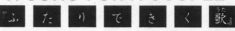

『ふたりできく歌』

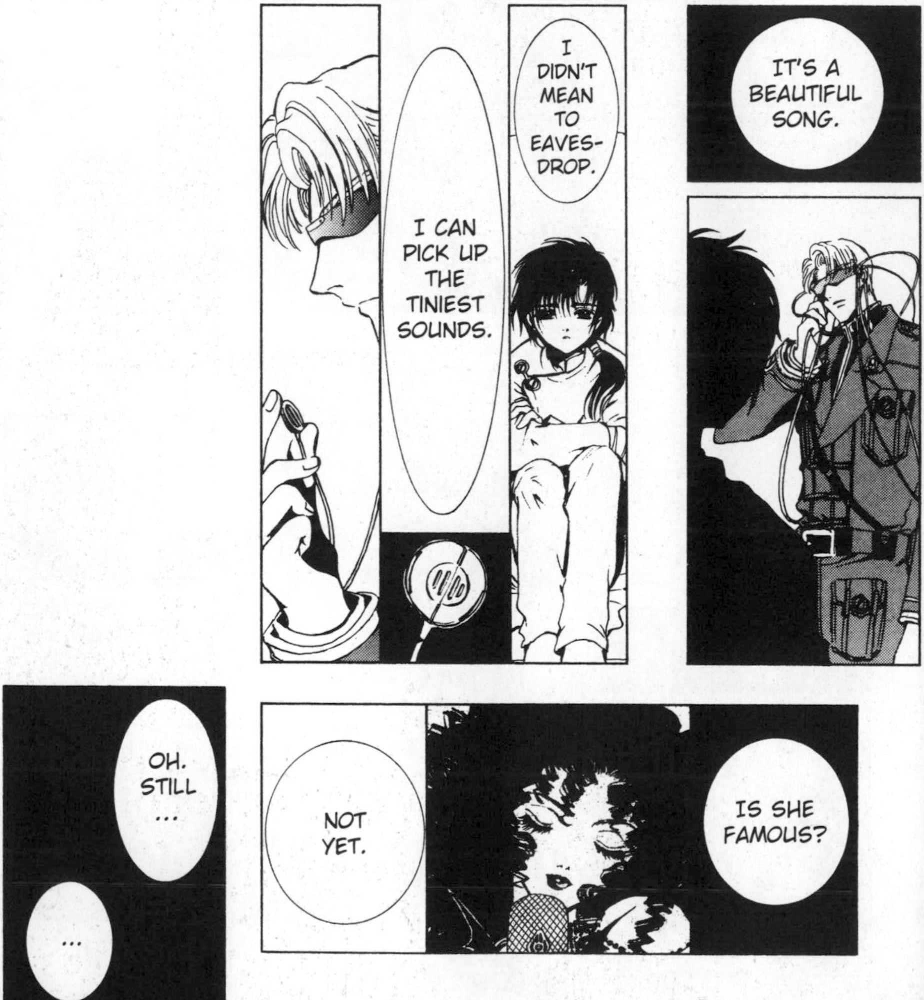
IT'S A BEAUTIFUL SONG.
I DIDN'T MEAN TO EAVES-DROP.
I CAN PICK UP THE TINIEST SOUNDS.
IS SHE FAMOUS?
NOT YET.
OH. STILL ...
...

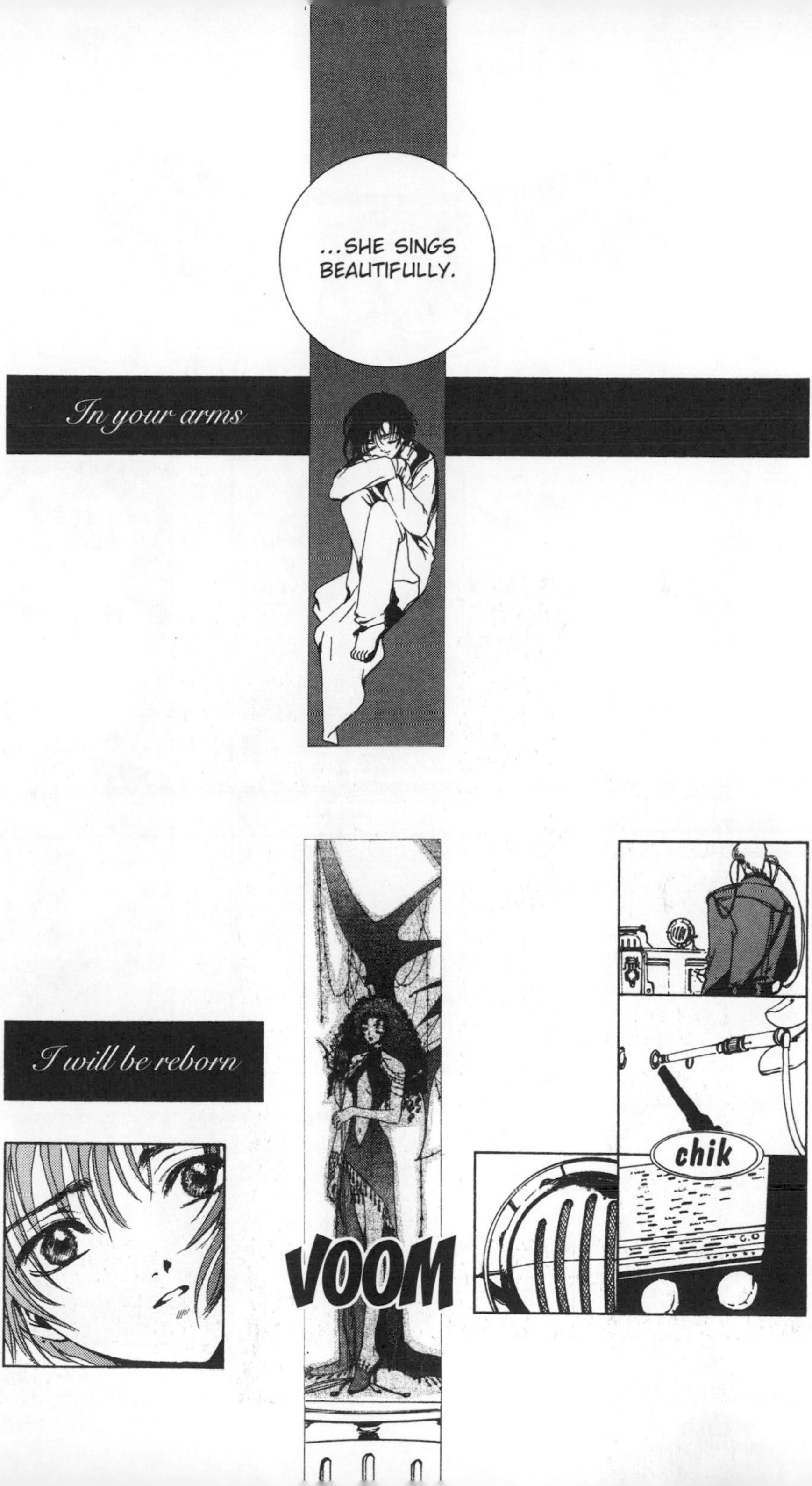
...SHE SINGS BEAUTIFULLY.
In your arms
chik
VOOM
I will be reborn

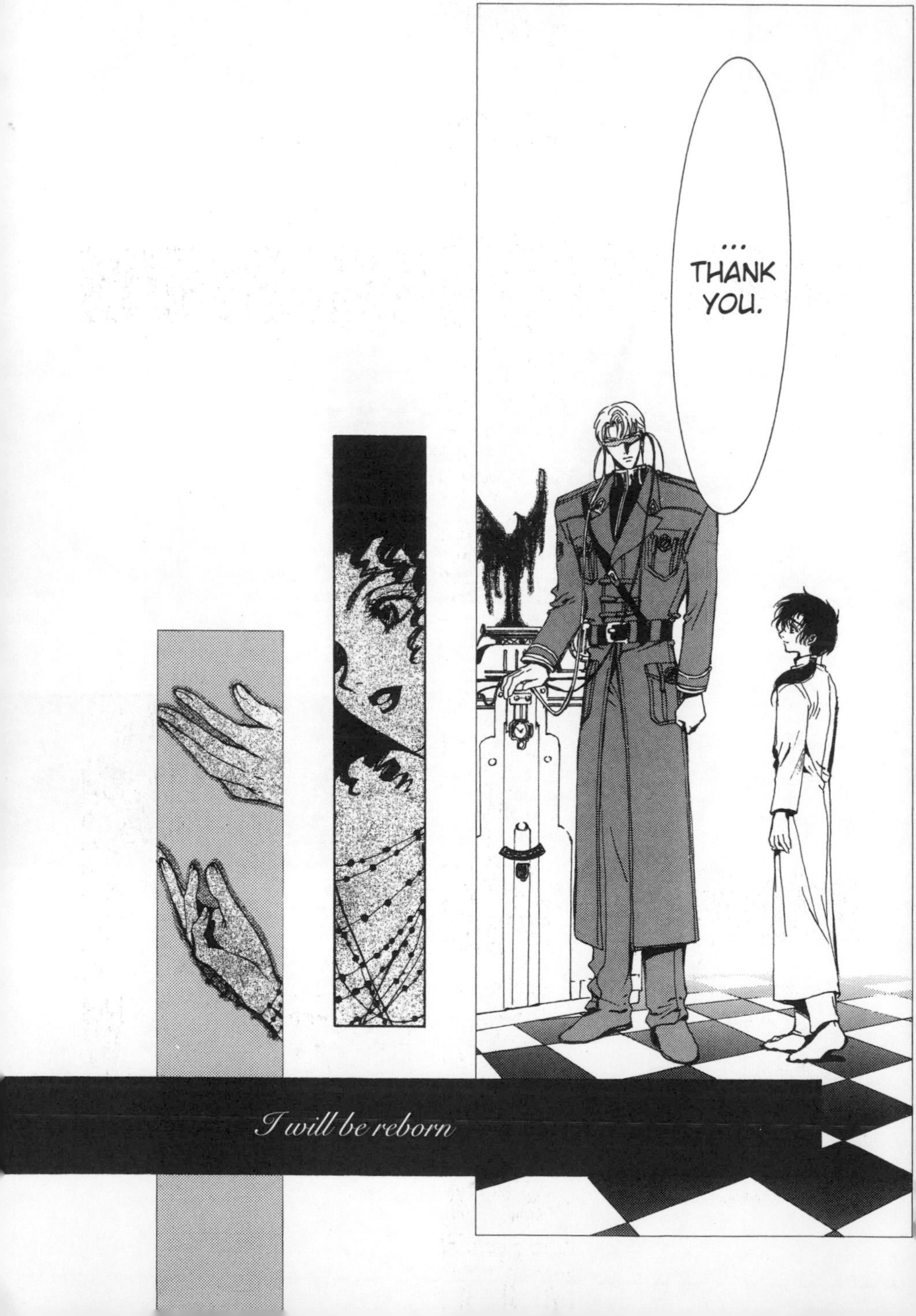
... THANK YOU.
I will be reborn

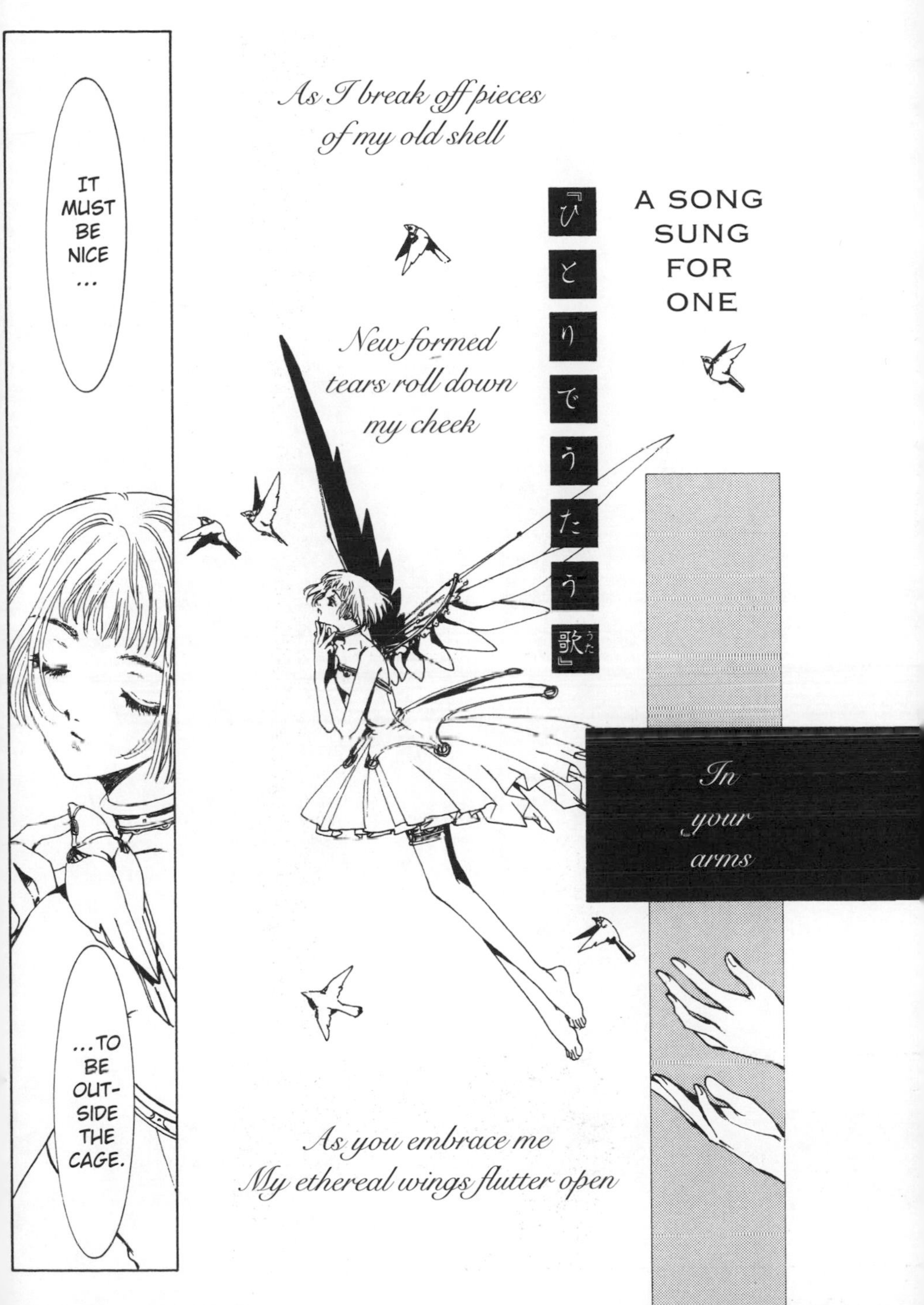

A SONG SUNG FOR ONE
『ひとりでうたう歌』
As I break off pieces of my old shell
New formed tears roll down my cheek
In your arms
As you embrace me My ethereal wings flutter open
IT MUST BE NICE...
...TO BE OUTSIDE THE CAGE.

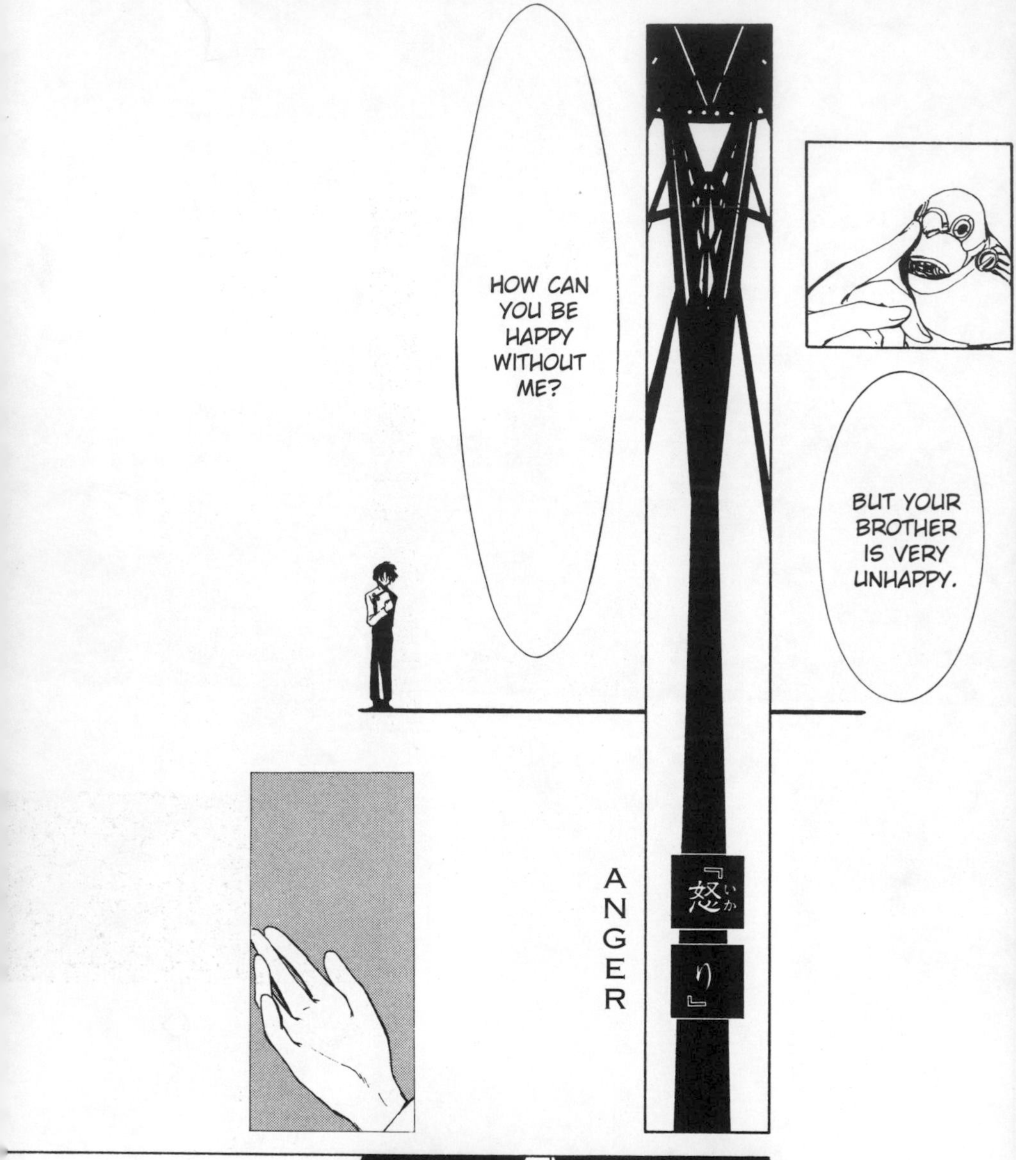
BUT YOUR BROTHER IS VERY UNHAPPY.
『怒り』
ANGER
HOW CAN YOU BE HAPPY WITHOUT ME?
...WHY?

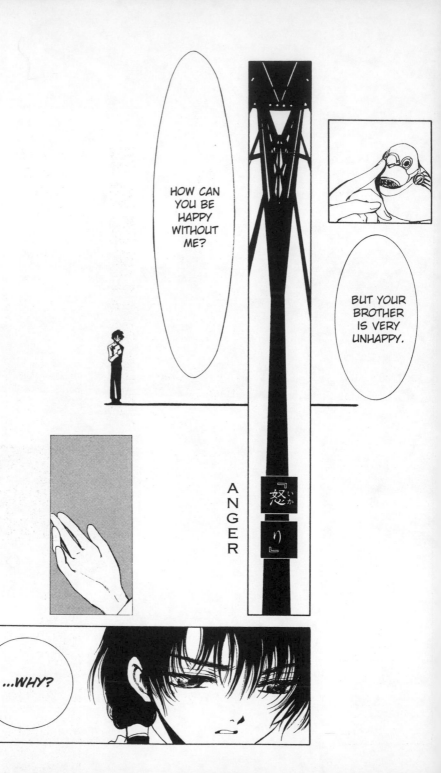

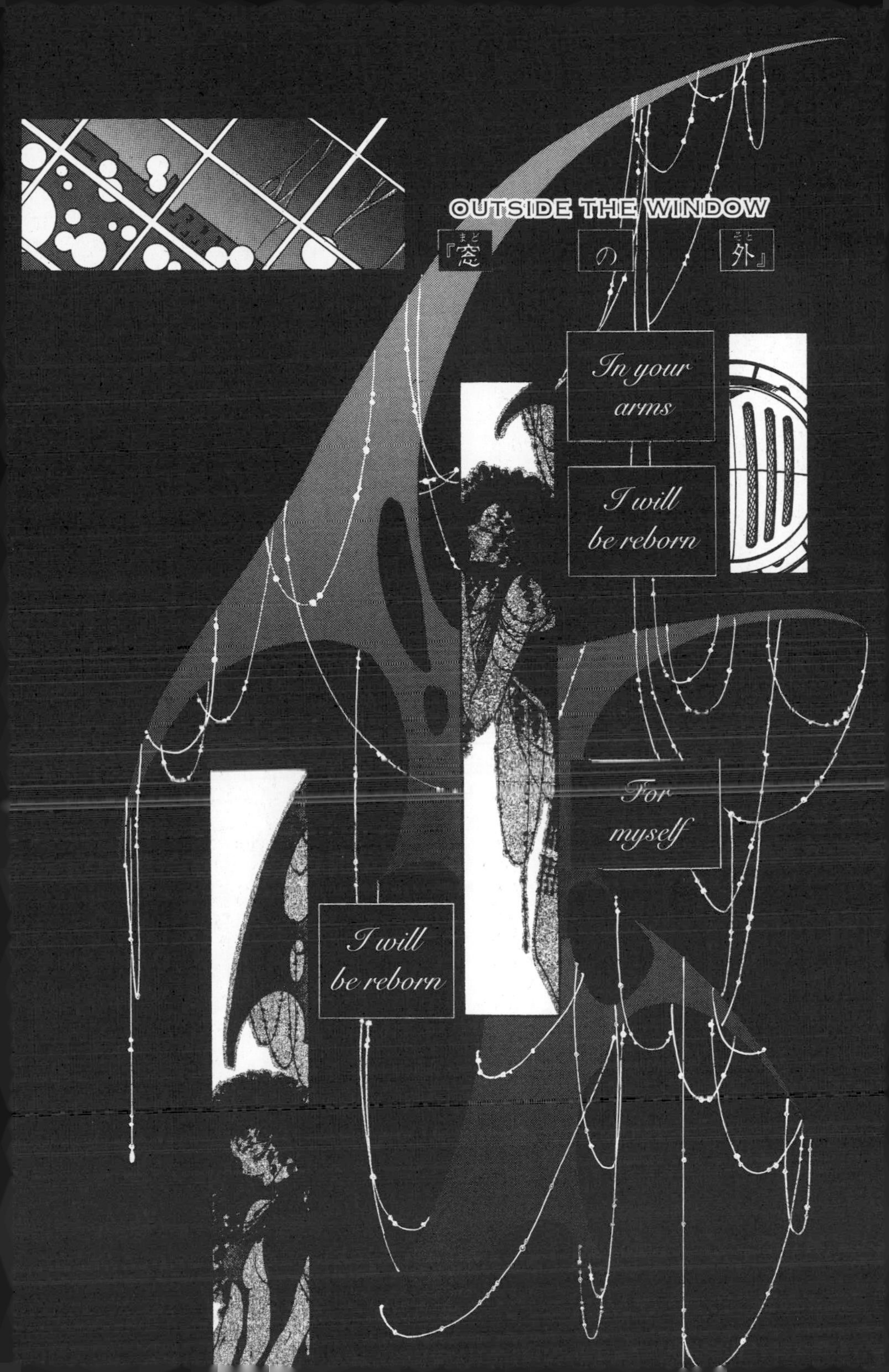
OUTSIDE THE WINDOW
『窓の外』
In your arms
I will be reborn
For myself
I will be reborn

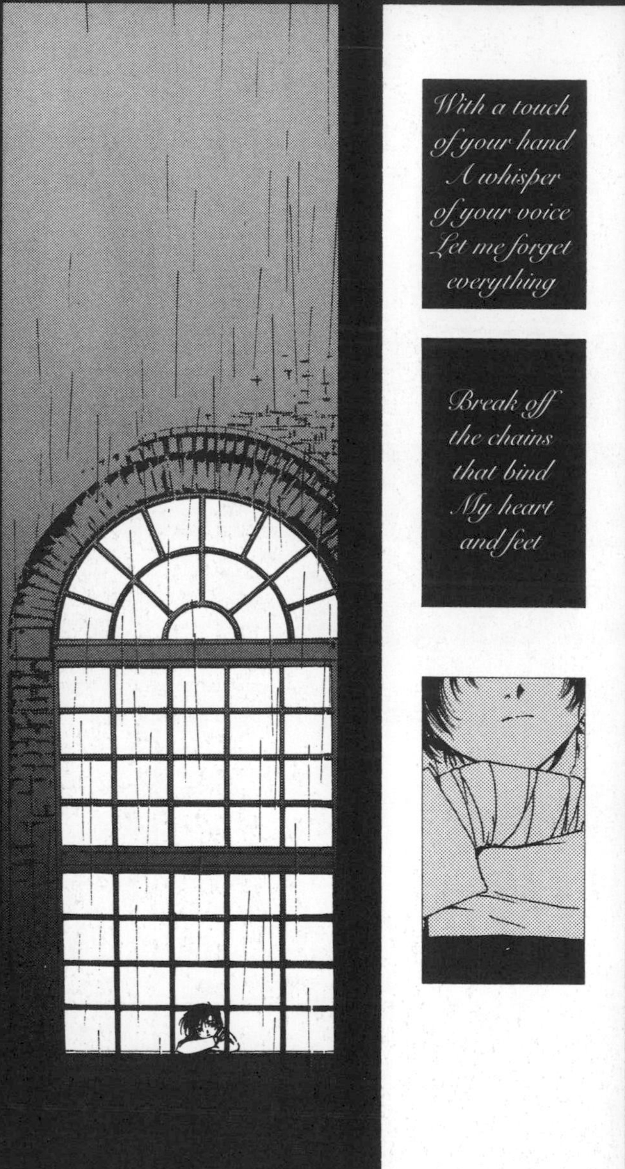
With a touch of your hand A whisper of your voice Let me forget everything
Break off the chains that bind My heart and feet

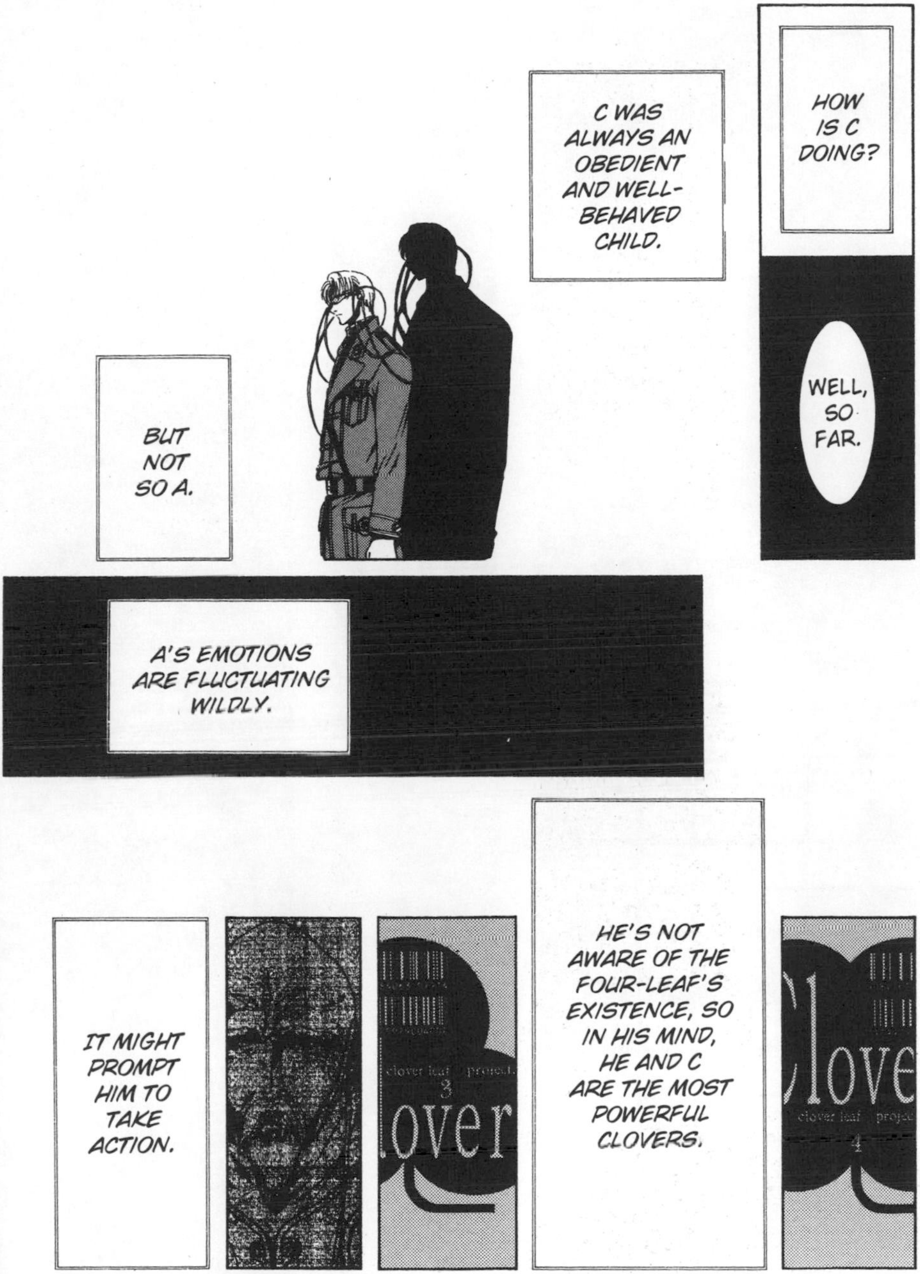
HOW IS C DOING?
WELL, SO FAR.
C WAS ALWAYS AN OBEDIENT AND WELL-BEHAVED CHILD.
BUT NOT SO A.
A'S EMOTIONS ARE FLUCTUATING WILDLY.
HE'S NOT AWARE OF THE FOUR-LEAF'S EXISTENCE, SO IN HIS MIND, HE AND C ARE THE MOST POWERFUL CLOVERS.
IT MIGHT PROMPT HIM TO TAKE ACTION.

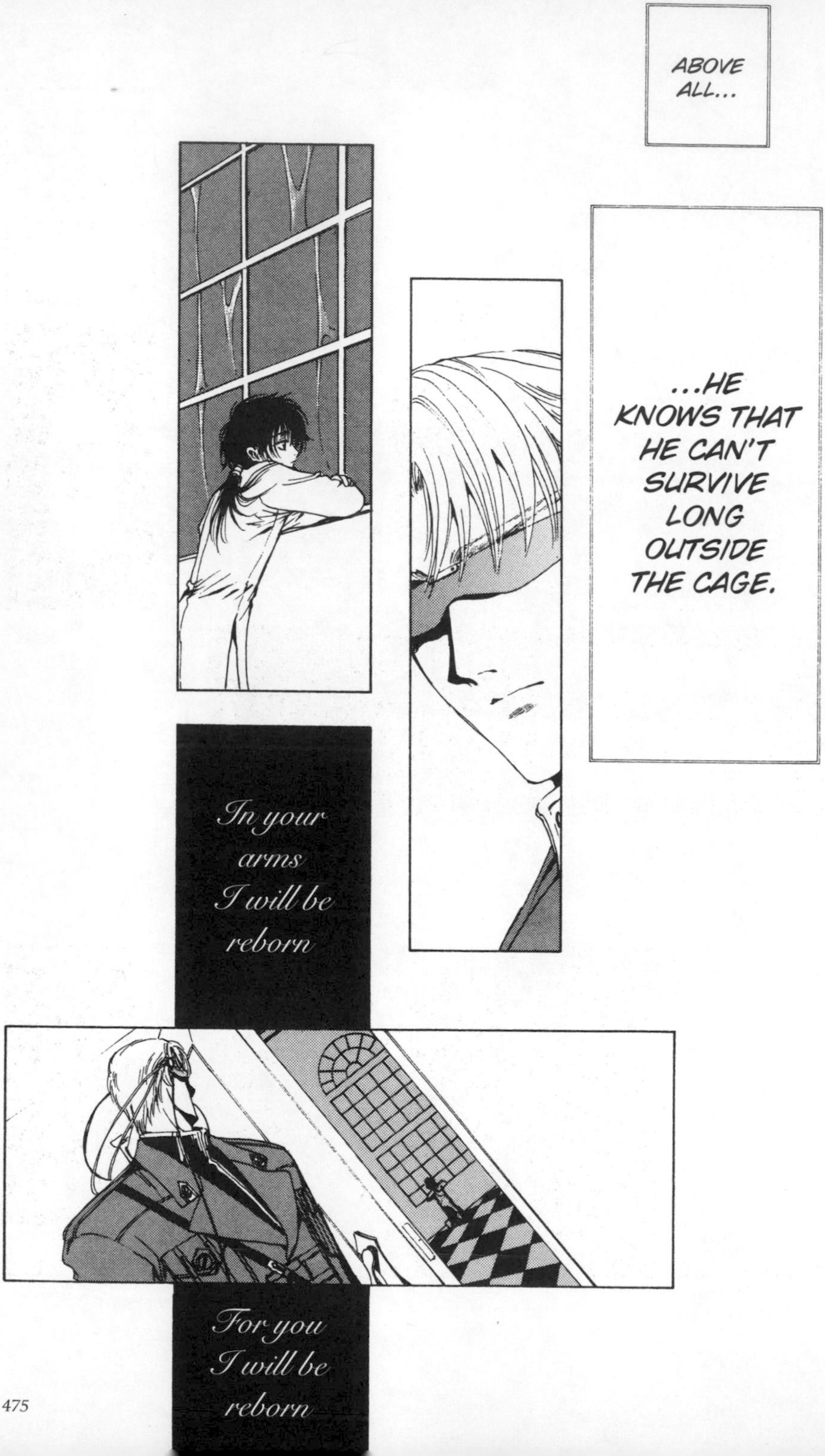
ABOVE ALL...
...HE KNOWS THAT HE CAN'T SURVIVE LONG OUTSIDE THE CAGE.
In your arms I will be reborn
For you I will be reborn

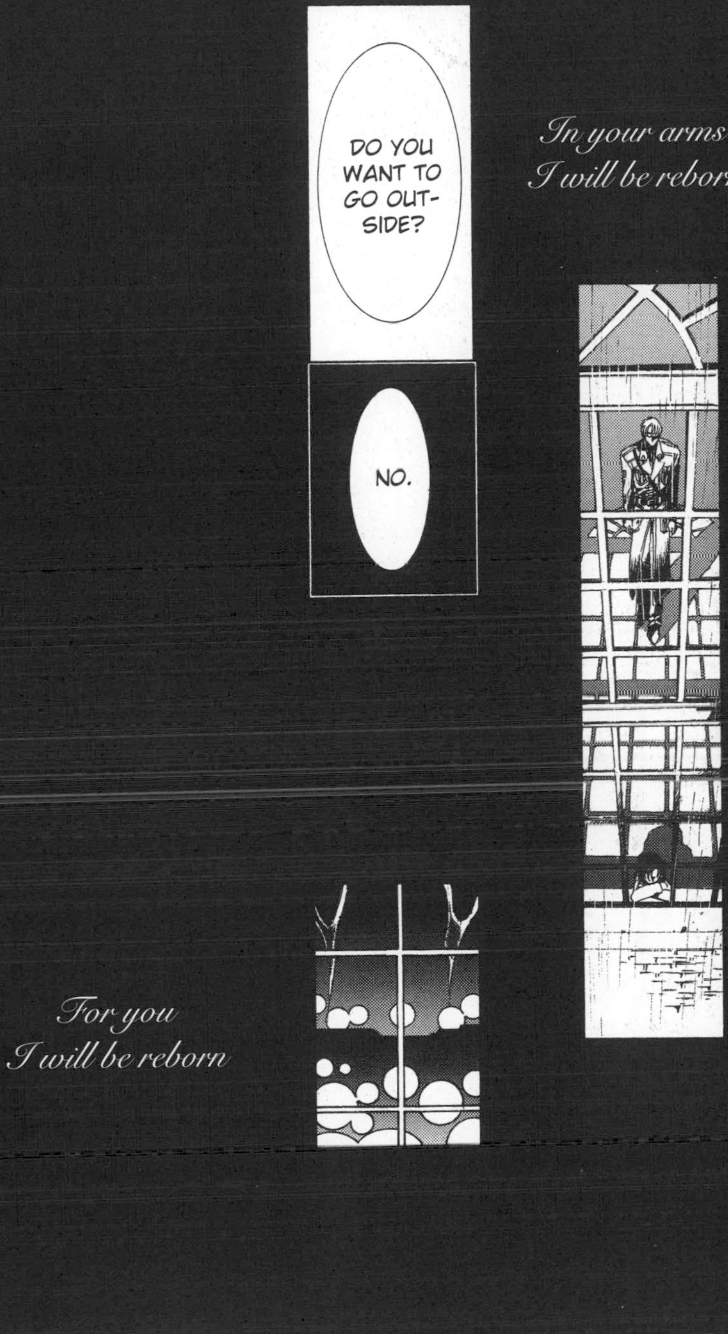
In your arms I will be reborn
DO YOU WANT TO GO OUT-SIDE?
NO.
For you I will be reborn

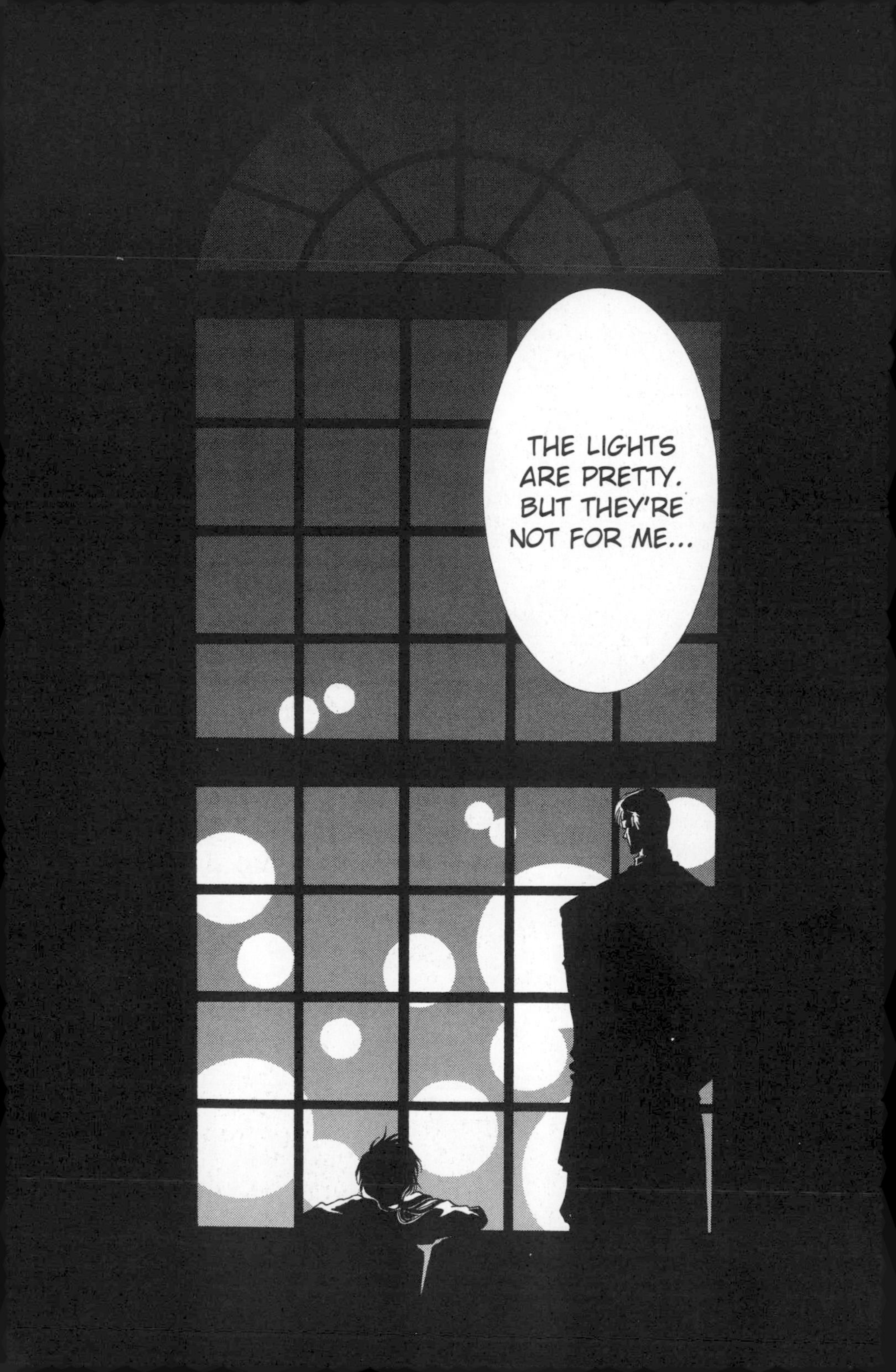
THE LIGHTS ARE PRETTY. BUT THEY'RE NOT FOR ME...

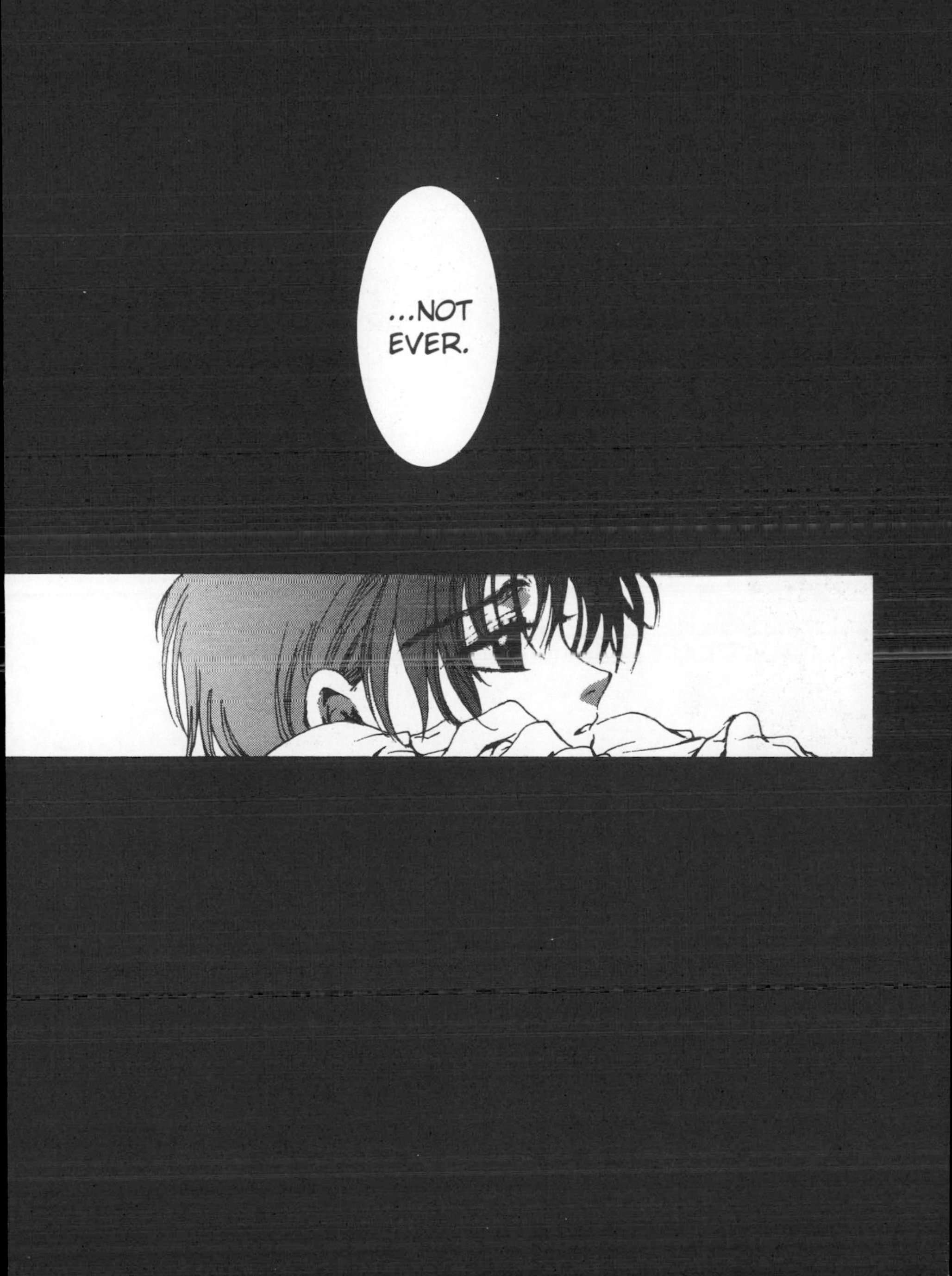
...NOT EVER.

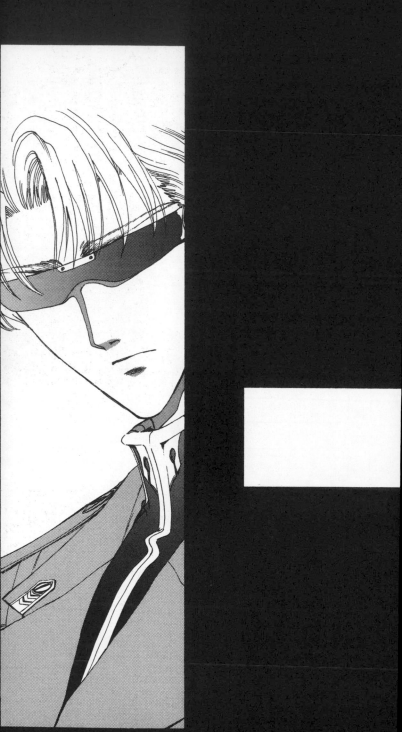

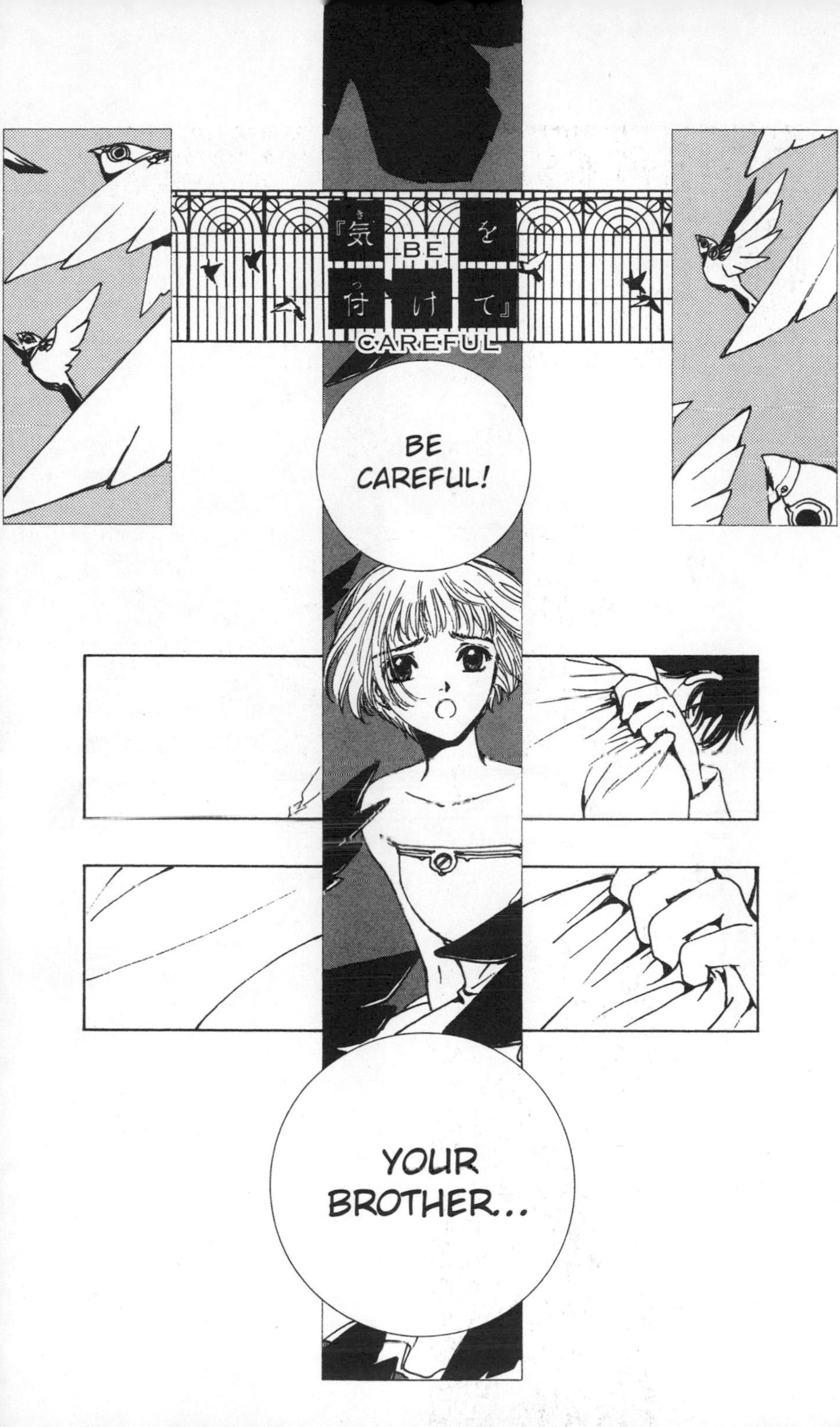
『気を付けて』
BE CAREFUL
BE CAREFUL!
YOUR BROTHER...

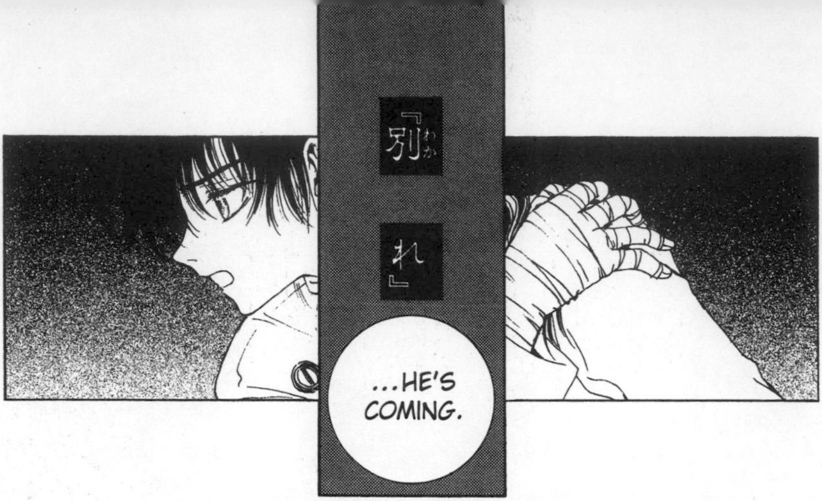
『別れ』
...HE'S COMING.

FAREWELL

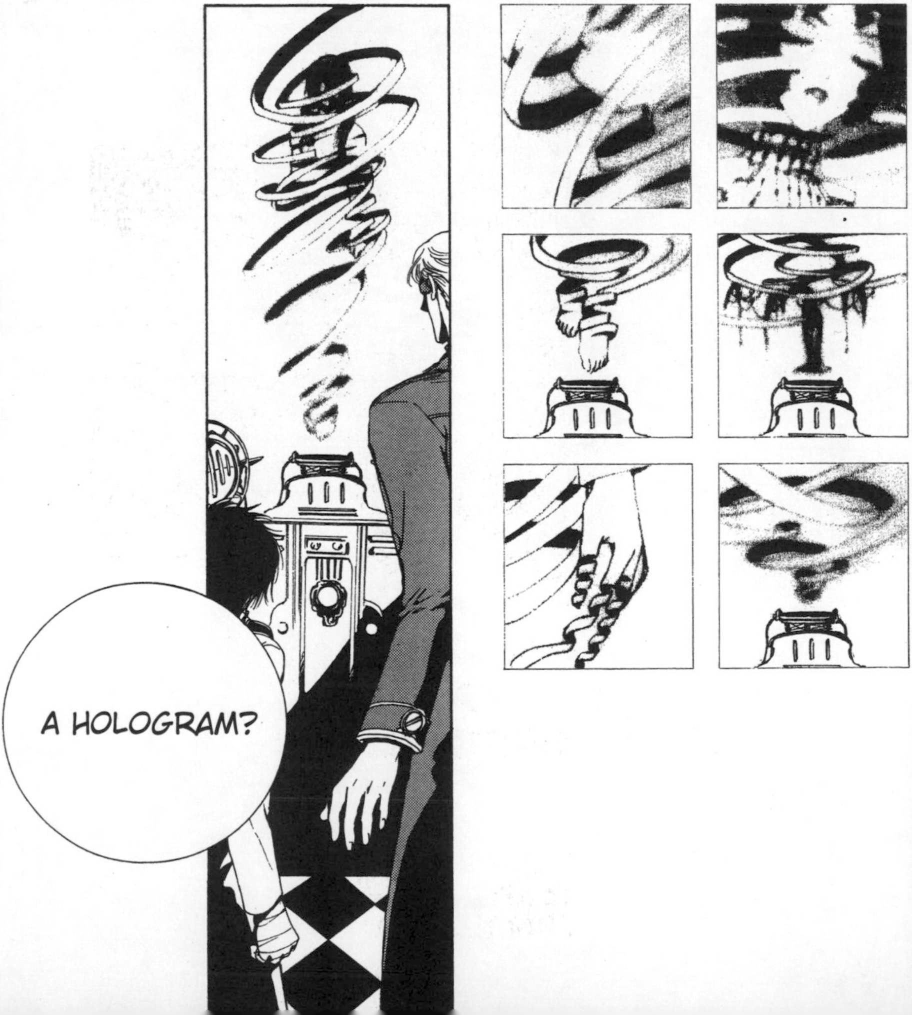
A HOLOGRAM?

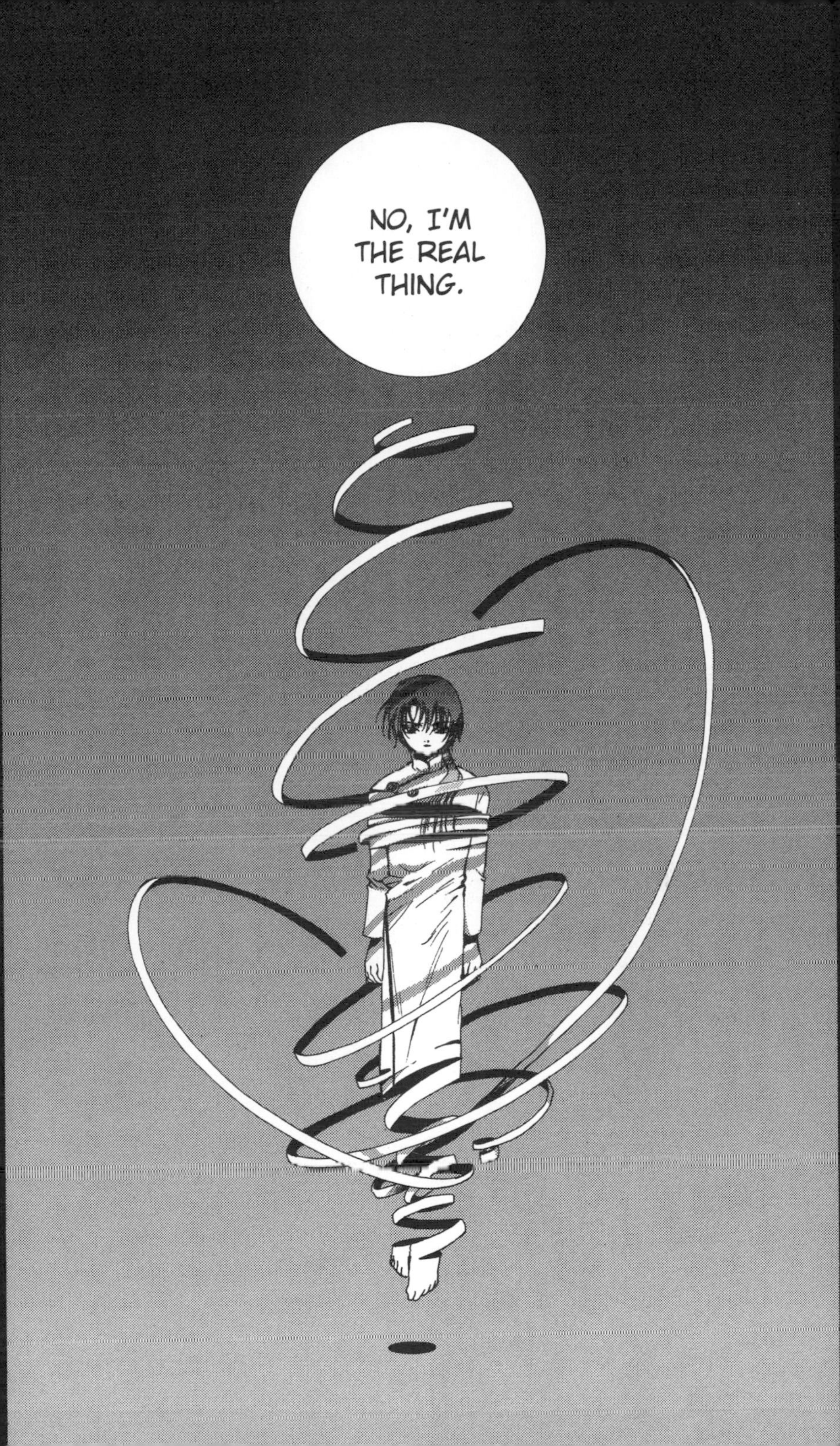
NO, I'M THE REAL THING.

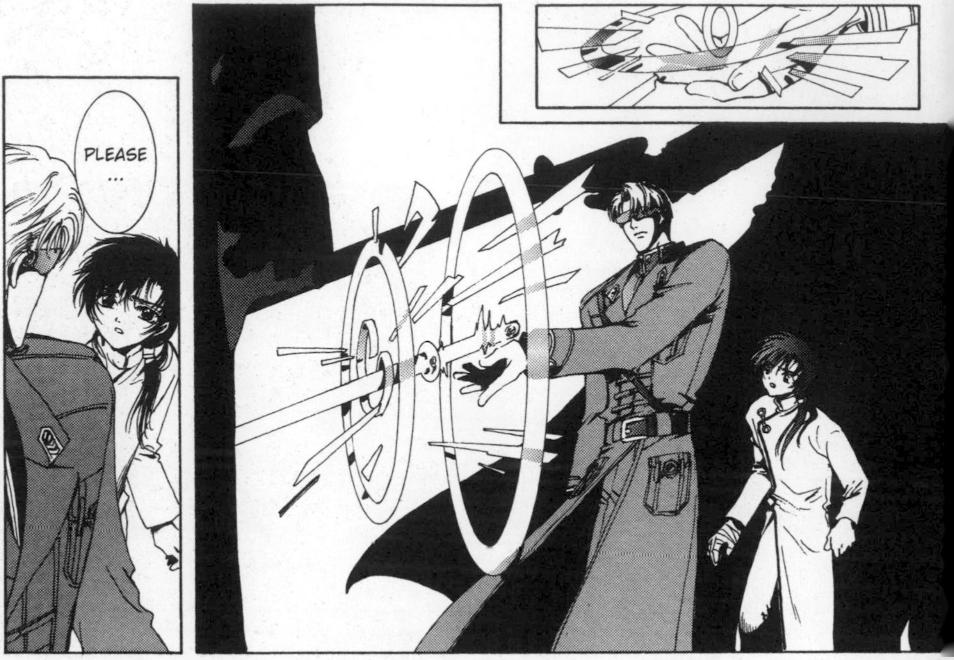
PLEASE ...

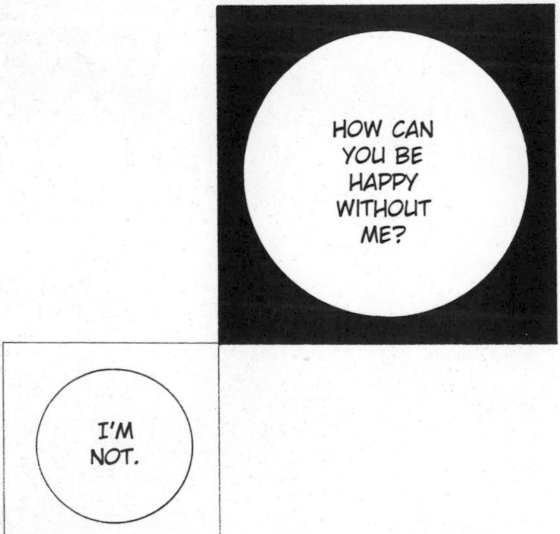
HOW CAN YOU BE HAPPY WITHOUT ME?
I'M NOT.

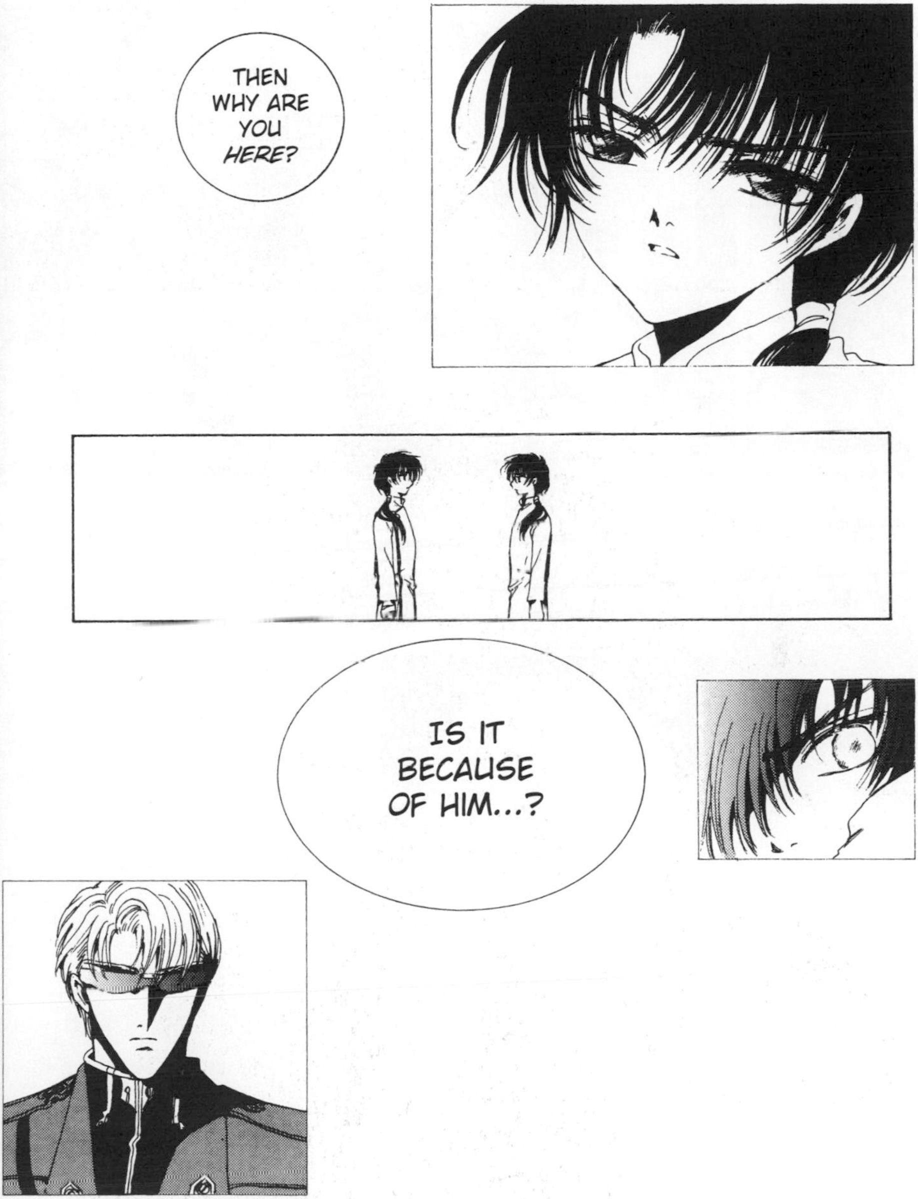
THEN WHY ARE YOU *HERE?*
IS IT BECAUSE OF HIM...?

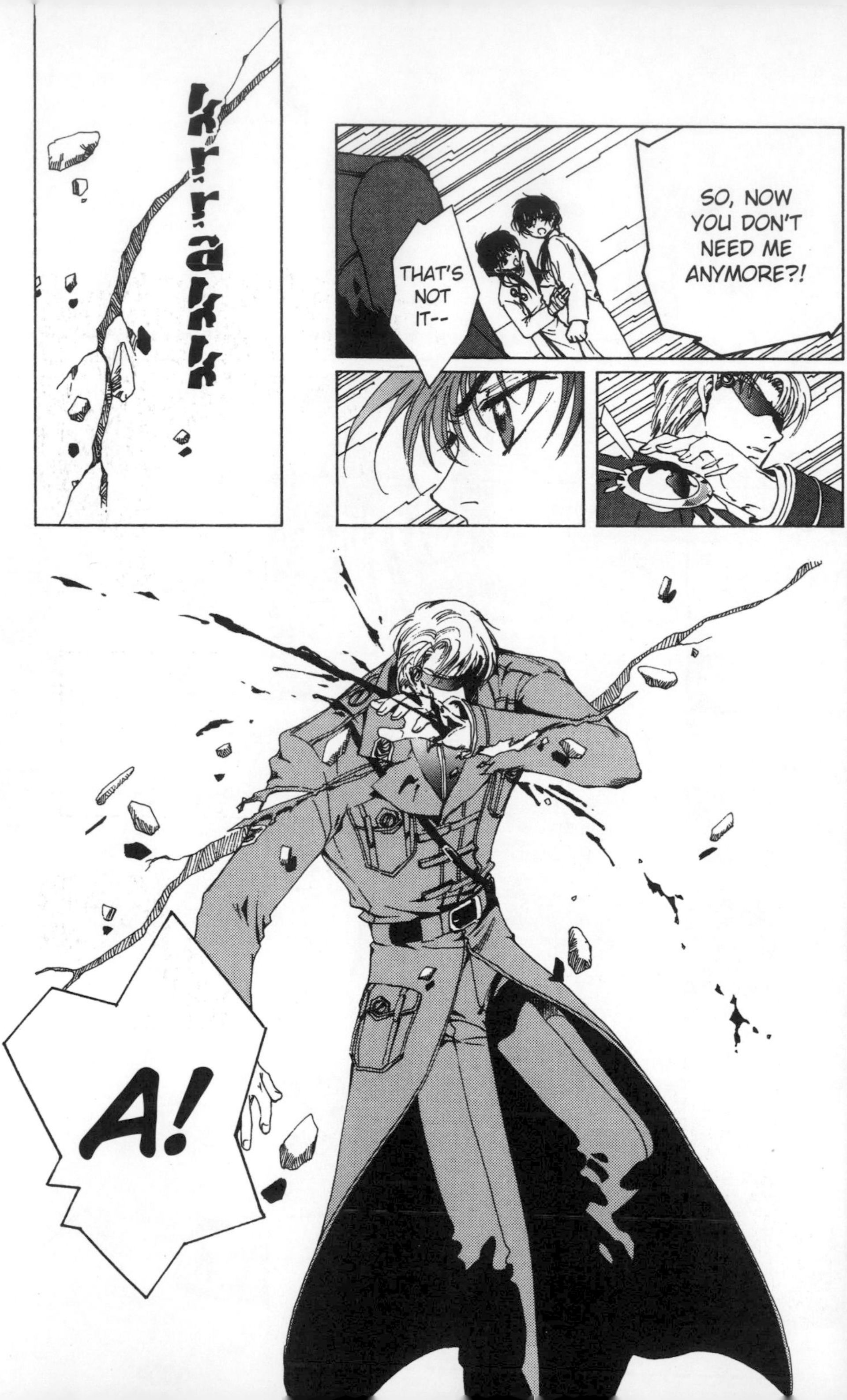
SO, NOW YOU DON'T NEED ME ANYMORE?!
THAT'S NOT IT--
A!

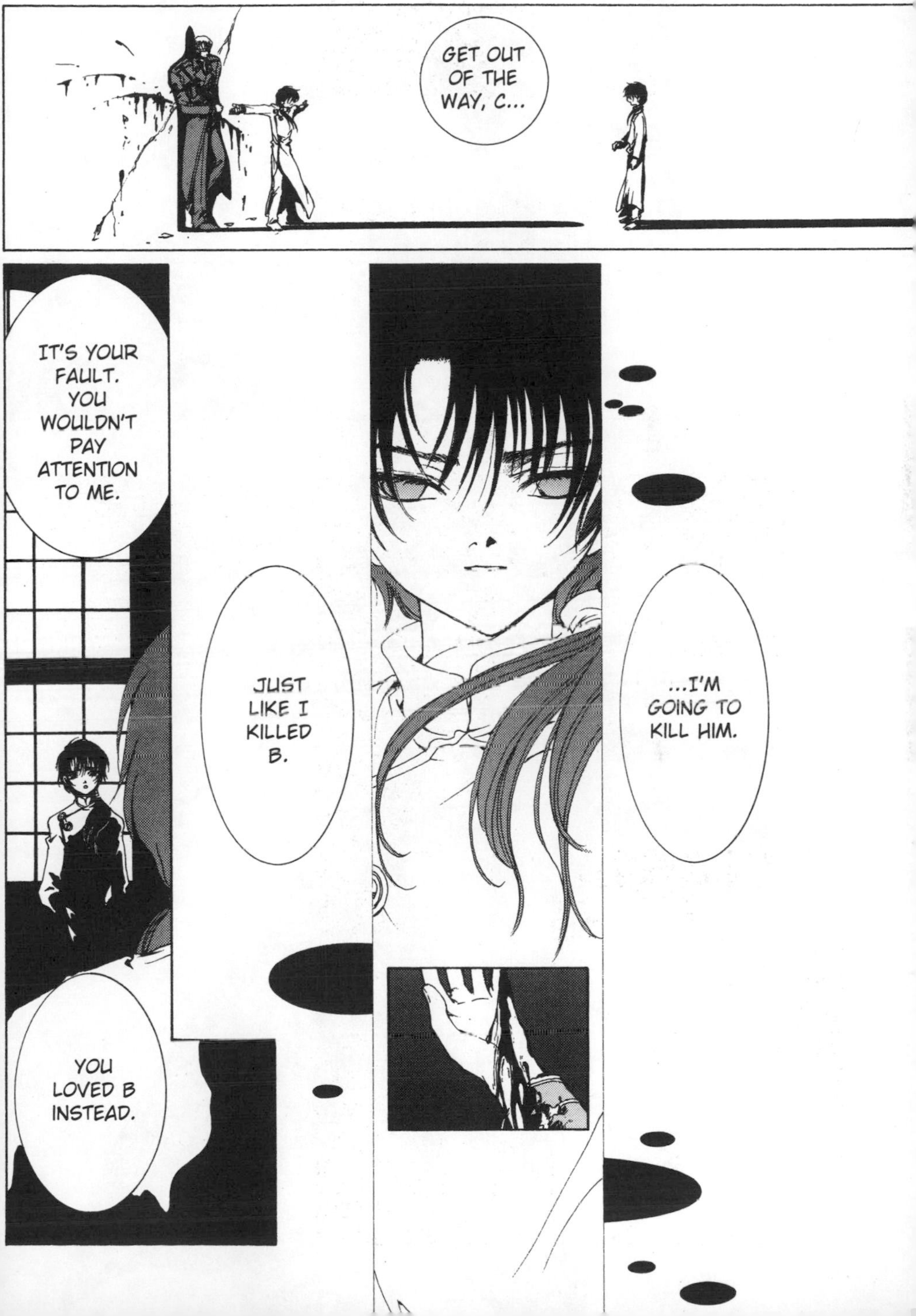
GET OUT OF THE WAY, C...
...I'M GOING TO KILL HIM.
JUST LIKE I KILLED B.
IT'S YOUR FAULT. YOU WOULDN'T PAY ATTENTION TO ME.
YOU LOVED B INSTEAD.

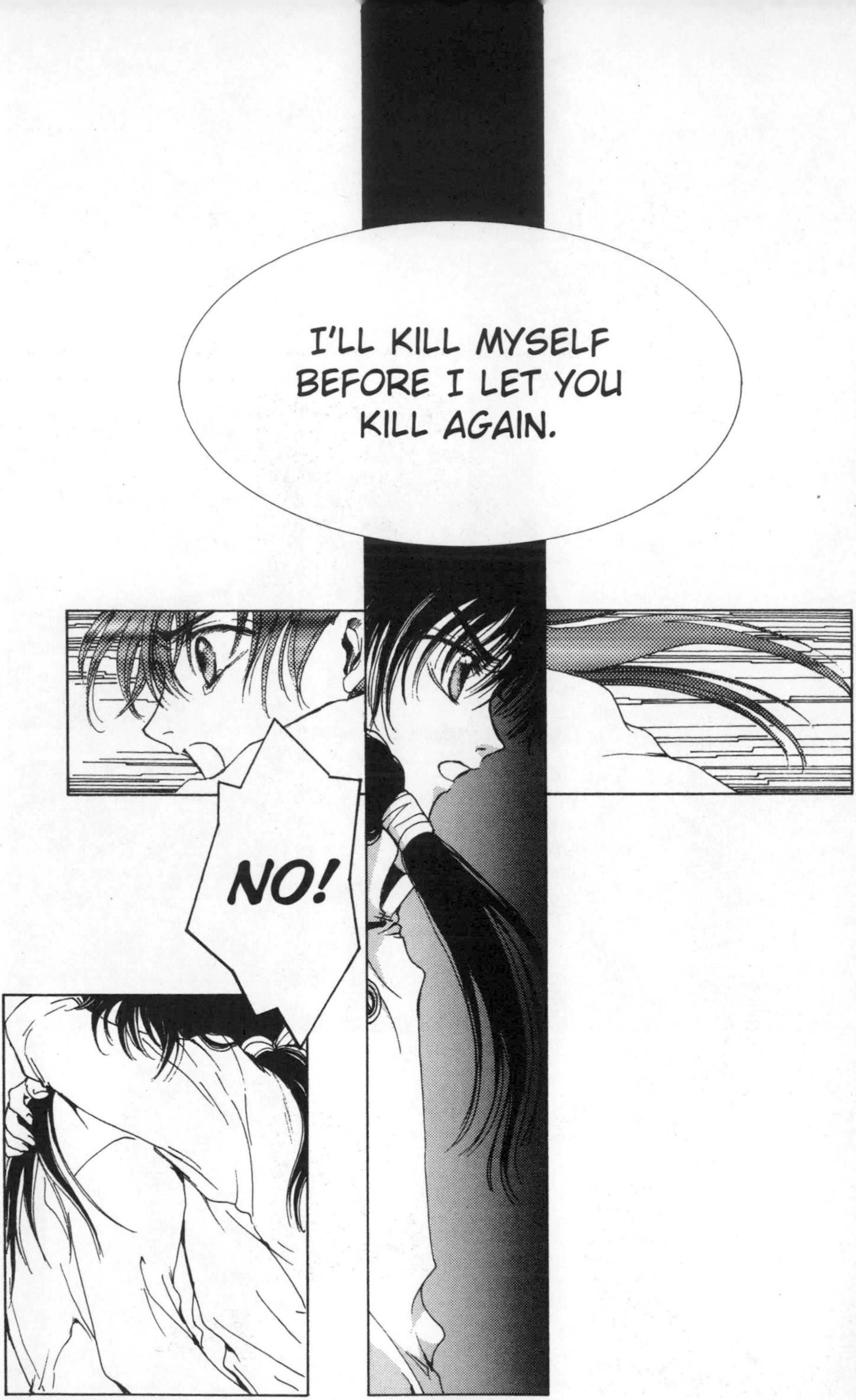
I'LL KILL MYSELF BEFORE I LET YOU KILL AGAIN.
NO!

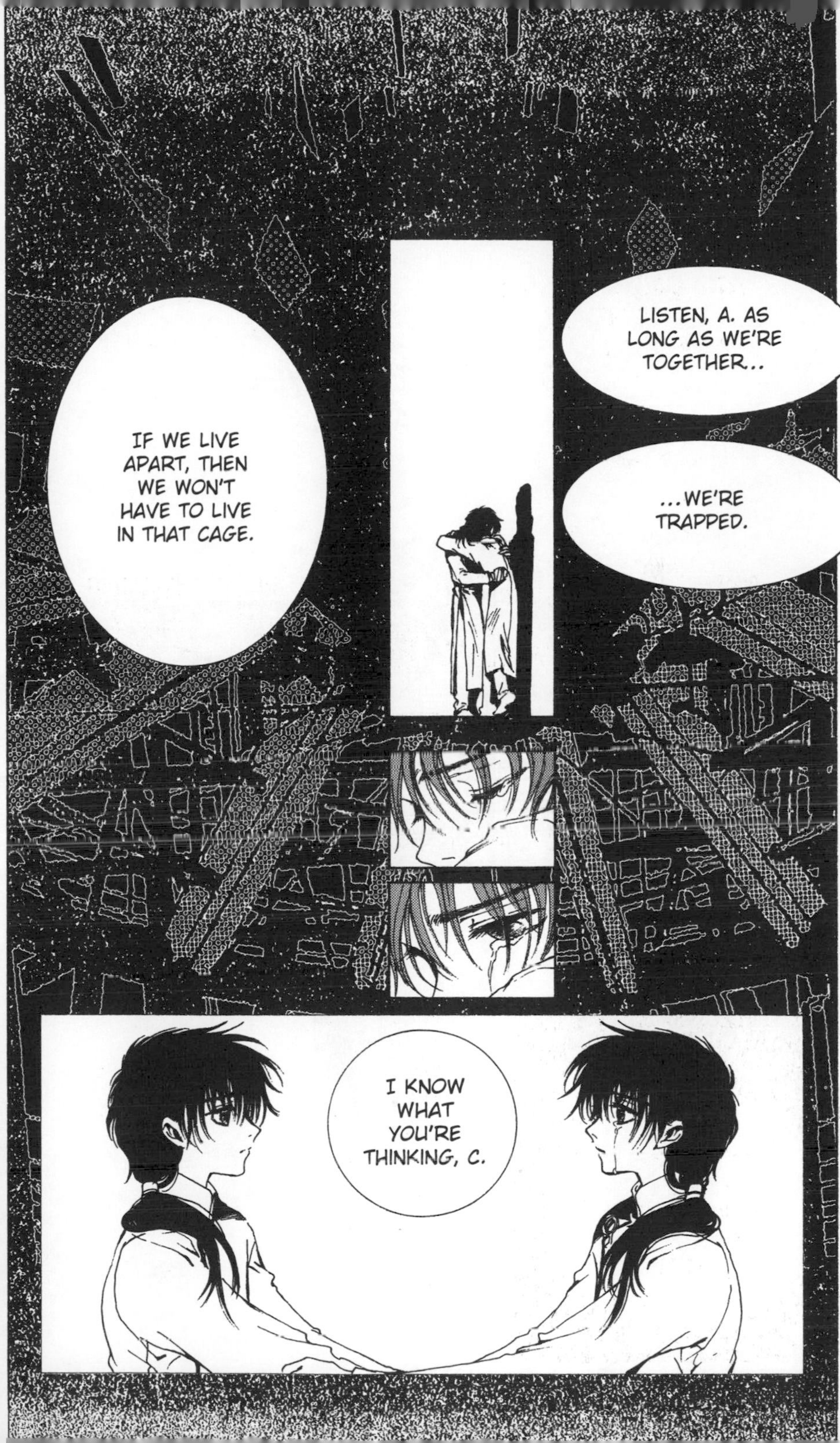
LISTEN, A. AS LONG AS WE'RE TOGETHER...
...WE'RE TRAPPED.
IF WE LIVE APART, THEN WE WON'T HAVE TO LIVE IN THAT CAGE.
I KNOW WHAT YOU'RE THINKING, C.

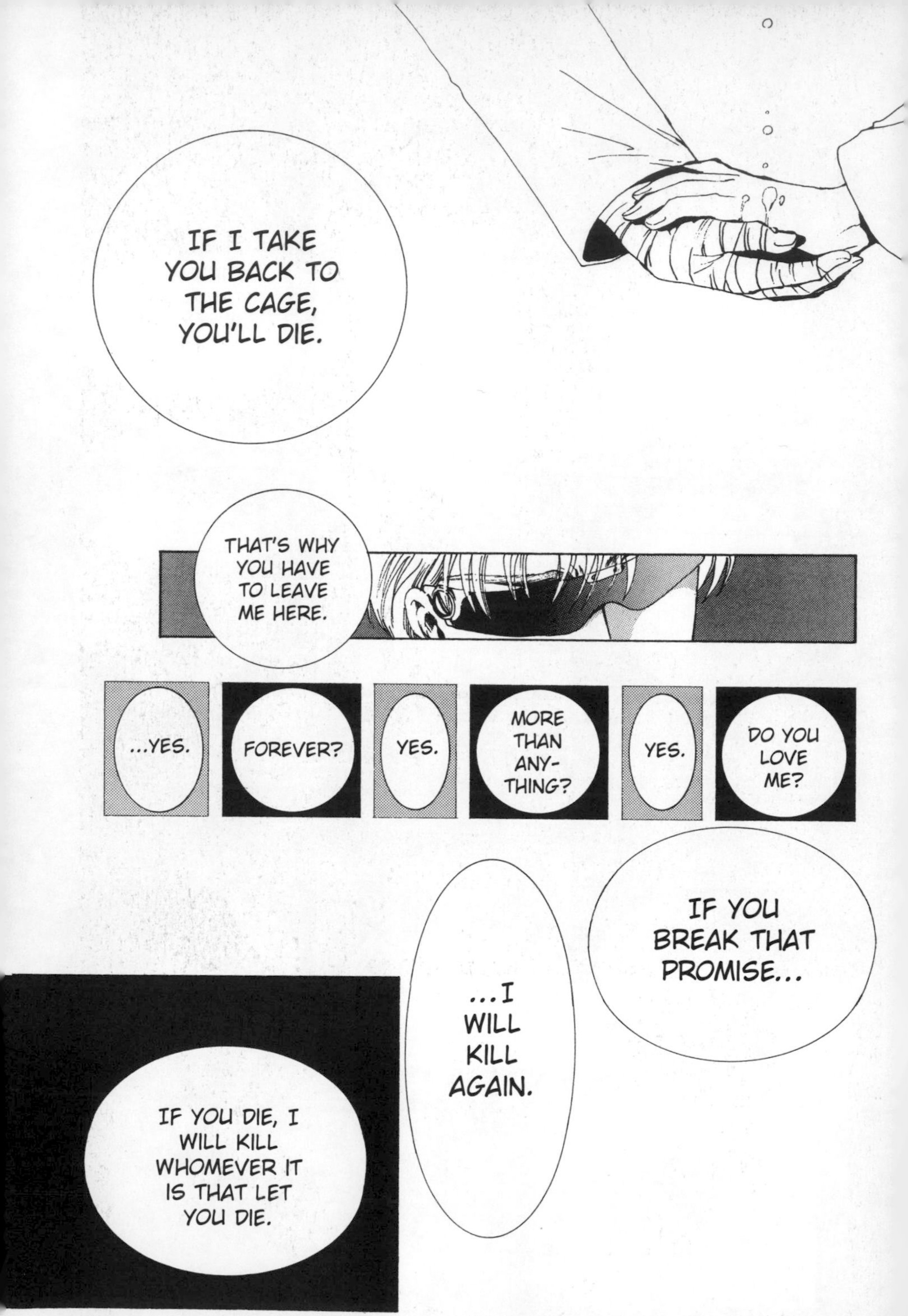
IF I TAKE YOU BACK TO THE CAGE, YOU'LL DIE.
THAT'S WHY YOU HAVE TO LEAVE ME HERE.
DO YOU LOVE ME?
YES.
MORE THAN ANY-THING?
YES.
FOREVER?
...YES.
IF YOU BREAK THAT PROMISE...
...I WILL KILL AGAIN.
IF YOU DIE, I WILL KILL WHOMEVER IT IS THAT LET YOU DIE.

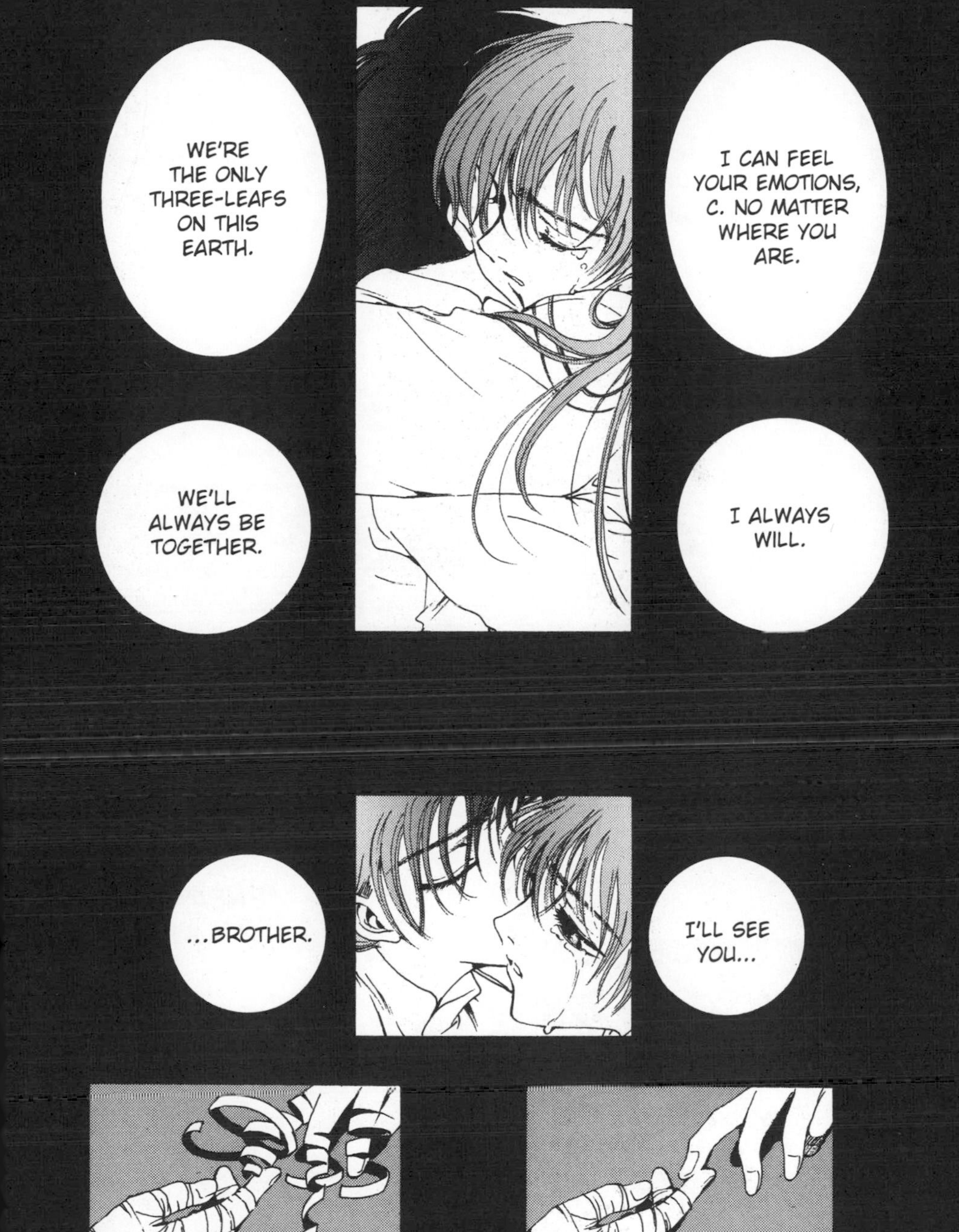
I CAN FEEL YOUR EMOTIONS, C. NO MATTER WHERE YOU ARE.
WE'RE THE ONLY THREE-LEAFS ON THIS EARTH.
I ALWAYS WILL.
WE'LL ALWAYS BE TOGETHER.
I'LL SEE YOU...
...BROTHER.

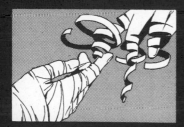

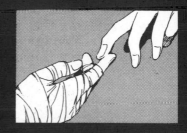

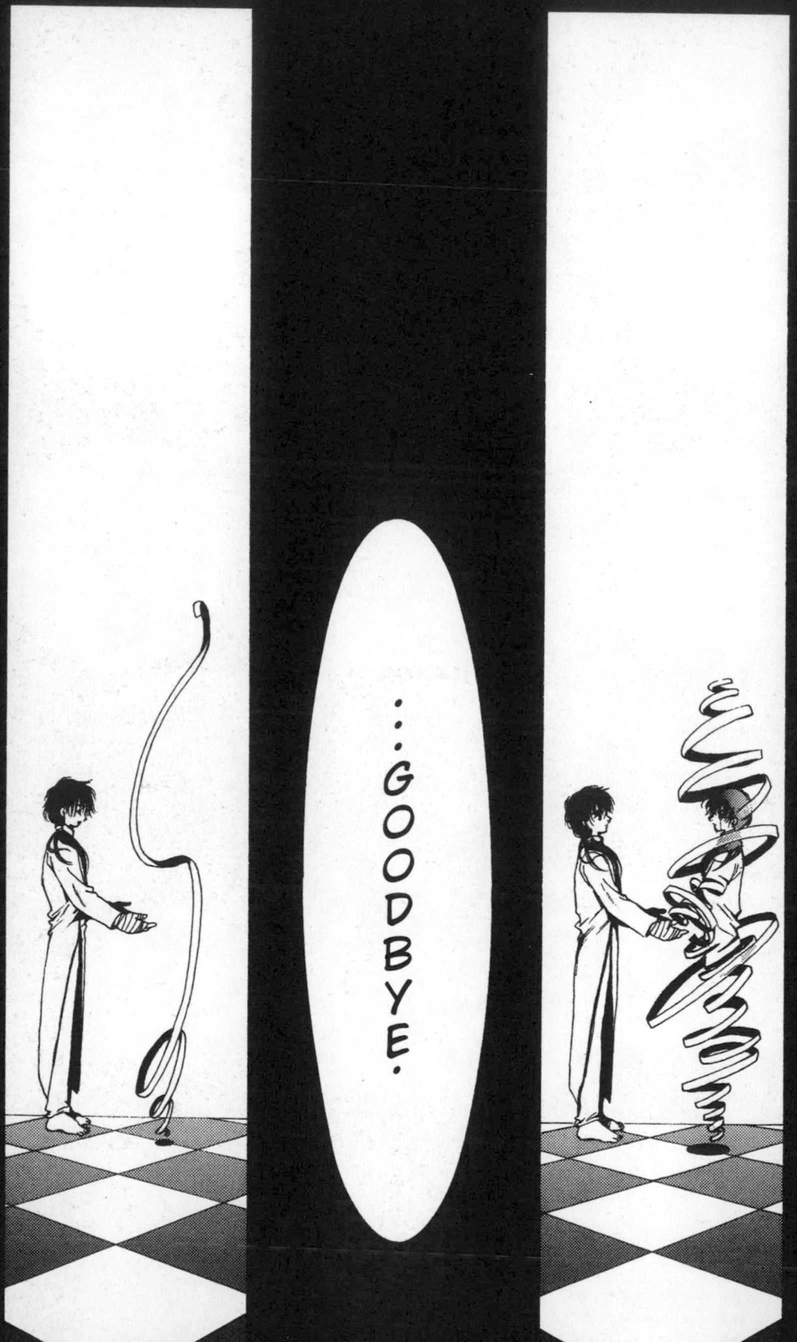
...GOODBYE.

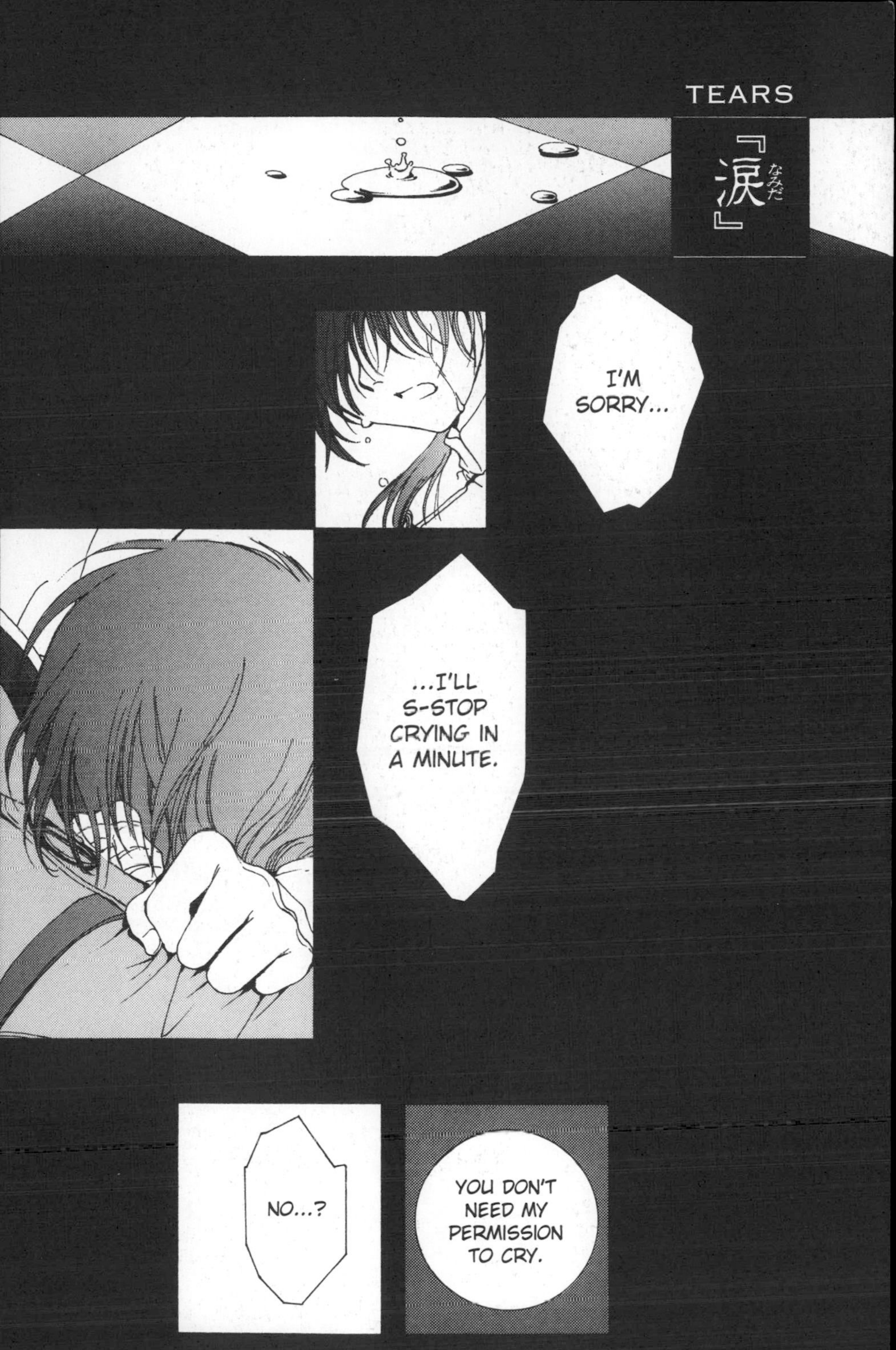
TEARS
『涙』
なみだ
I'M SORRY...
...I'LL S-STOP CRYING IN A MINUTE.
YOU DON'T NEED MY PERMISSION TO CRY.
NO...?

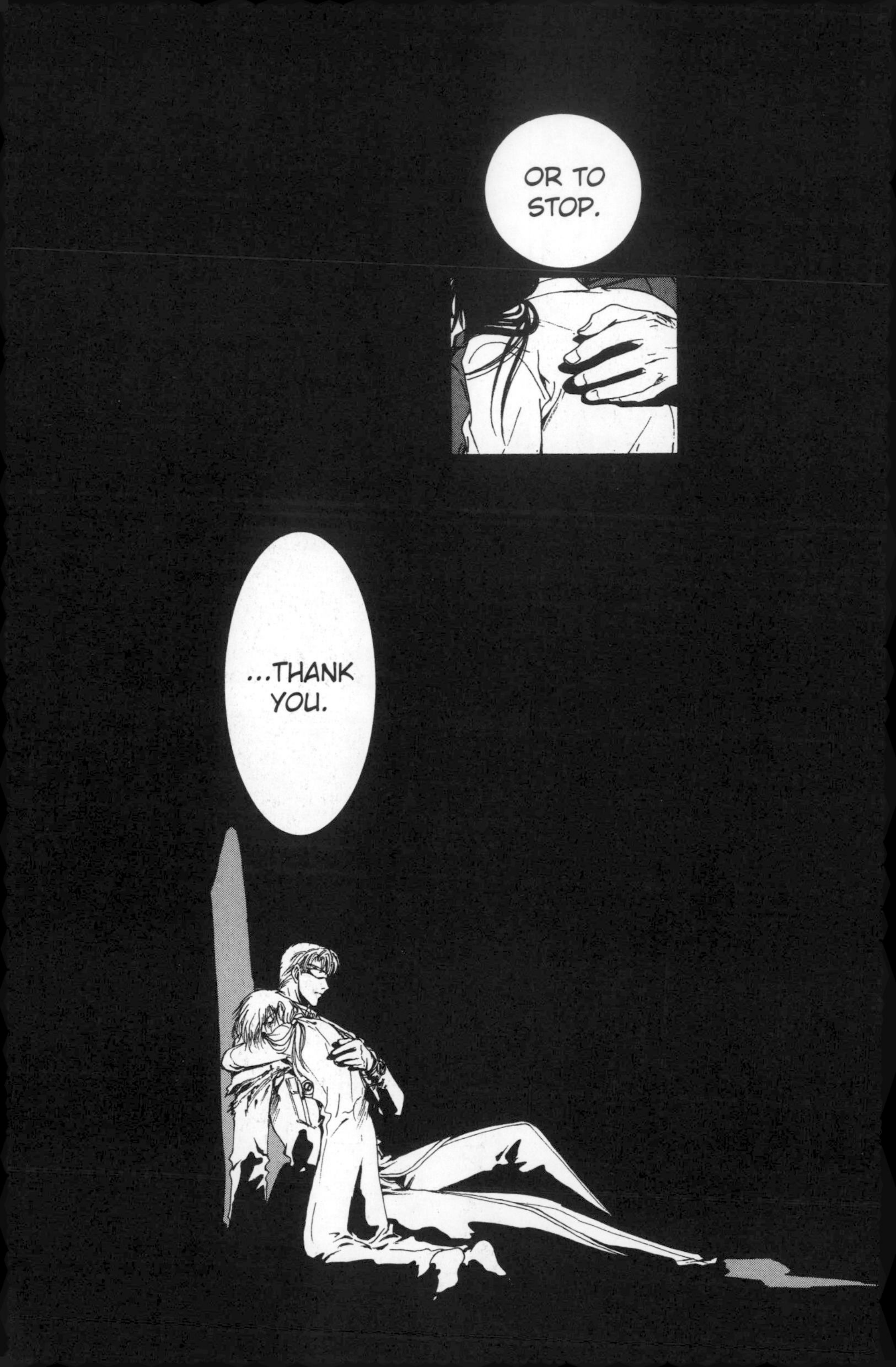
OR TO STOP.
...THANK YOU.

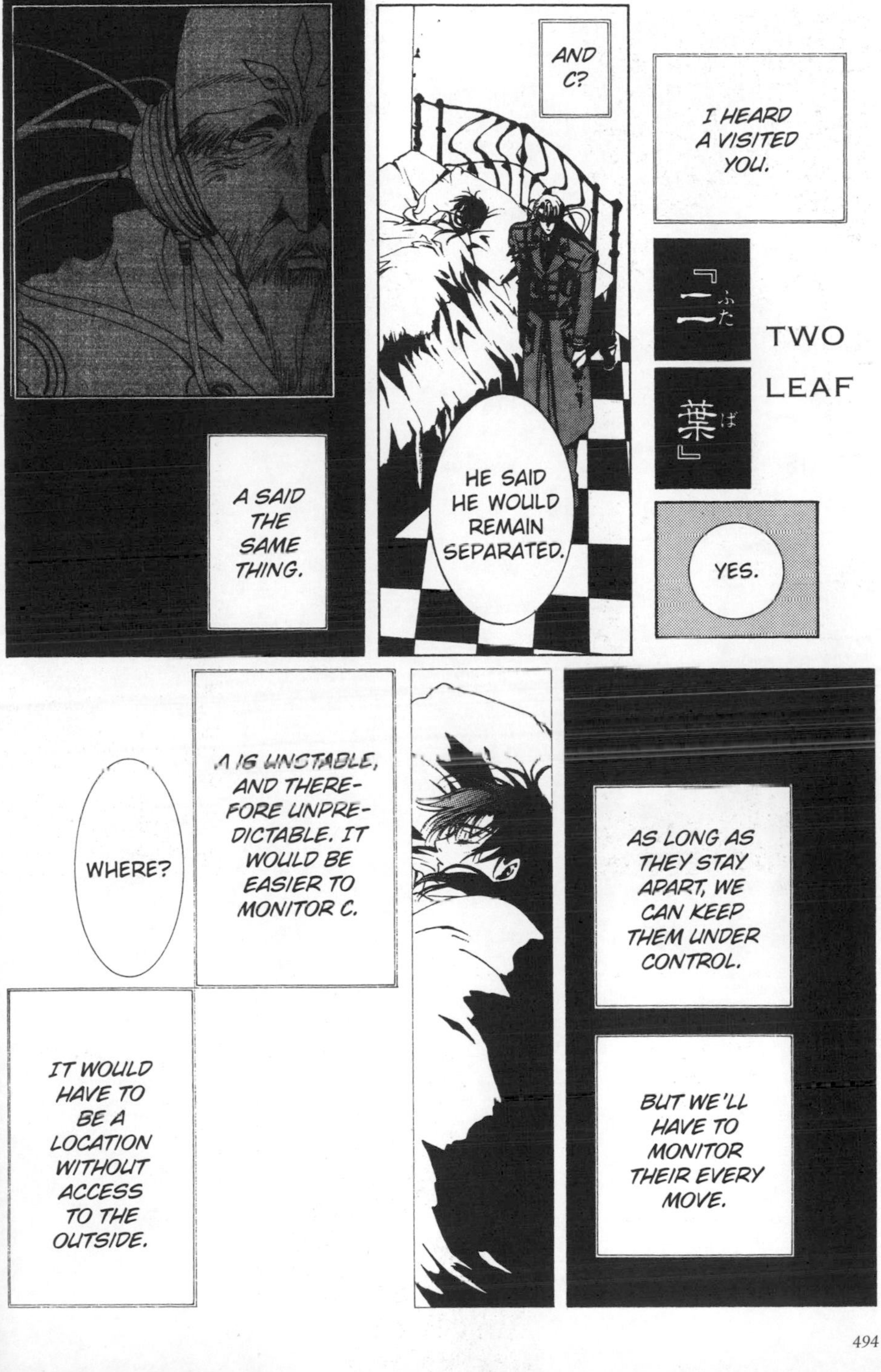
I HEARD A VISITED YOU.
『二葉』
TWO LEAF
YES.
AND C?
HE SAID HE WOULD REMAIN SEPARATED.
A SAID THE SAME THING.
AS LONG AS THEY STAY APART, WE CAN KEEP THEM UNDER CONTROL.
BUT WE'LL HAVE TO MONITOR THEIR EVERY MOVE.
A IS UNSTABLE, AND THEREFORE UNPREDICTABLE. IT WOULD BE EASIER TO MONITOR C.
WHERE?
IT WOULD HAVE TO BE A LOCATION WITHOUT ACCESS TO THE OUTSIDE.

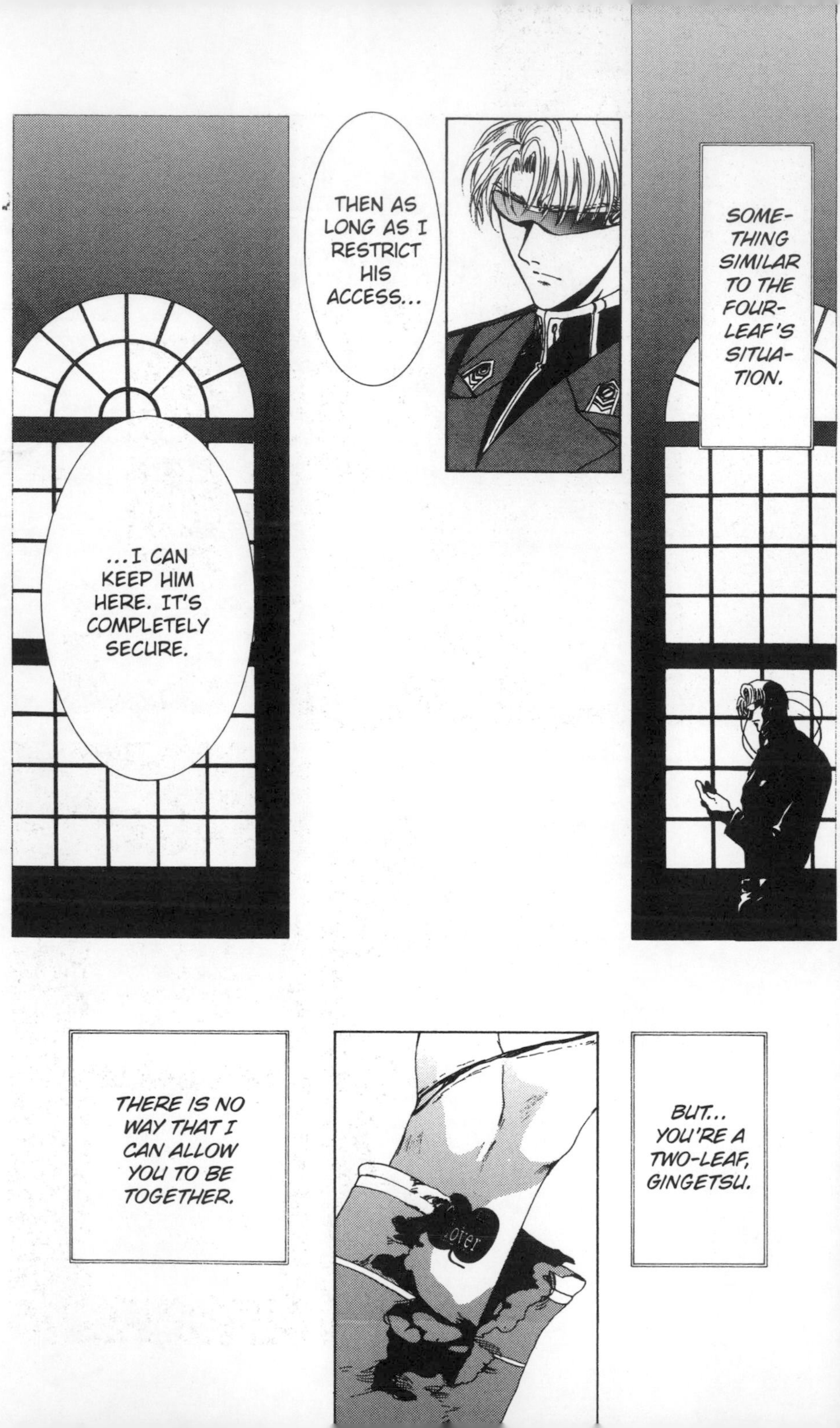
SOME-THING SIMILAR TO THE FOUR-LEAF'S SITUA-TION.
THEN AS LONG AS I RESTRICT HIS ACCESS...
...I CAN KEEP HIM HERE. IT'S COMPLETELY SECURE.
BUT... YOU'RE A TWO-LEAF, GINGETSU.
THERE IS NO WAY THAT I CAN ALLOW YOU TO BE TOGETHER.

TWO PLUS THREE EQUALS FIVE.

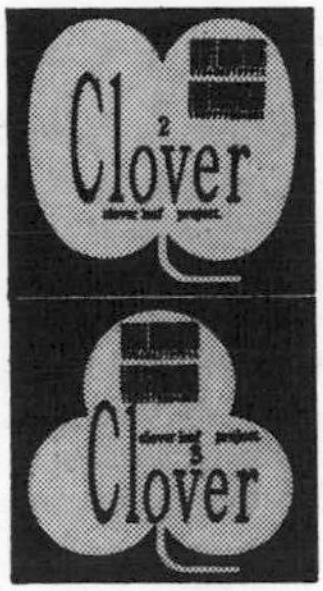
Clover
Clover

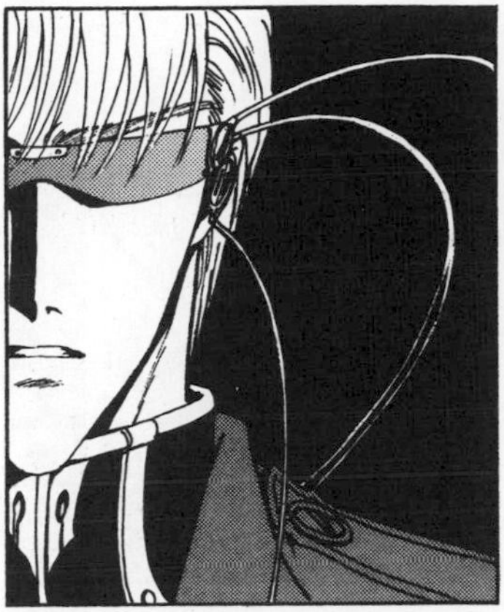

COMBINED, YOU TWO COULD OVER-POWER THE COUNCIL.

THEN IMPLANT A KILL DEVICE.

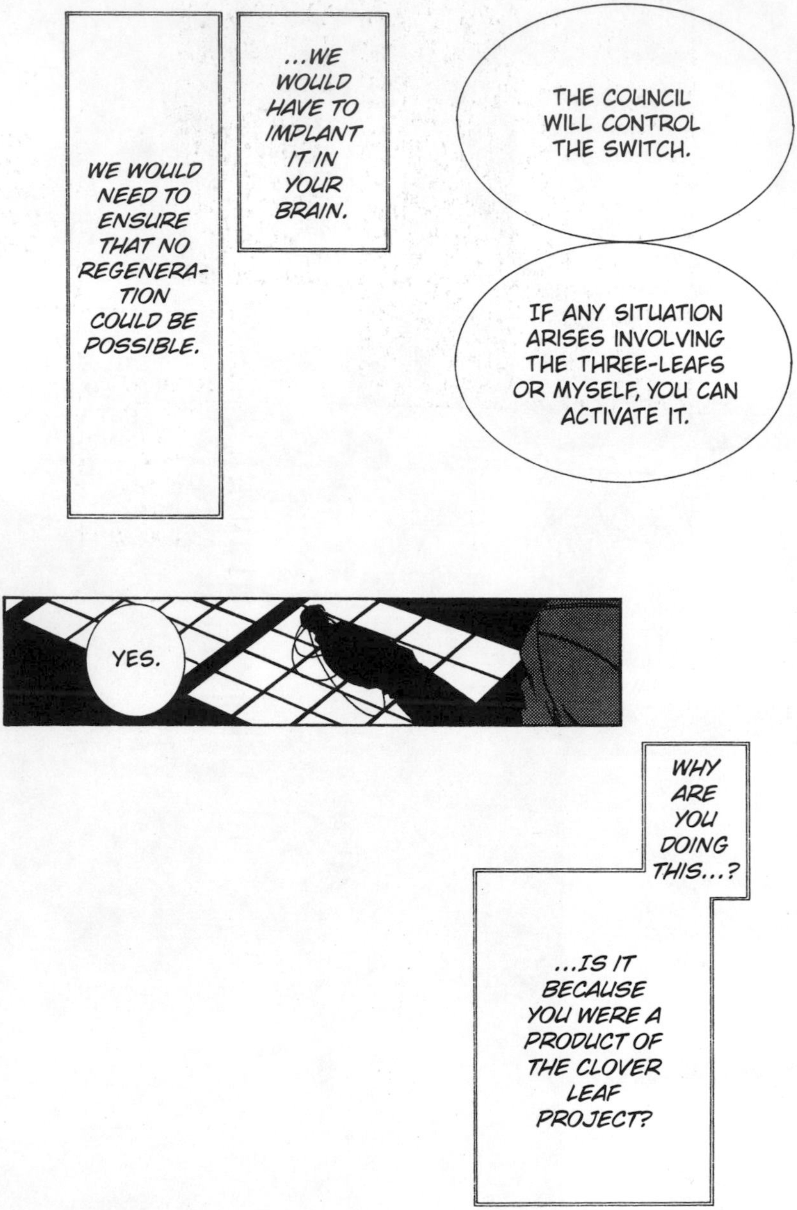
WE WOULD NEED TO ENSURE THAT NO REGENERA-TION COULD BE POSSIBLE.
...WE WOULD HAVE TO IMPLANT IT IN YOUR BRAIN.
THE COUNCIL WILL CONTROL THE SWITCH.
IF ANY SITUATION ARISES INVOLVING THE THREE-LEAFS OR MYSELF, YOU CAN ACTIVATE IT.
YES.
WHY ARE YOU DOING THIS...?
...IS IT BECAUSE YOU WERE A PRODUCT OF THE CLOVER LEAF PROJECT?

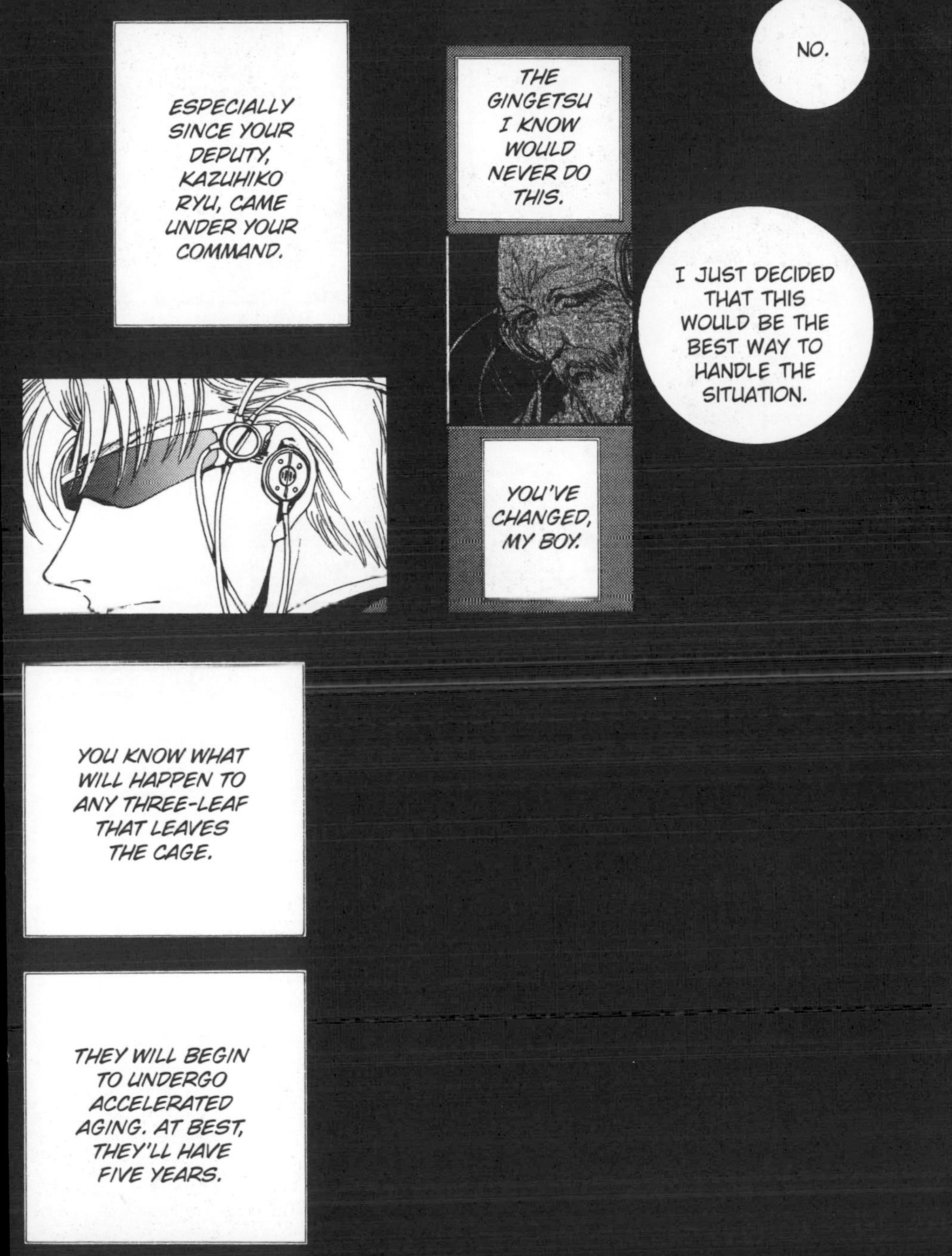
ESPECIALLY SINCE YOUR DEPUTY, KAZUHIKO RYU, CAME UNDER YOUR COMMAND.
THE GINGETSU I KNOW WOULD NEVER DO THIS.
NO.
I JUST DECIDED THAT THIS WOULD BE THE BEST WAY TO HANDLE THE SITUATION.
YOU'VE CHANGED, MY BOY.
YOU KNOW WHAT WILL HAPPEN TO ANY THREE-LEAF THAT LEAVES THE CAGE.
THEY WILL BEGIN TO UNDERGO ACCELERATED AGING. AT BEST, THEY'LL HAVE FIVE YEARS.

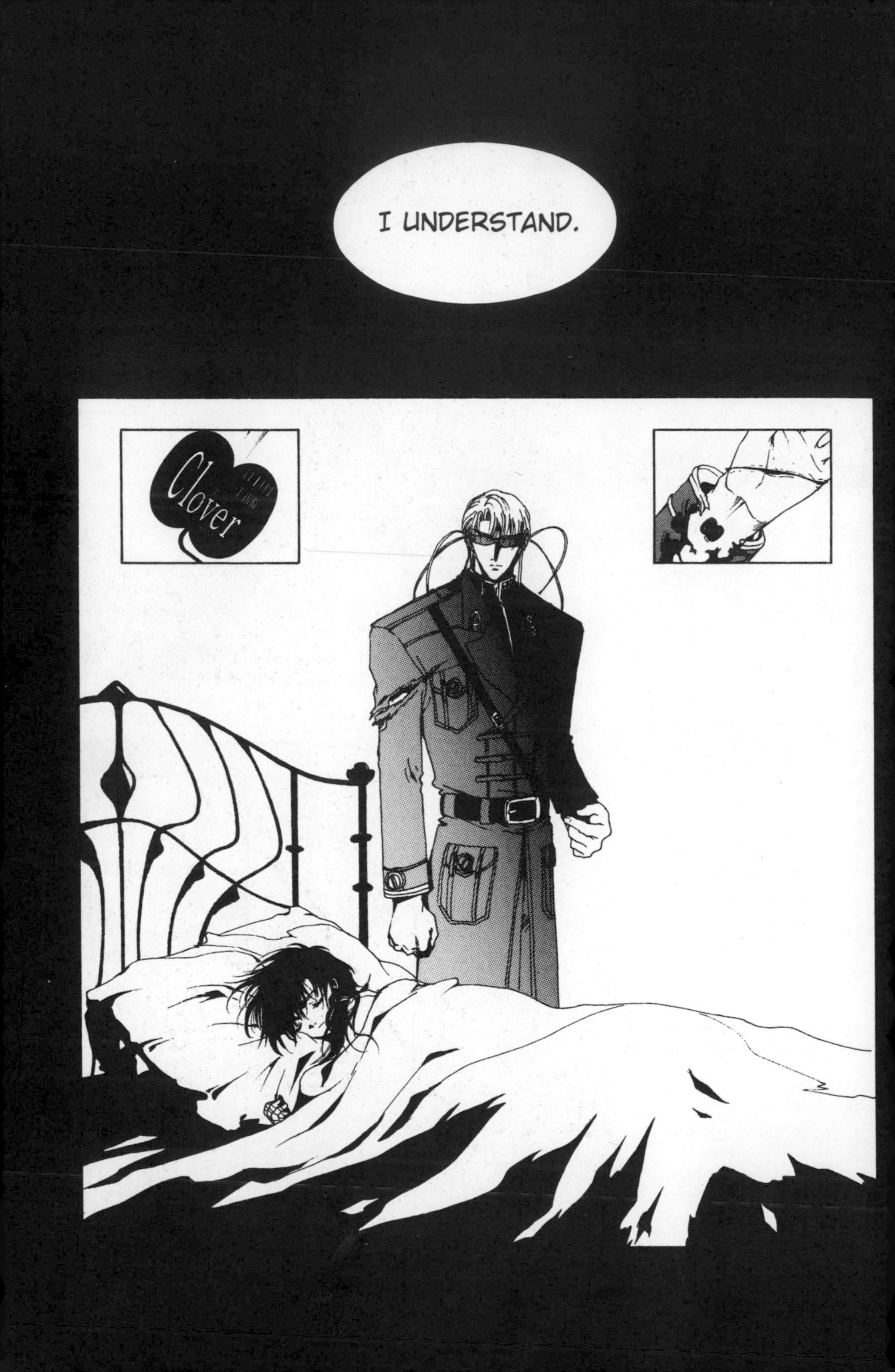
I UNDERSTAND.
Clover

BEING REBORN

『生まれ変わる』

THANK YOU FOR EVERY-THING.

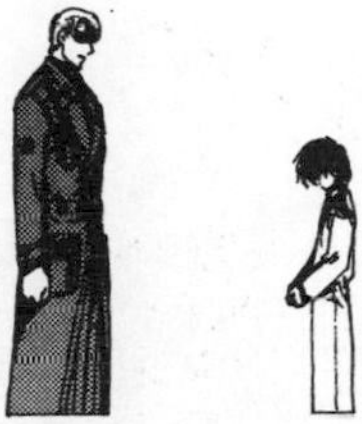

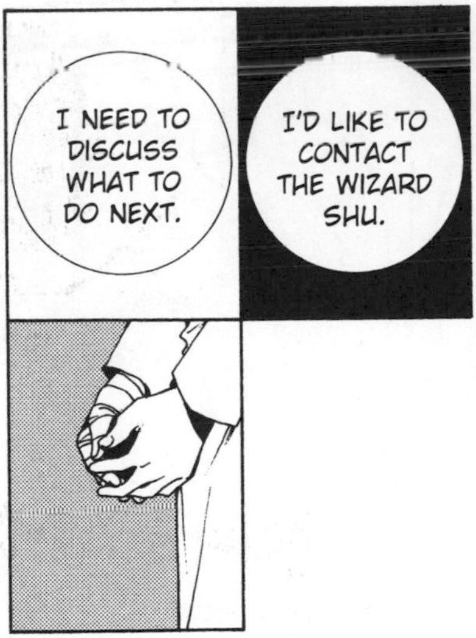
I'D LIKE TO CONTACT THE WIZARD SHU.
I NEED TO DISCUSS WHAT TO DO NEXT.

STAY HERE.

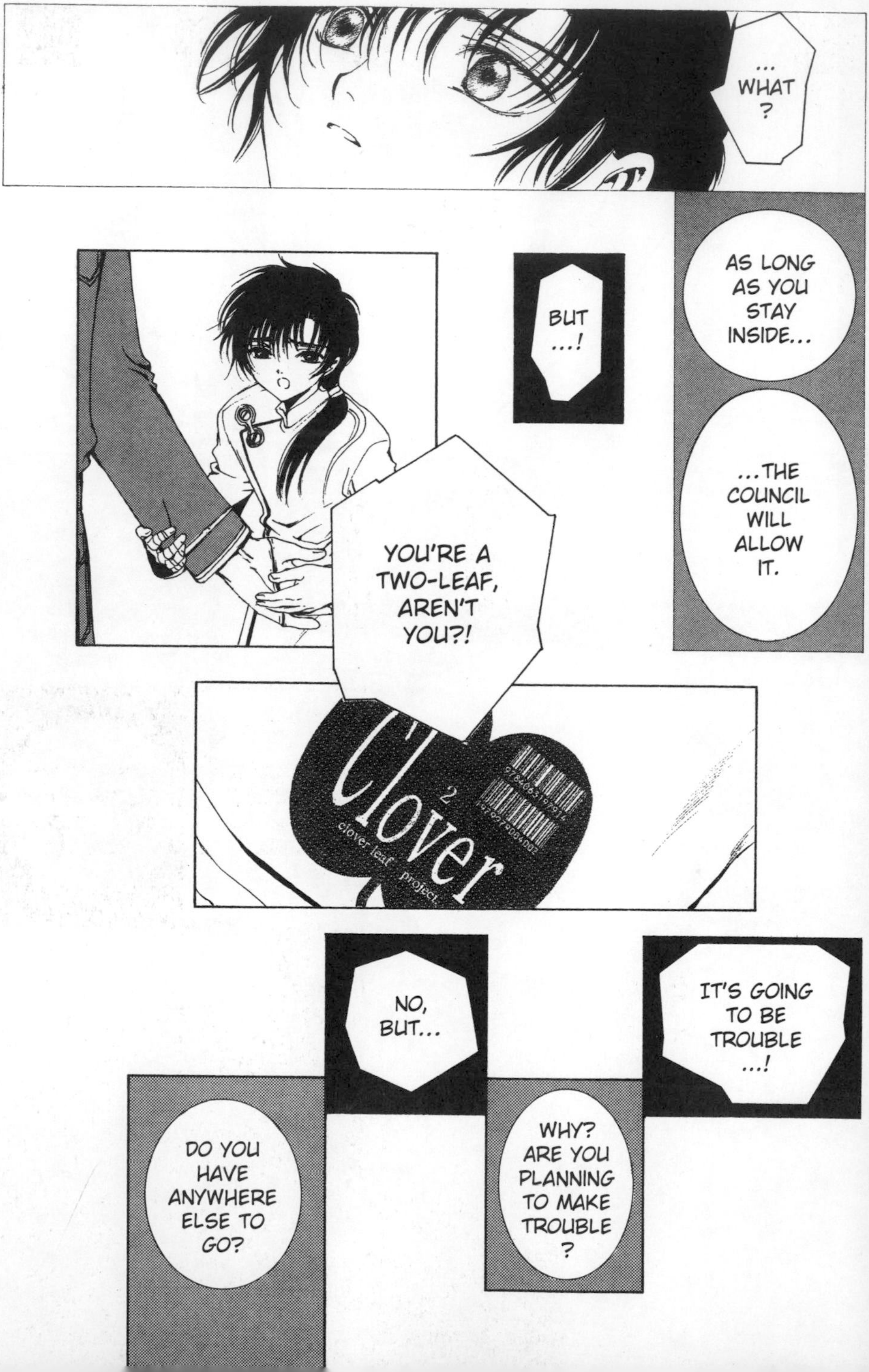
...WHAT?
AS LONG AS YOU STAY INSIDE...
...THE COUNCIL WILL ALLOW IT.
BUT...!
YOU'RE A TWO-LEAF, AREN'T YOU?!
Clover
2
clover leaf project.
IT'S GOING TO BE TROUBLE...!
WHY? ARE YOU PLANNING TO MAKE TROUBLE?
NO, BUT...
DO YOU HAVE ANYWHERE ELSE TO GO?

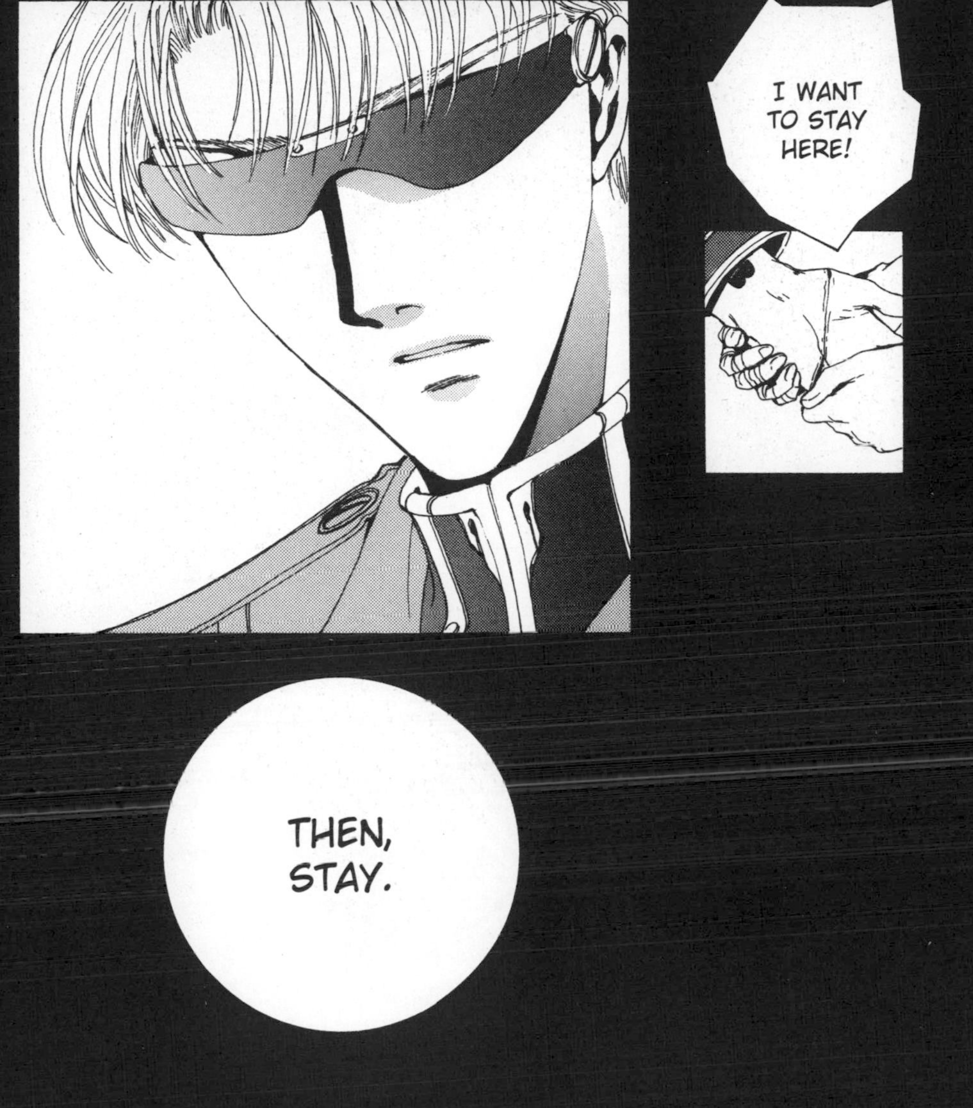
I WANT TO STAY HERE!
THEN, STAY.

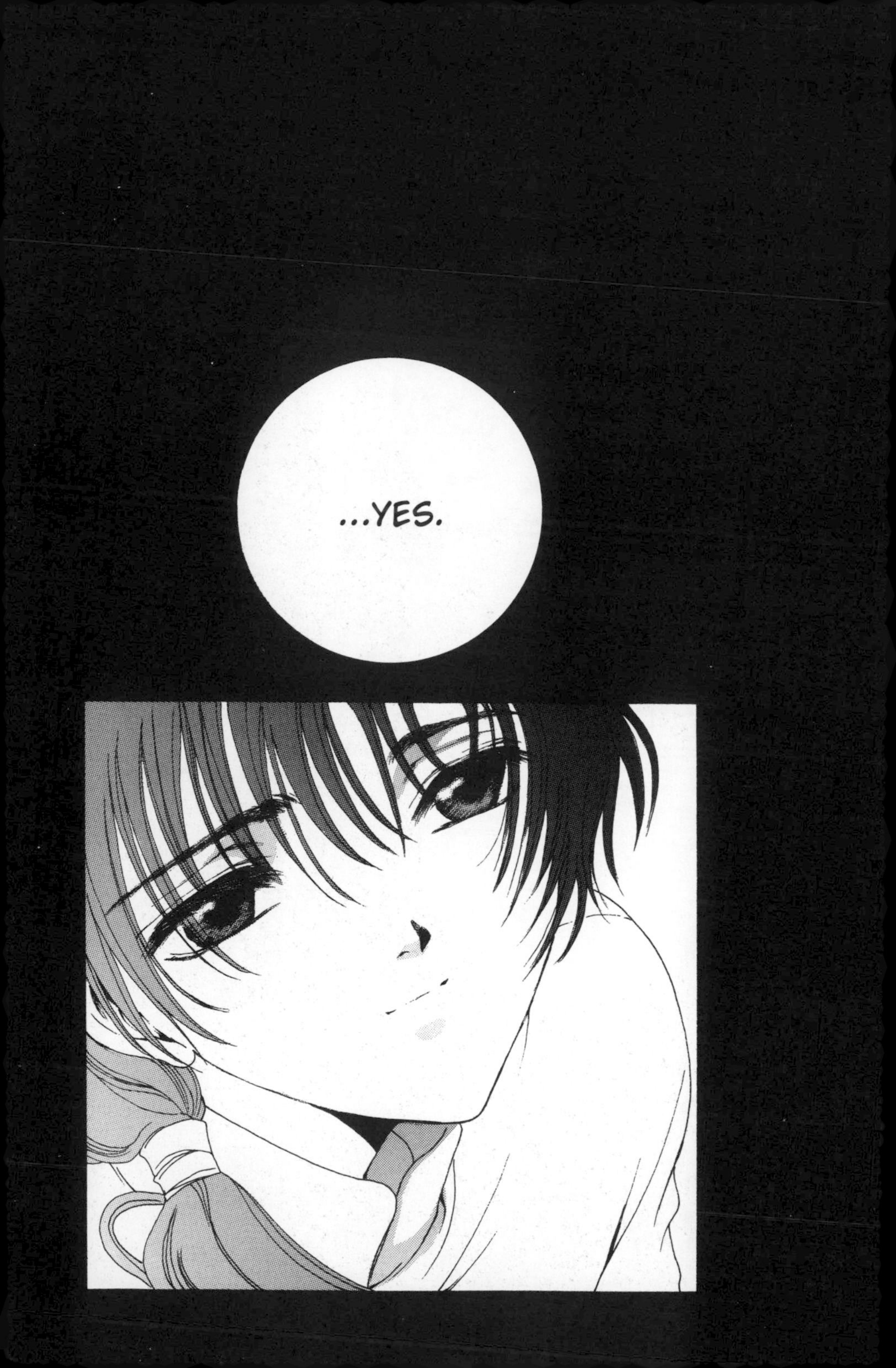
...YES.

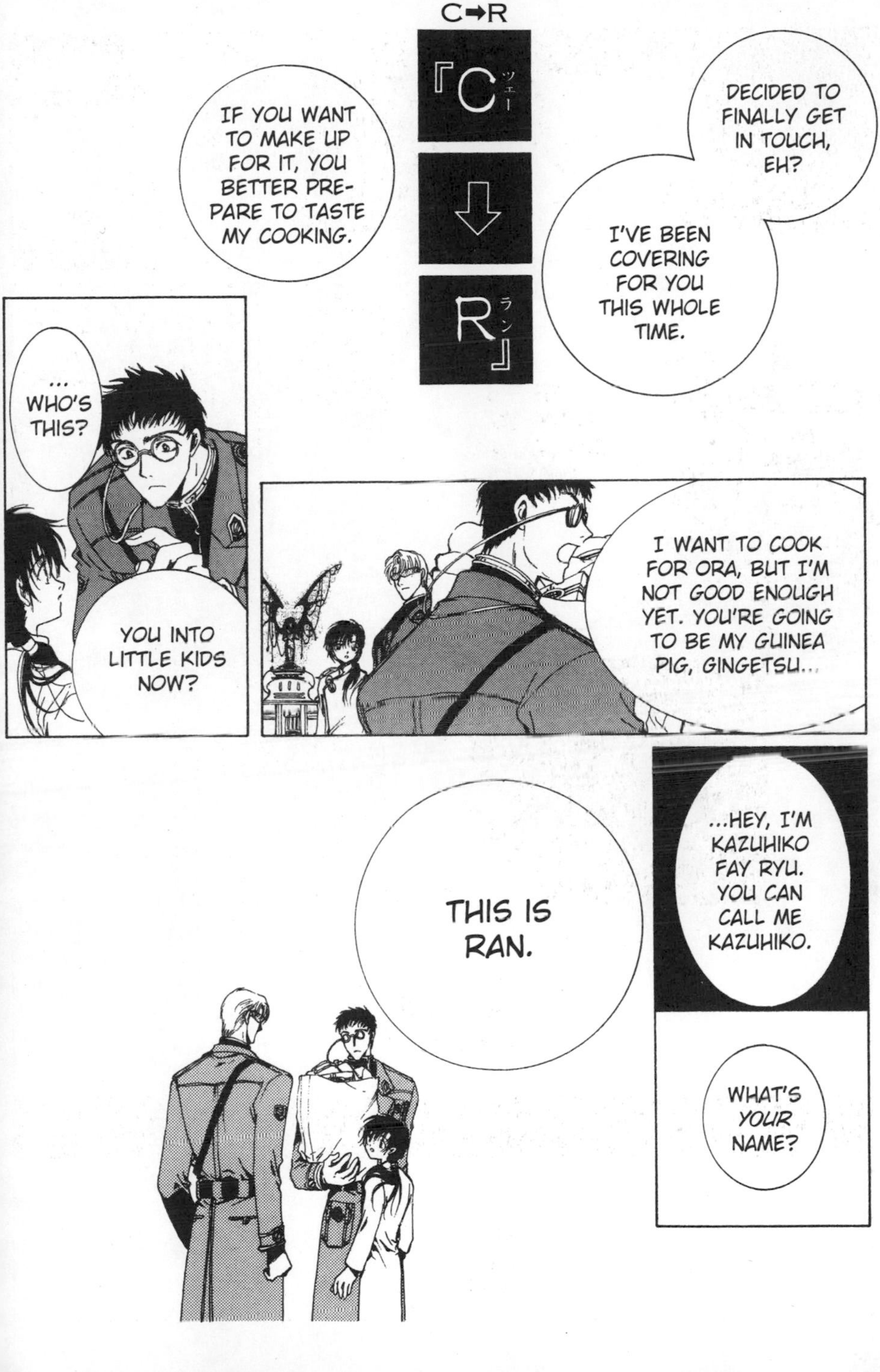
C➡R
『C ツェー ⇩ R ラン』
DECIDED TO FINALLY GET IN TOUCH, EH?
I'VE BEEN COVERING FOR YOU THIS WHOLE TIME.
IF YOU WANT TO MAKE UP FOR IT, YOU BETTER PRE- PARE TO TASTE MY COOKING.
I WANT TO COOK FOR ORA, BUT I'M NOT GOOD ENOUGH YET. YOU'RE GOING TO BE MY GUINEA PIG, GINGETSU...
... WHO'S THIS?
YOU INTO LITTLE KIDS NOW?
...HEY, I'M KAZUHIKO FAY RYU. YOU CAN CALL ME KAZUHIKO.
WHAT'S *YOUR* NAME?
THIS IS RAN.

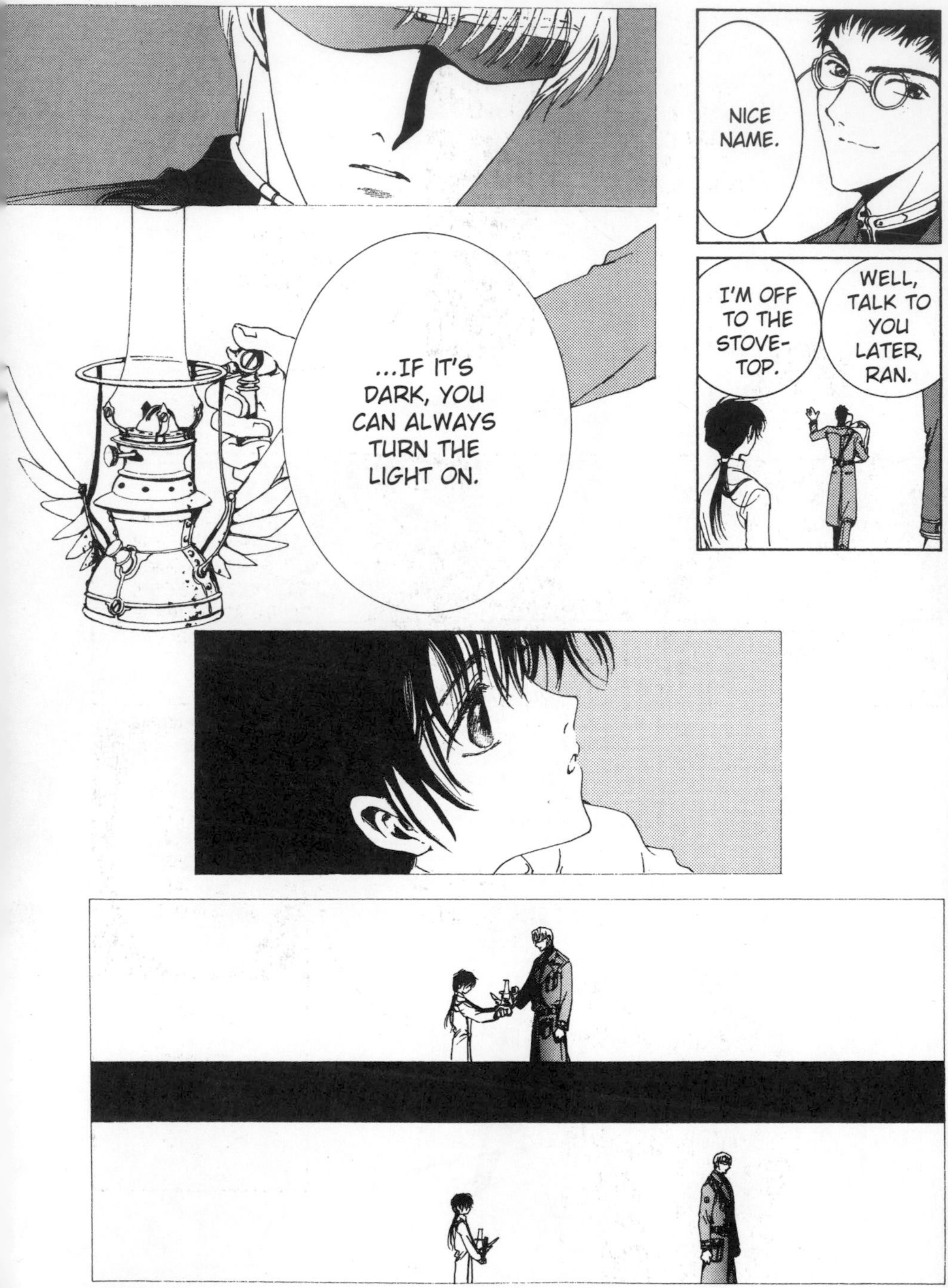
NICE NAME.
WELL, TALK TO YOU LATER, RAN.
I'M OFF TO THE STOVE-TOP.
...IF IT'S DARK, YOU CAN ALWAYS TURN THE LIGHT ON.

In your arms,
I will be reborn

For you
I will be reborn
An ember just lit
Let it not be put out

My thoughts
just created
May they not
be forgotten

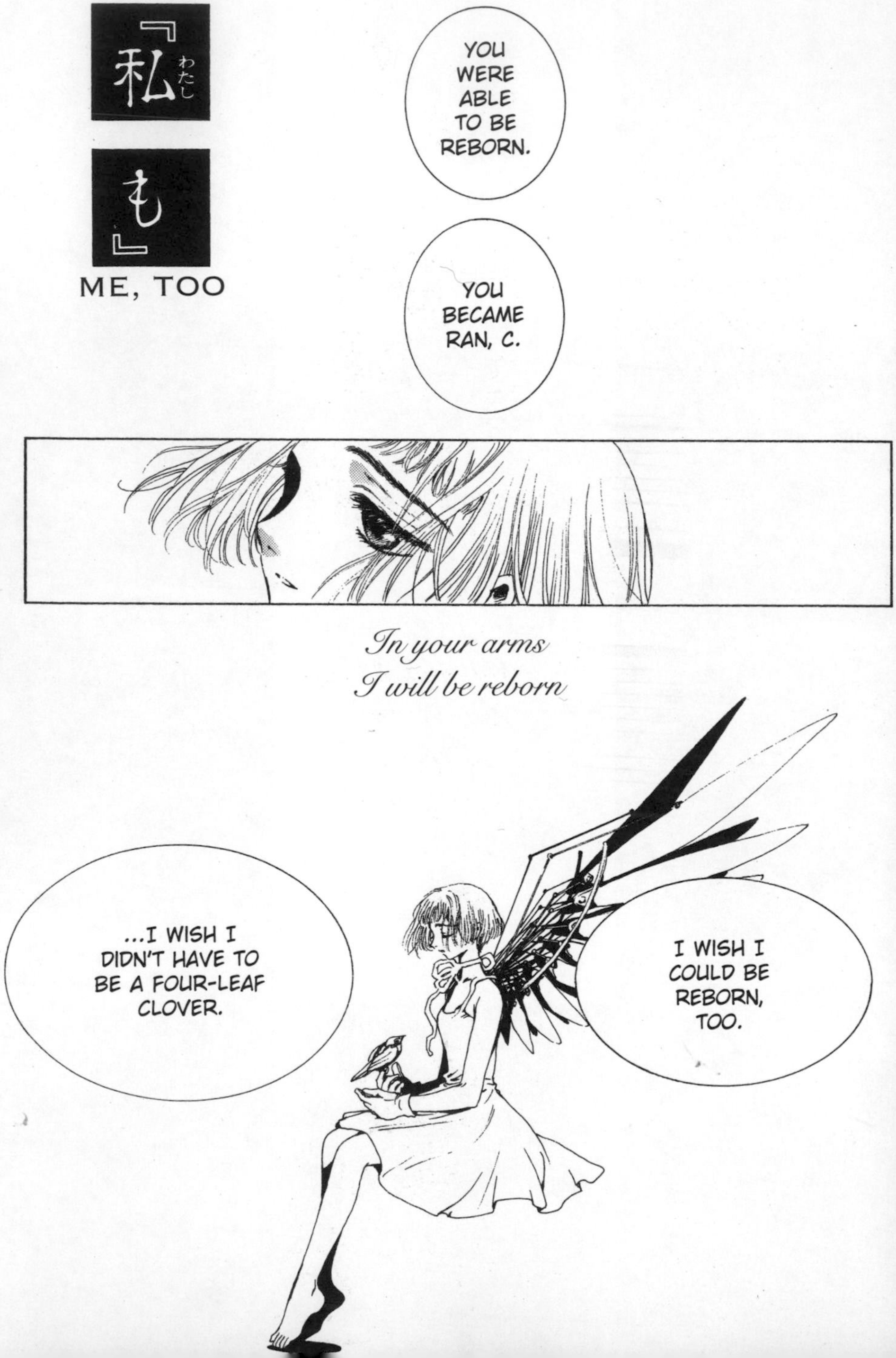
『私も』
わたし
ME, TOO
YOU WERE ABLE TO BE REBORN.
YOU BECAME RAN, C.
In your arms
I will be reborn
I WISH I COULD BE REBORN, TOO.
...I WISH I DIDN'T HAVE TO BE A FOUR-LEAF CLOVER.

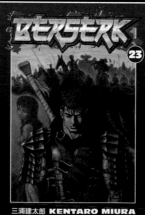

B U R S T

Don't miss the latest adventures of the most fun-loving, well-armed bounty hunters in Chicago! Rally Vincent and Minnie-May Hopkins return with Kenichi Sonoda's *Gunsmith Cats: Burst*, back in action and back in trouble!

Presented in the authentic right-to-left reading format, and packed full of bounty-hunting, gun-slinging, property-damaging action, *Gunsmith Cats: Burst* aims to please.

VOLUME 1
ISBN 978-59307-750-1

VOLUME 2
ISBN 978-1-59307-767-9

VOLUME 3
ISBN 978-1-59307-803-4

$10.95 EACH!

DARK HORSE MANGA

AVAILABLE AT YOUR LOCAL COMICS SHOP OR BOOKSTORE!

To find a comics shop in your area, call 1-888-266-4226. For more information or to order direct visit darkhorse.com or call 1-800-862-0052 Mon.–Fri. 9 AM to 5 PM Pacific Time.
*Prices and availability subject to change without notice.

GUNSMITH CATS

Kosuke Fujishima's Oh My Goddess!

Dark Horse is proud to re-present *Oh My Goddess!* in the much-requested, affordable, Japanese-reading, right-to-left format, complete with color sections, informative bonus notes, and your letters!

Volume 1
ISBN 978-1-59307-387-9

Volume 2
ISBN 978-1-59307-457-9

Volume 3
ISBN 978-1-59307-539-2

Volume 4
ISBN 978-1-59307-623-8

Volume 5
ISBN 978-1-59307-708-2

Volume 6
ISBN 978-1-59307-772-3

Volume 7
ISBN 978-1-59307-850-8

Volume 8
ISBN 978-1-59307-889-8

Volume 22
ISBN 978-1-59307-400-5

Volume 23
ISBN 978-1-59307-463-0

Volume 24
ISBN 978-1-59307-545-3

Volume 25
ISBN 978-1-59307-644-3

Volume 26
ISBN 978-1-59307-715-0

Volume 27
ISBN 978-1-59307-788-4

Volume 28
ISBN 978-1-59307-857-7

Volume 29
ISBN 978-1-59307-912-3

Volume 30
ISBN 978-1-59307-979-6

Volume 31
ISBN 978-1-59582-233-8

Volume 32
ISBN 978-1-59582-303-8

$10.95 each!

AVAILABLE AT YOUR LOCAL COMICS SHOP OR BOOKSTORE
*To find a comics shop in your area, call 1-888-266-4226

For more information or to order direct:
• On the web: darkhorse.com • E-mail: mailorder@darkhorse.com
• Phone: 1-800-862-0052 Mon.–Fri. 9 AM to 5 PM Pacific Time.

【 トゥランスルーセント 】
translucent

Can you see right through her?

By *Kazuhiro Okamoto*

Shizuka is an introverted girl dealing with schoolwork, boys, and a medical condition that has begun to turn her invisible! She finds support with Mamoru, a boy who is falling for Shizuka despite her condition, and with Keiko, a woman who suffers from the same illness and has finally turned *completely* invisible! *Translucent's* exploration of what people see, what people think they see, and what people wish to see in themselves, and others, makes for an emotionally sensitive manga peppered with moments of surprising humor, heartbreak, and drama.

VOLUME 1
ISBN 978-1-59307-647-4

VOLUME 2
ISBN 978-1-59307-677-1

VOLUME 3
ISBN 978-1-59307-679-5

VOLUME 4
ISBN 978-1-59582-218-5

$9.95 Each!

**Previews for *TRANSLUCENT* and other
DARK HORSE MANGA titles can be found
at darkhorse.com!**

AVAILABLE AT YOUR LOCAL COMICS SHOP OR BOOKSTORE
To find a comics shop in your area, call 1-888-266-4226. For more information or
to order direct: • On the web: darkhorse.com • E-mail: mailorder@darkhorse.com
• Phone: 1-800-862-0052 Mon.–Fri. 9 AM to 5 PM Pacific Time.

DARK HORSE MANGA

the KUROSAGI corpse delivery service
黒鷺死体宅配便

If you enjoyed this book, be sure to check out *The Kurosagi Corpse Delivery Service*, a new mature-readers manga series from the creator of *Mail*!

Five young students at a Buddhist university find there's little call for their job skills in today's Tokyo . . . among the *living*, that is! But their studies give them a direct line to the dead—the dead who are still trapped in their corpses, and can't move on to the next reincarnation! Whether you died from suicide, murder, sickness, or madness, they'll carry your body anywhere it needs to go to free your soul! Written by Eiji Otsuka of the notorious *MPD-Psycho*!

Volume 1:
ISBN 978-1-59307-555-2

Volume 2:
ISBN 978-1-59307-593-4

Volume 3:
ISBN 978-1-59307-594-1

Volume 4:
ISBN 978-1-59307-595-8

Volume 5:
ISBN 978-1-59307-596-5

Volume 6:
ISBN 978-1-59307-892-8

Volume 7:
ISBN 978-1-59307-982-6

Volume 8:
ISBN 978-1-59582-235-2

Volume 9:
ISBN 978-1-59582-306-9

$10.95 each!

EDEN

It's an Endless World!

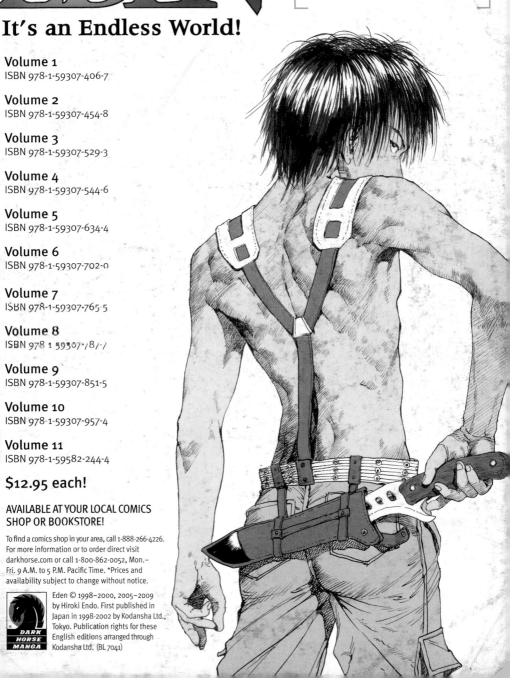

Be sure to check out *Tanpenshu*, Hiroki Endo's incredible slice-of-life short story collections! Volumes one and two available now from Dark Horse Manga!

Volume 1
ISBN 978-1-59307-406-7

Volume 2
ISBN 978-1-59307-454-8

Volume 3
ISBN 978-1-59307-529-3

Volume 4
ISBN 978-1-59307-544-6

Volume 5
ISBN 978-1-59307-634-4

Volume 6
ISBN 978-1-59307-702-0

Volume 7
ISBN 978-1-59307-765-5

Volume 8
ISBN 978-1-59307-787-7

Volume 9
ISBN 978-1-59307-851-5

Volume 10
ISBN 978-1-59307-957-4

Volume 11
ISBN 978-1-59582-244-4

$12.95 each!

AVAILABLE AT YOUR LOCAL COMICS SHOP OR BOOKSTORE!

To find a comics shop in your area, call 1-888-266-4226. For more information or to order direct visit darkhorse.com or call 1-800-862-0052, Mon.–Fri. 9 A.M. to 5 P.M. Pacific Time. *Prices and availability subject to change without notice.

S A T S U M A

—THE LEGEND OF THE SATSUMA SAMURAI—

G I S H I D E N

Master *gekiga* artist Hiroshi Hirata's art and calligraphy represent art at its most expressive, accentuating his classic stoic samurai characters as, in this quasi-historical tale of social caste and brutal reprisal, they cope with what it is like to be warriors without a war.

Volume 1
ISBN 978-1-59307-517-0

Volume 2
ISBN 978-1-59307-518-7

Volume 3
ISBN 978-1-59307-519-4

$14.95 each!

"Satsuma Gishiden" © 1977, 2006, 2007 by HIROSHI HIRATA. All rights reserved. First published in Japan by LEED PUBLISHING CO., LTD. TOKYO English translation rights arranged with LEED PUBLISHING CO., LTD. (BL7031)

THIS IS THE BACK OF THE BOOK!

...ft reading format to
in Japan. If you've
...rself an idea of how
will read each word
...t you should get the
...is way, never mind.

1
HER NAME IS SUE.
2
I DON'T KNOW HER LAST NAME.
3
GENERAL KO IS MAKING ME TAKE CARE OF HER.
4
OH...A GENERAL KO JOB.
5
I'M SUPPOSED TO DELIVER HER.
6
WHERE?
7
Somewhere far from here
8
I DON'T KNOW.
9
BUT SHE SEEMS TO.

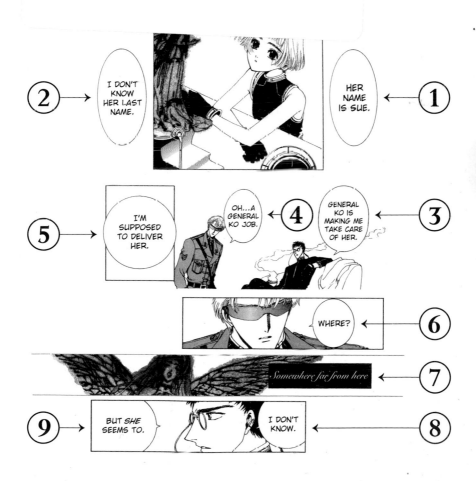